THE INSIDERS' GUIDE

TO

CHARLOTTE

by

Dawn O'Brien
and
Robin A. Smith

Published and distributed by:

Becklyn Publishing Group, Inc.
P.O. Box 14154
Research Triangle Park, NC
27709
(919) 467-4035

•

Sixth Edition
1st Printing

•

Copyright 1994
by
Becklyn Publishing Group,
Inc.

•

Printed in the United States
of America

•

•

ISBN 0-9623690-6-3

Publisher/Managing Editor
Carolyn Clifton

President
Barbara King

Vice President
Sales and Marketing
Pamela B. Myers

Editorial Consultant
David McNally

Account Executive
Theresa Y. Graham

This book is produced under a
license granted by:

The Insiders' Guides, Inc.
P.O. box 2057
Manteo, NC 27954
(919) 473-6100

Cover Color Photos

Charlotte Skyline:
Courtesy Muhleman Marketing, Inc.

Paramount's Carowinds:
Courtesy N.C. Travel and Tourism

Charlotte Motor Speedway:
Courtesy N.C. Travel and Tourism

Maps

By Fraser Van Asch

Preface

One of the hottest markets in the U.S., Charlotte is uniquely positioned for not only the success it is currently enjoying but for the future as a major leader in commerce, education and quality of life issues. Through the visionary and fiscally responsible guidance of community citizens willing to "roll their sleeves up and get the job done, Charlotte's "Can Do" spirit has allowed it to take full advantage of a growing Southeast, a moderate climate and a pro-business environment.

These are some of the reasons *Newsweek* named the Queen City as one of the ten most desirable cities in the nation to live. Charlotte is the third largest financial center in the United States, with two of the top ten banks headquartered here. This certainly played a part in Charlotte's being ranked as the "best city for economic development in the United States," by Financial World Magazine.

Charlotte is poised for the future. But, as with most things, to understand the present and gain insight into the future, it is helpful to look at the past. Through an "insiders' perspective," we have given you a brief glimpse at the early development of the area and an in-depth look at the city of today. The Guide attempts to provide a one-stop source of information about Charlotte and her neighboring communities. We try to provide needed information for visitors or a variety of professional sports. Our Sports Section gives you "inside insights" into the Carolina Panthers, the Hornets, the Knights, the Vipers, the NASCAR Racing, the Rage, the Checkers, and the Express.

A visitor will appreciate the chapters on Accommodations, Airport, Attractions, Night Life, Restaurants and Shopping. If you're considering relocating your business, you might be interested in Banking, Commercial Development, Local Government and Uptown. A newcomer will find Homes (with information on buying, building or renting a home), Neighbors, Neighborhoods, Colleges and Universities, Government Services and Utilities, Retirement and Worship especially helpful in making all the decisions associated with moving to a new area. For parents, we added a chapter on Kidstuff in addition to the chapter on Schools and Child Care.

As a special gift to you our reader, we have added valuable coupons to the back of the book to assist you in your exploration of Charlotte and the Carolinas. We hope you will enjoy our newest edition and look forward to receiving your comments and suggestions on our More Products Information Card.

About The Authors

DAWN O'BRIEN

Dawn O'Brien did her undergraduae work at Stephens College in Missouri and at the University of North Carolina at Chapel Hill, then received her master's degree in communications from Wake Forest University.

She produced and directed, "Scrunch," a syndicated teenage television program for Multi Media and has worked as a television reporter, anchor and host. A freelance writer for numerous magazines, O'Brien has authored or coauthored seven cookbook/travel guides on historic restaurants. She was the host and creative force for the PBS series, "A Taste of Adventure." Her most recent travel publication is *Down The Road In The Carolinas (Daytrips and Weekend Vacations)*.

ROBIN A. SMITH

Robin A. Smith is President of Robin A. Smith Communications, a Charlotte-based corporate communications, public relations and marketing firm. She has lived in the city for ten years. A graduate of Appalachian State University, she received the M.A. in English from the University of North Carolina at Charlotte.

Smith is active in the community, serving on various service organization boards. Her work includes *SouthPark Update* magazine which she edited and published for seven years. She is also the former associate editor of the *ACC Basketball Handbook* and the author of *A Presidential Visit to The Park*.

Acknowledgements

This INSIDERS' GUIDE offers suggestions, opinions and ideas from many area residents, all of whom provided help, expertise and guidance. We thank each of our contributors.

Dawn would like to acknowledge Terry Hoover's invaluable help in her research on the "Neighbors" section and Ann Wicker's great advice and aid in establishing those "insider" contacts. Esther Wesley with Brevard/Transylvania Chamber of Commerce, Sheri Moretz with High Country Hosts and Oren Coin with Smoky Mountain Hosts provided expertise and assistance with research for the "Daytrips and Weekends" section.

Robin would like to acknowledge the following contributors:

Tish Atkins and Nicole Cohen, Associates with Robin A. Smith Communications for their invaluable assistance with research and editing, as well as tying up all those loose ends which tend to dangle from a project of this magnitude.

The publishers wish to express special thanks to Manuel Kennedy at Central Piedmont Community College for his assistance in obtaining photographs; Katherine Kopp for her assistance in compiling information for the Kidstuff chapter; Gil Capps, Publisher and Editor of *Metrolina Golf* magazine for his contributions to the chapter on Golf; Marie Hyder for assistance on banking; Regina Atkins for assistance with fact checking.

Table of Contents

Directory of Maps

The North Carolina State Seal

From the Governor...

STATE OF NORTH CAROLINA
OFFICE OF THE GOVERNOR
RALEIGH 27603-8001

JAMES B. HUNT JR.
GOVERNOR

Dear Friends:

As Governor of the State of North Carolina, it is indeed my pleasure to welcome you to Charlotte, our state's largest city.

Nearly 250 years ago, a Scotch-Irish settler named Thomas Polk built a cabin on a spot along a ridge at the crossing of two old Indian trading paths. Where he once lived is now the Trade and Tryon intersection, the historic heart of the city. This busy intersection is home today to the 60-story NationsBank Corporate Center!

Charlotteans do not call their central business district downtown, as in most cities. Rather, they refer to it as "Uptown" because the center city is on a ridge and you must travel "up" from surrounding areas to get there. And getting there is certainly worthwhile as you explore the Performing Arts Center, Spirit Square Center for the Arts, Discovery Place, and the Omnimax Theatre, just to name a few exciting attractions.

If you are a sports enthusiast, Charlotte is the place to be. The NCAA Final Four Men's Basketball Championship finds its way to Charlotte in 1994, and the Charlotte Hornets NBA team is incredibly popular. Charlotte hosts the Coca-Cola 600, a major NASCAR race, and just recently, Charlotte was selected for an NFL expansion team--the Charlotte Panthers--and Charlotteans eagerly await North Carolina's entry into the professional football arena.

A large city, yes, but also a city that knows no stranger. Southern Hospitality is a way of life in Charlotte.

On behalf of all our citizens, I again welcome you and invite you to enjoy all that the Charlotte area has to offer.

My warmest personal regards.

Sincerely,

James B. Hunt Jr.

Charlotte Area Map

Greensboro
77
Durham Raleigh
40
17
Manteo
Asheville **Charlotte** 85
95
New
Bern
Fayetteville 40
Wilmington

MT. HOLLY HUNTERSVILLE ROAD
Latta
Plantation
Davidson
Energy Emporium
Charlotte Motor
Speedway
29

BEATTIES FORD ROAD
77
W.T. HARRIS BLVD.

16
N.C.
Zoo
49

MT. HOLLY ROAD
BELHAVEN BLVD.
Metrolina Expo
27
21
85
Blockbuster
Pavillion

THRIFT ROAD
J.C.
Smith
Univ.
UNCC

TRYON STREET
PLAZA RD.

74
85
FREEDOM ROAD
277
Hezekiah Alexander
Homesite

WILKINSON BLVD.
Mecklenburg Aquatic Center

Charlotte-
Douglas
Internat'l
Airport
Central YMCA
CPCC
Merchandise Mart
Ovens Auditorium
27

BILLY GRAHAM PKWY.
SOUTH BLVD.
PARK ROAD
Freedom
Park
Queens
College
Mint Museum
of Art
RANDOLPH
Reed
Gold
Mine

Charlotte Coliseum

TYVOLA
ROAD
FAIRVIEW

49
77
SOUTH BLVD.
PARK ROAD
SHARON ROAD
Harris
YMCA
CARMEL ROAD
PROVIDENCE ROAD
SARDIS ROAD
74

521

Paramount's
Carowinds

Heritage USA
PINEVILLE-MATTHEWS ROAD
16

SOUTH
CAROLINA
James K. Polk Memorial

From the Mayor...

CHARLOTTE

Greetings:

As Mayor and on behalf of the City of Charlotte, I am delighted to welcome you to the Queen City! We are so pleased that you've chosen to relocate to our beautiful progressive city.

Charlotte is the largest city in North Carolina and is named in honor of Queen Charlotte, wife of King George III of England. Our city began as a tiny settlement of Scotch-Irish colonists in 1748.

We are blessed with a wealth of social, cultural and recreational amenities. You will enjoy exploring Discovery Place and the Omnimax Theatre, Spirit Square Center for the Arts, the Performing Arts Center and the Mint Museum to name a few.

Charlotte is a sports enthusiast's dream. We are home to the NBA basketball team, The Charlotte Hornets; the NFL expansion team, The Carolina Panthers; NASCAR's Coca-Cola 600 at Charlotte Motor Speedway; and numerous other sporting activities in which to participate.

We are delighted to welcome you to our city and know you will find Charlotte a great place to call home!

Sincerely,

RICHARD VINROOT

*The early 1800s plantation home of merchant James L. Latta
is on the National Register of Historic Places.*

Inside
Charlotte

To understand Charlotte's personality today, it's important to understand how past events shaped the area. In his description of the South, University of North Carolina at Charlotte Professor and Historian David Goldfield said, "Soil, rivers, and climate determined whether counties would flourish or decline, whether railroads and manufacturing would arrive, whether people would come or leave." True, luck and location were the incentive tools, but vision, character and risk are the determining catalysts that made Charlotte go this century.

A city's success usually boils down to people doing the best they can with what they are given. But that wasn't the case with the settlers of the 1700s. Charlotte wasn't an inherited gift. Our early pioneers chose to come here and **paid** for the privilege. Inexpensive, fertile land near rivers brought them down the Old Wagon Road from Pennsylvania. They arrived not to an established community, but to beautiful forests inhabited by Native Americans. What you see today arose from the efforts of those stalwart, stub-

born, God-fearing pioneers. They weren't afraid to take the risky steps that made Charlotte bloom. Since many early North Carolina communities had the same potential for growth, why did Charlotte prosper where others either retained their status quo or dwindled?

You can get a quick overview of Charlotte's character at the newly unveiled **Museum of the New South** at Founder's Hall in the NationsBank building Uptown. Some might flinch at calling this a museum, but the touch-video obelisk, called a museum without walls, is an innovative concept that delivers Charlotte's history. This "museum" offers tangible proof that, in the words of First Union's CEO, Ed Crutchfield, "A new person coming to town or the presentation of a new idea (such as a museum without walls) has a very good chance of being accepted in Charlotte." This is the distinctive type of character trait that sets Charlotte apart from many Southern cities.

That character was influenced by the Scotch-Irish Presbyterians who began to settle here in the 1730s. A devout religious group, the character of those original settlers is best illustrated by the prayer attributed to them: "Lord, grant that I may always be right, for Thou knowest that I am hard to turn." No one was more acutely aware of their inability to turn than General Earl Cornwallis who invaded Charlotte/Mecklenburg on September 26, 1780. After staying a mere 18 days, the general had racked up humiliating losses. Owing this to the "obstinate integrity" of those cantankerous early Mecklenburgers, he unwittingly coined the phrase, "...this rebellious country, the hornet's nest of America." You can find the term "hornets" or "hornets nest" on our county seal as well as part of the name of an elementary school, a park and Charlotte's NBA team.

And though a hornet is not a bee, the irritated Cornwallis soon drew his conclusion about Charlotte. It occurred the day he dispatched "one of his majors with 450 cavalry and 40 wagons to McIntyre's farm eight miles north of Charlotte Town (Charlotte's earlier name, also called Charlotteburg) on the Beatties Ford Road. Here, British foragers began loading their wagons with every available commodity. McIntyre turned loose his dogs, which in turn, upset a bee hive. The bees swarmed the British soldiers who, in their confusion, "ran helter-skelter about the yard seeking refuge not only from the sting of the bees but from the sting of American-fired shots as well."

Charlotteans have always been a might testy when someone comes riding into town and decides to take-over. Some historians describe this as "a contentious independence of spirit"—that was the nature of Mecklenburg's Scotch-Irish settlers. These settlers who, a century and a half earlier, had immigrated from Scotland and England to Ulster in Ireland, then to the Piedmont from Pennsylvania. Because they differed in background and religion from the Irish, there had been little blending. Set in their ways they were "strongly Presbyterian in their determination to have both freedom of religion and government, along with freedom of the one from the other." Charlotte has a rich diversification of religious denominations today, still a strong Scotch-Irish Presbyterian influence remains intact.

Long before Cornwallis marched in, Mecklenburgers were at odds with British rule. The settlers had been extremely loyal and had already gone the extra mile. They named the county Mecklenburg after the new Queen's German birthplace and their town Charlotte after the Queen. (This is why you'll hear Charlotte called the "Queen City," and why the top of the new NationsBank wears a crown). Still, the colonists, who already had serious cash flow problems, felt the continuing sting of escalating British taxes in what had become an increasingly corrupt government. Does any of this sound like 20th century politics? The Crown steadfastly refused to listen to the colonists' economic plight. This provoked Commander of the County Militia, Thomas Polk, to call citizens to elect two representatives from each militia district to meet in the Charlotte Town Courthouse on May

19, 1775. The story goes that these men framed the first document "declaring the citizens of Mecklenburg free and independent of the Crown of Great Britain." They read the **Mecklenburg Declaration of Independence** to the assembled town at noon the following day. Unfortunately, they didn't have time to present it to the congress, and worse still, the document burned in a fire. Although historians are skeptical, Charlotteans believe that the declaration existed. They celebrate that first demand for freedom each May 20th at the Hezekiah Alexander house, the oldest standing house in Charlotte. Two years ago the kick-off speaker for the event was none other than Hezekiah Alexander's sister Elizabeth's descendant, Elizabeth Dole. Ms. Dole, a Salisbury native, is president of the American Red Cross.

If you look at the roster for businesses in Charlotte, you'll find that a sizable proportion of them have German origins. In the 1800s French Huguenots, Swiss, Highland Scots and a large migration of Germans left Germany for many of the same reasons as the Scotch-Irish, and traveled from Pennsylvania along the same route. They moved from expensive Pennsylvania lands to the fertile Piedmont through land agents. They advertised, "come south where it's cheap" (not that different from current lures to companies that Charlotte wants to add to the tax base).

According to Historian David Goldfield, " . . . the South still engages in untrammeled boosterism. The South also sells its nonunion,

relatively low-wage work force . . . and is also not particularly protective of its natural environment." Yet it is North Carolina's beautiful environment, picturesque towns and "right-to-work" laws that keep North Carolina wages low by barring the doors to unions. These incentives have convinced Hollywood movie makers to make North Carolina the third most productive movie-producing state in the union. Not all those movies are filmed in Charlotte, but a high percentage of actors and technicians involved in these productions are based here.

Back in the 1700s the lure of a pleasant climate in a fertile environment worked to bring settlers. Unlike the Scotch-Irish, the Germans wanted to move to establish independent communities on a religious basis (e.g., Moravians in Winston-Salem). The Germans also wanted to do missionary work among the Indians. The German sects, predominantly Lutheran and German Reformed (now part of the United Church of Christ), moved into the eastern section of Mecklenburg County. This section of Mecklenburg split in 1792 to become Cabarrus and Rowan Counties. Because the predominant spoken language was English, the German minority so struggled with new language and customs that many chose to anglicize their names. There remain strong remnants of the eastern section's distinctive identity tangible in the Eastern Cabarrus Historical Society Museum in Mount Pleasant. The German people were known as brave, industrious people who became innovative and successful farmers. Perhaps it is that pull of those early pioneers that continues to entice German companies to relocate with us.

Charlotte didn't grow appreciably after the American Revolution, as noted in South Carolinian William Loughton Smith's reflective description: "This place does not deserve the name of a town, it consists only of a wretched Court House and a few dwellings falling into decay. There is a good tavern kept by Mason, where, however, I paid the dearest bill on the road." Liquor was then such a staple that families made it just as often as they made bread. Liquor was offered at not only celebrations but even "at the graveside." And although President George Washington's diary did not describe the food or drink at the gala picnic supper at Thomas Polk's home on the corner of Tryon and Trade streets, you may be sure that he imbibed his share of home brew on that May 28, 1791.

The previous morning the President recorded his meeting with Mecklenburgers: "... in the midst of a beautiful and celebrated grove (where a victory was gained over Tarleton's dragoons) . . . they are about as obstinate and noisy a set of gentlemen as I have ever met, or ever wish to meet again—especially when in a hurry." A later diary entry dusted Charlotte off as "a trifling place." Our president preferred the more sophisticated Salisbury. Of course, that was prior to the discovery of gold in 1799, an event that would catapult Charlotte from village to city status. Gold made Mecklenburg the mining capital of the United States, and the discovery became the first building plank in constructing the city as a financial center.

In 1837 city fathers built a United States Mint on West Trade Street to process gold instead of sending it to Rutherfordton for private coinage. Then some clever public relations person wrote that our streets were "paved with gold," borrowing liberally from the network of old gold mining shafts lying "beneath midtown streets." In fact, people do believe that low-value gold ore from the gold mines was used as part of the mixture to pave the main streets of Uptown.

Just prior to this period, our eleventh president, James Knox Polk, was born in 1795 in either Pineville or Huntersville. Historians disagree on location as they do on the birthplace of seventh president Andrew Jackson. Waxhaw historians claim that Jackson was born in "the McKemey cabin in North Carolina or across the road at the Crawford plantation in South Carolina." Jackson said he was born in South Carolina in 1767, but the question is clouded by miscalculated North Carolina and South Carolina boundaries, which were laid out in 1735 and again in 1737.

The 1800s blossomed into a prosperous era with gold and iron ore operations, but the invention of the cotton gin soon overtook the difficult-to-mine gold. "King cotton" transformed Mecklenburg into a textile leader, but nothing so changed the way Charlotte did business as the arrival of the railroad. Our ideal location, connected by rail between Columbia and Greensboro, eventually turned Charlotte into a distribution hub. Today, Charlotte is at the center of the largest consolidated rail system in the nation, offering two major rail systems—Norfolk Southern Railway and CSX Transportation—that links 27,000 miles of rail systems between Charlotte and 22 of the states in the eastern United States.

And to Amtrak officials, trains aren't passenger transportation of the past. A couple of years ago, Charlotte and Raleigh signed on for the experimental X2000 high-speed passenger train. If funded by the federal government, the train could trim a three-and-a-half-hour trip from Charlotte to Raleigh to two hours. But even if this comes to pass, this train won't equate with the phenomena of October 21, 1852, when the first train chugged into town. Over 20,000 citizens celebrated its arrival with a dance, fireworks and a barbecue. And even though mega celebrations and cocktail parties seem to dominate the party scene these days, old fashioned open-houses at Christmas and all-day barbecues, similar to the one held the day the train arrived, are still popular methods of celebration with the citizens of Charlotte.

Charlotte had begun to take off economically in the 1800s, but the Civil War curtailed steady development. Although the city never saw military action, Charlotte families suffered huge casualties and the city hospitalized many wounded soldiers.

Historian Burke Davis *et al.*, have documented the mysterious disappearance of the Confederate Treasury during a fateful wagon caravan trip through Charlotte. Don't go digging up your back yard be-

The James K. Polk Memorial State Historic site is located in Pineville on the site of the birthplace of the 11th U.S. President.

Photo by William Russ. Courtesy N.C. Travel and Tourism Division.

cause the treasury was intact when it left Charlotte. It arrived accompanied by Jefferson Davis, Confederate Cabinet members and naval cadets. In Charlotte the caravan picked up the additional protection of Confederate cavalry and naval yard workers, making a total of 2,000 men. But soon, disillusioned and mutinous soldiers demanded and received their share of back wages from the treasury. When a Union attack appeared imminent, some of the money was secretly buried or hiden at Southern plantations. What happened to the rest of the money? Some of it was placed in a bank; large sums of it were entrusted to two Confederate officers (to take out of the country) to use for continuing the war when reinforcements were received from the west; and some of it was confiscated by Union soldiers. But still, a sizable sum has never been accounted for.

When you pass by the southwest corner of Tryon and Fourth Streets, note the plaque that reads: "Jefferson Davis was standing here when informed of Lincoln's death April 18, 1865." The horrified Davis knew that without Lincoln reconstruction was going to be an uphill task. Charlotte was spared the worst of reconstruction nightmares, and because of a you're-not-going-to-beat-us spirit, eventually recovered to become a major production center in the 1900s. The city advanced economically in the early part of the century, although some historians feel that the Mecklenburg area did not regain true momentum until after World War II.

In the latter part of the 19th century Charlotte's way of doing business changed when visionary, Daniel Augustus Tompkins, came on the scene in 1883. This aristocratic South Carolinian duly noted that Charlotte was "an extremely dull place...but a town disposed to improve." He did a great deal to promote improvement, not only for Charlotte with his Southern Cotton Oil Manufacturing Company, which made cooking oil and other products from cotton seeds, but for the Southern textile region. Tompkins outlined a way for communities to build their textile mills in his book *A Plan To Raise Capital*. Tompkins spawned the idea of stock subscription to guarantee local ownership instead of English and Northern industrialist ownership.

Tompkins saw textiles as the engine that would drive the New South. It did, bringing men, women and children out of the fields and into the mills. In all changing social patterns, history records both good and bad effects: mills breathed spirit and independence into an impoverished economy giving families a mill home and a somewhat better economic life with regular pay and easier work, "yet at a cost that they (mill workers) could not have foreseen." Tompkins advised new manufacturers: "a mill . . . can operate its own store and thereby get back in mercantile profit much of the money paid for wages." And mill-owned church ministers tended to preach "work ethic" sermons acceptable to capitalistic employers in order to keep the operatives, as they were called, in line. The mills furnished

Line Drawing by Jerry Miller.

The historical Hezekiah Alexander House.

schools . . . but, "The mill came first always, school after . . ."

Menial, poorly paid labor was the only work offered to blacks, which meant that few blacks worked in the area's mills. A job at the mill could be called the precursor that changed women's work status. But, it also robbed many children of a childhood, and in general fostered a cradle to grave, paternalistic mentality that is slow to erode in some mill areas even today.

Textile manufacturing hummed and purred but cranked to full throttle when tobacco giant James B. "Buck" Duke had the Catawba River dammed to build his hydroelectric plant in the early 1900s. With the advantage of good roads, the railroad, electricity and stable government, Charlotte "attracted many desirable citizens." Today, our mild weather and healthy business climate (low tax base) continue to attract desirable companies

to relocate here. In the past 10 years we have become home or second home to industries such as micro-electronics, metal working and vehicle assembly, research and development, high-tech and service-oriented international and domestic firms. Over 324 foreign-owned companies now have Charlotte facilities, and aggressive planning promises that this trend will continue.

The early pioneers had only private education, usually taught by ministers or teachers who traveled from home to home. Instruction involved strictly practical ideas about learning. Schooling in religion, rudimentary skills and the learning of a trade constituted the curriculum. Even President Polk went to a private home academy where he received poor marks for "bad handwriting, poor grammar and awful spelling." Something akin to public education didn't begin until 1839 when $750,000 was appropriated for North Carolina schools. Mill-owned schools provided free education through the seventh grade, though the "school work of the child from 12 to 16 years of age is frequently interrupted by a hurry call from the mill superintendent...these conditions improved only in the mid-1910s after schooling was made mandatory for all children under twelve.

And though law dictated "...seven years of elementary education and four years of high school, yet in a majority of the state's mill villages, schools provided only the first seven grades free of charge." Because mill schools enjoyed a separate tax status, "students who attended them were not entitled to a high school education at public expense" and few mill parents could afford the high school tuition.

In the 1920s the school system expanded, even adding such perks as a school dentist and nurses, etc. But, the extras came to a halt in the Great Depression. At one point funds were so short that the twelfth grade had to be canceled for a short period. The educational system soon rebounded.

A few decades ago when the Supreme Court mandated integration, Charlotte carried out controversial cross-town busing, which in the end, achieved fair and uncommonly peaceful integration. The 1990s educational direction has focused on creating five magnet high schools, with each magnet school concentrated in a specific learning discipline. Future plans include adding two magnet schools, one at the elementary level and one at the

junior high level. In our higher education system, you'll find a number of excellent old colleges such as Queens, Johnson C. Smith and Central Piedmont Community College, plus the newer, "best academic bargain"—the University of North Carolina at Charlotte, which draws students from across the United States.

Banking began in the Mecklenburg area with the early settlers but stayed a private business until 1865 when it became nationalized. During the Civil War, a branch of the Bank of Charlotte transported 3,000 pounds of gold bullion 18 miles away to Grasshopper Springs where it remained buried until the war's end. It would not be until 1927 that a branch of the Federal Reserve Bank of Richmond was established in Charlotte, which was another building plank toward making Charlotte an important financial center. After the Second World War, American Trust Company and Commercial National Bank merged. This eventually became NCNB, which merged a couple of years ago with C & S Sovran in Atlanta to become NationsBank, the fourth largest bank in America and first in Charlotte. The second largest in Charlotte is First Union followed by Winston-Salem-based Wachovia, and 14 smaller banks, as well as the Federal Reserve Branch, which coalesces to make Charlotte the third largest financial center in the nation.

It was during the late 1970s and early 1980s that Uptown's Fourth Ward, an area of quaint and charming Victorian homes, was rehabilitated. This brought people back to city living at a time when

Photo courtesy 601 Poplar Bed & Breakfast Inn.

Uptown's Fourth Ward, an area of quaint and charming Victorian homes, was rehabilitated during the late 1970s and early 1980s.

people were moving to the suburbs. Lake Norman emerged from weekend cabin status to year-round luxury homes and condominiums, with highway traffic reflecting the flight. And you couldn't throw a rock without hitting an apartment or condominium that wasn't there yesterday, on just about any free lot in town. The down side is that some of these multi-complexes caused severe traffic problems. The upside is the city is widening some congested roads and cutting roads through new residential areas to give relief to the traffic flow. Yet, crime became so endemic in west Charlotte, and in other problem areas, that the city hired an additional 100 police officers last year, and added two new jails to the system (one Uptown is under construction and the other on Spector Drive opened in the summer of 1994).

Charlotte did not grow in earnest until the 1980s, following IBM's 1978 arrival, which Insiders say caused the city to perk up and residential property prices to edge upward. Then Charlotte became an international city in the late '80s when USAir won the London route. The '90s international connection spread to a different connection when Charlotte's NBC News channel WCCB began to broadcast headline news to viewers from Mexico to Argentina, designating it as the first U.S. based Spanish language news network to cover the entire region. In addition, in 1991, WCCB became home to an overnight newscast for U.S. night owls, which added a new service for another untapped audience.

Due to loss of government funding, the arts went through a period of crisis in the '80s. But thanks to enthusiastic arts supporters and a strong Charlotte Arts and Science Council, the arts community enthusiastically supports the newly named "Cultural District." It consists of our new N.C. Blumenthal Performing Arts Center, Spirit Square, Discovery Place, the Afro-American Cultural Center, and out in the neighborhoods, Ovens Auditorium, Johnson C. Smith University, Queens College's Dana Auditorium and other varied entertainment options. A couple of years ago our hands-on Discovery Place science museum was named the top tourist attraction in the southeast by the South East Tourism Society. The museum continues to provide exciting programs and films in its Omnimax Theater. Each year, sponsored by the Charlotte Arts and Science Council, Uptown plays host to a First Night New Year's Eve Celebration of alcohol-free entertainment. Last year drew an estimated 65,000. And each April our popular SpringFest, an Uptown festival of juried arts and crafts, with the accompaniment of regional and national bands, has become a rite of Spring as eagerly awaited as the opening of the first daffodils.

Charlotte may be poised to become the arts center of North Carolina, but sports is in undisputed first place. We have the new coliseum where the NBA Hornets consistently sell out all 23,000 seats; the new Knights Castle baseball field with its AAA Cleveland Indians baseball team and the improved Charlotte Motor Speed Way. The last glittering stone in Charlotte's crown is the under-construction football stadium for Charlotte's NFL team—Charlotte Panthers. For many, this enthusiasm for sports makes Charlotte a name synonymous with spectator sports. And, our temperate climate also encourages year-round participation in a variety of outdoor sports.

No matter from what vantage point you view the city today, NationsBank's glistening crown acts as a beacon. Nothing dwarfs Uptown's glass and steel skyscrapers, many of which replaced valued historic architecture denying citizens what urban designer, Kevin Lynch calls "windows in time." "It is not just buildings," as UNC Charlotte history professor Dan Morrill points out, "it's being able to look out from the present and to gain a perspective by seeing things that come from a different era. The important thing is not what that does for the past, because the past is fixed, but what it does for the process of living today."

Though we no longer have as many physical visual reminders, our process of living today in Charlotte is good—not perfect, but good. One reason that it is so good can be traced back to the character of our early pioneers. Yes, good luck, location and natural resources contributed heavily to Charlotte's prosperity. But our city has also known economic stagnation and failure: the long battle with England's unfair rulings, the end of gold mining, the Civil War, and in this century, the closing of the big textile mills. Each took its toll. But it's been said that the test of character shouldn't be measured solely by success; it's how we deal with failure that tells the final story.

When you drive through this beautiful city designated as "the city of trees," some almost as old as those early ancestors, think back to the types of people who've refused to knuckle under to failure throughout the centuries. Their character built the kind of foundation that was willing to change—change not only for the sake of prosperity, but change for a better quality of life. You'll find that in Charlotte. It's a great place to live and raise children because our economic disadvantages taught us, as Wake Forest University's Paul D. Escott says in his observance of the South, "to appreciate family, friends, nature, and the human rather than the material riches of life . . . The world needs these Southern values, especially the sense of place or rootedness that is vital to Southern culture."

Note: Historical research for this chapter was found in LeGette Blythe and Charles Raven Brockman's *Hornet's Nest*; Mary Norton Kratt's *Charlotte: Spirit of the New South*; Hugh Leffler and Patricia Stanford's *History of North Carolina*; Daniel Augustus Tompkins' *History of Mecklenburg and City of Charlotte: 1740 - 1903*; Dannye Romaine's *Mecklenburg: A Bicentennial Story* and Annette Burgert's *German Speaking Lands to North America*. Paul D. Escott and David R. Goldfield's *The South For New Southerners*. Jacquelyn Dowd Hall, James Leloudis, Robert Korstad, Mary Murphy, Lu Ann Jones, and Christopher B. Daly's *Like A Family*.

Photo by John Cress.

*It's difficult to distinguish art from reality in front of
the Charlotte Marriott City Center in Uptown.*

Inside

Accommodations

*C*harlotteans know how to make overnight guests feel comfortable, and that spills over to our many accommodations. An authentic dose of that hospitality should be evident if you choose to stay for a night or longer in any one of our luxury hotels, economy lodgings or historic bed and breakfast inns. A new resident to the city put it this way: "I wouldn't say that my decision to move here was based entirely on the hotel where we stayed, but they were the first people that I came in contact with after leaving the airport. They were really nice...you know, warm. Then, in the course of doing business here, I kept running into that same kind of attitude. No, we didn't choose Charlotte because of the hotel, but the truth of the matter is—the hotel did get us off on the right foot."

When deciding on where you want to park your toothbrush for a few days, comfort and safety are factors that often weigh just as heavily as a location convenient to the business district and recreation centers. There are more alternative accommodations open for travelers too, such as almost-like-home suites with kitchens, exercise rooms, VCRs and full breakfasts, bed and breakfast inns with their homey pampering, or apartment motels for those who plan to stay awhile. Many health-conscious business travelers and tourists are attracted by amenities like jogging trails through the woods or boat rides on a lake.

Where you lay your head at night may also depend on how much time you'll be spending there during the day; whether there are conference rooms, food facilities, a fitness area and airport shuttle service. If you are a first-time visitor and want to bring your pet, you need to be aware that under North Carolina law, pets are not allowed in hotels and motels, although there are some places that make provisions or allowances for them.

For the purposes of comparing prices, we have categorized

accommodations with one to four dollar signs ($), based on the typical daily rates charged for a standard room with two double beds—weekend rates are usually less and some hotels offer very attractive weekend packages. Keep in mind that these rates are subject to change. But to give you a rough idea of what to expect we offer the following guide:

$31 to $50	$
$51 to $75	$$
$76 to $100	$$$
$101 and up	$$$$

Hotels and Motels

ADAMS MARK

555 S. McDowell St.　　　　372-4100
$$$

This large convention hotel overlooks Marshall Park and is within short commuting distance of the Uptown financial district. It's very spacious with 598 rooms, 38 suites and large meeting spaces, plus it boasts the best view of the Charlotte skyline anywhere in town. **Bravo!** and **Appleby's** are well-known restaurants, and the hotel's high-energy night club, **CJ's**, is one of the city's most popular late night spots. Guests enjoy the Nautilus-equipped health club, indoor and outdoor pools, whirlpools and saunas and free parking.

BEST WESTERN LUXBURY INN

4904 N. I-85　　　　　　　596-9229
9701 E. Independence Blvd.　845-5911
$-$$

A 98-room/suite corporate property, the Best Western Luxbury offers luxury accommodations at economy prices. Guests enjoy a complimentary breakfast in the pink marble lobby, free local calls, Cable TV, free USA Today, a swimming pool and small meeting rooms.

CHARLOTTE MARRIOTT CITY CENTER

100 W. Trade St.　　　　　333-9000
$$ - $$$$

A four-diamond hotel, the Marriott City Center sits on the corner of Trade and Tryon in the heart of the city on the spot once occupied by North Carolina's first skyscraper. It's one of Charlotte's most elegant hotels with an atrium linking shops and offices in **Independence Center**. The hotel has 431 guest rooms and suites, a health club, indoor pool and two of Charlotte's classiest restaurants—**J.W.'s Steakhouse** and **Uptown Gourmet**. Guests also enjoy **Champions** sports bar.

CHARLOTTE MARRIOTT EXECUTIVE PARK

I-77 and Tyvola Rd.　　　　527-9650
$$$- $$$$

This hotel, like its sister hotel, the Charlotte Marriott City Center, is a four-diamond hotel. Designed with both large and small meetings in mind, the Executive Park hotel has 298 rooms, 8 parlors plus the Presidential suite, an indoor/outdoor pool, an exercise room, and tennis courts. Locals and out-of-towners mix during after hours in **Cahoots** night club as well as the **Gratzi** restaurant. Non-refundable, reduced rates are available with 14-day advance bookings.

THE COMFORT INN
LAKE NORMAN
20740 Torrence Chapel Rd.
Davidson/Cornelius 892-3500
THE COMFORT INN
WOODLAWN/COLISEUM
4416 South Tryon Street 525-0456
$$-$$$

These two Comfort Inns and their sister Inns in Monroe, Matthews and Concord/Kannapolis, are all recognized as Choice Hotels award-winning properties, but the Lake Norman property has been chosen "Inn of the Year." The award is based on an evaluation of the hotel property, guest services and other criteria including attitude and spirit of cooperation among staff.

The Inns are owned and operated by **Parkway Management Corporation** of Charlotte. All five Inns offer good service and quite a few amenities that you won't find elsewhere, such as: in-room coffee makers, in-room refrigerators, some in-room Jacuzzi's, a free deluxe continental breakfast with more than just juice, coffee and a roll. The Inns also offer free popcorn, apples, newspapers and a lot more. At the Lake Norman Inn, you'll appreciate the jogging trails and the fact that it's only 3 miles to the lake.

COURTYARD BY MARRIOTT
800 E. Arrowood Rd. 527-5055
$ - $$

This economy to mid-priced motel was built with the business traveler in mind. The Courtyard features an attractive small lobby and lounge, the **Courtyard Cafe** restaurant, a swimming pool, whirlpool and exercise room. There are 146 rooms and suites. Attractive week-end rates are available. Two other Courtyards are also in the area: SouthPark location 552-7333 and University City location 549-4888.

DAYS INN
1408 Sugar Creek Rd. 597-8110
$

This 150-room economy motel on I-85 North is convenient to the Charlotte Motor Speedway and University City; other Days Inns are located at the Airport, at Carowinds, on Woodlawn Road and Uptown on North Tryon Street. The Sugar Creek location has a **Spoons Restaurant** and all have outdoor pools.

DOUBLETREE HOTEL
895 W. Trade Street 347-0070
$ - $$$

Located just north of Uptown, the Doubletree has 187 rooms. This modern hotel offers a full-service health club, outdoor pool and meeting rooms. Casual dining is available in the **Doubletree Club**. All guests receive free Doubletree chocolate chip cookies. Free shuttle to Uptown and shopping is available weekdays.

DUNHILL HOTEL
237 North Tryon St. 332-4141
$$$$

The 1929 Dunhill Hotel (opened as Mayfair Manor) is one of Charlotte's few remaining landmark hotels. Completely updated in 1987, it had the distinction of housing Beatle, Paul McCartney, a couple of years ago. Its 60 guest rooms are elegantly furnished to 18th century decor. Some rooms have Jacuzzis and sitting areas. Room service is available from its **Monticello Res-**

taurant. It has computer compatible phones and FAX capabilities. The hotel is equipped for in-room exercise. It also provides chauffeur-driven limousine service by prior arrangement.

ECONO LODGE

I-85 at Sugar Creek Rd.   597-0470
$

This is an economy motel—one of four in the city and one of 400 in the nation, for which Charlotte serves as headquarters. (Other properties are located on Clanton Road, on Westpark Drive and I-85 at Little Rock Road.)

EMBASSY SUITES

4800 S. Tryon St.   527-8400
$$$$

Embassy Suites features 274 two-room suites and 10,000-square-feet of meeting space. The hotel features P. J. McKenzie's restaurant and lounge, indoor pool, whirlpool, sauna and health club. Guest suites have 2 TVs, 2 telephones, a coffee maker with coffee, a microwave and a mini refrigerator. Guests receive a complimentary cooked-to-order breakfast, the manager's reception each evening and complimentary airport shuttle service.

FAIRFIELD INN BY MARRIOTT

I-85 and Sugar Creek Rd.   596-2999
$

This new concept is Marriott's version of the economy motel, but with some special touches such as large, well-lit work areas in the rooms. Guests receive complimentary coffee and tea each morning, free local calls and cable TV.

There's also an outdoor pool for relaxation. Frequent travelers often join the INNsiders Club, which gives them special privileges. Another Fairfield Inn is located near the airport (392-0600).

GUEST QUARTERS SUITE HOTEL

6300 Morrison Blvd.   364-2400
$$$$

Guests at this three-diamond, full-service luxury suite hotel can buy a few grocery items downstairs in the Market Cafe for the one- or two-bedroom suites, which come with a living room, dining area and fully-equipped kitchen. Guests can enjoy a health center, outdoor pool, meeting rooms and dining in the Market Cafe. Airport limousine service is available. Special weekend packages are offered.

HAMPTON INN

I-77 Executive Park	525-0747
I-85 and Billy Graham Pkwy.	392-1600
University Place	
8419 U.S. 29	548-0905
Statesville Rd., Cornelius	
(Lake Norman)	892-9900
$-$$	

These four hotel economy inns offer quality accommodations, value pricing, free extras and a 100 % Satisfaction Guarantee. Free extras include an outstanding continental breakfast, local telephone calls and airport transportation. The I-77 Executive Park location has an exercise facility and an outdoor pool.

HILTON UNIVERSITY PLACE

University Place   547-7444
$$ - $$$$

This modern property is located in the center of University Place, a European-style village of shops, theaters and restaurants. It offers 243 rooms (including exclusive club rooms on the 11th and 12th floors), meeting rooms, lake-side lounges, an exercise room and outdoor pool and continental breakfast on weekends. It is very convenient to the new **Blockbuster Pavilion**.

Holiday Inn-Airport
2707 Little Rock Rd.   *394-4301*
$$
The Holiday Inn-Airport is a 217-room chain motel catering to corporate clients. It houses a lively lounge called **Razzles** and an attractive dining room, **The Greenery**, which features piano music. All guests receive free airport limousine service, and **Priority Club** members (frequent guests) receive complimentary coffee and newspaper.

Holiday Inn-Center City
230 North College St.   *335-5400*
$$-$$$
Center City, adjoining the **Charlotte International Trade Center**, has 300 guest rooms, 28 suites, a complimentary fitness room and jogging track, indoor parking, a rooftop pool and spa. Complete dining facilities are available at **College Street Station Deli & Grill** and guests can relax at the **INSIDERS** lobby lounge. You can pick up something special in the hotel gift shop and make travel arrangements through the travel agency.

Holiday Inn-Woodlawn
212 Woodlawn   *525-8350*
$$
With 425 guests rooms and over 17,000 square feet of meeting

and banquet facilities, this hotel is Charlotte's second largest. One of the most outstanding features of the hotel is the Atrium. Characterized by tranquil gardens and reflection pools, it houses both a casual restaurant and a lovely pre-function area. Fine dining is also offered in **Carlyle's**, while **O'Hara's**, one of Charlotte's liveliest nightspots, features live entertainment and complimentary hors d'oeuvres. Other amenities include a state-of-the-art exercise facility, swimming pool, airline ticket office and complimentary limousine service to and from the airport.

Homewood Suites
8340 U.S. Highway 29   *549-8800*
$$$
This spacious, apartment-style suite hotel is comfortably furnished with all the features and amenities you expect, and some that may surprise you. Separate sleeping and living areas, two remote controlled color TVs and a video cassette player are the standard. A complimentary Deluxe Breakfast Buffet is served daily with an evening social hour with a light meal Monday through Thursday. You can work off stress by working out at the exercise center, sports/activity court, swimming pool or whirlpool.

Howard Johnson Lodge
118 E. Woodlawn Rd.   *525-5500*
$-$$
One of four Charlotte properties in the Howard Johnson chain, this 91-room motel is located just off I-77. The location is convenient to the Coliseum and also of-

Photo by John Cress.

The Hyatt Hotel in SouthPark has 262 rooms and one of the best
four-star Italian restaurants in town, Scalini.

fers an outdoor pool. There is a **Howard Johnson Plaza Hotel** at 4419 Tuckaseegee Road (393-9881), and two **Ho Jo Inns**, one at 6426 N. Tryon Street near the University (596-0042) and another at 1-77 and Sunset Road (598-7710).

HYATT HOTEL

5501 Carnegie Blvd.   554-1234
$$$$

All 262 rooms of this SouthPark area Hyatt are beautifully appointed. The hotel has an indoor pool, hot tub, sauna and fitness club. There is no fee for hair dryers, which may be obtained upon request. The Hyatt also boasts one of the best four star Italian restaurants in town, **Scalini**, and has 24-hour room service. You will like the hotel's free valet parking and complimentary airport shuttle service. This is an elegant place to stay, and you'll enjoy the helpful and friendly staff.

LA QUINTA INN-AIRPORT

3100 S. I-85 Service Rd.
393-5306
$

This economy motel on the west side of town is close to restaurants and the airport and is within easy distance of major Charlotte attractions. Guests receive free, unlimited local calls, satellite TV, continental breakfast and 24-hour coffee in the lobby, a courtesy van to

and from the airport, plus other specials. There is an outdoor pool and restaurant nearby. The La Quinta chain has been approved by AAA. Another La Quinta is located on Nations Ford Road near I-77 (522-7110).

MANOR HOUSE APTEL

2800 Selwyn Ave.   377-2621
$-$$

Neither an apartment nor a motel, this lodging facility in one of Charlotte's most exclusive areas, Myers Park, provides a homelike setting at prices almost anyone can afford. It's ideal for people who may be relocating to Charlotte, have relatives in the hospital or need a place for an extended stay without having to sign a lease or install a telephone. There is an outdoor pool and you'll find a grocery store, drugstore, restaurant and shops across the street. Guests staying a week or longer get a discount.

McDONALD'S
INTERNATIONAL PARK INN

2812 Beatties Ford Rd.   399-2378
$

McDonald's is a well-known, black-owned cafeteria in Charlotte. Owner John McDonald, building on his success in business, opened a 105-room, $3 million luxury hotel next door to his eating establishment. Amenities include an exercise room, Jacuzzi, meeting rooms, free airport shuttle and "corporate VIP club" benefits. It also has an outdoor pool and a travel agency. Across the street is the new **Fun City Amusement Center**, with batting range, Putt - Putt Golf, video games and rides. Limousine service is available upon request. Located between I-85 and I-77, the Inn is minutes away from the airport.

OMNI CHARLOTTE HOTEL
222 E. Third Street   *377-6664*
$$$$

     Charlotte's third largest hotel is also one of the most striking and boasts the city's largest ballroom. Located directly across from the new convention center site, the Omni caters to a mostly business clientele, providing complimentary coffee and newspaper for Omni Club members. The 411 rooms, plus privileges with the YMCA Health Club, meeting facilities and the popular **C. Banknight's Bistro & Bar** make this hotel a good Uptown choice.

THE PARK HOTEL
2200 Rexford Rd.   *364-8220*
$$$$

     The Park Hotel's extraordinary staff, dedicated to personal service and attention to detail, makes

Located in the heart of SouthPark, the four-star, four-diamond Park Hotel exemplifies gracious living.

every stay memorable. Located in the heart of SouthPark, this four-star, four-diamond Preferred Hotel property exemplifies gracious living. Although the hotel has 194 rooms and space for small meetings, there's an intimacy here you don't find in a regular hotel. Oversized guest rooms are decorated with 18th-century pieces and original lithography commissioned by the hotel. Guests dine in the authentic New York-style, **Morrocrofts** restaurant and lunch is served on the patio. The hotel features a full-service fitness center, and outdoor swimming pool, complimentary daily newspapers, airport limousine service and turn-down service with chocolates left on the down pillows. It also features live weekend entertainment on the patio.

QUEEN ARMS
20 locations in Charlotte   362-3800
Prices Vary

Every one- and two-bedroom apartment is full-sized, fully furnished and includes cable TV, a private phone, dinnerware, utensils, linens and weekly maid service. Many have pools, exercise rooms, tennis courts. There is no lease and you can stay as long as you like.

THE RADISSON HOTEL AND SUITES EXECUTIVE PARK
5624 Westpark Dr.   527-8000
$$-$$$$

Located at Tyvola Road Exit 5 off I-77, The Radisson Hotel & Suites Executive Park is a full-service hotel with 178 spacious guest rooms that include 34 one-bedroom suites. The **Veranda Restaurant** serves breakfast,

lunch and dinner and **Gershwin Lobby Bar** is available for cocktails and piano music. The Radisson offers 9,600 square feet of meeting space with a beautiful courtyard area for outdoor functions. An exercise facility is available as well as a heated outdoor pool and Jacuzzi. A full breakfast buffet is offered complimentary for all hotel guests. Located only 6 miles from the airport, complimentary airport transportation is provided.

RADISSON PLAZA HOTEL
Two NationsBank Plaza   377-0400
$$$-$$$$

The Radisson is a three-diamond property in the heart of the city. All public rooms and 365 guest rooms, including the deluxe Tower Suite have been refurbished. The hotel offers airport limousine service and its newly renovated restaurant, **Azaleas**. Charlotteans who want to get away, but not too far away, enjoy the Radisson's weekends on the Plaza floor. The **Plaza Club Weekend** includes chilled champagne, chocolates, continental breakfast and complimentary newspaper.

RAMADA INN CAROWINDS
225 Carowinds Blvd.
Ft. Mill, SC   334-4450

This 210-room Ramada Inn is conveniently located near Paramount's Carowinds theme park and Outlet Marketplace shopping center—and shuttle service is offered to both. Amenities include a swimming pool and a game room, cable TV with remote and pay-per-view. Nonsmoking and handicap-accessible rooms are available, as is air-port transportation. Children younger than 18 stay free and this Inn welcomes small pets. **Chow's** restaurant is a great oriental restaurant on the premises and there is a lounge for relaxing after a hard day of work or sight-seeing. Breakfast is free Monday through Friday for guests of the Inn.

RED ROOF INN
I-85 at Billy Graham Pkwy.   *392-2316*
$

At the Red Roof Inn, you get a few extras that most economy motels don't offer—free morning coffee and a weekday newspaper, free ESPN, CNN and first-run movies, unlimited local calls and other extras. This 85-room inn, one of three in Charlotte, is near the airport. Others are located at I-85 and Sugar Creek Road (596-8222) and I-77 at Nation's Ford Road (529-1020).

THE RESIDENCE INN BY MARRIOTT
5800 Westpark Dr.   *527-8110*
$$-$$$

This 80-suite hotel near Tyvola Road and I-77 doesn't look like a hotel, but it's a great place to hang your hat for a few days. Each one- and two-bedroom suite comes with a fully-equipped kitchen, living room, wood burning fireplace, one or two baths, private entrance, plus there is an outdoor heated pool, a spa and a sports court. Continental breakfast, satellite television, grocery shopping service and morning newspaper are all complimentary at this Marriott-franchise hotel. Another Marriott property by the same name is located near University Place (547-1122).

Photo by John Cress.

In addition to 178 guest rooms, The Radisson Hotel and Suites Executive Park offers 9,600 square feet of meeting space with a beautiful courtyard area for outdoor functions.

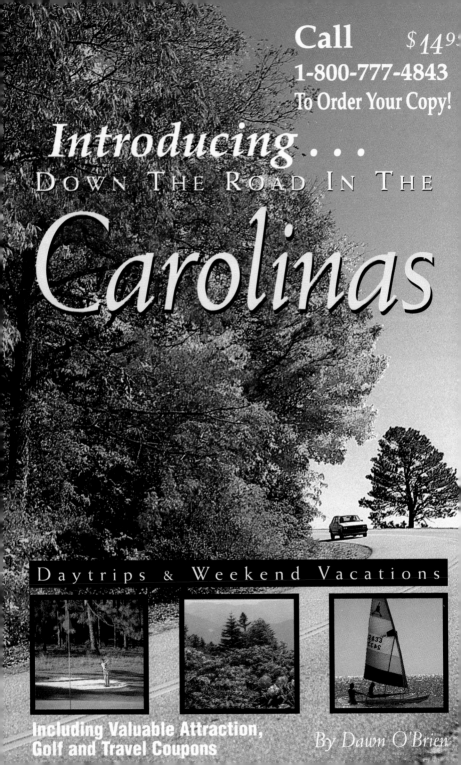

Introducing . . .

DOWN THE ROAD IN THE

Carolinas

Daytrips & Weekend Vacations

Including Valuable Attraction,
Golf and Travel Coupons

By Dawn O'Brien

SHERATON AIRPORT PLAZA HOTEL

I-85 at Billy Graham Pkwy.   392-1200
$$$

    The bright, well-appointed luxury hotel is close to the airport and the new Coliseum. It offers 220 rooms, executive suites and a Presidential suite; a number of meeting rooms; complimentary airport shuttle; fitness center and indoor/outdoor pool. A daily copy of USA Today and a fruit bar are complimentary. **Miami's Bar** offers lively evening entertainment; **Oscar's Restaurant** and the **Atrium Piano Bar** are for quieter moments.

STERLING INN

242 Woodlawn Rd.   525-5454
$

    This upscale economy motel may well be one of Charlotte's best-kept secrets. In lieu of meeting rooms and restaurants, Sterling Inn focuses on large, comfortable rooms that are tastefully decorated. Guests receive USA Today on weekdays. You'll enjoy complimentary morning coffee and Danish in the elegant sunken parlor and wine and coffee from 7 to 9 in the evening. A conference room is available upon request. The Inn, just off I-77, is near a number of nice restaurants.

Bed and Breakfast Inns

601 POPLAR STREET BED & BREAKFAST

601 N. Poplar St.   358-1464
                    (800) 545-2851
    An 1890's landmark in the historic Fourth Ward, this inn features stained glass, antique furnishings, ceiling fans, romantic fireplaces and a wrap-around porch that overlooks a splashing stone fountain. Conveniently located, guests can walk to restaurants, galleries, theaters, museums, shops and offices in Uptown. Innkeepers Ashley Parlier and John McJunkin go that extra mile to make guests feel welcome with complimentary beer and wine in the afternoon and a full breakfast to start the day.

ELIZABETH BED & BREAKFAST

2145 E. 5th St.   358-1368
$$

    This quaint home offering antique brass beds and Laura Ashley decor is conveniently located (5 minutes to Uptown) in the historic Elizabeth community, the only Charlotte neighborhood named for a woman. Old-style Southern hospitality welcomes you, and you'll appreciate a hearty continental breakfast in the courtyard.

THE HOMEPLACE

5901 Sardis Rd.   365-1936
$$-$$$

    You can take a real trip down memory lane during a visit to The Homeplace at the corner of Sardis and Rama roads. Sleep under a comfy quilt in a four-poster surrounded by family heirlooms, including paintings by John Gentry, owner Peggy Dearien's father. Then wake up to the sounds of birds just as the first owner, the Rev. R.G. Miller, did at the turn of the century in what was then rural countryside. Enjoy one of Peggy's full breakfasts and discuss the morning news with her husband Frank. The Homeplace has four guest rooms, two with private baths, plus a two-bedroom unit with bath. The perfect place for your wedding night!

THE INN ON PROVIDENCE
6700 Providence Rd.   366-6700
$$-$$$

You won't find a more charming hostess than Darlene McNeill, who operates this bed and breakfast in Southeast Charlotte with her husband Dan. Choose one of five rooms, including Scarlet's Victorian lair. Enjoy reading a book in the warm, cozy living room or chatting with Dan and Darlene in the evening – or simply relax on the verandah. One of Darlene's full breakfasts will round out your memorable stay.

THE INN UPTOWN
129 North Poplar St.   342-2800
                               (800) 959-1990
$$$-$$$$

Hornet's Nest Liniment, concocted by one of the original owners, Walter Mullen, in 1897 is no longer available at this beautifully restored Bed and Breakfast. However, the whirlpool bath, at the top of a spiral iron staircase in the Tower Suite is bound to soothe your muscle aches. A recent groom delivered a half bushel of rose petals that were spread over this room's Queen-size bed. Less romantic souls will appreciate the Inn's showers (with three body sprays), which kind of gives the feeling of being in an automatic car wash. Four of the handsomely appointed rooms have fireplaces, and all have writing desks and phones with modem capabilities. Fax (704-342-2222) and copier machines are

available along with a dry cleaning service, a morning newspaper and a meeting room. Guests receive a complimentary full breakfast at this three-story brick home, historically known as the Bagley-Mullen house.

THE MOREHEAD INN
1122 East Morehead Street
376-3357
$$-$$$

If you are looking for a return to more gracious times, this 1917 Inn located in the Dilworth area is a splendid cross between a 1700's Pennsylvania farmhouse and bungalow-style white clapboard. The Inn has gone through a major metamorphosis since its happy marriage with Churchill Galleries. There are now 10 richly appointed antique filled rooms, some with private balconies, sun rooms and whirlpools. Breakfast is served in the cheerful but elegant dining room overlooking the courtyard. Once the private home of wealthy automobile dis-

The Inn Uptown

tributor Charles and Marjorie Coddington, the home hosts numerous receptions, and the carriage house at the rear is frequently used for corporate retreats.

ROSWELL INN

2320 Roswell Avenue   332-4915
$$

You can wake up to the appetizing smell of homemade biscuits and rolls, or maybe coffee cake being prepared by effervescent innkeeper Lea Harrison from her own special (passed down from generations) recipe. During the warmer season you can dine on the terrace in one of Charlotte's loveliest gardens, then walk beneath towering trees through Myers Park, one of the city's oldest neighborhoods. This beautifully decorated, family heirloom-filled home is an inviting place to loll over afternoon Russian tea or old fashioned lemonade with warm-from-the-oven cookies. .

STILL WATERS

6221 Amos Smith Road   399-6299
$-$$$

Since a boat ramp and boat slips are part of the Still Waters property, bring a boat if you have one. If you don't, just sit on the dock or the deck or walk through the woods. Tennis, volleyball, basketball, etc., can be enjoyed on the new Sport Court where you can work up an appetite for the full breakfast served daily. Located on Lake Wylie, this rustic, log-sided 1930's home provides the perfect escape for world weary travelers. The home has two bedrooms plus a bedroom suite.

Photo by John Cress.

In less than ten years, the Charlotte-Douglas International Airport terminal has expanded two concourses and added a third with moving walkways.

Inside
Airports

Charlotte/Douglas International

Since many out-of-towners' first introduction to Charlotte is through their arrival at **Charlotte/ Douglas International Airport**, their first impression "...should be a good one," says Airport Horticulturist Joy McCain. "This is Charlotte's front door...and when travelers get off that plane, we want the landscaping to let them know where they are. People are usually tired after their trip, and walking out of the terminal to see green grass, Southern camellias and colorful flowers makes them happy. It lifts their spirits, calms their nerves and prepares them to go on their way."

Rising to the upper level terminal entrance, Raymond Kaskey's fluid-like stone sculpture of Queen Charlotte grabs your attention through the sheer drama of the piece. Equally enticing is McCain's garden-type landscaping. The handsome magnolia trees and bright flower beds tucked into manicured green lawns work as a welcoming appetizer to this beautiful city. Whether you're coming home or going away, the airport's landscaping acts as a "We're glad you're here" message to travelers.

Charlotte/Douglas International completed a 1,000 foot runway extension in late '93. The extension crosses part of West Boulevard, and Wilmont Road-Terminal Drive was extended to provide direct access to the airport's air cargo area and USAir's maintenance hangar and training facilities.

During the next several years, the airport will spend about $21 million to build additional aircraft parking ramps and warehouse space, adjacent to the new runway extension, for cargo airlines. Two new cargo buildings opened in the fall of '93, bringing the total on-airport warehouse space to more than 500,000 square feet. Also planned are facilities to accommodate U.S. Customs, cold storage cargo and livestock.

In less than ten years, the terminal has expanded two concourses and added a third with moving walkways. The newest concourse, Concourse D, opened in 1990 and includes 16 commuter gates and four international gates. The airport's South Terminal expansion includes additional moving walkways and two new domestic gates, scheduled for completion in the fall of '94.

And you'll see a brand new look inside the terminal. A gazebo-shaped crown is the centerpiece of a newly remodeled 195,000-square-foot area called "Queen's Court." Taking pride in the region's handiworks, there are regional gift boutiques as well as specialty shops, familiar fast-food places and even a gourmet coffee shop.

Travelers now pass through three central security checkpoints along the shopping mall as they make their way to the departure gates.

Another new and welcome perk for business travelers is a carpeted public lounge behind the gazebo that gives the feel of a quiet hotel lobby. The lounge is attended by food and beverage wait persons. In addition, desks, phones and other business paraphernalia make the lounge a convenient place to nail down some ideas or make contact with a client while waiting for a flight.

Charlotte/Douglas International has around 500 daily scheduled flights, with 147 non-stop services offered to approximately 150 cities. Non-stop flights are offered to and from London, Frankfort, Nassau, Bahamas, Bermuda, Ontario and the Grand Caymans, a newly acquired route. And ticketed international travelers can shop in the duty-free shop.

The airport is easily accessible from all of Mecklenburg County, via either I-85 or I-77, the Billy Graham Parkway or Wilkinson Boulevard. From Uptown, it's only a 15-minute drive to the airport.

Charlotte's airport ranks 21st among U.S. airports and 33rd world-wide in total passenger traffic. And this past year, USAir's 30 additional flights made Charlotte/Douglas the airline's largest hub.

These recent airport expansions and remodelings have been a clear signal to economic development people that our airport has been the catalytic impetus for the area's healthy growth.

Frequently Called Numbers

If you need information, here are a few of the most frequently called numbers for the Airport.

Aviation Dept.	359-4000
Advisory Commission	359-4848
Emergency Medical & Lost and Found	359-4012
Public Parking	359-4055
Terminal Information	359-4013
Paging & Welcome Center	359-4027

Major Carriers

Eight major carriers serve the Charlotte/Douglas facility:

American	800-433-7300
British Airways	800-247-9297
Delta	372-3000
Lufthansa	800-645-3800
Northwest Air Lines-Domestic	800-225-2525
Northwest Air Lines-International	800-447-4747
TWA	343-0366
United	800-241-6522
USAir	376-0235

Ticketing

For your convenience, most of the airlines maintain ticketing offices in the Uptown area and USAir, the airline with the most flights out of Charlotte/Douglas, has five ticket offices scattered throughout the city. Check with the airline to find the office most convenient for you.

Airport Transportation Services

When arriving by car, you have several options for parking. The short-term lot costs $.75 per half hour, to a maximum of $6.00 in a 24-hour period. There are two long-term parking facilities which charge $4.00 for each 24-hour period. Some of the rental car companies also offer long term parking for a nominal fee.

There is no city bus service. But, rental cars, taxis, limousine services and the new airport shuttle (Grayline Shuttle Express) are available. Listed below are the rental car and taxi companies, plus a representative list of some of the limousine services. To get to Uptown, cab fare will run you about $12; limousine service is charged according to the number of people in your party.

AIRPORT SHUTTLE	
Grayline Shuttle Express	359-8687

TAXIS	
American Cab Company	375-1010
A A Prestige Taxi	332-8001
Charlotte Checker Inc.	333-1111
Crown Cab Company	334-6666
Diamond Cab Company	333-3030
Eagle Cab	525-2990
Nations Cab Inc.	377-8066
Yellow Cab Airport Shuttle	391-1111

LIMOUSINE SERVICES	
Cameo Limousine Inc.	846-8483
Charlotte Limousine	377-2999
K & K Limo & Shuttle	394-6919
Rose Limousine Ltd.	522-8258

CAR RENTALS	
Avis	359-4586
Budget	359-5000
Dollar	359-4700
General	392-5593
Hertz	359-0114
National	800-227-7368
Thrifty	394-6588

Many hotels offer complimentary transportation and you can call them from courtesy phones in the baggage area of the terminal.

Other Airports

WILGROVE AIRPORT
10525 ParktonRd. 545-1875

It's a well-kept secret, but there is another airport in Mecklenburg County. Located due east of the city off Albemarle Road, Wilgrove Airport has served private and commercial planes since the early 1970s. The facility has two runways totaling 3,200 feet and offers hangars and tie-down services, maintenance, fuel, flying lessons and airplane charters and leasing. The **Metrolina Flying Club**, based here, has a staff of professional instructors and offers qualifying for all pilot ratings from private through ATP.

Photo by Kendra Grubb, CPCC © 1994.

The Carillon Building in Uptown houses the Hans and Walter Bechtler Gallery.
"The Garden" by Jerry Peart, is a permanent installation of the Gallery.

Inside
Arts

*I*n Charlotte, art is taking on a serendipitous image—showing up where you'd least expect to find it. You know you're going to find art in every discipline from theater to music and dance at **Spirit Square** and in our new **North Carolina Blumenthal Performing Arts Center**. It's a given that you'll find art at the **Mint Museum**, art galleries, on our college campuses, and to some extent at our varied outdoor festivals.

The surprise occurs when you run across a fresco by renowned artist, Ben Long, in the **NationsBank Corporate Center** at 100 N. Tryon. After all, banks are where people transact business. And while it may not be surprising to see sculpture in a private park, you might be surprised to find that Steven Siegel's work in the Carillon Building Park, entitled "Bridge," is actually a biodegradable newspaper sculpture that you can walk across.

You don't usually anticipate discovering an art gallery in the lobby of a business. But the Carillon Building is where you'll find the Hans and Walter Bechtler Gallery that staged "Our Public Image," an exhibit with a video of regional sculptures, monuments, buildings, obelisks and landmarks. In the same gallery, hanging from the Carillon's three-story ceiling, is Jean Tinguely's light flashing mobile, guaranteed to bring out at least one chuckle. As concluded in the video by painter and poet, Willie Stratford, Sr., "Art is not what you do with your hands. It's what you do with your heart. It represents the soul of a city."

You certainly don't expect to be driving along the expressways and find art, bigger than life, on a billboard. This daring incongruity can make you scratch your head and wonder, "What kind of a town is this that puts the work of regional painters on billboards?"

It's the kind of town that isn't afraid to use nontraditional methods to get the word out on art in Charlotte. Since not everyone attends performances or even goes to the library or movies, a different strategy had to be found to reach these citizens. A couple of years ago, the Artscape billboards, as they were referred to, became the project of Adams Outdoor Advertising in partnership with the Charlotte/ Mecklenburg Arts and Science Council and the Mint Museum of Art. The billboards, initially slated to remain in place for two months, stayed up for six months buoyed by such positive comments as, "Thanks, for bringing art into my day." These, and other comments were heard from some of the 202,000 motorists who viewed these rotating billboards appearing daily along Brookshire, South and Independence Boulevards. Needless to say, a repeat performance was scheduled for the next year.

For many summers Uptown business people and shoppers have spent lunch outside listening to the free **SummerStage** lunch time concert series featuring everything from jazz to beach music. The shows rotate among Two First Union (301 S. Tryon), Carillon's Park (201 W. Trade) and NationsBank Plaza (101 S. Tryon), which is another way to sandwich a little art into the workaday world in unusual places.

Do you expect to run into art on New Year's Eve? Every year the Arts and Science Council throws a tremendous performing arts party in the heart of Uptown's cultural zone. For a mere $5 and free parking, you can celebrate at this alcohol-free event. You can attend short programs of music, theatrical vignettes, storytelling, dance, etc., performed in various churches, business and hotel lobbies and stages. Thousands of people crowd the area

to watch the New Year's Ball descend over Charlotte at midnight.

A few years back, under the **Charlotte Public Art Program**, city government passed a law requiring that one percent of all new public building costs be allocated to some form of artistic expression. Usually, but not always, this has manifested itself in a statue. It is also why you'll see artistic variety gracing our buildings. As you might imagine, the public has not always agreed with the judges' choice of art or the artist's concept for these buildings. In fact, such a loud outcry arose concerning one artist's concept for the new coliseum that perturbed citizens forced the judges to change artists. This incident tells you how citizens feel about art (or how they feel about how their tax dollars are spent). Either way, Charlotteans care about art, say so, and are heard.

Shopping Malls are where you go to shop, not be entertained, right? SouthPark Mall will play more than that traditional role beginning in the summer of 1994 when one of the Charlotte Symphony's most relaxing programs—**Summer Pops in the Park**—will move from Freedom Park to SouthPark Mall. The Pops will perform during selected weekends in June and July. Once again, due to SouthPark's sponsorship, the concerts are free.

Unquestionably, one of the most exciting things happening on the art scene today is the infusion of art into every school subject (yes, math and science, too) in our Charlotte/Mecklenburg School System. The plan was initially targeted at

Charlotte's two arts magnet schools, but will spill over into the traditional school system now that funding has been received.

Educators have long believed that art may provide the catalyst to help students learn difficult subjects. An artistic introduction to a traditional subject can somehow access a different area of the brain. When something is fun to do (art), then rigid learning barriers can be lessened. This first step in implementing the Charlotte Arts and Science Council Plan to make Charlotte part of a national model arts education program began last summer in a Teacher Training Institute at Spirit Square. In the past students were exposed to art only through band or traditional art classes. No more. Artists and arts organizations will be part of the resource package that endeavors to expand a variety of programs in the public schools. The phasing in of this new educational concept will introduce children to a different, more creative way of learning.

The **Charlotte Arts and Science Council** (official watchdog of the arts that raises and disburses money to affiliated arts groups) continues to raise more money each year. And now that most of the classic arts are climbing out of debt (Charlotte Repertory Theatre repaid its $40,000 loan from the Council; the Charlotte Symphony's new programs and financial direction is moving out of red ink), the Council is now working toward developing a major endowment program. This two-year endowment campaign envisions raising between $18 and $30

million dollars in order to bring long-term stability to the arts community.

You could say that preparation for today's cultural climate actually began pre-recession, back in 1975 with the first Cultural Action Plan's building program. In those days, we were talent rich but had insufficient places to show it off. Now, $105 million later, the results show in our new and refurbished buildings.

The first is the twice renovated First Baptist Church, located in Uptown Charlotte, now known as **Spirit Square**. This historic building has become a multipurpose arts facility.

Across the street is **Discovery Place**, named by *Good Housekeeping* as one of the ten best hands-on science museums in the country and awarded the honor of top tourist attraction of the year by the Southeast Tourism Society. The museum offers a tropical rain forest, Planetarium and hi-tech Omnimax Theater, reminiscent of Cinerama of the '50s.

A few blocks away you'll see the restoration of the former 1907 Little Rock AME Zion Church that evolved into the **Afro-American Cultural Center**. Here the focus is on preserving African-American culture through multi-cultural events of theater, dance and music.

The circa 1836 **Mint Museum**, is yet another building that tripled in size during its restoration.

Then our *creme de la creme* of art buildings debuted in November 1992 when the dazzling **North Carolina Blumenthal Center for the Per-**

forming Arts opened in the Uptown NationsBank Complex. Everyone got in on the act of erecting this building. Charlotteans voted $15 million in bonds for the project and the state allocated an additional $15 million. Over 67,000 children contributed a quarter each to the Performing Arts Campaign and corporate and private donations fused this dream into reality. The foundation has raised a significant general endowment fund to supplement operating expenses and subsidize lower rents for performing groups. This awesome, five-level building with its dramatic marble and mosaic tile interior includes the 2,100-seat **Belk Theatre** performance hall for the symphony and opera and the 440-seat smaller **Booth Theatre** for local and regional theatrical productions. For convenience, a glass walkway connects the center to a guarded parking garage.

Now that our buildings are in place in what has become designated as the Cultural District, the onus is on all of the groups to pull out all the quality stops. That's where the second 1990 Cultural Action Plan has begun to take over. This plan, which was based on a study done in Charlotte by Dr. Thomas Wolf, an art consultant from Cambridge, Massachusetts, recommended better programming and administrative and financial accountability. This means that arts groups have got to make their dollars count and improve their operations, or their funding will be axed. As might be expected, the appearance of sacrificing art for bookkeeping has gone to the mat several times since its implementa-

tion. The good news is that in order to trim costs and provide better programming, the **Charlotte Symphony** has merged with the **Charlotte Oratorio** and the **Charlotte City Ballet** has merged with the **North Carolina Dance Theatre**.

Don't get us wrong, although the Arts and Science Council (ASC) is the prime arts organization, it is not the only game in town. For over thirty years, the **Golden Circle Theatre**, formerly of the Mint Museum (one of Charlotte's oldest theatrical groups), was self-supporting before its merger with the **Charlotte Repertory Theatre**. Other groups such as the **Charlotte Philharmonic**, the **Charlotte Choir Boys** and other art groups may not be thriving players without ASC funding, but they are still very much in the game.

Some of this is pretty heady stuff. Okay, it's downright exciting to be touted as a hub of culture, particularly when you look at the next plank in the second Cultural Action Plan—Arts Education. That plan stipulated that "Charlotte/Mecklenburg could become a national model in arts education with proper monitoring and support." This spurred the Arts and Science Council to ask for and receive a $1 million challenge grant for arts education programs in our public schools from the National Endowment for the Arts, (the most money ever awarded by the NEA to a local arts council). This dovetailed beautifully with Charlotte School Superintendent John Murphy's new plan of 7 magnet schools (specialized schools), two of which are for arts education. Northwest joins the other

*The dazzling North Carolina Blumenthal Center for the Performing Arts
opened in November 1992.*

magnet schools in becoming Charlotte's first arts-oriented magnet high school.

Before Charlotte had an inkling that the city was being considered as "a national model for arts education," our arts organizations were already at work instilling art appreciation on two levels: First, by making it possible for over 75,000 school children to attend performances of the **Charlotte Symphony**; for **Opera Carolina** to perform for over 100,000 children in classrooms throughout the county; for thousands of high school and college students to attend the **Golden Circle Theatre** and **Charlotte Repertory Theatre**, not to forget the **Children's Theatre** and **Afro-American Children's Theatre**, two groups that train, perform and tour exclusively for and with children. Fortunately, this spectator list goes on.

On the second level, arts organizations have established programs that instill art through participation. For example, Opera Carolina's **OperaFest**, a one week summer program for minority teens, encourages them to develop skills essential for individual achievement, lets them be a part of decision-making and problem-solving as they learn the techniques involved in creating an opera or musical theater work of their own. Then too, the Charlotte Symphony offers two separate programs—the **Junior Youth Symphony** for younger children and the **Charlotte Youth Symphony** for teenagers. Both groups of youngsters are admitted through auditions judged by symphony musicians. The 50 to 60 member groups perform throughout the community at churches, colleges and at the Symphony's Designer House. From this exposure, it is not unusual for a youth member to graduate to Symphony Orchestra status.

Three years ago, the Golden Circle Theatre Series (of the Charlotte Repertory Theatre) in a joint venture with Charlotte/ Mecklenburg Schools sponsored a contest based on student research of *A Man For All Seasons*—the theater's opening production at the Performing Arts Center. Senior high school contestants were judged on best essay or sculpture. The incentive to stimulate student creativity was an all-expense-paid weekend trip to London.

A community is unique that holds the arts in such high regard. It is willing to go to unprecedented lengths to safeguard its artistic heritage while nurturing future incubation via nontraditional marketing strategies.

On a weekly basis, one of the best ways to find out what's happening in the arts is through the *Charlotte Observer's* extensive listings, indepth features and interviews in its Sunday Arts Section and on Friday in the Extra section you'll find out what's going on around town and in the Carolinas. You might want to call **Charlotte Arts and Science Council** at 372-9667. The offices are located at 227 W. Trade Street in Suite 250 in the Carillon Building.

The following is a guide broken down into sections on theater, dance, music, visual arts and writing. Enjoy!

Theater

Theater has never before had such a promising future in Charlotte. Though High Point's Shakespeare Festival Stage Company is a fierce statewide competitor, the past mergers of the **Charlotte Repertory Company** with **PlayWorks** and the **Golden Circle Theatre** may very well place North Carolina as a worthy entry on the national level. To fill out this bouquet, new companies are sprouting all over the place, such as **Innovative Theatre**. This group commands a following among teens and others who may be into unconventional theater fare. Three years ago, **Matthews Community Theatre** was organized from seed money provided by the Matthews City Council and is going into its fourth season, adding a special production for children. **Theatre Charlotte**, formerly known as the Little Theatre, remains at the forefront of community theater and in recent years has added more musicals and classics to its slate. Another theater group with a different focus is **People First Players**, an improvisational group sponsored by the Mental Health Association. The audience (church, civic and mental health associated groups) suggests the characters and situations to a cast of performers who are individuals diagnosed with mental illness.

On the whole, the scene is pretty diverse with musicals at **Central Piedmont Community College** (CPCC), **Theatre Charlotte**, touring companies and high schools. Light to sophisticated comedies, including contemporary dramas are found at **Charlotte Repertory Theatre**; new and experimental offerings at **PlayWorks,** and vintage to classical comedies and dramas at **Golden Circle. Children's Theatre**, **Omimeo Mime Theatre** and **African-American Children's Theatre**, as well as public and private schools offer plays appropriate for young audiences. You might also want to check into the **First Friday of the Month Club for Working Actors**. Paul Kronsberg (535-5775) is the contact for this organization.

AFRICAN-AMERICAN CHILDREN'S THEATRE
372-7410 or 372-5000

Children from the ages of 5 to 18 are given the opportunity to express their unique creativeness in a series of workshops that include dance, storytelling, juggling, writing and exploring Africa. Each year, the workshops work toward a central theme that culminates in a theatrical production that is performed at the Afro-American Cultural Center, Spirit Square, churches and schools.

CENTRAL PIEDMONT COMMUNITY COLLEGE
1201 Elizabeth Ave. 342-6534

Theater performances of Broadway-style shows in Pease Auditorium on campus are a treat for locals and visitors alike. Each summer a show is included for children, such as *Aladdin*. And its popular, professionally staged productions of summer musicals and comedies, which now bring in some of the talent, are often sold out.

CHARLOTTE REPERTORY THEATRE
345 North College St.
Box Office   333-8587

This professional theater company was established in 1977 to provide entertainment and to heighten appreciation of professional theater. As the area's only repertory company, it presents a cycle of new, contemporary and classical works. The Repertory Theatre provides a professional opportunity for area artists as well as providing the community with wonderful diverse professional theater from a contemporized version of Robert Bolt's *A Man For All Seasons* to last season's popular *Breaking Legs*. An additional benefit is its new play festival of staged readings of new plays in progress. Under the same umbrella, Charlotte Repertory now offers both the Playworks and the Golden Circle Theatre Series. Performances are held at the Blumenthal Performing Arts Center. The 1994/95 season will stage *The Sisters Rosensweig, Signature*, a musical, *Five Guys Named Moe* on the Centerstage series; *Someone Who'll Watch Over Me, Oleanna* and *Three Hotels* on the Playworks series of contemporary works; and *Lost In Yonkers, A Midsummer Night's Dream* and *Inherit The Wind* on the classical Golden Circle series.

CHILDREN'S THEATRE
OF CHARLOTTE
1017 E. Morehead St.   333-8983

With both a production and education program, The Children's Theatre is the place for burgeoning Sarah Bernhardts and Lawrence Oliviers. The production program has four components—Mainstage,

productions geared for the entire family; Second Stage, a series of plays performed by and for young actors and audiences in the eighth grade and up; Tarradiddle Players, the touring component of the theater and Special Events, productions not produced by the Theatre. The education program offers kids aged 3 to 18 classes and workshops in theater arts, creative drama and dance. Founded in 1948 by the Junior League, the Children's Theatre became independent in 1952. Programs and performances are held in its 300-seat facility on East Morehead. Next year children and adults can see: *Stuart Little, Tom Sawyer, Teeny Tiny Tales, A Christmas Carol, Tis The Season, The Glass Menagerie, The Ice Wolf, Cinderella's Of The World* and *Pinocchio*, as well as performances of the Gray Seal Puppets that will stage *The Emperor's New Clothes* and *Gnomes At Christmas*. Storyteller Joyce Greer is also on the schedule, and the Omimeo Mime Theatre will perform *Mime Time*.

DAVIDSON COLLEGE
P.O. Box 340
Davidson, NC 28036   892-2000

The Davidson Theatre Department puts on three major productions each year. Performances are held at Hodson Hall in the John Cunningham Fine Arts Building.

DAVIDSON COMMUNITY PLAYERS
P.O. Box 76
Davidson, NC 28036
Contact: Kim Beard   892-7953

Founded in 1965, this community theater for the North Mecklenburg area presents two major summer productions, a winter children's play, "fireside" readings, dinner theater productions and receptions.

THE ENSEMBLE COMPANY
333-8983

This company is cosponsored by Children's Theatre and Charlotte/Mecklenburg Schools, and students receive school credit for their work. The company is cast only by audition and is open to all high school students, but it is intended for the very serious drama student. Students engage in intense study and acting techniques for nine-month classes with theatre professional teachers and directors. Two productions are staged each year in Children's Theatre's downstairs **Black Box Theatre**. The Ensemble Company is Charlotte's only pre-professional training program for young actors.

COMEDY MYSTERY THEATRE
DINNER THEATRE

Grapevine Cafe
Behind Park Road Shopping Ctr.   *523-5600*
This professional, for-profit dinner theater writes and produces its own comic/farce mystery productions. These are text book murder mysteries that involve the audience in solving the crime. Productions change on a 12-week basis. Theatre and dinner is $29.95 per person.

HISTORICAL OUTDOOR DRAMA
843-2300

Performed annually each weekend evening in June, the Historical Outdoor Drama *Listen and Remember*, staged in the outdoor amphitheater of Waxhaw (off N.C. 75), portrays American history lived by early pioneers of the Old Waxhaw Settlement, among them the family of young Andrew Jackson. The audience watches a reenactment of the Revolutionary War and the thrust for freedom from those early settlers.

INNOVATIVE THEATRE
342-1889

This theater company, now in its seventh year, has made giant inroads with the college, high school and young professional sets with such imaginative productions as *The Search For Signs Of Intelligent Life In The Universe*. The purpose of the theater lies in experimentation with written material and its dramatic presentation. The company believes that truly exciting theater comes from the independence of the artist to pursue artistic passion in addressing various social, political and religious concerns of contemporary society, presenting theater that's entertaining as well as relevant. Innovative Theatre reaches out to a larger audience than that which currently attends local theater, thus sustaining the life of theater in our community. The *Charlotte Observer* cited two of the company's jobbed-in plays in its top ten list of best touring plays, and *Creative Loafing* chose one of its directors, Alan Poindexter, as Theatre Person of the Year.

You can catch this company's performances at Spirit Square for less money than some other theater productions around town.

JOHNSON C. SMITH UNIVERSITY
100 Beatties Ford Rd.   *378-1177*

Performing in historic Biddle Hall, JCSU puts on two plays a year, plus a Christmas program. The productions are diverse, ranging from Neil Simon comedies to ancient Greek tragedies.

MATTHEWS COMMUNITY THEATRE
100 McDowell St.
Matthews
Contact: Chuck Haley   *847-5480*

Now in its third year of production, the Matthews Community Theatre, organized as the result of a Matthews survey, is self supporting and branching out in its new season. Having been successful with Broadway comedies done with a slightly different twist, the all-volunteer company will be staging more plays using these techniques this season. Volunteers are always needed for set building, costumes and the many other tasks involved in play production.

METROLINA THEATRE ASSOCIATION
Contact: Keith Marti   *333-8587*

This is the umbrella agency for theater in the region. It supports and promotes growth of dramatic arts in the Metrolina area. It debuted in 1984, and currently serves 50 members and maintains contact with 50 additional theater companies.

OMIMEO MIME THEATRE
Contact: Hardin Minor   *375-4012*

Mime and clown theatre performances are given here for both adults and children. Each January, the theatre sponsors a mime festival and circus, offering shows and workshops. Tours and residencies are available to educational institutions.

OVENS AUDITORIUM
2700 E. Independence Blvd.   *372-3600*

Ovens Auditorium, formerly the city's main performing arts center with 2,603 seats, books arts-oriented productions locally, but also offers touring Broadway plays as well as musical productions and other commercial events. In addition, Ovens provides space for such community events as dance recitals and graduations, etc. It is located on the major thoroughfare of Independence Boulevard and is easily accessible.

PEOPLE FIRST PLAYERS
Contact: Frank Dominguez   *365-3454*

An improvisational group whose focus is on reducing the stigma of mental illness, the players are made up of a group of individuals diagnosed with mental illness. The players rehearse through improvisational oriented workshops, then carry their message to the community. Organized since '91, the players have performed for over 45 different civic, church and mental health associated agencies, while touring throughout North Carolina. Each production is original, calling for the audience to suggest the characters and topic within special guidelines.

QUEENS COLLEGE THEATRE
1900 Selwyn Ave.   *332-7121*

Queens puts on two major plays each year, plus a variety of smaller productions presented around campus.

Spirit Square is an Uptown center for community and performing arts.

TARRADIDDLE PLAYERS

1017 E. Morehead St.   *342-0730*

Since 1971, The Tarradiddle Players, founded by the late Connie Welch, has provided the experience of quality theatre to young people throughout the Carolinas. The troupe, now the touring arm of Children's Theatre, performs at its theater and at other Charlotte facilities, as well as at schools, to community groups and at festivals. It also offers children's theater workshops for groups.

THEATRE CHARLOTTE

501 Queens Rd.
Box Office   *334-9128*

Theatre Charlotte, founded in 1927 as the Little Theatre of Charlotte, is the grande dame of theater in Charlotte—and North Carolina—as the oldest community theater in the state. Over the years, it has performed more than 350 main stage productions to more than 500,000 people. The company produces six plays a year and has a full-time staff of four, plus hundreds of volunteers. Celebrating its 68th consecutive season, Theatre Charlotte is a nonprofessional theater company. Workshops, musicals and classic Broadway plays are given every other month, year round. Next year's slate includes: *Assassins, Comedy of Errors, The Cemetery Club, A Raisin In The Sun* and *A Funny Thing Happened On The Way To The Forum.*

UNIVERSITY OF NORTH CAROLINA AT CHARLOTTE

Department of Performing Arts   *547-2599*

The Performing Arts Department produces four to five major productions during the school year, as well as occasional student productions. Held at Rowe Auditorium, the plays range from Shakespeare to modern comedies and from dramas to musicals.

Dance

In recent years Charlotteans have come to respect and appreciate dance as an art form. Original, innovative dances that might premiere in New York can now be seen right here in the Queen City—something that would never have occurred a dozen years ago. Much of the change in attitude toward dance can be attributed to Katharyn Horne and Mary Ann Mee who organized **Dance Central**, a professional repertory company, about ten years ago. (**Catchin' On**, a jazz company, evolved as a division of Dance Central.) You can start training for Dance Central and other companies as a youngster.

The Ballet School, home of the **Charlotte City Ballet** is under the direction of Claudia Folts Mercury. This excellent school offering dance opportunities that are hard to duplicate anywhere in the country, except in the larger cities, is in constant demand to perform at festivals and private schools. The Charlotte School of Ballet is an outgrowth of the Charlotte Regional Ballet Company of the 1970s. Performers are selected by audition.

There are dance studios and schools for children all over the city and the suburbs. Insiders agree that some of the best training is given by **The Ballet School**, Barbara Morgan's **Rhythm Dance Studio, Ltd.**, and **Charlotte School of Ballet**. Children may also take classes through **QUILL** at Queens College, **Spirit Square**, **Community School of the Arts** and **Children's Theatre**. Adult classes are available at **Central Piedmont Community College, Queens**, the **YWCAs**, **Spirit Square** and **Community School of the Arts**.

North Carolina Dance Theatre, founded in 1970, moved to Charlotte from Winston-Salem in 1990 and has enjoyed a warm and enthusiastic welcome in the community. Touring extensively through Europe and America, NCDT has performed at Spoleto, American Dance Festival in Durham and the Aspen Dance Festival in Colorado. It has become one of the most sought after and highly-acclaimed professional dance companies performing today and is probably the state's most widely known cultural ambassador. Under the artistic direction of Salvatore Aiello, the Dance Theatre has developed an exciting and versatile repertoire that ranges in style from breathtaking interpretations of full-length classical ballets to bold, witty and moving contemporary pieces. Performances

planned for the 1994/95 season include *Feast Of Ashes, Concerto Barocco* and *Rite Of Spring* done in repertory in October. *The Nutcracker* performed at Christmas, *Carmina Burana, Bach Brandenburg Three, Rodeo, Homage*. Tickets to the performances are available through the Performing Arts Center Box Office, 372-1000 or call NCDT at 372-0101.

A couple of years ago NCDT opened **DancePlace**, the official school of North Carolina Dance Theatre. DancePlace offers a wide range of the classes and dance-related educational activities for all ages and abilities; however, the school's primary focus is to train aspiring young professional dancers. Its studios are located at 800 N. College Street.

Clogging and square dancing have become very popular in recent years. These dance forms, indigenous to the Appalachian Mountains, are now performed all over the Southeast. Square dances are usually executed by four couples in a set who perform various moves that are given by a "caller." Dancers use a smooth step, a clogging step, or a combination of both. Men and women usually wear matching western outfits. Clogging—a foot-stomping dance that combines shuffles and taps—can be done with a partner or independently. International folk dancing is also an option in Charlotte.

If you are interested in finding out more about dance in Charlotte, just contact any of the groups listed below:

CLASSICAL BALLET AND MODERN DANCE GROUPS

Companies

CHARLOTTE CITY BALLET COMPANY
8612 Monroe Rd.   536-0615

NORTH CAROLINA DANCE THEATRE
P.O. Box 32667   372-0101

DANCE CENTRAL-CATCHIN' ON
1201 Elizabeth Ave.   342-6982

Schools

THE BALLET SCHOOL
8612 Monroe Rd.   536-0615

THE CHARLOTTE SCHOOL OF BALLET
627 S. Sharon Amity Rd.   366-9675

BARBARA MORGAN'S RHYTHM DANCE STUDIO, LTD.
9506-C Monroe Rd.   845-5260

COMMUNITY SCHOOL OF THE ARTS
200 W. Trade St.   377-4187

DANCE UNLIMITED
5606 E. Independence Blvd.   536-2293

Music

Charlotte celebrates through music. You can even have it for lunch in the summer. We're not kidding. The Charlotte Chamber of Commerce shells out good money so that you can take in a two-hour long **SummerStage Concert** while you munch away. Different Uptown locations play host to everything from jazz (Daryle Ryce) to exotic steel guitars (Don Baptiste).

The summer also brings the Symphony Orchestra's lighter musical offerings in the **Summer Pops Concert** series that has now been moved to SouthPark. Everyone usually brings a blanket and picnic food. Each summer heralds the popular **Folk Music Festival**, now held at Paramount Carowinds, where sing-a-longs mix well with Scottish, Blue Grass and Spirituals. Edging toward fall, you'll enjoy the September 10th and 11th weekend Jazz Festival that has also moved to Paramount Carowinds. Or drop in any Thursday night at **The Celtic Trader**, the international music store that has moved to 645-G in Pressley Park, off South Tryon Street (527-3800). This is where you'll hear local folk artists roll out their repertoire.

In the classical vein the city offers our over-60-year-old **Charlotte Symphony Orchestra and Oratorio Singers**, the **Charlotte Philharmonic Orchestra, Opera Carolina**, **Charlotte Community Concerts** and many other worthwhile groups. Traditional and nontraditional are part of the scene with liberal doses of country, pop and rhythm and blues—you'll find a lot on our musical plate.

If it's musical instruction you want, check out **Spirit Square, Community School of the Arts, CPCC, UNC Charlotte, Queens College** and other music clubs. Only a few of the city's diverse collection of musical groups have been noted below. Call the public library or the Arts and Science Council for more detailed information.

BLOCKBUSTER PAVILION
707 Blockbuster Blvd.   *549-5555*

An amphitheater, capable of seating 19,000, the Blockbuster Pavilion opened in 1991 to rave reviews. Located near UNC Charlotte, and easily accessible from all points of the region, the new facility offers both reserved seating as well as lawn seating. Open from mid-April through October, the amphitheater is versatile in the shows it is able to feature. From rock concerts with Paul McCartney to Broadway hits and classical orchestral programs, the Blockbuster Pavilion is a terrific addition to the city's cultural community.

PALADIUM AMPHITHEATRE AT PARAMOUNT'S CAROWINDS
I-77 & Carowinds Blvd.   *588-2606*

Paramount's Carowinds theme park, 10 miles south of Charlotte on the North Carolina/South Carolina border, is also the home of the Paladium Amphitheatre. The Paladium has featured such top-name performers as Billy Ray Cyrus, the Temptations and Four Tops, Sting, and Reba McEntire. It has also become a popular place to host local jazz and blues festivals. Visitors can look forward to new special events taking the Paladium Amphitheatre stage.

SOCIETY FOR THE PRESERVATION AND ENCOURAGEMENT OF BARBERSHOP QUARTET SINGING IN AMERICA
Contact: Carl deBrosse   *334-6631*

Chartered in 1950, the Charlotte Chapter of the Society for the Preservation and Encouragement of Barber Shop Quartet Singing in America (S.P.E.B.S.Q.S.A.) consists of a chorus (**Carolina Chord Company**) and several quartets. The chapter produces its own annual shows, participates in civic functions, performs for numerous audiences around the Metrolina region and is supportive of area charity organizations. The chorus has competed on an international level and has won many regional competitions.

The Carolina Chord Company is composed of men of all ages, from all walks of life. Men who enjoy

The Paladium Amphitheatre at Paramount's Carowinds features top-name performers, festivals and special events.

Photo courtesy of Paramount's Carowinds.

singing and performing, and who may wish to share in the unique camaraderie of one of Charlotte's finest singing organizations, are encouraged to pursue membership. Guests are always welcome at the rehearsals, to listen or to sing. Rehearsals are held each Monday evening from 7:30 to 10:00 PM at Piedmont Natural Gas Headquarters Building on Rexford Drive. Call for more information.

CAROLINA PRO MUSICA
2516 E. 5th St. 334-3468

This group offers concerts in St. Mary's Chapel and elsewhere in the community and the Carolinas. It features voices and historic instruments.

CHAMBER MUSIC OF CHARLOTTE
P.O. Box 9453
Charlotte, NC 28299 535-3024

This musical group is a nonprofit organization of approximately 85 musicians who play early and modern instruments. The group includes string quartets, Baroque ensembles, dance bands, jazz groups and other combinations of instruments. It annually sponsors more than 100 performances in a concert series and at public, private and business events. The organization also attempts to find places for musicians of all levels to play in chamber ensembles. Two series of public performances, plus in-school and outreach concerts are given annually.

CHARLOTTE CHILDREN'S CHOIR
Contact: Aimee Kennedy-Starnes 337-2248

This week-long day camp for students from ages 8 to 13 aids and prods them to discover their hidden talents in music. Almost 150 youngsters gather at Dana Auditorium on the Queens College campus to learn how to access and express their gifts with children possessing the same interests. The students take musicianship and Orff classes, in which they play small xylophones to help sharpen their sense of pitch and rhythm. They also get a feel for other art forms through presentations by the Light Factory Photographic Arts Center, Afro-American Cultural Center and Tarradiddle Players. The week's finale celebrates with a free concert known as *A Children's Celebration In Song.*

CHARLOTTE CHOIR BOYS
Contact: Kathy Edds 377-4187 or 344-0255
(Spirit Square)

Open to boys third grade through voice change, the Choir presents two public concerts each year in addition to other community group appearances. Charlotte Choir Boys goes on a national tour each summer.

CHARLOTTE CHORAL SOCIETY
374-1564

This nonprofit society made up of more than 100 volunteer singers has become a nationally recognized chorus. The Choral Society annually produces "The Singing Christmas Tree" and "On The Town," a spring pop performance. It frequently performs at community events and sponsors an annual Vocal Performance Award scholarship for a local student. Membership is open to any community singer who qualifies through audition.

CHARLOTTE COMMUNITY CONCERT ASSOCIATION, INC.
527-6680

Founded in 1930, this group is Charlotte's oldest concert organization. Each year the association offers a season of classical music by outstanding orchestras, dance companies, soloists and instrumentalists from around the world. Season membership is available and is usually sold out every year. Next season you can expect to see: Itzhak Perlman, Smithsonian Jazz Masterworkks Orchestra, Russian National Orchestra, Thomas Hampson and the Monte Carlo Philharmonic.

COMMUNITY SCHOOL OF THE ARTS
200 W. Trade St.   377-4187

In his work as church organist and choir director at First Presbyterian Church, Henry Bridges realized that the vacant Sunday school rooms and idle pianos could be put to good use. In 1969 he organized what would later become Community School of the Arts, a flourishing school that now reaches 4,000 students throughout the Charlotte-Mecklenburg area. The school—which offers courses in music (piano, strings, brass, woodwinds, guitar, voice, Suzuki violin, Orff), dance (beginning through classical ballet, jazz and tap) and visual arts (beginning to intermediate drawing, images and materials)—is currently directed by Gene C. Wenner. The outreach program is free to all participants and is presented through Community School of the Arts and various agencies. A number of scholarships are available for classes at the school.

CHARLOTTE'S CAROLINA CROWN DRUM AND BUGLE CORPS
Contact: Doug Madar or Kevin Smith   333-3351

This outstanding group of 60 high school students, ages 15 to 21, come from all over the Carolinas, with a few from Georgia. Last year, it won the World Championship in Division II in a week-long competition in Jackson, Mississippi. This all volunteer organization rehearses and performs with the drum corps relying solely on brass and percussion instruments. But the color guard unit (descendant of the units formed by veterans' groups after World War I) is not what you'd expect, and the music isn't of the John Philip Sousa variety either. You'll hear musical selections that run the gamut from jazzy show-business numbers to light classical. There are two local performances, but the Corps travels 15,000 miles a year to competitions throughout the United States. Auditions are held in late November and early December.

CHARLOTTE FLUTE ASSOCIATION
Contact: Irene Maddox   537-9592

This group sponsors the Charlotte Flute Choir and brings to Charlotte some of the world's finest flutists for concert performances and master classes.

CHARLOTTE FOLK MUSIC SOCIETY
5301 Alexa Rd.   846-5508

A fair-sized section of Charlotte's population is comprised of North Carolina, Tennessee and Virginia mountain people who migrated here in search of jobs. They brought their traditional mountain music, dances, crafts and folk lore with them. The Charlotte Folk Music Society formed to preserve their music and has expanded to include other elements of mountain life. The society sponsors and/or participates in many area festivals, including the annual **Folk Music Festival**. This annual festival is moving from its former June date to September 30th and October 1st at Blockbuster Pavilion and will feature Doc Watson. Call founder, Marilyn Price at 846-1899 for additional information on workshops and classes. Last year marked the second **Carolina Heritage Music Celebration** at the Paladium at Paramount's Carowinds. This celebration concentrated on honoring the best of Appalachian, bluegrass, Celtic, black string, minstrel, children's folk and blues musicians in a fun setting. It included clogging, storytelling and a finale that brought pickers of all types on stage to pick along with their idols.

This 500-member organization has monthly meetings and publishes a magazine for its members, listing workshops, classes, and concerts sponsored by the society.

Through Central Piedmont Community College, classes are held on folk instruments such as the Appalachian dulcimer, old-time banjo, fiddle, folk music guitar, recorder and autoharp. On Sunday evenings at 6:00 PM the **Old-Time Music Jam** class meets at Bryant Music Building on the CPCC campus to jam and play and sing the old-time music—jigs, reels, old-time Gospel are part of the fun.

American Harp Society

Contact: Marion Redd   372-6827

Promoting the appreciation of the harp as a musical instrument through public concerts and in-school programs is one of the main purposes of the society. Members of the group regularly perform for children in the Charlotte/Mecklenburg Schools. An annual event you don't want to miss is the society's free Christmas concert at Christ Lutheran Church on Providence Road in December. Heavenly sounds are performed by more than two dozen harpists, accompanied by various Charlotte musicians.

Charlotte Jazz Society

P.O. Box 37002
Charlotte, NC 28237525-9346 or 522-1234

This 300-member group, organized in 1985, promotes awareness of America's native musical form—jazz. The society promotes local and regional jazz musicians through such events as **Jazz-a-thon**, which is an 8-hour event held in the spring, and other well-received special programs. Each year the organization supports **Jazz Charlotte** by providing a free prelude concert the week prior to the event at First Union Plaza. The society, in cooperation with UNC Charlotte, sponsors a high school and college jazz competition and scholarship fund. The society also sponsors a club crawl at varied locations.

Charlotte Music Club

Contact: Richard Boward   376-1366

This group has monthly meetings with musical programs. The club also sponsors the annual performance of Handel's *Messiah* at Ovens Auditorium. This performance is free to the public, but donations, which go toward musical scholarships for Mecklenburg students, are appreciated.

METROPOLITAN MUSIC MINISTRIES
1615 E. 5th St.   *377-1352*

The goal of this organization, founded in 1984, is to complement the work of churches, crisis assistance and social service agencies by taking music to the "forgotten ones" in the community. The group presents live musical performances and devotional services to the homeless, elderly, handicapped, prisoners, hospital patients, nursing home residents and others. Already, it has enriched the lives of more than 60,000 people.

OPERA CAROLINA
345 North College St.   *332-7177*

Opera Carolina is the oldest and largest professional opera company in the state. The company mounts four annual productions, featuring world-famous singers. Performances take place at the Blumenthal Performing Arts Center.

The Company's Touring and Education Division presents smaller operas to community groups and schools throughout the Southeast. Next year's schedule includes performances of *Madama Butterfly, Salome, The Mikado* and *The Marriage of Figaro*. In addition, Opera Carolina provides **OperaFest** for Charlotte's minority and underserved teenage community. For one

week during the summer, a program is designed to stimulate musical self-awareness and appreciation through sessions in singing, dancing, music composition, set design, stage directing and acting in order that students can create an opera on their own.

OPERA COMPANY OF CHARLOTTE
Contact: Tim Levan   *372-5643*

You must audition for this professional group that offers two to three performances of scenes and arias from the standard operatic repertoire. Opera Company of Charlotte's training program holds regularly scheduled auditions for eight- to ten-week periods of master class/rehearsals, culminating in some fully costumed and staged performances accompanied by orchestra. Local promotional mini-performances are also available for groups.

ORATORIO SINGERS OF CHARLOTTE
345 N. College St.   *332-0468*

The 150-member Oratorio Singers of Charlotte merged last year with the Charlotte Symphony Orchestra. Together, they present three major concerts each season—including Handel's *Messiah*—joined by nationally recognized guest soloists. Also included in the organization is the 34-member **Oratorio Singers Chamber Chorus**, which performs throughout the Carolinas at locations such as the Piccolo Spoleto Festival in Charleston, S.C., and the 60-member **Charlotte Youth Oratorio Singers**, which provides an important educational program to students from over 15 area high schools.

CHARLOTTE
PHILHARMONIC ORCHESTRA

P. O. Box 470987
Charlotte, NC 28247-0987   846-2788

Charlotte Philharmonic Orchestra, a 65- to 70-piece professional orchestra now in its fourth season, has grown from three to 12 concerts per season. It began with a small following and has blossomed to fill Dana Auditorium's 1,000-seat house at Queen's College. By staying in touch with what concert goers want to hear, the Philharmonic added more pops concerts with its **Cabaret Concert Series**, retained low prices even though its opening concert moved to North Carolina Blumenthal Performing Arts Center and the Christmas concert to Ovens Auditorium to accommodate demand. A theme is devised for every concert, so don't be surprised to see the Pink Panther or the Phantom (*Phantom of the Opera*) doing the conducting. The Philharmonic gives 10% of its seating capacity for each performance to a variety of deserv-ing agencies, thus allowing many people to attend who might never have had the opportunity otherwise. This has become one of Charlotte's best classical and pops musical bargains.

QUEENS COLLEGE
COMMUNITY ORCHESTRA

Contact: Jean Lent   553-0314

Made up of professional and amateur musicians, this orchestra presents two concerts a year.

CHARLOTTE PIANO TEACHERS
FORUM

Contact: Gloria Stipp   542-1630

This group with 170 members from the Carolinas holds monthly meetings and programs during the school year and sponsors monthly recitals, and an annual workshop a professional clinician is brought annually with **Friends of Music** at Queens College. It also sponsors the Charlotte Piano teacher's forum audition each spring. The group also participates in the North Carolina

Photo courtesy Charlotte Symphony Orchestra.

The Charlotte Symphony Orchestra is considered one of the nation's finest.

Federation of Music Clubs. If you're looking for a piano teacher, this is a good place to find one.

QUEEN CHARLOTTE CHORUS OF HARMONY INTERNATIONAL CHORUS & QUARTETS

Contact: Susan Scott   *542-1266*

The Charlotte chapter of Harmony International Chorus & Quartets (formerly Sweet Adelines) trains its members in musical harmony, barbershop style, without instrumental accompaniment. An 85-voice chorus presents an annual show at Ovens Auditorium and performs for private groups, civic and community groups and others. Call for audition information.

CHARLOTTE SYMPHONY ORCHESTRA

1415 S. Church St.   *332-6136*

Considered one of the nation's finest, the Charlotte Symphony was the only regional orchestra to be invited to participate in the 1987 **Summer European Music Festival**. The orchestra received rave reviews everywhere it played and returned to Charlotte as an internationally recognized orchestra. Last year Charlotte Symphony merged with Charlotte Oratorio Singers.

The musical scope of the symphonic group is varied, ranging from a comprehensive in-schools music program to performances that include the Oratorio Singers and Opera Carolina. Two co-productions will be: North Carolina Dance Theatre's *Carmina Burana* and Charlotte Repertory's Golden Circle Series production of *A Midsummer Night's Dream*. The 41-week concert season is September through May.

The group offers a subscription season with a glittering array of the world's great artists. Next year Charlotte will be entertained by the following guest conductors: Marin Alsop, Kay George Roberts, Jahja Ling and Hermann Micael. Guest artists will include violinist Joshua Bell and flutist Marina Piccinini. In support of Women In The Arts, the symphony will performs the works of Libby Larsen and Joan Tower. There are multiple musical options for subscribers; two Mini Series (A and B) each with seven concerts or the full 14 concert series; a Friday night Gourmet Dinner concert series of eight concerts; or a Sunday Family matinee series of six concerts. The Winter Pops has two series, the C series with eight concerts or the D series with six concerts.

The Summer Pops series of four concerts is free. Three of these concerts are to be performed at SouthPark Mall and one at Memorial Stadium. The Oratorio Singers series includes three performances. Next year it will perform Handel's *Messiah, Carmina Burano* and the *German Requiem* by Brahms. In addition, the orchestra is noted for its five Saturday morning concerts for Young People (age 10 and younger), plus the annual performances of *The Nutcracker*. With the exception of the Summer Pops, all concerts are performed at the Belk Theatre in the North Carolina Blumenthal Performing Arts Center.

Visual Arts

There are, as we've noted all along, a lot of free things to do in

Charlotte, but probably none of the arts is as free to see or as approachable as the visual arts. You can even get in free at the Mint Museum on certain days. Around Uptown and on Davidson Street between 34th and 36th streets, you can visit galleries on the first Friday of the month from September through May in what is called **The Gallery Crawl**. You'll have a good time, bump into people you haven't seen in years (or meet someone you'd like to know) and sip a little wine that many of the galleries supply.

You don't have to spend a dime at these galleries or at the art festivals held around town throughout the year. You just browse until you find that certain *object d'art* that catches your eye and awakens something in your soul (or matches the colors in your bedroom). Of course, this is the point at which that free experience can be as costly as a season subscription to any arts group. But, it can add beauty to your life. After all, didn't someone famous say that art is what separates us from animals?—A distinction that is sometimes difficult to discern at The Gallery Crawl. We've outlined a few of the many visual arts outlets in town.

AFRO-AMERICAN CULTURAL CENTER
401 North Myers St.   *374-1565*

The Center is headquartered in a fully restored church near McDowell Street and Seventh in an area of the city known as First Ward. Its purpose is to preserve African-American history and culture and offer a forum for multi-cultural events, performances and exhibitions. With a gallery of changing art exhibits, dance presentations and theater, the Center offers much.

THE ANNEX GALLERY OF COFFEY AND THOMPSON
1423 E. 4th St.   *334-4332*

This gallery features original art by artists from around the country, from contemporary to traditional, plus it has a wide selection of signed limited prints. It also features bronze sculptures and wood carvings.

CENTER OF THE EARTH
3204 N. Davidson St.   *375-5756*

Center of the Earth, the first art gallery in historic North Charlotte, opened in 1989. Owner/sculptor, J. Paul Siers and owner/artist, Ruth Lyons have the largest offering of contemporary sculpture in Charlotte. A few figurative pieces stand among abstract works of stone, steel and wood. Many narrative pieces convey simple to complex messages. This gallery differs from the usual mainstream commercial galleries in that it became an outgrowth of the owners' search for a good place to work, educate the art community and carry the work of other artists. The distinctive difference in their approach focuses toward the work's integrity, not its marketability. Always a favorite on the gallery art crawls, the Center is open 1 PM to 5 PM Thursday through Saturday, or by appointment.

FARVAN & CO.
220 N. Tryon St.   *375-1424*

Farida Sweezy once worked with the U.S. State Department to

help develop private enterprise in Third World countries, and, with both her Uptown gallery and new satellite gallery at Atherton Mill on South Boulevard, she's now doing that on a personal level. Farvan & Co., which opened in early 1987, features museum-quality collectibles and better gifts from East Africa, Egypt, Morocco, Afghanistan, Guatemala, Indonesia and Turkey. You'll find etched gourds, ebony sculptures, musical instruments, masks, ceremonial pieces, jewelry, clothing and collections from private estates. The **Atherton Mill Farvan Gallery** has a slightly different personality with architectural pieces from Morocco, etc., but remains a good representative.

HODGES TAYLOR GALLERY
227 N. Tryon St.   *334-3799*
Owners Dot Hodges and Christie Taylor exhibit work in all media primarily by Southeastern artists. They stress that their gallery, the oldest in Uptown Charlotte, is not just for buyers, and they sponsor gallery talks and informal discussions with their artists the Saturday after a show opening. Their mission is to have the artists of the Southeast known and appreciated by the public. They have an active exhibition schedule from September through May and work with corporations and individuals.

JERALD MELBERG GALLERY
Morrocroft Village
3900 Colony Rd.   *365-3000*
The gallery's primary focus is paintings, drawings, prints and sculptures by living American artists with national and international reputations. Owner Jerald Melberg has an eclectic taste, and the gallery demonstrates that he looks for works with an inner spiritual quality that take them a step beyond. The gallery opened in 1984 and in October 1986 featured an exhibit of Picasso prints, drawings, paintings and ceramics, the first exhibit in North Carolina ever devoted solely to Picasso. It drew 20,000 people. The Melberg Gallery moved last year to Morrocroft Village.

KNIGHT GALLERY
110 E. Seventh St.   *372-9664*
Part of the Spirit Square Center for the Arts, Knight Gallery opened in 1983 with the goal to highlight pivotal developments in visual arts since 1960. The gallery has now matured into a major center for contemporary art in the Southeast, with a national reputation for the range and depth of its exhibits, its cutting edge attitude and its scholarly work. It publishes several catalogs. Other art galleries in the Spirit Square Complex are: First Union, Middleton Mc Millan, Dixon and Loch Walker.

THE LIGHT FACTORY
311 Arlington Ave.
(1300 block of South Blvd.)   *333-9755*
The Light Factory Photographic Arts Center was formed in 1972 and incorporated as a nonprofit arts organization dedicated to promoting photography as a fine art and communications medium. Since that time, The Light Factory has evolved into the foremost photographic resource facility in the South-

east. Its unique gallery has exhibited fine art and documentary photography by many outstanding artists. Continuing its long-term commitment to photographic education, it sponsors exhibitions, classes, lectures and workshops and community outreach programs.

McNEAL GALLERY
226 E. Tremont Ave.
333-9201

McNeal Gallery opened in the early '70s, making it one of the oldest galleries in Charlotte. It features an outstanding collection of reproduction prints (about 85-90 in all) by Andrew Wyeth and his family, many of them collectors' items. Owner Mark McNeal also has original art in all media.

MINT MUSEUM
2730 Randolph Rd.   *337-2000*
Taped Highlights   *333-6468*

The reason one of the Southeast's most prominent museum is known as the Mint Museum owes to the building's original function. Built in 1836 on West Trade Street, the building processed gold that came from 75 to 100 gold mines discovered around Charlotte in the early 1800s. Piece by numbered piece, the building was moved to its Eastover location in 1933 when preservationist, Mrs. Harold C. Dwelle, fought successfully to save this significant chapter in Charlotte's history. Reconstructed, the classic structure opened in 1936 as the first art museum in North Carolina.

In the past, only the artistic elite were apt to be found at Mint exhibits, openings, lectures and theatre performances, but since 1983's reconstruction, programming emphasis has changed to entice a wider spectrum of mainstream interests. No longer will you only see the expected type of museum goers, you'll now also rub shoulders with people who'd never dreamed of being part of a museum's activities. Why? The building's expansion opened the doors to larger and more nationally prominent exhibits as well as mounting its own shows, and that's certainly one part of the reason for the "new blood" infusion. Other reasons point to innovative educational approaches and a diversified programming schedule that serves up tantalizing artistic exhibits.

The museum offers a summer series of weekly workshops for elementary-age children to senior high students. These sessions let students explore the history and themes of the museum's collection through five studio art experiences. In addition, students are served through a year-round **Student Artist Gallery**. School teachers can earn a part of their recertification through an intense summer program introducing them to current and future exhibits. Those teachers also utilize their new knowledge by weaving art into their curricula. A high percentage of those teachers return throughout the school year with their students at no charge. In fact, all school groups throughout the Carolinas and neighboring states are now admitted free.

Everyone loves a good party with a theme. Maybe that accounts for the Young Affiliates success of the outdoor **Jazzy Ladies** series during the summer, entertaining with

Charlotte's Mint Museum of Art is one of the Southeast's most prominent museums.

live jazz blended with Hollywood film classics. It's a, "You bring a lawn chair and *hors d'oeuvres*—the mint supplies (for purchase) the soft and harder beverages." The **Faux Ball** in the fall swings into more imaginative socializing and the **Kentucky Derby Party** is kind of the "coming out" event for spring, now attracting up to 15,000 guests. Other social focuses are family festivals; seminars led by world-renowned art figures; and the most enthusiastic exhibition opening parties found anywhere

in the Carolinas. These are but a taste of the many social, educational and cultural interests that entice along with great art.

Seven museum affiliate groups cater to specific interests, ranging from the socially oriented Young Affiliates to the Delhom Service League for ceramics enthusiasts. It's been said that the museum couldn't run without its strong volunteer base who play an active role as docents, researchers and gift shop personnel.

The current and future agenda presents: **North Carolina Collects**, from July 9 through September 18, 1994; **Southwestern Native American Ceramics**, August 20 through January 15, 1995; **Japan: The Nature of Now**, (Japanese video feature called A I U E O NN SIX Features), September 3 through November 6, 1994. **French Oil Sketches and the Academic Tradition** presents works from the 17th, 18th and 19th centuries, which will no doubt acquaint us with French masters before their works go into the final rendering, October 15 through December 11, 1994; **Project Face to Face**, November 26 through January 22, 1995; **Partial Recall**, January 14 through March 12, 1995; The Mint's own **Southern Arts and Crafts Movement 1890-1940: Native Material and Designing Women** will debut November 1995 and run until it begins its travel tour throughout the United States.

Also, coming in 1995 will be **II X Immortal: Elvis + Marilyn** (Elvis Pressley and Marilyn Monroe). Like the popular Rameses Exhibit, Elvis and Marilyn will draw crowds from far and wide, but probably not the same crowds as did the Egyptian Exhibit.

You'll always find something fun to see or do at the Mint. Admission is $4 for adults, $2 for students ages 13 to 18, free for children younger than 12, and free on Tuesday evenings from 5 PM to 10 PM, and on the second Sunday of each month. (For more information on the Mint's collections, see the listing under "Attractions.")

THE NATURE MUSEUM

1658 Sterling Rd.   *372-6261*

This museum offers visitors hands-on experiences with animals and plants. It features an earth science hall, a live animal room, a puppet theatre and a nature trail. One of Charlotte's earliest educational institutions, this is a small urban nature center.

PICTURE HOUSE

1520 E. Fourth St.   *333-8235*

This shop, run by Bob Griffin, offers original art, art reproductions, posters and limited edition prints. It also does fine custom framing as well as period framing. If you have an old piece of art in need of restoration, the Picture House can supply the expertise.

POPE'S GALLERY

1029 Providence Rd.   *342-1774*

POPE'S GALLERY FOUNDERS HALL

100 N. Tryon St.   *339-0450*

POPE'S GALLERY AT THE ARBORETUM

8016 Providence Rd.   *541-3199*

In business for 25 years, Pope's sells original watercolors, oils, original paintings by Carolina artists, posters, serigraphs, pottery, statuary, limited edition prints and British restrikes from old antique steel plates and botanicals. Custom framing is also offered.

QUEENS GALLERY & ART CENTER

1212 The Plaza   *372-2993*

The gallery features mostly local young artists, many of them students, to provide them with a springboard, but it also works with professionals. Queen's doesn't have formal exhibits, but the gallery, housed in an old church, can be rented for local art exhibits and other functions such as wedding receptions and parties. It also provides framing services and sells arts supplies.

MIXED MEDIA STUDIO AND GALLERY

1620 S. Boulevard   *342-4481*

The goal of this gallery is to create a place where people feel comfortable. The gallery makes an effort to carry items no one else does, primarily contemporary American crafts and fine art at affordable prices. It also features many regional artists, as well as unusual and very special jewelry, much of it one-of-a-kind items. Shows rotate about every two months.

SPIRIT SQUARE CENTER FOR THE ARTS

345 N. College St.   *372-9664*

This multi-arts complex offers classrooms, studios, exhibits and 3 performance areas, not to forget its seven art galleries, a splendid gift shop and office space for small arts organizations. This center opened in 1975 in the renovated First Baptist Church and has since added two adjoining buildings. Adults and children can take classes in clay, fiber arts, drawing, printmaking and theater. Spirit Square offers a year-round performing season that includes Innovative Theatre and showcases small musical and comedy touring groups such as Emmylou Harris and the Smothers Brothers, plus a summer program for its **Interdisciplinary Arts Camp**. **Summerfest**, a celebration of German traditions, is held annually at the complex as well as a variety of other family-oriented and cultural festivals such as the **Native American Festival** and the **Japanese Festival**. Many of these festivals are usually free.

WALDEN GALLERY
4607 Parview Dr.   *541-8575*

Diana Walden opened her first gallery in August 1987. There are Southwestern American native lithographs, etchings and engravings; works by local artists and photographers, including fine art reproduction posters.

If you are interested in honing your artistic skills or finding instruction for your child prodigy, you'll almost surely find what you're looking for at either of the following schools.

CENTRAL PIEDMONT COMMUNITY COLLEGE
P.O. Box 35009
Charlotte, NC 28235   *342-6956*

CPCC offers classes in most of the visual arts, during the day or at night, for personal enrichment or to earn a degree.

COMMUNITY SCHOOL OF THE ARTS
200 W. Trade St.   *377-4187*

Founded in 1969, CSA offers classes in music, dance, visual arts, piano and violin for children aged three up to senior citizens. A variety of classes are held at its facility. Scholarships are available.

Writing

Charlotte Public Library's **NOVELLO** is a week-long festival held each year in mid-October. This year's agenda will bring such famous authors as: *Race Matters'* Dr. Cornel West, John Naisbitt speaking about his new book, *Global Paradox*; women's publisher of *Lear*, Frances Lear, and many other local and regional writers who give workshops and speak at other functions.

Charlotte has had its share of literati through the years—the unforgettable Harry Golden, creator of *The Carolina Israelite* and author of *Only in America* and Carson McCullars who wrote *The Heart Is a Lonely Hunter*. Charles Kuralt, best known for his *On the Road* stories that aired over CBS, is probably Charlotte's best known contemporary writer. WBTV's news anchor Bob Inman, known for *Home Fires Burning*, which was later produced on the *Hallmark Hall of Fame*, has gained national prominence. Frye Gaillard and Ruth Moose also get national attention. Noteworthy poets include Dannye Romaine, Irene Honeycutt, Judy Goldman, Rebecca McClanahan and others.

Charlotte is kind to writers and has quite a colony of them who produce everything from travel stories to science fiction to romances to mainstream novels. If you want to enjoy the company of other writers, there are many opportunities for doing so through writing classes offered in local colleges and workshops sponsored by writers' groups.

CAROLINA ROMANCE WRITERS
P.O. Box 470761
Charlotte, NC 28226   *332-8214*

Affiliated with Romance Writers of America, Carolina Romance

Writers meets the third Saturday of the month for a luncheon discussion and program. Open to published and unpublished writers, this active group sponsored a romance conference last year with professional guest speaker writers and editors. Its monthly newsletter, *A Final Draft*, offers helpful industry news, tips concerning writing problems, editors and agents. If you are interested in writing category or mainstream romance, you'll find CRW a helpful organization.

CHARLOTTE WRITERS' CLUB

Charlotte Writers' Club is Charlotte's oldest writing organization. Open to professional and amateur writers, this club holds monthly dinner meetings that feature well-known speakers and authors. The club also sponsors four writing workshops per year. All activities, including regular meetings, are open to both members and nonmembers. In addition, there are seven contests each year, which include writing for: article, short story, juvenile story, short story by student only, children's story, long short story and poetry. Members can submit without cost, but nonmembers are charged a nominal fee. Meetings are held the last Monday of each month for a dutch treat dinner with speaker.

INTERNATIONAL BLACK WRITERS CHARLOTTE, INC.
345 N. College St.
Contact: Maria Macon   *333-9605*
Founded in 1985, this group pulls together accomplished writers to serve as a support group for other new and emerging Black writers in the community. IBWC's mission is to encourage, develop and display new writing talent by providing a program of services including assistance in preparing manuscripts, poems and plays for production and publication. The group continually challenges writers to use their skills and talents to promote change.

Out of this group, playwright, athan Ross Freeman wrote, *Winter Isn't Over Yet*; poet, Ivey Dixon wrote, *The Heart Alone* and poet, Frankie Rolfe Johnson received the Play of the Year Award for her *I'll Grieve In The Morning*. Annual membership dues are $25.00. IBWC is an affiliate of the Arts and Science Council.

N.C. WRITER'S NETWORK
c/o Marsha Warren
P.O. Box 954
Carrboro, NC 27510   (919) 967-9540
This nonprofit, statewide organization has over 800 members who are writers of every type. Annual membership dues are $20 and include six issues of the 20-page *Network News*. Write for details.

WOMEN IN COMMUNICATIONS, INC.
P.O. Box 11952
Charlotte, NC 28220   846-4640
The Charlotte chapter of WICI, an organization for professional communicators, holds monthly meetings, including an annual spring luncheon that features a national speaker and honors local communicators. Men interested in joining the group shouldn't let the name discourage them. Rest assured, they are welcome and can become members.

Photo by William Russ. Courtesy N.C. Travel and Tourism Division.

Charlotte's Discovery Place is one of the Top Ten science Museums in America.

Inside
Attractions

Cut the whining about nothing to do in Charlotte! That may have been a legitimate lament a few years ago, but the scene has changed. Once upon a time, the circus, a carnival or a rodeo was about the extent of what the Queen City could attract. No more. Now, on any given day or night, there are more exciting things to try, places to go and celebrities to entertain us than most budgets can afford. Today, the question is not "where to go" but "which place to choose."

We're no longer content to stay home as perhaps our parents were. We want to go...to be part of the attraction, either as a participant or a spectator. And one of the best things about Charlotte attractions is that many are free, such as **Springfest** each April, or the nearly-free **First Night Charlotte** on New Year's Eve. Others can impact your wallet, but the dent isn't as severe as in other major cities. In that sense you'll discover that you can have the same type of fun here for a lot less.

What you choose is going to depend on your taste or mood that day. Charlotte has a sack full of attractions from the "rockem-sockem" participant family kind found at **Paramount's Carowinds** theme park, to the visually exhilarating type at **Discovery Place's Omnimax Theatre** (similar to the old Cinerama experience, just more so), and the **Blockbuster Pavilion** that brings in name talent for concerts and Broadway productions. For chilling excitement the **Charlotte Motor Speedway** will fill your bill, but if you're in the mood for something quieter, then take yourself out to **Reed Gold Mine** where you can spend a day panning for gold or try a little sight-seeing at the **Mint Museum of Art** or **Historic Rosedale.**

We have annual events and festivals at different seasons of the year (detailed in the calendar of events section at the end of this chapter), and many ongoing attractions that are here for us to enjoy any time we take the notion.

As the name implies, one of the main objectives of the **Charlotte Convention and Visitors Bureau** (CCVB), established in 1984, is to attract conventions and travelers to the area. However, the bureau is also concentrating its marketing efforts on targeting the individual traveler, as evidenced by its walk-in **Visitor Information Center** (331-2700), located at 128 East Stonewall Street until November 1994 when it will move to 201 South College Street (332-5051). The CCVB is open from 8:30 AM until 5 PM Monday through Friday, from 10 AM until 4 PM on Saturday and from 1 until 4 PM on Sunday. The office can supply you with brochures and information on any of the attractions listed in this section.

More suggestions on things to do and places to visit in the Metrolina area are given in the chapters on **NEIGHBORS** and **DAY TRIPS AND WEEKENDS**.

AFRO-AMERICAN CULTURAL CENTER
401 N. Myers St.　　　　　*374-1565*

Saved from demolition and beautifully restored, this former Little Rock AME Zion Church in the heart of First Ward promotes, presents, and preserves Afro-American cultural history. The center includes an art gallery, theater, resource and research center and offers educational classes. It is open from 10 AM until 6 PM Tuesday through Saturday, from 1 until 5 PM on Sunday, and no admission is charged.

ANDREW JACKSON MEMORIAL & MUSEUM OF THE WAXHAWS
N.C. 16 South
Waxhaw　　　　　*843-1832*

Through an audio/visual program you'll discover the Backcountry and pioneering life-style of the

Scotch-Irish who settled in this area. This memorial features exhibits and other educational programming.

BLOCKBUSTER PAVILION
707 Blockbuster Blvd.　　　　*549-5555*

Blockbuster Pavilion, located 11 miles from Uptown on U.S. 29 North promotes, as its name implies, spectacle-type, state-of-the-art, star-studded entertainment. Performances run from April through October at this outdoor amphitheater. Since it opened, the Pavilion has showcased world class concerts, Broadway shows, opera and ballet as well as the most popular rock, country and pop stars.

Guests can bring a blanket or lawn chair and relax outside with refreshment from the concessions (guests aren't allowed to bring their own food). The $14.5 million, 19,000-capacity facility offers great acoustics and good sight lines. For business needs, the Pavilion offers private boxes, club seating, hospitality tents and VIP parking.

BON ODORI DANCE FESTIVAL
　　　　　366-7835

The Bon Odori Dance Festival is a celebration of Japanese ethnic dances performed on a ceremonial platform. At the festival you'll hear a Japanese-American drum team and everyone is invited to join in the dance contest. There are exhibitions and demonstrations of origami paper folding and Shuji caligraphy. Children's activities include games and face-painting.

This is a great opportunity to taste Japanese food, including Sushi and other exotic dishes, plus an authentic Japanese tea ceremony. Last year the festival was held at Spirit Square in August, but check for time and place. A nominal admission is charged.

CAROLINA SHOWS

Charlotte Convention Center
101 S. College Street   *332-5051*

Each fall and spring Carolina Shows produces the **Carolina Christmas Craft Show** and **Carolina Spring Craft Show** which feature over 400 master craftspeople exhibiting their work.

CELEBRATION STATION

10400 Cadillac St.
Pineville   *552-7888*

If you're looking for family fun on a slightly smaller scale than Paramount's Carowinds, take a ride out to Celebration Station in Pineville. For the young, and young at heart, this place has something for everyone—batting cages, go-karts, bumper boats, arcade

games, Adventure Golf and more. And if you're in a less active mood, you can eat yourself into oblivion while you watch the fun around you.

CHARLOTTE COLISEUM

100 Paul Buck Blvd.   *357-4700*
Ticketron   *1-800-543-3041*

This 24,000-seat facility is the home of the NBA Charlotte Hornets. ACC basketball, Charlotte Heat tennis, the circus and the Ice Capades are big crowd pleasers here each year, as well as other sporting events, pageants, concerts, rodeos, horse shows and big name entertainment.

CHARLOTTE MOTOR SPEEDWAY

P.O. Box 600
Concord , NC 28026   *455-3200*

America's premier NASCAR facility is home to the **Coca-Cola 600** and the **Winston Select 300** each May, and the **Mello Yello 500** and **All Pro Auto Parts 300** each October. Another biannual event held at the

Photo by Vivi Kanellos, CPCC © 1994.

The 24,000-seat Charlotte Coliseum is the home of the NBA Charlotte Hornets.

speedway is the "AutoFair," the largest antique car show and flea market in the South, held in April and September. Group and individual tours are available, and a gift shop is open year round. (For more information on the Charlotte Motor Speedway and speedway events, see "Racing" in the **SPORTS** chapter.

DISCOVERY PLACE
301 N. Tryon St.   *372-6261*

Year before last, Discovery Place was named the Southeast Travel attraction of the year by the Southeast Tourism Society, and has long been considered one of the top ten science museums in the country. The museum brings in over 400,000 visitors annually. With lights

flashing and a continual stream of school children chattering enthusiastically about what they've just seen or are on their way to see, excitement rivets through this science and technology museum.

Its $18-million expansion has made this hands-on museum as much fun for adults as for children. Almost every exhibit is designed to be interactive—from the **Aquarium Touch Pool** to the **Science Circus** to the **Computer Center**. And for many, the museum's *piece de resistance* is its **Observer/Omnimax Theatre** featuring a tilted-dome screen and wraparound sound system that surrounds you with sight, sound and motion. The **Space Voyager Planetarium**, sharing the same space, features a

Photo courtesy of the Charlotte Motor Speedway.

Charlotte Motor Speedway attracts millions of visitors to the Charlotte area annually.

"Starball" that projects over 10,000 stars on the largest dome in the United States, and promises to take you on an incredible journey through space. In the downstairs section of the museum, birds and sea life thrive in the **Knight Rain Forest**. On the bottom floor you can really imagine yourself in a forest jungle with birds flying overhead. In addition, the expansion includes a new traveling exhibit hall, an early childhood learning center, a full service restaurant named **Food for Thought**, and a gift shop.

Playing until December 3, '94 at the Omnimax is *Africa: The Serengeti*, from December '94 through May '95 you can see *Tropical Rain Forest*, and from May '95 through August '95, the theater will show *Grand Canyon: The Hidden Secret*. The Planetarium show *Frontiers in Space*, a tour of the solar system as seen from various spacecrafts will play until November '94 when the Christmas show, *Season of Light*, a show that illustrates the beauty of the season plays until January 15, '95. *Starseekers*, a novice's guide to the stars, will begin in January and play until June '95.

The museum has also hosted some outstanding traveling exhibits—Dinosaurs, Robots and Beyond, Splice of Life, Special Effects, and Super Heroes. Discovery Place sponsors regular workshops, field trips, camps and learning vacations.

The museum is open every day of the year except Thanksgiving and Christmas. Hours are 9 AM until 5 PM weekdays (9 AM until 6 PM June through August), 9 AM until 6 PM Saturday, and from 1 until 6 PM Sunday. Admission is $5.50 for adults, $4.50 for students 6 to 18 years of age and senior citizens 60 and older. When accompanied by a parent, admission for children ages 3 to 5 is $2.75 and children younger than 3 get in free. Admission is free on "Wonderful Wednesday", the first Wednesday of each month after 2 PM. Annual family memberships entitle holders to unlimited visits and special benefits. On "Wonderful Wednesday," your ticket to the Omnimax Theater is reduced to member prices.

ENERGY EXPLORIUM
AT LAKE NORMAN

Off N.C. 73, P.O. Box 820
Cornelius, NC   875-5600

Operated by Duke Power Company and located near the McGuire Nuclear Station and Cowans Ford Dam, this energy information center is free. Here you can learn all about electricity through hands-on exhibits of model nuclear and coal-fired power plants, find out which appliances require the most energy, play computer games, or watch the film *Lake Norman—the Great Inland Sea*.

For diversion, you can walk through the wildflower garden or enjoy a picnic lunch. The Energy Explorium is accessible via boat and car and is open every day of the year except Thanksgiving, Christmas Eve, Christmas and New Year's Day. Hours are 9 AM until 5 PM Monday through Saturday and noon until 5 PM Sunday. Inquire about tours for **McGuire's Control Room Simulator** and **Duke's Environmental Labs**. No admission is charged.

Fresco at St. Peter's Catholic Church

The ancient art form of fresco, which mean fresh, can be seen in the magnificent work of North Carolina native Ben Long in this beautiful old 1893 Charlotte church. The fresco is a triptych depicting: The Agony, The Resurrection, and Pentecost. Long apprenticed with Pietro Annigoni of Florence, Italy, for seven years. This artist has two fresco works in Italy, several in West Jefferson and Glendale Springs, North Carolina (one of the largest tourist attractions in North Carolina) and in the NationsBank Corporate Center in Uptown Charlotte. The church is open to visitors from 10 AM until noon, and from 1 until 4 PM on Sunday. Visitors are asked to respect masses and weddings. No admission is charged.

Fourth Ward
Uptown Charlotte

In the mid 1800s, Charlotte was divided into four political wards. The northwest Quadrant, called Fourth Ward, was a prosperous area containing the homes of merchants, ministers, physicians and others. In the early 1900s, the trolley expanded Charlotte, and Dilworth and Myers Park became the prestigious places to live. By the '50s, Fourth Ward was becoming an undesirable area with abandoned or substandard housing, scattered businesses and crime.

When by 1970 many homes had been destroyed by fire, vandals and neglect, the Junior League, UNC Charlotte and a few other farsighted people had a dream. It was to interest the city, banks and, most importantly, the people in saving Fourth Ward and making it a desirable residential area once again. By 1978 most of the homes had been bought by adventurous, modern-day pioneers. The restoration was strictly governed by the home owners association and now this is a beautiful, active community which has increased the tax revenue to the city tenfold. This turn-of-the-century Victorian neighborhood in the heart of Uptown is a nice spot for strolling during the day or for taking the tour of homes at Christmas time.

Hezekiah Alexander Homesite & History Museum
3500 Shamrock Drive   *568-1774*

Charlotte's oldest home, built in 1774, served as the home of Hezekiah and Mary Alexander and their 10 children. Alexander was a blacksmith and planter by trade and assumed a leadership role in the new community called Charlotte. He eventually became a signer of the **Mecklenburg Declaration of Independence**.

Today his homesite, plus a replicated kitchen and reconstructed spring house, is the site of two special annual events: **Colonial Christmas** with weekends devoted to music, crafts and food, and **Rites of Spring** that features the way colonials celebrated with sheep shearing, music, etc.

Changing exhibits in the adjacent History Museum focus on local, regional and state history, as well as on special collections. Guided tours are given by the active docents who serve the homesite. Groups are encouraged to make arrangements for morning tours. The house and museum are open from 10 AM until 5 PM Tuesday through Friday and from 2 until 5 PM on weekends. Tours of the homesite are given at 1:15 and 3:15 PM Tuesday through Friday; 2:15 and 3:15 PM Saturday and Sunday. You can see the museum free of charge, but there is a $2 charge to adults and $1 for children ages 6 to 16 for an hour-long guided tour of the homesite.

HISTORIC ROSEDALE

3247 N. Tryon Street   335-0325

In the early 1800s, builders of fine homes called upon their artistic imaginations to produce elegant results. Not always able to find or afford exotic woods such as rosewood and mahogany, the builders became skilled at painting substituted wood to look like the pricey, real thing. These faux (fake) finishes, as they were called, grace many of America's most famous homes. At Rosedale, the 1815 private home of Archibald Frew, you'll need to stand within eight inches of the mahogany-looking paneling before you discover that the wood is painted.

Frew's diverse occupations as merchant, post master and tax collector took him throughout coastal areas where he became enamored of classic architectural styles with plantation overtones. When you visit the restored home you'll see Frew's taste in carved Adams mantels, elaborate cornices, detailed moldings, a classic porch and dormers.

Unfortunately, Frew lost his home in 1819 to his brother-in-law, William Davidson, in a federal bankruptcy case, but Davidson's descen-

dants kept the stately home in the same family for 180 years. In 1985 Rosedale was sold to the **Historic Preservations Foundation of North Carolina**. After an extensive restoration, the home opened to the public in November 1993 in conjunction with the Mint Museum's exhibit, **Classical Taste In America**. Today, you can take the 45-minute, docent-led tour through the home that is furnished with a mixture of originals and reproduction pieces.

You can also tour the restored boxwood garden where you'll see "treasured trees," some thought to have been planted by Archibald Frew and considered to be the largest known of their species in this area. Rosedale is open Sunday afternoon from 1 until 4 PM and during the week by appointment. Tours during the week must include a minimum of 10 people. Admission is $5 for adults, $4 for seniors and students. Children younger than 12 and Friends of Historic Rosedale are admitted free.

LATTA PLACE

5225 Sample Rd.
Huntersville
House   875-2312
Visitors Center   875-1391

Return to the early 1800's river plantation of James Latta, a prosperous traveling merchant who bought wares in Charleston and Philadelphia and peddled them to Carolina Piedmont neighbors. Costumed guides give tours of the two-story house, which is on the National Register of Historic Places. The plantation comes complete with farm animals and a unique equestrian center.

Tours are given at 1:30 and 3:30 PM Tuesday through Friday and at 1:30, 2:30 and 3:30 PM on Saturday and Sunday, and other events held here throughout the year. Admission for the tour is $2 for adults and $1 for children.

(For details on Latta Plantation Park, check the chapter on **PARKS AND RECREATION**.)

LOCH NORMAN

Rural Hill Plantation
Contact: Dick Taylor   875-3113

Do you want to be a Scot for a weekend? You can do it right outside Charlotte on April 22 and 23, 1995. That's when bagpipers from far and wide will sound the opening of Mecklenburg's own Scottish celebration. Since 1954, Grandfather Mountain has drawn throngs of true Scots and Scotish "wannabes" to the Highland Games to watch and participate in dancing the Highland Fling, tossing the cabel and watching Border Collie dogs bring errant sheep back into the fold just as they have since 1100 AD when the athletic games began in Scotland.

Mecklenburg's festival is smaller but characterizes the strong family nature of Scottish gatherings and really brings out the crowds. There's plenty to see, do and eat at the Highland Games, so don your kilt or jeans and listen to Celtic music traditional to the Highlands, Ireland, Wales and Brittany right here near Lake Norman. On Saturday evening at 8:30 (after the games) a Ceilidh will be held at the Holiday Inn on Woodlawn. This event promises to be an entertaining evening of Scot music and dancing. Admission

for the Ceilidh is $5. Admission for the games is $15 for both Saturday and Sunday or $10 for Saturday and $8 for Sunday. The games are held from 9 AM until 5 PM both days. Rural Hill Plantation is located off Beatties Ford Road, about one mile past Latta. Turn left onto Neck Road and follow it to the games.

McINTYRE HISTORIC SITE

Off Beatties Ford Rd.   875-1391

This green spot in northern Mecklenburg marks the place where the famous Battle of the Bees occurred in 1780 when 14 farmer/soldiers drove off a regiment of General Cornwallis with the help of an overturned bee's nest that targeted the Tories. A self-guided trail interprets the battle. Information on this attraction is available from the Latta Plantation Visitors Center.

N.C. TRANSPORTATION MUSEUM/ HISTORIC SPENCER SHOPS

411 S. Salisbury Avenue
Spencer   704-636-2889

This former repair shop for Southern Railway features a 45-minute train ride that allows visitors to tour the 57-acre site. Two of the 13 buildings are open and contain transportation displays. You'll see N.C.'s first Highway Patrol car. The former Flue shop building offers "Bumper to Bumper," an antique car display. There are various railway car displays. An intriguing museum for railroad buffs, it is open from April through October, from 9 AM until 5 PM Monday through Saturday. The hours are from 10 AM until 4 PM November through March. The site has a terrific gift shop with railroad items not found elsewhere. To get to Spencer Shops from Charlotte, take I-85 North to exit 70. Admission is charged for the train ride.

MECKLENBURG AQUATIC CENTER
800 East Second St.   *336-3483*

The Mecklenburg County Aquatic Center located in Uptown Charlotte is owned and operated by the Charlotte/Mecklenburg County Parks and Recreation Department. The Aquatic Center is a state-of-the-art swimming complex seating approximately 1,300 spectators. The facility includes a 50-meter swimming pool, two three-meter diving boards and two one-meter diving boards. The main pool includes a hydraulic floor that allows the depth of the water to be adjusted for various activities and instruction. This accessible facility also includes a 25-yard hydra-therapy pool, a 16-foot in-ground spa and an exercise/fitness room. The Aquatic Center is the site of **Charlotte Ultraswim**, an amateur swimming competition that has featured Olympians, world record holders and teams from around the world.

METROLINA EXPO CENTER
7100 Statesville Rd.   *596-4643*

On rainy days when you can't get outside to play your favorite sport, walking around at the "flea market" is a good cure for cabin fever. In 1971, a small number of vendors set up their tables and sold their wares at the Charlotte Fairgrounds. As "flea markets" became the rage of the times, the **Fairground Flea Market** grew rapidly. Savvy entrepreneurs use the market as a place to bring in a little extra cash, or unload overruns from local factories. It's a great place to pick up some terrific buys if you have a discerning eye, and bet-

Photo courtesy of Historic Spencer Shops.

The North Carolina Transportation Museum and Historic Spencer shops feature a 45-minute train ride that allows visitors to tour the 57-acre site.

ter than running all over town to yard sales. These are two reasons why the variety of this market continues to be a vital part of the new "Metrolina Expo Center" and floods the 147-acre site with bargain hunters on the third weekend of each month.

On the first weekend of every month, the country's largest monthly antiques and collectibles flea market is held at the Metrolina Expo Center. Antique dealers converge from Maine, Iowa, California, Texas, Florida and many states in between. They bring with them some of the finest antique furniture available as well as old farm implements and rare tools. Every conceivable type of old glassware, crystal and china passes through the gates, along with all kinds of memorabilia. For the shopper, Metrolina Expo is a fun-time fantasia filled with old-fashioned nostalgia amidst a happy carnival-like atmosphere. The first weekends of April and November feature an "**Antique Spectacular**" which last April drew 4,000 dealers and over 63,000 shoppers.

In addition to the incredible first and third weekends of each month, a special **Summer Craft Show** and a **Christmas Country Show** draw thousands of shoppers. General admission on the first weekend is $2.50, senior citizens are admitted for half-price, and children younger than 12 are admitted free. Third weekend admission is $1.50, half-price for seniors, and children younger than 12 are admitted free. Hours are from 8 AM to 5 PM on Saturday and from 9 AM to 5 PM on Sunday. Plentiful, free parking

makes this a fun place to explore and discover hidden treasures.

MINT MUSEUM OF ART

2730 Randolph Rd.	337-2000
Taped Highlights	333-6468

The Mint served the region as the first branch of the Philadelphia Mint, coining $5 million in gold from 1836 until the outbreak of the Civil War. A grassroots effort during the Depression saved the original Strickland building from demolition and moved it to its present Randolph Road site where, in 1936, it opened as the state's first art museum. The Mint has since grown to become one of the Southeast's leading art museums.

The collections include important holdings of American and European painting and sculpture, Pre-Colombian, African and Spanish Colonial art, historic costumes, regional crafts and one of America's premiere collections of pottery and porcelain. The permanent collection is enhanced by special changing exhibitions, including major exhibitions on national tour. Highlights have included 1989's "Rameses the Great: The Pharaoh and His Time" and 1994's "Classical Taste in America."

Throughout the year you can expect lectures, seminars, teaching programs for children and adults, films, festivals and other activities supplement exhibitions. The Mint is open 10 AM until 10 PM on Tuesdays, 10 AM until 5 PM Wednesday through Saturday and from 12 until 5 PM on Sunday. Admission is $4 for adults—members and children younger than 12 are admitted free.

Admission is free on Tuesday evenings from 5 until 10 PM, and the second Sunday of each month. For more in-depth information, check the **ARTS** section.

THE MUSEUM OF THE ALPHABET
Davis Road at JAARS Center
Waxhaw   843-6066
Reading and writing seems very basic to most of us; in fact, we take it for granted, but few of us realize that approximately half the world's 5,000 plus languages are still without a written form. The Museum of the Alphabet focuses on the written language and where it began and how alphabets developed by tracing the history of alphabets and other writing systems from the beginning to the present. Both ancient and modern alphabet makers are highlighted in the picturesque settings of the museum displays. You'll see the Chinese alphabet (oldest system, unchanged in 4,000 years) as well as Hebrew, Greek, Aramaic, Arabic and American. Due to the scholarly presentation of the displays, children younger than 12 are not encouraged to visit. The museum is open from 9 AM until noon, and 1:30 until 3:30 PM Monday through Saturday. No admission is charged, but a $2 donation is appreciated.

MUSEUM OF YORK COUNTY
4621 Mount Gallant Road   803-329-2121
Rock Hill, S.C.   800-968-2762
This museum is a true find for children and adults as well. The museum's phenomenal animal exhibits are reminiscent, though on a smaller scale, of New York's Natural History Museum. The museum also features a planetarium, art and astronomy exhibits. Teaching projects with the school system is another interesting feature of this well-rounded museum. It offers an excellent gift shop and is open from 10 AM until 5 PM Monday through Saturday, and from 1 until 5 PM on Sunday. From Charlotte take I-77 South to S.C. 161 (exit 82A), turn right onto Celanese Road and right on Mount Gallant. Admission is $3 for adults and $2 for students and seniors. Children younger than 5 are free.

NATURE MUSEUM
1658 Sterling Rd.   332-4140 or 372-6261
Founded in 1946, The Nature Museum is one of Charlotte's finest educational and recreational resources, aimed at developing an awareness and appreciation of nature through programs and exhibits designed particularly for young children. Adjacent to Freedom Park in an attractive natural setting, the museum offers visitors an opportunity to learn about the changing world we live in through a live animal room, the **Kelly Planetarium**, a nature trail, a puppet theater and exciting hands-on displays.

NEW HERITAGE USA
3000 Heritage Pkwy.   803-548-7800
Fort Mill, S.C.   800-374-1234
Reopened in June 1992, this Christian resort and theme park features its famous water park, a working farm, horseback riding, carriage rides, tennis courts, swimming pools, game rooms, miniature golf, fishing, canoeing, go-cart rides, batting

cages and a Passion Play. Admission is charged for individual rides and attractions. Campsites as well as hotel and motel accommodations are available.

OLE TIME FIDDLER'S & BLUEGRASS FESTIVAL

Fiddler's Grove
Exit 65 off I-77   *704-539-4417*

This event was begun in 1924 by Harper Van Hoy as a community project to support the local school. On Memorial weekend, folks have continued to gather for this annual, three-day celebration of dancing and playing authentic old-time music. This isn't the place you'll see musicians in sequined costumes. Here, you'll find down-to-earth people who spread their quilts in the sloping meadow to hear musicians, some famous such as "Doc" Watson, but

The Ole Time Fiddler's & Bluegrass Festival is an annual, three-day celebration of dancing and playing authentic old-time music.

most not, amble on stage in T-shirts and jeans and play their hearts out. The yearly regulars swap jokes as they eat homemade barbecue and ice cream, while sometimes clapping in rhythm and chiming in on the chorus of *Tennessee Stud* as their children sail frisbees nearby.

You can also join in at the competitions or workshops for autoharp, hammered dulcimer, bass fiddle, dobro, harmonica, banjo and guitar, or be a part of the clogging and storytelling programs. You're surrounded by private jammings where a musical exchange occurs that results in a blending of our musical heritage. It's family entertainment promoting a bonding of traditional family values that brings people from nearby states. The spacious grove, now equipped with electricity and hookup for RVs has complete facilities. Admission is charged. For reservations: P.O. Box 11, Union Grove, NC 28689.

PALADIUM AMPHITHEATRE AT PARAMOUNT'S CAROWINDS

Exit 90 off I-77 South
Tickets   *522-6500*

The Paladium Amphitheatre is located adjacent to Paramount's Carowinds theme park at the North Carolina/South Carolina border, just 10 miles from Charlotte. Staging some of the top musical concerts in the country, this outdoor amphitheater seats 13,000 guests and is easily accessible from I-77.

Regularly scheduled concerts run from April through September and supply the area with every kind of entertainment from Patti Labelle to the B-52's. It is not necessary to purchase a theme park ticket to attend a Paladium concert.

PARAMOUNT'S CAROWINDS

Exit 90 off I-77 South   588-2600

Paramount's Carowinds has gone Hollywood—literally. It's more fun than ever because we timid types have another reason, other than the park's celebrity drawing concerts, to entice us to the park. Guests can roam in WAYNE'S WORLD, eight new acres that are themed after the *Wayne's World* motion pictures and feature a rock music shop, a replica of Wayne's basement studio and the Scream Weaver ride. You add that to its heart-pounding roller coasters such as the **Hurler**, located in WAYNE'S WORLD, **Thunder Road**, **Frenzoid** and **VORTEX**, then cool off with **Rip Roarin' Rapids** and **White Water Falls** or the **wave pool** and you're off to a thrilling start.

This new park marriage with Hollywood has incorporated a professional ice skating show, an MTV-style choreographed show and Richard Scarry's *Huckle, The Cat*. The park has a new restaurant called Stan Mikita's diner, specializing in giant-size hamburgers and hot dogs and jelly doughnuts, slurped Garth-style with a straw. Walking around the park you'll see such characters as Star Trek Klingons, Romulans, and Vulcans, along with Wayne and Garth. You'll also find scads of movie paraphernalia to buy in the stores. Look for the **Paramount Walk of Fame** that lists prominent movies and their stars. The park's new motto is: "The only place thrills are paramount!" They could be right. Check it out.

Paramount's Carowinds continues as a world-class theme park with 91 acres of excitement, and now glamour. Paramount's Carowinds' popular one-price ticket covers all rides and park shows. Paladium concerts, featuring big-name entertainers, are extra. In 1994, general admission to Paramount's Carowinds for ages 7 to 59 is $24.95 and $13.50 for children ages 4 to 6 and senior citizens 60 and older. Children 3 and younger are admitted free. Groups, family and individual season passes are available, as are camp sites. Call (704) 588-2606.

PHILIP MORRIS

U.S. Highway 29 South
Concord   704-788-5698 or 5699

This manufacturing center in Cabarrus County, set in an area of pastures, woods and lakes, works effectively to enhance the quality of life in the communities where it operates. You'll find an extensive collection of North Carolina folk art with good representatives of pottery, earthenware, baskets, paintings and the world's largest hanging quilted tapestry, which was hand-stitched in Franklin, North Carolina. Another interesting exhibit is its collection of over 1,500 postcards depicting every region of the state from the beaches to the mountains.

In addition, you can tour this 1.8-million-square-foot manufacturing center where you'll discover every facet of cigarette production. Free tours are conducted hourly from 9 AM until 3 PM Monday through Friday, with the exception of Christmas, summer shutdown periods and other recognized holidays.

JAMES K. POLK MEMORIAL
P.O. Box 475
Pineville, N.C. 28134   *889-7145*

James K. Polk came into this world in a log cabin near Pineville in 1795. His homeplace has been reconstructed and is now a state historic site. Guided tours of the buildings are available anytime but are especially beautiful when the candles are lit at Christmas time. The Polk Memorial is open from 9 AM until 5 PM Monday through Saturday, April through October; and from 10 AM until 4 PM Tuesday through Saturday, November through March. Sunday hours are 1 until 5 PM April through October and 1 until 4 PM November through March. Admission is free.

REED GOLD MINE
Rt. 2, Box 101
Stanfield, N.C.   *(704) 786-8337*

Reed Gold Mine is the site of the first authenticated gold find in the United States. Residents of the area know well the story of young Conrad Reed who discovered a 17-pound gold nugget in 1799, and how his family used it for a doorstop for several years before selling it at the ridiculous price of $3.50 to a Fayetteville jeweler.

Today, Reed Gold Mine is one of the state's great treasures. Visitors flock to the remote Cabarrus County spot where they can tour the underground mine, walk the nature trails, enjoy a picnic, or learn more about gold mining in the museum. There is a 20-minute film that serves as a great introduction. April through October you can pan for gold (about $3 for two pans of dirt or $1 per pan for groups of 10). Hours are from 9 AM until 5 PM Monday through Saturday, from April through October, and 10 AM until 4 PM Tuesday through Saturday, from November through March. Sunday hours are 1 to 5 PM during the summer season, but are one hour shorter during the winter. No admission is required at this wonderful historic site.

SCHIELE MUSEUM
1500 Garrison Blvd.   *704-866-6900*

This museum has the distinction of being the most visited museum in North Carolina. It features an outstanding exhibit of the state's natural history, an extensive collection of North American land mammals, plus a Planetarium. It is a museum that will excite both children and adults who visit the pioneer site where living history demonstrations are staged throughout the year. The museum's nature trail is designed to illustrate man's bond with the land. The museum is open from 9 AM until 5 PM Tuesday through Friday

Charlotte's Family Fourth Celebration at Memorial Stadium is by far the best place in town to enjoy 4th of July fireworks.

Insiders' Tip

and 2 until 5 PM on Saturday and Sunday. To get to the Schiele Museum from Charlotte, take I-85 South to Gastonia's New Hope Road exit. Follow New Hope Road to Garrison Boulevard. No admission is charged.

SPIRIT SQUARE
CENTER FOR THE ARTS

345 N. College St.   *372-9664*
Box Office   *376-8883*

Once the home of First Baptist Church, this beautiful arts center, has brought vitality to Uptown Charlotte for over a decade. The interdisciplinary center design makes for a very intimate setting for the various groups who perform here. Spirit Square features seven art galleries, three performance spaces, studios and educational opportunities in a variety of visual and performing arts.

SOUTHERN SHOWS, INC.

810 Baxter Street   *376-6594*

Southern Shows, founded by Robert and Joan Zimmerman in 1959, is Charlotte's homegrown producer of consumer and trade shows held throughout the Southeast. Attending these shows is a Charlotte tradition and you can't call yourself a real Charlottean until you've attended at least one: the **Southern Spring Show** in February/March; the **Southern Women's Show** in September; the **Southern Ideal Home Show** in October and the **Southern Christmas Show** in December. Each show features exhibits, special events and speakers based around the show's theme plus oodles of booths selling food, books, gifts, jewelry, handicrafts, household items, services—you name it. All four shows are held at the Charlotte Merchandise Mart on Independence Boulevard.

DANIEL STOWE BOTANICAL GARDEN

6500 S. New Hope Rd.
Belmont, NC 28012   *(704) 825-4490*

Located on a 480-acre site on Lake Wylie, just outside of Belmont, the Daniel Stowe Botanical Garden is being developed over the next 25

Visitors flock to the Reed Gold Mine where they can tour the underground mine, walk the nature trails, enjoy a picnic, or pan for gold.

years to become one of the leading botanic gardens in the United States. The master plan will begin to unfold in late 1994 with the construction of the major gardens and a permanent Visitor Pavilion. Designed by the premiere garden designer, Geoffrey Rausch Environmental Planning & Design in Pittsburgh, the garden is expected to attract upwards of 1,000,000 visitors annually.

At the present time, you will find over 10 acres of perennials, daylilies, annuals and herbs surrounded by rolling meadows. There is an interim visitor Center and a unique gift shop. The gardens are open from 9 AM until 5 PM Monday through Saturday and from 12 noon until 5 PM on Sunday.

UNCC BOTANICAL GARDENS

UNC Charlotte   *547-4055*

This is a beautiful way to escape any time, but especially on those rainy days when you feel cooped up. Entering the tropics of the **McMillan Greenhouse** will revitalize your sagging spirits. The UNCC Botanical Gardens are located in the northeast area of the university campus. You can stroll through the Van Landingham Glen amidst the profusion of rhododendron and enjoy the plants in the **Susie Harwood Garden**. The gardens are open every day; the greenhouse, from 9 AM until 4 PM weekdays. Special tours can be arranged.

WING HAVEN GARDEN & BIRD SANCTUARY

248 Ridgewood Ave.   *331-0664*

Wing Haven was only a bare three-acre patch of land in 1927 when Edwin and Elizabeth Clarkson built their home and began working on their garden in this quiet pocket of Myers Park. Now, over 60 years later, despite the ravages of hurricane "Hugo" that downed over a hundred trees, the fruits of their labors are enjoyed by more than 4,000 visitors each year. The garden, in fact, represents the inspiration of spring with its more than 142 species of birds that have been sighted here.

The late Dorothy Doughty sculpted the myrtle warblers for the Royal Worcester Doughty Bird Series here, and naturalist/artist Roger Tory Peterson has also visited the sanctuary. The gardens are now the responsibility of the **Wing Haven Foundation**, a nonprofit corporation. Support also comes from the **Wing Haven Society**, and membership in the organization is open to anyone. The gardens are open from 3 PM until 5 PM Tuesday and Wednesday, and from 2 until 5 PM Sunday. Guided tours may be arranged Tuesdays through Fridays. Admission is free.

Annual Events

In addition to attractions, Charlotte offers a full calendar of special events such as the major events listed below. More detailed calendars are available upon request from the **Charlotte Convention & Visitors Bureau Information Center**. The state's annual "Calendar of Events" booklet, available at N.C. Welcome Centers or by writing the N.C. Division of Travel and Tourism, is also a handy reference and area newspapers are always a good way to keep well informed.

JANUARY

First Night New Year's Eve Celebration. This event draws thousands to The Square in Uptown Charlotte to begin the new year. Prior to the raising of the lighted crown at midnight, local entertainment groups perform at various locations. An admission of $5 includes parking. A variety of food is available from food venders.

Charlotte Observer **Marathon.** This marathon attracts runners and spectators from all the country. An entry fee is charged if you want to participate, but it is free to spectators.

FEBRUARY

Southern Spring Show. One of Charlotte's most popular events, the Spring Show draws thousands of visitors from across the state and beyond to see the latest in home, gardening and outdoor exhibits and merchandise. Admission is charged.

MARCH

St. Patrick's Day Parade & Fest. An old tradition in Uptown Charlotte, this parade brings out the Irish and the wearing of the green.

Rites of Spring. Held at the Hezekiah Alexander Homesite, this festival greets spring with demonstrations of how things were done in the 18th century. Admission is charged.

Springtime Made in The South. This arts and crafts show and sale is held at the Charlotte Convention Center.

APRIL

Antique Spectacular at the Metrolina Expo. This huge event attracts antique dealers and shoppers from all over the country. Nominal admission.

Elizabeth Association Festival. This annual neighborhood festival is held at Independence Park and attracts people from all over the city.

Loch Norman Highland Games. Held on Neck Road off Beatties Ford Road, 1 mile past Latta Plantation. April 22 and 23.

First Presbyterian Church and Memorial Garden. This lovely garden has a spring display of tulips, azaleas, dogwood, pansies among pretty fountains. The church is located in Concord at 50 Spring Street, SW. Exit I-85 at 29-601 South.

Glencairn Garden. Enjoy beautiful spring flowers, shrubs and trees including azaleas, flowering trees, pansies and tulips. The gardens are located at Charlotte Avenue and Crest Street in Rock Hill.

Mint Museum Home and Garden Tour. This event provides an opportunity to see some of Charlotte's more beautiful homes. Admission is charged.

SpringFest. Held in Uptown Charlotte, this festival features the arts and cuisine in the city's biggest street party of the year.

Stowe Botanical Gardens. See three acres of wild flowers interspersed with pansies, tulips and azaleas. Stowe Botanical Gardens is located at 6500 S. New Hope Road in Belmont.

MAY

GaribaldiFest. This festival is now held on Saturday the middle of May at both Stowe Park and on Main Street in Belmont. The town's former Spring Showcase was renamed GaribaldiFest a couple of years ago after John Garibaldi who built Garibaldi Station in the 1870s. You will be entertained with Bluegrass bands, Gospel Singers and sidewalks lined with arts and crafts. For a taste of the past try a horse and buggy ride, or have fun with jugglers and clowns roaming the festivities. There is also an antique car show. The festival ends with a downtown street dance. Take I-85 South to the Belmont exit.

Town Day. Davidson celebrates its annual festival the first Saturday in May on the Village Green with varied entertainment choices for children with games and demonstrations and lots of good food. You can also take an old fashioned carriage ride around town and participate in the merchant sponsored Treasure Trek. Bring your walking shoes and sign up for the 45-minute stroll to raise money for Habitat for Humanity. Take the Davidson exit 30, off I-77. For further information call (704) 892-3349.

The Winston Championship Race, Goody's Pole Day and Winn Dixie 300. These exciting racing events lead up to the **Coca-Cola 600** at the Charlotte Motor Speedway. Admission is charged.

Lake Norman Festival. This 13th annual festival, two weekends prior to Memorial weekend, begins with dancing in the streets. You'll see T-shirts that read: "Families Can Be Forever," and the beer truck dispenses only nonalcoholic beer. The Beach Jam and Shag Contest is held in downtown Mooresville on Friday evening beginning at 6:30 PM. The festival begins in earnest on Saturday where Main Street is closed to traffic to make room for arts and crafts booths, a children's fun fair, a flea circus and a lot more delicious goodies. If you've always wondered what it's like to fly around a race track at outrageous speeds, you can check out the Maxwell House Race Car Simulator. And you can register for a free ride in the *Lake Norman Magazine* hot air balloon or fly in the tethered hot air balloon of Lincoln Bank. Take the Mooresville exit 36 off I-77.

Denver Strawberry Festival. On Saturday of Memorial weekend, you can begin breakfast at 8 AM with strawberry pancakes at the eighth annual Denver Strawberry Festival. It's held at Country Accents next to Rock Springs Elementary School on N.C. 16. You can get your strawberry "fix" with the unimaginable supply of baked foods with strawberries offered by local churches. You can also take a hayride or wander among the local crafts and other planned entertainments for a delicious way to relax. For more information, call (704) 483-2281.

Ole Time Fiddler's & Bluegrass Festival. This three-day annual event on Memorial weekend, founded by Harper Van Hoy in 1924, is held at Union Grove, north of Statesville. Old time folk musicians, cloggers and storytellers gather and camp here for musical competitions, workshops and wholesome family fun. Drugs and alcohol are strictly forbidden. For more information, write P.O. Box 11, Union Grove, NC 28689 or call: (704) 539-4417. Take exit 65, off I-77, 1 1/2 miles west on N.C. 901. Admission is charged.

JUNE

Afro-American Art Expo. This expo will feature artwork, African artifacts, jewelry, cloth, shirts, books, card and other items related to African culture made by artists from throughout the Southeast. For more information, call 535-3247 or 392-0391. Friendship Missionary Baptist Church, 3301 Beatties Ford Road.

Juneteenth. This is the celebration of the true Independence Day for African-Americans. It commemorates June 19th, 1862, the first act prohibiting slavery, and in 1865 when Union troops arrived in Galveston, Texas, to enforce the end of slavery; and in 1964 when the Civil Rights Act was passed. Charlotteans celebrate with a banquet and dance on June 19 and Family Day on June 20th at Johnson

C. Smith University. For more information, call 373-1808.

Listen and Remember. This outdoor drama recalls the days of Andrew Jackson and the Waxhaw Indians. It is held each weekend in June. Admission is charged.

Charlotte Orchestra Pops Concerts. Now held at SouthPark Mall, these concerts offer residents a chance to spread a picnic and enjoy light music outside near the mall. The concerts continue through July. The concerts are free.

Charlotte Express Tennis. Charlotte Express tennis matches feature top tennis players from around the world and continue into August. Admission is charged.

Summerfest at Spirit Square. This event is a showcase for Charlotte's German speaking community that rolls entertainment, food and education into one tasty and appealing cultural event. Spirit Square is located at 345 N. College Street in Uptown Charlotte. Admission is charged.

WestFest. West Charlotte High School holds the annual day of good food, fun, games and arts and crafts.

Stumptown Festival. No longer held during Labor Day weekend, this festival is now held in mid-June on the grounds of Carolina Lanes near Matthew-Mint Hill Road and East Independence Boulevard. It offers a carnival, an arts and crafts show, music, an 8 K race, a petting zoo, a street dance and an aerial show, plus staged entertainment. Admission is free before 4 PM. For more information, call 847-8899.

July

Family Fourth Celebration at Memorial Stadium. This is by far the best place in town to see fireworks and renew one's patriotism.

The Reenactment of the Battle of Huck's Defeat. This drama of the American Revolution is held on the second Saturday in July, at Historic Brattonsville, South Carolina, in York County. For information, call (803-684-2327). Admission is charged.

August

Charlotte Observer **Carolina Moonride.** This event provides an opportunity to join other bicyclists in a safe ride on a hot summer night through Uptown Charlotte. The Moonride is free.

Dilworth Jubilee. Held in Latta Park, the second weekend Saturday in August, this is a neighborhood get-together that has grown in popularity and draws visitors from all over the city. The Dilworth Home Tour is held on both Friday and Saturday of that weekend.

Women's Equality Day Celebration. This event spotlights the city's women leaders and offers good food, fellowship and inspiring speeches.

Bon Odori Festival. A celebration of Japanese culture, this festival includes food, dance and music at Two First Union Atrium and Plaza. Hours are from 1 PM to 5 PM and admission is charged. For more information, call 336-8888.

SEPTEMBER

ASID (American Society of Interior Designers) Designer House. Held in a different location each year, this is where Charlotte decorators show off their talents and lookers pick up some great ideas.

Jazz Charlotte. This is a popular annual event that is now in its fifth year. Formerly held Uptown it has moved to Paramount's Carowinds Paladium. Admission is charged.

UNCC International Festival. This festival showcases the worldwide countries that are represented in Charlotte through arts, crafts, food and entertainment.

Greek Yaisou Festival. Greek food, music and dancing, arts and crafts are featured at this authentic event sponsored by Charlotte's large Greek community. The festival is held at the Greek Orthodox Church each year and a nominal admission fee is charged. No admission is charged for seniors and children younger than 12.

National Balloon Rally. Held at the Statesville Municipal Airport, this is a three-day event that paints our skies with colorful expressions of beauty and whimsy. The extravaganza features balloon rides, contests, arts and crafts, military displays, activities for children and food. Admission is charged.

Serenade to Autumn Fashion Show. Hosted by Belk Stores at Ovens Auditorium, Serenade to Autumn is a preview of fall fashions and attracts top designers such as Alexander Julian. Admission is charged.

Southern Women's Show. This event abounds with exhibits, merchandise and information of special interest to women. Admission is charged.

Annual Folk Music Festival. Normally scheduled for the second weekend in June, this two-day festival of traditional music, set last year at Paramount's Carowinds Paladium was a big success. Bring your own acoustic instrument and you can sign up for morning workshops in fiddle, banjo, autoharp, dulcimer, pennywhistle and storytelling. Afternoon concerts feature local groups. Admission is charged.

OCTOBER

Latta Folklife Festival. Historic Latta Place is the setting for this festival that recalls the old days with a day of festive folk music and crafts. Nominal admission is charged.

Mint Museum Antique Show. Held at Park Center, this show provides a good opportunity to view quality antiques.

Winston Pole Day, All Pro Auto Parts 300 and Oakwood Homes 500. These exciting race events fill the month of October with excitement at the Charlotte Motor Speedway. Admission is charged.

Mallard Creek Barbecue. This old-fashioned barbecue, held at Mallard Creek Baptist Church near UNC Charlotte, is the place to see and be seen with local and state politicians and enjoy good home-cooked barbecue at the same time. Food fee charged.

Southern Ideal Home Show. Exhibits and merchandise of interest to homeowners and would-be homeowners are featured here. Admission is charged.

Waxhaw Scottish Games. These traditional games are held at the Waxhaw Amphitheater. Admission is charged.

NOVEMBER

Shrine Bowl Game. This is the annual showdown between high school all-star football players from the two Carolinas. It is held at Memorial Stadium. Admission is charged.

Carolinas Carousel Festival and Parade. Held in Uptown Charlotte, this event officially heralds the Christmas season in Charlotte.

SouthPark Turkey Trot. This annual 8K roadrace is run on Thanksgiving Day. All proceeds go to charity. The event begins at the Hyatt Charlotte.

Southern Antique Spectacular. The Metrolina Expo Center hosts dealers and antique buffs from across the country for a three-day antique extravaganza. Admission is charged.

Southern Christmas Show. Truly a winter wonderland of crafts, gifts, exhibits, food and anything remotely connected with the Christmas season, this show is a Charlotte tradition. Thousands of visitors arrive by car or tour bus to get a head start on their Christmas shopping. Admission is charged.

DECEMBER

A Celebration of Christmas. The Hezekiah Alexander Homesite provides a unique way to get into the Christmas spirit with the singing of Christmas carols, the arrival of the minister on horseback and the serving of cider and gingerbread. Admission is charged.

Singing Christmas Tree. This celebration of Christmas in song is held at Ovens Auditorium and is a Charlotte tradition. Admission is charged.

Christmas Town USA. Neighboring McAdenville is the site of this spectacular Christmas light show. It has been staged by Stowe-Pharr Yarns for decades in the quaint mill village near Gastonia.

Security matters.
Yours. And ours.

At First Union, security means a lot of things. It means doing business for more than 86 years without ever reporting an annual loss. It means paying dividends to shareholders for the last 16 consecutive years — recession or no recession. It means having a capital reserve that far exceeds federal regulatory minimums. It means we take care of your money.

If you bank at First Union, you can be sure that your money is in one of the strongest banks in the country. And one of the most valuable services we will offer you is to safeguard your money, to protect it and help you to help it grow. We look forward to working with you to meet all your finanicial needs. So come talk. We like to listen. And we want to earn your business.

First Union National Banks℠

When it comes to service,
everything matters.®

Inside
Banking

There's no denying it: the jewel in Charlotte's commercial crown is banking. This is a banking town, first and foremost. One of Charlotte's many assets as a leading business center is the fact that more banking resources are headquartered in Charlotte than in all but three other U.S. cities. Six of the nation's top 200 banks operate in Charlotte, and two of the top 25 banks are headquartered here. Charlotte's concentration of financial institutions provides a wide variety of size, expertise and services to the city's industries.

Charlotte presents some amazing numbers when it comes to banking. With $105 billion in assets, it is only behind New York, San Francisco and Los Angeles. Charlotte ranks second with Chicago and San Francisco in the table of the 200 largest banks represented in the leading U.S. Distribution Centers. There are 17 banks operating here, along with 78 commercial finance and factoring firms, 64 leasing corporations, 139 mortgage companies and 12 savings and loans. Eleven of the nations 25 largest mortgage lenders have facilities in Charlotte with two of those headquartered here. Adding to Charlotte's financial variety is a branch of the Federal Reserve Bank of Richmond. All in all, there's a whole lot of bankin' going on.

Our banks provide a wealth of services to commercial and retail customers and are always leading the nation in the development of new and innovative ways to provide better services. The arrival of interstate banking and more liberal nationwide banking laws means that Charlotte's banks are poised for a financial invasion of other states. None of this ever would have been possible without North Carolina's aggressive banking laws and the motivation of Charlotte's banking leadership.

Charlotte's banks continue to grow. **NationsBank**, formerly NCNB, and C&S Sovran merged December 31, 1991, becoming the fourth largest bank in the country. NationsBank is headquartered in Charlotte in the new **NationsBank Corporate Center**, the largest office building in the Southeast. **First Union National Bank** announced in September 1992 an agreement to acquire Dominion Bankshares. First Union's combination with the Roanoke, Virginia-based Dominion produced the nation's ninth largest bank holding company with assets of $61.3 billion and more than 1,200 offices serving approximately seven million customers from Washington to Miami. **Wachovia**, although it is headquartered in Winston-Salem, has many locations throughout Charlotte and is one of the most profitable banks in the country.

With the abundance of banks in the area, competition is a given factor. Banks work hard to develop business in Charlotte as well as around the country. If a company in Kansas needs a big loan, you can be certain that one or more of Charlotte's banks will be there to bid for the account.

The competitiveness among banks in Charlotte produces a wide range of services and rates available to consumers. With over 175 banking offices all over the city, the city boasts one of the highest ratios of bank branches to population in the nation. There is no point in the city that is more than 2 1/2 miles away from a branch!

Competition has also led to the building war in Uptown. It all began in 1954 when First Union built what is now called the First Union Bank Building which was the first new structure Uptown in 25 years. NCNB (now NationsBank) countered in 1961 when it built what

is now the BB&T Center. Then, in 1971, First Union built the 32-story First Union Plaza. NCNB countered First Union again in 1974 by constructing a 40-story building at Trade and Tryon. This NCNB building remained the tallest structure in the city until 1987, when First Union built its new 42-story building on College Street. It became the largest building between Atlanta and Philadelphia. Once again, NCNB made the move to top First Union by announcing in late 1986 its plan to build a 60-story office tower which was completed in 1992. Christened with the bank's new corporate name, the NationsBank Corporate Center is the largest building in the Southeast, with well over one million square feet of office space. First Union's response to the NationsBank Corporate Center is yet to be seen.

The dominance of the banking industry in Charlotte heavily influences the local economy and the sociological makeup of the city. Banks in the area are based on steady profit growth and conservative business practices. The conservativeness of the area's banks has most likely contributed to the fact that Charlotte is a conservative but forward thinking city.

Banks in the Queen City deserve credit for contributing to Charlotte's impressive standard of living. The banks have been outstanding corporate citizens, with a long history of giving money and time to all sorts of projects to benefit the community at large. This has set a standard for community service that most every corporation here

Staff photo.

Signs of the banking industry are visible in almost every aspect of life in Charlotte.

follows: if you do business in Charlotte-Mecklenburg, you give generously to the community.

When outsiders think of Charlotte's banks, they immediately think about the giants such as NationsBank, First Union and Wachovia. But Charlotte is also home to some excellent smaller and medium-sized banks that offer the same sense of security of the larger banks. These smaller banks can be found throughout the Charlotte area, and most offer services similar to the ones available at the larger banks.

Mid-size banks include **First Citizens**, which is based in Raleigh, and **BB&T**, which is based in Wilson, N.C. Another mid-size bank, **SouthTrust**, just moved to Charlotte in 1992. Small local banks include the **Bank of Mecklenburg, Park Meridian** and **Home Federal. First Charlotte**, another of the city's smaller local banks was purchased last year by Centura Bank, which headquartered in Rocky Mount, North Carolina,

Charlotte banks have fueled the phenomenal growth of Uptown and other areas in the region. The presence of these large corporations creates the need for support services and attracts other large businesses-the result being that banks and related businesses are a major source of employment in the region. The next few years will be extremely interesting for the banks as they venture into some uncharted territories. With USAir's recent addition of a direct route to the Grand Caymans, which is a large Swiss banking center, Charlotte could see the addition of more banks which now have easy access to the area. It looks like in the near future big banks will become even bigger, while smaller institutions will actively chip away at niche markets. So even if you don't work directly for a bank or for a company that works for one, your life in Charlotte-Mecklenburg is still highly influenced by these financial giants. It may mean conservative business attire, but it also means a healthy, thriving economy.

For information on specific banks in Charlotte and the services they offer, simply call the bank. Many offer newcomer services and all will be glad to assist you in opening accounts or other transactions.

The following banks are among those that provide newcomer information:

BB&T
Newcomer Services　　*(704) 342-7054*

FIRST UNION NATIONAL BANK
Newcomer Representative　*(704) 374-6148*
(800) 473-3568

HOME FEDERAL
Newcomer Services　　*(704) 373-0400*

NATIONSBANK
Newcomer Representative　*(800) 275-6262*

UNITED CAROLINA BANK
Newcomer Services　　*(704) 554-7677*

WACHOVIA BANK OF NORTH CAROLINA
Newcomer Services　　*(704) 378-5235*

Photo by Bill Giduz. Courtesy of Davidson Cololege.

Davidson College, one of the nation's most respected private liberal arts schools, is less than 25 minutes from Uptown Charlotte.

Inside
Colleges and Universities

Whether you are interested in getting your undergraduate degree, your masters, or simply taking a class on computer programming or music, Charlotte has it. Now, the city also offers Ph.D. programs in several areas, thanks to the growth at University of North Carolina at Charlotte. There are 18 institutions of higher learning that currently serve over 60,000 full-time students in Charlotte. A wide variety of educational opportunities exists, ranging from technical and vocational schools to major colleges and universities. All of these institutions strengthen the economic, cultural and social life of the community.

A cooperative agreement has been established that allows the individual institutions to share in each others' resources, further enhancing educational opportunities in the area. Charlotte's higher education system serves dual roles, as it provides knowledge and training for vocational necessities and emphasizes as well as promotes arts and culture.

Several of the area's colleges and universities enjoy national visibility and recognition. **Central Piedmont Community College**, near Uptown, is one of the top five community colleges in the nation. The **University of North Carolina at Charlotte**, part of the University of North Carolina system and located just north of the city, has recently been rated as one of the best educational values in America by *U.S. News & World Report*. **Davidson College**, one of the nation's most respected private liberal arts schools, is less than 25 minutes from Uptown. **Queens College**, which has recently opened its doors to men, offers many evening programs designed for the nontraditional student.

Educational opportunities in Charlotte continue to grow. UNC Charlotte has three approved doctoral programs in Applied Mathematics, Electrical Engineering and Mechanical Engineering. All of the higher learning institutions in the area are constantly updating and adding programs to stay consistent with current educational needs of the expanding population.

Here is an overview of the many educational opportunities that exist in the Charlotte area. If you have further questions, do not hesitate to call the schools' offices.

Four-Year Institutions

BELMONT ABBEY COLLEGE
100 Belmont-Mt. Holly Rd.
Belmont, N.C.   (800) 523-2355
                       (704) 825-6665
Founded in 1876 by the Order of Saint Benedict, Belmont Abbey College offers a unique combination of the old and the new. The Belmont Abbey education, rooted in the 1,500-year-old Benedictine tradition of value-based teaching, helps students learn timeless values and whole-life skills. Located just minutes from Charlotte on I-85 South, the college offers many opportunities for contemporary learning and professional development.

More than 25 undergraduate majors and five pre-professional programs prepare students for graduate school and a variety of careers. Since 1993, the college has offered a Masters Degree in Middle Grades Education. Drawing students from 29 states and 18 foreign countries, Belmont Abbey College has a diverse population of approximately 1,000 students.

DAVIDSON COLLEGE
Davidson, N.C.   892-2000
Davidson College is a private, four-year, coeducational liberal arts college located 20 miles north of Charlotte. Founded by The Presbyterian Church USA, the college is intentionally small, with an enrollment of approximately 1,550 men and women, and is governed by an Honor Code that stresses honesty and integrity. Admission is highly selective, and students come from 43 states and 21 foreign countries.

In the past eight years, Davidson has had seven professors honored with silver and gold medals by the Council for the Advancement and Support of Education. Included in these honorees were one national professor of the year and three state professors of the year.

Davidson alumni are known for their community service, responsible leadership and passion for life-long learning. Among the college's 16,000 alumni there are approximately 1,900 doctors, 1,300 attorneys, 750 ministers, 10 former or current members of the U.S. Congress and two of the last three governors of North Carolina.

The **Campaign for Davidson**, the largest fund-raising drive in the college's history, was launched in 1989 with the primary goal of raising $150 million to increase endowment and ensure financial stability for the next decade and beyond. The Campaign surpassed the $118 million mark in June 1993.

JOHNSON C. SMITH UNIVERSITY
100 Beatties Ford Rd.   378-1000
Founded in 1867, Johnson C. Smith is one of the nation's oldest and most respected black colleges. It currently serves approximately 1,300 students and offers bachelor degrees in 26 fields. The University has developed four Centers of Ex-

Photo by Lance Anderson, CPCC © 1994.

Belmont Abbey College offers a unique combination of the old and the new.

cellence: Freshman Studies, Honors College, Banking and Finance Education and Natural Sciences. In recent years, the school has joined hands with UNC Charlotte, Duke University, Davidson College and Howard University to develop a cooperative program to better prepare its students for the future.

PFEIFFER COLLEGE
CHARLOTTE CAMPUS
1040 E. Woodlawn Rd.   *521-9116*

Pfeiffer's main campus is located in Misenheimer, N.C., but the college offers some special opportunities for those who attend its Charlotte Campus. In Charlotte, the college works closely with Central Piedmont Community College graduates and others who wish to continue their education by taking junior and senior courses in accounting, business administration and criminal justice. Pfeiffer also offers Masters Degrees in Business Administration and Christian Education.

QUEENS COLLEGE
1900 Selwyn Ave.   *337-2200*

Queens College, located in historic Myers Park, is a private college with close ties to the Presbyterian Church. Since its founding in 1857, Queens has evolved into a diversified institution of higher education serving a variety of learners. More than 1,600 degree-seeking men and women of all ages are enrolled in Queens' three colleges: **The College of Arts and Sciences**, a coed undergraduate program that emphasizes the traditional liberal arts; **The New College at Queens**, a program for working men and women who want to earn undergraduate degrees in evening or Saturday classes; **The Graduate School**, offering mostly evening and Saturday courses leading to a Masters Degree in Business or Education and Charlotte's only Executive MBA program. The **McColl School of Business** serves all of the business students in the three components of the college.

In addition, Queens provides lifelong learning opportunities through three non-degree programs. **Queens Compute** offers personal computer training in evening and day-long workshops, **Queens Excel** provides professional seminars for local businesses, and **Queens Continuing Education Program** offers a wide variety of personal enrichment courses for the Charlotte community.

Of all the elements that combine to make Queens' undergraduate program distinctive, three in particular deserve special mention. The award-winning required core curriculum, **Foundations of Liberal Learning**, emphasizes the interconnectedness of all knowledge, and the **International Experience** program guarantees every full-time student an opportunity for travel abroad, at no extra cost. Queens also offers internships, both professional and exploratory, that allow students to learn more about the world of work. The College enjoys unusually close ties with the Charlotte community. The **Learning Society of Queens College** sponsors a public speakers series, and the **Very International People Society** promotes a global outlook.

Belk Chapel at Queens is a popular place for weddings, and the Charlotte Repertory Orchestra, the Charlotte Philharmonic Orchestra and the Oratorio Singers perform periodically in Dana Auditorium.

UNIVERSITY OF NORTH CAROLINA AT CHARLOTTE

N.C.. 49 N.   *547-2000*

The University of North Carolina at Charlotte is a comprehensive university on a 957-acre campus in northeastern Charlotte. With nearly 16,000 students, it is now the 146th largest of the nation's 3,712 colleges and universities.

More than 60 undergraduate degree options are offered in six academic divisions: Architecture, Arts and Sciences, Business Administration, Education and Allied Professions, Engineering and Nursing.

A graduate school with an enrollment of more than 2,400 students offers a broad array of masters degrees, and the University is embarking on additional doctoral degrees within the year.

UNC Charlotte is ranked a top comprehensive university for quality and value by *U.S. News & World Report* and in 1990 was listed as a best value in America by *Barrons 300* and a new book, *A Guide to the 75 Best College Values in America.* It is also one of two universities in North Carolina featured in *How to Get an Ivy League Education at a State University.* The University now ranks 146th

The University has distinguished itself for its outreach to business and industry, and for its role as a catalyst in the development of what amounts to a "new town" surrounding the campus called **University**

The beautifully landscaped campus of The University of North Carolina at Charlotte covers 957 acres in the northeastern section of the city.

Photo by Wade Burton. Courtesy UNCC Information and Public Relations.

City. This area includes **University Research Park**, the nation's sixth largest research park, and the **Ben Craig Center**, a university business incubator. On campus, the University houses the **C.C. Cameron Applied Research Center** where faculty and students work jointly with businesses on research projects.

As an NCAA Division 1 school, UNC Charlotte offers 13 varsity sports, giving the city a wide variety of interests for local sports fans. The most visible program is men's basketball, which now plays its home schedule at the Charlotte Coliseum. Eventually games will move on campus to the James H. Barnhardt Student Center, scheduled for completion in the fall of 1995. Twelve of the 13 sports offered compete in the Metro Conference.

As a regional attraction, UNC Charlotte offers outstanding botanical gardens. These include the **Van Landingham Glen**, a collection of hybrid and native rhododendrons and wild flowers; the **Susie Harwood Garden**, a setting with an oriental motif that features ornamental plants from around the world; and the **McMillan Greenhouse**, which features collections of orchids, cactuses and carnivorous plants in addition to a simulated tropical rain forest.

The campus grounds are beautifully landscaped. Features for the visitor include a panoramic view of Northeast Charlotte from the 10th floor of the Dalton Tower the University's library, an outdoor sculpture garden, several art galleries and theaters and a performance hall in the Rowe Building.

Over 60,000 students are served annually in the Charlotte area's 18 institutions of higher learning.

Photo by Wade Bruton. Courtesy UNCC Information and Public Relations.

WINGATE COLLEGE

220 N. Camden Rd.
Wingate, N.C.   (800) 755-5550
                     (704) 233-8000

Wingate is an accredited liberal arts, church-affiliated institution, offering bachelors degrees in 40 majors, and masters degrees through its schools of business and education. Wingate's pioneering international study/travel program has made it possible for thousands of Wingate students to participate in the program before graduation. Another outstanding program, the **United Collegiate Assistance Network**, has been recognized nationally, statewide and regionally for its student volunteer record. Last year Wingate was given the John Templeton Honor Roll award for being a character-building college. The college now operates a center in nearby Matthews, N.C.

WINTHROP UNIVERSITY

Oakland Ave.
Rock Hill, S.C.   (803) 323-2211

Winthrop, founded in 1886, is a competitive, comprehensive, coeducational university committed to being a model of excellence in public higher education. Winthrop's 5,000 students may choose among 56 undergraduate and 44 graduate programs of study in the College of Arts and Sciences, and in the professional Schools of Business Administration, Education and Visual and Performing Arts. The University also offers the **New Start Program** for students age 22 and older, and a nationally accredited Executive MBA program.

Two-Year Institutions

CENTRAL PIEDMONT COMMUNITY COLLEGE

Elizabeth Ave. at Kings Dr.   342-6633

Rated as one of the top five community colleges in the nation, CPCC offers courses in just about every subject imaginable. Students may pursue more than 70 career programs and earn a diploma or associate degree. Many choose to take classes simply for personal enrichment or professional advancement. The beauty of CPCC is that it is an open-door institution that will accept students regardless of their educational attainment. Classes are affordable too—$13.25 per credit hour (to a maximum of $190.50) for N.C. residents; $107.50 (to a maximum of $1,510.00) for nonresidents.

The college, which is 30 years old, provides business and industry training in state-of-the-art laboratories to meet the needs of the Charlotte community. The school's **Adult Basic Literacy Education** program is a national model. Serving over 60,000 students annually, the school is the largest of the 58 community colleges in the state. The main campus is located in the heart of the city, with satellite learning centers on N.C. 51, in Huntersville and on Freedom Drive. Classes are also held at many other locations in Charlotte.

GASTON COLLEGE

N.C. 321
Dallas, N.C.   (704) 922-6200

Serving both Gaston and Lincoln Counties, this community col-

lege outside of Gastonia enrolls approximately 4,000 students each quarter in curriculum programs, and averages 12,000 students annually in its Continuing Education and Community Service programs. Students may pursue associate degrees in the arts and applied science. It also offers a B.S. in Technology through Appalachian State University in Boone and a Masters in Public Administration through UNC Charlotte.

YORK TECHNICAL COLLEGE
Rock Hill, S.C.   *(803) 327-8008*

Just south of Charlotte in Rock Hill, York Technical College offers technical training in business, health, computers, industrial and engineering technologies, in addition to associate degrees in the arts and sciences.

Business Colleges

AMERICAN BUSINESS AND FASHION INSTITUTE
1515 Mockingbird Ln.   *523-3738*

This business college offers full-time and part-time career training in interior design, fashion merchandising, secretarial science, travel/business/hospitality, and retail management. Courses of study, available days or evenings, take nine to 18 months to complete. Opportunities include internships, employ-

ment assistance, financial assistance and scholarships.

The college, located in Southeast Charlotte, boasts a graduation rate of over 80% and places virtually all of its graduates in their field of training. This 20-year-old institution is approved for Veteran's benefits and vocational rehabilitation.

BROOKSTONE COLLEGE OF BUSINESS
8307 University Executive Park Dr.547-8600

This business college specializes in high-tech secretarial training, computerized accounting and administrative and accounting software with hands-on experience. Financial aid and job placement assistance are available.

KING'S COLLEGE
332 Lamar Ave.   *372-0266*

You can prepare for some careers in less than a year at this well-established Charlotte institution. King's college was founded in 1901, making it the oldest business college in the Carolinas. King's offers a full-time job placement service with contacts throughout the business and professional community.

Courses of study include administrative assistant, accounting, computer programming, computer specialist, graphic design, legal secretary, medical-office assistant, paralegal, retail merchandising, secretarial science and travel and leisure.

Photo by Mitchell Kearney. Courtesy of Marketing Consortium Group.

Almost half of Charlotte's approximately 21.9 million square feet of office space is located Uptown in buildings like the 1991 Carillon Building.

Inside
Commercial
Real Estate

Charlotte has usually been able to remain stable and even grow in times of recession. The city is not immune from recessions, but it does have many dynamic companies that prosper in any economy, helping the commercial real estate market to remain secure.

Charlotte's considerable growth and its ability to attract new industries to the area has resulted in an increase in the size of the city's office, industrial and retail markets. In each case, the amount of square feet available in Charlotte has at least doubled since 1980. The rapid increase in the amount of commercial space contributed to a high vacancy rate during the recession, but the vacancy rate is now decreasing at a remarkable pace. The market has absorbed 1.1 million square feet of available space over the past year.

Charlotte's office market contains approximately 21.9 million square feet of space including about 9.7 million square feet located Uptown. Other major office concentrations are located along I-77 in the southwest, on N.C. 51 in the far southeast, in the Midtown area east and south of Uptown, and in SouthPark. Some of the newest office centers in Charlotte are the CrownPoint/Matthews area, along Billy Graham Parkway and the northeast submarket around University Place.

Although most people think of Charlotte mainly as an office center, the industrial category is far larger. About 85 million square feet of manufacturing, warehouse and business-park space exist in Charlotte. The largest concentrations of industrial space are in the central, southwest and northwest areas. Newly emerging as popular warehouse and/or business park locations are the I-77 area in northern Mecklenburg County including Huntersville and Lake Norman, the CrownPoint/Matthews area along East Independence Boulevard and Monroe Road and in the Southwest along Westinghouse Boulevard.

Retailers have been drawn to Charlotte because of the city's growth in population, households and incomes. Construction has been

Retailers have been drawn to Charlotte because of the city's growth in population, households and incomes.

especially active in neighborhood shopping ventures traditionally anchored by supermarkets and drugstores. With the recent completion of Carolina Place Mall in Pineville, the Charlotte area now has three regional malls.

A new trend occurring in Charlotte is the development of large power centers. These retail properties are generally over 250,000 square feet in size and heavily pre-leased to large anchor tenants like Wal-Mart, Kmart, Marshall's, Home Depot, Office Max, Service Merchandise, MediaPlay, etc.

Charlotte's long-term growth should continue to justify new office, industrial and retail development, although at a pace considerably reduced from the overbuilding experienced in the '80s that will take some time to absorb into the economy. But, if you are looking to lease or buy a site, times are great for you. The outlook for Charlotte's commercial development is positive. In fact, Charlotte was chosen by more of the nation's top business leaders as a good place for future business locations.

Here are some of the more visible commercial real estate companies in Charlotte:

AAC MANAGEMENT, INC.
5970 Fairview Rd., Ste. 600   556-0975

Developers of SouthPark landmarks such as the classic Fairview I, II and III office buildings, AAC Management, Inc. specializes in asset management, commercial and retail property management and commercial and retail leasing. The company holds many interests throughout Charlotte and offers Class A corporate space to discriminating companies in the area.

ATLANTIC PROPERTIES
4525 Hedgemore Dr.   525-5565

This commercial Realtor specializes in warehouse and manufacturing office space and retail locations. In addition, it is a full-service brokerage firm.

JAMES M. ALEXANDER REALTY, INC.
4400-A Stuart Andrew Blvd.   523-8753

Focusing primarily on industrial and office space, James M. Alexander Realty is a major developer of industrial and business parks. The company handles leasing, development, sales, investments and land sales.

THE BINSWANGER COMPANY
230 S. Tryon St., Ste. 1200   377-0801

One of the leading office-space brokers in town, Binswanger offers complete commercial real estate services. From tenant representation, to real estate investment and loan consulting, to building management and development, this company handles it all.

THE BISSELL COMPANIES, INC.
2115 Rexford Rd.   366-9841

Privately held and based in Charlotte, The Bissell Companies is responsible for more than 6 million square feet of developed retail, hotel and office space throughout the Southeast. Listed as one of the Top 100 developers in the country, the company is best known for developing much of what is now SouthPark.

CHARTER PROPERTIES
129 W. Trade St.   377-4172

Charter Properties manages, leases and develops a variety of properties in the area. It manages the distinguished Commerce Center in Uptown Charlotte and is partners with NationsBank in the new 60-story NationsBank Corporate Center.

CHARTWELL PROPERTIES

1800-J Associates Ln.   *357-1220*

This company represents properties with superb locations in the Charlotte metropolitan area. Some of the business centers it handles include Coffey Creek, Cornelius, Hickory Grove, East Harris Boulevard and Independence Pointe. Chartwell properties also handles properties in Greensboro, N.C. and Greenville, S.C.

CHILDRESS KLEIN PROPERTIES

301 S. College St.   *342-9000*

One of Charlotte's premier players, Childress Klein is the developer of LakePointe on Billy Graham Parkway and also One First Union Center, one of the most recognizable landmarks of the Uptown area. Childress Klein also handles industrial properties and retail shopping centers such as The Arboretum and The Centrum.

CB COMMERCIAL

1900 Charlotte Plaza   *376-7979*

A national real estate company since 1906, CB Commercial underwent a name change when it was sold by Sears in 1989. It has been active in Charlotte for 14 years and specializes in retail, industrial, office and investment sales, leasing and management.

COLLETT & ASSOCIATES

100 N. Tryon St., Ste. 4170   *376-6523*

Collett & Associates offers complete corporate, commercial and industrial real estate services, including brokerage, fee management and development, counseling and tenant representation.

CRESCENT RESOURCES

400 S. Tryon St., Ste. 1300   *373-3012*

This company is involved in all areas of residential and commercial real estate development, leasing

IBM is one of the many impressive tenants of University Research Park located north of Uptown near UNC Charlotte.

and management. Crescent Resources handles The Peninsula, Coliseum Center, Lakemont Business Park and many other prestigious properties throughout the region.

CROSLAND GROUP
125 Scaleybark Rd.   *523-0272*

Crosland Group is a full-service company. From corporate relocations to retail centers, the company prides itself on its quality service and reputation. CrownPoint is leased, developed and managed by the firm.

ERWIN CAPITAL
200 N. College St., Ste. 2035   *335-9579*

Investors and developers of commercial properties, this firm's projects include Northcross, CrownPoint and numerous shopping centers in the Charlotte area.

FAISON ASSOCIATES, INC.
1900 Interstate Tower
122 W. Trade Street   *331-2500*

Charlotte-based, Faison Associates is a full-service commercial real estate management, leasing and development company organized along project responsibility lines. Faison's first full service regional office opened in Richmond, Virginia, in 1993 followed by regional offices in Tampa, Jacksonville, Atlanta, Orlando, Milwaukee, Cincinnati, Dallas, Naples and Washington, DC. Faison's portfolio exceeds $3.2 billion in value and spans 12 states. The company has grown to over 800 people who manage over 38 million square feet of retail, office, apartment/condominium and hotel properties.

FIRST COLONY CORPORATION
6853 Fairview Rd., Ste. 200   *362-5000*

Developer and leasing agent for such well-known projects as Colony on Fairview in SouthPark and Colony Court, First Colony is a Charlotte-based firm.

FORSYTH PARTNERS
200-H W. Woodlawn Rd.   *525-6295*

A full-service commercial real estate company based in Winston-Salem with offices in Charlotte and Greensboro, Forsyth Partners has four divisions: development, brokerage, property management and construction. The company is actively involved in the office and warehouse/distribution markets in all of the major cities of North Carolina.

GIBSON-SMITH REALTY
301 S. College St., Ste. 3490   *333-7151*

The company handles commercial and industrial real estate. Gibson-Smith also deals with investment properties, office space and land.

HARRIS GROUP
4201 Congress St., Ste. 200   *556-1717*

Johnny Harris, Peter Pappas, and Benjamin Trotter founded the Harris Group in 1992. It offers comprehensive real estate services and developing to corporations, institutions and investors. The Harris Group focuses on tenant counseling, brokerage development and project management.

HESTA PROPERTIES, INC.
227 W. Trade Street, Ste. 2320   *343-9334*

Developer, owner and leasing agent of the Carillon office tower, Hesta Properties is poised for more development in the Uptown area in the future. Hesta Properties, Inc. is a full-service brokerage, leasing, investment and management firm.

THE KEITH CORPORATION
2719 Coltsgate Rd.   *365-6000*

The Keith Corporation is a full-service commercial real estate company offering brokerage, development and property management. It handles industrial, office and retail properties, including the revitalized, mixed-use CityFair in Uptown.

LAT PURSER & ASSOCIATES, INC.
901 S. Kings Dr.   *374-0999*

Established in 1961, this Charlotte-headquartered firm is involved in six major areas of commercial real estate: development, commercial brokerage, financial services, property management, leasing and construction management.

LEVINE PROPERTIES
8510 McAlpine Park Dr.   *366-1981*

Developers of affordable commercial space, Levine Properties is responsible for the leasing and management of Greylyn Business Park and the McAlpine Business Centre.

LINCOLN PROPERTY COMPANY
100 N. Tryon St., Ste. 4150   *331-0917*

Leasing agents for one of Charlotte's hottest new properties, the NationsBank Corporate Center, Lincoln Property Company is well-known in the area. The company is currently leasing NationsBank Center, the city's newest landmark.

MECA PROPERTIES, INC.
908 S. Tryon St.   *372-0005*

MECA Properties, Inc. is a full-service commercial investment real estate firm that offers brokerage, development and management services for the Charlotte area. Two of its more notable recent projects are Olmstead Park and Atherton Mill.

NORCOM DEVELOPMENT, INC.
1512 E. 4th St.   *332-4146*

Owned and operated from headquarters here in Charlotte, NORCOM leases, manages and de-

velops retail and office properties throughout the Southeast United States.

PERCIVAL'S, INC.
301 S. McDowell St.　　　*333-1535*

A longtime player in the local commercial market, Percival's leases and manages many area properties.

THE J.S. PROCTOR COMPANY
1610 E. Morehead St.　　　*372-0847*

This privately-held company is a full-service commercial real estate development and management firm headquartered in Charlotte. It was founded in 1977.

QUEENS PROPERTIES, INC.
6060 J.A. Jones Dr.　　　*553-3293*

Queens Properties is responsible for major developments in the SouthPark area of the city. SouthExecutive Park is a 50-acre campus-setting office location for which the company is responsible. In addition to the leasing and management of its own properties, Queens Properties provides a wide variety of development, consulting and real estate brokerage services.

THE REID COMPANY
P.O. Box 33396
Charlotte, NC 28233　　　*376-8133*

The Reid company is a full-service brokerage firm handling all facets of commercial and investment real estate. The firm places special emphasis on site selection and acquisition of premier properties available in the marketplace. Established in 1987, The Reid Company serves both North and South Carolina.

SOUTHERN REAL ESTATE
139 S. Tryon St., Ste. 500　　　*375-1000*

Expertise and integrity express what this company has stood for since 1899. Southern Real Estate specializes in the sale, leasing and property management of industrial, office, retail and land properties. Currently, Southern Real Estate manages more than 1.5 million square feet of office and retail space and 1.5 million square feet of industrial/warehouse space.

SPECTRUM PROPERTIES
Two First Union Ctr., Ste. 1910　　　*358-1000*

Headquartered in Charlotte, Spectrum Properties handles a full range of commercial real estate services including leasing, development and brokerage.

TRAMMELL CROW COMPANY
1450 Charlotte Plaza　　　*342-7900*

Of national acclaim, the Trammell Crow Company has had its influence in this market, since the early '80s and beyond. The company handles brokerage, leasing and industrial development.

WORLDSPAN COMMERCIAL PROPERTIES
6302 Fairview Rd., Ste. 100　　　*362-7777*

This Charlotte-based company leases, develops, and manages property throughout the Carolinas. It handles retail leasing, restaurant brokerage, acreage, investment sales and build to suit opportunities.

Photo by Clay Nolen. N.C. Travel and Tourism Division.

*Sliding Rock, in the Pisgah National Forest, is a 60-foot slide
down a sloping rock formation that drops into a pool of water.*

Inside
Daytrips

Stress doesn't take time off, but you can. There's no good reason, including money and children, you can't take a little holiday from stress. A "getaway" weekend is a great antidote. Even getting away for a day helps to lighten your mood. Then, too, there are those who don't "need" to get away; they simply "want" to get away and have some fun. The good part is that Charlotte is so well located that you don't have to go very far away from home to do it. From our location, you can drive to either mountains, beaches or sand hills in a matter of hours. And if your budget so dictates, you need spend little more than a tank of gas to do it because most areas have good camping facilities year-round. When the cold, gray doldrums of winter beset you, think: in two and a half to four hours you could be slicing golf balls in Pinehurst or Myrtle Beach or shushing down sparkling snow-covered slopes from Boone to Beech Mountain. When summer temperatures arrive and you feel perspiration indelicately tickling down your spine, remember: in just a couple of hours you could be enjoying the invigorating chill of the water as you scoot down nature's water slide at Slippery Rock, located a few miles out of Brevard. Or, in around three to four hours, you could be diving into an ocean wave, tasting salt water as you surface at one of North or South Carolina's beaches.

North Carolina has beautiful parks tucked away throughout the mountains. Come late spring, when mountain laurel spreads its lacy mantel around waterfalls and old wooden bridges, you can pack your picnic basket for a daytrip. You can spread your quilt on a mountain slope or use park tables spaced throughout the mountain overlooks and parks. That's not a bad idea for the fall either, when most "leaf lookers" are threading their way from Asheville to Blowing Rock enjoying the fiery red to gold brilliance of the Blue Ridge Parkway. Fall may be too late for swimming, but feeling the cooler sand of the beach crunching under your toes is a great lift to the spirit, particularly at remote Bird Island, in wading distance of North Carolina's Sunset Beach.

During the winter, North Carolina provides the best snow skiing in the South (not counting West Virginia). **Appalachian Ski Mountain**, just outside Boone, offers a good French-Swiss Ski School for beginners. Another 45 minutes from Boone, can find you "hotdogging" down the major ski slopes of **Sugar Mountain**, and an additional 20 minutes can have you shushing down the slopes of **Beech Mountain**. Skiing is not inexpensive, especially when ski rentals, lodging and a little *apres* is figured in, but the **Charlotte Ski Bees Ski Club** (552-2588), an all-season club, offers quite affordable day and weekend trips by bus to these and other major ski resorts. For an inexpensive winter weekend, winter rate packages at the beach or sand hills, which are frequently warmer than Charlotte, are ideal getaways.

This book would be too heavy to carry around if we included all the places and activities that you can enjoy in these areas, but we're going to recommend some of the well-known ones and some that are not, but are more than worth the trip. As noted in both the **Accommodations** and **Restaurants** sections, the same price codes apply.

Beaches

Ninety percent of the surveyed beach-going public say they go to the beach to rest, especially if it's a getaway weekend. For longer, vacation-type excursions, folks look for fun, interesting and occasionally educational things to do. We'll try to cover these points objectively, but

we're admitting up front that to some degree it is bound to slip into subjectivity.

MYRTLE BEACH, SOUTH CAROLINA

Myrtle Beach has been the beach of choice for Charlotteans for as long as anyone can remember. It's the closest for one thing, about a three-hour drive, and for those looking for fun and excitement, the North Carolina beaches just don't compare. For years sun-seekers have prayed for the building of a direct highway to Myrtle Beach, but that hasn't happened and we continue to go in droves every year anyway.

Now known as the Grand Strand, Myrtle Beach is the place that the "Shag" was born—on Ocean Drive. But as those youngsters grew up, entertainment changed and the dance scene dwindled. A few years back, some nostalgic souls sent the word out that a shag reunion would be held at the beach. Four to five hundred people were expected—thousands showed up, and folks of all ages have been shagging up and down the Strand (especially on the second weekend after Labor Day) ever since.

Years ago, families packed up their belongings, including sheets and towels, and moved to the beach for a week or a month. We still do that. The difference now is that instead of staying in weathered beach cottages, we stay in luxurious condos and hotels that furnish linens—along with almost every other amenity you could possibly need or want. The pace at Myrtle Beach has changed too, as more shops, restaurants, entertainment centers, golf courses (over 90 at last count) and the like have been built. At one time, the beach was pretty much a late-spring and summer activity. No more. Although the other seasons may attract fewer "laying on the beach" types, it has become an affordable golfer's paradise for fall and winter.

If you go south or north of Myrtle Beach, you can still find less crowded, less touristy conditions. Not much has changed at Murrells Inlet or Pawley's Island (for the arrogantly shabby as they call themselves) except for the increase in restaurants and shopping.

Staying at the beach is affordable, but the rates will reflect the seasons. You can camp at **Myrtle Beach** ($, 803-238-5325) or at **Huntington Beach State Park** ($, 803-237-4440).

For rental properties, try **Beach Rental** (800-255-5997). There are literally thousands of hotels and motels, but one of our favorites is

The Carolina Reef ($$, 800-633-9679) at 1501 S. Ocean Boulevard in North Myrtle Beach. It offers one- and two-bedroom condos on the ocean front and the widest beach on the Grand Strand. Or, try the **Flagship Motor Inn** ($-$$, 800-321-7556) at 1800 South Ocean Boulevard. The **Myrtle Beach Resort** ($-$$$, 800-845-0629) between Myrtle and Surfside is an all-ocean-front, family resort with six swimming pools, tennis courts and a pool bar. **Litchfield By The Sea** ($$-$$$$, 800-845-1895) is a lovely, full resort offering three golf courses, 26 tennis courts, 10 pools, a spa sauna, three restaurants and seven miles of beach. This is a super choice.

There's no lack of restaurants in the area either, especially between **The Carolina Opry** and **The Dixie Jubilee**, off U.S. 17 where you'll find the area known as Restaurant Row. Some of the following are not in this area, but so special that we wanted you to know about them, too.

Photo by Daintry O'Brien.

The beaches of North Myrtle Beach attract thousands of Charlotteans each year..

The day can begin at **Dino's House of Pancakes** ($-$$) at 2120 U.S. 17 south—directly across from the entrance to Azalea Sands Golf Course. It serves everything from croissants to corn beef hash.

When you ask about good seafood restaurants, one of the first places you'll hear about is Little River, a few miles north of Myrtle, where the fishing boats dock. Many good restaurants are in this area, but **The Parson's Table** ($$-$$$$), located off U.S. 17 is special. In a converted old church with stained-glass windows, the atmosphere provides a perfect setting for the extraordinary food.

A visit to Myrtle Beach is not complete without a visit to **Rice Planter's Restaurant** at 6707 Kings Highway. Other than exceptionally fine dining, perhaps the most stunning feature of the Rice Planter's Restaurant is the display of antiques, tools and implements representative of the period during which rice plantations flourished in the area. The restaurant seats 350 people in 13 dining areas on two floors. Seafood, pork, chicken, steaks, calves' liver, wonderful baked goods and salad dressings are just a few of the treats awaiting you.

There are many good restaurants that are also relatively easy on the wallet. A favorite is **Preston's** ($) at 4530 U.S. 17 in North Myrtle Beach. This is a super place for family dining due to its fun atmosphere and pure country-style buffet table that provides a mountain of foods like your mamma used to make.

The old reliable **Sea Captain's House** ($$-$$$) at 3000 North Ocean Boulevard provides a good breakfast, lunch or dinner, along with a view of the ocean. Try the She-crab soup.

For a veritable trip back in time, visit **Planter's Back Porch Restaurant** in Murrells Inlet, located on the corner of U.S. 17 south and Wachesaw Road. Planter's Back Porch opened in 1972 in an 1850's residence and meticulous care has been given to preserving the authenticity of the house and grounds. Enjoy music, have a libation in **Gibby's Patio & Bar**, rock on the porch or just take time to stop and smell the flowers. The restaurant bakes its own desserts and makes its own salad dressings, and pampers you like you haven't been pampered since you had the mumps.

Another popular eating spot in Murrells Inlet is **Lee's Inlet Kitchen** ($) located 1/2 mile south of **Captain Dick's Marina** on U.S. 17 Business. The restaurant serves dishes made from old family recipes.

Oliver's Lodge ($-$$), located off U.S. 17 in Murrells Inlet, is a very casual place that has been a favorite to generations of beach goers who love good seafood. The corn dodgers and hush puppies are terrific.

Outback at Frank's ($-$$$), located at the stoplight in downtown Pawley's Island, is a unique restaurant that combines unusual food bedfellows to produce sensational results.

Latif's ($$) at 506 61st Avenue, off U.S. 17 in Myrtle Beach, is the Insiders' pick for Sunday brunch. It serves great pastries and good lunches.

North Carolina Coast

SUNSET BEACH/
BIRD ISLAND

You don't have to go out of state to get to the beach, and you can make it to Sunset Beach, crossing over its one-lane floating bridge (a hop and skip across the border from South Carolina), or to Ocean Isle almost as fast as you can to Myrtle Beach. Working on the premise of "rest," these homey, family-type beaches are the place to go to relax and maybe build a few sand castles, play a little golf or do some fishing from the pier.

At Sunset Beach, action comes from surfers and kite flyers. This beach is so laid-back that the heaviest action some folks exert is burrowing their bodies into the sand—sculpting it to the perfect, relaxed contours of their torsos. Bird watching the 200 species of birds found on these barrier islands, including white ibis, osprey, egret and painted bunting, make this an interesting pastime when you get into the wind-down mode.

If you are looking for a place where you can talk to nature, wait for low tide, head to the west end of Sunset Beach and walk across Mad Inlet. It will take you 30 minutes or so to get to Bird Island, one of the last undeveloped islands on the Carolina beaches. Stand at the base of the windswept dunes for a good vantage point to watch pelicans, sea gulls and oyster catchers, some of the species that give the island its name.

One of the two remnants of mankind that you'll find on Bird Island is an ordinary looking mail box atop a weathered post with the words, "KINDRED SPIRIT" written across its side. Inside the box are several notebooks that you may read and one notebook in which you may record reflections of your experience. It touches a deep chord to sit and read what others before you have written. Don't stay long over an hour or you'll have to roll up your pant legs to wade back.

From Sunset, go back across the bridge and turn west on N.C. 179 to reach **Sea Trail Plantation & Golf Course** (910-579-4350). A golf haven if there ever was one, Sea Trail Plantation has three different and challenging golf courses, that are environmentally designed to preserve the marshes and wetlands. Other popular golf courses in the area are **Oyster Bay Golf Links** (910-579-3528) and **Pearl Golf Links** (910-579-3528).

Many golfers and beach goers schedule trips to the little fishing village of **Calabash**. Restaurants ($$) line up, each one promising either more or better. Your best plan is to come before five so you won't have to stand in line. Fried fish, hushpuppies, cole slaw and French fries have made the area famous. You'll have to pay about $1.50 extra if you prefer broiled.

Insiders like the Christmas Shop adjoined to **Calabash Nautical Gifts** on N.C. 179 (where you'll find the restaurants) for a fanciful departure from the usual beach scene.

If you didn't know about it, you'd probably never stop at **Big Nell's Pit Stop**, ($) on N.C. 179 between Ocean Isle and Seaside. This race car-oriented restaurant is the place to come for breakfast. Big Nell says, "This is the place to bring your joys and problems." Nell's Belgian Waffles are bigger than normal, and real good under strawberry whipped cream served with spiced hot apples.

For dinner, go west to 310 Sunset Boulevard, the corner to make the turn to the bridge. This is **Crabby Oddwaters** ($$), thought by many Insiders to have the best seafood in the area. Nothing is cooked before you arrive.

Sea Trail Plantation & Golf Course is located off N.C. 179 west ($$$$, 800-624-6601). You can rent one of the Plantations's luxurious condos, many of which overlook one of its three golf courses. This 200 - acre full resort offers swimming, tennis and volleyball along with its two clubhouses and restaurants.

Beach house rentals are mostly by the week, but there are a few condos and motels around for weekend-only guests. Try **Williamson Realty** (910-579-2373) for house rentals in Sunset. **Carolina Beach & Golf Resort** (800-222-1524) or the **Sunset Beach Motel** (910-579-7093) are good choices for short-term accommodations.

OCEAN ISLE

Ocean Isle stretches for eight uncrowded miles of clean beach with good boat docks and marinas for those who arrive by water. You'll see shark-shaped kites flying overhead as you bird watch or "bait up" to surf fish. Many anglers go on a head boat or charter a boat. It's only 35 miles out to the warmer Gulf Stream where you can fight with sailfish and catch

red snapper and grouper. Spring and summer are the months when blue fish, drum, summer and small flounder are biting. These months are also a good time to go shrimping or clamming. Fall and winter is the time to land large Spanish mackerel, spots, puppy drum, blue fish, gray and speckled trout, Virginia mullet and do some serious oyster harvesting. To find out what is biting, call the North Carolina Marine Fisheries in Wilmington (800-248-4536), or in Morehead City (800-682-2632).

The distinctive difference at this beach is the **Ocean Isle Museum of Coastal Carolina** on East 3rd Street. Take a left at the waterslide to find the museum. Now in its fifth year, this nonprofit museum displays a wealth of things to see and experience. You'll find artifacts of Tucorora and Lumbee Native Americans as well as reproduced weapons and tools used before recorded time. You'll see native animals in the habitat diarama, but perhaps the best room in the museum is the under sea diarama. Also, look for the Civil War memorabilia salvaged from the underwater wreckage of the blockade runner **Ranger** that sank off Holden Beach. Admission for adults is $2, $1 for children.

At all of the South Brunswick beaches, you can scuba dive and deep sea fish or fish from rebuilt piers. **Ocean Isle Marina** (910-579-0848) is a good place to rent boats or bikes—even jet skis.

To rent a cottage or condo in Ocean Isle, call **Cooke Realty** (910-579-3535). For a weekend, try the

Ocean Isle Motel ($$$, 800-352-5988) or **The Winds Clarion Inn** ($$$, 800-334-3581).

HOLDEN BEACH

Holden is a wooded island beach framed by dogwood, palmetto and live oak trees where, even in high-season summer months, you can still find a patch of beach all to yourself. This 11-mile-long beach, located between Lockwood Folly and the Shallotte River, falls into the "rest" category, except for the first weekend in October. This is when Holden Beach hosts its annual three-day **North Carolina Festival By The Sea**.

Golfers will enjoy **Lockwood Golf Links** at 100 Club House Drive in Holden Beach (910-579-8132) and the growing summertime population has brought about more activities for youngsters. The **Super Track Go-Cart Raceway** (910-842-5050), a waterslide and a miniature golf course all offer fun alternatives.

A number of pleasure boats have scenic and ocean cruises available from the **Holden Beach Marina**, located at 3238 Pompano Street, S.W., near the high-rise bridge on N.C. 130. You can charter deep sea fishing boats here, too (910-842-8002).

For accommodations at Holden, contact **Craig Realty** (910-842-2777). The only motel in Holden is the **Gray Gull Motel** ($, 910-842-6775)

OAK ISLAND

Oak Island sits at the confluence of the Intracoastal Waterway, Atlantic Ocean and Cape Fear River. The island is linked to the mainland by a modern high-level bridge, and includes the communities of **Long Beach, Yaupon Beach** and **Caswell Beach**. Like Holden Beach, the island is swathed in live oaks and has not replaced nature with neon.

The obvious activities are soaking up rays, fishing and playing golf at **The Oak Island Golf and Country Club** on Oak Island at 928 Caswell Beach Road (910-278-5275). But on Long Beach Road, you'll find something a bit different—**Brunswick County Airport** at 380 Long Beach Road (910-457-6483). On the face of it, this may not sound too exciting, but have you ever been up in an ultra lite aircraft? You can at this airport. Or you can take an aerial view tour of the barrier islands or flight instruction.

On rainy days or at sunset, you can zip over to the corner of Ocean and Barbie Boulevard in Yaupon to **Flagship Amusement Park**. It's right across from the **Yaupon Fishing Pier**. Let the kids release some of their pent-up energy in a bumper car while you take in an ocean sunset on the boardwalk beside the pier.

Scruggs and Morrison Realty (910-278-5405) or **Shirly Fowler and Associates** (800-637-4383) can help you with rental accommodations on Oak Island.

Jones' Seafood House at 6404 Oak Island Drive in Long Beach is not where the tourists go, because few of them know about it. However, just ask islanders and they'll point you to "the best seafood in town." Another favorite, because you can eat until you pop, is **Lucky Fisher-**

man at 4419 Long Beach Road, S.E. It has a great salad bar and good country cooking with country-style steak and terrific shrimp Creole, too. If you have a sweet tooth, stop by the **Fudge Factory** on East Oak Island Drive. The Amaretto Fudge is the Insiders' pick.

BALD HEAD ISLAND

In many ways, Bald Head Island is a throwback to primitive times. Until a few years ago, there were no telephones or electricity, and guests had to wade ashore to this 12,000-acre island. Today, there is no crime, no traffic and no noise— only the hum of golf carts to break the occasional honk of Canada geese. A trip here can refine your definition of "natural wild" and "pristine beauty." This island is ecologically controlled by the Bald Head Island Conservancy; walking isn't allowed on the windswept dunes that form a spine across the island and even residents can plant only flowers indigenous to the land. An Insider describes Bald Head's beaches as: "...a place of wonder...a kind of

The North Carolina Aquarium at Fort Fisher
is one of three nationally accredited state aquariums along the coast.

religious experience." Fishermen also consider the area's Frying Pan Shoals a religious experience of blessed abundance.

Bald Head will not be on the list of inexpensive getaways ($$$$). That's because of its inaccessibility. You can only get there by a 20 minute boat ride, and cars aren't allowed either. Residents and guests use rented golf carts. No fast foods, movies, water slides or motels here. Bald Head attracts a rugged group, who could probably afford to stay anywhere they want, but choose the solitude of unshackled nature.

There are a few rentals, so call ahead to **Bald Head Island Club** ($$$, 800-722-6450) if you want to spend the weekend. You'll find a small grocery store, the **River Pilot Cafe**.

FORT FISHER

In Fort Fisher, there's a beautiful cove with once-barricaded beaches where the Union Navy played its most important card of the Civil War. Fort Fisher, a Confederate-controlled earthenworks fortification, was the major link that defended Wilmington. The Fort kept Federal blockade ships at a distance from the Cape Fear River, allowing the Confederate blockade runners to supply provisions to General Lee's army. Following Wilmington's defeat on January 15, 1865, the Confederate supply line was cut, which sped the Union victory.

Much of the original beach has been eroded, but you can visit the museum (free) and see displays of items from blockade-running ships, plus an informative audiovi-

sual presentation and other interpretive exhibits as well as a gift shop.

Just north of the fort is the **North Carolina Aquarium at Fort Fisher**. This is a busy, program-packed museum that promotes a unique awareness of the coast and its resources. It has touch-tanks that let children stroke living starfish, hermit and horseshoe crabs, and other creatures.

The aquarium, on U.S. 421, is open from 9 AM to 5 PM Monday through Saturday and from 1 until 5 PM on Sunday. Admission is $3 for adults; $2 for seniors and active military personnel and $1 for children (910-458-8257).

PLEASURE ISLAND BEACHES

Kure Beach, the southernmost of the Pleasure Island Beaches, is a pleasant place to try your hand at some surf fishing, fishing from the pier (in the center of town) or just swimming and sunning. To add a different spice to your beach getaway, sign up for one of the programs at the aquarium. Environmental coastal programs have instituted a committed resolve to protect the mysterious life of the loggerhead turtle with field-trip classes. Find out about the alligators in North Carolina (which are all over the place) and discover just which are the edible marine life in culinary workshops. Take a hands-on sand castle class or venture out to sea on board collecting trips; explore the world of marsh birds, wildflowers, etc. The list goes on.

A little north on U.S. 421, you'll be hard-pressed to know when you travel from **Carolina Beach** to

Wilmington Beach as the two naturally flow together. If education on any level is what you're trying to escape, the beaches in this area offer fun for the entire family. You can visit a family amusement park or try more daring rides at the Boardwalk.

Sports enthusiasts can tackle deep sea fishing, and everyone needs to include a stop at **Carolina Beach State Park**, where you may glimpse the Venus Fly Trap in this small region of the world where it grows naturally.

If you're trying to weekend on a budget, campsites are available in the park adjacent to Snow's Cut. **Carolina Beach Family Campground** ($, 910-392-3322) has hot showers, wooded tent sites and a swimming pool. If you are looking for a rental, **Coastal Condo-lets** (910-458-5658) covers the Intercoastal Waterway beaches, or you could try **Cabana Del Mar Oceanfront** (800-333-8499) or check with **Walker Realty** (910-458-3388).

There is no shortage of fast-food restaurants on any of these beaches, but with shrimp and fishing boats lining the docks offering fresh shrimp, oysters, Atlantic blue crab and king mackerel, the seafood restaurants are the big enticement here.

WILMINGTON

You know that you've come to a city of old-world charm when you come upon 5th and Market streets and find a working old stone fountain in the middle of a downtown street. Although Wilmington has grown, declined, and now bustles again with its new movie industry,

the city has not lost its good-mannered, Southern dignity. By 1850, Wilmington had become the largest city in North Carolina. Impressive buildings rose in the downtown area that are still here, such as the old 1892 red brick courthouse at 24 North 3rd Street where you're apt to see TV actor Andy Griffith climbing the stairs for his *Matlock* film crew. The building is also the home of the **Cape Fear Convention and Visitors Bureau** (800-222-4757), which can supply you with tour times, maps and a short comprehensive film on the area.

Across the way on Chestnut Street are both **City Hall** and **Thalian Hall**. The ornate Thalian Hall opened in 1858 and remains one of the oldest continually operating performing arts theaters in the state. This often restored magnificent turn-of-the-century theatre is home to a number of performing art theatre companies, and local support is impressive. So check out what's playing (910-763-3398) while you're in the area.

Wilmington's **Historic District** covers 200 blocks. During the day, you can hit the high points, beginning at the flagpole at Market and Water streets, with Bob Jenkins' insightfully narrated walking tour (fee charged, 910-763-1785) or take a more leisurely approach in a horse and buggy tour around the central historic district (910-251-8889). You can also explore the renovated dock area on your own, pausing for the best frozen yogurt this writer's ever tasted at the **Water Street Market**. Outside, you can sit on the boardwalk and watch skilled river boat

pilots ferrying large boats through the harbor.

Take a stroll through the **Cotton Exchange** across the street from the Hilton. This two-block area of historic downtown derived its name from the original Cotton Exchange building which once housed the largest purchasers and shippers of cotton in the world. It has now been restored and adapted for shops and restaurants that provide neat pickin's for a rainy day or a respite from the beach. Another not-to-miss is **Chandler's Wharf**, located on the corner of Water and Ann Streets with its quaint picket fences and over-spilling flowers.

The **Cape Fear Museum** (910-341-7413) located at 214 Market Street is an upbeat and beautiful museum that has the state's oldest collection of history. With its many unique exhibits it is, however, anything but a stuffy museum. It's open Tuesday through Saturday from 9 AM to 5 PM and Sunday from 2 until 5 PM.

One of Wilmington's most popular attractions is **Orton Plantation** with its 1735 *Gone With The Wind* Greek Revival home and gardens. The difference between this plantation and Tara is that the principal crop was rice instead of cotton. In the spring, the garden's walking paths swirl and curl through acres of azaleas and camellias like a paisley design.

A few years ago, a replica of the antebellum house was burned for the movie *Firestarter*. Because of the home's authenticity, location scouts chose Wilmington for the filming. This helped establish the area

and persuaded Dino de Laurentis to locate his studio here (now Carolco). You can go into the quaint chapel, and even get married there, but you can't go in the private Orton home. Admission for adults is $7 and $3.50 for children ages six to 11.

Probably the best-known of Wilmington's attractions is the **Battleship** *North Carolina*. You can spend two or more hours on a self-guided tour, including a 10-minute orientation film explaining the battleship's important role in 57 WWII battles. Climbing through the hatch down into the ship's belly gives a hands-on feel to what daily life must have been like. But homesick letters of brave 18-year-old kids who handled deadly torpedoes evoke pride and admiration in most visitors.

Wilmington has a varied assortment of accommodations and restaurants. **Catherine's Inn** ($$-$$$, 910-763-5555), located on the waterfront at 410 South Front Street, is an 1883 bed & breakfast inn where you'll feel right at home. Soon after you've checked in, you'll have refreshments brought to you. A wonderful breakfast is also served.

The **Hilton** ($$$-$$$$, 800-662-9338), located at 301 N. Water Street, ranks as one of the city's best places to stay and is ideally convenient to good shopping and sightseeing. An economical option is **Park Inn International** ($, 800-437-7275) at 311 North 3rd Street. For a suite with kitchen, try **The Inn at St. Thomas Court** ($$, 800-525-0909).

If your dining taste runs to the upscale, dinner at **Crooks** by the river at 138 South Front Street is an excellent choice (try the cheese and shrimp grits). The old **Pilot House** ($$-$$$) is a good place for seafood, and **Elijah's** ($$) is outstanding too. Both are located in Chandler's Wharf at the corner of Water and Ann streets.

WRIGHTSVILLE BEACH

It's time to plop on the beach. Unpack the kid's sand pails and inflatable monsters, grab that slightly trashy "beach book," and park your brain for awhile. If this is a getaway weekend, you may not feel like venturing off the beach. But, if you're here longer, and you've overdosed on sun fun, the time may be ripe to try something more adventurous. You can sign up for wreck and reef diving with **Captain Chris Klingenberger** (910-350-0039), or explore the coast on your own with his boat rental service off Towles Road near Wrightsville Beach. You can go out for deep-sea fishing with the "**Sea Lady**" charters (800-242-2493) and reel in a marlin or sailfish and never leave Wrightsville Beach.

If golf is your game, there are plenty of nearby courses from which to choose. You might try the public course at **The Cape** on N.C. 421 South (910-799-3110). **Porter's Neck**, at 1202 Porter's Neck Road (800-423-5695), just minutes from

Battleship North Carolina is permanently berthed in Wilmington.

Wrightsville Beach is an 18-hole championship course designed by Tom Fazio.

For great accommodations, turn either right onto Waynick Boulevard or left onto Lumina Avenue. On either side you'll find good condos, motels and resort hotels. A good choice is **Shell Island Resort** (\$\$\$\$, 800-522-8575) located at the end of Lumina Avenue. This all-suite hotel offers miles of private and picturesque beach because of its secluded location. In cooler months, you can take advantage of the resort's indoor pool, but it is the wide beach that lures Insiders who like nothing more challenging than long evening walks watching the sun take a gentle nose-dive. The hottest local Insiders' pick is the **Blockade Runner Resort Hotel and Conference Center** (\$\$\$\$, 800-541-1161). Truly elegant, the Blockade Runner offers oceanfront dining and entertainment along with plentiful amenities.

For dining at the beach, local folk think **The Oceanic Restaurant & Grill** (\$\$-\$\$\$) located at 703 South Lumina Avenue on the ocean at Wrightsville is the finest with the freshest seafood. Order the cheesecake—than's an order!

TOPSAIL BEACH/DEL MAR BEACH

If you travel north from Wilmington on U.S. 17, you can detour onto Topsail (pronounced Top'suhl) or Del Mar Beach. These are quiet, family-oriented beaches with cottage rentals and motels. A little further north, off Old Folkstone Road, you will find **Lo-Di Farms**

where you can take a scenic horseback ride through wooded trails (910-327-2040). **The Jolly Roger** (\$\$, 910-328-4616) is on the ocean and has efficiencies and weekly rates.

SWANSBORO

An idyllic old seaside village, Swansboro is located north of Wilmington on N.C. 24. Don't sail right through this tiny 1730 historic town. Turn left onto Front Street (right before the bridge over White Oak River), park and walk down the street. Antique and country-oriented shops in restored brick buildings with geraniums popping over window boxes dot this quaint street. It's not that you'll make great "finds" at these shops, it's just a nostalgic little street opposite the waterfront that makes you think you've got all the time in the world. There are several restaurants on the waterfront that might interest you, but the Insiders' pick is **Yana's Ye Olde Drugstore Restaurant** (\$), located in an old '50's drugstore. It serves food reminiscent of the era such as burgers, salads, huge ice cream sodas and banana splits.

Swansboro is the perfect setting for the new outdoor drama, "Worthy Is The Lamb." This musical drama of the life of Christ is set in an amphitheater with the river as a backdrop to re-create the Sea of Galilee (800-662-5960).

BOGUE BANKS

The Banks is a 30-mile-long, narrow island that stretches from Emerald Isle to Atlantic Beach with Indian Beach/Salter Path and Pine

Knoll Shores sandwiched in between. From the topography, you won't know when you leave one beach for the next. It's funny that we all want to go to the beach, yet we want peopleless beaches. Well, Bogue Banks comes nearer to unspoiled beaches than any you'll find in North Carolina, with the possible exception of Bald Head and Ocracoke on the Outer Banks. And we're talking high season—mid-July.

Emerald Isle, part of the original Theodore Roosevelt estate, was incorporated as a resort town in the mid-50s with an emphasis placed on the beauty of the island and the ocean. A family beach, Emerald Isle got its name from the gorgeous green color of the ocean, owed to the effect of a sand bar just off the beach that gradually transforms the water's green color to a deep blue. Originally, the main road down Island stopped at Salter Path, but in 1955 it was extended to the fishing pier at Emerald Isle and later to the ferry landing at the end of the island.

If you didn't see the sign you wouldn't know that you'd arrived in **Indian Beach/Salter Path**. This area is kind of confusing because Indian Beach surrounds Salter Path. Today, it is both a residential and vacation spot for those who enjoy swimming, surf and pier fishing. The **Pine Knoll Shores** beach area was planned by Theodore Roosevelt's heirs and combines two special offerings: the **North Carolina Aquarium** and the **Theodore Roosevelt Natural Area**, a 265-acre state-owned maritime forest which lies around the aquarium.

Atlantic Beach, long a favorite beach for repeat visitors, is at the eastern tip of the island. Atlantic is probably the most action-oriented of the Bogue Beaches. **The Circle**, originally the site of its first arcade, is now a central stop to find out what is going on. And entertainment is diversified. You'll find some amusement-park rides, a terrific volleyball court and a number of night clubs that provide live music and a place to dance until the wee hours.

North of Atlantic Beach, on N.C. 58, is **Fort Macon**. Over 1.5 million people come to this fort each year, making it the most visited state park in North Carolina. It seems that protection from the likes of Blackbeard and other pirates who passed through and raided Beaufort, plus plunderings from both the British and Spanish, convinced North Carolinians that some sort of fortification had to be erected. Two forts, Dobbs and Hampton, were built and destroyed. Fort Macon was completed in 1834. The fort is open from 9 AM to 5:30 PM (919-726-3775).

For a list of vacation rentals, call **Emerald Isle Realty** (919-354-3315), **Realty World Clark Realty** (800-722-3006) or **Look Realty** (800-826-6226), all in Emerald Isle. There are a number of condos (2-3-4 bedrooms) for weekly rentals. One is **The Genesis** ($$$-$$$$, 919-247-0388), located just across from the state aquarium. It has some units on the ocean. There are scores of accommodations on Atlantic Beach from weekend rentals to longer. Try **Alan Shelor Rentals** (800-786-7368).

The **Sheraton Resort & Conference Center** on Salter Path Road in Pine Knoll Shores ($$$-$$$$, 919-

240-1155) offers refrigerators, microwaves and some Jacuzzis. The **Iron Steamer Oceanfront Family Resort** ($$, 800-332-4221), also on Salter Path Road, has oceanfront rooms, and at low tide, parts of the *Prevensey*, the Civil War blockade runner, can be seen from the pier. The **William-Garland Motel** in Salter Path ($, 919-247-3733) is a clean, no-frills motel with efficiencies and access to the ocean by a lovely nature trail. It also has access to the 20-acre Salter Path Natural Area.

The **Islander Motor Inn** ($$-$$$, 919-354-3464) located by but not on the ocean in Emerald Isle, the **Sandra Dee Motel** ($$, 919-354-2755), which faces the ocean and Bogue Inlet Fishing Pier, and the **Holiday Inn** at Atlantic Beach ($$$, 800-726-6570), also on the ocean, are good choices.

The **Show Boat Motel** ($-$$, 919-726-6163) in Atlantic Beach overlooks Bogue Sound, and guests can fish from the motel wharf, rent jet skis and waverunners on-site or board the custom dive boat for a day off shore. All rooms have refrigerators. Also in Atlantic Beach, the **Oceana Family Resort Motel and Fishing Pier** ($$, 919-726-4111) has oceanfront rooms with refrigerators and is near Fort Macon, fishing and the beach. The **John Yancey Motor Hotel** ($$-$$$, 800-682-3700) is located on Salter Path Road. You can

have an oceanfront room with a balcony or an efficiency that has a small kitchen.

The **Salter Path Family Campground** ($, 919-247-3525) offers camping on the ocean or the sound and has clam rakes available. The **Beachfront RV Park** ($, 919-354-6400) is on the ocean beside Bogue Inlet Fishing Pier or try **Holiday Trav-L-Park** ($, 919-354-2250) also on the ocean.

There are a number of excellent seafood restaurants in the Bogue Banks area, but one favorite is **Rucker John's** ($$) at 140 Fairview Drive in Emerald Isle. It offers a bit of everything, including seafood and pasta, but the fried calamari and alligator are really popular.

The **Big Oak Drive-In** ($) beside the William-Garland Motel in Salter Path has perfected the shrimp burger. And if oceanfront dining is what you're looking for, you can literally hang over the water while you swill down steamed clams at the **Crab Shack** ($$) off Salter Path Road. Also in Salter Path, the **Palms Restaurant** in the Holiday Inn is always a good choice and the **Clamdigger Restaurant** at the Ramada Inn is a tasty suggestion for breakfast, lunch or dinner.

Across from the Oceanana is **Man Chun House Restaurant** ($$) just in case you'd like to try the best Chinese food on the island. There's also the **New York Deli** ($) for a great New York Cheesesteak, big fat sandwiches or deli meats that you can take home. And it isn't too far to Morehead City and the legendary **Sanitary Restaurant** that's been here since 1938. Seafood is served (any way you like it) to its 600 guests who come back every year to this not fancy, but wholesome restaurant on the waterfront.

BEAUFORT

The first thing you'll notice as you pass the courthouse in Beaufort is that the statue of a Confederate soldier has his back turned to the north: symbolizing what eastern North Carolinians refer to as "The War of Northern Aggression." There are over 100 historic homes here that seafaring men built as early as 1698 with pegs instead of nails. You can take a daily double-decker bus tour of the homes with the Historical Society at 305 Turner Street for $5 (a good deal).

Gazing across Taylor's Creek, you'll see the Rachel Carson Component of the **North Carolina Estuarine Research Reserve** known locally as **Carrot Island.** Some forty feral ponies were taken there a hundred years ago and their offspring are the only residents on this island of uncluttered beaches. You can spend a day there swimming, fishing, bird watching, shell collecting, oystering and surfing. Since the island is accessible only by boat, a pleasant way to get there is by ferry. A roundtrip ferry ride for $8 leaves from the south end of Orange Street daily at 10 AM and 1 PM except during the winter (919-728-5247).

And to find out how this active little fishing village thrived through the years, a visit to the free **Maritime Museum** on Front Street is informative. This museum has an outstanding international shell collection as well as interesting maritime navigational equipment.

If you really want to get close to nature, then camping on Cape Lookout National Seashore may be for you. The only cost will be your roundtrip ferry fare. **Cape Lookout Tours** (919-728-3491) leaves from Morehead City. There are no developed campsites and you'll need to bring everything with you, including water.

Then again, you won't have any trouble unwinding at the **Inlet Inn Bed & Breakfast** at 601 Front and Queen streets ($$$, 919-728-3600), located right across from the waterfront with a view of Carrot Island. If you want to stay in one of Beaufort's restored B&B's, then try **The Pecan Tree Inn** at 116 Queen Street ($$-$$$$, 919-728-6733). This Victorian home preserves a sense of history and has great breakfasts. Or select **The Cedar's Inn**, circa 1855 ($$$-$$$$, 919-728-7036) at 305 Front Street. Next door is its charming restaurant ($$$) in a restored 1768 home that serves innovative gourmet dinners.

The best Insiders' tip for lunch or dinner is the **Beaufort Grocery Co. Restaurant** catty-corner to the Inlet Inn ($$-$$$) at 117 Queen Street. In the evening, catch the last rays of the day as you have a drink on the upstairs balcony of the **Dock House** ($) overlooking the water at 500 Front Street.

You'll be intrigued by the ambience at **Clawson's 1905 Restaurant** ($$) at 429 Front Street. This former grocery store and bakery wears its age with 1900's memorabilia. Order the Derigible (a yummy packed potato).

NEW BERN

Ideally juxtaposed between the sea and one of North Carolina's most beautiful national forests—the Croatan—makes this historic little town of lacy crepe myrtle trees appealing to both history buffs and rugged naturalists. The town of New Bern sits at the confluence of the Neuse and Trent Rivers, which is now known as Union Point Park, and where most of the waterfront activity buzzes.

In 1770, Royal Governor William Tryon began building his residence/ government capitol offices, which took on more the appearance of a palace than a modest government home with offices. The original palace burned in 1798, only 28 years after its completion, but was completely rebuilt from architect John Hawks' blueprints. It has been refurbished to its former splendor with a crystal chandelier, a spinet piano like the one Margaret Tryon used for entertaining and furnishings authentic to the period. You can take a tour with costumed hosts daily throughout the year, but Insiders vote for spring as the best time to visit as the royal English gardens are abloom with tulips.

During the summer months, historical drama tours are conducted. Actors portray Governor Tryon, cabinet members, his wife and their servants talking about the everyday happenings in the 1700s. The restoration includes the **Tryon**

Photo by Clay Nolen. Courtesy N.C. Travel and Tourism Division.

The Tryon Palace and Gardens is one of North Carolina's premier attractions.

135

Palace, the **John Wright Stanly House** (another handsome house thought to have been designed by Hawks as well), the Dixon-Stevenson House that was occupied by Union troops during the Civil War and the **New Bern Academy Museum** that portrays the town's history during the Civil War. The Tryon Palace is located at Pollock and George streets. Open from 9:30 AM to 4:30 PM Monday through Saturday and from 1:30 to 4 PM on Sundays. A combination admission that includes the Palace and Museum is $8 for adults; $4 for children, and a ticket that also includes the Stanly House and the Dixon-Stevenson House is $12 for adults and $6 for children (638-1560).

There are two rustic campsites for an economical stay in the area. The **Yogi Bear Jellystone Park** on N.C. 17 north ($, 919-638-2556) is located on the Neuse River. **Fisher's Landing** on N.C. 70 east in Riverdale ($, 919-638-5628) is the more rustic, but affords you the opportunity to walk along the crescent-shaped beach and do some special communing with wildlife. In New Bern, you'll find the **Ziegler Motel** at 1914 Trent Boulevard ($, 919-637-4498). This small older motel is set among azaleas and dogwoods in a residential community. If you are thinking B&B's, the beautifully restored historic ones in town are all excellent selections. **The New Bern House Inn** at 709 Broad Street ($$, 800-842-7688) is one block from Tryon Palace and you can walk or use their tandem bicycles to get around. **King's Arms Inn** at 212 Pollock Street (638-4409), built in 1847,

once hosted members of the First Continental Congress as a tavern.

Next door is the 1799 **Henderson House Restaurant**, which is our Insiders' tip for lunch or dinner. The food and history of this beautifully restored, award-winning restaurant tie in excellence. The home is reputed to have ghosts and a secret floor where it is thought British loyalists hid when the colonists got the upper hand. The home was later requisitioned by the Union Army during the Civil War. Try Chef Weaver's seafood casserole or carpetbagger steak.

The Bagel Cottage at 712 Pollack Street is another that combines unique food in an old-fashioned setting. It's located at the back of an old cottage and you can sit inside or outside at a table that overlooks **Tryon Palace Cutting Gardens**. Bagel lovers appreciate the daily baked variety of bagels with great soups and salads.

The **Harvey Mansion**, circa 1791, at 221 Tryon Palace Drive was the home and offices of John Harvey. The commanding old home on the Trent River is a romantic place for an elegant dinner of "Scallops a la Menthe" or "Flounder Captain Harvey," deliciously prepared by Chef Beat Zutter of Bern, Switzerland.

The **Sheraton Hotel and Marina** ($$-$$$, 800-325-3535) is arrayed along the shore of the Trent River in the historic heart of the city. The 165 rooms and suites are lavishly appointed and each offers a spectacular view. Within easy walking distance are antique and specialty shops, the Tryon Palace and

Gardens, a variety of restaurants and museums, plus many of the city's historic homes.

Mountains

Cashiers

This may be one of North Carolina's most God-kissed areas. If you really want to slow down and inhale mountain scenery—this is it! High in the Blue Ridge Mountains, Cashiers is a resort town, known for its many beautiful waterfalls, including **Toxaway Falls** (123 feet), **High Falls** (135 feet) and the beautiful Rainbow Falls that plunges some 200 feet.

Don't miss **Whitewater Falls**, the longest waterfall in the Eastern United States that swirls down 411 feet and straddles the border between North and South Carolina. Outdoor recreations span the seasons with golf in the lead and hiking or driving to the region's multiple waterfalls a close second. Fly fishers might argue that ranking because abundant mountain streams make fishing and boating mighty attractive, too.

The **High Hampton Inn** ($$-$$$, 800-334-2551) is located in Cashiers on N.C. 107 south. The inn was once the 2,300-acre estate of Confederate General and state Governor Wade Hampton. It is now a rustic resort that offers something for everyone. It has an impressive 18-hole, par-71 golf course, excellent hiking trails with many dramatic mountain views, and a private fishing lake where you may choose a canoe, fishing boat, sail boat, or, for timid souls like this writer, a gentle paddle boat. Guest rooms are in the main inn, and also in the surrounding guest houses. For dining, the High Hampton offers three buffet, country-style meals a day with a view of dramatic stone-faced Rock Mountain.

Sapphire Valley Resort ($$$-$$$$, 800-533-8268) at 4000 U.S. 64 west in Sapphire is about as gorgeous as a place gets. You can ride horses, ski, fish, play tennis and golf on the resort's course and dine in its

Photo courtesy N.C. Travel and Tourism Division.

The 411-foot Whitewater Falls is the highest waterfall in the Eastern United States.

fine restaurant. Needless to say, these beautifully equipped bedrooms and suites make one smile on just about every need or whim.

From the area's many wonderful bed and breakfasts, an Insiders' pick for the ideal one is **Millstone Inn** ($$-$$$, 704-743-2737). The inn is located 1 mile west of Cashiers on U.S. 64. Bedrooms and breakfast are handsome and delicious, but the view can take your breath away.

Singing Waters Camping Resort ($, 704-293-5872) is ten miles north of Cashiers on Trout Creek Road off N.C. 107. You'll find hot showers, heated bath houses and laundry facilities here. An ideal place to fish, swim and hike.

You'll find **Oakmont Lodge & White Goose Cafe** ($$, 704-743-5410) just north of the Cashiers intersection on N.C. 107. Bill Boswell and his family acquired Oakmont about 12 years ago and have successfully created a peaceful, relaxed hideaway that is like taking a stroll through past memories of mountain living. Four buildings, each with five big rooms and a front porch with rocking chairs, are available for guests, as is the 100-year-old log cabin with its wood-burning stove and claw-footed bath tub (still in working order). Antique farm tools fill the grounds, and you are welcome to take a snooze in the hammock or spread a tablecloth in the picnic areas.

In 1989, the **White Goose Cafe** opened in a remodeled barn overlooking a nearby pond that is home to mallard ducks and, what else but— a white goose (still going strong).

The cafe, too, carries the ambiance of yesteryear, and prides itself on its fresh foods and homemade creations. A player piano, presided over by a gigantic, stuffed bear, provides entertainment for guests during the evening hours.

A new Insiders' favorite is **The Hot Rocks Cafe at the Market Basket**, ($$-$$$) at the intersection of U.S. 64 and N.C. 107 south. If you choose, you can cook your own dinner at your table on hot rocks. It's the fat-free rage at this gourmet/ grocery that also cooks for you and prepares a great mountain trout. Brown bagging is allowed.

HIGHLANDS

Close to 60 % of this quaint mountain top town, which has never bothered with street numbers or had much crime, lies in the Nantahala National Forest. Although gorgeous mountains and waterfalls make this picturesque hamlet a vacationers' haven, it has a robust life of its own. The summer month-long **Highland Chamber Music Festival**, **Highland Playhouse**, a professional summer stock theater, art galleries and the **Highlands Forum**, a center for the study of current critical international issues, give citizens and visitors more to do than play golf, go mountain biking, ski, fish, ride horseback and tube the Cullasaja River.

Accommodations in the area run the gamut. You can spend next to nothing to camp, a moderate amount at a motel, or a little more for an inn or historic bed and breakfast. Expect to pay a reasonable figure to rent a rustic cabin and mega dollars to rent an elaborate chalet-like mansion with every possible need accounted for.

The Highland Inn ($$-$$$, 704-526-5036) and **The Old Edwards Inn** ($$-$$$$), located on Main Street and across from each other are owned by the same people. The Highland dates to 1880s and both are on the National Register of Historic Places. Each has a dining room that serves a continental breakfast with delicious strawberry butter to coat homemade rolls as well as lunch and dinner. Each has been renovated and decorated with hand-stenciling in the rustic mountain style of yesteryear.

Drive on down Main Street to 1885 **The Phelps House Bed & Breakfast Inn** ($, 704-526-2590). Bedrooms are a bit smaller here, but the inn's full breakfast makes this a real find if your wallet needs stretching.

In the Nantahala National Forest, you'll find both **Cliffside Lake** and **Van Hook Glade** ($, 704-526-3765). Cliffside is located 1.5 miles off U.S. 64 (4.4 miles west of Highlands) and Van Hook is at the turnoff prior to Cliffside. Combined, there are 29 campsites and a bathhouse at Cliffside Lake.

The Mountaineer Restaurant ($) is one of the local hangouts that is good for breakfast and to find out what's going on around town. If you don't know from straight-up what a catfish sandwich is, try one at the **Hilltop Grill** ($) at 4th Street on the hill. **Hildegard's Restaurant** ($$$$) on East Main Street serves authentic German food with Bavarian favorites. Order the potato dumplings.

BREVARD

From the entrance to Pisgah National Forest, it's about 7-8 miles to **Sliding Rock**. Put on a pair of worn out jeans to slide 150 feet down through the icy water's natural cascade. It doesn't cost a dime and is the most invigorating way to cool off and have fun that you probably can remember. Another cool wind-down activity is tubing. You can rent tubes at **Shorty's** on U.S. 74 and float down the Davidson River.

If you're not up to that kind of exhilaration, you can spend the day locating a few of Brevard/Transylvania County's 250 waterfalls. The best way is to take the scenic 79 mile drive that loops through the Pisgah National Forest past camera-demanding shots. You also could hike through the designated trails, (trail maps are available at the U.S. Forestry Service office on U.S. 276) and then you could make this a truly frugal weekend by fishing in one of the trout-filled streams for your dinner. There are horseback riding trails to give you one more way to explore the forest.

When you've had enough of communing with nature, check out the **Brevard Music Center**. There is an annual summer **Brevard Music Festival** with international stars. Call the Chamber of Commerce (800-648-4523) for dates or spend a Thursday evening listening to original mountain music and bluegrass at **Silvermont** on East Main Street in Brevard. Drive back down 64 to Flat Rock and you can take in a play at the **Flat Rock Playhouse**, which is the state theatre of North Carolina.

Throughout the mountains

you'll find handmade quilts, mountain furniture and toys. Insiders like the **Curb Market** (Farmer's Market) in downtown Hendersonville on Tuesday and Saturday mornings. You'll find reasonable to downright cheap handmade articles, jellies, fresh vegetables and the like.

For an inexpensive and fun family weekend near Brevard, call ahead to the **Davidson River Campground** ($, 800-283-2267 or 704-877-4910 or the Ranger Station at 704-877-3265) for a campsite in the Pisgah National Forest, just off the parkway near Asheville.

In case you had in mind a more pampered "getaway", the area is spilling over with motels and great bed and breakfast inns in every price range. The **Penrose Motel** (704-884-2691) in Penrose, boasts the best rates in the area and is conveniently located four minutes from Pisgah National Forest and five minutes from the Etowah Valley Golf Club. The **Womble Inn** in Brevard ($, 704-884-4770) serves your breakfast on a silver tray in your room—which will make going home hard to get used to. The 1851 **Red House** ($$, 704-884-9349) was here before Brevard of Transylvania County was established. It has been restored with period antiques to its former elegance, and is well-located in Brevard. For a stay in an 1862 Victorian farmhouse on the edge of the Pisgah National Forest, **Key Falls Inn** ($, 704-884-7559) will fit the bill with a full breakfast.

Now maybe you were thinking—mountains—log cabin. You can bring the family and stay in a log cabin at **The Pines Country Inn**

Photo courtesy buncombe County, N.C. Tourism Development Authority.

Visitors find blue Ridge Parkway vistas near Asheville irresistible.

(prices at inn $$ and up for cabins, 704-877-3131).

Most folks go to the mountains to rest, but there is a special place that emphasizes some unusual exercise. It is **Earthshine Mountain Lodge** at Lake Toxaway ($80 per person, including meals, which makes it hard to stay home (704-862-4207). They offer a program that allows you to invest in empowerment. One of the adventures is known as High Ropes, a sensitivity exercise that is dependent on inner rather than physical strength. This beautiful lodge also has horseback riding through the Pisgah National Forest, mountain-music evenings and good, made-from-scratch food.

If you are looking for a deluxe lakeside resort with a full complement of outdoor activities, try the **Greystone Inn** in Lake Toxaway off

U.S. 64 midway between Cashiers and Brevard ($$$$, 800-824-5766). The refurbished 1915 mansion situated on the banks of Lake Toxaway, has nineteen luxurious accommodations located on six levels. In the mansion, you can choose various sized rooms, some with balconies, fireplaces, oversize Jacuzzi baths and spectacular views. The Presidential suite, created from the former library, is the ultimate. The king-size bed, set in front of the wall of windows overlooking the lake, is dwarfed by the expanse of this enormous room which has a twenty-five foot ceiling with exposed oak beams, massive stone fireplace, matching upholstered chintz-covered chaise lounge, couch, easy chairs and draperies. There is a double marble Jacuzzi and a separate room with a full bath. Meals equal, and some say excel, the understated elegance of the decor.

In addition, the Inn offers golf, tennis, water sports and hiking. You would have difficulty finding a more romantic setting for your getaway.

If you opt not to cook out, try **The Carriage House Restaurant** ($-$$) on Country Club Road in Brevard. Another good choice is **Oh Susanna's** on West Main Street in Brevard. The **Inn at Brevard** ($$$) (a terrific place to stay) also has great food and **The Raintree** ($$$) is positively exceptional.

CHIMNEY ROCK/LAKE LURE

Three movies have been made in this picturesque area in the past few years. Remember "Dirty Dancing"? It was shot in Lake Lure. This makes a great daytrip because it isn't that far from Charlotte and is a pretty ride with mountain sides drenched in kudzu and snowball bushes adorning mountain homes. Lake Lure is a tranquil lake that is ideal for swimming, fishing and boating. A must in the area is a climb to **Chimney Rock Park** (admission is charged).

The town, with a river running beside it, gives a nice rural atmosphere, but is a touch on the touristy side. You can forgive a lot, though, as you wind up to the spectacular Chimney Rock or ride in a 26-story elevator inside the mountain. It deposits you at the top, rendering a panoramic view that is worth the trip all by itself. Below is **Hickory Nut Gorge**, which includes the **Rocky Broad River** and **Lake Lure**. Pack a picnic lunch or grab some takeout food to enjoy at one of the park's many picnic areas. Admission to Chimney Rock Park is $9 for adults and $4.50 for children ages 6 to 15.

You can stay at the refurbished art deco-esque **Lake Lure Inn** ($$$, 704-625-2525) for a truly restful weekend. Or, a favorite bed and breakfast stay in Chimney Rock is the **Ginger Bread Inn** ($$, 704-625-4038) right on Main Street, with every room looking like a page out of *County Magazine*.

FRANKLIN CORUNDUM MINES

Rule #1: Bring old clothes and patience. To get the rockhound fever, stop first at the **Franklin Gem and Mineral Society** located in a recycled 150-year-old jail. The all-volunteer museum (free, but donations appreciated) is located at 2 West Main Street. This is a small building that is packed with fascinating gems. A display case (in a former solitary cell) now springs into glowing magical colors when activated in the black-lighted Fluorescent Room. A tape explains that it's the rock's impurities that give off energy under a black light. Upstairs, you'll see models of stone writings from 701 B.C. found in Hezekiah's tunnel in Jerusalem. In this museum you'll find beautiful stones you're probably unfamiliar with, and other strange stones in the shape of ram's horns. You'll also see a 218 pound aquamarine and a 48-pound ruby; learn that sapphires and rubies are both corundum and that a ruby isn't a thing in the world but a red sapphire.

The prettiest rubies are said to come from India. But that's a hard sell to someone who's just found one in Franklin's Cowee Valley. It's difficult to equal the kind of excitement you feel when that hexagonal shaped red stone winks up at you. You may have spent hours digging out buckets of clay and gunk. Then stood or sat at a trough with fresh spring water circulating through its flume while you sifted dirt and gravel from potential gems. When a vein is hit, you'll find everything from chips to stones weighing several carats. You can also find garnets (dark red), rhodolite (purplish-red), kyanite (blue) and other beautiful minerals in that bucket of muck.

Insiders have had luck at **Mason's Ruby & Sapphire Mine** (704-524-4570). Go north on N.C. 28 to airport sign and turn left, bypass the airport and continue several miles to the mine. The mine supplies tools and allows you to dig your own for $8 a day. There are scores of mines in the area, but most have buckets that have been salted or enriched with a few chips. Another good bet is **Shuler's Mine** further north on N.C. 28 turning off at Cowee Valley Road (known as Ruby Mine Road). Its largest ruby find weighed in at 163 carats. You can have your rough stones cut into gems and mounted at the Cowee Valley Lapidary on Ruby Mine Road. For additional information, free maps, etc., call **Smoky Mountain Host of North Carolina** (800-432-4678).

Campers can be near the action at the **Cowee Valley Campground** ($, 704-524-2321) within walking distance of the Lapidary at 168 Ruby Mine Road. Or you can stay in Franklin at the **Franklin Terrace Bed & Breakfast** ($-$$, 800-633-2431) at 67 Harrison Avenue. For some good ol' country food stop in at the **Sunset** ($) on Harrison Avenue, **Luciose** at 150 Highlands Road for Italian ($$) and **Tallent's Steak Barn** at 130 Palmer Street ($$) for steaks, **MiCasa's** at 75 Porter Street ($$) for gourmet Mexican.

FONTANA VILLAGE/BRYSON CITY

"A little mountain cabin... something in the woods." To many out-of-staters, mountain cabin and North Carolina are synonymous. And it sounds pretty good to natives, too. Insiders appreciate rocking on the front porch in Fontana Village listening to the clip-clop of horses' hooves as rider's wind through the mountain trails below them. The vegetation is so lush that you'll get no more than a glimmer of fellow vacationers unless you sign up for a day of punching through white water rapids (**Great Smokies Rafting Company**, 800-277-6302) on the Nantahala River or a day of tubing on the Ocoee River in Tennessee. Another fun option is doing a half or full guided day of mountain bike cycling (**Euchella Mountain Bikes** 800-446-1603) through secluded mountain trails and along white water streams. The Appalachian Trail, only 3 miles away, follows a sylvan wilderness, providing some of the most beautiful hiking trails in the nation, and you can go at your own speed. Then again, we'd opt for a delicious meal prepared with fresh mountain vegetables, fruits and mountain stream fish in the Village's restaurant.

Take U.S. 74/19 east into Bryson City (elevation of 1800 feet) and listen for the train whistle. Just

100 years ago that was the sound that linked the isolated Smoky Mountains to the rest of the nation. The **Great Smoky Mountain Railroad** (800-872-4681) carries passengers through the soaring Nantahala Gorge in open-air cars. You'll find that these steep mountains lend credibility to the Indian name "nantahala"—meaning land of the noonday sun, where only the overhead sun can reach down deep enough to play along the gorge's toes. The ride will take you into remote wildflower and fern areas accessible only by foot, almost letting you touch the wilderness with your fingertips. You'll cross Fontana Lake where birds skim the still lake beside floating pontoon boats. From Bryson City, it's a four-hour excursion round trip, but Insiders like to take the train ride to the luncheon

Photo by William Russ. Courtesy N.C. Travel and Tourism Division.

The Great Smoky Mountain Railroad carries passengers through the soaring Nantahala Gorge in open-air cars.

destination, then spend the afternoon shooting through white water rapids for a guided return trip down the Nantahala River.

At **Nantahala Village** ($$, 704-488-2826), the first thing to do before unpacking is—inhale. Urbanites forget the clean fragrance of mountain air invigorated with the scent of pine. A great B&B that also serves delicious dinners is the **Randolph House** ($-$$, 704-488-3472) in Bryson City.

CHEROKEE

Who has grown up in America without hearing the saga of the great Cherokee Indians? It is a story of intelligence, skill, hardship, betrayal, sadness and more recently—success. Today, the 58,000-acre reservation, known as the Qualla Boundary, is a success story which you will discover by stopping at the **Cherokee Historical Association**. Across the street on Drama Road is the **Museum of the Cherokee Indian**. This is a modern museum displaying over 10,000-year-old artifacts and explanatory audio/visual programs that chronicle the history of the Cherokee. It's a worthwhile stop. Admission is $4 for adults and $2 for children six to 12 years old (704-497-3481).

It must be said that the level of commercialism in some, but not all, areas of Cherokee is not what you might expect in the midst of this little town banded by the magnificent Smokies. What you would expect to find—an authentic Indian Village—is here, however. It's the not-to-be-missed **Oconoluftee Indian Village**, a reproduction of how the Eastern Band of the Cherokees

lived 200 years ago. Admission is $8 for adults and $4 for children six to 13 years old (704-497-2315). The **Qualla Arts and Crafts Mutual** is a shop that looks more like a museum. This shop of artisans' works is responsible for keeping alive the authentic arts and crafts of the Cherokees. It is also the only place that you'll find these distinct crafts.

No trip to Cherokee would be complete without attending *Unto These Hills*, now in its 45th season at the renovated **Mountainside Theatre**. The outdoor drama professionally blends drama, music and dance to unfold the tragic story of how the proud and misunderstood Cherokees were driven west on the "Trail of Tears" from their Smoky Mountain homeland. It also shows how a few remained and, with sympathetic settlers' help, were able to rebuild into a race of productive American citizens. Admission is $9 to $11 for adults and $5 for children, call 704-497-2111.

Before leaving the area, drive north a half mile on U.S. 441 to the entrance of the **Great Smoky Mountains National Park**. Just inside is the recreation of the **Pioneer Homestead**. This is not just a log cabin, it's a series of 15 buildings that settlers needed to survive in the mountain wilderness. Placed beside a rushing river, the homestead is an interesting and picturesque place to visit and picnic in this beautiful park.

Trout fishing in the bountiful streams and rivers on the ancestral lands of the Cherokee Reservation is, for fishing enthusiasts, the best part of the trip. For fishing permits and maps, call (800-438-1601).

A principal reason that the Cherokee Reservation is such a success is that the businesses are tribal-owned. That includes motels, campgrounds and restaurants. For camping enthusiasts, there are many options. You could try the **Cherokee KOA Campground** (800-825-8352), or call for information on camping in the Great Smoky Mountain National Park (615-436-5615).

Inside Cherokee, the **Holiday Inn-Cherokee** ($$, 800-465-4329) on U.S. 19 south is a good bet with its North American Indian motif and convenient services. Holiday Inn's **Chestnut Tree Restaurant** is also a good option for dinner.

MAGGIE VALLEY

If you like gunfights in a mile-high **Ghost Town** theme park and warm mountain hospitality, go to Maggie Valley. There isn't a friendlier place anywhere, thanks in part to octogenarian Miss Jennie Reninger, the town's goodwill ambassador who dresses as "Miss Maggie" and waves to the passing tourists. There's also a first-rate zoo in the town called **Soco Gardens Zoo**. Maggie Valley is abuzz with activity from May through October.

Rustic but elegant lodges can be found next to the Great Smoky Mountains National Park at the 5,000-plus elevation. If you want to stay in town, **Twin Brook Resort** is ideal.

Maggie Valley Resort, ($$$$, 800-438-3861) has an 18-hole, championship golf course that is a scenically beautiful course with the Blue Ridge and Great Smoky Mountains as a backdrop for streams, lakes, rock formations and ancient trees. The resort also has tennis courts and a swimming pool, but for the non-golfer its greatest attraction may well be the food. Its International cuisine is prepared by a highly skilled and respected staff, and there is frequently entertainment in the restaurant. For reservations, call 704-926-1616 or 800-438-3861.

ASHEVILLE

Called the "Land of the Sky," this mountain city where wealthy 1900's vacationers once came for relief from the summer heat, is still compelling vacationers to visit, but now it's throughout the year. Golfers and tennis players have been coming to Grove Park Inn and Country Club, at the foot of Sunset Mountain, since it was hewn out of the mountain in 1913.

Asheville's traditional Fourth of July celebration took on added significance in the summer of 1992 with the long-awaited opening of **Pack Place Education, Arts and Science Center**, the new centerpiece of the historic district in downtown. Pack Place is dedicated to providing a culturally vibrant Asheville for the people of Western North Carolina and visitors to the area. And a constantly varied and changing menu of programs meets the challenge by offering something of interest for everyone. This bustling complex contains four museums, a performing arts theatre, courtyards, permanent exhibitions, a gift shop, restaurant and lobby galleries.

Tickets are required for admission to theatre events and to each of the four museums: the **Asheville**

Photo courtesy N.C. Travel and tourism Division.

Called "The Land of the Sky," the beautiful city of Asheville offers year-round activities for visitors.

Art Museum, The Colburn Gem and Mineral Museum, The Health Adventure and the **YMI Cultural Center**. You can buy a one-day pass which is good for all four, or you can buy single tickets. No admission charge is required for visitors to enter Pack Place and view the historic exhibit "Here is the Square," visit the **Craft Gallery** which spotlights regional crafts or shop in the **Museum Gift Store**. The fourth Friday of each month is "Free Day" when you may visit all of the museums with no charge for admission. Call 704-257-4500 for further ticket information and hours.

A landmark in itself, Pack Place also serves as the logical starting point for a number of walking tours of downtown Asheville featuring buildings of architectural and historic significance, including the home of Thomas Wolfe. A popular retreat into the past, this is the Dixieland Boarding House readers will remember from Wolfe's novel *Look Homeward, Angel.*

Unquestionably, one of the best daytrip excursions is to the **Biltmore Estate and Gardens and Winery** (admission is charged). The architectural style is that of a French chateau designed by Richard Morris Hunt and modeled on a chateau in France's Loire Valley, and could easily rival the grandest palace abroad. Built by George Vanderbilt, whose grandfather was a wealthy railroad magnate, the castle-like house contains 250 rooms which took 1,000 artisans (many imported from Europe) 5 years to build for 6 people (not including the 100 servants). In fact, the workers built their own housing which is known today as Biltmore Village, that houses shops and restaurants. A railroad was built from the village up to the chateau site to transport materials. The English and Italian gardens were designed by Frederick Law

Olmstead, and Biltmore hired Gifford Pinchot, the great American forester, to plan and redirect the badly eroded forest in the 1880s. Dr. Carl Schenck was brought from Germany to be the chief forester. And it was here that Schenck founded the Biltmore School of Forestry that developed the "land use" concept of forestry and conservation.

A favorite visit is Christmas season when the house is made resplendent with thousands of poinsettias, Christmas trees are trimmed with many original ornaments, and musical concerts fill the magnificent halls. The estate is open from 9-5 year round except Thanksgiving, Christmas and New Year's.

You can tour the main house with its beautiful antique furnishings, priceless paintings and ceiling frescoes that are kept in good repair. But the servant's quarters, where even the butler had his own servant, will give you a better clue as to how life was lived in 1895. Several movies have been filmed here.

Another enjoyable, as well as tasty, tour is that of the estate's winery. The rolling terrain of the vineyards is reminiscent of the cotes of Burgundy, and that blue haze dangling over the mountains brings to mind the mists that nestle the hilly vineyards along the Rhine and Mosel. And with the 16th-century Biltmore Chateau in the background, it's enough to convince you that you're in Europe rather than a unique corner of North Carolina. The old dairy barn has also been recycled into a lovely open-air restaurant—**Deerpark**, where at the

right time of the evening you can see herds of deer roaming the land. Biltmore Estate is located on U.S. 25, three blocks north of Exit 50 on I-40. The estate is open daily from 9 AM to 6 PM. Admission for adults is $22.95; for students ten to 15, $17.95.

After visiting the estate, stop in the **Biltmore Village** for a browse through a craft shop of handmade treasures—New Morning Gallery at 7 Boston Way. For more information on Asheville, call the **Asheville Area Convention and Visitors Bureau** at (704) 258-3858.

A terrific place to stay in Asheville is the recently renovated 1889 **Richmond Hill B&B** ($$$$, 800-545-9238). The B&B is located three miles from downtown Asheville on Richmond Hill Drive. This gracious hilltop mansion was built for U.S. Congressman Richmond Pearson. It has the reputation of

The Banquet Hall at the historic Biltmore Estate.

being one of the most pampering bed and breakfasts in the South as the staff is extraordinary. You'll enjoy the daily afternoon teas. **Gabrielle's** ($$-$$$) is its restaurant that serves outstanding breakfasts and dinners. Try the mountain apple and onion soup.

Probably the most well-known place to stay in Asheville is **Grove Park Inn & Country Club** ($$$$, 704-252-2711) on Macon Street. Even today, this continually renovated inn is awesome to enter. Truly, one of the playgrounds of the rich and famous, Grove Park is a rustically beautiful place to play and stay. You can also stay in the **Old Reynolds Mansion** ($$-$$$, 704-254-0496) and play a little golf.

For a more economical stay, there are RV campsites and apartments at the **Bear Creek RV Park & Apartments** ($-$$, 704-253-0798).

There are many dining options in Asheville to choose from. Insiders recommend **The Market Place** ($$-$$$) downtown at 20 Wall Street, **Deerpark** ($-$$$) on Biltmore Estate, **The Greenery** ($$) on Tunnel Road and **Magnolia's** ($) downtown.

BLUE RIDGE PARKWAY

The Blue Ridge Mountains formed about a billion years ago from "sediment at the bottom of a long-vanished sea." Then, just 300 million years back, the "continents collided and our ridges and mountains rose from the depths" to provide a ridge that has become one of America's most scenic parkways. The frequent overlooks afford breathtaking panoramas of high peeks,

waterfalls and lakes tucked into verdant valleys. Today, even at the peak of the summer season, driving down the parkway is like driving down your own highway. Spring is a different story with mountain laurel and red rhododendron in awesome abundance. Fall plays the same game with "leaf lookers" drinking in every ounce of red and gold beauty. An excellent day trip is to **Mount Mitchell State Park** at milepost 355. Mount Mitchell is the highest peak east of the Mississippi River, and you can hike through the park's many nature trails. But if you want to camp here, call (704) 675-4611 to reserve one of the nine campsites.

Exit at milepost 331 of the Parkway to reach the **North Carolina Mineral Museum**. This is a small, self-guided museum with explanatory information on many native minerals that are used in products that benefit all of us everyday. The museum offers detailed information on feldspar, kaolin and mica. The mica is referred to as a "book" of mica due to its slender page-like sheets of silver mica. The museum has over 300 varieties of minerals on display.

In Little Switzerland (milepost 334), you will find the **North Carolina Mining Museum at Emerald Village.** The museum tour (admission is charged) takes three hours, which breaks down to a 45-minute underground tour of the mine; a gallery gemstone identification explanation (20 minutes) and an hour to do some prospecting of your own. Working at the flume, you can unearth gemstones from a salted bucket. This is a truly fun way to have a hands-on educational experience, and who knows, you could come home with one of North Carolina's emerald's, rubies, sapphires, aquamarines or garnets as well as the native mix of feldspar, mica and smoky quartz.

In addition, Emerald Village has a tobacco and music exhibit as well as a gift shop full of reasonably priced native gemstone jewelry just in case its "finds" are preferable to yours. To reach the museum, turn left onto McKinney Mine Road at Chestnut Grove Church.

PENLAND SCHOOL AND THE PENLAND GALLERY

This is a great day trip. The Penland Gallery, now located in the newly renovated Horner Hall, houses representative works of Penland School artists and instructors. You are welcome to picnic on the grounds or rock on the front porch chatting with instructors and students. But you won't want to spend time rocking when the "for sale" gallery is just inside. This gallery collection of glass, fiber, pottery, woodworking, metal and jewelry is like walking through a contemporary art museum with a wish list in hand. The work is so exceptional that it gives you goosebumps.

It's obvious that this 1929 school, started by Lucy Morgan, nurtures and challenges serious artists to focus their individuality in this hard working but enchanted environment. It's a good idea to view the Penland audio/visual film that explains the history and mission of this unique art school tucked away in a secluded mountain community of artists. After visiting the gallery, if you want to see more of an individual artist's work, a map of community artists' studios is available.

Photo courtesy N.C. Travel and Tourism Division.

The Black Mountains in North Carolina, as seen from the Blue Ridge Parkway.

And you can take a tour of the school on Tuesdays and Thursdays at 10:30 AM or 1 PM from March 15 through November 20.

To find the Penland School and Gallery, follow N.C. 226 north from Spruce Pine for about two miles, turn left and follow the signs.

For those who want to spend the night, the **Pinebridge Inn and Executive Center** ($$, 800-356-5059) at 101 Pinebridge Avenue in Spruce Pine complements the school environment you've experienced at Penland, because it is a recycled and totally renovated elementary school. After a day of touring, you can get discount tickets to the fitness center on the property with its indoor pool, hot tub and ice rink that will let you play some more. The Inn's restaurant, **The Meeting Place,** is a nice but casual place for dinner and breakfast.

If you are on a budget or like to camp, the area has several good recreational options. **Springmaid Mountain Lodging and Campground** ($, 704-547-1006) on Henredon Road in Spruce Pine offers horseback riding, canoeing, hiking and tubing. The **Blue Ridge Gemstone Mine and Campground** ($, 704-765-5264) on McKinney Mine Road in Little Switzerland is close to the gem mines. The **Mountain Cove Campground and Trout Pond** ($, 704-675-5362) on U.S. 80 at 800 Still Fork Road in Burnsville provides bait and tackle.

LINVILLE FALLS

At Linville Falls and Gorge, there are three trail options from easy to rugged, depending on your energy and time. Money is not a concern, the trails are free. All are exquisite windows of nature that date back a half billion years. That was when the great rock folds tipped so far that they broke and pushed older sandstone beds on top of quartz. Then erosion cut through the older rocks leaving openings to expose nature's handiwork. The gorge is the deepest slash in the earth's crust east of the Grand Canyon. And the river tumbles into the gorge from its head to form a 90-foot fall of water.

To reach the falls, you'll walk through a half-mile tunnel of towering trees so dense that spatters of sunlight are rare. Waterfalls take on many personalities—these are gushing high-drama ones, particularly at the peak, which affords an unparalleled view. This is not a picnic area—you'll have to go further up the parkway for food—but rest rooms are available and the park is open year round, depending on weather.

From Spruce Pine, take N.C. 226 south to Little Switzerland and get on the Blue Ridge Parkway going north to milepost 316. From Charlotte, take I-77 north to I-40 west to Marion to N.C. 226/U.S 221 to the parkway.

LINVILLE CAVERNS

There are probably undiscovered caves all through the mountains. But Linville, like others, was discovered by accident in 1822 when curious fishermen followed trout disappearing into the side of a mountain. The current trout in this 20 million year old limestone cave have become blind due to low light source.

The mile-high swinging bridge spans two peaks at Grandfather Mountain.

Photo by William Russ. Courtesy N.C. Travel and Tourism Division.

Both Confederate and Union soldiers hid out in this cave during the Civil War, but it wasn't opened to the public until 1939. The knowledgeable tour guide shows the difference between stalagmite and stalactite formations. Don't expect Carlsbad or Luray splendors, but the cavern, on 3 levels, is an interesting and enjoyable half hour experience. Open year round, but check times by calling (704) 756-4171.

Admission for adults is $4 and $2.50 for children ages six to 12. From Linville Falls, take the parkway south for 1 mile, then take U.S. 221 south for 4 miles.

Old Hampton Store

This neat old 1921 general store, restaurant and gristmill has been refurbished only to the point of keeping it from caving in. The store offers a wide assortment of notions that you need and some that you probably don't, such as horse-hoof medication. Churns and washtubs hang from the ceiling and the back screened door is perpetually in motion. The gristmill, out back, stone grinds cornmeal and grits nearly every afternoon, and these products are sold with apple butter, local jams and old-fashioned tin cookware. Kids can buy their marbles by the pound and sturdy clothes are available upstairs. Best of all, though, is lunch. It serves the leanest and most delicious barbecue around, and its root beer isn't bad either. Top this off with a slice of terrific carrot cake or assorted cheesecakes.

To reach the Old Hampton Store, continue north on U.S. 221 to a stop sign just outside Linville, turn right and go for almost a mile to the sign for the Old Hampton Store.

Grandfather Mountain

This is a perfect daytrip choice that mixes scenery, animal habitats and a museum. One of the most enjoyable Grandfather Mountain experiences is the annual **Highland Games** the second weekend in July. You don't have to be a Scot to enjoy bagpipes, dancing, cable toss and watching Border Collies return lost sheep to the herd, as well as other games of skill. Another popular yearly event that comes the fourth Sunday in June is Singing on the Mountain.

Famed 6,000-foot Grandfather Mountain, seen from miles around, looks like a giant sleeping grandfather, and is considered North Carolina's top scenic attraction. You won't want to miss the celebrated **Mile High Swinging Bridge** which connects Linville's peak with the Visitor's Center. This bridge, for those brave enough to cross it, rewards you with a spectacular view.

You'll want to visit the natural habitats for native black bear, white-tailed deer, cougars, bald and golden eagles. Stop in at the new nature museum that offers state-of-the-art displays and entertaining movies filmed at Grandfather on native wildlife—especially the red-tailed hawk film. The museum's restaurant is a good bet for lunch featuring—what else? A dynamite view. You can also picnic on the mountain. Grandfather Mountain is open daily from 8 AM until 7 PM. Admission for adults is $9 and $5 for children ages four to 12 (800-468-7325).

Ski Country

Remember those "Think Snow" bumper stickers? Those are from thousands of Georgia, Tennes-

see, North and South Carolina skiers who listen to weather reports, watch the sky, send up snow prayers and wax skis in the hope of bringing on the first winter's snow. And when Mother Nature cooperates, snow guns whirl into action adding and packing ski resort bases. That's when you'll see packed car ski racks headed for one of our high country's downhill ski resorts. If you are new to the sport, you can rent equipment at any of the resorts, but Insiders like to save time by renting locally before they go.

Appalachian Ski Mountain, home of the French/Swiss Ski College, off U.S. 321 between Blowing Rock and Boone, has one of the best teaching schools for beginners around. It has 8 slopes with a peak elevation of 4,000 feet. Of course, both Beech and Sugar have good ski schools, particularly for very young children, and both offer more challenging slopes.

Ski Beech (704-387-2011), north of Banner Elk has 14 slopes and a peak elevation of 5,505 feet, making it the highest in the East with a vertical drop of 830 feet. The resort also has a charming Swiss-type village appearance with an outdoor ice skating rink encircled with shops and restaurants.

Sugar Mountain Ski Resort (704-898-4521), just to the south of Banner Elk on N.C. 184, boasts 18 slopes, peak elevation of 5,300 feet with a vertical drop of 1,200 feet, and needless to say, fairyland views.

Ski Hawksnest (704-963-6561), reopened last year, is sometimes less crowded than the other ski resorts and has seven slopes, a

*When the first snow falls, you'll see packed car ski racks
headed for one of North Carolinas downhill ski resorts.*

peak of 4,819 feet, and vertical drop of 619 feet, plus night skiing. All of these resorts have chair lifts, rope tows, lockers and restaurants, plus nurseries on Beech and Sugar. You can get a ski report by calling **High Country Hosts** at (800-438-7500), also a good source of mountain area information.

You can cross-country ski at **Moses Cone Park** on the parkway just outside of Blowing Rock and other gated-off areas by calling the Ranger's office: (704-295-7591); or on **Roan Mountain** ski with cross-country guided trips, including instruction (615-772-3303).

What skier has not dreamed of that idyllic mountain ski lodge with roaring fireplace and happy apres-ski bums tippling hot cider. You and yours can do just that at the **Beech Alpen Inn** ($$$-$$$$, 704-387-2252) near the top of Beech Mountain, or bring your family to an on-the-slopes condo at **Sugar Ski and Country Club,** outside Banner Elk ($$$-$$$$, 800-634-1320).

On Beech, **Kat's Overlook Pub** ($$) is a good place to dine with an enviable mountain view. And a few yards down Beech Mountain Road is **Fred's General Mercantile Store. Fred's Backside Deli** ($) offers good deli food and a smattering of general store vacationer type needs. A flavorful dining option in Banner Elk is the **Louisiana Purchase** ($$) that has good and spicy Cajun and Creole food.

From Banner Elk take N.C. 194 east to Valle Crucis. The **Mast Farm Inn** ($$$, 704-963-5857) serves fabulous, from scratch country dinners included in the lodging price.

And while you're in Valle Crucis, make it a point to check out the over-100-year-old **Mast Store**. The original post office is still inside along with a trap door in the floor where bartered chickens were once deposited. Locals still play checkers with Coke and Pepsi bottle tops beside an original potbellied stove. Their motto is "If we don't have it, you don't need it anyway." Very few browsers leave empty-handed as the Mast Store's prices are better than any known to this writer anywhere.

BLOWING ROCK

A lot of towns are dressed up to look quaint these days—Blowing Rock is the genuine thing. In summer the main street is lined with pyramid-shaped planters spilling over with pink and white begonias. Since the days the rambling hundred-year-old Green Park Inn was built over the center of the Continental Divide, the town took on an aristocratic appeal. Window-shopping down Main Street is a favorite pursuit with lots of antiques, oriental-rug houses and classy mountain wear. Evenings find folks at the auction house, which is a show in itself. The park on Main Street is a gathering place for tennis, people-watching, craft shows, etc.

The more athletically inclined can enjoy horseback riding along the trails of Moses Cone Estate on the Blue Ridge Parkway. Make reservations with **Blowing Rock Stables** (704-295-7847). The more adventurous will enjoy canoeing and white water rafting through Class III to V rapids down the Nolichucky. Check with **Wahoo's Adventures** (800-444-

Photo courtesy Buncombe County, N.C. Tourism Development Authority.

North Carolina's rivers lure the adventurous for whitewater rafting.

RAFT) on U.S. 321 between Blowing Rock and Boone.

Children in North Carolina grow up on trips to **Tweetsie Railroad** (admission is charged) on U.S. 321/221 in Blowing Rock. The drawing card is a three-mile adventurous train ride on an original mountain train with interruptions of Indian attack and settler rescue. The attraction has amusement rides, live entertainment, crafts, shops and picnic tables. It is open from May through October and on weekends only in November. Admission for adults is $12.95 and $10.95 for seniors and children from ages four to 12 (800-526-5740).

The **Green Park Inn** ($$$$, 704-295-3141) is on U.S. 321 Bypass, just south of Blowing Rock. It is a great place to stay as many of our U.S. presidents will attest. Another romantic bed and breakfast that serves dinner is the **Ragged Garden Inn** ($$-$$$$, 704-295-9703), located one block off Blowing Rock's Main Street on Sunset Drive. It also has great food and is a comfortable and convenient place to stay. Insiders' favorite restaurant for some of the best food in the mountains is **Best Cellars** located off the U.S. 321 Bypass in Blowing Rock ($$-$$$).

BOONE

Boone, home to the beautiful, rolling campus of Appalachian State University, also houses the **Appalachian Cultural Museum**. Here, the evolving life-style of mountain people is attractively displayed with artifacts plus information on Appalachia's abundant variety of rare and unusual herbs and plants—some medicinal. The relationship between (not versus) man and environment is a prevailing theme. An eight-minute film is accompanied by sweet mountain music. Admission for adults is $2, $1.75 for seniors and $1 for children from ages 12 to 18 (704-262-3117).

During the summer, make reservations for the outdoor drama, *Horn In The West*, now going into its 41st season. The musical drama revolves around life in Appalachia during the days of Daniel Boone. For reservations, call (704) 264-2120. Admission for adults is $8 and $4.50 for children. Adjacent to *Horn In The West* you'll find **Hickory Ridge Homestead**, which is an interesting tour of 5 representative home sites of the 1800s. Admission is $2.

A comfortable bed and breakfast in Boone is **Overlook Lodge** ($$-$$$, 704-963-5785) outside Boone off U.S. 105 on Poplar Grove Road; or try **Lovill House Inn** ($$-$$$, 704-264-4204) at 404 Old Bristol Road.

The place the natives go for a quick snack is the **Appalachian Soda Shop** ($). Insiders ask for the Carolina Pharmacy Doughnuts. Vacationers like the **Daniel Boone Inn** ($$) for lots of food served country-style for the whole family to enjoy.

GLENDALE SPRINGS

It's a toss-up to know whether people go to Glendale Springs ($$-$$$, 910-982-2101) for the wonderful gourmet food at the inn or to see the frescoes. The 1895 **Glendale Springs Inn**, intact with convivial ghost, is a sophisticated country inn

that attracts discriminating visitors from around the country. The restaurant serves a marvelous *prixe fixe* dinner on weekends and has an *a la carte* menu on week days.

And, Ben Long's controversial frescoes at **Episcopal Holy Trinity Chapel**, a block away, are among the most highly visited in the state. A number of craft shops have sprung up, which changes the area's once "hidden away" flavor, but does not diminish its overall appeal.

LAUREL SPRINGS

Some Hurricane Hugo victims overcame disaster ingeniously. Because Tom and Nancy Burgiss' 200-year-old farm yielded enough "Hugo" lumber to build a dancing barn, the popular **Mountain Music Jamboree** took up new residence here. Folks from near and far come to dance the Texas Two-Step, and old-time mountain dances. Staying at this bed and breakfast ($$, 919-359-2995) can be restful or exhilarating, and no matter your choice, it's a win-win deal. Overnight guests are treated to a two-bedroom suite with private hot tub, and private den with fireplace and piped in spring-fed water that lulls you to sleep like a trickling brook. Full breakfast offers a unique menu of choices. Dance classes are Monday and Tuesday nights; Texas Two-Step dances on Friday and two live alternating Blue Grass and Old Time Music on Saturday.

To reach the Burgiss Farm, exit the Blue Ridge Parkway at milepost 246, turn right onto N.C. 1143 for 3 miles and follow signs.

CROWDER'S MOUNTAIN STATE PARK

This free park in the Kings Mountain range in Gaston and Cleveland counties is a favorite weekend haunt of rock climbers and hikers. You can practice rappelling on the sheer precipice, study nature, go fishing, or enjoy primitive camping in this 2,148-acre park. For more information, contact Crowder's Mountain State Park, U.S. 1, Box 159, Kings Mountain, NC 28086, or call (704) 867-1181.

KINGS MOUNTAIN NATIONAL MILITARY PARK

Many brave Charlotteans were among the soldiers, known as "Over the Mountain" men, who triumphantly beat the Loyalists in a decisive battle in 1780 which signaled a turning point in the Revolutionary War. Today you can study the battle and see where Colonel Patrick Ferguson, the Loyalist leader, was killed. A short film serves as a good introduction to the battle, and artifacts from the historic event are displayed in the free museum.

Each year proud descendants of the mountain men reenact the famous march from Southwest Virginia, East Tennessee, and Western North Carolina to the battle site. Camping is available in nearby Kings Mountain State Park, located in South Carolina. For more information, contact the Department of Transportation, P.O. Box 25201, Raleigh, N.C. 27611.

The Sandhills

PINEHURST/SOUTHERN PINES

Few people realize that this golfer's utopia was once barren wilderness. The tract was nothing but leveled tree stumps when James G. Tufts bought the land in 1895 and hired landscape architect Frederick Law Olmstead to design a resort for convalescents. Olmstead was already famous for his design of New York's Central Park and the gardens of Biltmore House in Asheville. You might say that golf was born in Pinehurst when Tufts found his healthier patrons disturbing the cattle in his fields by hitting little white balls with clubs. Swimming against the tide that viewed golf as a passing fad, Tufts built a nine-hole golf course, and the rest is history.

In 1900, Scottish golf pro Donald Ross came to Pinehurst and designed more courses that eventually earned the area an international reputation. Today, it is considered the "golf capital of the world." For many years, the Pinehurst-Southern Pines area has been a favorite with Charlotte residents who enjoy golf, tennis, horseback riding, polo, croquet, water sports, trap and skeet shooting and other sports. Like Camden, Southern Pines has a long

Southern Pines has a long tradition of steeplechase and harness racing and is the site of the annual Stoneybrook Race.

Insiders' Tip

tradition of harness racing and steeplechases as well. The annual **Stoneybrook Race** is here.

We are happy to report that in our fast-track world the area has retained its quiet charm. There are approximately 35 golf courses, including Pinehurst's Number 2 which was voted by *Golf Magazine* as one of the "golden dozen" golf courses in the world. Other sites include historic Aberdeen, the Malcom Blue Farm, Weymouth Center and the House in the Horseshoe near Carthage.

For golfers, ideal stays are: **Pinehurst Resort and Country Club** ($$$$, 800-ITS-GOLF) on Carolina Vista or **Mid Pines Resort** ($$$-$$$$, 800-323-2114) at 1010 Midland Road in Southern Pines. Another long-time favorite since it opened its doors in 1895 is the **Holly Inn** ($$$, 800-682-6901) on Cherokee Road.

Two Insiders' favorites are the **Pine Crest Inn** on Dogwood Road in Pinehurst ($$-$$$, 910-295-6121), which is so comfortable it's like slipping on an old shoe, and the **Manor Inn** on Magnolia Road in Pinehurst ($$-$$$, 910-295-2700) for Sandhills charm and great food.

If you'd rather stay in a bed and breakfast, you might try the lovely **Pine Cone Manner** at 450 E. Philadelphia Street in Pine Bluff ($, 910-281-5301). Another excellent choice in nearby Aberdeen is the **Inn at the Bryant House** at 214 N. Poplar Street ($-$$$, 910-944-3300) with continental breakfast in a beautifully refurbished 1914 home. A super choice is **The Magnolia Inn** in Pinehurst ($$$-$$$$, 910-295-6900) that offers a complete country break-

fast. The inn also has an on-site restaurant—the **726 Pub**, open for lunch and dinner.

Other recommended restaurants in the area include **Barrister's Steak House & Pub** at 1500 on U.S. 1 in Southern Pines, the **Lob Steer** on U.S. 1 Bypass in Southern Pines and **The Barn** at 305 Rothney Road off U.S. 1.

SEAGROVE AREA POTTERIES

If you love handmade crafts and adventure, you'll love a trip to the Seagrove area to hunt down jugs and vases at the more than 90 potteries in the Sandhills. Some of the potters are carrying on the tradition of pottery that has been in the family for generations. Others are newcomers to the craft who have chosen to set up shops in the area because of its rich tradition.

Photo by William Russ. Courtesy N.C. Travel and Tourism Division.

Ken Poole at work at Rockhouse Pottery in Seagrove, North Carolina..

First-timers should begin any visit at the **North Carolina Museum of Traditional Potters** in Seagrove (910-873-7887), where you can see the variety of pieces that are produced in the area. Maps of the area are available at the museum or Seagrove Pottery. Believe us, you will need the map to find your way around. Potters are very modest people and don't hang out neon signs. And you might as well plan to make this a day—it will take that long to visit all the shops.

Don't miss Cole Pottery, Jugtown, Ben Owen Pottery and Westmoore, which produces Old Salem designs. Take along a picnic lunch—restaurants are few and far between. Seagrove Pottery has a picnic table and an old-fashioned drink machine. For more information on this area, contact the **Pinehurst Area Convention and Visitors Bureau**, P.O. Box 2270, Southern Pines, N.C. 28387, 800-346-5362 or 910-692-3330.

The Triad

About an hour north of Charlotte you will find Winston-Salem, Greensboro and High Point, the section of the state called the Triad. The area is rich in history and well worth a day trip.

OLD SALEM

This quaint village began in 1766 when the Moravians of Pennsylvania, an industrious religious group from Germany, traveled the Old Wagon Road in search of a new home. They came to this area and enacted commune-type living until they could become established. Today, the original village (admission is charged) has been completely restored and is, in effect, a miniature Williamsburg. Visitors often prefer Old Salem as they can tour the entire community in one day.

There is a 17-minute film in the Visitors Center that will give you a good introduction to what you are about to see. The costumed guides introduce you to craftsmen and women at work in their shops producing everything from tinware to woven cloth. You will visit the home of the clock maker as well as other distinguished artisans. Perhaps, the favorite visit is to the bakery, which almost always has homemade bread or delicious Moravian cookies baking in the old ovens. All of their goodies are for sale.

The Moravians enjoyed music, a fact borne out in their music and education building, as well as the festive Christmas and Easter celebrations each year. During the Christmas season, the event is heralded by the town crier who stands on the corner to officially ring in the event. Homes in the village are decorated in the style of yesteryear and there are special foods, music and worship services, which includes the candlelight Love Feast on Christmas Eve.

The Easter Sunrise Service that begins on the Old Salem square, is a worship service that now draws crowds of 5,000. The Moravian minister opens the service with a brief sermon. Then Moravian brass bands, which are stationed along the two block route to the Moravian cemetery, play and answer each other as the congregation silently walks to the cemetery. This is an awe-inspiring pilgrimage that takes you to the cemetery where you'll see fresh-scrubbed gravestones, each adorned with flowers. People of all faiths are welcome, but if you are going, Insiders recommend that you get there by 5:30 AM in order to find a place.

Old Salem is open Monday through Saturday from 9:30 AM to 4:30 PM and from 1:30 PM to 4:30 PM Sunday. Admission for adults is $12 and $6 for children from ages six to 14. Old Salem is located in Winston-Salem (910-721-7300).

MUSEUM OF EARLY SOUTHERN DECORATIVE ARTS (MESDA)

MESDA is adjacent to Old Salem, and features 19 furnished rooms, demonstrating the varied styles of Southern furnishings. Many rooms have been reassembled here, just as they were in their original locations. Hour-long guided tours are avaiable. It is open Monday through Saturday from 10:30 AM to 4:30 PM, and from 1:30 to 4:30 PM on Sunday. Admission for adults is $6 and $3 for children. MESDA is located at 924 S. Main St. in Winston-Salem (910) 721-7360.

REYNOLDA HOUSE

Reynolda House, the bungalow-style former home of R.J. Reynolds of tobacco fame, is now a museum of American art offering guided tours. The collection features paintings by diverse artists ranging from 19th-century landscape painter Frederic Church to Thomas Eakin and Mary Cassatt. Also represented are contemporary painters, including Georgia O'Keeffe, Andrew Wyeth and Frank Stella. The house contains many of its original furnishings, and you're sure to appreciate the bottom floor complete with bowling alley, shooting range, night club area and enclosed swimming pool.

You may tour the gardens on the grounds, which are a mass of daffodils in springtime, and the formal gardens' roses are a fragrant delight throughout the summer. When the Reynolds family lived here, there was an underground passage to the church across the street, and Reynolda was a self-contained estate with its own dairy barn (which you can visit), boiler room and other shops of Reynolda Village. Just down the road you'll see Polo Road, once the Reynolds' private polo field. Reynolda is open Monday through Saturday from 9:30 AM to 4:30 PM and from 1:30 to 4:30 PM on Sunday. Admission is $6 for adults, $5 for seniors and $3 for children. Reynolda House is located on Reynolda Road in Winston-Salem (910-725-5325).

SOUTHEASTERN CENTER FOR CONTEMPORARY ART (SECCA)

SECCA is just down the road from Reynolda House and well worth a visit. It is a complex of galleries with rotating exhibits by contemporary Southern artists and has an excellent gift shop. It is located on the former estate of the Hanes family, and many of the galleries are in the Hanes home. It is open Tuesday through Saturday 10:00 AM to 5 PM and Sunday 1:00 to 5:00 PM SECCA is open Tuesday through Saturday from 10 AM to 5 PM and from 1:30 PM until 5 PM Sunday. Admission is $3 for adults, $2 for seniors and students, children under 12 are free. SECCA is located off Reynolda Road at 750 Marguerite Drive in Winston-Salem (910-725-1904).

SciWorks

It's become overworked to say, "Children of all ages will enjoy ... " but in the case of SciWorks, the phrase is true. Adults need to be as willing to tap into fun as are children. So, don't be afraid to try out the procedure that lets you make a shadow and then walk away from it. Oh, sure, SciWorks is educational, but not the boring lecture variety. You won't hear someone **tell** you what a tornado is, you press a button and watch the elements go into action that whirl a mass of fluid to build into a vortex. You can whisper into a parabolic whisper dish and be heard clearly by someone standing 40 feet away. Or stand up close and watch how the Foucault Pendulum demonstrates the rotation of the earth.

Norman Tuck's different magnetic sculptures bring a chuckle from all types in this interactive, "touch me" museum. Be sure to take a trip through the African exhibit and the Carolina Piedmont Wildlife exhibit that offers an upclose video look at special animal exhibits. Before scheduling a trip here, be sure to call first for Planetarium show times. The Planetarium theatre is a 50-foot tilted dome with a Spitz star machine that produces eye-boggling laser effects.

This museum isn't geared only for older children. There's a huge room for toddlers and preschool children filled with big, floppy climbing bars, slides and cushions to roll around upon. And outside you can become acquainted with Jacob sheep, an otter swimming in its tank and a few other animal exhibits.

SciWorks is located north of downtown. Take U.S. 52 north, exit at Hanes Mill Road and follow the signs. It's across from Sara Lee Offices on Museum Drive. It is open Monday through Saturday from 10 AM to 5 PM and on Sunday from 1 to 5:00 PM. Admission: adults, $3.50, students and seniors, $2.50, children under 3 are free (910-767-6730).

Tanglewood Park

Tanglewood's hardwood forest was so tangled with gnarled overgrowth back in the 1900s that it looked like a mythical place from Hawthorne's *Tanglewood—Tales*. The idyllic lake, now called Mallard Lake, completed this fantasy setting for Margaret Griffith who gave the park its name. In 1921, new owners Kate and William Reynolds, added wings onto the original 1848 home, now known as the **Manor House Bed and Breakfast Inn**.

Thirty years later, Tanglewood was left to the people of Forsyth County for use as a park. Tanglewood's brambling undergrowth has now been cut back to provide for horseback riding trails, a swimming pool, 9 tennis courts, a fenced area for deer, a steeplechase course, nature trails, a rose garden, a lake filled with canoes and paddleboats, camp grounds, golf

Staff Photo.

Costumed guides introduce you to craftsmen and craftswomen at work
in their shops in Old Salem.

driving ranges, a **Championship Golf Course** where the Senior PGA Vantage is played and the popular **William Neal Reynolds Golf Course** that runs along the forest.

This park has a multitude of events from lavish tailgate parties for the annual **Spring Steeplechase** to the new **Festival of Lights** program during the Christmas season. Begun in 1992, the Festival of Lights more than quadrupled by 1993. There are now 45 fanciful light exhibits. It's worth a trip to the area just to drive through the fantasy snow storm. Golfers and equestrians will love the ingenious, moving light representations of their sports. To be sure, children will enjoy snowmen, candy cane figures, etc., that are liberally sprinkled over the drive.

One of the best things about Tanglewood is that people of a variety of incomes can enjoy staying here. You can camp out ($) at one of the 100 tent and trailer sites that offer good camping facilities, including hot water showers, firewood and picnic tables. Camping is conveniently located near nature trails and the riding stable, or you could stay at one of the secluded cottages ($$$) that overlook the lake, or in the historic Reynolds Manor House Bed and Breakfast Inn ($$$-$$$$). The Inn's bedrooms have private baths, TVs, telephones, and attractive decor. You can breakfast beside the original old stone fireplace with a big continental breakfast of fruit muffins, cereals, and a large fruit plate.

Tanglewood Park is open year-round from dawn to dusk. Admission to the park is $1. Golf fees for the Championship Course range from $24 to $50; for the Reynolds Course, $8 to $26. Tennis fees are from $6 to $8 per hour. Horseback riding fees are $14 per hour (910-766-0591).

Winston-Salem has a number of other interesting sites, including **Bethabara** (the original Moravian settlement), **Piedmont Craftsmen**, **Tanglewood Park**, and the **Stevens Center for the Performing Arts**. Tours of **R.J. Reynolds Tobacco Company** and the **Stroh Brewery Company** are also available.

GUILFORD COURTHOUSE NATIONAL MILITARY PARK

This is the site of a Revolutionary War battle that pitted General Nathaniel Greene (for whom the city of Greensboro is named) against General Lord Charles Cornwallis, commander of the British troops. Although the American troops eventually withdrew, Cornwallis' losses were heavy, and this led to his surrender at Yorktown seven months later. The battlefield is now a national park, with a number of monuments (including one of Nathaniel Greene) and a Visitors Center. It is open daily from 8:30 AM to 5 PM. Admission is free. The Park is located off U.S. 220 on New Garden Road in Greensboro (910-288-1776).

THE NATURAL SCIENCE CENTER

Behind the Guilford battleground is Country Park, site of this fine museum for children. There are reproductions of dinosaur skeletons, rocks and mineral exhibits, a planetarium and a small zoo. It is open Monday through Saturday from 9:00 AM to 5:00 PM and from 12:30 PM to 5 PM on Sunday. Admission is $3.50 for adults and $2.50 for children. Children under three are free. The Center is in Country Park at 4301 Lawndale Drive in Greensboro (910-288-3769).

Other Places of Note

CAMDEN, S.C.

Steeplechase fans know this town well. It's the scene of the **Carolina Cup Race** in the spring and the **Colonial Cup** in the fall. Charlotte families have been attending these events for so long that they use the same parking spot year after year. People-watching and tailgating are almost as much fun as the races.

People dress to the nines for these events, and the tailgate picnics are elaborate affairs complete with silver, china, linens and flowers. The events are open to anyone, regardless of family affiliation, and don't really cost that much if you park in the general parking area and pay general admission.

Horses aside, Camden is an interesting place to visit any time of the year. Traditionally a playground for the rich and famous, the town has many beautiful historical homes and estates dating to the 18th and 19th centuries. Some buildings in **Historic Camden**, such as the reconstructed Kershaw-Cornwallis House and others in the historic complex are open to the public; others can be seen during home and garden tours during the year. Historic Camden is

Photo courtesy of Olde English District Tourism Commission.

Steeplechase fans converge on Camden for the Carolina Cup Race in the spring and the Colonial Cup in the fall.

open from 10 AM to 4 PM Tuesday through Saturday and from 1 until 4 PM on Sunday. Admission for adults is $4.50 and $1.50 for students (803) 432-9841). Write to the **Kershaw County Historical Society**, P.O. Box 501, Camden, SC 29020 for more information. Insiders advise the **Paddock Restaurant** at 514 Rutledge Street for good food.

HANGING ROCK STATE PARK

This nearly 6,000-acre state park in Stokes County (north of Winston-Salem) is the preferred getaway for mountain climbers who enjoy rappelling off the mountain's walls. From the summit, climbers can see three states—and this is also a dandy spot for a picnic. Hanging Rock, with its waterfalls and vast variety of wildflowers is a natural for hikers.

You'll also enjoy the natural swim area on hot summer days. Explorers have found a cave that once housed Tory soldiers and there is evidence that the park was a favorite hunting ground for Indian tribes. This is a great spot for campers. For information on vacation cabins and tent/trailer campsites call or write the park at P.O. Box 186, Danbury, NC 27016.

MORROW MOUNTAIN STATE PARK

A favorite haunt for Charlotteans and certainly easily accessible, this state park near Albemarle offers 4,641 acres of enjoyment in the Uwharrie Mountains. There's a myriad of outdoor sports to participate in here. Hiking through the mountains is a favorite, but you can also swim, boat and fish

The Hamadryas Baboon enjoys watching his watchers at the N.C. Zoological Park in Asheboro.

on Lake Tillery. And you can investigate the nature study museum. Camping is available or you can stay in vacation cabins. There's also a nature study museum. For details, contact Morrow Mountain State Park, N.C. 5, Box 430, Albemarle, NC 28001 (704-982-4402).

NORTH CAROLINA ZOOLOGICAL PARK

Zoos aren't just for children anymore. Adults also enjoy watching and studying animals roaming about in cageless habitats similar to their native environments. You can do just that at N.C.'s Zoological Park, which was patterned after the San Diego, California concept. This gives the animals a healthy measure of freedom and lets you watch from a safe place. You are separated from the animals by ditches, waterways and other physical barriers worked into the landscape.

This is a perfect outing for the whole family. Here you can observe more than 625 wild animals and over 10,000 exotic plants. By the year 2000, this ever-expanding facility is expected to be the largest natural-habitat zoo in the world. You won't want to miss the **R.J. Reynolds Forest Aviary**, the only one of its kind anywhere. A 55-foot-high glass dome houses exotic plants and birds from all over the world. Walking through the aviary is like exploring a tropical forest, complete with all the sights, sounds and smells. While you're gawking at the African snake plants, don't be surprised if an Indian thrush lands at your feet.

The zoo is located off N.C. 220, south of Asheboro. From April 1 through October 15, the zoo is open from 9 AM to 5 PM Monday through Friday, and 10 AM to 6 PM weekends and holidays. From October 16 through March 31, the hours are 9 AM to 4 PM daily. Admission is $4 for children ages 2 to 15, and $6 for adults. For more information, write the N.C. Zoological Park Route 4, Box 83, Asheboro, NC 27203 (910-879-7000).

PINEVILLE, N.C.

If you live in Charlotte, you may not think of Pineville as a daytrip, but you can certainly spend the day and more if you visit all the shops here. With 20-plus shops, Pineville has rapidly risen to one of the area's premiere antique meccas. This charming small town also offers many other shopping opportunities such as accessories, oriental rugs and collectibles. There are even designers on hand in one shop to give you ideas on the latest home and office decorating trends. There are excellent restaurants nearby, ample free parking and most shops are open from 10 AM until 5 PM daily, and from 1 PM until 5 PM on Sundays. Pineville is located south of Charlotte with convenient access from I-77, N.C. 51 or South Boulevard. For more information, call 889-4387 or write P.A.D.M.A., P.O. Box 1079, Pineville, NC 28134.

SPENCER SHOPS
N.C. TRANSPORTATION MUSEUM

Unlike Steve Brody, the famous brakeman in the "Wreck of the Old 97," you can get to Spencer on time from Charlotte. In no time at all, you can see what was once Southern Railway's largest repair facility between Washington, D.C., and Atlanta, Georgia. You might even be lucky enough to run into some old engineers who work on the rusty engines and meet for coffee in the Spencer Ties Room. In the last few years, diesel and steam engines have been put into service on a limited-track run, giving visitors the opportunity of "riding the rails" from Spencer to Salisbury.

The museum also houses other artifacts that relate to transportation. The gift shop offers rail and transportation memorabilia you won't find many other places. This state historic site is open year-round except for major holidays. Hours are 9 AM until 5 PM Monday through

Saturday, and 1 PM until 5 PM on Sunday, April through October; 9 AM until 4 PM Monday through Saturday, and 1 until 4 PM on Sunday, November through March. Train rides are offered at 11, 1, 2, and 3 Monday through Saturday and 1:30, 2:30, and 3:30 on Sunday. There is a nominal fee of $1 - $3 for train rides, but no admission is charged. Spencer Shops is located about one hour north of Charlotte off I-85 (704-636-2889).

TOWN CREEK INDIAN MOUND

This state historic site near Mount Gilead in the Uwharrie Mountains commemorates the life of the Pee Dee Indians who inhabited the area hundreds of years ago. Town Creek was a fortified place of refuge and counsel where religious ceremonies and feasts took place. The reconstruction is based on archaeological excavations. A Visitors Center provides more insight into this Indian culture. Guided tours are available. The trip to Town Creek takes about two hours. For information, contact Town Creek Indian Mound, Route 3, Box 50, Mount Gilead, NC 27306 (919-439-6802).

UWHARRIE NATIONAL FOREST

The Uwharries are said to be the oldest mountains on the North American continent and the name is thought to come from a Native American tribe indigenous to the area. They were pushed out by French, German, English and Irish who chose the area to build stone quarries and for its excellent logging opportunities. President John

F. Kennedy established the area as a National Forest in 1961.

The wilderness area encompasses 47,000 acres, which provides plenty of space to enjoy nature's beauty while boating, fishing, swimming, hiking, picnicking, camping, hunting, horseback riding and two, three and four-wheel driving. Good camping is available here at three different camp grounds: **Badin Lake Campground, Uwharrie Hunt Camp** and **Uwharrie Hunt Camp**. For more details on camping and reservations call the above number or write to the Uwharrie National Forest District Ranger, U.S. Forest Service, Route 3, Box 470, Troy, NC 27371 (919-576-6391).

WEST VIRGINIA

Mother Nature put her energy into scenic beauty when she painted West Virginia. Tall, craggy mountain peaks and rushing white water rivers combine to offer exciting outdoor activities and breathtakingly beautiful sight-seeing. Rock climbing, mountain biking, skiing, golf and white water rafting are just a few of the activities available in West Virginia—about a four-hour drive from Charlotte.

If white water rafting is your sport, check out Rivers Resort (800-TRY-RIVERS). This resort offers special packages for rafters and has other activities such as horseback riding, kayaking, float trips, etc. for those in your group who may be interested in a little less excitement.

Photo courtesy of N.C. Travel and Tourism Division.

Golf is the unofficial sport of the Carolinas.

Inside
Golf

With the utmost respect to basketball, golf is the unofficial sport of the Carolinas. Eleven percent of all Carolinians play golf, not to mention the millions of players who visit our courses each year and pump untold amounts of money into the region's economy. While not a golf destination, yet, Charlotte has a rich golf history with the 1990s adding a new and exciting chapter.

Charlotte's first golf course, Charlotte Country Club, was designed by noted course architect Donald Ross in 1918 and is still recognized as one of the country's top layouts. The club hosted one of many notable tournaments that have come to the Queen City, the 1972 U.S. Amateur Championship. Prior to the Second World War, the Charlotte Open attracted many professional stars to Myers Park Country Club. The PGA Tour returned to Charlotte with the Kemper Open played at Quail Hollow Country Club from 1969-1979. Tom Weiskopf, Raymond Floyd, and Andy Bean were among the event's champions.

Today, many of those same players come to Charlotte annually for the Senior PGA Tour's PaineWebber Invitational. Held at the TPC at Piper Glen in southeast Charlotte, the tournament is hosted by Arnold Palmer and attracts the top stars of yesteryear.

Over the years, some of those stars have been from Charlotte. Clayton Heafner was a PGA Tour star in the 1940s and 1950s. He played on two Ryder Cup teams and twice finished second in the U.S. Open. In 1961, Charlie Sifford became the first black golfer to play on the PGA Tour full-time and the first black member of the PGA of America. He won two events and displayed enormous courage and determination throughout his career. Currently, Charlotte native Davis Love III is a superstar on the PGA Tour with eight victories to his credit.

In their attempt to emulate these greats, golfers across Charlotte have numerous facilities from which to choose. Within a 30-mile radius of downtown Charlotte, they can swing their clubs at one of 30 public golf courses, 23 private courses, three par-three courses, and 16 practice ranges.

While Charlotte's growth rate has taken off in the past decade, golf has actually lagged behind—not the popularity of golf, but the number of quality public golf facilities. That is now changing with more than a half dozen new courses on the drawing board to meet the demand for better conditioned and more challenging public layouts. From the scratch golf to the beginner, from the six-figure earner to the cash-starved college student, there is now a golf course for everyone in Charlotte.

Public Golf Courses

CHARLOTTE GOLF LINKS
11500 Providence Rd.   *846-7990*

Located in populous southeast Charlotte, this course represents the next best thing to playing the links of Scotland, and at a fraction of the cost. Noted architect Tom Doak designed the par-71, 6,520-yard links course which opened in the spring of 1993. The tract is virtually wide-open, except for the high rough guarding the fairways. You can try your bump-and-run shot around pot bunkers here. This highly regarded course is as close as you'll get to playing in the British Open.

EAGLE CHASE GOLF CLUB
N.C. 205, Marshville   *385-9000*

Scheduled to open in September 1994, this par-72, 6,800-yard layout is being built by a group of local investors who saw the need for an upscale public facility in Union County. They'll get just that with this Tom Jackson design. Located ten miles northeast of Monroe, the course is set along a rugged ridge and will feature many elevation changes and spectacular views.

EASTWOOD GOLF COURSE
Eastway Dr. & The Plaza   *537-7904*

This course is one of Charlotte's oldest public facilities and was once owned and operated by famed golfer Clayton Heafner. Under new ownership, the layout has undergone numerous on-course improvements over the past two years. Although a short course at only 5,850 yards, many locals play here and enjoy the old-fashioned design and small, crowned greens.

HIGHLAND CREEK GOLF CLUB
Ridge Rd.   *875-9000*

Charlotte's newest, and arguably best, public golf course is well worth the drive into the ever-developing countryside of northeast Mecklenburg County. Maintained

---

Insiders' Tip

There are 30 public golf courses within a 30-mile radius of Uptown Charlotte.

better than many private clubs, Highland Creek offers a variety of holes which are balanced, fair, aesthetically pleasing, and tough. It has the highest slope rating of any area public facility at 133. You'll have no problem recalling each hole of the par-72, 7,008-yard course. The climax doesn't come until the finishing hole, a reachable par-four with a lake running down the entire right side.

MALLARD HEAD GOLF CLUB
Brawley School Rd.
Moorseville   *664-7031*

Located north of Charlotte on Lake Norman, this rolling course of 6,900 yards is known for its well-kept greens. The front nine is relatively tight with the long, downhill par-three 7th hole playing over water and being a potential card wrecker. The back nine is kinder to wayward shots, but it ends with the tough 18th hole requiring a long

and precise tee shot to a small landing area.

REGENT PARK GOLF CLUB
U.S. 21
Fort Mill, S.C.   *(803) 547-8334*

Scheduled to open in the autumn of 1994, this course will be a much welcomed upscale facility south of the border. Multiple teeing grounds, generous landing areas, and removed undergrowth will allow all levels of golfers to compete, but well-positioned hazards and multi-level greens will challenge their games. The layout, designed by Ron Garl, actually crosses over both states and three different counties.

RENAISSANCE PARK GOLF COURSE
Tyvola Rd.   *357-3373*

The most convenient course in Charlotte is definitely one of its most popular as well. Located on Tyvola Road a 3-iron away from the

Photo by John Cress.

The spectacular Peninsula Club on Lake Norman was designed by Rees Jones.

Charlotte Coliseum, Renaissance Park may well be the area's most difficult course, too. Tight landing areas and sloping greens characterize this par-72, 6,880-yard layout. It also offers four of the area's best par threes ranging from 140 to 200 yards. The course annually hosts the Mecklenburg County amateur championships.

SUNSET HILLS GOLF COURSE
800 Radio Rd.   *399-0980*

Their slogan "Maximum Golf, Minimum Cost" is highly accurate. Sunset Hills is one of the least expensive courses in town. While there are few challenges from tee to green on this 6,400-yard tract, it offers many crowned and sloped greens which challenge all golfers. It's a great place to bring the family.

TEGA CAY COUNTRY CLUB
Gold Hill Rd.
Tega Cay, S.C.   *(803) 548-2918*

Tucked into a private community on Lake Wylie in South Carolina, this public-access course offers a private club setting. The 6,400-yard course offers a wide variety of holes and is a favorite among locals.

WESTPORT GOLF COURSE
N.C. 16   *483-5604*

On the western side of Lake Norman, Westport presents a straight-forward, challenging layout which stretches to 6,800 yards. The par-four 4th hole quickly get one's attention at 424 yards—one of the area's toughest holes. Golfers must lay up in front of a pond and then face a 200-yard approach shot to an

GOLFING

Charlotte Style!

Convenient to downtown and all points around Charlotte, "Golfing Charlotte Style" presents three well-manicured golf courses, and all related golf amenities, to enjoy your round of golf. A professional and friendly staff await your every golfing need with services to include snack bars, well-stocked pro shops, the American Golf Club, and clean, well-maintained facilities.

CHARLES T. MYERS
PUBLIC GOLF COURSE
7017 Harrisburg Rd
536-1692

REVOLUTION
PARK
2661 Barringer
342-1946

RENAIS-
SANCE PARK
1536 W. Tyvola Rd
357-3376

Mecklenburg County
Park and Recreation

American Golf ™

elevated green. Its greens are usually in superb condition, and the course offers a quiet getaway from busier Charlotte facilities.

Other public courses of note:

CHARLES T. MYERS GOLF COURSE
(NINE HOLES)
Charlotte 536-1692

LARKHAVEN GOLF CLUB
Charlotte 545-4653

OAK HILLS GOLF COURSE
Charlotte 394-2834

PARADISE VALLEY GOLF COURSE
(NINE HOLES)
Charlotte 547-0222

PAWTUCKETT GOLF CLUB
Charlotte 394-5890

REVOLUTION PARK GOLF COURSE
(NINE HOLES)
Charlotte 342-1946

SPRING LAKE COUNTRY CLUB
York, S.C. *(803) 684-4898*

Private Club Courses

The Charlotte area is also blessed with a spectacular set of private golf clubs. Unfortunately, many golfers aren't blessed enough to be members. If you want to play, call a club's head professional and inquire about their guest policy. If you're a member of another private club, ask your professional about any reciprocal agreements they might have with Charlotte area clubs.

It's worth a try when you consider being able to play venerable courses such as **Charlotte Country Club, Quail Hollow Country Club, Carmel Country Club, Myers Park Country Club,** and **Carolina Golf &**

Country Club. Other noted Charlotte clubs include **Raintree Country Club, Cedarwood Country Club, Pine Lake Country Club,** and **Pine Island Country Club**. Outside the city, there's **Cramer Mountain Country Club** located on its namesake in Gaston County and **River Hills Country Club** on the South Carolina side of Lake Wylie.

Some newer private courses have been built in the last five years as the centerpieces of residential developments. Two are in southeast Charlotte: **Providence Country Club**, designed by Dan Maples, and the **TPC at Piper Glen**, designed by Arnold Palmer. In north Mecklenburg County, the spectacular **Peninsula Club** on Lake Norman was designed by Rees Jones, and Raymond Floyd served as a consultant on the tough **River Run Golf & Country Club** in Davidson.

Carolina Courses

Being smack in the middle of the Carolinas, Charlotte offers golfers the convenient opportunity to play some of the finest tracts in the world. It's just two hours to the mountains, two hours to Pinehurst/Southern Pines, three hours to Myrtle Beach, and four hours to Hilton Head Island.

Before adventuring too far from Charlotte, though, an easy daytrip to **Tanglewood Park** (910-766-5082) would be worthwhile. An hour's drive from Charlotte, the 1,200-acre park and its Championship Course sit just west of Winston-Salem. It's not often a golfer gets to

Photo courtesy of Pinehurst Area Convention and Visitors Bureau.

The tradition of excellence continues on the more than
30 courses in the Pinehurst area.

tee it up at the site of a Senior PGA Tour event and former host of a major championship—the 1974 PGA Championship. Obviously, the course is extremely demanding with several long par fours and 110 bunkers. But with water on only three holes and little undergrowth, the average golfer can scrap it around with enjoyment quite easily. Its companion, the Reynolds Course, is no slouch either. Many regulars consider its tight, tree-lined back nine the park's toughest.

The Appalachian Mountains of North Carolina offer golfers the challenges of dramatic elevation changes and wildlife-filled forests along with the pleasures of scenic beauty and cool temperatures. Patrons of **Springdale Country Club** (800-553-3027) can take advantage of all these aspects. Thirty minutes southwest of Asheville, Springdale actually has a split personality. The front nine of this family-owned resort is wooded and mountainous while the back nine is open and flat.

Fifteen minutes north of Asheville, **Reems Creek Golf Club** (704-645-4393) features a rare treat of immaculately kept bentgrass tees, fairways, and greens. It's very much a target golf course with lay-up and blind shots the norm. Large, tiered greens add to the challenge.

Golfers can let loose a little more on its sister course, **Mt. Mitchell Golf Course** (704-675-5454). Sitting at the base of the highest peak east of the Rockies, the course is actually relatively flat and features bentgrass from tee to green. The natural hazards of streams and forests have been wonderfully incorporated into the

course to form another major distraction—breathtaking scenery. Beware especially of the picturesque 10th and 14th holes.

In the northwest corner of the state, **Jefferson Landing** (800-292-6274) opened three years ago along the New River, the world's second oldest. Former U.S. Open and PGA champion Larry Nelson designed this 7,111-yard layout. Its gently rolling, open terrain would allow golfers a larger margin of error if it were not for the creeks and ponds which are in play on 15 holes.

Moore County, North Carolina, is home to 34 golf courses and the world famous **Pinehurst Resort and Country Club** (800-659-4653). Guests have seven courses from which to choose, but the most frequent pick is Course No. 2. Designed by Donald Ross, No. 2's trademark is its crowned greens characterized by humps, bumps, and greenside

The N.C. mountains provide many scenic and challenging courses.

swales. Ben Hogan, Jack Nicklaus, and Paul Azinger have all won on this course. Another name will be added to the list at the U.S. Open to be played here in 1999.

The sandhills of North Carolina are full of other top-notch courses, as well. South of Aberdeen, **Legacy Golf Links** (800-344-8825) is a newer public layout designed by Jack Nicklaus II. The label "challenging, yet enjoyable" fits this course perfectly. Picturesque par threes, reachable par fives, and testing par fours naturally flow over former pasture land. Legacy is one of the most fun courses to play in the Carolinas.

Just west of Pinehurst, **Foxfire Resort & Country Club** (800-736-9347) has two courses, the East and West, designed by Gene Hamm. Although the East is longer and rated more difficult, the West is favored by locals because of its variety of holes and rustic feel. You can't go wrong with either one, though.

If your beggar turns into a chooser, take him/her to Myrtle Beach, South Carolina, and the Grand Strand. Here, golfers have more than 80 courses from which to choose. At the top of the list is the **Dunes Golf & Beach Club** (803-449-5914), site of the Senior Tour Championship. Although semi-private, the course has guest privileges at several area hotels. Test the par-five 13th hole, a sharp dogleg right around water. It's not reachable, but the hole's name "Waterloo" reveals past failures to heed similar warnings.

In North Myrtle Beach, **Bay Tree Golf Plantation** (800-845-6191) stands as a long-time favorite. With three 18-hole courses created by George Fazio and Russell Breeden, the complex has a design for every golfer: the rolling Gold Course, site of the 1977 LPGA Championship; the 7,044-yard Green Course, nicknamed "the Green Monster"; and the diverse Silver Course.

Photo by John Cress.

Providence Country Club Golf Course is a Dan Maples designed course.

A newer course in the Cherry Grove area, **Tidewater Golf Club** (803-249-3829), has garnered tremendous praise for its playability and straight-forward test of golfing skills. Ten holes run along the waterway, and all of them feature fast, sloping bentgrass greens.

Sliding down the coast to the South Carolina Lowcountry, **Wild Dunes** (803-886-6000) was one of the original island developments, and its Tom Fazio-designed Links Course has withstood both newer courses and Hurricane Hugo. Seaside golf doesn't get any better, especially when the 17th and 18th are true links holes which run right beside the ocean.

On the other side of Charleston, **Kiawah Island** (803-768-2121) offers four top-rate courses. The most famous is the Ocean Course, designed by Pete Dye and host to the memorable 1991 Ryder Cup Matches. Set hard by the Atlantic, if the wind blows, the course becomes the most difficult you'll ever play. Try parring the 205-yard 17th hole, or just try getting it over the water.

If you don't tire of playing world-famous courses, then continue down to Hilton Head Island and **Harbour Town Golf Links** (803-671-2436). When opened in 1969, the course's small greens, railroad tie-supported bunkers, and tight fairways were considered radical. Today, professionals rave about the course each year at the MCI Heritage Classic.

ASK DUKE POWER WHY THE HOUSE ON THE TOP IS A SMARTER MOVE.

They'll show you the energy-efficient features that really make a difference.

The Comfort Machine® is just one of them. It's Duke Power's high-efficiency heat pump. The more temperate the climate, the better it works. So the Comfort Machine's perfect for the Carolinas' mild weather.

If you plan on building or purchasing a new house, ask your builder or Realtor about The MAX®, an all-electric home featuring the Comfort Machine. The MAX is designed to meet Duke Power's strict energy-efficient guidelines. So it's also sure to meet your strong desire for lower power bills.

Before heading off on the house hunt, save yourself a lot of energy and call Duke Power at (800) 786-3853. They know some tips you can't afford to live without.

DUKE POWER
Smart People With Energy

Inside

Government Services and Utilities

When you move to a new area, there are some services you just can't do without—some provided by the government, some by public utilities and some by private business.

Because they are readily available and, in most cases, efficiently provided, the citizens of Charlotte often take for granted the services provided by the city. The garbage gets picked up on time, the streets are paved on schedule (continuously), the water is clean and drinkable, and the police and emergency services respond in a timely manner. That doesn't mean that Charlotte is problem-free.

Like many Sunbelt cities, it suffers from growing pains, but local government attempts to address the problems even though at times the solutions seem to cause problems of their own. For example, when rampant growth to the south of the city caused area residents to have low (or no) water pressure, the construction of a new pipeline turned the south Charlotte traffic problem into a real nightmare. But all things

considered, the city does a good job of planning and managing, as well as being responsive to the needs of its citizens.

The following is a short guide to some of the services you need to know about as a citizen of Charlotte. Included here are both state and local government services as well as public utilities. A directory of professional and miscellaneous services that you may want to know about is provided in a later chapter of this book.

Telephone Service

Southern Bell serves most of Charlotte-Mecklenburg, except for some of the small incorporated towns, which operate their own service or use other companies. Call 780-2355 to arrange for new service or request disconnection. If the property has had service in the past, you can probably take advantage of Southern Bell's Quick service plan. If you plug in your phone at the new residence and get a dial tone, just call 780-2355 before 3:00 PM and your service will be working the same day. For a new home, installation may require a couple of days.

If you have been a Southern Bell customer before, there is usually no deposit required. Your monthly charges will depend on where you live and the number of options you choose. A complete listing of service fees, installation fees and other miscellaneous charges can be found in the front of the current Southern Bell directory.

Electric Power

Thanks to tobacco magnate James B. Duke, Charlotte has one of the nation's top utility companies, **Duke Power**. Service may be initiated by calling 594-9400, Monday through Friday, between 8:00 AM and 5:00 PM, or you may apply in person at the office at 500 S. Church Street. If a deposit is required, it will normally run between $100 and $175, depending on the type of service. The fee is returned after one year of prompt payments. No deposit is required from previous customers who have established a good payment record.

Gas Service

City and county residents may obtain service by calling **Piedmont Natural Gas** at 365-2660, Monday through Friday, between 8:30 AM and 5:00 PM. Renters are required to pay a deposit, based on the history of the residence. The deposit is refundable with interest after 12 prompt payments. Home buyers are

usually not required to pay a deposit.

Water and Sewer

To secure water and sewer connections, apply in writing or in person at the **Charlotte-Mecklenburg Utility Department** at City Hall, 600 E. Fourth St. New customers must pay a non-refundable service charge of $32.00, which will be included in the first month's bill. The sewer charge is 100 percent of the water bill. The city also furnishes water and sewer to some parts of the county. To obtain new service or transfer service, call 336-2211. For emergency water service, call 336-2564; emergency sewer service, call 357-6064. If you have questions about your bill, call 336-2211.

Cable Television

Cablevision of Charlotte (377-9600) serves the city and **Vision Cable** (545-0136) serves homes in the county. Both offer a variety of optional services and equipment, and your monthly fee will depend on what you choose. Standard service is about $20.00 per month with both companies.

Garbage Collection

Regular garbage is picked up from backyards once a week and again from curbside later in the week. Furniture and appliances are collected by appointment only. Charlotte also provides a curbside recycling service. For information on

collection days in your neighborhood or for recycling information, call 336-2673.

Auto Tags and Drivers Licenses

When you move to the Charlotte-Mecklenburg area, you should report your change of address to the **North Carolina Department of Motor Vehicles**. To register a vehicle, it is necessary to have proof of ownership—either the title from the state in which the car was formerly registered or the manufacturer's certificate of origin if the car is new. You must also have liability insurance.

If you are transferring the title of a used vehicle already registered in North Carolina, it must be signed and notarized. Within 10 days of purchasing a North Carolina tag, the vehicle must be inspected. This can be done at an authorized service station or automotive repair shop and is required annually.

To purchase license plates, you must provide the name of your insurance company and the policy number. The cost of each plate is $20 and renewal stickers are purchased annually, during the month in which you initially bought the tag. Department of Motor Vehicles locations for tags are:

6058 E. Independence Blvd.	535-2525
6016 Brookshire Blvd.	399-8306
4751 South Blvd.	525-3832

You have 30 days to obtain a North Carolina driver's license after establishing residency. The license is good for four years and expires on your birthday. You will be notified about renewal. If you've moved within the state, report your new address to the DMV within 60 days. New drivers must be at least 16 years old and have successfully completed a driver's education course, or be 18 years old if they lack driver's education certification.

During the examination, you will be tested on vision, traffic signs, safe driving practices and, possibly, driving ability. The driver's test is usually waived when a license is renewed, as is the written test if the applicant has not had a traffic violation in the previous four years. If you have a physical or mental impairment, you can expect to be tested and may receive a restricted license. The regular license fee is $10, payable in cash only.

To study for the exam, get a free handbook from the Department of Motor Vehicles at the following locations:

N.C. 29 North	547-5787
6016 Brookshire Blvd.	392-3266
W. Arrowood at Nations Ford Road	527-2562

Insiders' Tip

To register your auto, you must provide a vehicle title, your insurance company's name and a policy number, your odometer reading and photo identification.

City-County Service Directory

The following directory lists some of the most frequently called, or difficult to find, local government offices. If you don't find the number you need here or in the blue pages of your telephone directory, try the City-County Action Line at 336-2040.

Frequently Called Numbers

Emergencies	*911*
Police, Fire, Ambulance (TDD)	*334-3323*
Water (24-hour service)	*336-2564*
Sewer (24-hour service)	*357-6064*
Building Permits	*336-2831*
Bus/Car/Van Pool	*336-RIDE*
Garbage/Trash Collection	*336-2673*
Information (Action Line)	*336-2040*
Parks Information	*336-4200*
Recreation Programs	*336-2884*
Tax Office	*336-4600*
Water/Sewer Bills	*336-2211*

Other City Services

ANIMAL LICENSES
336-3786

All cats and dogs four months of age or older and horses six months or older must have an animal license, renewed annually. Mail-in applications are available at the Animal Shelter or at local veterinarians offices.

ANIMAL SHELTER
2700 Toomey Ave. 336-3786

Citizens may obtain animals as pets for a reasonable fee that includes spay-neutering and inoculations.

ATTIC SALE PERMIT
Tax Office, 720 E. 4th St. 336-6315

Citizens are required to obtain permits to hold attic or garage sales.

BLOCK PARTY PERMIT
Department of Transportation
Government Center
600 E. 4th St. 336-3893

Permits are needed to close a street or road temporarily, or to have a block party.

BURNING TRASH
336-2101

Charlotte prohibits the burning of trash within the city limits.

CABLE CHANNEL 16
336-4246

Citizens can receive continuous information regarding city government on this channel.

COMMISSIONS AND BOARDS
City Clerks Office, Government Center
600 E. 4th St. 336-2247

Citizens are encouraged to apply for appointment to serve on the city's boards and commissions. Call the City Clerks Office for a list of open positions.

COMMUNITY IMPROVEMENT DIVISION
336-2587

The CID works to rid Charlotte's neighborhoods of unsightly litter, abandoned cars, and overgrown weeds and grass.

CRIME PREVENTION
336-2310

This office can help you organize a Neighborhood Watch program or learn about educational opportunities in crime prevention.

CRIME STOPPERS

334-1600

Call here with information that could possibly help solve a crime.

DANGEROUS DOGS

336-3786

Emergency Hotline   *336-3840*

If you have questions or want to report a potentially dangerous situation involving a dog, use this number. For immediate response, call the EMERGENCY DOG HOTLINE.

ECONOMIC DEVELOPMENT DEPARTMENT

336-3399

The EDD coordinates the city's involvement in selected public/private ventures, assists in planning and coordinating special events and festivals, and provides information on economic and business development.

GRADING PERMITS

336-2291

The Engineering Department issues permits to grade on private property.

HORTICULTURIST

336-4262

Charlotte employs a full-time horticulturist to coordinate the design, planting and maintenance of flowers and shrubs in the city's parks, medians and city-owned rights of way.

HOUSE NUMBERS

336-2173

The county Engineering Department assigns house numbers.

LEASH LAW

336-3786

A city ordinance requires that dogs be under physical constraint on the owners property unless accompanied by an adult, 18 years or older.

LIVESTOCK PERMITS

336-3786

A permit is required in order to keep livestock, domestic fowl or wild animals within the city limits.

MAPS

336-3624

The Engineering Department is responsible for updating the official city map. Copies (5' x 5' wall maps) are available from this office for $5. (If you just want a city map to help you find your way through the maze of Charlottes streets, head for the nearest convenience store.)

PARADE PERMITS

Government Center
600 E. 4th St.   *336-2247*

The City Clerks Office issues permits for a parade or picket.

Insiders' Tip

Owned and operated by the city, historic St. Mary's Chapel is a popular spot for weddings, receptions and parties.

PARKING TICKETS

Revenue Division
P.O. Box 31032
Charlotte, NC 28231   *336-4295*

Parking tickets may be paid by mailing a check or money order to the above address.

PLANNING COMMISSION

336-2205

The Charlotte-Mecklenburg Planning Commission identifies land use issues relating to housing, zoning, urban expansion and open space.

PROPERTY TAX

720 E. 4th St.   *336-5733*

Property taxes must be paid on real property, automobiles, boats, trailers and income-producing personal property. Real property includes land and buildings. Personal property taxes can be paid by mail or in person. The combined city-county tax rate in 1992 was $1.196 per $100 assessed valuation.

RECYCLING

336-2673

All single-family residences and duplexes in Charlotte should have red Curb It containers. Recyclable items should be placed in the container and placed at the curb on the specified pickup day.

ROAD CONSTRUCTION

336-2291 or 336-3893

With all the road construction around town, it's no wonder the Transportation Department has two numbers. Call here with questions or suggestions.

ST. MARY'S CHAPEL

336-4200

Owned and operated by the city, this historic chapel in the midtown area is a popular site for weddings, receptions and parties. Call for information and reservations.

SANITATION DIVISION

336-2673

The Sanitation Division provides backyard garbage pickup once a week. Also weekly, on a different day, the city has curbside collection of leaves and trash.

SIGNS

To report illegally posted signs, call 336-2587.

To obtain a permit to erect a permanent sign, call 336-3570.

To report damage to a street sign, call 336-3893.

SPEAKERS BUREAU

336-7600

A list of speakers available to talk about a variety of city issues and services can be obtained by calling here.

UTILITY DEPARTMENT

399-2221

The Utility Department is responsible for supplying purified water to Charlotte-Mecklenburg residents, and collecting and treating wastewater. The department maintains more than 4,000 miles of water and sewer lines.

WE'LL OPEN
THE DOOR TO YOUR
NEW HOME.

Whether you're moving across the country, or just across town, The Huntington Mortgage Company can help make your move easier. We offer competitive rates on a wide variety of loans and we're committed to serving your needs. Which means providing personalized attention. Working within your schedule. And being involved from the first step through the last. So if you're house hunting, call us. We'll help you feel at home.

**Huntington
Mortgage
Company**

A Smarter Way to Finance

4500 Cameron Valley Parkway, Suite 380
Charlotte, N.C. 28211
(704) 365-2770

The Huntington Mortgage Company is a subsidiary of The Huntington National Bank.

Inside
Homes

Charlotte offers a wide variety of housing options for every age and preferred life-style, from historic Fourth Ward in busy Uptown to quiet homes in the country. You can get a home in the country, city or suburbs as well as lake and river front homes. Charlotte has something to offer everyone. For example, if a new home in a planned neighborhood is your desire, you can live in southern Charlotte. If you would rather have a home away from it all, you can live up I-77, north of Charlotte. During rush hour, it takes the same amount of time, around half an hour, to get from South Charlotte to Uptown, as it does to get from the lake area to Uptown. Whatever you prefer, you can be assured that Charlotte has it.

Mid-year sales reports show a surprisingly healthy real estate market in the first half of 1994. In fact, sales were phenomenal. Through June, residential sales were up 23.4% from the same time in 1993—and '93 was a record year! At the end of June 1994 there were 6,364 houses on the market to be sold, down 20% from the same month in 1993. Be-cause the supply of houses is down, and the demand is strong it is reasonable to expect that house prices will begin to rise.

The average home cost $125,303 as of July 1994, with prices ranging from $30,000 on up. The typical home has three or four bedrooms, two or three baths, and either a family room, den or separate dining room. Many Charlotte homes have beautiful lawns. Make sure you drive through historic Myers Park and Dilworth to view some of the lush lawns sheltered by old trees. Not all lawns are as large as those, with the average lot measuring 85 feet by 180 feet.

Traditionally, Charlotteans have taken great pride in their homes, home furnishings and landscaping, and this city does not lack for beautiful homes, both old and new. Most of the older sections of the city have countless large homes that have been preserved to the finest detail with antiques eclectically intermingled with modern fabrics and furniture. This is also one of the few markets in the country where developers continue to build and sell new homes ranging from 3,500 to 6,000 square feet.

To make looking for a home a little easier, the **Multiple Listing Service** (MLS) divides Charlotte into nine areas. The fastest growing are primarily to the southeast and north of the city. University City, Area 2, is growing by leaps and bounds with University Place, a European-style community with shops, theaters, restaurants, hotel accommodations and housing as its nucleus. Southeast Charlotte, Areas 5 and 6, traditionally the place to which newcomers are directed, continues to offer the largest number of homes. East Charlotte, Areas 3 and 4 (Matthews and Mint Hill), is also a popular choice.

The **Charlotte Association of Realtors**, a volunteer professional organization with a paid staff, is the watchdog of the industry and benefits the community in a number of ways. The organization is pledged to protect the rights of property owners, help members solve common problems, provide opportunities for agents to continue with educational programs and promote the interest of real estate matters by involvement in national and local political issues. The board's Ethics Committee hears business disputes between parties, often a successful alternative to litigation, and does so free-of-charge. It also offers arbitration services. The Association is located at 1201 Greenwood Cliff and may be reached at 372-0911.

Space does not permit a complete listing of all the Realtors and builders in the area, but our suggestions can get you started in the right direction. Names of builders, land-

scapers, interior decorators and other home helpers are also listed. *The Charlotte Observer's* Real Estate section should be your first stop for up-to-the minute market offerings.

Relocating

Most everyone has had to go through the inconveniences of moving. Though it can be exciting, moving can also be traumatic for families. To ease some of the anxiety, most of the larger realty companies in the area offer some type of relocation services. Usually, one or more of their agents specialize in helping clients with relocation. Many companies will provide tours of Charlotte, maps, brochures, school information and a complimentary newspaper prior to your move. When moving to Charlotte, always carry a map in the car. Too many people who like to feel their way around a city get lost at the intersection of Queens and Queens or Sharon and Sharon, etc.!

The Charlotte Chamber of Commerce sends out information on the city to residents and potential residents. And don't forget the relocation services offered by local banks. In addition, there are several private relocation companies. If you are new to the area, the offices below should be able to provide you with objective relocation information.

EXECUTIVE RELOCATION SERVICES
900 Huntington Park Dr.   *364-9040*

This relocation and home-finding service, founded by Carolyn Sachsenmaier, is known for its personal approach. Consultants make

"Moving doesn't have to be a puzzling experience. Let us fit the pieces together and find your new home."

Executive Relocation Services

704/364-9040

Licensed in real estate since 1973
Call today for our Newcomer's Packet.

hotel reservations, meet planes, give tours of Charlotte, find temporary housing, help the spouse with job searching, seek out schools and day-care facilities, provide mortgage-assistance counseling, fill special needs and requests such as locating a horseback-riding facility or a junior soccer program or do whatever is necessary to meet the specific needs of their transferees. There is no charge for these services, but the company does receive a real estate commission when transferees purchase a home. Executive Relocation Services belongs to the Multiple Listing Service, Charlotte Board of Realtors, North and South Carolina Association of Realtors and Employee Relocation Council, a national organization.

KRES & CO.
2130 Queens Rd. W.   *344-9211*
574-3270

Kres & Company, a relocation rental assistance company, works with individuals and families to find suitable apartment housing. A na-tive Charlottean, Keith Jones is knowledgeable about areas, price ranges and amenities available in different complexes. This is a welcome service for renters who don't have the time or the inclination to search all over town for that perfect apartment.

MAKING CONNECTIONS
229 N. Church St.   *374-0669*

This highly regarded company custom-designs services to suit the client. This includes arranging short-term, fully-furnished corporate apartments, apartment-finding, utility connections and VIP personal tours of the city. Making Connections also serves companies on a contractual basis.

ALLEN TATE RELOCATION CENTER
6620 Fairview Rd.   *365-6900*

If you are considering a move to Charlotte, this is an excellent place to start. A division of the Allen Tate Company, it's the only walk-in facility of its kind in the area, designed solely to assist home buyers moving

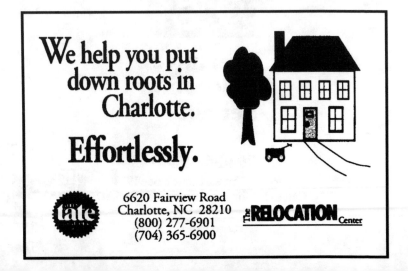

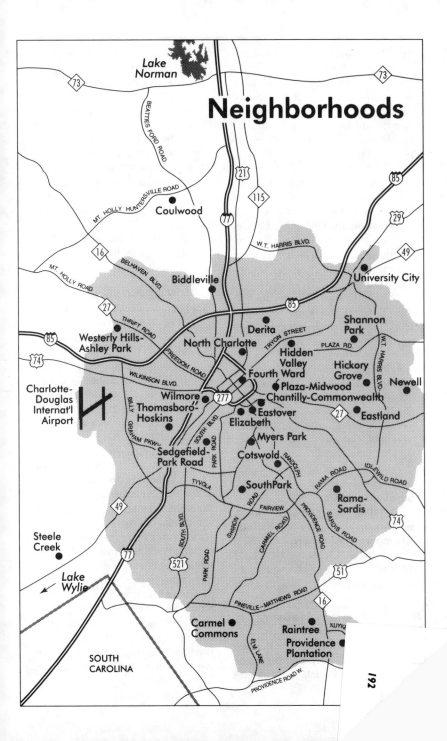

Neighborhoods

Lake Norman

Coulwood

Biddleville

University City

Derita

Shannon Park

Westerly Hills-Ashley Park

North Charlotte

Hidden Valley

Hickory Grove

Newell

Fourth Ward

Plaza-Midwood

Chantilly-Commonwealth

Charlotte-Douglas Internat'l Airport

Wilmore

Thomasboro-Hoskins

Eastover

Eastland

Elizabeth

Myers Park

Sedgefield-Park Road

Cotswold

SouthPark

Rama-Sardis

Steele Creek

Lake Wylie

Carmel Commons

Raintree

Providence Plantation

SOUTH CAROLINA

into the Charlotte metropolitan area. The center not only concentrates on preparing a family to make the right home selection decision, but its staff of 14 full-time professionals will help the individual or family reestablish those other important life focuses.

A phone call will get you a personally tailored relocation kit containing city maps, Chamber of Commerce statistics and reports, information on cultural amenities and activities, recreation, area attractions within driving distance, marine services and home and apartment guides.

The Center's Corporate Services Division also works with companies of all sizes who are relocating to the area. It will plan and present an on-site presentation for employees as well as counsel employees and provide valuable information packets and home-finding assistance. When you visit the Center, be sure to ask to see the multimedia presentation on Charlotte.

Many area banks also offer newcomer information. (See **Banking** chapter of this Guide.)

Always a great source of information on the city, the **Charlotte Chamber of Commerce**, 129 West Trade Street, Charlotte, NC 28203 (377-6911), also provides newcomer information.

Temporary Housing

When you're moving to a new location, the first few months can be ie toughest, especially if you haven't found a permanent home yet. There are several good temporary housing resources in Charlotte.

SELWYN AVENUE APARTMENTS
3400 Selwyn Ave. 527-3400

This 129-unit property allows month-to-month leases for corporations or offers a three-, six- or 12-month lease to private individuals. A variety of amenities are optional—maid service, coffee maker, cable TV, etc., and there are both furnished and unfurnished units. Rates vary according to the amenities provided and the length of stay.

MANOR HOUSE APTEL
2800 Selwyn Ave. 377-2621

Located in Myers Park, this property is another option for families moving to Charlotte. Neither an apartment nor a motel, the Manor House provides a homelike setting at prices almost anyone can afford. No lease is required, and guests staying a week or longer get a discount.

OAKWOOD CORPORATE HOUSING
(800) 888-0808

Oakwood Corporate Housing is the one solution for temporary housing throughout the greater Charlotte area and in over 400 cities nationwide. Fully furnished apartments, condominiums and townhouses come complete with linens, housewares, cable TV, telephone and maid service. Everything is billed on one convenient monthly invoice. This is the perfect solution for those on extended business travel, in training, relocating or between homes for one month or longer.

Look For A Charlotte Apartment On Your Own...And You'll End Up All Over The Map.

You can wander for hours looking for an apartment in Charlotte — from the intersection of Queens Road and Queens Road to Sharon Road, or Sharon Amity, or Sharon Lane, or 10 other streets named Sharon-something.

You can quickly drive yourself crazy. Or you can use our official apartment map of Charlotte. It's the fastest way to find a home in any part of town. And it's free. Just call us at (704) 529-6098.

Crosland Properties
P. O. Box 11797, Charlotte NC 28220
(704)529-6098

The **Only** map you'll ever need
In Charlotte

Crosland

QUEEN ARMS CORPORATE APARTMENTS

233 S. Sharon Amity   *362-3800*

With locations throughout Charlotte, the Queen Arms offers convenience as well as comfort. It caters to corporate transferees and offers one- and two-bedroom apartments with a variety of amenities from which to choose. No lease is required, and pets are allowed.

Rentals

Rentals account for only about 30 percent of the housing stock in Charlotte/Mecklenburg, but that doesn't mean you don't have a variety of options to choose from. There are approximately 312 different apartment communities and 64,000 apartment units in Mecklenburg County. In April 1994, the average month's rent for a one-bedroom apartment was $441, two-bedroom $512 and three-bedroom $608.

The vacancy rate in the Charlotte apartment market is a low 4.2 percent, which is down from 6.1 percent in the May of 1993. This low vacancy rate is due in part to the lowest construction rate in the apartment industry since 1976. New construction has accelerated, however, with several communities currently under way and planned for opening in 1995.

There are two free guides to Charlotte's apartment communities, which are available in a variety of outlets all over town.

THE APARTMENT FINDER

528 East Blvd.   *373-0051*
(800) 277-5679

The Apartment Finder is published four times a year by Southeast Publishing Ventures, Inc. Although this is a free publication, you will occasionally see them for sale with a rebate coupon enclosed in the guidebook. It also offers the *Apartment Finder Map Guide*, a detailed area map including apartment community information with color photos.

GREATER CHARLOTTE APARTMENT GUIDE

1515 Mockingbird Ln.   *523-0900*

This guide, published by Haas Publishing, features over 200 shop-and-compare listings with maps, photos, features and prices. It is also offered free of charge at many area grocery stores, drug stores and convenience centers.

CHARLOTTE APARTMENT ASSOCIATION

711 E. Morehead St.
Ste. 201   *334-9511*

CAA is a trade organization of landlords, developers and others involved in all aspects of the apartment business. The goal of the orga-

Insiders' Tip

There are approximately 312 different apartment communities and 64,000 apartment units in Mecklenburg County.

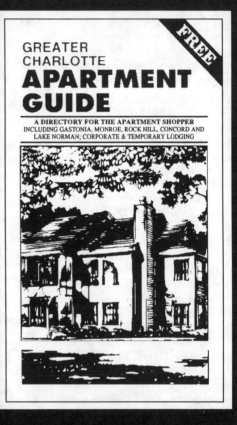

nization is to increase the professionalism of its members through education.

Property Management Companies

Whether you are looking to rent an apartment or a house, you want a reputable landlord who takes pride in the property and will live up to the terms of your rental agreement. Here are a few of the property management companies in Charlotte who have good track records.

CROSLAND PROPERTIES
4 Scaleybark Rd.   *529-6098*

Once affiliated with the single-family-home builder, the John Crosland Co., Crosland Properties manages eleven apartment complexes, primarily in southeast Charlotte. Rents range from $415 to $785 a month, with an average of $600. All accept families with children and have swimming pools. The communities vary in price and amenities offered.

FIRST UNITED REALTY
1132 Greenwood Cliff   *372-6667*

If you are looking for a house to rent, Denny Henson and his staff at First United Realty manage properties throughout the county and in various price ranges. If they don't manage one that suits your needs, they will go the extra mile to help you find it.

INSIGNIA MANAGEMENT GROUP
5970 Fairview Rd.   *541-0307*

INSIGNIA has nine complexes in Mecklenburg County:

Habersham Point and Pine Manor in South Charlotte are all-adult communities, while Countryside in the northeast and Barcelona and Foxfire in the east accept families with children.

MECA PROPERTIES
908 S. Tryon St.   *333-5300*

MECA is a good place to go if you're looking to rent a house. Its main areas are Myers Park and Dilworth, but MECA has properties located all over the county, which range in size from 1,000 to 6,500 square feet and rent from about $400 to $2,200 a month. The company has been in business since 1972, and there is no fee for its services.

OXFORD MANAGEMENT CORP., INC.
4801 E. Independence Blvd.
Ste. 901   *567-1039*

Oxford, the third largest multifamily developer in the U.S., manages four luxury complexes geared for singles in Charlotte, with rents starting at $415 a month. The communities feature complete recreational facilities and social programs as well as completely furnished corporate apartments.

PARAGON GROUP, INC.
5821 Fairview Rd.
Ste. 302   *556-9319*

This is the Mid-Atlantic Division of a national firm—one of the largest investment builders in the country based in Dallas. It has been in Charlotte since 1972 and currently has four apartment communities here: The Falls, Park South, East Chase and Copper Creek. The properties are geared for young singles. All feature extensive recreational facilities.

SUMMIT PROPERTIES
212 S. Tryon St.   *331-0470*

Founded as McGuire Properties in 1972, the firm changed its name to Summit in 1985. Its six complexes, located in the east and southeast, feature contemporary Victorian architecture and are all-adult and upscale, with a full package of recreational amenities such as spas and exercise rooms. They are McMillan Place, Alexander Place, Charleston Place, The Arbors, The Fairington, The Villages at Forest Ridge and McAlpine Place. Monthly rents start at $510. The company is based in Charlotte and has apartment communities from Florida to New Jersey.

YAGER PROPERTIES
600 Town Center Blvd., Ste. 110
Pineville   *889-2500*

Yager Properties is locally owned and has been in the Charlotte market for about 10 years. The company manages the Hamiltons Bay apartment complex at Lake Wylie as well as residential homes and commercial office buildings in both Charlotte and Lake Wylie.

Apartment Complexes

The following is a sampling of some of the apartment complexes available in the area:

CEDAR RIDGE
4012 Quail Forest Dr.   *542-6232*

Cedar Ridge is a reasonably priced apartment community in a beautiful neighborhood setting. As the only apartment community on Carmel Road, Cedar Ridge is part of a stable, upscale residential area and is within walking distance of excellent shopping and dining. Spacious one-, two- and three-bedroom garden and townhouse apartments feature private patios and an abundance of storage space. Amenities include a children's playground, tennis courts and an oversized pool.

CHATEAU VILLA
8940 E. University City Blvd.   *549-1474*

Located directly across from UNC Charlotte, Chateau Villa offers students affordable apartment living within walking distance of the university. This relatively small community offers one-bedroom apartments, two-bedroom garden apartments and two-bedroom town homes.

FOXCROFT EAST
4612 Simsbury Rd.   *365-1903*

This fine apartment community is a great value in the prestigious SouthPark area. Located on the corner of Fairview and Simsbury Roads between Charlotte Country Day School and the Foxcroft East Shopping Center, Foxcroft East offers convenience as well as spacious apartments with great storage space. Other features of note include fireplaces, a swimming pool, tennis courts and a jogging/biking trail. This complex has one- and two-bedroom garden apartments, one-bedroom loft apartments and one- and two-bedroom town homes.

LAUREL WALK

908-201 Summit Walk Dr.   366-1162

The neighbors stop and say hello as you drive through Laurel Walk, a small, lushly landscaped apartment community conveniently located just off Providence Road. The energy-efficient apartments feature large, spacious rooms, wood-burning fireplaces, built-in bookcases, oversized sunrooms and eat-in kitchens. Just 15 minutes from Uptown and moments away from the Arboretum Shopping Complex, SouthPark Mall, and major parks and tennis clubs, the community has a surprisingly quiet, serene atmosphere. Immaculate grounds, friendly and efficient management and an active social program give Laurel Walk a real home-like feeling.

OLD TOWNE

4738 Sharon Rd., #43   552-8094

Conveniently located in the SouthPark area within walking distance of some of the city's best shopping and dining, Old Towne is distinguished by its traditional architecture with wrought iron, dormers, copper-roofed doorways and par-quet floors. If a courtyard setting and the privacy of town home living appeal to you, you will love this 40-unit apartment community. Each spacious two-bedroom unit features an oversized kitchen, big windows, large closets, a private entrance and a large patio with a gate.

OLMSTED PARK

500 Meacham St.   358-3003

This brand new, upscale apartment community offers the charm of historic Dilworth and the convenience of being located just minutes from Uptown and some of the city's most popular shopping and entertainment. Notable features include dramatic vaulted ceilings, microwaves, fireplaces, ceiling fans, ceramic tile bathrooms and alarm systems. This community of one- and two-bedroom apartments is a good choice for those with active professional and social lives.

PARKWOOD EAST

7108 Wallace Rd.   536-5352

Parkwood East is a quiet residential apartment community with a convenient location. Located just off Independence Blvd., it is a quick

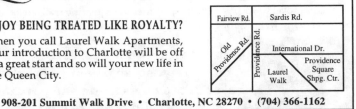

trip to shopping, schools, entertainment and work. The neighborly atmosphere makes it extremely popular with working parents. Parkwood East offers one- and two-bedroom apartments and is just the right size to provide personal attention and a strong sense of community.

SIMSBURY PLACE
4428 Simsbury Rd.   364-8762

Located in the heart of SouthPark, Simsbury Place boasts such exceptional features as indoor and outdoor pools, a gazebo-style clubhouse, private brick-enclosed entrances, microwaves, fireplaces, a jogging trail and a sophisticated electronic security system. Elegant one- and two-bedroom garden apartments offer luxurious living in one of the city's most exclusive communities.

THE VILLAGES
1600 Village Brook Dr.   552-9660

Convenient to Uptown, SouthPark and Carolina Place Mall, The Villages offers one- and two-bedroom apartments. The deluxe one-bedroom features a private screened deck and the two-bedroom apartments feature an L-shaped screened deck and double master bedrooms. Other features include microwaves, fireplaces with raised brick hearths, refrigerators with icemakers, oversized bay windows, courtyards, a weight room and a

Jacuzzi—a real value at a less than exorbitant price.

WATERFORD LAKES
8000 Waterford Lakes Dr.   552-5446

If resort-style living appeals to you, take a look at the new Waterford Lakes Apartments. These luxurious one-bedroom/one-bath and two-bedroom/two-bath apartments offer excellent roommate floor plans along with an impressive list of features such as fireplaces, ceiling fans, mini-blinds, walk-in closets, refrigerators with ice makers, vaulted ceilings on upper floors, balconies/patios and more. There is an elaborate pool, whirlpool spa, a clubroom, racquetball court, a complete workout and fitness center and planned social activities. Located just off Sharon Lakes Drive in south Charlotte, the community is convenient to shopping, restaurants and entertainment.

WESTBURY LAKE
3209 Westbury Lake Dr.   598-1313

Winner of the Pillar of Industry Award for the best garden apartment in the entire United States, Westbury Lake combines excellent design and architecture with the best in resort-style living. The natural focus of this community is its beautiful 4-acre lake, complete with dock and gazebo. Additional amenities include a jogging trail, an expansive natural area, fireplaces and an exer-

Insiders' Tip

The latest trend in real estate is the Buyers Agent, who represents the buyer in the negotiation and purchase of homes and other real estate.

Photo by John Cress.

This brand new, upscale Olmsted Park apartment community offers the charm of historic Dilworth and the convenience of being located just minutes from Uptown.

cise room. The north Charlotte location provides easy access to UNC Charlotte, University Research Park, Uptown Charlotte, I-85 and I-77. Westbury Lake features one- and two-bedroom garden apartments, one-bedroom garden apartments with den, and three-bedroom town homes.

WESTBURY PARK
8850 Park Rd. 552-9884

Located on Park Road, a short distance from the Quail Corners Shopping Center, Westbury Park is set apart by its attractive architecture and cheerful atmosphere. Both single professionals and couples with children are attracted by the convenient location and open floor plans. Add beautiful landscaping, quality construction, convenience and an active social program and it is easy to

see why Westbury Park is a popular choice in south Charlotte. Floor plans include one- and two-bedroom garden apartments as well as two-bedroom garden apartments with twin master bedrooms.

WESTBURY WOODS
9200 Westbury Woods Dr. 541-3573

Hard-working professionals who recognize and demand the best can take refuge from their hectic workday and relax in style at Westbury Woods. With sun rooms, screened porches, vaulted ceilings and walk-in closets, these apartments provide luxury living in a quiet, wooded setting. The community is located just off N.C. 51, within walking distance of grocery stores, drugstores and restaurants. Amenities include a swimming pool with a multitiered sun deck, an exercise room, lighted tennis courts and a

jogging trail. Westbury Woods offers one-, two- and three-bedroom apartments.

WILLOW RIDGE
9200 Willow Ridge Rd.   *541-5479*

Located off Park Road Extension next to Mercy South Hospital, this community is convenient to south Charlotte and Uptown. Willow Ridge offers 6- and 12-month leases as well as corporate leases. It also provides a host of amenities, including washers and dryers, an activities director, tanning bed, exercise room, four swimming pools and two hot tubs.

Buying A Home

Charlotte continues to be one of the hottest real estate markets in the country. The recent downturn in the economy had an impact here as well as the rest of the country. But all in all, the Charlotte market withstood the storm, and is now setting sales records. Charlotte's status as a leading financial center makes it possible for local Realtors to choose from a wide variety of financing options. It also contributes to the healthy real estate market. The competitive market is a plus for buyers and sellers. Home buyers who make wise investments can usually make a profit when they sell. Competition also keeps real estate salespersons on their toes, willing and eager to please their clients.

There are several local publications that can be helpful if you are buying a home.

THE NEW HOME FINDER GUIDEBOOK
528 E. Blvd.   *704-373-0051*
(800) 277-5679

If you are looking for a newly constructed home, *The New Home Finder Guidebook* will introduce the metro area's homebuilders and their new subdivisions. Published bimonthly by Southeast Publishing Ventures, Inc., it is the area's only comprehensive new housing guide, complete with color photos, maps, community and builder listings and prices.

For the resale housing market there are two publications that can be of assistance: ***Homes & Land*** (366-8799) or ***The Real Estate Book*** (845-5800).

Buyers' Agents

The fastest growing trend in real estate—buyers' agents—has hit Charlotte with a bang. These agents represent the buyer in the negotiation and purchase of homes and other real estate. Some real estate companies now provide buyer representation exclusively, while other traditional listing companies offer both buyer and seller services. Buyers' agents are licensed in the full spectrum of real estate transactions and provide Multiple Listing Services as all Realtors do.

CAMPBELL PROPERTIES
576-7792
Relocation Department   *(800) 745-5661*

Always on the cutting edge, Joe Campbell was one of Charlotte's first buyers' agents. The company specializes in residential real estate

and can assist in the purchase of a
new home or a re-sale. This company has no listings of its own and
provides buyer representation exclusively. It co-brokers through the
Charlotte Multiple Listing Service,
which has over 7,000 listings and
serves the Metro Charlotte area, Lake
Norman and Lake Wylie.

OFF SITE
NEW HOME SALES
Eastland Promenade
5534 Albemarle Rd.   *531-4089*
Another twist on the traditional real estate company, Off Site
New Home Sales deals only in new
construction. If you know that you
want a new home rather than a re-
sale, this company represents 300

builders in 200 different communities all over the area. It helps take the
confusion and the pressure out of
buying a new home by providing
information on most of the area's
major builders—as well as what's
available in the market—in one convenient location.

Realtors

There are approximately
2,500 licensed real estate agents in
Charlotte's Multiple Listing Service,
as well as 300 to 400 commercial
agents.

According to the National
Association of Realtors, a Realtor is
expected to perform the following
services for clients: have the most

current information about what is on the market, including homes listed by other Realtors; help determine how much home you can afford, how you can acquire the down payment, and what financing options are available; help find a home that best suits your needs—size, style, features, location, etc.; suggest simple ways to make a prospective home more suitable for you and improve its utility and value; supply information on real estate values, taxes, utility costs, municipal services and utilities; point out advantages and disadvantages of a home in an objective manner; act as a liaison between you and the seller to present offers and counter-offers; inform you if an attorney is needed at closing and provide a list to choose from; be familiar with the local money market and financing and let you know the personal and financial data that will be needed for a loan application; and explain the closing process in advance.

The companies selected for this guide are known to be some of the best, but they are not the only ones to consider. If you want a complete list, check with the **Charlotte Association of Realtors** (372-0911) or the Yellow Pages. Keep in mind also that a number of builders in town have their own realty companies. You'll find them under Builders in this section.

HELEN ADAMS REALTY
2301 Randolph Rd. 375-8598

Personalized service is the watchword for this small company that has only nine agents. The firm specializes in property in the Myers Park, Eastover and Southeast areas of Charlotte. It also offers property management services and represents Myers Park Manor, a 41-unit apartment complex.

Photo by John Cress.

Many people find the life-style at Lake Norman worth the commute to Charlotte.

THE ALLEN TATE COMPANY

6618 Fairview Rd., Ste. 100	364-6400
Carmel Office	
7824 Pineville-Matthews Rd.	541-6200
East Charlotte Office	
7212 Albemarle Rd.	563-6000
Lake Norman Office	
N.C. 73, Jetton Rd.	896-8283
Matthews Office	
165 S. Trade St.	847-6400
University City Office	
145 W. W.T. Harris Blvd.	547-8900

Charlotte's largest locally owned independent Realtor, the company was founded in 1957 by Allen Tate upon the premise that every client should be treated as if he or she were the company's only client. Known for its specialization in residential property, the company has played a strategic role in the development of new neighborhoods near UNCC. Allen Tate Builder Services is considered one of Charlotte's quality builders.

BISSELL-HAYES REALTORS

4515 Sharon Rd.	364-4515

Founded in 1964 by Charlotte natives Betty Hayes and Smoky Bissell, this realty company is still locally owned and operated. "We know Charlotte like the back of our hand," says Hayes. "Our roots are here." The firm offers a variety of services, including relocation. The company is very active in community agencies and arts organizations.

BRAWLEY & ASSOCIATES

P.O. Box 221037	
Charlotte, NC 28222	364-5222

Brawley & Associates, Inc., is a leader in both residential and commercial real estate in the Charlotte area. The company is a forward-moving firm in the business of finding just the right home for you and your family and turning the trauma of uprooting your family into a pleasant, exciting opportunity. Backed up with sound credentials, the sales staff prides itself on friendly, efficient service.

CENTURY 21
OF THE SOUTHEAST, INC.

4401 E. Independence Blvd.	568-2121

There are five independently owned and operated Century 21 office in Mecklenburg County.

Century 21 At the University

8401 University Exec. Park Dr.	547-0210

Century 21 Gary Cooper Realty

10801 Johnston Rd.	541-6306

Century 21 Vision Realty

5101 Central Ave.	568-5134

Century 21 Westside Realty

Coulwood Shopping Ctr.	399-4848

Century 21 Hecht Realty

Lake Norman	
Davidson	892-6556

COLDWELL BANKER
FLOUHOUSE REALTORS

Relocation Center	(800) 325-0986
Corporate Offices	362-7800
Carmel Road Office	541-5111
SouthPark Office	552-6116
Sardis Road Office	845-2900

Locally owned and operated, Coldwell Banker Flouhouse Realtors delivers all of the resources of an international company with a personal touch throughout the Greater Charlotte Metropolitan area. Coldwell Banker Flouhouse offers a full range of services, including sales, marketing properties and financing. Through its affiliation with Relocation One, a nationwide relocation service, the company assists many families and companies with corporate relocation.

COTTINGHAM CHALK & ASSOCIATES
6846 Morrison Blvd.   *364-1700*

This community-spirited company has dozens of experienced sales professionals and a full-service relocation division. The company's expertise is evident by its affiliation with RELO, the world leader in relocation. The company has been heavily involved in assisting transferring families whose firms have relocated to Charlotte.

FIRST CHARLOTTE PROPERTIES, INC.
1366 E. Morehead St.   *377-9000*
Relocation Services   *(800) 262-8715*

First Charlotte Properties, active in the Charlotte market for about 13 years, prides itself on sound business principles and practices, a history of solid growth and deep community involvement. All the firm's agents have the REALTOR designation, and a comprehensive Relocation Department is dedicated to providing first class service to its customers and clients.

MULVANEY HOMES
1229 Greenwood Cliff   *375-9373*

An offshoot of The First Colony Group, First Colony Realty specializes in new homes priced from $80,000 to $175,000. Founded by well-known Charlotte developer Michael J. Mulvaney, this young company is filled with local Charlotte people who focus on attention to detail and service to their customers.

HARDING REALTY, INC.
2727 Selwyn Ave.   *377-4927*

Founded years ago by John and Donna Harding, this small Charlotte firm handles residential real estate primarily in the southeast area and represents several home builders. "About 50 percent of our business is relocation," notes John Harding, who serves as vice president while his wife Donna heads up the 25-agent company.

HARRINGTON DOWD REALTY
6701 Fairview Rd.   *364-3541*

Founded by builders Gene Harrington and Ken Dowd, this full-service realty company specializes in new homes, in the higher price brackets. The firm offers a helpful relocation packet to its clients.

KNOX REALTY

Cornelius
Hwy 73   892-7802
Davidson
103 N. Main St.   892-0196
Mooresville
141 N. Main St.   7(04) 663-5776

Founded in 1973, this family-owned company is headed by Russell B. Knox. The company, which employs 25 agents, serves North Mecklenburg, Lake Norman and South Iredell, offering residential and commercial brokerage and appraising.

LAKE NORMAN REALTY

Mooresville
I-77 and N.C. 150   (704) 663-3655
Cornelius
I-77 and N.C. 73   (704) 892-9673
Charlotte Number   332-6464

As the name implies, Lake Norman Realty knows about Lake Norman Real Estate. One of the largest real estate firms in the area, its motto is "Lake Norman, we've got you covered," and from the northern tip to the southern end it has hundreds of listings. Lake Norman Realty was founded 14 years ago and has grown to meet the exciting new development needs of the area. The Mooresville office is home to an extensive Property Management division. Other services offered are a Relocation Division, Development Service and a Commercial Division.

LAKE PROPERTIES LTD.

Davidson
19700 N.C. 73 W.   892-5518
                             (800) 232-6447
Denver   483-6574

Established in 1984 by experienced real estate professional Mary Ann Drag, Lake Properties serves Lake Norman, North Mecklenburg and South Iredell County properties. The 19 agents live in the lake area, so they know their product well. Only a 20-minute drive from Charlotte, lake lots and homes are a wonderful investment as well as a perfect first or second home.

MARY RYDER REALTY COMPANY

SouthPark Center	*364-3300*
Carmel Center	*541-4160*
Arboretum Center	*541-6100*
Relocation Services	*(800) 876-3300*

Owned locally by Pat and Bill O'Connor, Mary Ryder has been serving Charlotte's real estate needs since 1965. As one of Charlotte's largest locally owned real estate firms, the Mary Ryder associates are professional Realtors and have the experience and training to offer the highest quality service. They know their city and the surrounding Metrolina area, and have been a part of its tremendous growth. Mary Ryder's relocation department facilitates numerous corporate moves to this area every year and all three offices offer full services, including home sales, complete market analyses, relocation and sales agent training.

PRENDERGAST, INC. REALTY

6733-A Fairview Rd.   *364-8580*

An established real estate company, founded about 20 years ago, this firm offers clients a wide range of personalized services. It specializes in fine residential properties.

THE PRUDENTIAL CAROLINAS REALTY INC.

7301 Carmel Executive Park	*542-1100*
2034-A Randolph Rd.	*334-6677*
4529 Sharon Rd.	*364-1580*
8320 University Execuive Pk. Dr.	*548-8700*
Relocation Service Center	
4529 Sharon Rd.	*366-5545*
Gastonia	
514 S. Union Rd., Ste. A	
Charlotte Tel. No.	*333-8161*
Mint Hill	
7521 Matthews-Mint Hill Rd.	*545-9600*
Monroe	
2605-A W. Roosevelt Blvd.	
Charlotte Tel. No.	*372-7378*

Merrill Lynch became The Prudential Greater Charlotte Real Estate Company when it was acquired in 1989. Now known as The Prudential Carolinas Realty, the company has a number of offices throughout the Mecklenburg area and offers full real estate services, including home sales, commercial sales and a relocation department.

REALTY PROFESSIONALS

1347 Harding Pl., #200	*372-6000*
Relocation Services	*1-800-422-2105*

Realty Professionals is a select group of experienced Realtors with proven abilities in assisting home buyers and sellers in maximizing their options and minimizing their problems. The firm offers services in the areas of new home sales, home buying and selling and commercial properties. It has a terrific Corporate Relocation Center that offers everything from courtesy tours of the area to special medical needs information.

FIRST PROPERTIES OF TEGA CAY
2222 Tega Cay Rd.
Tega Cay, S.C.   *(803) 335-8601*

When owner John Wilkerson bought River Hills Realty in 1977 from Sea Pines Plantation, which had developed River Hills Plantation on Lake Wylie, his expertise was in oil. He didn't even have a real estate license. Today he not only has his license but owns two real estate offices that have 25 agents. Other offices are located at River Hills Plan-

tation. Wilkerson's company is the largest realty company in York County.

WANDA SMITH & ASSOCIATES
423 S. Sharon Amity Rd.   *366-6667*
Lake Wylie
4052 Charlotte Hwy.   *(803) 831-9330*

Wanda Smith is one of the best known names in the Charlotte real estate market. During eight of her nine years with Merrill Lynch Realty, Smith was the top sales leader and in 1985 was named the corporation's top agent in the nation. The company serves as the exclusive sales agency for many of Charlotte's top home builders, as well as specializing in home resales.

Builders

When you're looking for a home you look for location and

Photo by John Cress.

New home construction is on the rise throughout the Charlotte/Mecklenburg area.

price, but you also look at the company that's building it. You want quality construction and a firm that stands behind its product. That's especially true if you are buying a custom-built home. What follows is a representative look at some custom-home builders as well as some information about tract builders.

CENTEX CROSLAND HOMES
145 Scaleybark Rd.   *523-8111*

Founded in 1937, John Crosland Homes is one of the oldest home builders in Charlotte and has been the largest for most of the last 10 years. In fall 1987, it was purchased by Centex Real Estate Corp. of Dallas, the country's largest home builder. Crosland has built about 12,000 homes throughout the area and has been a major influence on local residential construction. It generally accounts for about 15% of the new home market here. In the early 1980s, Crosland built primarily for first-time buyers, and still does, but has increasingly turned to the buy-up market, with homes ranging in price from the low 80s to upwards of $200,000. Its more than 20 communities are located all over Charlotte and surrounding areas.

FORTIS HOMES
7504 E. Independence Blvd.   *568-1144*

Fortis, once a subsidiary of the giant Daniel Construction Co. of South Carolina, has been building in the Charlotte market for about 15 years. The company develops, builds and markets its own properties and currently is selling in five communities in the Charlotte area— Claiborne, Willow Pond, Forest at Shelton, The Heathers and Habersham. Prices range from the 80s in Claiborne and Habersham up to $150,000 in The Heathers. Many special features such as crown moldings, six-panel doors and upgraded cabinetry are offered as standards in a Fortis home, along with generous allowances for such items as wallpaper and lighting fixtures. At the present time, Fortis is building primarily in North Charlotte and the Matthews area.

FULL HOUSE CONSTRUCTION CO.
7144 Moss Point Dr.   *846-3666*

Mac Petitt has 20 years of homebuilding and remodeling experience under his (carpenter's) belt. Mac and his team will custom design a home to fit your specifications or he can provide you with complete house plans. Whether its adding on a room or starting from scratch, Full House Construction will get the job done. Call for a free estimate.

HARRY GRIMMER & CO.
1312 Matthews-Mint Hill Rd.
Matthews, NC 28105   *847-8823*

Harry Grimmer builds about 60 homes a year priced from $200,000 to $450,000, making him the largest home builder in this price range in Charlotte. The firm, founded in 1974, has a large land inventory primarily in Southeast Charlotte, building in about a dozen locations, including Providence Plantation, Montibello and Providence Country Club. Doing both contemporary and traditional homes, Grimmer offers a turnkey operation to home buyers.

All brick homes $150's to $220's

You Can Too, Have It All...

• *The Latest Style* • *Enduring Quality* •
• *Excellent Location* • *Great Value* •

Builder With Integrity

William Trotter Company has been building in Charlotte and Mecklenburg County since 1959. A locally owned builder, known for dependability and pretty neighborhoods and winner of many awards. For example: Mecklenburg's first "Conservation Developer" awarded for a long record of conserving trees, and North Carolina Home Builder of the Year.

Fine Quality Homes

We specialize in all-brick exteriors (not just brick on the front of the house). You will find one and two story, 3 and 4 bedroom homes. These homes are designed for enduring value with a variety of features and styles for you. There are: luxurious master suites, spacious open kitchens, high ceilings, garages and daylight basements that appeal to various ages and family circumstances.

The Price Range

From the $150's to $220's. We know of no other Charlotte builders that offer such high quality, all-brick homes at prices this low.

Great Locations

There are five attractive new home neighborhoods representing the best areas of Mecklenburg County. At Matthews: Sardis Plantation and Matthews Plantation. At Huntersville: Wynfield. Near the University and the Research Park: Colvard Park. At Concord: Parkside at Oak Park. Near the Piper Glen PGA Golf Course, off Highway 51: Providence West.

For FREE Neighborhood and Plan Folder, write or call collect at (704) 525-1783.

SINCE 1959
1515 MOCKINGBIRD LANE
28209: TEL (704) 525-1783

JOHN R. POORE, BUILDER
P.O. Box 1437
Matthews, NC 28105   847-0496

Randy Poore builds homes, primarily in Southeast Charlotte, starting at about $250,000 to more than $1 million. He's built or sold several residences in Seven Eagles, all costing $600,000 and up. These are very customized homes, and Poore works closely with architects and designers to give you just what you want. Most homes are traditional on the outside, with transitional floor plans inside, and his bathrooms are unsurpassed for luxury.

SIMONINI BUILDERS
1600 Elizabeth Ave.   358-9940

For years Mr. Simonini was the preeminent builder on and around Lake Wylie. Sons David and Alan joined the firm and now this thriving family business builds some of the most beautiful residences in Charlotte and Lake Norman as well as in South Carolina. Priced from $300,000 to $600,000, these stately homes reflect the quality Simonini signature.

SOUTHERN TRENDS
8318 Pineville-Matthews Rd.
Ste. 281-F   542-0123

Mike Sikorski, president of Southern Trends Homebuilders, has made a commitment to excellence in the home building industry. Besides having house plans from which to choose, Mike offers the customer the option of a true custom-built home. He personally assists in the plan design, visits the site daily, meets with the customer regularly and provides ongoing creativity during the construction of each home. Mike has successfully built in Rosecliff, Wyndham, Greygate and Cobblestone and is among the select builders in Park Crossing and Providence Country Club.

JOHN THOMASSON CONSTRUCTION CO., INC.
4425 Randolph Rd.,
Ste. 215   365-3218

Now operated by brothers Sid and Jim, Thomasson builds homes priced around $150,000 and up, with the average running about $250,000. Most of the firm's homes are built in Stone Haven and Montibello, although it does build infill homes on spec in Myers Park and Eastover. In business for more than 30 years, Thomasson is one of the oldest builders in the area and has a proven track record for flexibility.

TROTTER BUILDERS
1515 Mockingbird Ln.,
Ste. 900   525-1783

The William Trotter Company has been a well-respected name in the Charlotte market for over 30 years, and a visit to one of its neighborhoods, such as Sardis Plantation or White Oak, will immediately tell you why. All brick homes with beautiful landscaping (William Trotter won Mecklenburg's first Conservation Developer award) combine to create a feeling of upscale quality well beyond the price range. Beautifully decorated model homes reflect a variety of unique floor plans that offer features normally found only in custom-built homes. And this level of quality is found throughout the neighborhoods. Model homes are the standard, not the high-end exception, so the integrity of the neighborhood and your property value remain intact. Priced from $110,000 to the 180s and up, a Trotter home is a true value in today's market.

Remodelers

If you need major work done on an existing house, start here:

CRAFTSMEN CONSTRUCTION, INC.
3811 Miriam Dr.   *377-2011*

Since 1951, Craftsmen has been providing quality residential remodeling and building additions primarily in Southeast Charlotte.

ANDREW HANES & CO.
109 West Blvd.   *375-8016*

Hanes takes on residential and commercial work, both large and small, from redoing rooms to adding them on. The firm started in 1975 and works all over Mecklenburg County, although much of its work is centered in the Southwest section of the city. It's known for strict attention to details.

KITCHEN MAGICIAN
216 Iverson Way   *523-2046*

This company really is the closest thing to magic when it comes to remodeling your kitchen or bath. It will do the whole job with floor plans,

elevations and a color board of the project, or it can furnish you with just the cabinets or other small items. Its designers are available to give you advice on how to change the total look of your room as an alternative to a complete remodeling job. Kitchen Magician and its management have 14 years experience in the design, furniture and cabinetry industries.

ANDREW ROBY, INC.
GENERAL CONTRACTOR
1131 Harding Pl.   *334-5477*

With more than 40 employees, Roby is one of the largest general contractors in the area. The firm, in business for nearly 40 years, does both additions and remodeling, primarily in the Myers Park-Eastover area of Charlotte.

REMBERT ROGERS III, INC.
2132 Floral Ave.   *375-8371*

Rembert A. Rogers III, is the remodeling contractor responsible for the renovation of The Brem House on East Boulevard, where his office is located. The charming archways, elegant railings and sophisticated cabinetry evident here are examples of the timeless quality which goes into his work. Whether replacing the kitchen faucet, renovating your kitchen, building that perfect addition or embarking upon a historic restoration, Rem Rogers can provide top-quality, professional assistance.

TRI-SQUARE CONSTRUCTION COMPANY

2012 Euclid Ave.   334-8850

David Young and his firm offer additions and remodeling, but their specialty is kitchens and baths. The firm started in 1984 and works primarily in Southeast Charlotte, Myers Park and Dilworth.

Interior Designers

Deciding to work with an interior designer can be a wise investment for a business person or a homeowner. Whether you are designing a new interior from the floor up or redesigning an existing space, a designer can be invaluable in helping you transform general ideas into functional realities.

No doubt you have seen the letters A.S.I.D following the name of an interior designer. These letters identify him or her as having met the highest professional standards required by the American Society of Interior Designers. To become a Professional Member of this group, a designer must meet rigorous criteria, including accredited education, years of proven experience and passage of the NCIDQ examination.

Most designers are found through word of mouth by client recommendation. If you decide to work with an interior designer, no matter how you make your choice, it is a good idea to interview the individual to be certain that your ideas and tastes are compatible. A good

place to see top area designers work showcased is at the A.S.I.D Symphony Designer House, sponsored by the Charlotte Symphony's Women's Association each September, or the Southern Spring Show held every February and March at the Charlotte Merchandise Mart on Independence Blvd. If you are more of a do-it-yourself type, you can get ideas and talk directly to suppliers at the Southern Ideal Home Show held at the Charlotte Convention Center each September.

INTERIOR DESIGN SOCIETY GREATER CHARLOTTE CHAPTER

I.D.S., the Interior Design Society, is the second largest accrediting organization for professional interior designers in this country. Qualification for membership as a designer is contingent on meeting very high standards of education and experience. I.D.S. designers specialize in quality residential interior design. Examples of their work can be seen at the I.D.S. Showhouse in May 1992, A.S.I.D Symphony Designer House, the Southern Spring Show, Homerama and, of course, in many of the finer residences in this area. Here is a selection of some of Charlotte's best known designers.

ACCESSIBLE ENVIRONMENTS, INC.

1327 Durwood Rd.   376-6641

Started by Carl Hefner, A.S.I.D., Accessible Environments specializes in designing and consulting services for people with all kinds of disabilities. It is expert at creating handsome barrier-free interiors that function well for people with any type of disability.

BECKY GILL INTERIORS

4007 Meadowridge Dr.   542-5583

Becky Gill has been active in residential design in the Charlotte area for ten years, specializing in traditional and transitional interiors. An Allied Member of A.S.I.D. and an Associate Member of I.D.S.,

Becky also teaches interior design at Central Piedmont Community College.

CALVIN HEFNER

1327 Durwood Dr.   376-6641

Calvin Hefner, A.S.I.D., has been in business in Charlotte since

Interiors Marketplace at Atherton Mill has 83 vignettes, subleased to interior designers, antique or architectural dealers, that are decorated with imports from around the world.

1977 and does high-end residential and contract interiors. Widely known for his contemporary designs, he also does traditional and eclectic interiors.

GEORGE W. PITMAN
438 Queens Rd.   *376-6661*

A Charlotte tradition, Pitman has been in business for about three decades and still works out of his home. His work can be seen at several area country clubs, including Carmel Country Club. Pitman's work includes residential and commercial.

EDWARD H. SPRINGS INTERIORS, INC.
1236 E. Morehead St.   *376-6461*

With a staff of 10, Ed Springs, A.S.I.D., has one of the largest and oldest design firms in Charlotte. He deals primarily with residential design and offers an eclectic mix of styles that include both the traditional and contemporary.

CAROL TROY INTERIORS, INC.
601-B Providence Rd.   *335-9963*

A Charlotte native, Carol Troy, Allied A.S.I.D., has been in business for 10 years. She specializes in residential and small commercial projects with a mix of contemporary and traditional styles designed to incorporate the home or business owners special treasures. Carol Troy's work includes many area restaurants.

ROBBIE A. WARREN INTERIORS
316 Main St.
Pineville   *889-4465*

Robbie Warren, Allied A.S.I.D. and Associate I.D.S., is a native Charlottean who brings the traditions of the past together with the current styles of today. This studio offers complete residential design services, specializing in incorporating antiques with other styles and decor.

Antiques and Home Furnishings

It used to be that Waxhaw was the place to go for antiques, and it still is a wonderful days outing for the serious shopper. But in the past few years Matthews and Pineville have come into their own as antique centers, and Main Street in Pineville is a shoppers paradise with about 16 shops within walking distance of each other. Here's a sample:

THE ANTIQUE CUPBOARD
331 Main St.
Pineville   *889-4387*

The Antique Cupboard has one of the area's largest collections of American and Continental antiques and collectibles, featuring English, Irish and French country pine. An adjoining warehouse is a must for the serious antique lover.

BREM HOUSE ANTIQUES
211 East Blvd.   *375-7800*

The Brem House buys old estates where heirlooms and oddities have been housed for years and helps you use them to create beautiful, affordable interiors. It has wonderful lamps, accessories and furnishings that will add interest and personality to any decor. If you love antiques, you must see its hand-carved, solid mahogany mantles!

With access to over 100 lines of fine furniture, locating a particular piece of furniture or that must-have accessory is its specialty.

THE CORNER COTTAGE
237 Main St.
Pineville   889-4385

This charming six-room cottage, decorated in the Victorian motif, has an outstanding collection of 18th- and 19th-century American and Continental antiques and accessories. While browsing, enjoy some light snacks from the Corner Cottage Coffee Shoppe.

MINT HOUSE GALLERY
320 Main St.
Pineville   889-4384

The Mint House Gallery is Pineville's newest antique shop, but the old pressed-tin ceiling and the feeling of yesteryear makes a visit to this shop like a step back into earlier days. It features American and Continental antiques and has a wonderful selection of original oil paintings in distinctive frames.

PERSIAN RUG HOUSE
312 Main St.
Pineville   889-2454

This family-owned European shop has been in business in this country for seven years, specializing in original Persian rugs. If you are worried about making the right choice from its huge selection, the firm will let you take the rug home on approval and if you're still worried, it offers a lifetime exchange policy. This is a great place to have your oriental rugs cleaned or repaired. The Persian Rug House also buys old pieces.

THE RED GERANIUM
316 Main St.
Pineville 889-4465

This nostalgic old shop with its hardwood plank floors and one-of-a-kind antiques also offers a wide variety of fabrics, wallpaper, home furnishings and accessories. It has interior designers on staff to help you with your decorating needs.

Of course, there are numerous other well-known antique shops in the area. **Churchill Galleries**, located in SouthPark Mall (364-3838), has a beautiful selection of fine antiques. **Treasures Unlimited** at 6401 Morrison Boulevard (366-7272), has wonderful porcelain and linen, as well as antique furniture. A little more than an hour's drive up I-85 will take you to **Byerly's Antiques** (919-299-6510), just this side of Greensboro. Wear comfortable shoes because this place is huge, filling up a 42,000-square-foot warehouse. And don't forget the antique extravaganzas every other weekend at **Metrolina Expo**. (See **Attractions**.)

Many area furniture stores and specialty shops also offer design services and antiques or antique reproductions:

BREM HOUSE RUG GALLERY
211 East Blvd. 358-3916

Here you will find the finest in handmade oriental rugs, custom design area rugs and designer-quality broadlooms. A visit here is like a tour of the world as you shop for that unique find to compliment your home. Designers love the collection, you'll love the prices.

COLONY FURNITURE SHOPS, INC.
811 Providence Rd. 333-8871

Colony is the area's oldest complete interior design showroom and features distinctive furnishings, period antiques and handmade rugs.

THE DESIGN PLACE
1820 South Blvd. 333-5208

Since 1979, The Design Place has been specializing in custom items for the home, and also does residential and commercial interior design. It has the largest selection of wallpaper and fabric under one roof between Miami and Washington, D.C., and if you are looking for unique or unusual accessories, this is the place to start. If you need some decorating help but want your home or office to reflect your taste, Jennie Day at the Design Place is a pro at blending the principles of color and design with your ideas and functional requirements.

MECKLENBURG FURNITURE
520 Providence Rd. 376-8401

This is a unique source for home furnishings, from traditional to contemporary. It offers furniture, accessories, fabrics, wallcoverings and specialty items, and has staff designers to assist you in making the right choices.

METRO

911 E. Morehead St.   *375-4563*

For "Designs for Modern Living" Metro is the place. Here you can find the contemporary and unusual in home furnishings. Metro has everything from furniture to jewelry and greeting cards.

IDEAL LIGHTING

9600 Monroe Rd.   *847-8765*

Ideal Lighting, located in East Charlotte, offers a wide selection of lighting fixtures, lamps and recessed lighting and other related products. If you are shopping for lighting for a new or remodeled home, you will appreciate the help of its trained consultants. Appointments can be made either in the showroom or in your home. Ideal Lighting offers wholesale pricing with excellent service.

Landscapers

If its yard maintenance you want, the best bet is to see who has the best-looking lawn in your neighborhood and then ask the owners who they use. A drive through Charlotte's neighborhoods will convince you of the pride Charlotteans take in maintaining their property. The mild climate helps, and spring brings about a veritable fairyland of dogwood and azalea blossoms. If you are a do-it-yourselfer, there are numerous nurseries about town that will not only sell you plants, but are quite helpful with advice on the types of plants and shrubs that do well in the area and how to nurture them. Here are a few of the best-known area nurseries and landscape designers:

Photo by John Cress.

Beautiful landscaping is the norm for Charlotte's new homes and neighborhoods.

EL EL, INC.

4901 Dwight Evans Rd.   *523-6785*

If your tastes run more to interior landscaping, Cindi Ballard and her staff can design it, install others' designs, work with you to create a plan and decide on the best plants for your home environment, provide the plants and planters and offer weekly maintenance. The firm has been providing these services throughout the Piedmont since 1976 and is one of the largest companies of its kind in the area.

GARDEN SECRETS

6705 Park South Dr.   *554-7856*

Formerly Park Road Garden Center, Cameron and Dee-Dee Harris now own Garden Secrets. Not only is theirs a full nursery but they also carry garden gift items. This English-style garden shop is the exclusive carrier of Haddonstone planters in Charlotte.

RANDY SIGG LANDSCAPE

1818 Graybark Ave.   *535-1587*

Randy has been in the landscape business in Charlotte since the early '70s and does both residential and commercial work. The firm is especially well-known for the design and maintenance of huge beds of annual flowers around local commercial properties, but its residential work is equally impressive.

SOUTHERN TREE AND LANDSCAPE COMPANY

2621 Bus. 21
Ft. Mill, S.C.   *375-7555*

Southern Tree, with 90 employees, has four divisions—landscape contracting, landscape maintenance, tree and shrub sales, and tree scraping—that provide and plant young trees on-site or transplant trees from one site to another. Owner Roger Braswell is a past president of the N.C. Landscape Contractors Association.

PRESBYTERIAN *has* HEART. AND *just* ABOUT EVERYTHING *else.*

- Presbyterian Hospital

- Presbyterian Hospital
  Matthews
  (opening 1994)

- Presbyterian Specialty
  Hospital

- Presbyterian-
  Orthopaedic Hospital

- SameDay Surgery
  Center

Presbyterian
Health Services Corp.

Belk Heart Center

Family Maternity Center

Eye Center

Presbyterian-Orthopaedic Hospital

Inside
Hospitals and Medical Care

*C*harlotte's hospitals offer the latest in medical techniques as well as some of the most qualified specialists. General hospitals and specialty hospitals offer a wide variety of services, and Charlotte's healthcare costs are below the national average, making medical services one of the best bargains in the Charlotte area.

Medical facilities are expanding at a rapid rate throughout the city and the region, so wherever you live in the area, you probably won't have to drive too far to find the services you need. The city is nationally and internationally known as a center for cardiac care and research. Three hospitals, Carolinas Medical Center, Presbyterian and Mercy, perform open-heart surgery as well as other highly specialized medical services. You will not have to leave Charlotte to find the best medical care available.

General Hospitals

CAROLINAS MEDICAL CENTER
1000 Blythe Blvd.   *355-2000*

Carolinas Medical Center, opened in 1940, is the flagship facility of the **Charlotte-Mecklenburg Hospital Authority**. With 843 beds, the Medical Center is the second largest hospital in North Carolina. In addition, the Medical Center also treats a significant number of patients from South Carolina and all over the Southeastern U.S.

There are seven specialized intensive care units, including the **Neonatal Intensive Care Nursery**. The Medical Center is the regional referral center for high-risk pregnancies. **MedCenter Air** serves as the area's only hospital-based air ambulance service with two helicopters and two fixed-wing aircraft.

A Level I Trauma Center and one of only five Academic Medical

221

Center Teaching Hospitals in North Carolina, Carolinas Medical Center offers 11 medical and dental residency programs and serves as an off-campus teaching facility of the University of North Carolina School of Medicine.

The **Carolinas Heart Institute** is the major center for heart transplantation in the two Carolinas, with more than 140 transplants. It is the only facility in the two states where pediatric and infant transplants are being performed. More than 10,000 coronary bypass operations have been performed at the Heart Institute, where laser techniques to correct heart rhythm problems have been pioneered. A liver and pancreas transplantation program began in 1994.

The **Children's Hospital** opened in May 1992, at Carolinas Medical Center. Also offered are the **Cancer Center, Carolinas Epilepsy Center, Carolinas Diabetes Center**, the **Hemby Pediatric Trauma Institute** and the **James G. Cannon Research Center**. The area's only **Multiple Sclerosis Clinic** offers multi-disciplinary services to patients at a single location.

The Charlotte-Mecklenburg Hospital Authority also includes **University Hospital**, the **Charlotte Institute of Rehabilitation** and **Carolinas Medical Center's Center for Mental Health**, all of which are listed separately in this section. Other facilities are: **Urgent Care Center at the Arboretum, The Women's Center, Charlotte Continence Center, Family Practice Center, Neighborhood Health Center, Sardis Nursing Home, Huntersville Oaks Nursing Home, Brookwood Senior Living Facility, CMHA School of Nursing** and **The Dilworth Inn**, a lodging facility for pre-admission patients and families of patients.

MERCY HOSPITAL
2001 Vail Ave.　　　　*379-5000*

Mercy Hospital opened in 1906 and offers a full array of acute care services to Charlotte residents. Mercy Health Services and the Charlotte-Mecklenburg Hospital authority are currently forming a collaborative partnership under which some aspects of the two health systems will work together and be jointly managed.

More than 700 physicians are on staff at Mercy. It has 336 beds and a nursing school. Its **Heart Center** provides cardiac surgery and procedures. A 29-bed rehabilitation center is also offered.

Mercy diversified geographically in 1982 by opening an urgent care center in heavily-populated southeast Mecklenburg County, followed by the 97-bed Mercy Hospital South (mentioned in this section) in 1987. The **Mercy Maternity Center** opened adjacent to Mercy Hospital South the following year.

Mercy Medical Group operations began in April 1992 as a network of primary care physicians located throughout the Charlotte Metropolitan area. As of July 1994, The Mercy Medical network consists of eight primary care physician offices located in Mecklenburg and Gaston Counties, North Carolina and York County, South Carolina.

Mercy operates the **Mercy Center for Outpatient Rehabilita-**

tion (MCOR), which specializes in comprehensive outpatient rehabilitation services, and the **Mercy Diagnostic Center**, which is a medical imaging center designed with patient care and comfort in mind. Both facilities are located on Billingsley Road in Charlotte.

Other services offered by Mercy include medical detoxification through a program called **Horizons**, adult day care at the **Selwyn Life Center** and in-home assistance through **Mercy Home Care**.

MERCY HOSPITAL SOUTH
10628 Park Rd.
N.C. 51 and Park Rd. Ext.   *543-2000*

Mercy Hospital South is an 85-bed general medical and surgical facility designed to serve the upscale population of southeast Mecklenburg County with quality healthcare. The hospital offers the only single-room maternity care within the region. Mercy South's location and accessibility make it the community hospital for residents of South Mecklenburg and Northern South Carolina.

PRESBYTERIAN HOSPITAL
200 Hawthorne Ln.   *384-4000*

Established in 1903, Presbyterian Hospital is a 593-bed regional referral, tertiary care medical center serving Charlotte-Mecklenburg and surrounding North and South Carolina counties. It offers a wide range of specialized diagnostic and therapeutic services.

The **Center for Women's Health** is an area leader in services for women. More than 5,000 babies are born annually in the **Family Maternity Center**. It is supported by the full service **Hemby Intensive Care Nursery** and other unique services

Photo courtesy Carolinas Medical Center.

Carolinas Medical Center, opened in 1940, is the flagship facility of the Charlotte-Mecklenburg Hospital Authority.

such as **Nursing Mothers' Place** lactation consulting service.

The 72-bed **Presbyterian Hemby Children's Hospital**, which opened in 1993 and 1994, is dedicated to family-centered care and child-right services to assure that all children's needs are met from the time of admission until they go home. The **Pediatric Intensive Care Unit** is supported by full-time physician pediatric intensivists.

The **Belk Heart Center** offers up-to-date care including heart catheterization and open-heart surgery. The **Cancer Center**, the first in North Carolina designated as a Community Hospital Comprehensive Cancer Center by the American College of Surgeons' Commission on Cancer, is home for the **Harris Hospice Unit**, the only such unit in the area. The Center is also the only

North Carolina affiliate of the Duke Comprehensive Cancer Center.

The **Center for Psychiatry** offers programs for adults, adolescents and children, plus the **Center for Mind-Body Health**. The 24-hour Emergency Department operates the area's only **Chest Pain Emergency Room** program. Other centers of excellence include surgery, medicine and neurosciences.

The hospital also offers a full range of in-home services including home care and the **Lifeline** personal emergency response system. The **School of Nursing** is the largest hospital-based program in the Carolinas. Free information and physician referral services are provided by **Presbyterian Care Connection** (384-4111).

Presbyterian is the flagship hospital of the not-for-profit Presby-

Photo courtesy Presbyterian Hospital.

Presbyterian is the oldest hospital in continuous operation in Charlotte-Mecklenburg.

Photo courtesy Presbyterian Hospital.

The new Presbyterian Hospital in Matthews.

terian Health Services Corp., an integrated health care system. It has four hospitals, outpatient facilities and a growing physician hospital organization with more than 90 primary care physicians and some 200 affiliated specialists.

PRESBYTERIAN HOSPITAL MATTHEWS
1500 Matthews Township Pkwy.
Matthews   *384-6500*

Opened in August, 1994, Presbyterian Hospital Matthews is a new kind of hospital, designed for efficiency and for greater user friendliness for patients and their families and visitors.

Located in Matthews, the new hospital offers a full range of diagnostic and treatment services including emergency, surgery (inpatient and outpatient) and maternity. All but the most specialized kinds of surgery are performed at Presbyterian Hospital Matthews.

Its user-friendly features include maternity rooms that are large and have Jacuzzi tubs, TVs, VCRs, refrigerators, balconies and a daybed for dad to spend the night, if he wishes.

All rooms in the new hospital have similar features, including a daybed. Even the critical care rooms encourage overnight visitors, assuming the physicians approve.

The new 24-hour Emergency Department has separate entrances for drive-in and ambulance patients. Like Presbyterian Hospital, the new hospital's Emergency Department houses a **Chest Pain ER** for early diagnosis and treatment.

Meals at the hospital are delivered to each patient at the time he or she specifies. The two inpatient wings each has a family medical resource center, an outside balcony and a large family kitchen.

The hospital serves the Matthews-Mint Hill-Pineville communities as well as other areas of south and east Mecklenburg and west Union counties.

UNIVERSITY HOSPITAL
U.S. 29 at W. T. Harris Blvd.   548-6000

University Hospital opened in 1985 to serve rapidly growing northern Mecklenburg, southern Iredell and western Cabarrus counties. The 130 private rooms are configured in the "snowflake" design, with every patient just a few feet from a nurses' station, yet isolated from much of the traffic in the traditional corridor arrangement.

University Hospital offers a wide range of healthcare services. The **Sleep Center** is the first in the Charlotte area to be fully accredited by the American Sleep Disorders Association. Physicians use sophisticated instrumentation to identify sleep problems and causes. Obstetric and Gynecology services offer five Labor and Delivery suites specifically designed to create a "home birthing" environment.

There is also an eight-bed intensive coronary care unit and six-bed telemetry unit for patients with more serious medical needs requiring closer supervision.

The Emergency Department is staffed 24 hours a day and is equipped to handle minor and life-threatening emergencies. University Hospital also offers rehabilitation, diagnostic radiology and mammography services along with a **Respiratory Diagnostic Center** and full-service laboratory for inpatients and outpatients. Adjoining the hospital is **University Medical Park**, a growing home for physician groups and satellite offices.

Specialty Hospitals and Centers

AMETHYST
1715 Sharon Rd. W.   554-8373

Amethyst is a 94-bed private, nonprofit facility that provides various levels of care, including outpatient, for the treatment of chemical dependency for adolescents (beginning at age 12) and adults. Amethyst also offers a wide range of family treatment services, including a program called **"For Kids Only"** designed for children ages 6-11 who have a parent or relative in treatment or who have been affected by chemical dependency. Other services include a **Cocaine Track, Women's Track, Relapse/Relapse Prevention Program, Referral**, DWI assessments, intervention, education classes and professional workshops and seminars. This facility is owned and operated by the Charlotte-Mecklenburg Hospital Authority.

CAROLINAS MEDICAL CENTER'S CENTER FOR MENTAL HEALTH
501 Billingsley Rd.   358-2700

Carolinas Medical Center's Center for Mental Health is the psychiatric medicine and behavioral sciences campus for the Charlotte-Mecklenburg Hospital Authority. It has 66 beds where inpatients receive therapy needed to help them recover from emotional and mental illnesses. Patients with emergency psychiatric needs have care available to them 24 hours a day from Emergency Services.

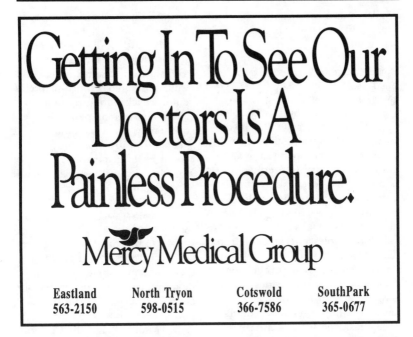

Getting In To See Our Doctors Is A Painless Procedure.

Mercy Medical Group

Eastland	North Tryon	Cotswold	SouthPark
563-2150	598-0515	366-7586	365-0677

Children, adolescents and adults may receive extensive outpatient therapy, which includes individual and group psychotherapy, comprehensive psychological testing and mental health evaluation and referral services.

CHARLOTTE INSTITUTE OF REHABILITATION
1100 Blythe Blvd.   *355-4300*

The Charlotte Institute of Rehabilitation, a 143 bed facility, is one of the premier facilities of its kind in the country. Focusing on patients suffering from stroke, brain injury and spinal cord trauma, the Charlotte Institution of Rehabilitation helps patients return to as normal a life-style as possible after illness or injury. Its specialists in rehabilitative medicine tailor programs to the physical and emotional needs of individual patients. Pediatric and adolescent patients are treated in a special unit with separate healthcare providers to meet their special needs. **Rehab Advantage** is a work hardening and industrial medicine satellite facility of the Institute. It is equipped with state of the art equipment and overseen by physiatrists, i.e., physicians skilled in physical rehabilitation.

CHARTER PINES HOSPITAL
3621 Randolph Rd.   *365-5368*
(800) 332-PINE

Founded in 1985, Charter Pines is a 60-bed psychiatric hospital offering both inpatient and partial hospitalization services for adolescents and adults. Outpatient treatment for chemical dependency is available and the hospital offers a free, confidential, no obligation consultation.

CPC CEDAR SPRING HOSPITAL
9600 Pineville-Matthews Rd.   541-6676
(N.C. 51)

CPC Cedar Spring Hospital, founded in 1985, is a 70-bed psychiatric and chemical dependency facility owned and operated by Community Psychiatric Centers, a worldwide hospital corporation. It offers inpatient and partial hospitalization serving the psychiatric/chemical dependency/dual diagnosis needs of adults, adolescents and children. Each program is housed in separate units that include semiprivate rooms. The hospital also provides a gym, swimming pool, outdoor recreation and an in-house school. It offers a free, on-site evaluation and referral service for psychiatric/chemical dependency problems, 24 hours a day, seven days a week, as well as free educational lectures and/or training for area groups.

PRESBYTERIAN-ORTHOPAEDIC HOSPITAL
1901 Randolph Rd.   375-6792

Presbyterian-Orthopaedic Hospital is a 166-bed regional specialty hospital dedicated to the diagnosis and treatment of injuries and diseases of the bones and joints. The facility offers inpatient and ambulatory surgery including total joint, major back and spine, microvascular hand, knee and shoulder surgeries. It also focuses on arthritis and provides other specialized care and procedures, such as pain manage-

ment, CT diagnostics, intensive care and laboratory services.

In addition, Presbyterian-Orthopaedic offers freestanding rehabilitative services, including a work evaluation center, a sports-medicine center, a back school, evening physical therapy sessions, pediatric physical therapy and occupational and speech therapy. The hospital is owned by a partnership of Health Trust Inc. and Presbyterian Health Services Corp.

PRESBYTERIAN SPECIALTY HOSPITAL
1600 E. 3rd St.   384-6000

Presbyterian Specialty Hospital is a private 15-bed facility that specializes in outpatient and inpatient eye, ear, nose and throat surgery. The hospital also offers oral, plastic and cosmetic surgery. Specialty Hospital is also the Charlotte home of the mobile lithotripter, operated by the **Stone Institute of the Carolinas**, which dissolves kidney stones without surgery; the **Presbyterian Sleep Medicine Center**; and the **Presbyterian Pain Therapy Center** of Charlotte, which offers programs for chronic pain rehabilitation, chronic headache, acute pain and back pain.

THE REHAB CENTER
2610 E. 7th St.   375-8900
(800) 968-6738

The Rehab Center is a regional outpatient multi-disciplinary pain rehabilitation facility, specializing in the rehabilitation of work-related injuries. The center employs a team approach in the provision of comprehensive rehabilitation services, including medical, psychological, neuropsychological and vocational. It also offers physical therapy evaluations and treatment along with work site analyses, work capacity evaluations, water therapy, hand therapy and work hardening. The Rehab Center's treatment goals are to restore human potential and to return the injured person to a more productive, functional life style.

Medical Care

The first physician known to have practiced in the area was Dr. John Newman Oglethorpe who settled south of Charlotte along McAlpine Creek around 1746, and the first recorded physician in the town of Charlotte was Dr. Ephraim Brevard. In those days, medical training was attained through apprenticeships or formal schooling, of which the closest was Baltimore, Maryland.

In the late 1800s, a group of women from Charlotte's First Presbyterian Church decided it was time for Charlotte to have its own medical school, so they outfitted the infirmary at Davidson College and hired a physician who taught biology in addition to practicing medicine. This program was the forerunner of the Davidson Medical School, which later was moved to Charlotte and was renamed the North Carolina Medical School. Originally housed in the building that recently served as Charlotte's Visitor Information Center, the school was closed when the Carnegie Foundation, in an effort to slow the boom of colleges

offering diplomas around the country, gave it an unacceptable rating.

Providing quality medical care and attracting qualified physicians to the area remained a priority of local citizens through the years. Credit for much of the progress must be given to the religious community. In fact, all of Charlotte's large hospitals were founded by religious organizations.

Today, medical care in Charlotte offers a wide distribution of specialties and physicians scattered throughout the city, but as in the rest of the nation, there are also major challenges. The two biggest problems the medical community faces today are drugs and the challenges of rising costs with diminishing resources.

As the city grows, so does its medical community, both in terms of services offered and in the geographic distribution. Doctors' offices and clinics are no longer clustered just around the hospitals, as satellite offices and new clinics are being opened all over the county. So unless you're looking for someone in a highly specialized field, you will probably be able to find a doctor you like located near your home or office.

If you are visiting or if you need medical help and haven't yet found a physician, there are numerous urgent-care centers around town that provide minor medical emergency services and walk-in healthcare. You don't need an appointment and most have extended hours, but they are not cheap, so your best bet is to make finding a personal physician a top priority.

As with anything else, word-of-mouth is usually a good way to find a physician. Your neighbors, friends or co-workers can give you advice on the doctor's personality, how well the staff treats you or how long you can expect to wait. However, Charlotte also has formal services that can refer you to physicians and other health professionals. These referral services can be a great help if you are new to the area, because the abundance and variety of medical care available can be overwhelming. Remember that for emergencies, Charlotte has a 911 system.

Referral Services

CARE CONNECTION

Presbyterian Hospital   384-4111
This service, open Monday through Friday, 9:00 AM to 4:00 PM, will give physician referrals, not only by specialty, but by geographic location and type of insurance accepted as well. Care Connection will even help you make an appointment. You can also call for information about the hospital's programs and other healthcare needs. For maternity information, call 384-4949.

MECKLENBURG COUNTY MEDICAL SOCIETY

1112 Harding Place
Ste. 200   376-3688
The Society gives physician referrals for family practitioners, internists or specialists by phone, 9 AM to 1 PM, Monday through Friday. It will usually give you three names.

UNITED WAY HOTLINE (FIRST CALL FOR HELP)

Mecklenburg County   377-1100
Cabarrus County   788-1156
Union County   289-8102
A United Way Service, the hotline is open 24 hours a day, seven days a week and is staffed by referral specialists who can answer questions or provide referrals on anything regarding human services in Mecklenburg, Cabarrus or Union counties.

Other Services and Numbers To Know

EMERGENCY AND FIRST AID NUMBERS

Ambulance Information	
Emergency	911
Non-emergency	523-9430
Charlotte Life Saving Crew	
Emergency	911
Non-emergency	332-7649
Poison Control Center	355-4000

DRUG ABUSE SERVICES

Drug Education Center	375-3784
Drug Information 24 hrs.	375-3784
Open House Counseling	332-9001
Hotline	(800) 234-0420

FAMILY PLANNING, PREGNANCY, NEWBORN SERVICES

Catholic Social Services	333-9954
Charlotte La Leche League	841-5491
Children's Home Society	334-2854
Crisis Pregnancy Center	372-5981
Florence Crittenton	372-4663
Health Dept. Maternity & Family Planning	336-6500
LDS Social Services Unwed Parents Council	535-2436
Mecklenburg Council on Adolescent Pregnancy	332-6721
Planned Parenthood	377-0841

PROFESSIONAL ORGANIZATIONS AND SUPPORT GROUPS

Al-Anon Family Group (Support group for alcoholics family)	333-9523
Alcoholics Anonymous	332-4387
Alzheimers Association	532-7392
American Cancer Society	376-1659
American Heart Assoc.	374-0632
American Lung Assoc.	537-5776
Arthritis Foundation	535-8303
Arthritis Patient Services	331-4878
Association for Retarded Citizens	535-4289
Association for Sickle Cell Disease	332-4184
CanCare Volunteer Cancer Service	372-1232
Charlotte Dental Society	841-2599
Compassionate Friends (Support group for bereaved parents)	366-9506
Cystic Fibrosis Found.	567-0329
Diabetes Services	375-0172
Downs Syndrome Assoc.	536-2163
Epilepsy Association	377-3262
Juvenile Diabetes Found.	377-2873
Kinder-Mourn (Support group for bereaved parents)	376-2580
Learning How (Support group for physically handicapped)	376-4735
Leukemia Society	535-8585
Lupus Foundation	375-8787
March of Dimes	377-2009
Mental Health Association	375-0176
Metrolina AIDS Project	333-1435
Metrolina Association for the Blind	372-3870
Multiple Sclerosis Society	525-2955
Muscular Dystrophy	567-2912
To Life (Bereavement and loss support)	332-5433

HOME HEALTH CARE SERVICES

Home Health Professionals	536-4930
Hospice at Charlotte	375-0100
Mecklenburg County Health Department	336-4700
Medical Personnel Pool	372-8230
Mercy Home Care	379-5200
Presbyterian HomeCare	384-4130
Total Care, Inc.	332-1121
Olsten Health Care	372-8184

MENTAL HEALTH SERVICES

Alliance for the Mentally Ill	333-8218
Central House	332-2314
Goodwill Industries	372-3434

Area Mental Health
  Authority of Mecklenburg
  County   336-2023
Youth Homes, Inc.   334-9954

TIPS FOR EVERY DAY LIVING
336-4632

This is a service of the Mecklenburg County Area Mental Health, Developmental Disabilities and Substance Abuse Authority. TIPS features mental health-related information. Messages on a variety of topics help you keep physically and mentally healthy, recognize early signs of illness and develop skills to cope with everyday living. For directory highlights, dial 333111 after you dial the main number (336-4832); for an updated list of messages, dial 333112.

PHARMACIES

Take your pick—you can have your prescription filled while you shop for groceries or household items, eat a burger, mail a letter, or pay your telephone bill. Yesterday's corner drug store has become a multi-service super-store. The price you pay for your prescription can vary widely, so it's a good idea to shop around. But it's also wise to establish a relationship with your pharmacist who can be a valuable source of advice for everything from what to take for your sore throat to how (or how not) to administer prescription drugs for yourself or your family members who may need assistance. Most drugstores offer senior citizens discounts. Many honor major credit cards. Some have home healthcare services, and there are even a few that still provide delivery service. If you get a headache or stomach ache in the middle of the night and have no medicine in the house, or if you suddenly need your prescription filled, Eckerd Drugs in the Park Road Shopping Center (523-3031) and at 3740 East Independence Blvd. (536-1010) are both open 24 hours.

Special Services

If you or your child need special assistance for physical, emotional or mental handicaps or disabilities, Charlotte offers many resources. Here are a few:

ALEXANDER CHILDREN'S CENTER
6220 Thermal Rd.   366-8712

This nonprofit center offers an intensive 24-hour-a-day treatment program for emotionally disturbed children ages six through 12 with parallel counseling for their families. Children in this program are given a therapeutic environment in which to learn and live. The Alexander Children's Center was founded over 100 years ago by the Presbyterian Church. Funds from churches, businesses, foundations and individuals has allowed the Center to continue to offer its services to children in the area. The Center also has a self-supporting Child Development Center that is aa AA-licensed program offering quality child development for children ages three months through kindergarten. The Child Development Center also provides a mainstreaming environment for special needs children. The Center provides a low staff/child ratio and an expanded curriculum.

CATHOLIC SOCIAL SERVICES
116 E. 1st St.   333-9954

This organization offers many services, including individual, family, adoption, marital and substance abuse counseling and pregnancy support. Fees are based on a sliding scale.

CHARLOTTE SPEECH AND HEARING CENTER
300 S. Caldwell St.   376-1342

Screening, evaluations, consultation, education and therapy are all a part of the total service available to the community at this nonprofit center. Funded, in part, by United Way, the Center is accredited by the Professional Services Board of the American Speech-Language-Hearing Association, and clinical staff are licensed by the state. Help is offered to anyone who has or may have a speech, language or hearing problem. Some services are free; others are on a sliding-fee scale. The Center operates a satellite service in Union County.

CHILD AND FAMILY DEVELOPMENT
1316 E. Morehead St.   332-4834
10801 Johnston Rd.
Pineville   542-0317

A private, for-profit practice, Child and Family Development offers a number of assessment services for children and their families such as monitoring of high-risk infants and preschoolers, developmental screenings, school readiness assessment, diagnostic evaluations and treatment services, plus special classes that assist children in their development.

COMMUNITY HEALTH SERVICES
1401 E. 7th St.   375-0172

CHS is a multi-service United Way agency that offers affordable (sometimes free) health screenings and educational programs. It has six program components: Diabetes Services, Emergency Services, Occupational Health, Senior Health Services, Parkinson's Disease and Anorexia/Bulimia Support Groups.

THE FLETCHER SCHOOL
1001 Queens Rd.   376-2032

The purpose of this special school for learning-disabled children in grades one through nine is to provide a structured, individualized academic program that will prepare them to return to the regular classroom environment whenever possible. The school has been approved by the N.C. Department of Public Instruction and the Governors Office of Nonpublic Instruction.

MECKLENBURG COUNTY CENTER FOR HUMAN DEVELOPMENT
3500 Ellington St.   336-7100

This county agency offers a number of services, including a developmental day preschool for mildly and moderately mentally retarded children, a parent-infant training program, and a developmental evaluation program to determine if an individual of any age has a disability or delayed development. Fees are based on the client's ability to pay.

MECKLENBURG COUNTY HEALTH DEPARTMENT

2845 Beatties Ford Rd.
Appointments   336-6500
249 Billingsley Rd.
Health Promotion Program & Home Health
                        336-6028 or 336-4650

The department functions to promote good health and to prevent and control disease by providing health education; maternity, family planning and well-child clinics; home and school health services; assistance to business and industry in developing employee health and safety programs; nursing services for new mothers and their infants; environmental services; and communicable and chronic disease control.

NEVINS CENTER, INC.

3523 Nevins Rd.   596-1372
3127 Kalynne St.   393-5910

This Adult Developmental Activity Program provides vocational training, academic training, supported employment and a sheltered workshop for mentally retarded and physically handicapped adults.

OPEN HOUSE COUNSELING SERVICES, INC.

145 Remount Rd.   332-9001

This community agency provides counseling and support groups for chemically dependent young people and adults and their families. Services are rendered through the Johnnie H. McLeod Treatment Center, Methadone Medical Services, Outpatient Clinic, Adolescent Outpatient Services and Treatment Alternative to Street Crime.

PERCEPTUAL MOTOR STUDIES

UNC Charlotte   547-4695

Dr. John Healey, a member of the UNC Charlotte faculty, coordinates this unique program for children up to the age of 18 who are experiencing difficulty in their perceptual motor development. Each child undergoes screening before acceptance into the program and is paired with two college students who, under the direction of the coordinator, assist him/her in various activities.

PRESCHOOL PROGRAM FOR THE HEARING IMPAIRED

North Carolina School for the Deaf
1000 E. Morehead St.   332-1881

This total child development program provides comprehensive speech and language development for hearing-impaired preschoolers, and newborns to five-year-olds, in Mecklenburg and surrounding counties. Instruction is given on-site and in the home.

ST. MARKS CENTER

1200 E. Morehead St.
Ste. 200   333-7107

This center, established in 1973, offers programs and services to approximately 230 Mecklenburg County residents who have severe or profound mental retardation or are at high risk for a severe disability. Preschool, special education and summer school programs for children and sheltered workshops, developmental activities programs and supported employment programs for adults are offered. In 1993, the Center began a child development program, **The Circle School**, that allows special needs children to be mainstreamed with other children.

UNITED CEREBRAL PALSY DEVELOPMENTAL CENTER

1900 Queens Rd.   377-6016

A branch of United Cerebral Palsy of North Carolina, this center, housed in Myers Park Baptist Church, provides education and therapy for children ages two through five with cerebral palsy or a similar neurologically based disorder, as well as training for parents in Mecklenburg and surrounding counties. Tuition is based on a sliding-fee scale.

*A magical world awaits kids at Paramount's Carowinds,
one of the Charlotte area's biggest attractions.*

Inside
Kidstuff

Charlotte boosters have been known to boast that "Our city has no limits!" And when you begin to explore the wealth of places, events and activities in the metropolitan Charlotte area that appeal to the kid in all of us, it's easy to agree. The possibilities here are indeed almost limitless.

Here's a smattering of what Insiders in the Queen City recommend to newcomers and visitors with kids in tow. Check out the Attractions, Daytrips and Weekends and Parks and Recreation sections for more ideas. Local newspaper dailies and free specialty publications (see *Charlotte Parent: Our Kids & Teens Magazine*) are good sources for information on upcoming family events and activities. In short, enjoy your children and enjoy Charlotte!

Museums and Historic Sites

AFRO-AMERICAN CULTURAL CENTER
401 N. Myers Street 3   74-1565

The Afro-American Cultural Center is located in Charlotte's First Ward district, in an old restored AME Zion church. It offers an art gallery with changing exhibits, theatre and musical productions and classes and programs for adults and children. Give the Center a call for information on upcoming exhibits and programs.

CHARLOTTE MUSEUM OF HISTORY & HEZEKIAH ALEXANDER HOMESITE
3500 Shamrock Dr.   568-1774

The Charlotte Museum of History gives you a "slice of life" of the North Carolina Piedmont region, with a special focus on the history of Charlotte and Mecklenburg County. The museum offfers exhibits, classes, arts and crafts demonstrations and occasional special events. Admission to the museum is free. The Hezekiah Alexander homesite, home to a signer of the 1775 Mecklenberg Declaration of Independence, was built in 1774 of stone quarried nearby. It is the oldest orignal dwelling still standing in Mecklenberg County, and is listed in the National Register of Historic Places. A reconstructed barn, a kitchen and a spring house are also on the property. The house has been restored and furnished with North Carolina antiques. Guided tours ($2 for adults/$1 for children) are given Tuesday through Sunday afternoons. The homesite hosts several events of interest to children throughout the year, including the Rites of Spring (where sheep shearing is a popular spectator sport), a Summer Sampler and a Colonial Christmas program.

DISCOVERY PLACE
301 N. Tryon Street   *372-6261*
(800) 935-0553

Discovery Place is one of the largest and most exciting science and nature museums in the country. It contains the OMNIMAX theatre, a planetarium, a replica of a tropical rainforest, aquariums, discovery areas for young children and much more. It's easy to spend a day or two inside the sprawling complex in downtown Charlotte. Annual memberships are available—you'll want to come multiple times a year—and the museum also honors memberships from other science museums throughout the country.

HISTORIC LATTA PLACE
Sample Road
Huntersville   *875-2312*

Historic Latta Place encompasses over 700 acres of land surrounding the restored and furnished house (circa 1800) of James Latta, a merchant and planter in the Catawba River region. Guided tours are available of the house, listed in the Na-

Panning for gold at the Reed Gold Mine has long been a favorite activity for area kids.

tional Register of Historic Places, and the replica of the old kitchen. There are outbuildings and gardens to explore, and farm animals graze nearby. The Carolina Raptor Center (see Science, Nature & the Outdoors section), the Latta Equestrian Center and a bird sanctuary are also on the park grounds by Mountain Island Lake just northwest of Charlotte. Plan to bring a picnic and spend a sunny afternoon hiking, canoeing or riding horses through the old plantation grounds. Call for more information on admission charges and activity fees.

MINT MUSEUM OF ART

2730 Randolph Rd. 337-2000

The Mint was originally built as the first branch of the U.S. Mint in 1836. The building was later used as a headquarters for the Confederacy and a hospital, among other uses. The Mint building was moved to its present location in 1933, and opened as North Carolina's first art museum in 1936. The Museum includes fine collections of PreColumbian art, American and European paintings, decorative arts and special collections such as North Carolina and African galleries. The Mint sponsors many programs for children and adults, including classes, workshops and family events. Exhibits change several times each year. Past favorites have included exhibits of treasures from ancient Egypt, costume displays and photography exhibits. There is an admission charge, but free admission is offered on the second Sunday of each month. Call for more information.

REED GOLD MINE STATE HISTORIC SITE

Route 2, Box 101
Stanfield, N.C. (704) 786-8337

The Reed Gold Mine is the site of the first documented discovery of gold in the United States. There is a museum, guided tours of the old mine, and - the favorite for children - panning for gold! Admission to the site is free; there is a small charge to pan for gold.

SCHIELE MUSEUM OF NATURAL HISTORY & PLANETARIUM

1500 E. Garrison Blvd.
Gastonia, N.C. 866-6900

The Schiele Museum has a fine collection of North Carolina natural history exhibits, including native mammals and flora of the Piedmont, as well as changing exhibits which have included favorites like Native American artifacts. The museum hosts living history programs several times a year, where kids and adults can see reenactments of life in North Carolina in earlier times. The planetarium shows change periodically, and may give a peek at the night sky or a look at comets and meteors. The Schiele is one of North Carolina's most popular science and discovery museums. Admission is free; there is a charge for the planetarium show.

Entertainment

CELEBRATION STATION

10400 Cadillac Street
Pineville, N.C. 552-7888

The name says it all: what a place to celebrate! This is a popular spot for birthday parties, family outings and more. There is miniature golf, bumper boats, go cart rides, batting cages and of course, a video arcade. When you're tired from all the activity, there's lots to eat and drink while you rest up for the next go round. And best of all, Celebration Station is open every day of the year!

CHARLOTTE CLIMBING CENTER

619 S. Cedar St.   333-ROCK

This is the first and largest fully equipped indoor climbing facility in the state. The indoor climbing programs teach valuable climbing skills while allowing kids to challenge themselves, stretch their limits, build self-confidence and, best of all, have a great time doing it! More advanced climbers can opt for

an outdoor trip to Crowder's Mountain, Table Rock or a variety of other climbing areas. For a really unique birthday party, check out the various packages offered by the center. Remember, it never rains indoors!

CHILDREN'S THEATRE OF CHARLOTTE

1017 E. Morehead St.   376-5745
Box office: 333-8983

The Children's Theatre of Charlotte has been producing professional performances by and for kids ages three to eighteen since 1948. The Theatre's Mainstage productions are for the whole family. The Second Stage shows are performed by kids in grades eight and up. The Theatre also hosts other productions by local and touring

theatre groups. The Children's Theatre also sponsors educational programs teaching drama, puppetry and creative movement to young thespians.

ICE CAPADES CHALET
5595 Central Ave.   *568-0772*
(Eastland Mall)

Though ice skating has never been the South's biggest sport, it's been growing in popularity in recent years. Displaced Northerners and local "polar bears" can enjoy skating all year long at the Ice Capades Chalet at Eastland Mall. Adults and children can take lessons or just skate for the pure pleasure of it. It's also a great place for a birthday party. There is an admission charge; you may rent skates or bring your own.

NEW HERITAGE USA
Fort Mill, S.C.   *(800) 374-1234*

The former playground for Jim and Tammy Faye Bakker, New Heritage USA, a Christian theme park and resort, was reopened in 1992. There are lots of activities, including a water park, a video game arcade, go cart rides, miniature golf and batting cages. There is also a conference center, hotel accomodations (with tennis and swimming) and camping facilities at New Heritage USA. A Passion Play drama rounds out your choices. Families come from all over for the day or for several days to have the chance to see it all!

PARAMOUNT'S CAROWINDS
I-77
South of Charlotte   *588-2606*

What better to fulfill a child's fantasy than a day in Hanna Barbera Land with Yogi and BooBoo Bear? Paramount's Carowinds has big fun for little visitors with several such themed areas. Kids have great fun at RipTide Reef water park or at the WaterWorks children's play area. For the older child, WAYNE'S WORLD and the Southeast's best selection of roller coasters will provide a day of fun and excitement. When it's time for a treat, drop in at the Richard Scarry Busytown Cafe where, if you're lucky, you might see Lowly Worm in his Applemobile! For more information on Paramount's Carowinds, see the **Attractions** section of this Guide.

SPIRIT SQUARE CENTER FOR THE ARTS
345 N. College St.   *372-9664*

There's just about everything associated with the arts here: galleries with a variety of changing exhibits, three theatres for dramatic and musical productions, and classes galore for adults and children! Spirit Square is located in a renovated church building, creating an unique setting for artistic expression. There are performances and classes just for kids all year long. Drop in for a look or call for more information.

Science, Nature & The Outdoors

CAROLINA RAPTOR CENTER AT HISTORIC LATTA PLACE
Sample Rd.
Huntersville   *875-6521*

The Raptor Center is a conservation and environmental education center. It is dedicated to the care and release back into the wild of injured birds of prey. The Edna S. Moretti Environmental Education Center is also here. (See Historic Sites & Museums section for more information on Historic Latta Place and its features). There is an admission charge for the Center.

CHARLOTTE NATURE MUSEUM
11658 Sterling Rd.   *372-6261*

The Charlotte Nature Museum is geared for somewhat younger children, with its live animal room, aquarium and puppet theatre shows. There are also nature trails to follow. It's a good place to visit with little ones fascinated with the natural world. Memberships are available; there is a small admission fee.

DISCOVERY PLACE
30 N. Tryon St.   *372-626*
(800) 935-0553

(See Museums and Historic Sites section)

ENERGY EXPLORIUM
N.C. 73
Davidson, N.C.   *875-5600*

The Energy Explorium, operated by Duke Power, gives a unique look at energy and electricity with its hands-on displays about nuclear and coal-produced energy. You can explore the exhibits, play an array of interactive video games or see a film, "The Inland Sea," about the creation of Lake Norman. There are nature trails and a wildflower walk on the grounds, giving a nice blend of indoor and outdoor things to do. Admission is free.

LAZY 5 RANCH
N.C. 150 E.
Mooresville   *663-5100*

Not your typical ranch, the Lazy 5 is more like a small zoo that stretches over 180 acres of rolling farmland. Visitors can take a leisurely ride along the gravel road in their own vehicles and view the animals, or opt for a horse-drawn wagon ride. There are over 400 species of animals, many of which come from different continents and have an assortment of exotic names. The animals roam freely and are not at all shy. They know the routine and will cautiously approach your vehicle— probably hoping that you stocked up on the feed available for purchase at the Welcome Center. Younger children will love the petting area where they can get up-close and personal with a variety of small and large critters, from baby goats and lambs to camels. The Lazy 5 Ranch opens at 9 AM Monday through Saturday, and at 1 PM on Sunday. It closes each day one hour before sunset. You and your children will be amazed by the beauty of the ranch and the peaceful nature of its inhabitants.

McDOWELL PARK AND NATURE PRESERVE
N.C. 49
Lake Wylie   *588-5224*

This 800-plus acre park is the largest in the area, and encompasses lots of activities. You can go boating or canoeing, fish, walk on the miles of nature trails or visit the indoor nature center. There are campsites and picnic facilities open all year long. The park sponsors special programs throughout the year: evening campfires and storytelling, moonlight hikes and nature classes for young and old. Call for more information.

REEDY CREEK PARK AND ENVIRONMENTAL CENTER
2900 Rocky River Rd.   372-6261

Most of this 700 acre nature preserve is in its natural wooded state, giving visitors a chance to disappear into the natural world. There are several lakes on the property, nature trails, as well as picnic sites, ball fields and a playground. The Environmental Center has exhibits and hands-on activities to enjoy and

The American Mastodon looks back 10,000 years to greet visitors as they enter the Hall of Earth and Man at the Schiele Museum of Natural History.

explore. There is an admission charge for the center.

WING HAVEN
248 Ridgewood Ave.   331-0664
                              or 332-5770

Wing Haven is a beautiful garden and bird sanctuary in the middle of Charlotte, the former home and grounds of Elizabeth and Edwin Clarkson. The three-plus acres are filled with woods, formal gardens and lovely walks. The home is also open. There is a garden shop, tours of the home and grounds, and special children's programs throughout the year. Wing Haven is open on Sunday from 2 to 5 p.m. and on Tuesday and Wednesday from 3 to 5 p.m; it is open at other times by appointment.

Camps

Mecklenburg County Park and Recreation offers extensive day camps and playground programs during the summer. Day camps with structured activities are available at 16 recreation centers including **Recreation On The Move**, which is a mobile recreational unit, fully-staffed and equipped to provide supervised experiences in athletics, arts and crafts, music, dance and special events. The cost varies, depending on the program.

Playground programs for which there is no charge are given at seven sites and feature planned activities as well as free time. A number of city-wide special events, such as **Junior Tennis Tournament**, are planned each summer at Renaissance Park.

You're invited

This is an opportunity for you and your family to come and check out the YMCA of your choice! You can visit any YMCA of Greater Charlotte for one free day of fun and exercise when you mention this ad.

The mission of the YMCA of Greater Charlotte is to put Christian principles into practice through programs that build a healthy body, mind and spirit for all.

The YMCA uses the different branches as energy centers thereby focusing on the following five major Association thrusts.

Membership

We are committed to creating exceptional, long-term member relationships with individuals and families that represent all segments of the community.

Community Development

We are committed to empowering disadvantaged families and individuals through flexible, long-term community development relationships within specific neighborhoods.

Healthy Lifestyles

We are committed to providing healthy lifestyles through preventive education and experiences for people of all ages and abilities.

Camping and Environmental Education

We are committed to providing year round camping experiences which emphasize Christian values and to teaching environmental stewardship in all YMCA programs.

Strengthening the Family

We are committed to helping families grow stronger by providing family programs and activities that build relationships.

To Mooresville YMCA
403 E. Statesville Ave.
PO Box 6035
Mooresville, NC 28115
664-9000

I-77

To Lake Norman YMCA
21300 Davidson St.
Cornelius, NC 28031
892-9622

I-85

McCrorey YMCA
3801 Beatties Ford Rd.
Charlotte, NC 28216
394-2356

Beatties Ford Rd.

University City YMCA
Ben Craig Center
8791 Mallard Creek Rd.
Charlotte, NC 28256
547-9622

I-85

Uptown YMCA
301 S. College St.
200 One First Union Center
Charlotte, NC 28202
333-9622

Davidson St.

Johnston Memorial YMCA
3025 N. Davidson St.
Charlotte, NC 28205
333-6206

Independence Blvd.

Albemarle Rd.

Central YMCA
400 E. Morehead St.
Charlotte NC 28202
333-7771

49

Simmons Family YMCA
6824 Democracy Dr.
Charlotte, NC 28212
536-1714

To Camp Thunderbird
One Thunderbird Ln.
Lake Wylie, SC 29710
(803) 831-2121

Providence Rd.

Harris Family YMCA
5900 Quail Hollow Rd.
Charlotte NC 28210
552-9622

Sharon Rd.

Quail Hollow Rd.

To Matthews/Union County YMCA
3104 Weddington Rd., Suite 400
Matthews, NC 28105
845-9622

16

I-77

Mecklenburg County Park and Recreation holds one-week day camps at five different sites, featuring special programs, field trips, games, athletics and arts and crafts. The David B. Waymer Complex offers a free playground program.

The Harris YMCA offers coed day camps at Queens College and on-site. The YWCA on Park Road holds an annual **Kamp-a-Long** for girls and boys. **Camp Arrowhead** at the Simmons YMCA is another choice. One of the finest coed boarding camps in the Southeast is YMCA-affiliated **Camp Thunderbird** on Lake Wylie, where kids learn to wa-ter ski, sail, swim and participate in competitive sports and other activities. (The camp is also a center for the YMCA's extensive **Y-Indian Guide program**.)

Most YMCA camps offer counselor-in-training programs for older young people. Since the YMCA camps are very popular, it's a good idea to register early. Some scholarships are available. The Jewish Community Center's day camp is **Camp Maccabee**, and a number of day care centers and learning/tutoring centers in the Charlotte area also offer summer programs.

Photo by John Cress.

The Charlotte City Council holds three open meetings each month in the meeting chamber of the Charlotte/Mecklenburg Government Center.

Inside
Local Government

*T*he citizens of Charlotte/ Mecklenburg pride themselves on their interactive government structure. There are opportunities for most everyone to be involved in some aspect of the local government. Charlotteans take their government very seriously, and citizen involvement is held in high esteem, both publicly and privately. Very open debate and discussion of government issues have led to the creation of a community consensus that enables everyone to move forward on a given problem. There is concern, however, that as Charlotte's population becomes larger and more diverse, its ability to reach a consensus will diminish.

Several years ago, the City adopted a new mission statement: Public Service Is Our Business. As part of this mission statement, employees identified six core values important in serving their community: quality and excellence, accountability, productivity, teamwork, openness and personal development. Loyalty to the community as a whole is a deeply ingrained tradition and will hopefully continue as we face a decade of growth.

Mecklenburg County Government has an adopted vision statement: "Mecklenburg County Government: An organization that cares and is perceived as caring about all those it serves as well as those it employs and that promotes an environment which nurtures and encourages innovation and creativity in pursuit of excellence; a governmental unit that is a professionally recognized leader with a trusting and enthusiastic partnership of elected officials, staff leaders, employees and the community."

Charlotte/Mecklenburg is served by a city-county form of government. Generally, the city provides urban services, such as water, sewer, trash disposal and recycling, while the county provides human services such as health and education. The other towns in Mecklenburg County, Pineville, Mint Hill, Davidson, Huntersville and Cornelius, each have their own town governments. Both Charlotte and the county use a manager form of government, with the manager hired by the city board of county commissioners. This system has been very successful here.

The council-manager system is designed to be responsive to citizens' needs. City Council is made up of 11 members, seven from districts and four at-large, elected every odd-numbered year in partisan elections. The mayor is also elected at this time. The mayor presides at City Council meetings and officially represents the City at special ceremonies and events. The mayor is generally responsible for the execution of local laws. The Mayor Pro Tempore, elected by a City Council vote, assumes all duties, powers and obligations of the office in the mayor's absence. Together the mayor and City Council are responsible for establishing the general policies under which the City operates. Their duties include: appointing the city manager, city attorney, city clerk and members of various boards and commissions; enacting ordinances, resolutions and orders; reviewing the annual budget and approving the financing of all city operations; and authorizing contracts on behalf of the City.

The City Council holds three open meetings each month in the meeting chamber of the Charlotte/Mecklenburg Government Center at 600 East Fourth Street. The meetings on the second and fourth Mondays are general business sessions that begin at 6:30 PM. On the third Monday at 6 PM, the meeting deals only with matters related to zoning.

All City Council meetings are open to the public. The general business sessions are broadcast live on Cable Channel 16, as is a calendar of meetings for all city boards and commissions. Contact the Office of the City Clerk (336-2247) for information about the City Council agenda or to speak at a City Council meeting.

In the council-manager form of government, the city manager administers the policy decisions made by the City Council. The manager is responsible for: assuring that all city departments provide services to citizens in an efficient and cost-effective manner; assuring that city laws are faithfully executed; attending City Council meetings; reporting to City Council on the affairs and financial condition of the City; and appointing all department heads except those appointed by City Council. The city manager oversees 26 departments that provide services to Charlotte residents. Working directly with him are a deputy manager and three assistant managers who direct specific areas of city administration.

The board of county commissioners, elected in partisan elections held in even-numbered years, consists of seven members, four elected from districts and three at-large. The chair and vice chair are elected by the members, and the chair is usually the top vote-getter of the majority party.

The commission holds its general business meetings on the first and third Mondays of each month in the meeting chamber of the Charlotte/Mecklenburg Government

Center, beginning at 8 AM. All commission meetings are open to the public and citizens are encouraged to attend. The Board of County Commissioner's meetings are broadcast live on Cablevision's government access Channel and rebroadcast during the week in which the meeting was held. For information on the commission meeting agenda, or to speak at a commission meeting, contact the Clerk to the Board at 336-2559.

During even-numbered years the county elects representatives to the General Assembly and, with Cabarrus County, four state senators. All of these are elected from districts. School board elections, also held in even-numbered years, are non-partisan. All nine members are elected at-large for four-year terms that are staggered.

Mecklenburg County government has initiated a process called "Pursuit of Excellence." This is a customer-oriented process that evaluates how county government is structured and operates and makes whatever changes are necessary to be responsive to the customers' (citizens) needs.

If you have a question or need information regarding city or county government, call the **City-County Action Line** at 336-2040. Elected officials are also very accessible, and

you can get numbers to reach them by calling the action line.

REGISTERING TO VOTE

In order to participate in the political process, of course, you must be sure to register to vote or change your address when you move. For questions regarding registering, call the **Voter Registration Office** at 336-2133. If you have been a resident for 30 days you are eligible to register to vote in the appropriate elections. You can register at the Voter Registration Office at 741 Kenilworth Avenue, Suite 202, in any branch of the Public Library, at town halls of Cornelius, Matthews and Pineville and in the Department of Motor Vehicles Drivers License Offices.

GETTING INVOLVED

It's also easy to get involved in civic activities here. Community involvement is a good way to meet people and make friends if you are a newcomer. One way to get involved is by serving on citizen advisory bodies. There are about 100 city, county and joint commissions and boards, some standing, some *ad hoc*, to which citizens can be appointed by the mayor, city council or county commission. These boards, made up of approximately 1,000 community volunteers include the Planning Commission, Airport Authority,

You can register to vote at the Voter Registration Office, in any branch of the Public Library, at town halls of Cornelius, Matthews and Pineville and in Drivers License Offices.

Insiders' Tip

Residents can register to vote in any branch of the Charlotte Public Library.

Tree Commission, Sister City Committee, Building Standards Advisory Committee, Minority Affairs Committee and Park and Recreation Commission.

All it takes is filling out a simple application and a little bit of lobbying (i.e., calling or writing council or commission members and making the appointment). Some appointments are powerful and very much sought after, so the process becomes highly political. In other cases, getting appointed is just a matter of letting the appropriate people know you want to serve.

To get an application, and to find out what appointments are coming up, call the **City Clerk's Office** at 336-2247 or the **County Clerk's Office** at 336-2559. *The Charlotte Observer* also runs lists of upcoming appointments as well as the schedule for board meetings. You might want to attend some meetings before you apply for a board in order to find out what serving on it entails. All meetings are open to the public. You can also pick up a brochure called *Citizen Participation in Mecklenburg County* at the Mecklenburg County Public Service & Information, 600 East Fourth Street, Charlotte, NC 28202, that describes the major citizen advisory boards.

Getting involved in politics is also easy, great fun and a good way to meet people. Both major political parties use precincts as their basic organizational structure, and attending the annual precinct meetings is a good way to start an involvement. Both parties also have clubs for men, women, old people, young people

and whoever else wants to form a group. There are also many nonpartisan groups, such as the **Black Political Caucus**, the **Women's Political Caucus**, the **League of Women Voters**, **Concerned Charlotteans** and the **N.C. Policy Council**.

If you would like to get politically involved on the state or local level, here's who to call:

LOCAL DEMOCRATIC HEADQUARTERS
334-1139
STATE DEMOCRATIC HEADQUARTERS
919-821-2777
LOCAL REPUBLICAN HEADQUARTERS
334-9127
STATE REPUBLICAN HEADQUARTERS
800-868-8849

If organized groups aren't quite your cup of tea, help in an election campaign. Grassroots support is very important, and candidates gladly make use of eager volunteers. If politics in any form is not for you, there are a myriad of community groups looking for volunteers. The **Volunteer Connection** at 301 South Brevard Street brings together eager helpers with needy groups. Call the United Way at 372-7170 and ask for the Volunteer Connection.

Another great resource about services available to you is *People, Pride, Progress—A Citizen's Guide to Government and Services.* The City puts out a similar brochure entitled *City and Government Services from A to Z.* Both of these guides are a must in order to learn about all the programs the city and county have to offer.

Turn On One Of These

So You Don't
Turn On One Of These

The best way to avoid turning onto a traffic nightmare is right at your fingertips. It's your car radio tuned to one of the network of stations who broadcast Traffic Patrol reports.

Traffic Patrol employs the most extensive traffic monitoring system in Charlotte and is the only one in the skies above the traffic. With multiple fixed-wing aircraft, six mobile units, a

police activity desk, and professional broadcasting support, you'll get the most complete and up-to-the-minute picture of traffic problems available on radio.

From 6 to 9:30 am and 3 to 6:30 pm, turn on one of the Traffic Patrol Broadcasting affiliates listed below, so you won't turn on a street or highway that's going nowhere.

WBAV-AM • WBAV-FM • WBT-AM • WBT-FM • WBTV-CHANNEL 3 • WCGC-AM • WEDJ-FM • WFAE-FM • WGSP-AM • WOGR-AM • WPEG-FM • WRDX-FM • WRFX-AM • WRFX-FM • WRHI-AM • WWMG-FM • WXRC-FM

Inside
Media

*C*harlotte is the home for many quality broadcast and print mediums. The Queen City has one daily paper, 20 radio stations, six commercial TV stations, three PBS TV stations, cable TV and six weekly newspapers to offer the community. A wide variety of information and programming is available in the Charlotte market, including Traffic Patrol reports broadcast daily on 17 local radio and TV stations. In addition to Charlotte's local media, there is also a national news program, The NBC News Channel, produced and broadcast from Charlotte.

Another sign of Charlotte's emergence as a media center was the announcement in 1990 that the Hearst Corp., one of the largest communications companies in the world and the largest monthly magazine publisher in the U.S., would relocate 250 accounting and administrative jobs to Uptown. Hearst's Service Center occupies space in the Carillon building.

Charlotte's media is first class. Whatever your viewing, reading or listening tastes, Charlotte can satisfy them.

Newspapers

BREAK
600 S. Tryon St.   *358-5910*

Break was started in 1987 by The Charlotte Observer to serve the 18-34 age group. The paper comes out every Wednesday and is circulated free via black boxes located throughout Charlotte. The tabloid-size newspaper is an excellent source of information on local entertainment, movies and restaurants. *Break* newspaper is "A free guide for your free time."

THE BUSINESS JOURNAL
128 S. Tryon St.
Ste. 2250   *347-2340*

Part of the American City Business Journals pack, *The Business Journal* arrived in Charlotte in 1986 and has made quite a mark in the business news market. Publisher Mark Ethridge's staff provides the city with breaking business news as well as interesting in-depth features and analyses on a weekly basis. You'll find regular columns by local business people and consultants on their area of expertise. A local business gossip column, "Table Talk," is very well-read.

THE CHARLOTTE OBSERVER

600 S. Tryon St.   *358-5000*

The Charlotte Observer is the oldest daily newspaper in the county and the single most powerful medium in the area. Its paid circulation is 300,000 on Sundays and 240,000 weekly. The paper is the 31st largest in the country and covers the central portion of both Carolinas.

The Charlotte Observer publishes seven regional local sections that cover neighborhoods and community events. The Charlotte Observer was founded in 1886 and became a part of the Knight-Ridder chain in 1955. The paper's high journalistic quality has been awarded with the Pulitzer Prize Gold Medal for Meritorious Public Service in 1981 and 1986. Detractors call the paper too liberal, but anyone north of the Mason-Dixon line would consider it moderate, at best.

THE CHARLOTTE POST

1531 Camden Rd.   *376-0496*

Covering the black community since 1918, *The Charlotte Post* is published every Thursday. It has a solid reputation in the community and reaches about 15,000 readers.

CREATIVE LOAFING

1620 South Blvd., Ste. 3-A   *375-2121*

Creative Loafing came to Charlotte from Atlanta in the spring of 1987. A weekly that comes out every Wednesday, it is free and distributed through boxes located around the area. Although primarily an entertainment newspaper, it carries on the tradition of alternative papers

with a different perspective on politics, business and the arts scene you're not apt to find elsewhere in Charlotte. *Creative Loafing's* Personals are always a hot topic of conversation.

THE LEADER

128 S. Tryon St., Ste. 2200   *331-4842*

A user-friendly tabloid with a circulation of almost 70,000, *The Leader* carries local stories by staff members as well as syndicated features. The society section is well-read by locals.

THE MATTHEWS NEWS

P.O. Box 2218
Matthews, NC 28106   *847-8484*

This weekly newspaper is published each Wednesday and reaches approximately 15,000 households. The paper focuses on community news within the Matthews town limits. *The Matthews News* is delivered free within the area and is also available by subscription.

MINT HILL TIMES

P.O. Box 2218
Matthews, NC 28106   *847-8484*

The *Mint Hill Times* is published weekly and has a circulation of about 5,000. The paper covers Mint Hill and focuses on community news.

Magazines

BUSINESS PROPERTIES

528 East Blvd.   *373-0051*

This quarterly magazine covers commercial real estate in Charlotte and the surrounding areas. *Business Properties* is a must for those in the Charlotte real estate market.

Photo by Pamela Myers.

The Queen City has one daily newspaper and six weekly newspapers to offer the community.

The magazine has the latest trends in real estate and also has interviews focusing on current market conditions. Guest editors frequently write articles for the magazine.

CHARLOTTE MAGAZINE
220 King Owen Ct. 366-5000

This colorful, upscale city magazine focuses on local business, entertainment, fine living, social gatherings, fashion, and the arts. The magazine also has an extensive restaurant guide. *Charlotte Magazine* has recently added coverage on medical breakthroughs and local sporting events. The magazine is available by subscription, direct mail and newsstand sales.

LAKE NORMAN MAGAZINE
147 N. Harbor Dr.
Davidson 892-7936

A tabloid-size monthly owned by *The Charlotte Observer*, this publication covers all the action on the lake from regattas to real estate. *Lake Norman Magazine* is distributed free in the four-county area surrounding Lake Norman.

SOUTHERN LIFESTYLES
9925 Hannon Rd. 545-1184

Southern Lifestyles is printed on newsprint and mailed once a month to subscribers. In addition to great local fare, the magazine offers upbeat editorials from Andy Rooney and Paul Harvey, as well as other syndicated columns such as the Frugal Gourmet.

SOUTHPARK UPDATE
2115 Rexford Rd. 362-3880

Every season brings a new edition of *SouthPark Update*. The

Bissell Companies produces this quarterly four-color magazine and distributes it free in the SouthPark area. The publication caters to businesses and homeowners in South Charlotte.

TRIP MAGAZINE
9222 Covedale Dr. 841-1355

This complimentary monthly playbill-sized magazine is found in hotels, USAir ticket counters and other visitor spots. *Trip* offers visitors tips on dining, shopping, attractions and entertainment in the area. The 12 pages of maps are helpful in finding your way around Charlotte and getting to local attractions.

Television

WBTV-3, CBS
One Julian Price Pl. 374-3500

Started in 1949, WBTV is the oldest TV station in the Carolinas and is one of the oldest CBS affiliates in the country. The local news operation is both sophisticated and competitive. A sister company, Jefferson Pilot Sports, owns the rights to ACC football and co-owns the basketball rights, so WBTV is the station to turn to for ACC coverage. The station recently won rights to broadcast NFL Carolina Panthers' football games. WBTV is owned by Jefferson Pilot Corp., which owns WBT-AM and WBT-SUNNY 107.9 FM in Charlotte, as well as eight other radio stations and another TV station in Richmond, Virginia.

WCCB-18, FOX
One Television Pl. 372-1800

WCCB features the Fox

network's hit programs. Other times, the 24-hour station shows movies, off-network reruns, lots of kids programming and college basketball. WCCB is privately owned by local, family-held Bahakel Communications, which also owns 15 television and radio stations and two cable systems outside of Charlotte.

WCNC-36, NBC
1001 Wood Ridge Center Dr.   329-3636
WCNC's news team was the winner of the 1992 Associated Press' Award for the best Newscast. The station is making great headway in the competitive news programming arena. Once owned by Ted Turner, WCNC has also been part of the Westinghouse chain and was purchased by Providence Journal Broadcasting out of Rhode Island in 1988. WCNC is also headquarters to the NBC News Nightside program.

WJZY-46, IND.
3501 Performance Rd.   398-0046
WJZY began broadcasting in Charlotte in 1987 and already is the third-most-viewed station in Charlotte. It is home to the NBA Hornets in 1994-95 and plans to broadcast many road and home games. WJZY boasts the second strongest market coverage and is Charlotte's movie station.

WSOC-9, ABC
1901 N. Tryon St.   338-9999
The WSOC-TV Eyewitness News team operates from one of the nation's most modern news rooms and brings viewers live reports from all over the Carolinas as well as the nation and abroad. Weekday news-

casts are scheduled at 6:00 AM, 12 noon, 5:00, 5:30, 6:00, and 11:00 PM. Weekend newscasts are aired at 12 noon, 6:00 and 11:00 PM.

In addition to Channel 9's Eyewitness News and the popular ABC news and information programs, WSOC-TV will premiere "American Journal," featuring in-depth coverage of breaking news stories on location. As a community outreach effort, Channel 9 created "Family Focus," a project dedicated to nurturing the family setting through community activities, television specials and public service announcements.

WSOC-TV is owned by Cox Enterprises, based in Atlanta, which also owns a number of TV and radio stations, newspapers and cable companies across the country.

WTVI-42, PBS
3242 Commonwealth Ave.   372-2442
WTVI is the only community-owned PBS station in the Carolinas and has a strong commitment to public affairs broadcasting and documentaries. It regularly broadcasts meetings of the Mecklenburg Board of County Commissioners and the Charlotte-Mecklenburg School Board, plus produces Final Edition, a weekly half-hour program that features a lively discussion of local events by area news and business people. The station also has a weekly business update program called "Carolina Business Review" that can be seen on Fridays.

Two other PBS stations WUNG (Channel 58, Concord) and WNSC (Channel 30, Rock Hill) also reach the Charlotte market. Not always, but often, the stations will broadcast PBS programs at different times or repeat past programs the others are not currently showing.

Radio

WEDJ-95.1 FM
400 Radio Rd.   *399-6195*

The Edge began broadcasting on January 1, 1992, under the call letters WAQQ. A Top 40 contemporary hit station, WEDJ is popular with the 18-34 age group. The station offers Charlotte a different angle on music with its alternative and progressive music programming on weeknights from 11:00 PM until 12:00 AM and on Sundays from 9:00 PM until 12:00 AM. The Edge also produces "Carolina Hit 30," which is a local countdown featuring hot hits in the Carolina area.

WBT-107.9 FM
One Julian Price Pl.   *374-3500*

Sunny FM is an adult contemporary station with a standard set of current hits and occasional oldies, with a leaning toward a softer sound. It is owned by Jefferson Pilot Corp., which also owns WBT-AM and WBTV in Charlotte, as well as eight other radio stations nationwide. Bob Lacey, former PM Magazine co-host, and Sheri Lynch heat up the morning with gags and giggles.

WBT-1110 AM
One Julian Price Pl.   *374-3500*

WBT celebrated its 70th anniversary this year, making it one of the oldest radio stations in the country. Consistently one of the area's top stations in the ratings, it features a news/talk format, along with strong sports coverage, with a daily sports talk show, and complete coverage of the Charlotte Hornets NBA basketball games. Because of its 50,000 watt signal, Hello, Henry, a nightly telephone talk show, attracts callers from up and down the East Coast.

WCKZ-102 FM
2303 W. Morehead St.   *536-2920*

This popular urban crossover station is already among the top five most-listened-to stations in the area. It features urban contemporary music with some Top 40. Kiss, as it is popularly known, is a favorite with teens.

WDAV-89.9 FM
207 Ridge Rd.
Davidson   *892-8900*

Based at Davidson College, WDAV plays classical music 24 hours a day. It broadcasts Charlotte Symphony Concerts as well as other syndicated concerts including the Metropolitan Opera series. On Thursday nights, WDAV features local concerts. During the month of December, Christmas favorites are extremely popular. The station celebrated its 15th Anniversary last year.

WEZC 102.9 FM
301 S. McDowell St.
Suite 210   *333-9690*

Easy FM features a light contemporary format. WEZC is a great station to listen to at work and at home. You can hear your favorite love songs nightly from 7 PM until 12 AM.

WFAE-90.7 FM

8801 J. M. Keynes Dr.
Suite 91   *549-9323*

Charlotte's National Public Radio (NPR) affiliate, WFAE also features strong local news coverage with Carolina Chronicle on weekday afternoons, and its award-winning correspondents are frequent contributors to NPR's national news service. WFAE operates 24 hours a day and features a contemporary jazz format. The highly acclaimed, nationally syndicated show, Thistle and Shamrock, is a WFAE original. The weekly show features Celtic music and is hosted by Fiona Ritchie. WFAE relies completely on public financial support.

WGSP-1310 AM

4209-F Stuart Andrew Dr.   *399-9477*

WGSP programs a traditional Christian format with emphasis on the new up-tempo, fully-orchestrated contemporary inspirational music that is not limited to the traditional religious mold. The station also serves a wide group of area Christian ministries by making available a variety of technical and administrative assistance, including live broadcasts.

WMXC-104.7 FM

4015 Stuart Andrew Blvd.   *372-1104*

Mix 104.7 plays energetic, adult contemporary music. Its main market is adults ages 25-54. The station concentrates on "superstars" of the 1970s, 1980s and 1990s. The station, along with its sister station FM103, recently moved into a new $2 million state-of-the-art studio on I-77 at Clanton Road.

WPEG-98 FM

520 U.S. 29 N.   *570-9898*

Based in Concord, Power 98 is one of the most popular stations in the area. It features an urban

This new state-of-the-art facility at I-77 and Clanton Road, houses MIX 104.7 and its sister station WSOC 103.7.

259

BEFORE LISTENING TO WFAE'S DRIVETIME NEWS.

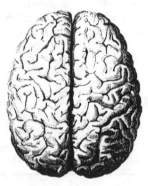

AFTER.

NATIONAL PUBLIC RADIO NEWS

6 TO 9 AM, 5 TO 6:30 PM.

NEWS OF THE WORLD.

AND ALL THAT JAZZ.

contemporary format with a mixture of rhythm and blues, rock, dance and jazz targeted at the black 18-34 year old audience.

WRFX-99.7 FM

915 E. 4th St.　　　　　*338-9970*

The Fox is best known for its infamous morning drive duo, John Boy & Billy, who are Number One in the morning show market. Their listeners have grown from 300,000 to 2.7 million with the addition of simulcast shows in four markets of the Carolinas. The Fox simulcasts John Boy & Billy to other parts of the United States, making the show well on its way to being the most listened to radio show in America. A visit or move to Charlotte would not be complete without listening to our own John Boy & Billy and "News and Opinionated Views" from Robert D. Raiford.

The Fox features classic album rock with an emphasis on mainstream album cuts. On Sunday nights you can catch live talk shows featuring rock artists.

WSOC-103.7 FM

4015 Stuart Andrew Blvd.　　　*522-1103*

WSOC has been the dominant country music station in the area for 15 years, and Bill Dollar has been the top DJ much of that time. The station plays hot, new country music. It also has a strong local news and sports staff and features NASCAR coverage. The station is currently ranked Number One in the area. WSOC sponsors a Family Reunion Concert annually at the Union County Fairgrounds that fea-

tures big stars in country music. Along with its sister station MIX 104.7, WSOC recently moved to a new, state-of-the-art $2 million studio.

WTDR-96.9 FM

301 S. McDowell St.　　　　*333-9690*

WTDR went on the air in January 1985 and has been successful ever since. It is currently the Number One station in its market. This contemporary country music station generally appeals to adults 25 to 54. For country music lovers, it allows you to kick up your heels and relax.

WWMG-96.1 FM

1437 E. Morehead St.　　　　*338-9600*

Magic 96.1 is Charlotte's only Oldies station playing all oldies all the time. The station bills itself as Charlotte's Oldies authority, focusing on music from the '50s and '60s with a lineup of popular, well-known air personalities. Magic 96.1 is a fun, promotionally active station with a strong commitment to community service.

WXRC-95.7 FM

1437 E. Morehead St.　　　　*465-0254*

Rock 95.7 programming includes the best new rock and roll as well as your favorite classic rock. Tune in on Wednesday nights f the Super Star Concert Series, wh includes live concerts and interv On Sunday nights you can lis the best new alternative mu Sonic Rendezvous. Rock welcomed to Charlotte in by rock and roll lovers station just for them.

Photo by John Cress.

or
ich
ews.
en to
sic on
5.7 was
arly 1992
seeking a

261   ...arlotte's neighborhoods include amenities
       ...urts, swimming pools and golf courses.

Inside
Neighborhoods

*T*he picture of kids waving to folks on their front porch swings as they skate down cracked sidewalks doesn't have to be a faded snapshot of Charlotte's past neighborhoods. You can still find front porches in the older neighborhoods, and on hot days you'll probably run across a few folks who prefer cranking out homemade ice cream on that porch to indoor air conditioning.

But in today's newer neighborhoods it's more probable that you'll see roller-blade-skating kids vying with joggers and walkers for a sliver of cement, and most of the people waving will be those out tending to their front yards. Throughout our neighborhoods, many of those porches, as well as doorways and balconies, will be sporting one of the beautiful flags that announce the changing of the seasons or an alumni's sports event. Last year Tarheel banners waved proudly during the Final Four as well as those bright teal and purple Hornets flags we saw adorning everything from flagpoles to cars during the NBA playoffs.

Even though we have many warmish, sunshiny days in winter, the first lawn mowing weekend of spring will probably mark your coming out party from winter's hibernation. Neighborhood Christmas parties and the few occasions when you accidentally bump into a neighbor as both of you are retrieving your curbside red recycling bins can provide a little "Hey, how are you?" time, but unless you're car-pooling or plan a night out at a sports or arts event, you just don't see as much of your neighbors as you do when weather removes its wintry cap. The same is true for apartment and condo dwellers who find themselves stopping to chat in the parking lot on a pretty spring day.

One is hard put to find neighborhoods more beautiful than Charlotte's when spring hesitantly unfurls the buds of white and pink dogwood trees; when whole avenues bloom with the Bradford pear trees and azaleas breathe vibrant color into the landscape in every neighborhood in town. Renewed by the wonder of it, you'll stand in the street comparing this year's flowering pear or cherry trees with last year's as you "catch up" with your neighbor. We thought after Hurricane Hugo it would be different. We would see more of each other; do more things together. But it isn't that different from before the disaster and we don't see that much more of each other, but that's okay. The difference is now we know our neighbors are there when the need arises—any need—and that's what counts.

That hearty spirit of community, spawned by Hurricane Hugo, revived our inner-connectedness and reminded us of who we are and where we sprang from. Our interdependence (no matter where we came from) turned out to be not so effectively different from the interdependence Mecklenburg's settlers experienced after they purchased this fertile land from Lord Selwyn in the 1700s. They, too, needed one another's skills and friendship to survive.

Being primarily agrarian, the settlers chose land near water sources. This is the reason that Charlotte's original neighborhoods formed near eight creeks and rivers. An early map would place these neighborhoods like eight almost equidistant points on a clock, radiating from the center of that Indian crossroads trading path which is now Uptown's Trade and Tryon Streets, and called the square. It was later divided into four sections called First, Second, Third and Fourth Wards.

And if you are confused by today's seemingly haphazard and meandering streets, remember that the settlers' laid them out along the high ridges in order to make traveling easier between their neighborhoods. In time, they built Presbyterian meeting houses (churches) within reasonable access to each neighborhood. The first was Rocky River in 1750, followed by Sugar Creek in 1755, Steel Creek in 1760, Hopewell in 1762, Poplar Tent in 1764, Centre Church in 1765, Providence in 1767 and Philadelphia in 1770. Though the churches have either been added onto or rebuilt, they remain on their original sites, two of which are now in Cabarrus County due to an early subdividing of Mecklenburg.

Charlotte's original eight neighborhoods have grown to over 128 which gives us many varied and diversified choices. Charlotteans (pronounced shar-la-tee-uns, never shar-luh-tons) are loyal to their neighborhoods and those in the north wouldn't think of moving to the east, west or south and vice versa. Finding the neighborhood where you belong—feel in sync with your neighbors—is the key.

In the past few years we've become very protective of our neighborhoods. We want to preserve our way of life and preserving our neighborhoods is part of the deal. Strong neighborhood associations have been key to binding many neighborhoods together. Some of our oldest neighborhoods like Dilworth, Elizabeth, Myers Park, Eastover, Plaza-Midwood, Fourth Ward and Biddleville have used several methods to maintain their character. The Charlotte-Mecklenburg Historic Properties Commission has developed some walking tours and worked toward historic designation for many homes and commercial buildings in these neighborhoods, while individual neighborhoods have held home tours and festivals. A few have written their histories, lending distinction and character to these grand old ladies.

Whereas magnificent new mansions are blanketing the landscapes toward Pineville and Matthews, older historic mansions built by the town's visionaries are where many of the new visionaries currently reside. The Duke mansion in Myers Park that legendary tobacco tycoon James "Buck" Duke purchased in the '20s and added to extensively has been returned from condominiums to a single-family home. Almost directly across Providence Road, the famous Reynolds-Gourmajenko Tuscan-styled home has been recycled as a restaurant. The house has many eccentricities, such as a room on the top floor with leather walls and a ceiling painted metallic silver. The room is said to have been used for holding seances. One wall of the room, when pressed at the right point, pivots to display a secret room. Uptown in Fourth Ward, where two of Charlotte's most recent mayors live, you will find fine examples of Victorian architecture.

You can find out a great deal about an area by contacting the neighborhood association, but remember that most of these people are "high" on their neighborhood, and probably wear brighter rose-colored glasses than real estate agents. The Planning Commission (336-2205) is another good source of information. The commission has statistics on all Charlotte/Mecklenburg neighborhoods, as well as studies on land use and development for certain areas. If you want to know about the future of the entire metropolitan area, ask for a copy of the 2005 Plan. Realtors can usually provide the "inside story" on neighborhoods. "Mecklenburg Neighbors" in the *Charlotte Observer* spotlights different neighborhoods from time to time. Other sources of neighborhood news are *The Leader* and neighborhood newsletters.

Biddleville Community

The area is still called Biddleville even though the 1871 black university, Biddle Institute, from which it derived its name had a name change in 1927. This well-preserved historic area, which successfully fought off demolition forces a few years ago, is anchored around what is called "Biddleville-Five Points."

After the Civil War citizens felt the need for education for freed black men—an ambitious undertaking in such economically impoverished times. Prime acreage was chosen off Beatties Ford Road, and with a $1,900 gift from Mrs. Henry Biddle of Philadelphia, the fledgling Biddle Institute was born. A thriving community grew up around it, especially after 1903 when the trolley was extended to the area.

Biddleville has always been an entity to itself even in the manner its post office operated. The story Insiders hear is that the postman would bring the mail to a house at 301 Mill Road, put the letters and packages on a rock in the front yard, and then rend an ear-splitting yell that could be heard from one corner of Biddleville to the other. People came running to see what the mailman had brought.

It was between 1921 and 1928 that the widow of Johnson C. Smith donated $700,000 to the university in her husband's name, resulting in the university's name change. The school is also a recipient of the Duke endowment. Many changes have been made through the years and the university is now coeducational. But some campus buildings that date to the Reconstruction era remain.

Biddleville's oldest neighborhoods are **Western Heights** and **Roslyn Heights**. The area has its own city park next to its cemetery with gravestones dating from 1908. A walking tour of the area has been developed by the Historic Properties Commission. Today new condos, apartments, and homes are being built on vacant lots, and old homes are being restored by young families.

Carmel Commons

Ten years ago most of the land in this area—along N.C. 51 and between N.C. 16 and U.S. 521 at Pineville—was pasture; now it is filled with luxurious mansions, middle-income homes and a wide selection of condos. The area is being chosen by the new elite movers and shakers as well as just plain folks who have found that they can have more house for the money in the country. Like so many of Charlotte's neighbor-

hoods, Carmel Commons is a complete community within itself, and far more so than most with shopping centers, restaurants, medical facilities and country clubs. The area takes its name from a strip shopping center that serves as a hub for the community, and neighborhoods have good access to the new Carolina Place Mall. The growth has been so phenomenal that a new high school, a junior high, three elementary schools and four parks are just putting on the finishing touches. A branch of the library has been built and CPCC has an area learning center there. Mercy Hospital operates a satellite facility in the neighborhood and the name "Carmel" (pronounced kar-muhl) is part of five neighborhood associations.

The Planning Commission has developed a district plan for the South Mecklenburg area (of which Carmel Commons is a part), including a much-needed plan for new roads that is being slowly implemented.

Chantilly-Commonwealth

Just five minutes from Uptown, the medium-priced neighborhoods in this area provide a powerful incentive to young home buyers who are looking for "fixer uppers." This neighborhood, which began in the 1930s, is really two neighborhoods in the old Coliseum area. After World War II, many veterans built homes in the area before Independence Boulevard came through and divided the area in half. Considered part of the inner city, both the

Commonwealth-Morningside and the **Chantilly** neighborhood associations have worked diligently to have many commercial establishments, located in former residences, "downzoned" to residential property. Neighborhood representatives have developed a small area plan to upgrade, preserve and enliven the spirit of the neighborhoods.

You'll find that these are neighborhoods where many of the original families still live and they work with new home owners to protect the neighborhoods with quite innovative Neighborhood Watch programs. At present, two residential streets in the Morningside-Commonwealth area have installed hidden video cameras that have cut the crime rate by almost 80%. Other streets have private-citizen patrols.

The Chantilly area now has new sidewalks, curbs and gutters installed, and hopes to have a new seven-acre Greenway Park completed soon. Before long, when you walk down its lovely tree-lined streets, you'll see proud neighbors sporting Chantilly T-shirts.

You'll find that both neighborhood associations are particularly strong and publish newsletters. Both sponsor spring and summer cookouts and covered dish gatherings and both participate in the August 4th National Night Out. This unified event acts to deter crime by designating an evening that asks neighbors to leave their porch lights on between 7 and 10 o'clock.

A small area plan has been developed to preserve and improve the life of the community.

Cotswold

This is a neighborhood that grew up in the '50s. You'll see more one-story ranch and semi-contemporary homes here than in the older neighborhoods, but some of the newer neighborhoods and apartments show a garden variety of architectural styles ranging from medium prices to more expensive offerings. Located in the center of Charlotte, makes Cotswold wonderfully convenient to just about everything. You are close to the city, SouthPark and Eastland malls, doctor's offices, restaurants, the old coliseum, Ovens Auditorium and all the handy businesses of Independence Boulevard, as well as good shopping and cultural activities at the Mint Museum of Art. Cotswold Shopping Center, renovated in recent years, serves as a center of activities. This is another neighborhood that is self-contained with an active neighborhood association.

Coulwood

On Charlotte's west side, this area is still semi-rural with open pasture land around homes that are situated on large lots. Coulwood is close to Oakdale, Mountain Island Lake and the Paw Creek Community. The Coulwood Community Council serves as a neighborhood group.

Derita

This old community has retained its rural flavor over the years in spite of urban growth all around it. Located near I-85 in the vicinity of N. Graham Street and Sugar Creek Road, Derita has a town center around which community life revolves. A plan for future development and land use has been adopted. Citizens of the area are active in the Derita-Statesville Road Neighborhood Association.

Dilworth

Dilworth was developed in 1891 by Edward Dilworth Latta to appeal to the moneyed gentry who wanted to live in the country. And, in order to get them there, Latta cleverly extended his electric streetcar to the area as an enticement. His entrepreneurial techniques further sweetened the appeal by creating Latta Park with a lake for boat rentals, pavilions, a racetrack and municipal fairgrounds where circuses and the like were held. Clarence Kuester recalls those halcyon days when, as a youth, he stood on the same large rock that remains in the park to recite the Gettysburg Address in an induction ceremony to a boy's club.

Latta Park was the first pleasure center in Charlotte's first suburb, and drew just about anyone who could scrape up a nickel for the ride. And Latta's unheard of proposal to "buy a house with the rent money" long before long-term mortgages were known, made this the place to live for the rich and middle-class home buyer.

Though the lake has been drained and the pavilions are gone, the once deteriorating neighborhood has again come to be the home of the better-off and want-to-be-better-off set. Dilworth was rediscovered about 15 years ago by energetic young families who have adapted and redecorated historic homes and businesses to look like pages out of *House Beautiful*. The century old trees that line the landscaped-design "hourglass" loop make this "country" setting (almost in walking distance of Uptown) a great place to live and play. Although former Hollywood actor Randolph Scott spent his boyhood in Fourth Ward, his last Charlotte home was at 1301 Dilworth Road where his proud mother always answered the telephone, "This is Randolph Scott's mother."

Life in the neighborhood still revolves around Latta Park and get-togethers such as the **Dilworth Criterium** bicycle race in April and the **Dilworth Jubilee** and home tour in August. The Jubilee has become not only a neighborhood event but a festival that draws residents from all over the city.

The fashionable East Boulevard is now a business district with offices in handsomely restored homes. The **Greek Orthodox Church**, **Covenant Presbyterian Church** and the **Dilworth United Methodist Church** are major presences in the community. The Dilworth Community Development Association offers many opportunities for neighborhood involvement.

Eastland

Another fast-growing part of Charlotte, this area thrives on the expanding Eastland Shopping Cen-

Many of Charlotte's neighborhoods are are noted for winding tree-shaded streets that are lined with beautiful flowering shrubs.

ter. Since the center was built about 15 years ago, development along Central Avenue and Albemarle Road has been brisk, as office complexes, apartments, restaurants, theaters and other shopping areas have been built. Eastland serves not only the immediate area but residents of the Rama area, Mint Hill, Matthews and Union County communities. Traffic is often a problem, and the Planning Commission has addressed the congestion in a study. Neighborhoods such as **Idlewild Farms**, **Olde Savannah**, **Bent Creek**, and **East Forest** in the Eastland area tend to be in the average price range.

Eastover

Developer E.C. Griffith accomplished exactly what he set out to do in 1927 when he envisioned a neighborhood of exclusive homes for the rich and noteworthy located between Providence and Randolph Roads. Insiders report that from the beginning Griffith planned Eastover as a competitor to the already established Myers Park just across Providence Road. He hired Earle Sumner Draper, an associate of John Nolen, designer of Myers Park, to design the gently curving drives in the former pastures of dairy farmer, Mc D. Watkins. Citizens of that era fondly remember it as the place that young boys went for rabbit hunting. No longer worried about trolley transportation, as were other neighborhoods, Griffith counted on Eastover being the first exclusive automobile suburb. His pitch was more toward family values, advertising: "Home is far more than four walls and a roof

that protects us from weather. It is the shrine of family life which will cluster the fondest memories after years."

Of course, if you weren't willing to accept the regal Colonial Revival and English Tudor tastes that his building restrictions stipulated, then you had to cluster your memories elsewhere. In succeeding years the restrictions have softened considerably, allowing Spanish and contemporary structures. Though known as the neighborhood of grand and expensive homes, the area does have pockets of upper-medium-priced cottages and bungalow styles.

Since fires were a great concern everywhere, **Charlotte Fire Station No. 6,** designed by C.C. Hook to blend with the neighborhood, was erected in 1929 and remains to this day on Laurel Avenue. In 1933 Mrs. John Dwelle persuaded Griffith to donate land in Eastover to house the **Mint** which would have been demolished had not this valiant lady interceded. The mint became the first art museum in North Carolina and remains the centerpiece of the area.

The area has all the conveniences of a small town—hardware stores, grocery stores, specialty shops, restaurants, and theaters—and is only two miles from Uptown. Villa Square with its lovely Tuscan courtyard, originally the Reynolds-Gourmajenko private residence, has been converted into shops and restaurants. Many residents have lived in the tree-shaded neighborhood for years, but young families make their home there as well. There is an active neighborhood association.

Housing is very expensive.

Elizabeth

Elizabeth, so accessible to Uptown, is Charlotte's second oldest streetcar neighborhood. Before the streetcar took people downtown to jobs, farmers worked the soil on the rolling hillside sloping toward Sugar Creek. That was in the 1880s when a spring-fed stream was damned to form a series of lakes (where Independence Park now stands). Historians relate that the "board of aldermen sternly forbade wading and fishing in the reservoir until two of them were caught one night in water up to their hips with fishing poles in hand."

This neighborhood has the distinction of being the only neighborhood in Charlotte that is named for a woman—Anne Elizabeth Watts. In 1897 Elizabeth College for women opened on the site where Presbyterian Hospital now stands. A second hospital—Mercy was located just a few blocks away, and that area now has a number of medical buildings in the hospital vicinity.

After 1891 the area was subdivided into **Piedmont Park**, **Highland Park**, **Oakhurst**, **Elizabeth Heights**, and **Rosemont**. Independence Park, which opened in 1907, was the city's first "pleasure ground." In 1918, department store magnate William Henry Belk commissioned noted architect, C.C. Hook to build his palatial home on Hawthorne Lane, which remains intact. Elizabeth Avenue is still lined with some fine examples of Victorian architecture that have been adapted for various businesses. They mix well with the modern buildings of CPCC located across the street from the sprawling campus.

Elizabeth Avenue was also the home of famous journalist and humorist Harry Golden who wrote in his newspaper the *Carolina Israelite* "Golden's Vertical Rule," concerning desegregation. Golden reported that "He observed a complete lack of segregation in the South as long as the black man remained standing. He shared grocery and bank lines with whites, paid his light and phone bills at the same window with them—no problem whatsoever. It was only when blacks sat down that there were problems." Therefore, Golden proposed the removal of all seats in public schools. Why he remained in Charlotte is uncertain, but perhaps it was because he so enjoyed "watching the Christians chase a buck" as he often said.

Most of the older homes have been renovated, and the commercial area along Seventh Street has salvaged its heritage by recycling homes to house antiques, consignment shops, a natural food store and several excellent restaurants. Some call the area around "Pecan Point" **Stanleyville**, acknowledging the Stanley Drugstore and Spoons Ice Cream as institutions. This is a laid back neighborhood where residents insist that it is not so much a place as a state of mind.

The Elizabeth Community Association puts on a festival every year in Independence Park, known for its beautiful roses. The association has also been successful in fighting to keep the Independence freeway project from impacting heavily on the neighborhood.

Fourth Ward

Today, Historic Fourth Ward is an upscale, homespun walk-to-work neighborhood with Victorian mansions and cottages and new condos. But this has not always been so. When Thomas Polk and other settlers purchased this tract of land we call Charlotte from Lord Selwyn, it was divided into four sections. They called each section a ward and each one originated from the center point of today's Uptown square. Fourth Ward began, not as a neighborhood, but as a political subsection created for electoral purposes. That changed within the following century to become a neighborhood of prominent families.

Neighborhoods grow and decline and then sometimes regain former prominence. That is the case of Fourth Ward. About 15 years ago, a plan was set fourth to revitalize these decaying signatures of the Victorian era. Special 3 % bank loans were lent for rehabilitation, and today the area shows off "can do" energy and resourcefulness. The old hospital was adapted for condominiums; a beautiful park is the neighborhood's centerpiece, and there is a new low-income residence for the elderly. The former Berryhill store has become Alexander Michael's restaurant on 9th Street. There are two outstanding bed and breakfasts and a number of attractive condominiums.

You'll find that **St. Peter's Episcopal Church, First Presbyterian Church** and the **Old Settlers Cemetery** anchor the community. But, to get the flavor of the neighborhood, check out **Alexander Michael's** or drop by **Poplar Street Books** on 10th Street. They sched-

Photo by John Cress.

Historic Fourth Ward is an upscale, homespun walk-to-work neighborhood with Victorian mansions and cottages and new condos.

ule poetry and short story readings on the 3rd Sunday of the month from September to June. And, if you ever wondered how your great-grandparents lived, then take the city's walking tour through Fourth Ward or join the **Holiday Home Tour at Christmas.**

Hickory Grove

It isn't uncommon here to find the person who is principal of your child's school to have gone to this same school when he or she was a youngster. It has always been a generational community that has been pretty unconcerned about status—no matter what the person's income. Folks here are described as closer to the earth, more inclined to take you as you are, not who your ancestors were.

The townspeople fought the Planning Commission tooth and nail over selling the Methodist's Church's lots for development, but lost their battle. Since then, development has run amok in this old community east of Charlotte, as new shopping centers and apartments fill up all the empty spaces. Dominating the area is the tall spire of the **Hickory Grove Baptist Church** sanctuary, one of the most active churches in North Carolina, and the bedrock of the community. Yet the original business district remains unscarred and old neighborhoods built around the many lakes in the area maintain a sense of the past.

An active community association has staged an annual **Fourth of July parade** for over 25 years. It offers such old-fashioned attractions

as a greased pole climb, a beauty contest, the induction of the neighborhood "mayor," a parade with two bands and free watermelon until it runs out.

Hickory Grove is a good place to find an inexpensive home that begs for some TLC, but there are several medium-priced and more affluent neighborhoods as well.

Hidden Valley

This primarily black neighborhood is located in the North Tryon-I-85 area of the city, with homes in the average price range. Because of its location, the neighborhood is very convenient to the city and the Hidden Valley Community Association takes an active role in decisions that affect the neighborhood.

Myers Park

Soaring trees shade Myers Park's gracefully curving streets, reminding residents of landscape designer John Nolen's promise of "outdoor art." Myers Park is the farmland of Jack Myers that was developed by his son-in-law, George Stephens, under Nolen's design as a garden suburb for Charlotte. It has been one of the few old neighborhoods that has never gone into decline. Possibly a strong neighborhood association has contributed to this effect, but the magnificent, park-like design, unknown in the South in 1911, has played the leading role. Stephens envisioned an upscale environment that would draw the city's wealth to the country, and he helped finance the streetcar extension (with massive stone wait stations) to the area to validate that purpose.

Nolen laid out the suburb so that no lot would be "farther than two blocks distant from a playground or park area. ...The plan featured grand boulevards 110 feet wide feeding a web of narrower residential byways. The street plan was intentionally confusing, for picturesque effect" (both points attested to by newcomers who see Queens Road intersecting Queens Road). Stephens went a step further by outbidding competitors for Presbyterian College for Women (located downtown) to relocate there. A contest decreed the college's new name to be Queens, after former Queen Charlotte of England for whom the city takes its name.

Myers Park has long been the home of the city's wheelers and dealers, noted by the beautifully restored presence of tobacco magnate's James "Buck" Duke's imposing mansion as well as such illustrious characters as the poetic Hugh McManaway, whose hobby was directing traffic at the busy intersection of Providence and Queens. And none can forget the imaginative parties given by Anne Quarles, who once filled her house with sand and palm trees for a beach party. There were poets and novelists (as there still are,) along with energetic political campaigners. And **Myers Park Country Club** on Roswell was and is the scene of many fun-filled tennis and golf excursions.

If you live in Myers Park, you need not venture out of the neighborhood as it is well supplied with a branch library, good shopping, churches and one of the city's most beautiful parks—Freedom Park.

Newell

This rural-suburban community near the University of North Carolina at Charlotte is beginning to change as development encroaches and more residents move in (5,000 to 7,000 families are estimated to live in the area). The railroad track and Newell-Hickory Grove Road run through the middle of the community, which boasts several restored homes. Community life centers around the post office and Newell Presbyterian Church. "Old Fashioned Days" are observed every fall.

The Newell Community Association is leading efforts to retain the area's rural character and permit controlled growth at the same time.

North Charlotte

Neighborhoods thrive, often because of neighboring industries, and wither when those industries down-size or close their doors for good. This is the story of the North Charlotte neighborhood until lately. Primarily, the neighborhood was made up of mill-owned homes with enough land for a vegetable garden and maybe a cow for milk. Almost everyone worked in one of the three mills (Highland Park, number 3, Johnston and Mercury,) and going Uptown (3 miles away) on the streetcar was a big event. Grocery stores were operated by the mill and a drug store, once operated by Mr. Jasper Kennedy Hand, still remains in the area.

Few of the original residents still live here, but Mr. Frank Hand still resides in the same two-story home that his pharmacist-father built in 1914. Mr. Hand remembers North Charlotte as a working person's neighborhood. And what did they do for fun in those days? Mr. Hand remembers taking the open air streetcar out to Lakewood Park off Tuckaseegee Road where families gathered at the Pavilion for all-day Saturday outings. They boated or swam on the lake and danced in the Pavilion while zoo animals, especially monkeys, entertained the children.

The neighborhood is finally experiencing a turnaround. The two-story **Johnston Mill**, on North Davidson Street near the corner of 36th Street, is breathing new life. After standing idle for twenty years, the almost-fireproof, indestructible walls have come to life as apartments for low-income people. Included in tenants' rent is membership in the Johnston Memorial YMCA. And another nearby building will become the new home of the **North Charlotte Boxing Club**, to be run by Charlotte Police Department Officers. The building will also serve as a day care and community center. In addition, Trenton Properties, the firm developing the apartments, is hiring a full-time family support person to work with new tenants to help involve them with the community.

The next project on the agenda is to turn the **Mecklenburg Mill** into live-in studios for artists. A common area will have a kiln for potters, and a gallery will serve as exhibition space. This will fit well into the row of art galleries on North Davidson between 34th and 36th Streets, already a popular stop on the ArtCrawl scene on Friday nights from September to June. A coffee house (a sixties/nineties mix) opened here last fall.

Plaza-Midwood

This midtown turn-of-the-century area off Central Avenue has not only made a comeback in recent years, it is now being touted as the "second Dilworth." The Plaza is known as one of Charlotte's most beautiful tree-lined streets. It is also one of the most eclectic neighborhoods in Charlotte. Developers began selling tracts of land as early as 1903 to form over 10 different subdivisions. The neighborhoods ranged from blue collar to white collar with a significant factory district growing up along the Seaboard Railroad. Later, pretty homes from cottages and bungalows to mansions were built along the Plaza and around the Mecklenburg Club, now the **Charlotte Country Club**, where everyone who was anyone in Charlotte's revered social circles, belonged. The lure of a prestigious golf club attracted this group of wealthy homeowners to **Club Acres**. Some of the notable residents were John Crosland, Sr. (home builder), textile leader George B. Cramer, for whose family Cramerton, North Carolina, was named and other distinguished city fathers.

Midwood-Plaza was also the site of experiments that led to WBT, one of the first radio stations licensed in the United States. But overall travel to and from the area was difficult as commuters had to cross the railroad at Central Avenue. The real problem arose when developer, Paul Chatham, unable to persuade Edward Dilworth Latta to extend his streetcar line to Plaza-Midwood, asked the City Board of Aldermen for a franchise to build his own streetcar line. Latta objected, feeling that Chatham was merely a front for the powerful tobacco magnate, James Duke. "...evidence abounds that the Dukes and Chatham were in collusion." Chatham was awarded his request and Plaza-Midwood was stuck with Chatham's tiny line that forced passengers to switch trolley cars to Latta's line, slowing their trip into Uptown and retarding Plaza-Midwood's growth. This caused the area to develop in a haphazard design despite the rise of automobile travel. Different developers used different sized lots and building plans to attract new home buyers and businesses.

The area is noted for its remarkable Queen Anne Victorian homes and C.C. Hook's imposing version of a bungalow in the **Van Landingham house** in Paul Chatham's, **Chatham Estates** in 1914.

There has been a neighborhood group since 1940 who were so community-minded that they scraped together $6,000 for a park. More recently when, in 1973, the city proposed a highway through the Club Acres section, affected citizens lobbied successfully against it, convincing the city council that their neighborhood was not expendable. The neighborhood has also requested that the **Neighborhood Housing Service** encourage local banks to offer low interest loans to revitalize older residences and businesses. Neighborhood efforts have produced beautiful medians of new trees and flowers, and there is a plan to add paving blocks, trees and benches along Central and the Plaza within the next five years.

Providence Country Club

The first family moved into this upscale golf community in the summer of 1988, and there are about 165 homes presently. When complete, the development will have about 500 single-family homes ranging in price from $250,000 up. A family-oriented neighborhood, the club offers tennis courts, a pool and an 18-hole golf course designed by Don Maples. Part of the booming south Charlotte market, the community is located off Providence Road (N.C. 16) about 4 minutes past the new Arboretum shopping center.

Providence Plantation

This large upscale neighborhood near Matthews is made up of 526 families who enjoy a variety of activities such as monthly newcomers' socials, barbecues in the fall and political parties. There are four active women's clubs in the neighborhood. Opportunities for community involvement are offered through the Greater Providence Area Homeowners Association.

Raintree

Located near the intersection of N.C. 51 and N.C. 16, this neighborhood was developed about 17 years ago. Many of the homes are contemporary in design and are clustered around the Raintree Country Club and golf course. Raintree Greens Homeowners Association, Deerpark Homeowners Association and other groups meet at the Village of Raintree. These organizations sponsor many social events, including block parties, pig roasts and Christmas get-togethers.

Rama-Sardis

Once in the country, the Rama-Sardis community on Charlotte's east side is now suburbia. Many of the older homes are located on large acreages and are in the upper-price range. The neighborhoods of **Olde Stonehaven**, **McClintock Woods**, **Medearis**, and others have active community groups. Sardis Presbyterian Church, The Homeplace and Rama Country Store, now a convenience mart, are familiar landmarks.

Photo by John Cress.

When complete, Providence Country Club will have about 500 single-family homes ranging in price from $250,000 up.

Sedgefield-Park Road

A number of developments clustered around the Park Road Shopping Center make up this community of shops, restaurants, churches, schools and homes. The area, home to about 2,500 families, includes a mixture of homes from the '40s, '50s and '60s in the average to upper price range. The YWCA offers many opportunities for residents, as does Park Road Park. Charlotte Catholic High School is also in this area. The Planning Commission has developed a Streetscape Plan for the area. The neighborhood group is Sedgefield-Park Road Association.

Shannon Park

Located in northeast Charlotte, off The Plaza between Eastway Drive and W.T. Harris Boulevard, many of the original families in this integrated, 1950's neighborhood still live in the rolling, wooded area. An extremely determined neighborhood association publishes a monthly eight-page newsletter filled with information about neighborhood happenings such as recycling efforts, block parties and its popular yard-of-the-month contest. These ice breakers help neighbors to get to know each other and take pride in the appearance of their homes. At Shannon Park the association has helped to make the neighborhood a good place to raise children. Integration aided in founding the neighborhood association and has made the neighborhood a model for other neighborhoods who are having a hard time engendering a sense of spirit. This neighborhood's success has been based on "reaching out to neighbors to try to get them involved."

SouthPark

This former farmland was pastoral country until SouthPark Shopping Mall opened in 1971. Although the area was originally referred to as Sharon, it is now called "Southeast Charlotte."

A drive or jog up Sharon Road provides a visual treat. The medium-priced to upscale-priced neighborhoods that make up this area are clustered around the Mall and Specialty Shops on the Park. They include developments such as **Foxcroft**, **Morrocroft**, **Mountainbrook**, **Olde Providence**, **Beverly Woods**, **Sharon Woods**, **Candlewyck** and others, plus numerous apartment complexes and condos. Each neighborhood has its own neighborhood association with newsletters, neighborhood block parties, garden clubs and Neighborhood Watch programs. These tree-shaded neighborhoods with well-kept lawns provide great places to bike or jog.

Colony Road has been cut through from Sharon to Sharon View Road opening Charlotte's newest and most exclusive privately guarded residential area. It is also the home of the magnificent new Morrison branch library, several banks and other stores. Because Southeast Charlotte encompasses such a big area and is growing so rapidly, residents tend to center activities around their neighborhoods, churches, schools, or swim clubs. As more and more office complexes have been built, the area has developed into a major business district rivaling Uptown. The area has plenty of upscale hotels and good restaurants that make this country setting an excellent place to live.

Steele Creek

Home of the 1760 Central Steele Creek Presbyterian Church, this was one of the original eight neighborhoods. Older than Mecklenburg County, this southwest community is home to many families whose roots date back over 200 years. You'll still run into generations of Boyds, McDowells, Prices, Hunters and Youngbloods whose forefathers were instrumental in shaping Mecklenburg.

You can't miss the rustic charm in this primarily agricultural community evidenced by this reflection overheard at the 1890 Byrum's General Store: "I love to see the seasons change, the harvest and the smell of grass and manure." These are the people who hold dear the virtues of simple living and hard

Photo by John Cress.

Park Crossing is a popular neighborhood in South Charlotte and convenient to South Mecklenburg High School.

work. It was considered the best place in the county for agricultural development because of its proximity to the Catawba River. But the area began to change during the Second World War when a Naval Munitions plant was located here. The navy abandoned the plant after the war, and it lay idle for a few years until several civic leaders made arrangements to develop it as Arrowood Industrial Park. Today, it is the second largest employment base in Charlotte. That has naturally produced new residential areas and currently 3,230 single- and multi-family residences are planned.

The neighborhood association is trying to stabilize the area by offering starter homes, medium-priced homes and some expensive homes around Lake Wylie in order to hold onto its residents. For years the lake was a weekend retreat to small lakeside cottages, but half-million-dollar mansions, such as Hornet's basketball star Larry Johnson's, have made lake living a year-round concern. Steele Creek is also the home of the North Carolina side of Paramount Carowinds Amusement Park that draws people from both Carolinas for thrilling rides and top-rated musical entertainment.

Outlet Marketplace is nearby, offering affordable shopping to local residents. Steele Creek is a community in transition and members of the Steele Creek Residents Association are trying to keep the rural atmosphere of the area by bringing land-use concerns to the attention of county officials. The area has to contend with mounting airport noise

and traffic, but still the life of the community revolves around schools, churches and a superb athletic association that was built solely by the community.

Thomasboro-Hoskins

Thomasboro and Hoskins were two of the earliest developments on Charlotte's west side and were for the most part mill villages. After World War II, the area declined. Today there are many abandoned homes in the area and only about half the residents own property. Yet those who have been in the area a long time have maintained their homes well and have a desire to upgrade the entire area. The Thomasboro-Hoskins area offers many opportunities for potential young homeowners who desire to have a part in restoring this once thriving community.

University City

Meadows and pasture lands have been transformed into what amounts to a new city near UNC Charlotte in only a few years. Anchored by University Place—a cluster of shops, restaurants, theaters, homes, a hospital and now several hotels—the area is changing dramatically day by day. New housing developments, condos and apartments are springing up all around. In the midst of all the changes however, some things remain the same— the annual **Mallard Creek Barbecue** at Mallard Creek Presbyterian Church still attracts people by the droves and every politician within miles.

The area also includes University Research Park, with such impressive occupants as IBM, AT&T, EDS, Sandoz Chemicals, Verbatim, Michelin Aircraft Tire, Union Oil of California, First Data Corporation HSG Health Systems, Duke Power, Wachovia Bank, Allstate, Collins & Aikman and the Wall Street Journal. If you're new to Charlotte, you might strongly consider living in this area. You have all the amenities of the university, the advantages of being located near University Research Park and the conveniences of a brand new town. It's definitely one of the city's most exciting neighborhoods.

Westerly Hills-Ashley Park

This west side neighborhood, near Freedom Drive, was developed between World War II and the 1960s. Today's residents are sprucing up the area, following suggestions made by the Planning Commission. **Ashley Park** and **Westerly Hills** neighborhood groups are very involved in the decisions of the community.

Wilmore

Wilmore was once the farms of Mr. Wilson and Mr. More until Dilworth builder A.C. Abbot bought the land and combined the names to become Wilmore in the early 1900s. Prior to that purchase the area was called Blandville. That was before the turn-of-the-century when it held two of Mecklenburg's largest gold mines. The older streets were western extensions of Dilworth with such names as Tremont, Worthington, East (West) Boulevard, and the early homes reflected the cottage style of the early 1900s. The neighborhood is located southwest of Uptown and across South Tryon Street from Dilworth, and its energized neighborhood association hopes to revitalize it in the way that Dilworth has been reawakened.

Today, it is a bustling mix of low- to mid-priced houses bringing in a younger, more mixed neighborhood. The Neighborhood Housing Services has been making improvements in the area for about five years, and the Wilmore Neighborhood Association meets monthly to talk about changes. The current thrust is toward finding the funding to renovate a vacant, boarded-up apartment house at West Boulevard and Cliffwood Place as a badly needed neighborhood community center.

The association has awarded its first $500 scholarship to Shaw University and for the past 14 years has held its annual **Wilmore Day**. It occurs in May to celebrate each of its 16 streets with a parade. The parade includes the House of Prayer Band, a Police float, floats from Dilworth and Latta Park and both the Charlotte and Wilmore clowns. The parade disburses at Abbot Park with a day of dancing, a variety of foods, crafts, sporting events, country store and gospel groups. There is a Christmas dinner each year, and a special lunch held yearly for the Adam 2 Police unit that diligently works with the neighborhood. A lively "**Back to School Jam**" is held each August.

Neighbors

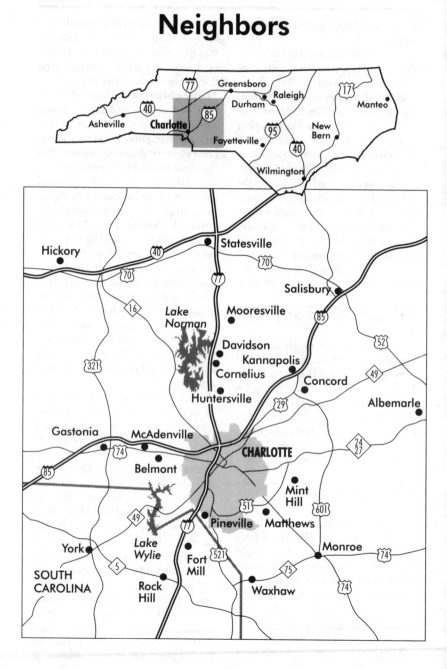

Inside
Neighbors

*F*ood, shelter and clothing may be our three primary needs to survive, but **belonging** also factors into that picture. If we don't feel that we fit into an area, we don't feel that we belong. And although belonging won't keep us from the three basic needs for staying alive, it can make considerable difference in the quality of our happiness. It's important to couple that basic need with where we're apt to feel most comfortable living.

Words such as "neighborhood" and "community" touch a warm note in most everyone's heart because that's where folks call home. A place where people know who you are or, in the fading Southern tradition, know "who your people were." Whether you're new to the area and nostalgic for your old neighborhood, or a native looking for a different life-style such as moving from the inner city to the lake or vice versa, or thrilled with your current neighborhood, most would agree that where you choose to live is almost as important as who you choose to live with (or without). Like finding a friend, the match needs to be mutual. Much

of this is because neighborhoods, like people, have identifiable personalities. Few folks get misty-eyed over asphalt and street lights or even the bricks and mortar of houses—it's what goes on in that neighborhood that gives it distinctiveness and makes us want to live there.

And where you choose to live isn't always dictated by convenience or your pocketbook. Again, it's dictated by where you feel most comfortable; how you want that neighborhood to impact your life-style. Considering the traffic on our surrounding highways, short or long commutes aren't out of the question to achieve that way of life that makes you happy. A neighborhood's appearance and price tag may be the initial selling points, but the area's activities, schools, churches, shopping, etc., are strong factors to be considered. Sure, we think of neighborhoods as houses and trees and streets but more important—neighborhoods mean people and activities.

When you're looking for that place to park your car or worries, you may be looking for a little town that's the updated version of Andy Griffith's fictional Mayberry. And to some extent, those little towns can be found in the Mecklenburg area. We still have small towns that rally to individual personal disasters. No more than a month passes when you'll hear about a group throwing a spaghetti dinner or bake sale to pay the hospital expenses for some local disaster victim. And it isn't unheard of or even surprising to find that that community has helped out or run a victim's business until permanent help could be found. We're talking involvement here, and you'll get a lot more in these communities than being able to walk down the street and have someone, who you've never met, greet you with "hey" in the classic Southern sense. The kind who will make you feel that this is a community where you'd fit in. Each person's idea for the perfect small town is individual, but many would agree that it should have people who don't shy from helping each other; the kind of people who will take you to the doctor when you're sick, the sort of merchant who'd call your home to let you know that you'd gone off and left something that you'd already paid for. A place where you could feel as comfortable with your doctor as your barber. For those among us who yearn for that less complicated way of living, the atmosphere and people of our small towns hold a great deal of appeal.

While, for economic reasons many Charlotte natives or newcomers may decide to work or locate their business in Charlotte, they are often choosing to live in one of our surrounding small towns within reasonable commuting distance. Because Charlotte's growth continues to push into these communities that lie within Metrolina, this has become the fifth largest urban area in the country with a population of over five million people in a five-mile radius.

The small town label brings to mind certain stereotypes, but the small towns near Charlotte such as Pineville, Matthews, Mint Hill, Cornelius, Davidson and Huntersville have their own distinct personalities as will be illustrated in the section devoted to each one. A few of these small towns in the metroplex took root as stage coach stops, others from being a stop on the railroad line or the location of a cotton gin. Evidence of those earlier beginnings is now in short supply, but a few historic buildings have been preserved and recycled into small museums, restaurants, stores and local government offices.

Each town has its own government and volunteer fire department, and some have their own police force, while others rely on county law enforcement. Satellite offices of some Charlotte-based medical groups give Pineville, Matthews and Mint Hill a good supply of doctors and dentists. Neighbors to the north are close to the University Memorial Hospital via Harris Boulevard off I-77. Charlotte/Mecklenburg Schools provide public education. Each town has a branch of the public library and shares in the amenities offered by county parks. Some of the towns get water and sewer from Charlotte, while others rely primarily on wells and septic systems.

As you might have guessed, residents of the neighboring towns pay both county and town taxes, but the total amounts are considerably less than that paid by Charlotteans (another small town perk). A lot of the towns have their own newspaper, but each is also served by the *Charlotte Observer's* "Mecklenburg Neighbors."

Of course the downside of living in the small town but working in Charlotte is the traffic commute. Still, when asked, most commuters feel that the quality and substance of their small-town life outweighs the traffic problems, giving them the best of both worlds.

The touches of modernization such as fast-foods, discount grocery chains and yes, even condos have branched into these once unsullied hamlets. In most instances these intruders have not driven stakes through the hearts of these communities, uglifying the town's architectural integrity. They've remained on the outskirts, and provide an undeniable convenience to many who would have to either "do without" (a hard if not impractical virtue to sell anymore) or travel many miles elsewhere, taking business and jobs away from the community.

A strong religious structure cements the foundation of all the towns, setting the tone for their quality of life. Social life centers around school activities, various clubs, sports, festivals and bazaars that include barbecues with brunswick stew or fish fries near the lake communities. In small communities you'll come upon the unexpected such as last year's Car and Truck Show held by a Baptist church because the parishioners said they wanted "...everybody to know a church does fun things, too...but we want God to get the glory out of it."

In the past, people had to come to Charlotte for the "action" or glitzier entertainment, but the new Blockbuster Pavilion near the University on U.S. 29 and the Paladium at Carowinds off I-77 on the South Carolina border, both offering popular rock star and country concerts, are now drawing the crowds to their doors from spring to fall. And as the small town attractions become more diversified or less of a hassle, they have begun to pull residents from the Queen city.

As Charlotte has grown, towns such as Gastonia, Monroe, Concord, Kannapolis and Rock Hill (S.C.) have absorbed new residents who have chosen to commute to work in the Queen City and live in another place. Likewise, many of the neighboring towns offer attractions and shopping that Charlotteans find worthy of a short drive.

Mecklenburg's Small Towns

Charlotte's rampant growth in recent years has spilled over into the six small, incorporated Mecklenburg towns that surround the city. One of them—Pineville—has been engulfed almost entirely by development. Mint Hill, Matthews, Davidson, Cornelius and

Huntersville are clinging to their identities, having pledged not to let the same thing happen to them. Each town has staked its claim to adjoining territory, having worked out a "sphere of influence" agreement with Charlotte on possible limits. Yet residents who live in those never-never lands beg to be annexed into the small towns before "Charlotte gets them," and annexation battles continue.

Life in Mecklenburg's small towns is still, shall we say, idyllic. You'll often hear people say that they live at Lake Norman. This means that they claim allegiance to either Cornelius, Huntersville, Davidson, Mooresville, Troutman or Denver but may live on the other side of I-77 at Lake Norman or across the lake at Troutman or Denver. If you want to know more about small town life in Mecklenburg County, read on....

CORNELIUS

A Confederate statue on the lawn of the Mount Zion Methodist Church, opposite the railroad tracks, reminds you that no matter how sophisticated this corner of Lake Norman has become, Cornelius remains Southern to the core. You can find out what's officially happening in this North Mecklenburg Community at the town hall, but you'll have to stop in at the library or a drugstore to get the low down on life in Cornelius.

In the period between 1883-1888, known as the "cotton battle" time, so much cotton was shipped to Liverpool, England, from here that this area was nicknamed "Liverpool." It was not until 1893 that the town

came into existence when J.R. Stough relocated part of his Davidson cotton business outside the Davidson town limit, where he could do his own cotton weighing unhampered by Davidson's newly hired town weigher. Local farmers, rather than trudge up a muddy hill to Davidson, came to Stough in such abundance that he and associate, C. J. Johnson, "conceived the idea of having a mill nearby so that cotton could be converted into cloth right there. They didn't have the money to spare but knew a man who did, Joe Cornelius of Davidson. Soon the cotton mill opened and the town took its name from the principal stockholder who apparently never made his home there but whose widow, nee Ann Sherill, did locate at Cornelius after his death." The town was incorporated in 1905.

Cornelius remains a strong manufacturing center, retaining its original cotton mill, now named Foamex. Cornelius's population is over 2,000, and it is governed by a mayor and a five-member council. Special committees and Charlotte/Mecklenburg planners have developed a growth plan. Growth, by the way, is welcome in this small town. Cornelius has a paid police department, but fire protection is provided by volunteer firemen. The town owns a part of the Catawba Nuclear Plant and its Utility Department manages electric power in the town. Water and sewer are furnished by the Charlotte/Mecklenburg Utility Department.

Nearby Davidson College provides many opportunities for educational and cultural enrichment. The

People like living on Lake Norman because even with its abundance of condos, new shopping centers and growing resident base, it's a beautiful place to live.

North Mecklenburg YMCA is located in Cornelius. From June through mid-October the **North Mecklenburg Farmers Market** is held every Saturday at Cornelius Elementary School. Many residents live in the surrounding countryside or on the lake and enjoy a variety of recreational pursuits. As the gateway to Lake Norman, Cornelius continues to show expansion in its retail and real estate markets due to its proximity to development at the lake where you're apt to hear more than one fish tale a day.

DAVIDSON

Davidson promises the best of two worlds: living in a small college town that looks as if it came off the cover of an old *Saturday Evening Post* magazine, or living on the lake (Lake Norman—straight across I-77 from the town). Whoever coined the phrase "Southern Hospitality" copied it from the townspeople of this quaint village.

Davidson College is of course the reason for the town and contributes heavily to its charm. Last year the college put the finishing touch on its new $9.1 million Visual Art Center at the corner of Main and Griffith Streets. Make a point of taking in the art gallery, which is open to the public free of charge. It is the first college building exclusively devoted to teaching and exhibition. A magnificent Auguste Rodin sculpture, commissioned by the town of Calais in 1884, presides over the atrium. This academically acclaimed Presbyterian college has been here so long (since 1837) that it does not pay property taxes. But, as a consci-

entious neighbor, the college frequently comes forward to help the town meet financial goals and has provided space on its campus to build a new public library.

The first thing you'll notice as you walk down Davidson's Main Street and through the campus is an **arboretum** of gigantic old trees. The idea for this horticultural effort formed back in 1869 when the Faculty recommended that the campus reflect ". . . the forest growth of the State . . . and the general botany of the region." So over the years a variety of trees and shrubs were planted. Then in 1982 the Director of the National Arboretum in Washington, D.C., urged the college to use its campus grounds "as a working arboretum." Today, you can take a self-guided tree tour and identify 40 different varieties from their metal tags.

Davidson casts a spell on those who come to visit, sometimes causing them to put down permanent roots. It's a cerebral atmosphere of friendly attitudes replacing phony ones existing on some college campuses. So friendly and natural, in fact, some visitors feel they've been dropped into a pre-WWII village. So, then it should come as no surprise to find Dr. Tom Clark's famous sculptures of woodspirits and gnomes right here on Main Street. This former religion and art professor turned sculptor of whimsical characters, displays hundreds of his forest-dweller figures at this Main Street museum. The top floor houses Clark's personal collection of "retired" statues (now commanding a hefty sum in the secondary collectors market,) but you may purchase Clark's and the works of sculptors, Jim Palmer, Timothy Wolfe, Lee Sievers and others on the first floor. Over a million people now collect and trade Clark's imp-like creatures crafted from their creator's puckish sense of humor.

And if you're hungry and like traditional French cuisine, try **Les Trois Faisans** at 101 Depot Street right around the corner. The food in this small restaurant is Gallic in both taste and presentation, which more than makes up for the restaurant's try at formal decor.

Or park yourself in one of the old wooden booths for breakfast, lunch or dinner at the **M&M Soda Shop** on Main Street. From a country ham breakfast to a root beer float and burger, this old Davidson Wildcat College-sweater decorated shop is **the** hangout.

The *Mecklenburg Gazette,* which carries the news of the northern end of the county, is also on the main drag. Another weekly newspaper, *Lake Norman Times,* also covers Davidson as does *Lake Norman Magazine.*

It isn't uncommon for Charlotteans and other neighbors to drive to Davidson to enjoy its many cultural amenities and sporting events. The Davidson Wildcats have had their share of basketball victories, led by some outstanding coaches, including Coach Lefty Dreisell. There's also a lot of activity at the Community Center. **Town Day**, observed on July 4th, is a big holiday.

Residents have a choice of in-town housing, some of the Victorian variety, countryside living, or homes on Lake Norman. In recent years a number of luxury condos have been built on the lake, a development that some citizens feel threatens the ambiance of the small town. Davidson, which adjoins Cornelius, is about 20 miles north of Charlotte via I-77. Incorporated in 1879, the town has a population of over 4,000 including 1,550 students.

Davidson is governed by a mayor and five commissioners, and citizens serve on a number of committees. The town has its own police force, and fire protection is provided by volunteers. Residents get their water from Charlotte/Mecklenburg. Surprisingly, there are a number of manufacturing facilities in and around Davidson.

HUNTERSVILLE

A lot of people continue to live, or upon moving to Mecklenburg, have chosen to live in Huntersville because they say, "It's one of the few places left that still has some country." If you can overlook the utility poles and the fact that you're driving on a paved highway, driving down Gilead Road in the springtime is almost like taking a step back into the past. There are rambling old homes and a subdivision or two that have crept in during the last couple of years, but mostly you'll notice the beautiful magnolias and stands of ancient hardwoods.

More important than what you'll see, will be the feel and smell of being in the country. This is one of Mecklenburg's oldest neighborhoods, particularly the **Hugh Torrance House and Store** that's been sitting on Gilead Road since the once itinerant peddler, Hugh Torrance, took ownership in 1779. Now a museum, the original log house and store is where neighbors once gathered to buy necessities while they no doubt exchanged dissenting talk of British rule. They had settled here near Long Creek where they farmed the bottom lands along river and creek banks where the richest soils lay. Sitting about 100 yards from the store, you'll see **Cedar Grove**, the beautifully restored 1831 brick plantation home built by Torrance's son, James.

Much history has occurred in the Huntersville area. One of its most famous residents—historian and novelist LeGette Blythe—has written about surrounding historic sites such as **Latta Plantation**, **Alexandriana**, the **McIntire Place** and **Hopewell Presbyterian Church**. **Midas Spring** (Mecklenburg's oldest manufacturer) and the **Silas Davis General Store** have changed very little since the turn of the century. Midas still pumps and sells spring water; the general store sells everything from farm implements to overalls to brogans. But the place to get a good cup of coffee and catch up on the town gossip is in **Neil's Drug Store** in the center of town.

Huntersville, 15 miles north of Charlotte, is easily accessible via I-77. The **Central Piedmont Community College North Area Learning Center** offers a variety of academic and recreational opportunities. Originally called Craighead after a fiery Presbyterian minister, the town was renamed for Robert B. Hunter when it incorporated in 1873. It is governed by a mayor and four commissioners. The town has its own police department, water and sewer system, and electrical department. Fire protection is provided by volunteers. The population is over 1,300. Residents enjoy in-town or countryside living. Unlike other areas of Mecklenburg, Huntersville has not yet experienced a building boom and has been able to maintain its rural character.

LAKE NORMAN

It's difficult to put into words just what it is that draws people to Lake Norman. It's more a state of mind than anything else. Its the kind of place where you can do business in shorts and docksiders and natives will look at you funny if you try it in a three-piece suit. As one recent lake dweller put it: "In the city you can't look out your window and watch an osprey swoop down and dive bomb a fish in the lake. It's fun just to see them catch their fish, and I want my kids to be a part of all that." In addition, the ospreys, relocated to the lake in the last six years, also serve as "environmental panic buttons" for the lake's health. Since ospreys eat the fish, their systems are the first to sound the alarm. If rain has washed too large a chemical dose from lawn and golf courses or treated wastewater into the lake, these birds respond. This helps to maintain the delicate balance between man and nature.

Another reason people like living on Lake Norman, even with its over abundance of condos, new shopping centers and growing resident base, is because it's a beautiful place to live. Beautiful because the lake brings peace to establishment types who are world weary and it brings a freer life-style to non-establishment types who move here because they want to have a good time and a simpler life. Although not incorporated as Lake Norman, the lake is claimed by Cornelius, Huntersville, Davidson, Mooresville, Troutman and Denver. These are towns from four counties: Mecklenburg, Iredell, Lincoln and Catawba.

Coming from headwaters high in the North Carolina mountains, the original Catawba River runs four hundred and fifty miles through the Carolinas, becoming the Wateree, then the Santee and, finally, the Cooper River, before blending into the Atlantic Ocean. Lake Norman is a "working" lake, created when Duke Power Company began construction in 1959 of the Cowan Ford Dam for the generation of hydroelectric power. Completed in 1963, it was named Lake Norman after Duke Power President, Norman Atwater Cocke.

I-77 slices through the lake area, separating Cornelius, Davidson and Mooresville to the east, Troutman to the north and Denver to the west. Lake dwellers in each area are supplied with such services as volunteer fire departments, police departments and separate governing bodies. As you might imagine, lakeside restaurants and shopping areas with a good representation of real estate firms are scattered about central areas of the lake, but it isn't uncommon to see corn fields sandwiched between expensive homes in this original farming community. Because Duke Power gave its employees first option on lake lots, you'll see many summertime mobile homes sitting compatibly beside luxury condos and spiffy developments. The *Lake Norman Magazine*, a free monthly publication, updates residents and neighbors on such coming events as the annual **Crappiethon** held in April, an event carrying different price tags on fish caught within a specified 60-day period. With national and local sponsors, the prizes range from $25 to $1,000, and the grand prize fish caught with a tangle-free-plus reel commands $65,000. Last year's Crappiethon branched out to include Mountain Island Lake and Lake Wylie.

MATTHEWS

If you don't want everybody to know your business, think twice about moving to a small town. Now this is not all bad. What Matthews folks refer to as "The Great Bank Robbery of 1976" is an excellent case in point. The story goes that after the police received a tip on the intended event, the bank's president along with quite a number of local towns people, watched from the plate glass windows of Renfrow's Hardware on North Trade Street as the would-be robbers cruised the deserted street in front of the bank. Unaware that federal officers carpeted the street's rooftops, the alleged robbers finally entered the bank and were startled to meet well-armed officers. That's what happens when word gets around.

If a movie company was looking for a quaint, last century "Country" village look, they'd need search no further than Matthews because the town looks and feels laid-back. It has the quaint touch and that plays well in its fast developing antique center.

In the center of downtown you'll find the 1900's institution of **Renfrow's Hardware** on North Trade Street. On any given morning, you can find the town elders gathered around the black potbellied stove discussing politics and problems. You can still buy seed and garden supplies, hardware items, clothing (even red long handles,) hoop cheese, soft drinks and pickles at the store which has served the community since the early 1900s.

Matthews was known as Stumptown when it was first settled in 1825 because of the stumps left from the forests that covered the section. In those days people said a wagon couldn't make a U-turn without running into a stump. The town later became Fullwood to honor John M. Fullwood who operated Stagecoach Inn and became the area's first postmaster in 1825. When incorporated in 1879, the townspeople renamed it Matthews for Edward Matthews, principal stockholder of the railroad. Eventually, 13 trains came through Matthews every day. One unusual benefit accidentally bestowed by the railroad was "water spilling over beneath the railroad's water tank that provided a swimming hole for kids and a baptismal for churches."

When gold was discovered in the early 1800s, Matthews shared in the bounty. The Rea Gold Mine was established where Sardis Road North is today, and the Tredenic Mine was located near McAlpine Creek in the present Stonehaven area. Unfortunately, the gold found at these mines was of such fine texture that it finally became too expensive to process.

Photo by Dawn O'Brien.

Matthews' Stumptown Festival, now held in mid-June, has retained its small town flavor.

Matthews has grown from its 91 residents in the town's first census in 1880 to over 15,000 today. And the antique and craft shops in turn-of-the-century buildings have made it something of a tourist town.

But even small towns aren't strangers to political problems. A storm of criticism blew in all directions after 1992's **Stumptown Festival**, held Labor Day weekend. Gun shots were fired through a local TV reporter's bedroom when investigative reporting got too close to revealing festival problems and it seemed that the annual festival, which attracted crowds of 75,000, would be canceled. When city officials scaled the event back for last year's festival, the small town flavor returned to the event.

The **Matthews Athletic and Recreation Association** involves over 1,000 children annually in sports programs. The Matthews Little League All Stars, winners of past years' state championships defended their title at **Arthur Goodman Memorial Park** year before last as two skydivers dropped from 3,500 feet to deliver the game ball to the pitchers' mound at the close of the national anthem. Need we add that this is a great place to raise kids?

Many people take classes at the **Central Piedmont Community College Area Learning Center**. And **Matthews Community Theatre** grows in talent and attendance every year. The **Matthews Community HELP Center** offers food, clothing and shelter to those in need. The *Southeast News* serves as a newspaper for Matthews, Mint Hill and Union County communities.

Today Matthews is home to some very prominent companies, including Family Dollar, Inc., Pic 'n Pay and PCA International, Conbraco Industries, Alltel Service Corporation, Harris Teeter, Rexham and many others. CrownPoint offers shopping, hotel, office and business space.

The town, about 12 miles east of Charlotte, offers a variety of housing options beginning at $100,000.

Citizens are governed by a mayor and six council members. Matthews' police force merged last year with Charlotte's. The town is served by two volunteer fire departments—Matthews-Morningstar and Idlewild. Water and sewer are provided by the Charlotte/Mecklenburg Utility Department.

MINT HILL

Few small towns anywhere have a white-columned brick hardware-furniture store as their focus. Mint Hill does. If you want to find out what's going on in town, stop in at **McEwen Furniture and Hardware Store** on the square. **Penny's Place** and **Shomar's** in the Mint Hill Festival offer camaraderie and good food. What really makes Mint Hill unique, however, is not its gathering places, but the superior overall quality of life it offers. Its wide open spaces, neat homes in all price ranges, and lack of strip development set Mint Hill apart from all the other Mecklenburg towns. It also has one of the lowest tax bases in Mecklenburg County. Through the years Mint Hill has perhaps had the most stringent zoning laws in the county and in 1986 adopted a land-use plan to steer and guide growth through the year 2000.

Mint Hill is currently the third largest town in Mecklenburg, with a population of 11,615. It was incorporated for the second time in its history in 1971. Settled in the mid-1700s by Scotch-Irish Presbyterians, Mint Hill has a rich heritage. **Philadelphia Presbyterian Church**, established in 1770 in one of Mecklenburg's eight original neighborhoods, makes it one of the area's oldest churches. Its chapel, built of handmade bricks made on the spot in 1826, may be the oldest church building in continuous use in the county. Nearby **Bain Academy** was established in 1889 as a prestigious boarding school and still serves as a public elementary school. Last year both Bain and Lebanon Road Elementary held a one-day festival to celebrate the students' year-long program of studying other cultures. Classrooms were turned into countries, and students visited the various nations to learn about other cultures. The program featured food from each country, art work and artifacts.

Mint Hill was an early military muster ground and had several industries, including gold mining. There are a few manufacturers in the area today, but Mint Hill is primarily a residential community with several stores. A number of fine developments have been built, including Farmwood, known for its large lots and houses. Commuting to Charlotte, 13 miles away, via Lawyers Road can be a headache, however.

Residents are governed by a mayor and four commissioners. Day-to-day operations of the town are carried out in an ultra-contemporary town hall. Mint Hill uses the services of the county police but provides its own fire and emergency protection through a volunteer fire department. Most residents rely on wells and septic tanks, but some developments have their own water and treatment systems.

The town has a number of very active civic clubs, including a historical society that has restored a turn-of-the-century doctor's building in a new park off N.C. 51. **Mint Hill Athletic Association** provides opportunities for youth sports year-round, and all residents enjoy the **Mint Hill Municipal Park** that has a softball field, tennis courts, basketball court, playground equipment and picnic tables. **Mint Hill Madness**, an arts and crafts fall festival, is a popular annual event.

PINEVILLE

This last year "old" Pineville took back its comfortable, easy going personality and look. You couldn't go so far as to say that you can hear the wind sweeping through the pines again—there's still a bit too much traffic for the sound of a country town—but Pineville is beginning to take on that yesteryear look again.

Pineville's first street lights were installed in the 1920s, using single light bulbs that old timers say gave off a shimmery glow. Back then, a police officer switched those lights on at the jail beside the railroad tracks each evening. At sunrise, a courier sent to get mail from the train, turned them off. Hanging baskets of flowers now adorn new, but old-looking black metal light posts along Pineville's four lane Main Street, but the new light models are activated by darkness. Last year's $200,000 prettification project also buried utility lines, repaved sidewalks and set out wooden barrels of colorful flowers. Crape myrtle trees now add a softer look to this town of 18 antique shops where you'll feel comfortable strolling down the street. And if you want to pass the time of day with folks, **Blankenship's Feed and Seed Store** is the place to do it.

This nostalgic-looking little village lies in sharp contrast to Carolina Place Mall and its many surrounding enterprises located, as the natives say, "down the road a piece" on U.S. 521. This former cotton patch is located about 12 miles from Uptown Charlotte. Boom times have brought the town more than its share of traffic since anyone traveling from South Charlotte to I-77, or to Carowinds, has to go through Pineville via N.C. 51. Traffic bottlenecked in the former downtown's two lanes, but recent changes in parking patterns have provided greater flow.

Pineville, originally inhabited by the Sugarees and the Catawbas, was the junction of two Indian paths and was called "The Turnout." In the 1760s, after white settlers moved in, it became Morrow's Turnout. When tracks were laid for the Charlotte, Columbia and Augusta railroad in 1852, so many large pines

had to be removed that it became known as Pineville. The railroad brought manufacturing, and Pineville became known then as a trading center for mules and for cotton, which was grown in the surrounding fields.

Pineville's most famous native son was James Knox Polk (1795-1849), 11th president of the United States. The **Polk Memorial**, south of town on U.S. 521, consists of several home and barn structures of the period. Each year Polk's birthday is celebrated on the site with demonstrations in weaving and cooking food of his era. The **Polk Education Center** warrants a trip to familiarize yourself with the way neither the rich nor famous lived in those golden times.

Pineville was incorporated in 1873. Today, Pineville has a population of approximately 2,500-plus residents. It is governed by a mayor and four council members and operates its own electrical distribution system and telephone company. Water and sewer are furnished by the Charlotte/Mecklenburg Utility Department. The town had its own police department which merged last year with Charlotte's police force. The Pineville Volunteer Fire Department, originally the Fire Brigade that was organized in the 1850s, provides fire protection.

The town's recreation department offers many activities for all ages at **Lake Park**, including a big **July 4th Celebration**, and team sports are handled by the **South Mecklenburg Athletic Association**.

Photo by Lance Anderson, CPCC © 1994.

The cathedral at Belmont Abbey College is the only abbey cathedral in the country.

Regional Neighbors

BELMONT

A few years back the spring festival in Belmont was renamed Garibaldi for the man who pioneered the town's beginnings. John Garibaldi built a railroad water tank two miles west of the Catawba River in the early 1870s that resulted in a station stop. Garibaldi's tank serviced trains on the Atlanta and Charlotte Railroad, which in turn opened the path for this area to become heavily industrialized with textiles.

A decade later, Catholic Bishop Leo Haid founded a site near the station for an abbey. To avoid the embarrassment of having a Catholic monastery in a town that people might mistakenly believe was linked to controversial Italian nationalist, Giuseppe Garibaldi, the famous general who had led a fight to unify Italy and win separation of church and state, Bishop Haid changed the site's name to Belmont. Historians disagree on the reasoning behind the name's selection. It may have been named after New York Congressional member, Perry Belmont (the Bishop's friend), or a sort of Latin version of "beautiful mountain," owing to the town's location near the foothills. For whatever reason, **Belmont Benedictine Monastery**, located in the heart of the town has shaped its personality.

The Monastery operates **Belmont Abbey College**, one of two educational institutions in the town—the other being the **North Carolina Vocational Textile School**. The cathedral at Belmont Abbey College is the only abbey cathedral in the country. The Abbot has jurisdiction over eight Western North Carolina counties. The stained glass windows in the cathedral are worth a visit. They came from Myers Brothers Studios in Bavaria and received a gold prize at the Chicago World's Fair in 1892. The college is also the site of an old slave block, a stone 3' x 4.5' in size, that was used during plantation days to exhibit and auction slaves.

Also worth a visit is the **Piedmont Carolina Railroad Museum**. You'll see two old boxcars and a club car. In addition, the museum has a Western Union display that demonstrates the old method of sending telegrams. The museum is open only on the weekends (704-825-4403).

Although the **Sisters of Mercy** closed **Sacred Heart College** in the late 80s, they remain a major presence in the area. Members of the order direct Mercy Hospital in Charlotte, Saint Joseph's Hospital in Asheville and Holy Angels Nursery in Belmont. They live in the Motherhouse, a huge stone building at Sacred Heart. As you might expect, Belmont is a very friendly town with civic-minded citizens and a cooperative business community. It has 25,000 residents.

CONCORD

Concord was settled by a resolute, if not cantankerous bunch of Scotch, Irish, Dutch and Germans. The story goes that in the dwindling days of the Civil War, a Yankee soldier was riding his horse along the dusty road that was known as Main Street in Concord. The Yankee stopped an old-timer and asked, "Is this Concord?" pronouncing it "conkerd" in his northern way. The old-timer spat, glared at him testily and said, "Hell, no. Ain't never been, ain't never gonna be!" Naturally no one can say whether the tale is true, but people who know Concord have little doubt that it is.

In 1887, after the economic hardships of Reconstruction, James W. Cannon started his cotton mill in order to take advantage of this strong cotton-farming region. That plant was the beginning of the textile manufacturing giant, **Fieldcrest-Cannon**. Mr. Cannon built a palatial white Victorian home on Union Street, and was later followed by his top managers who also built grand homes there. The street is now the historic district of the town. After Mr. Cannon died, his youngest son Charles took command of the enterprises. "Mr. Charlie," as he was paternalistically called, ruled his company and town with an uncompromising but kind hand for 50 years. His straightlaced policy brooked no drinking or infidelity, and all employees were expected to be at church every Sunday.

Concord may not be blessed with a cathedral like Belmont, but it is blessed with some of the area's most beautiful churches. Cannon's influence is still seen in the **Cannon Memorial Library** and the up-to-date **Cabarrus Memorial Hospital**. Like Belmont, much of its industry is traditionally related to textiles, but with the new major presence of **Philip Morris USA**, Concord is trying to shuck its mill town image. The plant has one of the largest collections of North Carolina arts and crafts, in-cluding the world's largest quilted tapestry, which can be seen during free tours of the plant. Another change has been brought about with **Concord Farms**, the single largest duck hatchery and the second largest duck processor in the world.

As the county seat of Cabarrus, Concord is about 20 miles from Charlotte, and grows nearer every year as Charlotte's boundaries become more elastic and Concord continues to annex large tracts of land such as the **Charlotte Motor Speedway**, just west of town. The speedway, which features NASCAR short track racing, has become very important to the economy of Concord.

Another major attraction in the area is the **Reed Gold Mine**. If you like barbecue, **Troutman's** is the place to chow down. Many cultural events are staged by the **Cabarrus Arts Council**, the **Cabarrus Art Guild**, and the **Old Courthouse Theatre**.

Concord is the second-fastest growing city in North Carolina, having doubled in population and tripled in land area (encompassing 23 square miles) during the past five years. The population of Concord is 28,250.

Note: A research source for this material is free-lance writer, Terry Hoover.

FORT MILL, S.C.

Like so many small towns that emerged because either the railroad made a stop there, or someone put in a cotton gin, Fort Mill was so named for two separate occurrences—a fort and a mill. The fort was built in 1740 by North Carolina's colonial governor to protect the

Photo by Ashlyn Beck, CPCC © 1993.

The Cabarrus County Courthouse
is one of many beautiful historical buildings found in Concord.

friendly Catawba Indians in the area from attacks by the Shawnee and Cherokee tribes. Later, in 1775, a gristmill was erected on Steele Creek.

The Catawbas, originally part of the northern tribe of Siouan, ventured south, splitting from their former group and taking the Catawba name, which in Choctaw means "separated." In 1763, after years of alternating peace and friction with the white settlers, "an agreement was reached whereby the white men set aside an area about fifteen miles square for the use of the Catawbas." However, through the years, much of this "Indian Nation" came back into settlers' hands, a point which has been bitterly disputed in the courts.

In addition to its Native American heritage, Fort Mill has an interesting colonial past that can be traced in the remaining historic sites. These include the **Spratt family graveyard**, **Spratt's Spring** where General Cornwallis camped during the American Revolution, **Confederate Park**, **Springfield Plantation**, **White Homestead**, **Springs Mills' first textile plant** and various other sites.

Today, due to the "green belt" girdling Fort Mill, the town remains fairly untouched by unwanted development. This crescent of land surrounding the town was purchased through clever planning of textile tycoon Elliott Springs to protect his labor force from invasion from other textile developers. The crescent remains with the Close family (Springs' descendants) who have agreed not to develop the land.

Rising from the ashes of the ministry of Jim and Tammy Bakker, who left behind them the sour taste of lemons, **New Heritage Village** took those lemons and made them into a refreshing lemonade. Success stories are rare these days, which is why they are such a pleasure to report. Today, Fort Mill can boast of its newly reorganized Heritage Village that has worked hard to reestablish religious values. The Christian theme park, with its campsites and hotel accommodations, has also reopened its doors and children of all ages are again enjoying the spectacular water park.

At Fort Mill's centennial celebration in 1973, organizers put together a "Coon Harris Memorial Contest" to remember W.T. "Coon" Harris, who, in 1923, with homemade wings, leaped from the top of an oak tree in an effort to fly, but fell short of being airborne. Fortunately, the contestants had it a bit easier when they landed in the municipal swimming pool. Only a small town would have the kind of free spirit that commemorates an event of that nature, which is why more and more Charlotteans are becoming suburbanites.

The town is internationally known for Springs Mills and just about as well-known for its marching band, which receives invitations to play far and wide every year.

Fort Mill has approximately 4,162 residents but is so close to the major population centers of Rock Hill and Charlotte (18 miles away) that it has become a shared bedroom community. Residents enjoy the amenities of the **Leroy Springs Recreation Complex**, which includes an indoor-outdoor swimming pool, tennis courts, handball courts, ball fields, billiard room, exercise rooms, saunas, whirlpool, hiking/jogging trails, picnic areas and arts and crafts instruction. **Paramount's Carowinds** and the **Museum of York County** are also nearby. Fort Mill is also the home of the **Charlotte Knights**, the AAA Cleveland Indians' baseball team. **Knights Stadium** is a $15 million facility that was opened for the 1990 season. It seats 10,000 and is located on I-77 South and Gold Hill Road, just one mile past Carowinds Boulevard.

Note: A research source for this material is free-lance writer, Terry Hoover. An additional research source for this material is novelist, Mignon Ballard, of Fort Mill.

GASTONIA

You can see the fabric for upholstered furniture and draperies purchased at either Luxury Fabrics or **Mary Jo's Fabric Store** all over North and South Carolina. That's how good the prices and selection are at these two Gastonia stores. But fabric material isn't Gastonia or Gaston County's only draw. The **Schiele Museum**, one of the most visited museums in the Carolinas, houses the largest collection of land mammal specimens in the Southeast. It has a reconstructed Catawba Indian village, and an 18th century farm. The museum also features a 360-degree Planetarium. An equally enticing draw is their newly opened 480-acre **Daniel Stowe Botanical Garden**, slated to become an all season attraction in the area.

Men will enjoy the **C. Grier Beam Truck Museum** located be-

tween Gastonia and Kings Mountain in the town of Cherryville. It has a good display of the original trucks (some from 1927) that transported foods and merchandise over our highways. The history of trucking is well-chronicled, explaining its growth and development from 1931 through the '90s by Carolina freight carriers.

Take a day to visit Cleveland County's **Kings Mountain National Military Park** (about 10 miles southwest in South Carolina). This marks the spot where our countrymen broke apart Britain's southern campaign, capturing 1,100 Tories. Then midway between Gastonia and Kings Mountain is **Crowders Mountain State Park**. You can get in a little rock climbing here, and wander through its beautiful hiking trails.

Close by, in Belmont, don't miss the **Piedmont Carolina Railroad Museum**. Here you'll see Western Union displays that demonstrate how telegrams were originally sent. Boxcars and a club car are also part of the exhibit.

Military buffs will want to take a Sunday afternoon to visit the (free) **American Military Museum of Gastonia**. Here you'll find uniforms and artifacts from every war from the Civil War to Desert Storm, plus a diorama of Pearl Harbor under Japanese attack.

A few miles away in Dallas, be sure to take in the **Gaston County Museum of Art & History**. This museum gives you a great insight into what life was like in the agricultural, then textile environment of the 19th century.

Originally, the town of Dallas held the county seat, but when the railroad placed the station in Gastonia, the county seat moved to Gastonia. As in so many other North Carolina towns where the railroad came through, textile mills and other manufacturing companies took root. The town blossomed into a city with current population of over 55,000 residents. Gastonia has 419 manufacturing firms today and Gaston County is one of the foremost counties in the country in the number of cotton bales and man-made fibers consumed in textile mills, as well as in number of operational textile spindles.

There's also wide emphasis on the arts in Gaston County. Theater groups include the **Gastonia Little Theatre**, **Belmont Playmakers**, **Gaston Children's Theatre** and **Cherryville Little Theatre**. Gastonia has a small symphony, as well as a choral society. The **Starving Artists Festival** in September and **Serendipity in the Park** in October draw thousands of visitors to the area. And if you wondered why many seafood restaurants are called Fish Camps, then take in the annual **Fish Camp Jam** in downtown Gastonia in October. Gastonia is a good place to visit or make your home.

INDIAN TRAIL

Indian Trail was so named for the Native American Indian path that ran straight through it from Petersburg, Virginia, to Waxhaw in the 1800s. It's east of Charlotte about one mile off N.C. 74 (Independence Boulevard) on Indian Trail Road. When the town incorporated in

1907, it was designed as a circle extending a half-mile in all directions from a point in the center of the railroad tracks at the intersection of the main street. But today the town stretches for miles and has a population of about 4,000 residents. Like so many tiny towns, Indian Trail was little more than a wide place in the road until the railroad came through in 1874 connecting it with Charlotte and Monroe. Cotton bales lined the railway platforms for many years and the town had a fine gin. Stores, churches, a sawmill and a brickyard made this a thriving community until the Great Depression of 1929. Then times were lean until World War II.

Today, if you want to know what's happening in Indian Trail or how life used to hum through here, then get up early and drop by **Indian Trail Pharmacy** (on Indian Trail Road next to the library) where seniors meet daily at what has been called the **Indian Trail Breakfast Club**. The **Indian Trail Athletic Association** plays a variety of sports at **Edna Love Park** throughout the year. And the **Arts Alive Program** is held in the spring at the library with artists and youngsters engaged in "hands-on" art work. Each spring the VFW sponsors its annual clean up and hosts different service groups with hot dogs and refreshments.

Although Indian Trail is considered a Charlotte bedroom community, it's actually located in Union County. The town has a mayor and five-member city council. A volunteer fire department services Indian Trail, Stallings and Hemby Bridge, and police protection is provided by Union County. Children attend In-

Photo by Ashlyn Beck, CPCC © 1993.

Kannapolis was restored to a New England-style village in the early '80s.

dian Trail Elementary Middle School and Sun Valley High School. The future is promising with the Indian Trail Medical Clinic, hardware stores, a modern post office, library, town hall and a couple of banks. Since annexation, Radiator Specialty and the Genwoze Veneer Plant are located in Indian Trail. Most of the stores are specialized and have replaced the old general stores where you once got as much variety of merchandise as conversation. Yet Indian Trail still retains its rural beauty and dedicated citizens, many who are third and fourth generation to the community.

KANNAPOLIS

Kannapolis was restored to a New England-style village in the early '80s, which breathed barrels of charm into this southern mill town. Like its neighbor Concord, Kannapolis was settled by the same wholesome Dutch, Irish, German and Scotch stock. These basically agrarian people were "tickled pink" when James Cannon bought a 600-acre former cotton plantation seven miles north of his first plant in Concord to build another textile plant. "Cannon laid out an entire village which he called Kannapolis, a combination of two Greek works, which mean 'City of Looms'." This meant steady employment for hundreds of families. As in Concord, the mill-town influence is becoming a thing of the past, but evidence is still around. For a glimpse of the past, visit the Fieldcrest Cannon Museum and Exhibition at the Cannon Village Visitor Center. This exhibit includes the world's largest towel, an antique hand loom, samples of textiles that are more than 1,200 years old, a hands-on demonstration of sheet fabric printing, an interactive touch-screen monitor that details textile manufacturing processes and a pictorial description that explains how a towel is made. The exhibit also includes a 20-minute multi-image show conducted in a 100-seat theater.

People used to go to Kannapolis to buy towels by the pound. Today they make a day of shopping for everything imaginable in **Cannon Village**, with its national outlets, boutiques, specialty shops and restaurants. There are 44 different stores, anchored by the **Cannon Bed and Bath Outlet**, the first outlet

store. As might be expected, Fieldcrest Cannon is the city's largest employer, providing jobs for 8,500 area residents.

The population of the city is approximately 41,000. Kannapolis is within 15 to 35 minutes of six colleges and universities, including **Rowan Technical College** and **Catawba College**, which are both in Salisbury and is now home to the Rowan-Cabarrus Community College South Campus.

Note: A research source for this material is free-lance writer, Terry Hoover.

LAKE WYLIE

Originally, mountain waters trickled stream-like down through eroding ditches. Creeks fed into these cascades of water to form rivers that ran south through the lands of North and South Carolina before flowing into the Atlantic Ocean. When Native American tribes of the Siouan separated from their parent tribes to move southward, they settled in the fertile river valley of that ancient river that lies between North and South Carolina borders. They called the river, "Eswa Taroa—The Great River." From that river the men fished and the women made clay pots from secret places in the river known only to themselves, (and passed down to present generations). These Native Americans called themselves Kawahcatawbas that translates to mean, "The People of the River." Today, the new settlers who make their homes on that river, now called Lake Wylie, are also "The People of the River." They don't draw their livelihood from the river as the Catawba Indians did, but they are drawn to the river for the sense of renewal and completeness that it gives their lives. As one river dweller said, "It's hard to describe how the river makes me feel...I don't know. I just drive home after a taxing day at work and there it is—so undemanding, so peaceful. That river just puts me at right with the world."

Lake Wylie is named for Dr. W. Gill Wylie, the doctor who convinced Ben and Buck Duke to invest in a hydroelectric power operation on the Catawba River. In 1904 Wylie brought in his engineer, William S. Lee, to design the $8 million project that would convert water power into energy from the proposed 12,455-acre lake. Hydroelectric power changed the way mills operated, and later brought electricity into peoples' homes.

The lake's waters were mud red in those early days when lots were leased to power company employees for $45 a year. Many families used their lake lots as weekend getaways for swimming and fishing. An early lake visitor remembers those early days: "There were no paved roads, electricity, telephones or anything on the lots. We usually came for a day of fishing and swimming and picnicking, but one Labor Day weekend we brought a tent to spend the weekend. That night it began to rain and continued for two days. The roads were so muddy our old Packard couldn't get through the four to five miles to a paved road. We were stuck. I was about twelve, so I threw my fishing pole line in the water, threw in a plug and caught a three pound bass. Was I excited? Gosh, yeah."

This same visitor continued to return to the lake, and when Duke Power offered the lots for sale in 1971, he purchased his family's leased lot. Until six years ago he lived in Charlotte, but the draw of the lake's waters, now matured to a deep blue, convinced him to build his permanent home at the place he loves. "Life is just too short to live in the city" he says.

The area has grown steadily, but unlike many recreation centers, it has no resorts or motels. There are good restaurants, marinas and two service-type shopping centers near the lake. You can sail or motor up to the lake entrance of last year's most ambitious ground breaking—the **Daniel Stowe Botanical Garden**. When completed, the formal and informal gardens will have cost $100,000,000. The garden is already a delight to behold, and expects to someday draw 1,000,000 visitors annually.

Lake Wylie really began to develop residentially in the '70s when two major developments were built giving area residents the option of living at the lake and working in Charlotte or Rock Hill. Many new neighborhoods have sprung up, but the first developments, **River Hills Plantation** and **Tega Cay**, continue to be sought after by "River People" who add golf and tennis to water recreation. A variety of living accommodations such as luxury apartments, condos, and a mobile home community complete with wooded lots and lighted and paved streets are also available.

Photo by William Russ. Courtesy N.C. Travel and Tourism Division.

Nearly two million people come to see the "lights" at McAdenville every Christmas.

Tega Cay is located on the east side of the lake just fifteen miles south of Charlotte. The name "Tega Cay" means "beautiful peninsula" in Polynesian and the South Seas theme was carried out in the street names and in the architecture of this picturesque area. Incorporated on July 4, 1982, the city has sixteen miles of shoreline, a rugged topography and is densely wooded with tall pines and hardwoods. Each Fourth of July, the city celebrates its birthday with ceremonies, parades, fireworks and the cutting of the ceremonial birthday cake.

Neighbors and visitors use Lake Wylie's beautiful 325 miles of shoreline to sail, water ski, swim and fish as well as participate in boat races and sailing regattas. One of the year's more popular competitions is the annual **Crappiethon** held in April. This year Lake Wylie, Mountain Island Lake and Lake Norman will be included in the nationally and locally sponsored competition. The prize winning fish bear price tags that range from $25 to $65,000. The latter is the grand prize fish that must be caught with a tangle-free-plus reel.

You'll find that marinas are a good source of information on activities in the area and offer a full range of services and storage facilities for your boat. There is a public access boat ramp at **McDowell Park**. And if you'd like to go boating, but would rather have someone else at the helm, try an outing with **Lake Charters** (564-9333). Or, you can rent a pontoon from **Pontoon Boat Rentals** (800-352-Lake or 803-329-4544 or 331-9027). You can drop anchor in a quiet cove and enjoy a picnic lunch. Either way, it's a great day for folks who want to experience a day on the lake.

McAdenville

Nearly two million people come to see the "lights" at McAdenville every Christmas. This tradition began over 35 years ago when the Men's Club of McAdenville asked for a meeting with the owners of Stowe-Pharr Mill. The members asked the mill owners what they thought about the idea of generating Christmas spirit by decorating a few trees around town. Both Mr. Stowe and Mr. Pharr not only supported the idea but offered to pay for the decorations and electricity. Those first nine decorated trees have grown every year to include almost every tree in town, making this tiny town of 830 people "**Christmastown USA.**" During the holidays the town is transformed by thousands of lights—a sight you shouldn't miss (only about 45 minutes away from Charlotte). You'll find the reflection of red, blue, green and white lights upon the little pond near the town's center especially beautiful.

This is a classic mill town located on the South Fork River, and it has changed very little since it was built in the 1880s. The entire town, complete with shops, churches, schools and houses, is owned by **Stowe-Pharr Yarns**.

Monroe

The vintage courthouse building, which dominates the town square, and "Old City Hall" have been restored to maintain the integ-

*The restored vintage courthouse building
dominates the town square of downtown Monroe.*

rity of the "home town" atmosphere of downtown Monroe. Whenever movie makers need authentic small town courthouses of yesteryear, they head for Monroe. The town has several other historic structures of note, including a Seaboard Railroad station and many residential structures.

The earliest inhabitants of the area were the Waxhaw Native Americans. They were followed by German, English and Scotch-Irish settlers in the 1750s. Union County was carved out of Anson and Mecklenburg Counties in 1842, and the city of Monroe was incorporated in 1844.

The area has many diverse industries—manufacturing facilities for heat-treated metal alloys, door closers, automobile and aircraft parts and textiles. The area is also known for its production of poultry, soybeans, corn, beef, swine, cotton and other products.

Wingate College, a four-year college with a unique approach to education, is located in nearby Wingate. Theater, music and the visual arts flourish in Monroe.

MOORESVILLE

In Iredell County, before 1857, twenty-five residents of a dusty little wide place in the road, known as Shepherd's Crossroads, were lured by Atlantic, Tennessee and Ohio Railroad into establishing a railroad depot in the center of their community. Since wealthy farmer and merchant, John Moore, offered land for the depot and a cotton weighing platform, the crossroads was renamed Moore's Siding (later changed to Mooresville.)

The North Carolina General Assembly appointed commissioners to lay out the town "with town limits one mile as the crow flies in every direction from said depot," which split the town evenly down the middle on either side of the railroad tracks. Moore insisted that the proposed 60-foot-wide streets be changed to 40-foot widths so they wouldn't cut into his cotton fields, and also insisted that Main Street curve away from the railroad tracks in order for him to sit on his front porch after lunch and see if passing wagons were stopping at his store across from the depot.

Except for the absence of wagons and the addition of utility poles, nothing much has changed the architecture or the atmosphere of downtown Mooresville. You'd never dream that the upscale Lake Norman area is but a few miles away. No, here the stores don't change; the same color awnings and glass front have remained at **D. E. Turner Hardware** since it moved to its "new location" across from the depot on Main Street in 1902. Inside, the original, now sagging wood floor, same wooden counters and rolling 20-foot wood ladder make you feel like time just decided not to move on here—and that's the way people like it.

The depot has been recycled into an arts center, but the other buildings remain the same. As one transplanted Chicago customer explained why she fell in love with the area: "When I first came to Mooresville, every time I went out these people, that I didn't know, would wave to me and say 'Hey'. I wasn't used to such open kindness...pretty soon I learned to respond. That's what I like about Mooresville—it brings out the best in you."

Another customer at **Mooresville Ice Cream Company** said: "I like living on the outskirts...It's the only place you can sit on the front porch in your underwear and listen to the birds." No question about it, this is a slow moving Southern town where nobody will ever die of stress. Nevertheless, the town's growth is, mercifully, a few miles north on N.C. 150 where shopping malls, fast-food establishments and motels have sprung up in the last few years. The influx of such new Japanese industries as Matsushita Hajima and NGK have added a cultural resource to the community's growing industrial sector.

Mooresville is also home to **Lake Norman Regional Medical Center**, which has greatly expanded medical service to the area in the past few years. Mooresville has its own police department, water and sewer system, volunteer fire department and governing body who work diligently to preserve its autonomous and less cluttered way of life.

MOUNT HOLLY

The town derives its name from the mill established there by the Rhyne family. This is where Gaston County's textile empire began. Today, textiles continue to dominate the town of over 7,710 residents. It now boasts several textile manufacturers and supports companies that make textile dyes and chemicals. As is true in many textile towns, loyalty to church and civic clubs is a reaffirmation of their fine work-ethnic values.

ROCK HILL, S.C.

Just 20 minutes south of Charlotte is Rock Hill, South Carolina, a growing community with an active business climate and educational opportunities. With a current population over 42,000, Rock Hill has four industrial parks and the busiest general aviation airport in the area. The city has approximately 90 businesses, producing everything from truck bodies to egg rolls to textiles. **York Technical College** provides training for many area industries. The city is also home to **Winthrop College**, a four-year college with undergraduate and graduate programs.

Settled in the 1850s and now a part of South Carolina's "Old English District," Rock Hill is rich in history. Two sites that Charlotteans enjoy visiting are **Glencairn Garden** and the **Museum of York County**. Once the private garden of Dr. and Mrs. David A. Bigger, Glencairn Garden was opened to the public in 1960. It is the site of the **"Come-See-Me" annual spring festival**, a 10-day event that features exhibits, concerts, gourmet gardens, crafts, road and bicycle races, children's events, a parade and fireworks. Vernon Grant, the creator of Kellogg's Rice Krispies' Snap, Crackle and Pop, designed the frog that serves as the festival's emblem.

At the Museum of York County you can see an Anderson Six 40 touring car, one of several models manufactured by the Anderson

Photo by Dawn O'Brien.

The *1896 water powered flour and feed roller mill*
is one of countless historic buildings in Salisbury.

Motor Company in Rock Hill in 1915. Apparently, the car was so well made it became too expensive to produce. The museum's wild animal collection is one of the most comprehensive anywhere. Featured are animals from Africa, North America and South America. The museum also devotes space to exhibits on York County, Indian tribes of the area, photography and traveling shows. The **Settlemyre Planetarium** is also popular with visitors.

SALISBURY

For over two-and-a-half centuries, Salisbury has been "on the leading edge of the American frontier—the jumping-off point for pioneers, visionaries and even a few scoundrels and fugitives." When General Nathanael Greene rode into Salisbury in 1781 he stopped off at Mrs. Elizabeth Maxwell Steel's tavern. After Mrs. Steel heard of the pitiful conditions of Greene's troops, she gave him two small sacks of money for provisions. As he accepted the gift, the General saw the portraits of King George III and Queen Charlotte on the tavern wall. He turned the picture of the king to the wall and wrote on the back with a piece of chalk: "O George! Hide thy face and mourne." Today, you can find those portraits, with the inscription still legible, hanging at the **Thyatira Presbyterian Church**. In the church cemetery, a monument marks the grave of Mrs. Steel.

Also worth a visit is **O.O. Rufty's General Store**, located on East Innes Street. You'll have fun in this store. It still carries everything from horseshoes to hunting caps.

Take note of the nails in the floor that once were used to measure the lengths of cord. And if you visit on a Saturday or Sunday afternoon, take a tour of **Dr. Josephus Hall's home**, the doctor for the nearby Confederate prison. The home was requisitioned by General Stoneman during the Civil War. Mrs. Hall, who cut her name in glass to prove ownership of this lovely mansion, also instructed Stoneman to keep his soldiers' horses off her boxwood path borders. Apparently, the General had been taught to mind because the boxwoods, as well as the home's interior, remain in mint condition.

Despite its small size, Salisbury abounds with culture, a point that attracted President George Washington when he visited the area in 1791. Had he come a century and a half later, he would have been treated to Cheerwine—a cherry flavored soft drink, unique to the area, along with Salisbury's famous barbecue. The barbecue is often used as a standard of comparison across the Carolinas.

This active community always has something going on such as **Mayfest** and **Autumn Jubilee**. There is also the **National Sportscasters & Sportswriters Hall of Fame Celebration** and a full season of concerts with a full-scale symphony orchestra. You'll also find an art gallery, sculpture garden, choral groups, community theater and three outstanding colleges: **Catawba**, **Livingstone** and **Rowan Tech**, not to mention countless historic buildings. Among them are the **1896 flour and feed roller mill, Rowan Museum** and a **stone house built in 1766**. The

1839 Salisbury Female Academy is now a fine restaurant known as **Miss Lucy's**, and **Spencer Shops**, once the largest repair facility between Washington, D.C., and Atlanta is now a state transportation museum. The largest mural in the state, painted on the side of a downtown building, depicts Salisbury's heritage at the turn of the century. A Spanish mission-style train station designed by Frank Pierce Milburn in 1907 is under restoration.

Twenty-three blocks comprise the **National Register Historic District** of this city, whose character has been saved by Historic Salisbury Foundation, Inc. Several historic buildings are open to the public anytime of the year, but you can get into private homes during the annual **Historic Salisbury October Tour**. Crafts are also demonstrated at this time. Another good time to visit the city is during the Christmas season when some of the historic buildings are decorated for the holidays.

Rowan County has some fine parks and recreational areas. One worth the drive from Charlotte is **Dan Nicholas Park**.

There's a lot of old money in Salisbury. Residents have made their fortunes in textiles and chemicals. **Stanback Headache Powders** is still being manufactured by the Stanback family. Salisbury is also where **Food Lion, Inc.**, the nationally known supermarket chain, began.

STATESVILLE

Today, Statesville is nationally known for the **Hot Air Balloon Rally** in September. What would the Catawba Native Americans, whose heritage dates back to 4000-6000 B.C. in this part of Iredell County, think if they could see the sky filled with this colorful explosion of graciously floating baubles? The balloons would probably have also upset the traditional religious thinking of the Presbyterian and Lutheran settlers who traveled down "the great wagon road" from Pennsylvania and Maryland to this former Indian Camp and buffalo licks. Most were headed toward the established Salisbury. But many found the fertile soil, plentiful rivers and creeks to the west of Salisbury a good place to put down roots.

Pioneer John Edwards purchased a land grant from the Earl of Granville in 1751 for this land. At first they described their new community as Fourth Creek, meaning the fourth creek west of Salisbury. The name is still retained in the **Fourth Creek Presbyterian Church and Burying Ground**. Four years later Governor Arthur Dobbs chose the area for a fort to safeguard settlers from French and Indian attacks. The fort, named after Dobbs, successfully repelled a Cherokee attack but was later abandoned and fell into ruin. You can see artifacts on display at the fort's Visitors Center.

In 1789, the town was incorporated as Statesville. The new name came from one of two reasons: one says the early pioneers desired to honor the original thirteen states; the other for the stopover for travelers on the then famous States Road. Take your pick.

The town prides itself with three historic districts and the historic downtown is centered at the square. The only original building still standing there is the **Statesville Drug Company**, with its signature clock on top. The clock, costing $500 in 1890, was renovated in 1990 and can be heard for miles around on the hour and half hour. Statesville has many homes and buildings listed in the National Register of Historic Places and is undergoing a Main Street transformation that has already made great progress in returning much of Statesville's original design.

Yet Statesville doesn't live in the past. The town has diversified to be viable in the present. The old textile plants have been replaced by German machinery manufacturers, Japanese engine manufacturers, a plastic recycling plant and movie making. Statesville is the largest manufacturer of hot air balloons (Balloon Works). What started out as a small pig pickin' for eight balloonists and 300 spectators in 1973 has become a national rally that draws 100 balloonists and a crowd of over 50,000. It's an event you don't want to miss.

On top of all that, Statesville is a nice place to live and educate children. **Mitchell Community College** is located in the heart of one historic district with 170 buildings.

Statesville's other claim to fame is that North Carolinian Zebulon Vance lived and practiced law here. His 1832 home served as headquarters for Governor Vance during his exile from the state capi-

Photo by William Russ. Courtesy N.C. Travel and Tourism Division.

What started out as a small pig pickin' for eight balloonists and 300 spectators in 1973 has become a national rally that draws 100 balloonists and a crowd of over 50,000.

tol during the last months of the Civil War. Stateville was North Carolina's temporary capitol while Raleigh was occupied by Union troops. The home now operates as a museum.

WAXHAW

Some folks take regular trips to Waxhaw to eat at the **Bridge and Rail Restaurant**. And if you like country food, this is the place to visit. The helpings are large and the atmosphere in this historic setting is ideal. The walls are filled with photographs of Waxhaw's past and lovely paintings by local artists grace the back dining room.

Of course, most people come to this quaint area of South Union County, near the South Carolina line, for the antiques. More than 18 antique shops are open just about every day year-round.

And if you tire of looking for treasures, consider some of the other sites. Six miles to the east is the **Mexico-Cardenas Museum at JAARS** (Jungle Aviation and Radio Service). The museum honors Lazaro Cardenas, Mexico's former president, who was a close associate of JAARS founder Cameron Townsend. The museum offers a glimpse into the work of this unique world organization that has about 250 specialists translating the Bible into languages all over the world. Or you might head to **Cane Creek Park**, a 1,000-acre recreation facility surrounding a large lake. It offers camping, boating, fishing and picnicking. An annual military reenactment is staged here.

A number of special events are also worth a visit: the **Waxhaw Woman's Club Antique Show** the last full weekend in February; "**Listen and Remember**," an outdoor drama that tells the story of President Andrew Jackson and the Waxhaw Native Americans, performed each weekend in June; the **Antique Car Show** in July; the **Old Hickory Classic Festival** in September; and the **Scottish Fair** in October.

YORK, S.C.

Years ago, if you felt the urge to get hitched and couldn't wait to get the results of the blood test, you drove across the state line to York and paid the justice of the peace to make it legal. It's still a marrying town—children and grandchildren of those who eloped years ago are now coming here to marry as a part of family tradition. In recent years, however, weddings have been played down a bit.

Residents like to tout their history these days. In fact, state brochures are now proclaiming York as the "Charleston of the Upcountry," and rightly so. York, which has over 6,000 residents, is a part of South Carolina's Olde English District and boasts 46 historic sites dating from 1790 to the early 1900s. The U.S. Department of the Interior has designated York as one of the largest historic districts in the country. Near York are **Kings Mountain National Military Park** and **Historic Brattonsville**, known for its early American architecture.

Manzetti's Bar & Grill is a popular after-work hangout in the SouthPark area..

Inside
Night Life

*I*t hasn't been long since Charlotteans complained about the lack of night life in the city. But now those complaints have faded because Charlotte's rapid growth has brought an increase in all types of night life. Whether you're looking for a Broadway play, a jazz club or an offbeat alternative club, you will find it in Charlotte.

The most innovative entertainment concept to date has to be **World Mardi Gras** scheduled to open in the fall of 1994 in Uptown. Utilizing the first and second floors of the CityFair atrium, World Mardi Gras will offer weekend and holiday entertainment complete with full-scale props, costumed employees, live music, theatrical lighting, and a large selection of food and beverages, all centered around a Mardi Gras theme.

Charlotte floats in the happy medium between being a town that never sleeps and one that goes to bed at 10:00 on a Friday night. While there are few party-till-dawn hot spots, there are many restaurants which, after dinner hours, cater to Charlotte's twenties crowd.

Liquor-by-the-drink arrived here only in 1978, so the city has yet to develop any old-time bars with long and interesting histories, but true neighborhood haunts are still in the making. You'll notice that a lot of the popular bars are restaurants as well. The law requires that all public restaurants and bars that serve mixed drinks must also serve food, and they must be able to prove that half of their income is derived from food sales.

Private clubs are not bound by the law, but don't be misled by the term private. Just about all of these clubs allow anyone who pays a nominal membership fee, usually around $10, to enter. If, by chance, they are restricting entrance to members only, you can usually get in by waiting outside and convincing a member to take you in as his or her guest. The guest fee is normally a couple of dollars, and you can settle up once you're inside.

During the warm months, many restaurants offer a bar in an outside patio area with live music; a relaxing way to spend time with friends during the summer. Usually different restaurants or bars are popular on certain nights, so don't be confused if a place you heard was great does not have a crowd when you go; you may be there on a Wednesday while its popular night is Friday. Sundays and Mondays (except during Football season) as well as Tuesdays are usually slow nights in Charlotte, but any other night you should not have a problem finding something going on.

Charlotte's night life does provide a diverse offering to suit varying musical tastes, life styles and drinking styles. For information on plays, concerts, etc., see the **Arts** chapter. Here's a selective directory of dance clubs, music bars, lounges and other notable places to give you some idea of what's out there.

Hangouts

BEAUREGARD'S TOO
8933 J.M. Keynes Dr. 547-0180

Located at University Place, Beauregard's Too is a favorite of those around the University area. This place is always hopping—especially when racing is in town!

DILWORTH BREWERY
1301 E. Blvd. 377-2739

Located in Charlotte's oldest neighborhood, this pub brews five different varieties of beer—this Insider's favorite is Reed's Gold. It also features a wide range of live music on Friday and Saturday, ranging from Celtic ballads to rock. A late night menu is offered until midnight Monday through Saturday.

THE GRADUATE
2014 Sharon Forest Dr. 532-2562

This bar, popular with UNC Charlotte students, is a great hangout. In fact, The Graduate was named Best College Bar by *Creative Loafing* two years in a row. Live music is played Thursday through Saturday nights; on other nights you can play your own from one of the best jukeboxes in the city. Mondays are $.99 Mexican beer nights. The Graduate is open 365 days a year.

THE CAROLINA MILL BAKERY AND BREWERY
122 W. Woodlawn 525-2530

The Mill is not only a restaurant and bakery, but a brewery as well. It makes five different styles of beer and adds special brews during holidays. Try the Hornet Tail ale for a beer with a kick! All its beers are named after Charlotte landmarks. Meet some friends at The Mill to enjoy some fine beer and bread! The Mill also offers live music a few nights a week.

MANZETTI'S BAR AND GRILL
6401 Morrison Blvd.   364-9334

Manzetti's is a popular spot in the SouthPark area to meet friends for a drink after work. It attracts a mixed crowd, but tends more toward the young professional group. Manzetti's has great food, too, and you can order anything from munchies to a full meal.

PROVIDENCE CAFE
110 Perrin Pl.   376-2008

Located in the Myers Park area, this restaurant has quickly become a popular hangout. The bar draws a big crowd during after-work hours and on weekends. A wide variety of great food and an extensive choice of beverages are offered. During the warm months, relax after work on the patio of this new popular restaurant.

RAINBOW DELI & CAFE
Town Center Plaza
1001 East W.T. Harris Blvd.   548-8989

This UNC Charlotte hangout is a small deli that doubles as a favorite night spot. Its patio offers a chance to enjoy the air and your friends. There are weekly drink specials and live acoustic rock is featured Thursday through Saturday nights.

SELWYN AVENUE PUB
2801 Selwyn Ave.   333-3443

This bar offers a great outdoor patio with a neighborhood feel. This cozy restaurant/bar is a great place to grab some friends and sip some beer under the trees on the patio. Selwyn also features different specials, such as two-for-one appetizers, Sunday through Thursday from 11 PM until 1:30 AM.

VILLAGE TAVERN
4201 Congress St.   553-7842

Located in the Rotunda Building at the corner of Morrison Boulevard and Barclay Downs in SouthPark, the Village Tavern offers great food as well as good night life. With a beautiful open-air patio, complete with wrought-iron furniture and umbrellas, this is not only a great place to get a meal, but also to meet some friends. It's no wonder you can find around a thousand people on Village Tavern's patio on Friday nights in the warm months. There is live music on the patio on Wednesday, Thursday and Friday nights.

Alternative

MILESTONE CLUB
3400 Tuckaseegee Rd.   398-0472

This place is a dive, but it features excellent up-and-coming bands you're unlikely to hear anywhere else in Charlotte. The walls are covered with graffiti, but it has a definite charm that attracts not only punks, but Yuppies, matrons and even some mainstream people. The Club serves only beer and soda (in cans), and there's a nightly cover.

MYTHOS
6th and College sts.   375-8765

Mythos is Charlotte's newest progressive dance club. Award-winning D.J.s spin Progressive House, Techno and European dance music, and the club puts on Carolina's best sound and laser light show. Each night brings a different theme: Tuesday is Rave night; Wednesday features Disco Trash Jam; Thursday is Rock Lobster night; Friday and Saturday nights feature progressive dance; and Sunday is Boys Night Out. The club offers drink specials nightly, and it's open from 10 PM to 4 AM. The entrance to the club is in the rear of the building as is parking.

THE PTERODACTYL CLUB
1600 Freedom Dr.   *342-3400*

Considered the closest thing to a New York club in Charlotte, The Pterodactyl is the place where you can dance until your face falls off. It plays only alternative dance music and, although a college crowd does dominate, you'll see a variety of people and dance styles here. Most people feel welcome and at ease, even if it does appear from the outside that leather and mohawks are mandatory. Only beer and wine are sold, and there's a nightly cover.

13-13
607 W. 5th St.   *347-3999*

The 13-13 Club has reopened in conjunction with the 607 Club. 13-13 is a private club that features a wide variety of live bands. A lot of well-known bands who are too large for small clubs, but too small for the coliseum, play here as do many local bands.

Dance Clubs and Lounges

BOPPERS BAR AND BOOGIE
5237 Albemarle Rd.   *537-3323*

If shagging to beach music is what you're after, this is the place to head for, especially on Tuesdays and Sundays. This private club plays music from the '50s to the '90s ranging from beach to country. Boppers crowds are fairly mixed and tend to be between 35 and 45 years old. Special events are offered weekly, so call Boppers to find out what's happening. On Wednesdays, ladies are admitted free of charge.

THE CELLAR
300 E. Morehead St.   *334-2655*

This private dance club plays dance music from the '50s to the present. The Cellar has long been a popular spot among college students. It has two good-sized dance floors and a D.J. who likes to interact with the audience. Live music is played in the attic Thursday through Saturday. During the warmer months, a large patio complete with bar and fiery fountain is open.

The Texas Two-Step has taken the Carolinas by storm.

CHAMPIONS
Marriott Hotel City Center
100 W. Trade St.   333-9000

Champions is a popular after-work and business traveler spot with Happy Hours from 5 PM until 7 PM.

CJ's
Adams Mark Hotel
555 S. McDowell St.   372-4100

This Uptown lounge is located in the lobby of Charlotte's largest hotel. Live Top 40 bands play throughout the week and on Saturday. CJ's crowds are usually professional and in the 25-and-older group.

COYOTE JOE'S
4621 Wilkinson Blvd.   399-4946

If you're looking for a night of fun and two-stepping, Coyote Joe's is the place to turn. Primarily a country/western bar, it features a large dance floor (always full) and live music Tuesday through Saturday. For those of us who aren't sure what the difference is between the Texas Two-Step and the Hokey-Pokey, Coyote Joe's offers dance classes on Tuesday, Wednesday and Thursday nights. Bring the kids for family dance classes on Sunday night. Beginner or professional, put on your jeans and boots and head out to Coyote Joe's. This is a private club but non-members are just charged $1 more.

EXCELSIOR CLUB
921 Beatties Ford Rd.   334-5709

In business for more than 45 years, The Excelsior is the oldest nightclub in the Carolinas. The bulk of its members are professionals between 30 and 40 years old. Music at this private club is usually disco and jazz with live bands on Sunday.

GOODTIMES BY THE LAKE
N.C. 49 South   *(803) 831-8232*

You can dance until the sun comes up at this private dance club by Lake Wylie. There's a D.J. flash from midnight until daylight on Friday night. It's open 7-days-a-week and memberships are available.

MIXER'S
5321 E. Independence Blvd.   535-7225

Mixer's is one of Charlotte's Top 40 dance clubs. This is a large, private club and memberships are available for $10.

O'HARAS
Holiday Inn
212 W. Woodlawn Rd.   525-8350

O'Haras features live entertainment beach sounds and Top 40 Monday through Saturday. It attracts a good local crowd as well as the usual out-of-towners staying at the hotel. Not surprisingly, Friday and Saturday nights are the busiest.

THE PALOMINO CLUB
9607 Albemarle Rd.   568-6104

The Palomino is primarily a country music club. The club has a large local following but many of its patrons also come from neighboring counties. This club often features big-name country talent and it has live music on Thursday, Friday and Saturday nights. The adjacent bar, The Roxy, plays Top 40, beach and rock and features a D.J on Friday and Saturday nights.

Music Bars

AMOS' BAR & BISTRO
4329 Park Rd.   527-6611

Amos', located just in front of Park Road Shopping Center. Not only does it serve great food, but it also features some of the best live local music seven days a week. The music varies, as does the cover charge.

BOURBON STREET STATION
6101 Old Pineville Rd.   522-0231

Tucked away off Old Pineville Road, this restaurant, housed in an old railroad car, has great atmosphere. Live music is played Wednesday, Friday and Saturday nights. Tuesday features Karaoke.

CAJUN QUEEN
1800 E. 7th St.   377-9017

Not only does the Cajun Queen serve great food, but it also has live Dixieland Jazz to entertain you! The Seventh Street Gator Band plays for your listening enjoyment nightly.

DOUBLE DOOR INN
218 E. Independence Blvd.   376-1446

This place is a Charlotte institution. Come here if you like the sound of blues, rock and zydeco. The concrete floors and plastic chairs that have seen better days only add to the aura, and they'll look at you funny if you wear anything fancier than jeans. There's also a game room. The Double Door is a private club, so it can serve beer, wine and mixed drinks. There's still a cover on most nights. There's no official dance floor but a small one is made by clearing some tables in front of the stage. The Double Door is closed most Sundays and offers bands Wednesday through Saturday nights.

FOUNDRY PUB & DELI
601 S. Cedar St.   347-1841

This place is big on rhythm and blues and acoustic rock. Friday nights have the larger bands that usually get the place moving. An impromptu dance floor usually appears at the front of the stage. The Foundry Pub & Deli is open Monday through Saturday and features live bands on Tuesday, Friday and Saturday. Cover charges apply on Friday nights.

JACK STRAW'S
1936 E. 7th St.   347-8960

For great food and live music, Jack Straw's is the place. It's open Monday through Saturday and features live music Monday, Tuesday and Saturday nights.

LIZZIE'S
4809 S. Tryon St.   527-3064

This cozy, intimate bar and restaurant features old musical standards, especially from the '60s, for both listening and dancing, meaning you get an older crowd here— usually 35 and up. During the week, Lizzie's draws mostly from Uptown business travelers. On weekends, the crowd is mixed. Lizzie's is open Monday through Saturday with live music nightly.

THE MEADOWVIEW STEAK HOUSE PIANO BAR
Windsor Square
9727 E. Independence Blvd.   847-3238

This European-style bar features David Panell, one of Charlotte's premier pianists. You can relax on one of the comfortable loveseats with your favorite drink or grab a table and a bite to eat while David plays your requests. The bar offers a tremendous selection of cocktails, munchies, entrees, savory homemade desserts and after dinner drinks and coffees, including espresso, cappuccino and frappe. Open Monday through Saturday, 5 to 11 PM, this intimate bar has it all!

THE MOON ROOM
433 S. Tryon St.   *342-2003*

This bar offers live jazz or acoustic music on the weekends. It advertises itself as being "A weekend beverage bar with live music, light food and funky things to do."

PEWTER ROSE
1820 South Blvd.   *332-8149*

Pewter Rose is a bistro style restaurant with live music in the bar

and patio area on weekends. It features more than 200 selections from an award winning wine list and an eclectic menu with international varieties. Check local entertainment listings for the weekend musicians.

PJ MCKENZIE'S
4800 S. Tryon St.   *529-1922*

Thursday Happy Hours are popular at this bar located in the Embassy Suites Hotel. Expect to find a different theme and drink specials nightly. D.J.s play Top 40 hits Wednesday, Thursday, Friday and Saturday nights.

QUEEN CITY OYSTER HOUSE
911 E. Morehead St.   *342-1497*

This seafood restaurant's bar area is filled with live jazz music on weekends. A late night menu is offered, allowing you to enjoy great seafood and jazz. There may be a cover charge.

Blockbuster Pavilion brings big-name concerts to the Charlotte area.

ROCKY'S
4220 E. Independence Blvd.   *532-9172*

Rocky's, in Simms Plaza, is open Thursday, Friday and Saturday nights. Thursday is Ladies Night. Rocky's has all ABC permits and features top name rock and roll live bands. The cover varies.

Exotic Entertainment

Charlotte has quite a few exotic dance bars. Some are classier than others, but all are a hit for bachelor parties.

CAROUSEL DOLLS
3114 South Blvd.   *525-2605*

LEATHER AND LACE
7327 N. Tryon St.   *596-7540*
2101 S. Blvd.   *334-8313*

VIP SHOW GIRLS
4205 Monroe Rd.   *342-1234*

PAPER DOLL LOUNGE
3221 Wilkinson Blvd.   *392-9647*

Sports Bars

For extraordinary sports consumption, there are many sports bars where you can watch your favorite teams play their way to glory or infamy in a rousing group setting. Tops are:

ALL SPORTS CAFE
6010 Fairview Rd.   *366-3663*

BAILEY'S SPORTS BAR & GRILL
5873 Albemarle Rd.   *532-1005*
8500 Pineville-Matthews Rd.   *541-0794*

KRISTOPHERS
250 N. Trade St.
Matthews   *845-6200*

LANNY'S
5856 Albemarle Rd.   *568-7165*

THE PRESS BOX
1627 Montford Dr.   *523-4981*

THE SCOREBOARD
2500 Crown Point Executive Dr.   *847-7678*

THE SPORTS PAGE
8400 Bellhaven Blvd.   *399-4417*

Comedy Clubs

If you prefer laughs to music, try **The Comedy Zone** located on Independence Boulevard (568-4242). Reservations are recommended, particularly on Friday and Saturday nights, and the cover varies depending on the show. National and local comedians are featured. Check the local newspapers for weekly schedules.

Karaoke

For those who like to express or test their singing abilities many bars and restaurants in the Charlotte area feature Karaoke on select nights. There are also a few places you can go that offer Karaoke all the time:

THE KARAOKE CAFE
5317 E. Independence Blvd.   *532-5608*

NICKYO'S
731 Providence Road   *331-9150*

Movies

Charlotte offers all kinds of atmospheres in which to enjoy a movie. From large multi-theatre cinemas to drive-ins, Charlotte has it all.

CARMIKE THEATERS

MATTHEWS FESTIVAL 10
10404 Independence Blvd.   *847-7469*

TOWN CINEMA 6
8640 University City Blvd.   *549-1629*

PARK TERRACE TRIPLE
Park Road Shopping Ctr.   *525-2121*

UNIVERSITY PLACE 6 CINEMAS
8925 J.M. Keynes Dr.   *547-1187*

CONSOLIDATED THEATERS

ARBORETUM CINEMA 10
8008 Providence Rd.   *556-6843*

EASTERN FEDERAL CORPORATION

DELTA ROAD 6 CINEMA
8800 E. W.T. Harris Blvd.   *532-9117*

MANOR THEATER
607 Providence Rd.   *334-2727*

MOVIES AT THE LAKE 8
Cornelius   *892-3841*

MOVIE AT SARDIS-8
9630 Monroe Rd.   *847-2024*

PARK 51 CINEMA
10621 Park Rd.   *542-5551*

GENERAL CINEMA

EASTLAND MALL CINEMAS-3
Central Ave. & Sharon Amity Rd.   *568-0408*

TOWER PLACE FESTIVAL 8
N.C. 51 & Park Rd.   *541-9010*

SOUTHPARK MALL CINEMAS
Sharon & Fairview rds.   *364-6622*

SECOND RUN MOVIE THEATERS

QUEEN PARK CINEMAS
3700 South Blvd.   *523-6600*

REGENCY THEATERS
6434 Albemarle Rd.   *536-5378*

Specialty Theaters

OMNIMAX THEATER
Discovery Place   *845-6664*

This state-of-the-art theater features a five-story, 79-foot-diameter tilted dome theater. Surround yourself with sight, sound and motion!

SILVER SCREEN CAFE
4120 E. Independence Blvd.   *535-8333*

This unique theater allows you to be served with food, beer and wine while you enjoy a movie. The menu has a wide variety of items, including pizza, burgers and wings. Domestic and imported beer as well as a selection of wines are available.

BELMONT DRIVE-IN THEATER
314 McAdenville Rd.   *825-6044*

Take a trip back to the '50s at this drive-in. Located in nearby Belmont, this theater offers first run movies as well as some second run movies.

Miscellaneous

CONCERTS
For big-name concert performances, there are three main venues in Charlotte. **The Paladium at Paramount's Carowinds** (588-2600), renovated and expanded in 1990 now seats 13,000. **Blockbuster Pavilion** (549-5555) opened in 1991 with a seating capacity of 19,000. **The Charlotte Coliseum** (357-4700) has a maximum seating capacity of 22,000.

THE GALLERY CRAWL

On the first Friday of the month, from September to June, several Uptown art galleries coordinate their openings and hold open house in what has become known as The Gallery Crawl. Not only do you get to view some fine exhibits, but you also get to see an interesting mix of Charlotteans, from well-dressed bankers to punks with orange hair. Some of the galleries serve wine and food. The Crawl generally runs from 6 to 9 PM. Call any of the Uptown galleries for more information.

Also, on Friday afternoons, there are several outdoor after-work parties during the spring and summer.

ALIVE AFTER FIVE

Uptown

Friday afternoons in the late spring and early fall, join several thousand Uptown workers at this after-work concert series. It's a respectable meet-market.

JUNE JAM

University Place

Located at University Place, June Jam is an outdoor concert around the lake. This series lasts from 5:30 to 9:30 PM for a ten-week season, May-July.

FOX'S AFTER FIVE

Uptown

This concert series is sponsored in part by radio station WRFX and held on Friday afternoons during the summer in the Hyatt parking garage at SouthPark.

FOX's After Five at the SouthPark Hyatt draws large summer crowds.

Photo by John Cress.

One of Charlotte's most heavily used parks, Freedom Park is scheduled to reopen in December 1994 after extensive renovation.

Inside
Parks and Recreation

*F*or most of us the words "park" and "play" can be almost interchangeable. Parks are one of the last places left where you can have fun for free. It's a time-out for us. Time to romp and relax. For adults, the park can provide a little escape where we leave all our problems behind for a few hours. For children, it can mean a place to swing or feed the ducks or maybe chase down the ice cream person; teens may view it as a place to play softball or a game of tennis; moms and dads may see it as a place to jog or reel in a fish. It can be a gathering place for picnics and festivals. It can be a place to go when you want to be alone—to walk, sunbathe, or simply commune with nature. When time won't allow a getaway weekend or day trip and you need to air out your brain for a bit, you are never far from a park in Charlotte.

The Mecklenburg County Park and Recreation Department (the city and county departments merged a couple of years ago) has a wide variety of programs. One lets you see (up-close) wildlife and fragile freshwater habitats while canoe-ing through the **Catawba Waterfowl Refuge** or wading into the marsh to search for aquatic plants and animals that live there. You can go horseback riding in some of our parks, learn to play golf at others or, if you have a boat, spend the day water-skiing or sailing. Our parks have special facilities for the handicapped, too.

While it's true, most parks are geared toward year-round physical recreation, Charlotte has some parks with a strong emphasis on nature. You'll find such special interests at the **Carolina Raptor Center's Audubon Sanctuary** at Latta Plantation Park, where injured birds are cared for. As you can see, the Mecklenburg County Parks and Recreation Department offers a generous variety of parks, located throughout the county, where folks do a lot more than skip pebbles across a lake.

Historically, Charlotteans have been serious about creating, rehabing and preserving our parks by voting support for park bonds. In '91, voters approved over $10 million for a parks bond package to fund four land-acquisition projects.

The largest acquisition, totaling 800 acres, is the **Mountain Island Lake Waterfowl Refuge** and surrounding property that has been developed to protect migratory waterfowl. The addition of 250 acres to **Latta Plantation Park** increases this nature preserve to more than 1000 acres. Both of these projects border northwestern Mecklenburg County. **Idlewild Road Park**, which serves the Mint Hill and Matthews communities, was expanded from 38 to over 100 acres. The park now has one softball field and additional planned recreation facilities are still in the design phase. In southwest Mecklenburg County, a 200-acre park will be developed in the Steele Creek community as soon as the site is selected.

Now in the second phase of building is the 180-acre **Statesville Community Park** near Ranson Junior High School off Statesville Road. When finished, this park will have a lake, four lighted ball fields, a picnic area and playground facilities. Nearing completion is a 100-acre park on N.C. 51, near Strawberry Lane (still unnamed at this writing), but rumor has it that the park will be named for North Carolina native Charles Kuralt. This park is being built in conjunction with South East Junior High School and will share four lighted ball fields with the school.

The $10.1 million **Jetton Park** on Lake Norman, opened in late summer of '92. Located on a peninsula, the 106-acre park is almost surrounded by Lake Norman. It's wrapped with quiet coves on two sides and a broad stretch of open water around its tip. There's something nostalgic about the white gazebos scattered throughout the woods, some a stone's throw from tennis courts. But most people believe it is the more than two miles of asphalt bike paths, many along the shore, that make this an appealing place to do a little communing with nature.

May 1994 saw the opening of the county's latest park—**Mallard Creek Community Park**, located at 3001 Johnston-Oehler Road. This brand new 300-acre park currently has four lighted softball fields and two soccer fields with more to come.

If you or someone in your family has a disability, you'll be pleased to know that the Mecklenburg County Park and Recreation Department offers equal access to all recreation programs for persons with special needs. If you are interested in one of the park's programs but need some assistance or modification, a trained volunteer from the **Marion Diehl Recreation Center** will be provided to assist with program inclusion. The Leisure Companion does not serve as a personal attendant, but for specialized needs, the support and encouragement provided by this trained volunteer may be the key to successful participation. For more information on the **Leisure Companion Service**, call 527-0237.

You can also find help for special needs when you join one of the following groups: the **YMCA**, **YWCA**, the **Jewish Community Center**, the new **Mecklenburg Aquatic Center**, churches, private health clubs and numerous neighborhood athletic associations surrounding Charlotte.

The city parks offer year-round activities, including summer programs centered around playgrounds, day camps and pools. You can find out about registering for team sports such as basketball and football by calling the Mecklenburg County Park and Recreation Department (336-2584), but you should also watch for signs in your neighborhood announcing sign-ups. Teams, divided into various age categories, play other teams in the city leagues. The Charlotte Chapter of **National Youth Sports Coaches Association Program** offers a six-hour video training program where volunteer coaches can gain valuable knowledge for coaching football, baseball, volleyball, hockey, and softball. Call 336-2584 to find out schedules.

The YMCA and YWCA both operate strong programs in Charlotte. In addition to its Main Branch on Park Road, the **YWCA** has several satellite sites, and the **YMCA** operates branches all over the area, including one in North Mecklenburg County and a summer camp on Lake Wylie. The YWCAs operate after-school and summer camp programs in addition to their children and adult classes that include: gymnastics, aquatics, aerobics, Yoga, martial arts with an emphasis on self-defense, tennis, dance classes from ballet to jazz. The YMCA also offers Community Education classes for English as a Second Language and a variety of bridge classes. Be sure to check out the excellent seminars that range from health and nutrition to financial planning. For a schedule, call (525-5770).

YWCA Day Care Centers

Alexander Street Center	372-6317
Belmont Center	372-6339
Piedmont Courts Center	333-6087
Uptown Center	375-9922

YMCA Locations

CAMP THUNDERBIRD
Lake Wylie, S.C. (803) 831-2121

CENTRAL BRANCH
400 E. Morehead St. 333-7771

CENTRAL BRANCH ABLE CENTER
400 E Morehead St. 335-7323

GEORGE SIMMONS FAMILY BRANCH
6824 Democracy Dr. 536-1714

HARRIS FAMILY BRANCH
5900 Quail Hollow Rd. 552-9622

JOHNSTON MEMORIAL
3025 N. Davidson St. 333-6206

LAKE NORMAN FAMILY BRANCH
21300 Davidson St., Cornelius 892-9622

MCCROREY FAMILY BRANCH
3801 Beatties Ford Rd. 394-2356

MATTHEWS/UNION COUNTY BRANCH
1433 W. John St., Matthews 845-9622

METROPOLITAN OFFICE
500 E. Morehead St. 339-0379

PROGRAM CENTER AND EAGLE ROCK DAY CAMP
Matthews 846-2477

SIMMONS BRANCH
6824 Democracy Dr. 536-1714

UPTOWN BRANCH
200 Two First Union Center 333-9622

UNIVERSITY CITY BRANCH
4701 Mallard Creek Rd. 547-9622

YWCA Locations

MAIN BRANCH
3420 Park Rd.   525-5770

SCATTERED SITES:

CEDARKNOLL
304 Green Needles Ct.   525-4258

GLADEDALE
5805 Old Providence Rd.   366-3413

LEAFCREST
6513 Leafcrest La.   552-9293

LIVE OAKS
6722 Oakengate La.   554-1907

MALLARD RIDGE
1428 Axminster Ct.   554-9191

SAVANNAH WOODS
3124 Leaside La.   376-0123

SUNRIDGE
4005 Sunridge La.   532-2244

Jewish Community Center

The **Jewish Community Center** in Shalom Park on Providence Road offers a full-range of services and activities that are open to all ages of the public, regardless of religious affiliation. The center has an aquatic program plus the following seven different day camps: K through 2 unit, third through fourth unit, a children's special needs group for the developmentally challenged, a boating camp, a horseback riding camp, a computer camp and a sports camp that specializes in certain sports. The center also has an arts center, cultural arts activities, senior adult program and other programs. For details, call 366-5007.

Mecklenburg Aquatic Center

The **Mecklenburg Aquatic Center** is the county's newest facility. It opened its doors to the public in April of 1991. Located on East Second Street in Uptown Charlotte, the Mecklenburg Aquatic Center (MAC) is a full-service swimming, diving and fitness center offering a wide variety of instructional, recreational and competitive aquatic programs. Call 336-DIVE for more information.

Not every park in the city and county is listed separately in this guide, except for the city recreation centers and county community centers. However, those parks that have a special attraction are highlighted. In addition, activities such as golf and tennis are itemized. Not included are spectator sports such as NASCAR racing, which are detailed in the chapters on "Attractions" and "Sports." For more information, contact the Mecklenburg County Park and Recreation Department, 700 North Tryon Street, 366-3854. To reserve ball fields and picnic shelters at city parks, call 366-4200. To reserve county facilities, call the individual park. Check *The Charlotte Observer* for the quarterly newsletter on park programs and schedules.

Recreation Centers

ALBEMARLE ROAD RECREATION CENTER
5027 N. Idlewild Rd.   567-1941

AMAY JAMES RECREATION CENTER
2425 Lester St.   336-3053

BOULEVARD HOMES RECREATION CENTER
1620 Brookvale St.   399-8166

CORDELIA SWIMMING POOL
2100 N. Davidson St.   336-2096

DOUBLE OAKS RECREATION CENTER
326 Woodward Ave.   336-2056

DOUBLE OAKS SWIMMING POOL
2600 Statesville Ave.   336-2653

EARLE VILLAGE RECREATION CENTER
610 E. 7th St.   336-2095

ENDERLY RECREATION CENTER
1220 Clay Ave.   393-7333

GREENVILLE RECREATION CENTER
1330 Spring St.   336-3367
Public Swimming Pool   336-2191

HAWTHORNE RECREATION CENTER
345 Hawthorn La.   336-2008

LATTA RECREATION CENTER
510 E. Park Ave.   336-2533

MARION DIEHL RECREATION CENTER
Special populations and senior citizens programs
2219 Tyvola Rd.   527-0237
IIndoor Swimming Pool   527-3175
TDD Equipped   527-6566

METHODIST HOME RECREATION CENTER
3200 Shamrock Dr.   568-3363

NAOMI DRENAN RECREATION CENTER
750 Beal St.   365-1265

REVOLUTION RECREATION CENTER
1201 Remount Rd.
Golf Course   336-3841
Swimming pool   336-2652

SUGAR CREEK RECREATION CENTER
943 W. Sugar Creek Rd.   596-0107

TUCKASEEGEE RECREATION CENTER
4820 Tuckaseegee Rd.   399-4492

WEST CHARLOTTE RECREATION CENTER
2400 Kendall Dr.   393-1560

YORK ROAD RENAISSANCE PARK
1536 W. Tyvola Rd.   357-3841
Tennis Courts   523-2862

City Parks

FREEDOM PARK
1900 East Blvd.   336-2663

This under-renovation park is scheduled to reopen December 1, 1994. It is one of Charlotte's most heavily used parks and has an old train that children love to explore, softball fields, several playgrounds, lighted tennis courts and paved walk ways. Activities are centered around the lake, which serves as the official residence of the local duck population. **Festival In The Park**, one of the park's most popular events is slated to return to a 4-day festival in September of 1995.

GRADY COLE CENTER
310 N. Kings Dr.   336-2462

The Grady Cole Center hosts a number of exciting events, plus antique and craft shows, political rallies and gospel sings. Adjacent is **Memorial Stadium**, the city's largest stadium and the home of the annual **Shrine Bowl**, which features the top high school football players from the two Carolinas.

HORNET'S NEST PARK
6301 Beatties Ford Rd.   399-4744

This 110-acre park boasts the area's only motorcross track and has hosted national tournaments. It also has softball, fishing, hiking, picnic shelters, a bicycle trail, a playground and tennis courts. A petting zoo featuring farm animals is open year-round except on Mondays.

MARSHALL PARK
Third and McDowell streets

Close to Uptown, this park is frequently used to kick off political events. A gushing 50-foot fountain and beautiful flowers, with the Charlotte skyline for a backdrop, make this an oasis in the city. A statue of Martin Luther King, Jr., is located in the park.

PARK ROAD PARK
5300 Closeburn Rd.   *552-7285*

This 124-acre park has a 12-acre fishing lake, plus ball fields, lighted tennis courts, a basketball court, playground, picnic shelters and nature trails. Located in Southeast Charlotte, the park is heavily used.

REEDY CREEK PARK
2900 Rocky River Rd.   *598-1803*

This park near Hickory Grove is unique because 85 percent of its 699 acres is natural and includes three lakes. It offers a new **Environmental Education Center**, nature trail studies, ball fields, picnic areas, a playground and a short walking path.

ST. MARY'S CHAPEL
Corner of King's Dr. and Fourth St. 336-4200

Near Uptown, this tiny park was chosen to honor those who lost their lives in Viet Nam. The memorial stands near the chapel. The chapel is the only remaining structure on the original site of Thompson Orphanage, which makes it an appealing setting for weddings and concerts.

VETRAN'S PARK
2136 Central Ave.

Built to honor Lt. Budd Harris Andrews who crashed his airplane in 1945 to avoid hitting a Charlotte neighborhood, the park serves the Plaza-Midwood area. It has ball fields, lighted tennis courts, a playground and an indoor shelter.

Community Centers

DAVID B. WAYMER RECREATION COMPLEX
14200 Holbrook Rd.
Huntersville, N.C.   *875-1549*

This program center, for young and old alike, features a gymnasium/weight room, activity rooms, basketball and indoor soccer, playground equipment, picnic tables and a softball field. A fun community festival is held here annually on the first Saturday in June.

HOLBROOK FLYING FIELD & PARK
15401 Holbrook Rd.
Huntersville, N.C.   *875-1549*

The Holbrook landfill is being put to good use as an aeromodeler flying field. There are three circle areas and a 600-foot grass runway for remote control model plane flying.

County Parks

COULWOOD DISTRICT PARK
Coulwood Park Rd.   *875-1391*

Located next to Coulwood Junior High School, this 27-acre park

The Vietnam Veterans Wall stands in the tiny park near St. Mary's Chapel.

includes an amphitheater, four lighted tennis courts, 2 softball fields, picnic shelter and concession stand. The 18-hole Sunset Hills Public Golf Course is also located here at 800 Radio Rd., 399-0980.

HARRISBURG ROAD PARK/ CHARLES MYERS GOLF COURSE

7817 Harrisburg Rd.   *536-1692*

Golf greens have replaced portions of the Harrisburg Road Landfill at this 10-year-old park. Plans are to expand the nine hole course to 18 holes by 1994. The park also features a playground and picnic shelter.

IDLEWILD ROAD PARK

10512 Idlewild Rd.   *568-4044*

This newly expanded 100-acre park serves residents in the Mint Hill/Matthews area. It offers a children's playground, softball field, and picnic shelters and sites.

JETTON PARK

Jetton Rd.
Outside Cornelius, off N.C. 73   *875-1391*

This new 106-acre park, already known as our premier park, abounds with trees and green meadows featuring Lake Norman as its centerpiece. The park is on a peninsula, with inviting coves on two sides and a broad stretch of water at its toe. A loop road winds through the oblong-shaped park, and there are over two miles of asphalt bike paths, plus another mile of gravel trails that dip in and out of the shoreline. Tennis courts are scattered among gazebos and picnic tables and canoes are available for rental. No swimming is allowed, and the park

has no boat launching ramps. The entry fee is $2 for county residents; $4 nonresidents on weekends from Easter through October.

LATTA PLANTATION PARK

5225 Sample Rd.
Huntersville   *875-1391*

This 760-acre nature preserve on Mountain Island Lake is unique. Centered around the restored 1800's river plantation home of James Latta, the park has an Audubon Sanctuary, the Carolina Raptor Center where injured wildlife is cared for, a canoe access area, Visitor Center and the only publicly owned Equestrian Center in the area. The latter features two horse arenas, 80 permanent stalls, and seven miles of bridle trails. Individuals may use the trails or school in the Equestrian Center free of charge. The park sponsors special events such as blackberry picking, photo safaris, night fishing, sunset canoeing, summer hayrides, and hunter safety courses. Annual special events include a triathalon held in June and Spooktacular Halloweek in October. At the new boat rental harbor, canoes and john boats are available for a small fee.

MCALPINE CREEK PARK

8711 Old Monroe Rd.   *568-4044*

The first developed greenway in the county's system, this 360-acre park stretches from Independence Boulevard to Sardis Road along McAlpine Creek. It is a wildlife sanctuary with nature trails. Park users enjoy several miles of bike paths and cross-country trails, soccer fields, picnic areas and a lake, and there

Photo by Di Ann Hasslock, CPCC © 1993.

Many parks in the Charlotte/Mecklenburg system
feature wildlife sanctuaries and nature trails.

are special events such as creek walks and fishing clinics.

McDowell Park and Nature Preserve
15222 York Rd.   588-5224

The county's largest park encompasses 800 acres on Lake Wylie. It offers year-round camping, hiking, fishing, picnicking and other activities. You can launch your boat free of charge or rent a paddleboat or canoe during the summer months. There are four miles of nature trails and a nature center with hands-on exhibits. Special programs include campfire programs and ghost stories, wildlife programs, stargazing and creek stompin'. From April through September on weekends and holidays, county residents are charged a $2 vehicle entry fee; non-county residents, $4.

North Mecklenburg Park
16131 Old Statesville Rd.
Huntersville   875-1549

Facilities at this 88-acre park in North Mecklenburg include ball fields for soccer, softball and baseball, as well as a picnic shelter and concession stand.

Ramsey Creek Park
18441 Nantz Rd.
Huntersville, N.C.   892-7852

If you don't own a place on Lake Norman—a popular spot for all types of boating—this 46-acre park is the place to launch your boat or enjoy a picnic. The park also offers a fishing pier, picnic tables, nature trails and a play area for small children. Sometimes there are special programs on ghost stories or live performances by musicians and jug-

glers. Sailboarding is taught at the park, and sailing regattas are popular.

Recreation, Arts & Crafts

Neighborhood Arts Program

This popular program is an ongoing (September through March), cooperative arts education and enrichment program involving the Community School of The Arts and Mecklenburg County Park & Recreation Department. These free classes are offered to all ages with a focus on serving those individuals who otherwise might not have the chance to discover their unique artistic talent or to work alongside a professional artist. The schedule includes classes from the areas of music, dance, drama, visual and media arts.

During the summer, another arts and crafts program is held on each Saturday from 10 AM to 12 PM. Children can go to their neighborhood park or to any of the participating parks for an exciting and fun-filled discovery. The **Community School of the Arts**, the **Mint Museum, Discovery Place, International House**, the **Public Library, Spirit Square, Theatre in the Park** and **Museum of the New South** all rotate to make each Saturday morning experience different. The child may be painting with water colors, guided by an instructor from the Mint Museum, one week and finding out how bubbles form from a Discovery Place teacher the next. Children can see Shakespeare performed live, or participate in various musical interests that may lead them to sign up for the Community School of the Arts enrichment classes. Classes are offered at the following 11 sites: Yorkmont Park in the southwest district; Hoskins Park in the northwest district; Allen Hill Park in the northeast district; Park Road Park in the south district; Idlewild and Kilborne alternate Saturday mornings in the east district; Archdale Park in the southeast district; L.C. Coleman Park and Jimmy Carter Park alternate with Christ the King Episcopal Church and Morgan Park to round out the central district parks.

At most of the recreation centers, students may choose a variety of courses: ceramics, sculpturing, woodcarving, drawing and painting, enameling, sewing and other crafts. For details, call the Parks and Recreation (336-2884).

Parks and Recreation programs aren't the only game in town when it comes to arts and crafts. **Spirit Square** (372-9664) has a generous offering of courses each quarter, and **Community School of the Arts** (377-4187), which specializes in music, has art classes other than the classes offered through the Neighborhood Arts Program. The county's Agricultural Extension Office sponsors classes through the **4-H Club** program (336-2082) and the **Home Economics** clubs (336-2692). You might also check **Central Piedmont Community Col-**

lege (342-6956), the **Jewish Community Center** (366-5007). and Charlotte/Mecklenburg Schools' **Summer Enrichment Programs** (343-5567) for arts and crafts classes.

Sports

BASKETBALL

Budding Atlantic Coast Conference athletes can get a headstart at any of the many basketball programs available through the city recreation centers, neighborhood athletic associations, **YMCA** programs or **Salvation Army Boys Clubs**. Sign-ups for organized **City League** play for youths, ages 7 to 17, begin in October at participating recreation centers. Team registration is held during October and November, with practice and exhibition games in December and regular season games in January. Qualifying teams participate in city-wide, regional and state tournaments. For more information, call 336-2884.

Bryan Adrian conducts annual **basketball camps** for young people at UNCC. Call 372-3236 for details. The YMCA sponsors a basketball league for players 18 and older, and the city offers organized league play for adult men and women as well as industrial teams. Registration for summer games (June through August) is held in May; for winter games

To find out about registering for team sports such as basketball and football, call the Mecklenburg County Park and Recreation Department at 336-2584.

Insiders' Tip

(December through April), in October. Call 336-2884.

BASEBALL

You can play baseball through a number of different avenues. Neighborhood athletic groups, Charlotte Parks and Recreation and the YMCAs have programs for all ages. The city offers organized league play for youths, ages 5 through 18. Participants are placed in compatible age divisions to provide proper training and skill development through organized practices and games. T-Ball and Coach Pitch programs are geared to children, ages 5 to 8, while baseball and girls' softball programs offer organized league play. For more information, call 336-2884. For county information call 875-9503.

BOATING

Boating is very popular in Charlotte-Mecklenburg because of the easy access to Lake Norman, Mountain Island Lake and Lake Wylie. Lake Norman has about 530 miles of shoreline; Lake Wylie, 325 miles. Residents enjoy sailing, water skiing, fishing and other water-associated activities, including boat races and sailing regattas. To find out where and when, check with one of the numerous marinas surrounding both lakes.

Most of the marinas provide the full range of services for boat owners including storage, supplies and repairs. At Lake Norman, you might check out **Holiday Harbor Marina** (892-0561) or **Outrigger Harbor** (892-8911). At Lake Wylie, check out **Lake Club Marina** (331-

Because of the easy access to area lakes, Charlotte/Mecklenburg residents enjoy sailing, water skiing, fishing and other water-associated activities, including boat races and sailing regattas.

9027) or **Outrigger Harbor** (892-8911). Also at Lake Wylie, try **Carolina Crossing Marina** at the Buster Boyd Bridge (588-5463). **Long Cove Marina & Yacht Club** (588-1467) and **Tega Cay Marina** (543-3328) are also popular choices at Lake Wylie.

Public boat ramps are available at McDowell Park Nature Preserve and Ramsey Creek Park.

BOWLING

Bowlers will find plenty of competition at Brunswick Lanes' two locations on East Independence Boulevard and Freedom Drive, Centennial Lanes near Park Road Shopping Center, University Lanes, and George Pappas Park Lanes. If you want to join a league, check with one of the above lanes which are listed in the Yellow Pages.

CAMPING

You can't pitch a tent just anywhere in Charlotte/Mecklenburg, but it's perfectly fine to do so at **McDowell Park and Nature Reserve**. Camping is also available at **Paramount's Carowinds, Duke Power State Park** on Lake Norman, **Morrow Mountain State Park** near Albemarle, and **Kings Mountain State Park** in South Carolina. A few of the marinas around Lake Wylie and Lake Norman also offer camping sites.

CRICKET

Cricket began in England over 300 years ago and eventually became the country's national sport. In American terms, cricket is most akin to baseball in that there are two teams, a bat, a ball, fielders, runs and outs—but that's where the similarity ends. The **Charlotte Cricket Club** is a great venue for locals to witness and learn the game first hand. The Charlotte Cricket Club (841-2555) was formed in 1990 by 2 transplanted gentleman—one from England, Michael Teden, and one from South Africa, Richard Davies—with a view to introducing a "new" sport to Charlotte. Like-minded enthusiasts provided the club with a nucleus of player-members, and a successful inaugural season, both on and off the field, was enjoyed by all. Matches are played against teams from surrounding cities and districts (there are over 360 registered cricket clubs in the United States). The season culminates in a one-day tournament match against a touring cricket club from either Philadelphia, Bermuda or New York. This finale is hosted as a spectacle to introduce the game to the local populace.

Cricket is best enjoyed as a family-day-out-in-the- sun affair, so pack a picnic and head out for either Olde Providence or the Charlotte Polo Club field.

The club is always looking for interested members, both of the playing and of the social variety. The games are usually played on Saturday or Sunday afternoons, depending on everyone's schedule. Admission to regular and tournament events is free.

CYCLING

The Charlotte area is rich in cycling opportunities for riders of all abilities. The gently rolling countryside offers pleasant routes for the

Photo courtesy N.C. Travel and Tourism Division.

Groups of colorfully clad cyclists are a common sight along Charlotte's back roads.

recreational road rider, while occasional longer climbs challenge the fitter cyclists. Groups of colorfully clad riders are a common sight along the back roads in the Waxhaw, Monroe and Huntersville areas on weekends. The local cycling club, the **Tarheel Cyclists** (523-6209) publishes a monthly newsletter with schedules of weekly rides held in Mecklenburg and surrounding counties. Area bike shops are also a gold mine of information. A permanent bike route, designated by oval signs with a bike symbol, makes a 10-mile loop between Southeast Charlotte and Uptown. Bike racks are stationed at most public buildings, and bike lockers are located beside Charlotte Transit shelters along Central Avenue. There is also a great biking opportunity at **McAlpine Creek Park** on a pit gravel trail.

Off-road riders new to the area will be pleasantly surprised to learn that trail riding is available within a short distance from Charlotte. **Cane Creek Park**, near Waxhaw, has many miles of highly prized "single track" trails ranging from fairly easy for the new rider, to fairly challenging for the more adventurous souls. Many area bicycle shops know of other off-road areas, and some, such as **Soft Spokin'** in Monroe, sponsor regular ATB rides. Other good bets are **Bicycles East** (535-3242) or **Bicycle Sport** (335-0333), which advise cyclists to get the Tarheel Cyclists map that highlights 16 different cycling areas throughout the area.

The annual **Moonride**, held in late August each year, is the city's premier cycling event and brings together cyclists of all persuasions for a popular midnight ride in downtown and suburban Charlotte. Sponsored by the *Charlotte Observer*, the ride attracts over 2500 riders. The races preceding the Moonride provide an exciting pageant of speed and color, and bring the excitement of criterium racing to downtown.

Other popular events include September's MS 150 ride to the beach, the **Catawba Valley Cyclists' Lake Norman Ride** in July, and the **Lung Association's Triathalon**. With so many activities for the cyclist, it's no wonder that bicycling is booming in Metrolina!

DAY CAMPS

Mecklenburg County Park and Recreation offers extensive day camps and playground programs during the summer. Day camps with structured activities are available at 16 recreation centers including **Recreation On The Move**, which is a mobile recreational unit, fully-staffed and equipped to provide supervised experiences in athletics, arts and crafts, music, dance and special events. The cost varies, depending on the program. Playground programs for which there is no charge are given at seven sites and feature planned activities as well as free time. A number of city-wide special events, such as **Junior Tennis Tournament**, are planned each summer at Renaissance Park. Mecklenburg County Park and Recreation holds one-week day camps at five different sites, featuring special programs, field trips, games, athletics and arts and crafts.

The David B. Waymer Complex offers a free playground program.

The Harris YMCA offers coed day camps at Queens College and on-site. The YWCA on Park Road holds an annual **Kamp-a-Long** for girls and boys. **Camp Arrowhead** at the Simmons YMCA is another choice. One of the finest coed boarding camps in the Southeast is YMCA-affiliated **Camp Thunderbird** on Lake Wylie, where kids learn to water ski, sail, swim and participate in competitive sports and other activities. (The camp is also a center for the YMCA's extensive **Y-Indian Guide program**.)

Most YMCA camps offer counselor-in-training programs for older young people. Since the YMCA camps are very popular, it's a good idea to register early. Some scholarships are available. The Jewish Community Center's day camp is **Camp Maccabee**, and a number of day care centers and learning/tutoring centers in the Charlotte area also offer summer programs.

FISHING

There are plenty of lakes and streams for throwing in your hook in the Charlotte/Mecklenburg area. If you use live bait, you can fish for free in your home county; lures require a $5.00 state license, available at any local bait and tackle shop. A number of parks—**Latta Plantation, Hornet's Nest, Park Road, McAlpine, McDowell, Ramsey Creek, Freedom** and **Pineville Park** in Pineville—offer excellent fishing (catfish, bream, bass and crappie). The county park fishing fee is $1 per day.

FITNESS

Beautiful bodies are in style, so you won't be hard-pressed to find a commercial or nonprofit organization that can help you attain one. Check the newspapers for special discounts at health centers, but shop before you sign on the dotted line. The **YMCA** and **YWCA** offer extensive exercise programs, including stroke clinics and special activities for cardiac patients. **CPCC** holds fitness classes in a number of locations around the city, and you'll also find classes at **Queens College**. The **Jewish Community Center** has exercise classes for all age groups, including a cardiac rehabilitation program.

FLYING

Want to fly? Several schools on the outskirts of the city will teach you the basics of how to fly an air-plane as well as provide the proper training for a private, instrument, commercial, or instructor license. (There's also a gliding school at Chester, S.C.) To get a private airline pilot's license, you must have at least 40 hours of instruction and be 17 years of age (you can start training and even do your solo at age 16). The cost of getting a private pilot's license in the area is about $2,500.

FOOTBALL

Even the pee wee set starts training early for football, and with the coming of the NFL Panthers, the sport can only get more popular. Many neighborhood athletic associations have programs. Late starters can get good experience through the Charlotte/Mecklenburg junior and senior high schools or through private school programs.

There are plenty of lakes and streams for throwing in your hook in the Charlotte/Mecklenburg area.

Photo courtesy N.C. Travel and Tourism Division.

GOLF

There are several very fine public golf courses in the area. Since Charlotte is located in the Golf State, there's no shortage of courses here, but you have to be a member or know a member to play at any of the private country clubs in town. You can play 36 holes at Carmel Country Club and Raintree Country Clubs; 18-hole private courses are Carolina Golf Club, a Donald Ross course built in the 1920s, Cedarwood Golf Club, Charlotte Country Club, Cramer Mountain Country Club, Quail Hollow Country Club, Myers Park Country Club, Pine Island Country Club, River Hills Golf Club, River Run, The Penninsula Club, Providence Country Club, St. Andrews at Piper Glen and Tega Cay.

For suggestions on where to play, ask some of your golfing buddies or check with the manager of a golf shop that is not affiliated with a club. And don't forget, you're only two hours away from Pinehurst and Southern Pines in the Sandhills, four hours away from the beautiful courses near Sunset Beach to the east, and four hours away to the 85 plus golf courses in Myrtle Beach's Grand Strand area. For in-depth information, see this Guide's chapter on **Golf In The Carolinas**.

GYMNASTICS

The city has several gymnastic schools. **Clemmer's** (523-5940) is the oldest, having been in business since 1935. A number of dance studios also teach gymnastics. The **YWCA** on Park Road and the **Harris YMCA** also offer instruction, and

Mecklenburg County Park and Recreation Department has classes, gym meets and competitions.

ICE HOCKEY

The **Charlotte Youth Hockey League** is open to boys and girls, ages 4 through 18. Players may opt for the House League (at-home games only) or for the Travel League, which plays opposing teams in the Southern Hockey League and the Mid-Atlantic League. The cost to play in the House League for the 1994-95 season is $100 per player for youngsters 9 and under and $175 for ages 10 and up. The fee includes ice time and a jersey; players must provide their own equipment. The season runs from early to mid September through late March with a 15-20 game schedule. The Travel League involves additional expenses. For information contact League President Jim Taylor at 536-5600. Adult hockey teams are also available. If you're interested contact **Ice Capades Chalet** at Eastland Mall, 568-0772.

HORSEBACK RIDING

Latta Equestrian Center is located in historic Latta Plantation Park in Northern Mecklenburg County (5225 Sample Rd. in Huntersville, (875-0808). First built by the County Park and Recreation Department as a horse show facility, Latta Equestrian Center has 194 stalls, 2 show rings, 2 practice rings and 10 miles of scenic trails, all available to the public for shows or use with privately owned horses. Horses are available at the center for guided trail rides (by reservation) and for group or private lessons. Latta Equestrian Center offers "Pig Pickin's" and hay rides for private parties, along with horse shows, Hunter Paces and other activities that are open to the public.

There are several good places to board your horse or take horseback riding lessons. Check **Providence Equestrian Center** in Waxhaw (843-5215), **Branch Hill Farm** (596-1910), where horses can be boarded only, **Cedarhill Farm** (843-5944) in Waxhaw or **Bill Medlin Stables** on Fairview Rd. (545-0782).

If you like hunting with the hounds, you might check out the **Mecklenburg Hounds Hunt Club**, which was established in 1956. Call Ron Brown at 764-7479 for information.

JOGGING, RUNNING, WALKING

Charlotte's mild climate makes it ideal for jogging, running, walking—even skipping—out of doors most of the year. You'll find trails and tracks in city and county parks, as well as at public junior and senior high schools. Many of the commercial health clubs and Y's have indoor tracks that become quite appealing during 20-degree or 100-degree days. Local runners train all year long for *The Charlotte Observer* **Marathon**, a January event that attracts participants from all over the United States. (You can buy a T-shirt or sweat shirt at the shop on the first floor of the Knight Publishing Building on South Tryon Street, whether you're a marathon runner or just a spectator.)

In late November, the annual **SouthPark Turkey Trot** takes place.

A Thanksgiving Day tradition, the 8K road race benefits local charities. Call the Hyatt Charlotte at SouthPark (554-1234 extension 2002) for more details. Most public schools and many private ones, offer the sport of Track to students. **McAlpine Creek Park** offers a 2-mile bike-jogging path and a 5-K Cross Country running course.

KARATE

There are more than two yellow pages in the telephone book listing schools in Charlotte that teach karate, martial arts and self defense. They can be found in almost every section of this area. Instruction is also available at some of the YMCAs. Unless you already know the specific sort of instruction you want, check at several of the studios and ask questions before you sign up. Many studios will let you observe a class.

ORIENTEERING

Map and compass classes are available through the **Carolina Orienteering Klubb**, which meets once a month from October through April at various locations, including McDowell Park, Latta Plantation Park, Crowder's Mountain State Park, and Kings Mountain National Park. For more information, call 332-1199.

PERFORMING ARTS

If you want to get in on the act—whether it's a dance act or theater production or concert—the city abounds with opportunities. **Spirit Square** has the longest list of offerings for children and adults and will

Photo by John Cress.

City and county parks are favorite places for walking, jogging or running.

be happy to put you on its mailing list to receive a class schedule each quarter. Just call 372-9664. **Community School of the Arts** (377-4187) offers a variety of musical instruction, plus classes in drama, dance and art. **Mecklenburg County Park and Recreation Department** is another option.

The **Children's Theatre** (376-5745) teaches drama, puppetry and related courses to children. Stage struck adults can find opportunities for acting at local theaters such as **Theatre Charlotte** (376-3777), **CPCC Summer Theatre** (342-6618), and **Charlotte Repertory Theatre** (375-4796).

If you want to learn tap, ballet, or jazz, check out the "Dance" section of this book. The Mecklenburg County Park and Recreation Department and the YWCA are other options for classes. (See the Guide's **ARTS** chapter for more ideas on performing arts opportunities.)

POLO

Located off Tom Short Rd., Southeast of Charlotte, is a unique opportunity for a day of family-oriented fun and festivities. The **Charlotte Polo Club** takes to the field against teams throughout the Carolinas for some "divot-stomping" excitement. The 9-week spring season runs from May through June, with the 10-week fall season running from September through November. Two matches are played each Sunday with the gates to **Cato Farms** opening at noon, allowing fans to picnic and tailgate before the 3 PM main event. The polo matches have proven to be a favored pastime for Charlotteans in the spring and fall, with each match attracting several thousand fans. Call 846-1010 for more information.

SKATING

Charlotte's ice rink is the **Ice Capades Chalet** located in Eastland Mall. Instruction is available—just call 568-0772. There are several roller skating rinks: **Kate's** on Central Avenue and on Old Pineville Road, **Roll-a-Round** on Delta Road, and **Skate Palace** on South Boulevard.

SKYDIVING

Charlotte Skydivers perform aerial tricks at the airport in Chester, S.C. Member John Ainsworth performs with the **Prism Skydiving Team**, national champions. For details on this daring sport, call **Skydive Carolina** at (803) 331-5131.

SOCCER

Although Charlotte lost its professional outdoor soccer team several years ago, the sport has remained extremely popular, and the new indoor soccer team will bolster the interest. A number of athletic associations offer soccer, and **Bryan Adrian** (372-3236) leads soccer camps. Programs are also available through **Mecklenburg County Park and Recreation Department** and the **YMCA**s. The city offers organized league play for youths, ages 7 to 18. The fall program is played outdoors and is geared to recreational teams in the 7 to 15 age group. The winter program is played indoors for recre-

ational and selected teams in the 7 through 18 age group. Leagues have been organized through recreation centers and neighborhood associations. Sign-ups are usually held at participating recreation centers. For details, call 336-2464. Adult indoor soccer is available at the **David B. Waymer Complex** in Huntersville (875-1549). Outdoor soccer is played at **McAlpine Creek** (568-4044).

SOFTBALL

Male and female players of all ages enjoy this sport, whether it's played in a sandlot or on a baseball diamond. Programs are offered by athletic associations, Mecklenburg County Park and Recreation Department, and various churches. The city offers organized league play for adult men and women through industrial and co-recreational teams. Registration for the spring/summer program is in January and February, with league play occurring from mid-April through early August. Registration for the fall program is during July and August, with games scheduled from early September through November. For more information, call 336-2584. The county has an Adult Men's Softball League at the **David B. Waymer Center** in Huntersville (875-1549) and at various county parks (336-3854).

SPECIAL POPULATIONS PROGRAMS

Mecklenburg County Park and Recreation Department offers recreational programs for all Mecklenburg citizens, but places a special emphasis on programs for the physically, mentally and emotionally challenged at the **Marion**

Diehl Recreation Center (527-0237). The center, among the few of its type in the nation and the only fully accessible center and playground for the developmentally challenged in the state, has a therapeutic playground and wheelchair fitness course. The center operates **Camp Spirit** during summer days.

SWIMMING

Mecklenburg County Park and Recreation Department operates five public pools, including an indoor facility at the **Marion Diehl Center**. It is also worth noting that the center's swimming pool and pool room's temperature is kept several degrees warmer than at other pools in order to aid working out sore muscles. Free swimming lessons are given to youth and adults at all pool sites in June; in addition, there is a city-wide two-week session, cosponsored by the American Red Cross, at **Revolution Pool**. The **YMCAs** and **YWCAs** all have pools and swimming classes year round, including life saving classes. The **Jewish Community Center** offers a full aquatic program.

The new **Mecklenburg Aquatic Center** (MAC) has brought swimming in Charlotte out of the deep. MAC is upfitted with an eight-lane, 50-meter competitive pool and a state-of-the-art timing system. Diving enthusiasts have access to two three-meter diving boards and two one-meter boards. The facility also offers a 25-yard hydra-therapy pool, a 16-foot in-ground spa, an exercise/fitness room, sunning deck, and meeting rooms...all for minimal daily or annual fees.

TENNIS

Tennis took Charlotte by storm a decade ago, and it's still going strong. Many of the city and county parks have excellent courts, and they're free! Those at country clubs and private swim-tennis clubs are yours for a membership fee. **Olde Providence Racquet Club** (366-9817) is the best known racquet club in town; another is **Charlotte Tennis Club** (554-7777). Most tennis clubs, including the Y's, belong to leagues.

VOLLEYBALL

This team sport is one of the hottest activities in town, particularly with singles. You can play at several locations including **Myers Park United Methodist Church**, the **Jewish Community Center** and **St. John's Baptist Church**. **Mecklenburg County Park and Recreation Department** has a league based on various ability levels. Leagues are divided into high, moderate and novice levels for team competition. There are three seasonal leagues—spring, fall, and winter. The winter program is for co-recreational teams only. To find out more about this exciting activity, call Mecklenburg County Park and Recreation Department at 336-2584.

Other not so well-known sporting activities exist in and around Charlotte as well. **Scuba Diving** and **Lacrosse** both have clubs in the area. For information on these and other "off the beaten path" recreational opportunities, you might try either *The Charlotte Observer* sports department or your local YMCA.

Photo by Michele Able, CPCC © 1994.

The beautiful Morrison Regional Library serves the Southern Mecklenburg Country area.

Inside

Professional and Miscellaneous Services

Finding service providers can be a major headache when you move. A referral from a trusted friend or neighbor is always the best route so try that first. The handy abbreviated directory that follows can save time and frustration, but it is not intended as a replacement for the Yellow Pages. Listings are arranged alphabetically except for Emergencies, which come first.

Emergencies

Ambulance, Fire, Police	911
Ambulance, Fire, Police TDD	334-3323
Drug Emergency (Open House)	332-9001
Emergency Mental Health Services	358-2800
Environmental Emergency	(800) 424-8802
N.C. Highway Patrol Office	547-0042
Poison Control Center	379-5827
Rape Crisis	375-9900
ReachLine, (Suicide Counseling)	333-6121

Accounting

McGladrey & Pullen	333-9003
Smith, Black & Co.	377-7631
Tinsley & Terry	364-8800

Alcohol/Drug Abuse Assistance

Alcoholics Anonymous	332-4387
Drug Education Center	375-3784
Open House	332-9001
Randolph Clinic	376-2431
Seventh Street Detoxification Center	336-3067

Adoption

Adoption Information Exchange/ Support Group	532-6827
Adoption Search Consultants	537-5919
Agape of N.C., Inc.	536-1743
Catholic Social Services	333-9954
Children's Home Society of N.C..	334-2854
Golden Cradle	1-800-327-2229
Lutheran Family Services	554-5862 or 342-9785
Department of Social Services	336-3150

Agriculture

Agricultural Extension Service	336-2561

Airlines

American	1-800-433-7300
Delta	372-3000

Lufthansa	1-800-645-3880
TWA	343-0366
United	1-800-241-6522
USAir	376-0235

Airport

Airport Manager	359-4000
Paging Service	359-4013

Animal Care

Animal Control	336-3786
Emergency Veterinary Clinic	376-9622
Park Cedar Animal Emergency/	
Urgent Care Center	541-3022
Pet Licenses	336-3786
Sharon Lakes Animal Hospital	552-0647
Spay-Neuter Clinic	33-4130
University Animal Clinic	455-5907

Arts and Culture

Arts & Science Council	372-9667
Spirit Square	376-8883

Auto Rental

Agency	537-7272
Alamo	392-8020
Avis	359-4586
Enterprise	553-8744
General	392-5593
Hertz	359-0114
Triangle	527-1900

Auto Repair

Independence Automotive	535-3830
Norris Auto Service, Inc.	376-2779

Blood Bank

American Red Cross	376-1661

Bus

Charlotte Transit	336-3366
Greyhound/Trailways	527-9393

Business

CPCC International Business Ctr.	342-543
CPCC Small Business Center	342-6900
Charlotte Chamber of Commerce	378-1300

Children's Services

Big Brothers/Big Sisters	377-3963
Child Care Resources	376-6697
Children's Law Center	331-9474
Council for Children	372-7961
Gatling Juvenile Diagnostic Ctr.	875-2922
Youth Services Bureau	336-2926

Community Relations and Services

Carolina Community Project	372-0675
Charlotte Area Fund	372-3010
Charlotte/Mecklenburg Community	
Relations Committee	336-2424

Consumer Services

Better Business Bureau	332-7151
Consumer Credit	
Counseling Service	332-4191

Crisis Intervention

American Red Cross	376-1661
Crisis Assistance Ministry	371-3000
The Salvation Army	332-1171
Travelers Aid Society	334-7288
Victim Assistance Program	336-2190

Driver's License

Driver's License	527-2562
	392-3266 or 547-5787

Employment

Charlotte/Mecklenburg Urban League	376-9834
Employment Security Comm.	342-6131

Family Services

A.D.A.M. (Support Group for Abusive Men)	332-8619
Catholic Social Services	333-9954
Christmas Bureau	372-7170
Family Support Center	376-7180
Planned Parenthood	377-0841
	or 536-7233
The Relatives-Youth Crisis Center	366-0602
To Life	332-5433
United Family Services	332-9034

Funeral Homes

Alexander Funeral Home	333-1167
Hankins and Whittington and Williams-Dearborn	333-6116
Harry and Bryant	332-7133
McEwen Funeral Service	334-6421
Wilson Funeral Service	568-2106

Handicapped Services

Goodwill Industries	372-3434
Handicapped Organized Women	376-4735
Programs for Accessible Living	375-3977

Historic Properties

Charlotte-Mecklenburg Historic Properties Commission	376-9115

Home Mortgages

CTX Mortgage	556-1300
The Huntington Mortgage Co.	365-2770

Hospitals

Amethyst	554-8373
Carolinas Medical Center	355-2000
Carolinas Medical Center's Ctr. for Mental Health	358-2700
Charlotte Inst. of Rehabilitation	355-4300
Charter Pines Hospital	365-5368
CPC Cedar Spring Hospital	541-6676
Mercy Hospital	379-5000
Mercy Hospital South	543-2000
Orthopaedic Hospital-Charlotte	375-6792
Presbyterian Hospital	384-4000
Presbyterian Specialty Hospital	384-6000
University Hospital and Medical Park	548-6000

Information

CCVB Visitor Information Center	371-8700
Census Bureau	371-6144
City-County Action Line	336-2040
United Way Information & Referral Service	372-7170

Insurance

H. B. Cantrell	552-1411
Edwards Church & Muse, Inc.	342-2341
Klenz-Mardirosian Agency	542-6427
Harry F. Lapham, Jr. Insurance	553-8888

Legal Assistance

Accident & Injury Referral Service	1-800-682-5909
Children's Law Center	331-9474
Ralph H. Daughtry, PA	527-7734
Lawyer Referral Service	375-0120
Legal Services for the Elderly	334-0400
Legal Services of Southern Piedmont	376-1608
North Carolina Lawyer Referral Service	1-800-992-4500
Weinstein & Sturges, P.A.	372-4800
Wishart, Norris, Henninger & Pittman, P.A.	364-0010

Library

Main Library	336-2725
Belmont Center	336-2470
Carmel	542-0401
Cornelius	892-8581
Coulwood	394-7820
Davidson	892-8557
Hickory Grove	563-9418
Huntersville	875-2412
Independence	568-3151
Matthews	847-6691
Mint Hill	545-3932
Morrison Regional	336-2109
Myers Park	336-2011
North	336-2882
Plaza-Midwood	336-2982
Scaleybark	529-0632
Tryon Mall	336-2469
West	336-2721
West Blvd.	373-1050

Limousine Service

A Magic Nite	541-5231
Mike's Limousines	532-6739
Rose Limousine Ltd.	522-8258

Newcomers Organizations

New Neighbors League	541-0402
Welcome Wagon International	563-4499

Recycling

General Recycling Information	336-6087
North Mecklenburg Mulch/Compost Facility	875-1563
North Mecklenburg Recycling Center	875-3707
Harrisburg Road Recycling Center	568-1588
University City Resource Recovery Facility	549-9738
Recycling Center	358-9875

Telephone Answering Service

Answering Charlotte	334-8666
Southeastern Answering Service	372-2768
TAS	523-6515
Voice Track	525-9796

Teen Services

Open House	332-9001
The Relatives Emergency Shelter & Crisis Counseling	377-0602
Toughlove	366-8712

Time/Temperature

Time/Temperature	375-6711

Train

Amtrak	376-4416 or 1-800-872-7245

Travel Agencies

Away We Go Travel	547-1454
LTA Travel Services	332-4378
Professional Travel	542-7513

Veterans Services

Veterans Service Office	336-2102
Vet Center	333-6107

Volunteer Organizations

Retired Senior Volunteer Program	372-7170
Volunteer Center	372-7170

Voter Registration

Elections Office	336-2133

Weather

Weather   359-8466

Western Union

Office   523-2008
Mailgram, Telegram
  or Cablegram   1-800-325-6000
Credit Card Money Transfers   1-800-225-5227

Women's Services

Crisis Pregnancy Center	372-5981
Hunter House	333-6233
Rape Crisis Center	375-9900
Shelter for Battered Women	332-2513
Woman Reach	334-3614
Women's Commission	336-3210

Alexander Michaels is one of Fourth Ward's favorite spots for a drink after work or a great dinner served in a friendly neighborhood atmosphere.

Inside
Restaurants

Doesn't anyone stay home and cook anymore? Not much. Not since on their way home from work, they can pick up dinner for less than it would cost to take the whole family out to eat. For years we've been taking home Chinese and Barbecue, but now the variety is diversifying. Even vegetarians get a break from that endless grind of chopping vegetables. **That Place Deli & Grill** on South Boulevard, **Pasta & Provisions** on Providence and at the Arboretum, **Rosemary's** in Shops on the Park, **The Takeaway Cafe** on Monroe, **Red Rocks Deli & Bakery** in the Strawberry Hill Shopping Center, the **Roasted Chicken** on Montford Drive, **Thai Cuisine Restaurant** on Central Avenue and a lot more like them, are a leg up on yesteryears' fast food, drive-by restaurants. Now dinner can be more nutritious and take no time to pick up if you call ahead. Baby back ribs, a dozen or more different types of fresh pastas with homemade sauces (ready to pop into the microwave), fresh homemade sausages, chicken

to die for, roasted vegetables, spicy Thai wonders and fresh baked bread are all part of the varied menus. Naturally, you can dine at these restaurants when you have more time or don't have children and homework and meetings to balance.

Pasta places, bistros and bakery cafes, coffee houses and ritzy deli's seem to be the latest restaurant trends in Charlotte. Most of these eateries pay some homage to the lite, fat-free healthy eating dialogues of the '90s. But, Insiders notice a great deal of not-so-low-cholesterol or calorie-conscience cheesecakes and other yummy to decadent-tasting dishes creeping back onto restaurant menus. Why? The general consensus seems to be that people are tired of being constantly bombarded with "what's good for them." When they go out they want to feel free to-have something "sinful" without feeling guilty. Hence, restaurants are striving to maintain that delicate balance.

Occasionally, you'll still hear grumbles about the lack of "good" restaurants in Charlotte. Don't believe it! Chances are the complainant hasn't tried **La Bibliotheque** on Roxborough, **Chez Daniel** on Lombardy, **Sonoma** on College, **Bistro 100**, a carbon copy of the renowned Chicago eatery located Uptown in Founders Hall or Charlotte's newest eatery—**Morton's Of Chicago** that moved into Uptown's elegant Carillon Building. Charlotte's culinary growth doesn't have the same meaning for folks who haven't watched the metamorphosis of our restaurant scene over the last thirty years.

Back in the '50s, going out to eat in Charlotte meant something entirely different than it does today. That was before "fast foods" and liquor-by-the-drink came about. People did go out once in a while—to hotel dining rooms, country clubs or, if they were a member, the **Charlotte City Club** (now moved to 121 W. Trade St. (334-4738). Ladies (women were called that then) lunched at downtown (as it was called then) department store restaurants and cafeterias. You hauled the kids off to fish camps and family-style restaurants. Drive-ins and barbecues were popular with teenagers, but if you didn't count Chinese or a couple of places where you could find decent Italian, and the only thing that resembled atmosphere, there were precious few ethnic establishments around.

Of course, chains and "fast food" places had begun to fracture the landscape, but Charlotte dining was defined by good Southern food (big helpings) served in comfortable, but rarely stylish restaurants. It was not until the '80s that Charlotte

began to support fine restaurants. Chefs came from Europe, the Culinary Institute in New York and Johnson and Wells in Rhode Island to perform their wizardry on both rare and common ingredients. That was when food become known as cuisine (and rightly so), and was savored in sophisticated settings of sublime ambience. Yes, a new day dawned and our palettes were the richer for it, even though our wallets were not.

Food has changed from being what you do to stay alive to providing a cultural recreation. This change in attitude is reflected in the curriculum at **Central Piedmont Community College** on Elizabeth Avenue at Kings Drive. At first, courses in everything from food preparation to ice sculpting were offered, then the school really became serious by building a teaching dining room called the **Quad**. This semicircle building with floor to ceiling glass windows allows diners a view of the city while they are served ambitious preparations. Because chefs and waitpersons are unpaid students and the building is their lab, you only pay for the actual food, making this the tastiest secret in Charlotte. The dining room is in operation only during school sessions and reservations are taken only on Fridays from 9:00 AM until noon. (342-6581). A word or caution: call early, the Quad can become booked in 45 minutes.

Restaurant yellow pages of yesteryear covered less than a page; 1995's restaurants take up 21 pages with divisions for locality and type of cuisine. In Charlotte, you can find

14 different ethnic foods represented and that doesn't include seven other categories that feature barely-out-of-the-water fresh seafood, along with specialty fruits and exotic meats and fowl flown in for continental offerings. You won't go hungry here, and some will discover ingredients indigenous to our area that will make your mouth water. You'll be ashamed that you ever bad-mouthed Southern cooking, particularly new Southern that removes the fat, leaving the taste intact.

With your pocketbook in mind, we have included a price code that gives you a general idea of how much a dinner for two, including appetizer, entree, dessert and coffee, will cost you. So if your appetite is smaller, your bill will be lower. The code can be translated this way:

Under $20 $
$21 to $35 $$
$36 to $50 $$$
$51 and up $$$$

Most places will accept credit cards, but it's a good idea to check ahead of time to be certain they honor the one you plan to use. And although we've included hours, they change often and a phone call could save you time and frustration. We've deliberately deleted chains from this listing because we want you to know what's unique and different about Charlotte. Some of the best food in the city can be found in out-of-the-way spots known only to those Insiders with a taste for "fine victuals." The following listing is admittedly a subjective guide to some of the area's most frequented restaurants. Trying to include every restaurant is a formidable task, so we may have missed your favorite. If so, let us know so we can be sure to check it out for next year's *Insiders' Guide.*

American Cuisine

BISTRO 100
Uptown in Founders Hall inside NationsBank Corporate Center
100 North Tryon Street   344-0515
$$-$$$

You can feel comfortable in jeans or a tuxedo in this upscale-but-relaxed French and American restaurant. In the bar, sage green wicker chairs give that homey, front porch feel with blackboard tips on theatre, airfares, headlines, sports and current event reminders such as, "Last day to register to vote." Although the Bistro seats 300, the floor plan wraps from one dining area to the next providing a cozier atmosphere. Judy Rifka's ceiling mural based on a whimsical vineyard provides a colorful theme for the Bistro's more formal dining room.

This is a comfortable place to lunch on any of the restaurant's herb-roasted entrees. You'll love the complimentary roasted elephant garlic served with hot-from-the-oven sour dough bread. And you can't go wrong with the wood-roasted chicken breast stuffed with goat cheese and wild mushrooms, or you might prefer one of their gourmet pasta dishes, or a sandwich that would make the Earl of Sandwich salivate. The chef has taken the best from both American and French culinary techniques by cooking with fresh herbs and roasting rather than frying. The result is wholesome and delicious, with the possible exception of homemade desserts, which may be more delicious than wholesome. Insiders like the Chocolate Paradise, but the Bistro does offer fresh berries and sorbets. Bistro 100 is open from 11:30 AM to 10 PM Monday through Thursday, until 11 PM Friday and Saturday and from 11:30 AM until 8 PM Sunday.

CAFE VERDE

Inside Talley's Green Grocery
Dilworth Gardens Shopping Center
1408 East Blvd.   *334-9200*
$ - $$

Busy, busy is the scene in this favorite market cafe inside Talley's Green Grocery. Cafe Verde features food that is often hard to find in other Charlotte restaurants. You'll get a full bouquet of natural, vegetarian and ethnic foods. The menu includes hot entrees such as vegetarian lasagna and Mexican dishes with black and red beans that are especially delicious. This is another take-away place to put on your list for home dining. The cafe offers homemade soups, sandwiches on whole grain breads, a fresh salad bar and its baked goods and desserts are made daily. It caters to people with special dietary needs including low fat, low cholesterol, low sugar, low salt and dairy-free. Talley's opens at 9 AM, but Cafe Verde's hours are from 11:30 AM to 8 PM, Monday through Saturday. On Sunday, only sandwiches and the salad bar are available.

Photo by John Cress

Although the Bistro seats 300, the floor plan wraps from one dining area to the next and provides a cozy atmosphere.

FENWICK'S

108 S. Sharon Amity Rd.   *333-2750*
$$

Fenwick's offers fine dining in a casual, intimate atmosphere. Fresh seafood and salads, grilled chicken and steaks are popular menu items, but the fabulous breads, muffins and desserts are worth the price of the meal. No reservations are accepted here. Fenwick's is open from 11 AM to 10 PM Monday through Thursday, from 11 AM until midnight on Friday. Saturday hours are from 11 AM until midnight and Sunday hours are from 9 AM until 3 PM. Brunch is served on Sunday.

FIFTH STREET CAFE

118 W. Fifth St.   *358-8334*
$$

This is a great Uptown getaway for lunch, dinner or a drink after work. It serves excellent pasta and fresh seafood. Entertainment is provided every Friday night and there is a room upstairs for private parties. Hours are from 11:30 AM until 9 PM Monday through Thursday, and from 5 PM until 10 PM on Friday and Saturday.

HOTEL CHARLOTTE

705 S. Sharon Amity Rd.   *364-8755*
$$

The furnishings and decor of the original Hotel Charlotte located Uptown were transported to the suburbs and serve as a backdrop for this old Charlotte tradition. For lunch, try burgers or po-boys with "add-ons" of your choice. For dinner, shrimp creole or the Steak Diane are long-time favorites. New is the Crawfish Etouffee and Jumbo Gumbo.

The restaurant's wine and beer clubs are just the thing for sampling a wide variety of beverages (it boasts of more than 100 varieties of beer). Live Maine lobster with New England clam chowder is featured the first full weekend of each month and two weekends later. Closed on Sunday, Hotel Charlotte is open for lunch from 11:45 AM until 2 PM Monday through Friday, for dinner from 6 PM until 10 PM Monday through Thursday and from 6 PM until 11 PM Friday and Saturday.

LIZZIE'S RESTAURANT

4809 S. Tryon St.   *527-3064*
$$ - $$$

Entrees here include prime rib, shrimp scampi and a selection of pasta dishes. And you should wind up every meal with the homemade peanut butter pie. Live bands play classic dance music from the '40s, '50s and '60s, six nights a week. Liz King sings at lunch on weekdays, which is available from 11:30 AM until 2 PM Monday through Friday. Dinner is served from 5:30 until 10 PM Sunday through Thursday, and from 5:30 until 11 PM on Friday and Saturday.

MORROCROFT RESTAURANT

The Park Hotel
2200 Rexford Rd.   *364-8220*
$$ - $$$

Located in Charlotte's only four-star, four-diamond hotel, this restaurant offers three meals a day, wonderfully prepared and presented. In nice weather, diners can enjoy entertainment outdoors Wednesday through Saturday evenings. Breakfast is served from 6:30 AM until 11 AM Monday through Friday and from 7 AM until 9:30 AM on Sunday. Lunch is available from 11:30 AM until 2:30 PM Monday through Saturday and dinner hours are from 6 PM until 10:30 PM Sunday through Thursday, from 6 PM until 11 PM on Friday and Saturday. A truly spectacular brunch is served on Sundays from 9:30 AM until 2 PM.

PROVIDENCE CAFE

110 Perrin Place   376-2008
(next to Leaf'N Petal on Providence Rd.)
$$-$$$

When the temperature begins to climb, Insiders head for the patio at the brand-spanking-new building housing the Providence Cafe. Neighbors in shorts or running clothes can peddle over to this upscale restaurant on their bikes and suit-types don't turn around to stare. Of course, most people prefer to dine inside in the open ceiling, two-story Artichoke Room bathed in high glass windows or the bistro-type setting opposite the mahogany bar.

The menu is the same for lunch or dinner, which uncomplicates decisions. Eggs Sardou, poached eggs in artichokes and creamed spinach accented with hollandaise, topped off with the Cafe's wondrous dessert, Tiramisu, made with Maiscapone cheese, marsala wine, espresso liqueur soaked lady fingers (kind of a liquid cheese cake) is an Insiders favorite for Sunday Brunch. The cafe's own version of pizza made with marinated artichokes, plum tomatoes, roasted red peppers, pesto and fontina cheese atop a focaccia crust, or a penne pasta enhanced with blackened chicken with gorgonzola cream are two good reasons that artist, Ben Long, calls this his favorite restaurant. And though the accent here is primarily Mediterranean, it's sufficiently eclectic to include Grilled Tuna Jambalaya and Blackened Filet of Tenderloin. Healthy, diet conscious dishes include Black Bean Cake on fresh greens with goat cheese dressing and hickory grilled brochette of seasonal vegetables.

Many folks like to make this a stop on their way home from work. Why? Because the customer is brought four different wines to sample before making a decision. Wine may also be ordered by the glass. And live jazz is featured on the patio on Wednesday night. Providence Cafe is open from 11 AM to 11 PM Monday through Thursday, from 11 AM to 12 PM Friday and Saturday. On Sunday brunch is served from 9 AM to 3 PM, and from 3 PM until 10 PM dinner is served.

30TH EDITION

Two First Union Center   372-7778
$$$

If you're looking for a romantic evening where you can watch from the 30th floor as the sun slides away and washes over the whole of Charlotte, then make reservations at 30th Edition. If you want to impress someone or pretend you're in a New York restaurant, then take them here. On the other hand, if you're simply hungry for exceptional food, then look no further.

Insiders like to begin their meal with Baked Brie with Raspberry Coulis Sauce, or Crabmeat stuffed mushrooms. For an entree, the Peppered Salmon in three peppercorn and mustard cream sauce is a standout, though the restaurant gained its reputation with Prime Rib. Vegetarians and those preferring something lighter will enjoy one of three different pasta dishes. It's hard to go wrong with Pasta Primavera accented with a Cajun Creole Sauce. Seafood lovers are in for a treat with the Low-Country-meets-the-Bayou dish consisting of jumbo prawns, sea scallops and andouille sausage served with a crawfish cream sauce. Desserts are wicked tempters, but none more so than the Charlottetown Sundae with ice cream rolled in granola and lathered in hot fudge, nuts, cherries and fresh fruit.

Dinner is served from 6 PM to 9:30 PM Monday through Thursday, from 6 PM to 10 PM Friday, from 6 PM to 10:30 PM Saturday, and from 6 PM to 9 PM on Sunday. It's a good idea to make reservations, but casual attire is welcomed.

THE TOWN HOUSE RESTAURANT
1011 Providence Rd. 335-1546
$$$$

If you used to stop by The Townhouse for breakfast, you have a big, delicious surprise in store for you. This restaurant has been a landmark at the intersection of Queens and Providence Roads for as long as most Charlotteans can remember (over fifty years), but old-timers remember it as the place where business deals were made and where after-theatre parties ended up. All that has changed. Today, it is a warm, casually elegant restaurant where regional American cuisine is expertly prepared and elegantly served. In addition to the extensive list of fine wines, the wine bar offers a choice of 12 to 15 different wines, including champagne and Port, by the glass. The Townhouse is open from 6 PM to 10 PM Monday through Saturday (lounge opens at 5 PM).

UNIVERSITY PLACE RESTAURANT
Hwy. 29 & W.T. Harris Blvd. 547-1985
$$$

Formerly Slug's University Place, the new management is keeping up the tradition of fine dining begun by its predecessors. Prime rib

is the signature item here but the restaurant also features a wide range of entrees such as aged western steacks, veal, chicken, and a variety of seafood dishes. The ideal destination for business and special occasion dining, University Place Restaurant is open for lunch Monday through Friday from 11 AM until 2 PM, for dinner Monday through Saturday from 5:30PM until 10 PM and from Noon until 9 PM on Sunday.

Barbecue

The barbecue debate will probably go on forever in North Carolina. Some think Lexington-style barbecue is the best, others say Eastern-style barbecue is the only barbecue they'd put in their mouth. Some like Texas-beef-style, others western or with pork. Then comes the discussion of whether barbecue should be sliced or chopped, and you'll get no more consensus on that than you would on style.

It is questionable whether anyone who's not a native Southerner can truly understand and appreciate fully the varieties and subtleties of barbecue. Natives and recent converts have been known to drive over a 100 miles for lunch at their favorite barbecue place. And, these restaurants are not usually known for the ambiance. A newcomer who'd heard of our famed barbecue rushed down to a local spot for dinner. "Ugh," she exclaimed, "the place was just awful. Thank goodness they have takeout." Fortunately, Charlotte offers a wide selection for you to sample before settling on your favorite. Try one of these:

BUBBA'S BARBECUE

4400 Sunset Road   393-2000
(Exit 16-B from I-77 North)
$$

It's all a matter of personal preference, but Insiders' votes go to the Eastern-style barbecue of Bubba's. Bubba's cooks the whole pig, using peppers and spices in a vinegar base. You can also order shrimp, barbecue chicken, barbecue beans, barbecue french fries, brunswick stew and, of course—hush puppies. And in true Southern tradition Bubba's offers sweet potato pie and key lime pie.

If you choose takeout, remember to purchase a bottle of Bubba's sauce—it's not included with a regular take-home order. Bubba's is open from 11 AM until 11 PM daily.

CAROLINA COUNTRY BARBECUE

838 Tyvola Rd.   525-0337
2501 Executive Dr. at Crown Pt.   847-4520
$$

Come hungry. This restaurant has fine Southern-style barbecue, pit cooked and hickory smoked. Expect big portions and good service. Both locations are open from 11 AM until 9 PM Monday through Saturday and from 11:30 AM to 8 PM Sunday.

HOG HEAVEN BARBECUE

1600 Purser Dr.   535-0154
(at Eastway and Sugar Creek)
$$

You'll get delicious Lexington-style barbecue that features pork, chicken, ribs and homemade brunswick stew. The atmosphere is great for family dinners, and Hog Heaven is open from 11 AM until 7 PM on Wednesday and from 11 AM until 9 PM Thursday, Friday and Saturday. It is open for lunch only on Monday and Tuesday from 11 AM until 3 PM.

OLD HICKORY HOUSE
6538 N. Tryon St.   *596-8014*
$$
The Old Hickory House serves terrific pit-cooked barbecue—pork, beef, ribs and chicken—and Brunswick stew, too. It has takeout and catering is available. The hours are 11 AM until 9 PM daily except for Sunday when this eatery is closed.

OLE SMOKEHOUSE #1
1513 Montford Dr.   *523-7222*
$$
This landmark serves great barbecue—ribs, chicken, beef and pork —but it also has steaks and fresh seafood for the non-barbecue lovers in your crowd. Be sure to inquire about the daily specials!

The Ole Smokehouse is open from 11 AM until 10 PM Tuesday through Saturday and from 11 AM until 9 PM on Sunday.

ROGERS BARBEQUE
901 N. Wendover Rd.   *364-2939*
$$
In addition to great barbeque for lunch or dinner, you can get a good old-fashioned breakfast here. On Monday. it is open for breakfast and lunch from 6 AM until 2 PM, on Tuesday through Saturday the hours are 6 AM until 8 PM, and on Sunday it serves breakfast only from 6 AM until 1 PM.

Bistros, Bars & Grills

ANNABELLE'S
5555 Central Ave.   *568-5392*
$$
Annabelle's specializes in chicken, quiche and burgers and has a large salad bar. It opens at 11:30 AM Monday through Thursday and closes at 11 PM. On Friday and Saturday it's open until midnight, and from noon until 9 PM on Sunday.

ALEXANDER MICHAEL'S
401 W. 9th St.   *332-6789*
$$
This is one of Fourth Ward's favorite spots. Drop by for a drink after work and a great dinner (or lunch) served in a friendly neighborhood atmosphere. It's open for lunch from 11:30 AM until 4 PM Monday through Saturday; for dinner from 4 until 10 PM Monday and Tuesday; from 4 PM to 11 PM Wednesday and Thursday; from 4 PM to midnight Friday and from 4 PM to 11 PM Saturday. On Sunday, brunch is served from 11:30 AM to 3 PM and dinner from 3 PM to 9 PM.

CAROLINA MILL AND BAKERY, INC.
122 W. Woodlawn Rd.   *525-2530*
$$ - $$$
Under new management, health sets the standard at this nutrition-conscious restaurant. The full country breakfast features all the good-for-you things that folks dream about. Many items on the menu are prepared under the dietary guidelines of the American Heart Association. The Mill offers everything from freshly baked

breads, muffins and sweets to a variety of homemade soups, salads, pizzas and sandwiches. It also brews its own beer on the premises. The restaurant is open from 6:30 AM to 11 PM Sunday through Wednesday and 6:30 AM to 1 AM Thursday through Saturday.

CHARLEY'S RESTAURANT
SouthPark Mall
Sharon Rd.   364-7475
$$

Charley's serves tasty soups, salads and sandwiches. Its most popular items include the "one great chicken sandwich" and the grilled chicken salad. A pleasant atmosphere makes this a good place to unwind when you "shop' til you drop" at SouthPark. The restaurant is open from 11 AM until 10:30 PM on Monday, 11:30 AM until 10:30 PM Tuesday through Thursday; Friday and Saturday from 11:30 AM to 11 PM, and from 11 AM until 9 PM on Sunday.

DILWORTH BREWING CO.
1301 East Blvd.   377-2739
$ - $$

Not only can you get the best brew in town here, but you can sample a new lighter fare as well. The burger and fries menu has been expanded to include pastas, soups and seasonal fruits and vegetables in salads or side orders. For a different taste, try the Fish Taco—fried perch wrapped with cabbage and topped with sour cream sauce. Dilworth Brewing Co. is open for lunch from 11 AM until 5 PM Monday through Saturday, for dinner from 5 PM until midnight Monday through Thursday and from 5 PM until 1 AM on Friday and Saturday. The restaurant is closed on Sunday.

Photo by Pamely Myers.

Charley's at SouthPark Mall is a South Charlotte favorite.

EAST BOULEVARD BAR & GRILL
1601 East Blvd.   332-2414
$ - $$

    This is one of those places where you can come in, sit back and just enjoy the food and your friends. Menu items run the gamut from burgers and chicken wings to soups and salads. Hours are 11:30 AM until 10 PM Sunday through Thursday; 11:30 AM until 10 PM on Friday and until 11 PM on Saturday.

THE FOUNDRY PUB & DELI
601 S. Cedar St.   347-1841
$ - $$

    Enjoy the Foundry's wide selection of imported beers with a tasty sandwich or salad for lunch, or try the grilled chicken or deli fare. Dinner offers interesting specials along with a variety of regular entrees plus pastas, Mexican dishes and steaks. The Foundry opens at 11:30 AM and closes at 11 PM on Monday and Wednesday. It's open until 2 AM Tuesday, Thursday, Friday and Saturday when live bands entertain. It opens at 6 PM on Saturday.

FRENCH QUARTER
321 S. Church St.   377-7415
$

    This restaurant began as a little lunch place in the heart of Uptown serving good food at a reasonable price. The salads (taco, chef's and Greek) are delicious or you might want to try a chicken sandwich. It's now open for dinner, but the menu is light with burgers and pastas. Meals are served from 11 AM until 7:30 PM Monday through Friday.

GLORIOUS CUISINE
131 E. John St.
Matthews   847-8331
$$$-$$$$

    This casual American bistro serves both European and American cuisine and is located in the heart of Matthews. Guests are comfortable in this newly renovated restaurant in either casual or dressier attire. The European bakery specializes in buttercream cakes and extraordinary wedding cakes. The restaurant is also known for corporate and family catering, and it was rated as #1 caterer in *Best Of Charlotte* last year.

    The Friday night seafood buffet is an eye-popping event, and Sunday brunch features a complete omelette and pancake bar, plus chef-carved ham and roast beef and other delicious surprises. Dinner may feature quail, lamb, and old standbys utilizing special culinary wizardry. Be sure to leave room for dessert—the baked goods, made on the premises, are out of this world. The restaurant is open from 11 AM until 10 PM Monday through Friday; from 11 AM to 10 PM Saturday; and from 9 AM to 2 PM Sunday.

GRADY'S GOODTIMES
5546 Albemarle Rd.   537-4663
$$$

    The menu here includes just about everything from soup to steaks. No reservations are accepted, but call-ahead seating is available. Open from 11 AM until 11 PM Sunday through Thursday and 11 AM until midnight on Friday and Saturday.

JACK STRAW'S

1936 E. 7th St.   *347-8960*
$ - $$

Jack Straw's is a great place to get anything from a burger to fine cuisine in a very casual atmosphere. The kitchen serves up homemade soups, salads, specialty sandwiches and a wide range of entrees, including pastas, fresh seafood, ribs and steaks. Live music is featured on Wednesday nights. Private parties are welcome and all menu items are available for take out. The restaurant is open for lunch from 11:30 AM until 2:30 PM and for dinner from 5 PM until 10:30 PM. It's closed on Sundays.

Photo by Pamela Myers.

Although relatively new, Trio has proven to be a welcome addition to the Highway 51 restaurant scene.

LOAFERS RESTAURANT & BAR

4715 E. Independence Blvd.   568-9209
$$

The creators of the original Hornets shuttle, Loafers serves American cuisine with a Tex-Mex flair. The restaurant is open Monday through Sunday from 11:30 AM until 2 AM. A late night menu is served from 11 PM until 1 AM every night, and there is live music Wednesday through Sunday from 10 PM until 2 AM.

MCGUFFEY'S

Windsor Square
9709 E. Independence Blvd.   845-2522
$$

The regular menu includes honey mustard chicken, pasta, seafood and stir fry and is served from 11 AM until 2 AM daily. It also has a late-night menu until 12:30 AM seven nights a week. The restaurant's low-calorie and low-fat entrees are approved by the American Heart Association. Try the "Classical Brunch" on Sunday.

NEW MARKET GRILLE

The Arboretum
8136 Providence Rd.   543-4656
$$ - $$$

New Market's specialty is cooking on the grill—particularly seafood. Pasta and chicken entrees are also available. Hours are 11:30 AM until 10 PM Monday through Thursday, 11:30 AM until 11 PM Friday and Saturday and 11 AM until 10 PM on Sunday.

P J MCKENZIE'S

4800 S. Tryon St.   529-1922
$$-$$$

Formerly Bobby McGee's, the same fun-type atmosphere still exists. The restaurant continues to serve seafood and steaks along with the salad bar, and it also has unique mix and match combinations with yummy desserts and specialty drinks. Don't miss the nightly specials. Lunch is served from 11 AM until 4:30 PM Monday through Thursday. On Friday and Saturday, meals are served from 11 AM to 11 PM, and on Sunday from 11 AM until 2:30 PM and from 5:30 PM until 10 PM.

PRICE'S CHICKEN COOP

1614 Camden Rd.   333-9866
$

This family-owned takeout food establishment, founded in 1962, is already a "legend in its own time." Though originally designed as a place for good food at reasonable prices for "blue collar" workers, "white collar" workers caught on to the deal. Price's Chicken Coop has become the place to stop to pick up lunch or take some good fried chicken home for dinner. Its principal product is fried chicken—by the piece, or the whole chicken. Business demands have pushed Price's to expand to fried fish, sandwiches, Eastern North Carolina Barbecue with all the trimmings of hush puppies, potato salad, slaw, and even pies. This is the best place around for instant parties or plan-ahead events. Food is available from 10 AM until 7 PM Monday through Friday, and until 6 PM on Saturday.

PROVIDENCE ROAD SUNDRIES

1522 Providence Rd.   366-4467

$$

Known simply as "Sundries," this is the place to go for great burgers and sandwiches. It's also the place to go to see or be seen by the local Yuppie crowd. Sundries is open from 11 AM until 2 AM Monday through Friday, and 8 AM until 2 AM Saturday and Sunday. It serves breakfast from 8 AM until noon on the weekend.

RED ROCKS CAFE & BAKERY

4223-8 Providence Rd.   364-0402

$$

The day of Bistro dining has arrived in Charlotte. Red Rocks Cafe & Bakery is a trendy, upscale restaurant that works hard to offer everything from deli to dinner to takeout in a substantive style. The interior is black and white slick without being cold and you won't feel out of place in casual attire or your spiffiest duds.

The new cuisine is health conscious without sacrificing taste. Roasting, grilling, steaming, as well as low-fat and low-salt, if you so desire, are menu options. The on-the-premises bakery has fresh daily offerings that you can take home with you, so don't load up on so much that you won't have room for the other offerings.

The menu sports Veggie Pasta Provencale right beside a Rib-eye steak. But the Insiders' choice entree is the Breast of Chicken "bencotto" with its spinach, mushrooms, jack cheese and red pepper filling in a hunter's sauce. You can also get Black Bean Chili or a Burger or stick-to-the-ribs salads laced with either chicken or fish. Wash these down with a selection from the extensive wine list or one of the imported beers. Yes, iced and herbal tea are both available, too.

Desserts are a rich European affair. White chocolate mousse wearing a dark chocolate coating and garnished with fruit is popular and the layered apple pie is more delicious than anything anybody's grandmother ever made. Top dessert off with a specialty coffee such as Parisian Bistro (Grand Marnier and Courvoisier, whipped cream and zest of orange).

Red Rocks serves lunch Monday through Thursday from 11:30 AM until 5:30 PM; dinner is served until 10:30 PM during the week and until 11 PM on Friday and Saturday. Brunch is served Saturday and Sunday from 8 AM until 5:30 PM, and Sunday dinner is served until 9 PM.

ROASTING COMPANY

1601-A Montford Dr.   521-8188
                             FAX 521-8288

$

The main feature at the Roasting Company is its "Rosti Pollos," rotisserie chicken that's injected with a special marinade from Costa Rica and then cooked to perfection in a brick-fired oven. From fresh vegetables (hot and cold) to appetizers, salads or tacos, you won't be disappointed in the quality of the food, which is served in a casual, pleasant atmosphere. Roasting Company is open Monday through Thursday from 11 AM until 10 PM, 11 AM until 10:30 PM on Friday and Saturday and from 9 AM to 10 PM on Sunday.

SPRATT'S KITCHEN & MARKET

Founders Hall in NationsBank Corporate Center
100 N. Tryon St.   334-0864
$

When you're Uptown shopping or on your lunch hour and don't have much time or money, Spratt's cafeteria-type deli is the place to go for a scrumptious quick meal. You can also pop in for breakfast. The clever floor plan moves in a circle with one offshoot for its mini-style gourmet grocery and another for the dining area.

The restaurant is named for Charlotte's first pioneer, Thomas Spratt, who no doubt tread the very Indian trading path (Trade Street) that the eating area overlooks. You can build your own sandwich or salad, charged by the pound, from a vast array of deli selections on homemade breads, or select from the hot vegetables including a squash medley, something called Mississippi Caviar (black-eyed peas with zing), a rice pilaf with personality and a meat bar that featured a baked Athenian Chicken.

The pasta bar has a tasty chicken with tarragon, Soba Noodles, Mediterranean Cous Cous, etc. The cold salad bar is adjacent, which makes it tempting to mix both bars. There is a wide assortment of imported beers and good selection of wines, plus tea and soft drinks. Afterwards, try something chocolatey and gooey such as the German Chocolate Cake from the Bistro 100 bakery, or if you're diet conscience enjoy the great nonfat frozen yogurt with one of the restaurant's espressos, capuccinos or gourmet coffees. Take a spin through the market where you can find all the fixins' for a no fuss dinner. And if it's one of those busy days

Photo by John Cress

Spratt's cafeteria-type deli is the place to go
for a scrumptious quick meal when you're Uptown..

Uptown, delivery service is also available. Spratt's is open Monday through Friday from 7 AM to 2:30 PM, Saturday from 8 AM until 2:30 PM.

300 EAST

300 East Blvd.   *332-6507*
$$

This place has it all—from pizzas to grinders—including a good chunky chicken salad. It's a great place to start Sunday morning off with a relaxed brunch in informal surroundings. The restaurant is open from 11:30 AM until 11 PM Monday through Thursday, 11 AM until 11 PM Sunday, and 11:30 AM until midnight on Friday and Saturday.

TOWNSHIP GRILLE

10400 E. Independence Blvd.
Matthews   *847-2480*
$$

Go for lunch or dinner and enjoy soups, sandwiches, burgers and charcoal-grilled chicken in a friendly neighborhood atmosphere. It has the largest selection of imported beer in the area—over 75 brands. And if you are a Buffalo Bills fan, this is the Charlotte Buffalo Bills Backers headquarters. Township Grille is open 11 AM until 10 PM Monday through Thursday, 11 AM until midnight on Friday and Saturday and from 11 AM until 9 PM on Sunday.

TROLLEY'S END GRILL & BAR

1933 South Blvd. at Tremont Ave. 377-3377
$$

At one time this was the end of the trolley line where the trolley cars actually turned around to change conductors, etc. The turn-of-the-century brick building served as a grill-type restaurant for those trolley employees. Today, it is where you want to be first in line for weekday lunch or for brunch on Sunday. This is one of the best architectural recycling jobs around town, and you won't be disappointed with the food either. Trolley's End serves a great turkey salad, good pastas, fresh seafood each evening, along with an occasional Mexican dish or whatever is the current food vogue. It's open from 11:30 AM until 10 PM Monday through Thursday, and it serves dinner until 11 PM on Friday and Saturday. Sunday brunch is from 11:30 AM until 3 PM, and dinner is served until 9 PM.

VILLAGE TAVERN

Rotunda Bldg., SouthPark
4201 Congress St.   *552-9983*
$$

The Tavern's huge outdoor patio is a great place to meet with friends for a drink when the weather is nice. The brunch menu offers several different omelettes and a variety of eggs benedicts. For a change of pace, try the Crab Cake Benedict or the Belgian Waffles. Nice crunchy salads and good sandwiches are available for lunch. The dinner menu offers a continental variety. The restaurant is open from 11:30 AM until midnight Monday through Thursday, 11:30 PM until 1 AM Friday and Saturday, and 11 AM until 10 PM on Sunday.

Coffee Houses

PEABODY'S COFFEE

Sharon Corners
4732 Sharon Rd.   556-1700

A coffee house should smell good, and Peabody's does. Someone once said that if coffee could only taste as good as it smells it would be fabulous. Insiders think Peabody's comes about as close as you can get to coffee actually tasting as good as it smells. Peabody's is the type of place where you "drop in" after visiting the performing arts center or a movie. Of course, it's a great "drop in" early in the morning to start your day.

With your coffee (there are 50 different varieties), or tea (15 different varieties), or hot chocolate (5 different selections), you can enjoy a croissant or to-die-for cinnamon bun. Iced coffees are offered in warmer weather as well as 15 different flavored sodas for that coffee alternative. From the pastry case, there are 8 different cheesecakes (Insiders vote for the Drunken Chocolate). It also offers other "sin-enticing" pies and cakes plus an Affogatto (double shot of espresso with Haagen-Dazs ice cream).

Peabody's has the look of a brand-spanking-new European coffee house and, by the time you read this, it will probably have received its license to offer liqueurs. Peabody's is open from Monday through Thursday from 7 AM until 10 PM; from 7 AM until midnight on Friday; from 8 AM until midnight on Saturday and from 8 AM to 8 PM on Sunday.

Caribbean Cuisine

ANNTONY'S CARIBBEAN CAFE
2001 E. 7th St.   *342-0749*
$$

Anntony's offers a variety of Caribbean cuisine, the most popular being the rotisserie-style Caribbean chicken served with your choice of greens, rice or potato salad. Live entertainment is featured on Friday and Saturday nights. Takeout is available. Lunch is served from 11:30 AM until 2:30 PM Monday through Friday, dinner from 5:30 until 9:30 PM Monday through Saturday.

Cajun & Creole Cuisine

BOURBON STREET STATION
6101 Old Pineville Rd.   *522-0231*
$$$

Great cajun cuisine is served here! Look for the old train car, and you've found the right place. Appetizers are served every night until 12:30 AM, and there is entertainment some nights. Lunch and dinner are served from 11 AM until 1 AM Monday through Wednesday and from 11 AM until midnight 2 AM Thursday, Friday and Saturday.

CAJUN QUEEN
1800 East 7th St.   *377-9017*
$$-$$$

Cajun Queen's Bayou-in-

spired kitchen turns out some of the most authentic New Orleans cajun in town. As might be guessed, it specializes in blackened fish and steaks but also offers crawfish, shrimp, Etouffee and its own homemade Oreo cheesecake and Bourbon Bread Pudding. Nightly, live dixieland jazz entertainment adds spice to your dining enjoyment in this attractive restaurant located in a charming old home. Dinner is served from 5:30 PM until 10 PM Monday through Thursday, until 10:30 PM Friday and Saturday and 9:30 PM on Sunday.

FAT TUESDAY
211 N. College St.   *375-3288*
(located in CityFair)
$-$$

Frozen daiquiris at their finest! Located in the center of Uptown Charlotte, Fat Tuesday serves up over twenty different flavors of specialty frozen drinks. Delicious appetizers and sandwiches are created from recipes direct from New Orleans. Fat Tuesday is open seven days a week from 11 AM until 2 AM and it serves free daiquiri samples all the time.

Continental Cuisine

CARPE DIEM
431 S. Tryon St.   *377-7976*
$$ - $$$

A fabulous little restaurant tucked into the old Radcliffe's Florist building on South Tryon, the quiet surroundings make for a comfortable place to enjoy a superb lunch or dinner. Lunch is served from 11:30 AM until 2 PM Tuesday through Friday, dinner from 5:30 until 10 PM Tuesday through Thursday and from 5:30 to 10:30 PM on Saturday.

THE LAMPLIGHTER

1065 E. Morehead St.　　　372-5343
$$$$

The Lamplighter name has been synonymous with good food and good service for years. It's the perfect place to impress, whether a business associate or a romantic dinner for two. Every guest is treated like royalty. The Lamplighter serves dinner from 6 PM until 10 PM daily.

THE MELTING POT

Kings Court Plaza
901 S. Kings Dr.　　　334-4400
$$$

Select cheddar or Swiss cheese fondue served with fruit and french bread, or choose to fondue the heartier beef, chicken or seafood. For dessert—chocolate fondue, of course. The Melting Pot is open for dinner from 5 until 11 PM Sunday through Thursday and from 5 PM until midnight on Friday and Saturday.

CASTALDI'S ITALIAN BISTRO

311 East Blvd.　　　333-6999
$$-$$$

A number of fine restaurants have occupied this old historic home where Carson McCuller wrote *The Heart Is A Lonely Hunter.* The new owners have redecorated the house to a more upbeat design than has been seen here before. The food falls more into the gourmet-Italian category with the use of fresh ingredients and new techniques. You can choose from 14 different varieties of pasta and four varieties of pizza. How about the restaurant's Pizza Sofisticata? This combines smoked chicken, caramelized onions, goat cheese and rosemary. Also known for its fish entrees, you can have yours baked, broiled, grilled or sauteed. Meals are served from 11 AM to 10 PM Monday through Thursday and from 11 AM to 11 PM on Friday and Saturday.

PEWTER ROSE BISTRO

1820 South Blvd.　　　332-8149
$$ - $$$

This bistro makes for a nice change from fast food for a quiet, expertly prepared lunch or dinner. Late night appetizers and desserts are served in the bar on weekends until 11 PM. Lunch hours are from 11 AM until 2 PM Monday through Friday and from 11 AM to 3 PM Saturday and Sunday. Dinner is served from 5 PM until 10 PM Monday through Thursday, from 5 PM to 11 PM on Friday and Saturday and from 5 PM to 9 PM on Sunday.

PRISMS RESTAURANT & THE BISTRO

Atrium of the Two First Union Center Bldg.
327 S. Tryon St.　　　335-9918
$$$

Upstairs, enjoy fine dining in beautifully decorated surroundings that provide a crystal clear view of the city. The wild mushroom fettucini is always good. Downstairs, the bistro offers more casual dining in addition to frequent entertainment. Prisms serves meals from 11:30 AM to 11:30 PM Monday through Thursday, from 11:30 AM to 10:30 PM on Friday and from 5:30 PM to 10:30 PM on Saturday.

The Bistro is open from 11:30 AM until 10 PM Sunday through Thursday and 11:30 AM until 11 PM Friday and Saturday.

Deli

THE BAGEL WORKS DELICATESSEN
4422 Colwick Rd.   *364-4000*
$

Come in and select a dozen or so of this deli's trademark freshly baked bagels or order one toasted with cream cheese to eat on the road. Bagel Works is open from 7 AM until 3 PM, seven days a week.

THE COUNTRY BOARDWALK
100 S. Kings Dr.   *342-4004*
$

For all those transplanted Yankees, this is a New York-style deli and bakery with several homemade specialties. Lunch delivery is available. It's open from 6:30 AM until 3 PM Monday through Friday and from 8 AM until 3 PM on Saturday.

DIKADEE'S DELI
Twin Oaks Shopping Center
East Blvd.   *333-3354*
$

This place offers fabulous soups, salads, sandwiches and incredible desserts. It's open from 11 AM until 3 PM on Monday, from 11 AM to 8:30 PM Tuesday through Friday and from 11 AM to 3:30 PM on Saturday.

PASTA & PROVISIONS
1528 Providence Rd.   *364-2622*
(next to Providence Sundries)
8016-100 Providence Rd.   *543-7595*
$

Technically speaking, Pasta &

Provisions is not a restaurant. It's more of a takeout place, but we put it in this section so you wouldn't miss it. When you're too tired or busy to cook, this is an excellent place to pick up dinner. Pasta and sauces are made fresh daily—over 12 different types of pastas, 10 raviolis and 4 tortellinis. You can get fresh baked bread, and Italian specialty items. Both locations are open Monday through Friday from 10 AM to 7 PM and from 10 AM to 6 PM on Saturday.

RUSTY'S
Quail Corners Shopping Center
Park Rd. and Sharon Rd. W.   *554-9012*
5445 77 Center Dr.   *527-2650*
320 S. Tryon St.   *374-1140*
$

There are three Rusty's—the one Uptown in the Latta Arcade is called Rusty's Burgers, Etc. Each provides a good place to grab a quick bite with great sandwiches and salads and an extensive selection of wines. Fax orders are accepted between 7 AM and 4 PM Monday through Friday. Hours and days open vary at each location. The Quail Corners Shopping Center location serves breakfast from 7 AM until 9 AM Monday through Saturday. Lunch and dinner are available from 10 AM until 9 PM Monday through Friday and 10 AM until 7 PM on Saturday.

THAT PLACE DELI & GRILL
Corner of East & South blvds.   *358-1516*
$

A classy but comfortable California-style deli decorated with dark prints and green tile—colors that don't yell at you as some deli color schemes do. Flowers are on the tables and there's a rack for newspapers for guests to enjoy with their meals. Stop by for a mid-morning snack of croissants, bagels, muffins and coffee. For lunch, you can have thick, thick Chicago-style deli hot or cold sandwiches served on pumpernickel, rye, pita, kaiser and whole wheat, but the neat surprise here is the salad bar. Or you can order one of the deli's 25 pasta combinations; either Italian or oriental stir fry, baby back ribs, and yes—barbecue. Of the homemade soup selection, chili is the standout. You can find a nice selection of desserts from yogurt to cheesecakes, and there's a reasonably priced kid's menu. That Place is open Monday through Friday from 10:30 AM to 4 PM. From 5:30 PM to 10 PM on Thursday, Friday and Saturday, a delicious vegetarian buffet is served.

Family-Style Dinning

ANDERSON'S RESTAURANT
1617 Elizabeth Ave.   *333-3491*
$

Family owned and operated, Anderson's has become an institution in Charlotte. If you are looking for your lawyer or accountant some morning, chances are he or she is eating breakfast here. The home fries are the best in town and the restaurant is famous for its pecan pie. Breakfast, lunch and dinner are served from 6 AM until 10 PM Monday through Saturday and from 7 AM to 3 PM on Sunday.

THE CHARLOTTE CAFE
Park Road Shopping Ctr.   *523-0431*
$

This is one of the best moderately priced places to go for breakfast. You can sit for hours hatching a business deal or catching up with a friend, and never find your coffee cup empty. The extensive menu includes everything from deli items to steaks, seafood, a variety of Italian dishes and 25 different home-cooked vegetables daily. The Cafe is open from 7 AM until 9 PM Monday through Friday, from 8 AM until 9 PM on Saturday and from 8 AM to 2:30 PM on Sunday.

THE COUNTRY INN OF MATTHEWS
341 Ames St.
Matthews   *847-1447*
$-$$

The Country Inn features fine family dining in the heart of Matthews. You can enjoy breakfast (only on Saturday), lunch and dinner in a casual, friendly atmosphere. Breakfast is served from 8:30 AM until 11 AM on Saturday. Lunch hours are 11:30 AM until 2 PM Monday through Friday, and from noon until 2 PM Saturday and Sunday. Dinner is served from 5:30 PM until 8:30 PM Thursday through Saturday.

THE CUPBOARD RESTAURANT
3005 South Blvd.   *523-9934*
$

Another Charlotte institution, the Cupboard offers no frills, family dining. Get there early for dinner because sometimes it's so busy that the restaurant runs out of its wonderful homemade rolls. The Cupboard is also famous for its delicious banana cream and coconut cream pies. It's open Monday through Friday, serving breakfast from 6 PM until 11 AM, lunch from 11 AM until 3 PM and dinner from 4:45 PM until 7:30 PM.

GUS'S ORIGINAL FORTY-NINER
10008 University City Blvd.   549-0968
$$

Since 1969 this attractive, family-owned restaurant in the University community, has served delicious American, Southern Italian and Greek cuisine in a casual atmosphere. An Italian specialty that you won't find elsewhere is the Braciole—a beef roll-up in Salsa Pomidori sauce. For dessert, you'll definitely appreciate the homemade Bisque Tortoni and Cannoli. If you can't decide, a good bet would be the Sampler Platter of Mixed Italian Cuisine for two. Meals are served from 11 AM until 10 PM Monday through Thursday, until 10:30 PM Friday, and 4:30 PM until 10:30 PM on Saturday.

GUS'S SIR BEEF RESTAURANT
4104 Monroe Rd.   377-3210
$

It's not unusual to see a line of people all the way to the parking lot of this family-style restaurant. It's been serving vegetables fresh from the garden for over 29 years. No fats are used to cook the delicious squash, greens and other good veggies, which is a heart healthy way to dine. You'll also appreciate the lean roast beef, and Elizabeth Taylor said that Gus's fried chicken was the best ever. Meals are served from 11 AM until 9 PM Monday through Saturday.

LUPIE'S CAFE
2118 Monroe Rd.   374-1232
$

From Lupie's time-worn exterior, you'd probably pass it by, but Insiders know better. The old, not made to look old, but old interior wooden booths, floors and walls aren't an appreciable improvement over the exterior, but the diverse clientele, vegetables with cornbread, hot, super hot and too hot chili is this otherwise dive's drawing card. This folksy place, which grows on you, is where you'll rub elbows with politicians and mill workers just hangin' out. Meals are served from 11 AM to 11 PM Monday through Friday and from noon until 11 PM on Saturday.

McDONALD'S CAFETERIA
I-85 & Beatties Ford Rd.   393-8823
$$

This cafeteria-style restaurant offers truly superb home-cooked food, from macaroni and cheese to a great assortment of vegetables and some great fried chicken. Banquet facilities are available for up to 500 people. Breakfast is served from 7 AM until 11 AM Monday through Saturday and from 7 AM until noon on Sunday. Lunch and dinner are available from 11 AM until 11 PM Monday through Thursday, 11 AM until midnight Friday and Saturday and from noon until 8 PM on Sunday.

French Cuisine

CHEZ DANIEL

1742 Lombardy Cr.   *332-3224*
$$ - $$$$

Elegant touches abound in this small, intimate dining spot located in a quaint, historic cottage. The authentically prepared French cuisine, combined with the background of folk and classical French music on tape, will make you feel like you're dining in Paris. Every item on the menu is exquisite, but this writer's favorite is salmon in a secret cream sauce. Insiders are partial to the restaurant's chocolate mousse. The restaurant's back room seats 12 people, allowing space for up to 50 people for private parties. Be sure to call for reservations for a night you will long remember. Specials change nightly. Dinner is served from 6 PM until 10:30 PM Monday through Saturday.

LA BIBLIOTHEQUE

1901 Roxborough Rd.   *365-5000*
$$-$$$$

Now under new management, even lunch is an elegant affair in this beautiful restaurant where table candles are lit even at the noon hour. La Bibliotheque means library in French, and the cuisine is mastered using traditional French techniques in a library setting. Book cases line most of the walls, making you feel like you're dining in a friend's lavish walnut library. Since the designers have utilized one wall with floor to ceiling windows, you never get that stuffy, closed-in feeling in this richly appointed room.

Your taste buds can enjoy a diversity of tastes from Escargot a la Chablisienne (snails baked in wine and garlic butter) as an appetizer to Tranche de Saumon Avec Sauce Montrachet (salmon with Montrachet sauce) as an entree.

379

D'agneau (lamb), Canard (duck), Boeuf (NY strip steak, filet of tenderloin, Poulet (chicken) and Homard Thermidore (Maine lobster with tarragon cream sauce) are a few of the dinner entrees. Lunch is a touch simpler, but no less divine. Flounder Filet broiled in caper butter is always great, or one of the five pastas (Insiders particularly like their House Chicken Pasta Penne with sauteed chicken in a rich tomato and mushroom sauce). But no matter what you order, the food presentation is outstanding (even the cream soups are presented in beautiful marble-swirled patterns). You can do light or heavy for dessert: indulge in Fraise a la Romanoff (strawberries in cognac), or Gateau aux amandes et a la Mousse au Chocolat avec coulis de Framboises (Almond and chocolate mousse cake with raspberry sauce), which should satisfy your sweet tooth for a week.

You'll find this elegant restaurant inside the Roxborough Building across from Specialty Shops on the Park. The food is excellent and sure to impress the most sophisticated connoisseur in both quality and presentation. Choose from an extensive international wine list to complement your meal.

For a change of pace, try dining the restaurants new patio. There is a separate menu here along with live entertainment.

Lunch is served from 11:30 AM to 2 PM, and dinner is served from 5:30 to 10:30 PM daily. La Bibliotheque is closed on Sunday.

THE SILVER CRICKET
4705 South Blvd.　　　　*525-0061*
$$$$

Unpretentious looking from the outside, this quiet, intimate restaurant serves outstanding New Orleans Creole and French country cooking in an authentic French Quarter decor. The atmosphere is romantic and the service is great. Dinner is served from 5 until 10 PM Sunday through Thursday and from 5 until 10:30 PM Friday and Saturday.

German Cuisine

BAVARIAN HAUS
Park Road Shopping Ctr.
Off Brandywine Ave.　　　*523-2406*
$$

German restaurants are usually filled with fun goings on, and the Bavarian Haus is no exception. You'll get excellent German food here. Don't get lost—the restaurant is located on the back side of the shopping center. Entertainment is offered on Friday and Saturday nights. Dinner is served from 5 PM until 10 PM Monday through Friday and from 5:30 PM until 10:30 PM Saturday.

THE RHEINLAND HAUS
2418 Park Rd.　　　　*376-3836*
$$

From the moment customers come through the door, owner James Emmanuel goes way out of his way to make them feel comfortable. Naturally, the primary accent is on German food, but you'll also find plenty of American-style choices as well. The atmosphere is robust and there's piano entertainment from Tuesday through Saturday, and on the first Monday of each month, a German Sauerkraut Band will get you into the spirit of a Hof Brau House in Europe. Hours are from 11:30 AM until 11 PM Monday through Saturday.

Greek Cuisine

GRAPEVINE CAFE
Behind Park Road Shopping Ctr.
540-B Brandywine Rd.   523-5600
$$

Even though Charlotte restaurants have been run by Greeks for years, what do we as customers really know about authentic Greek cooking? Not much because those restaurants have catered to American/ Southern style foods. Most of us know what a pita, Greek Salad or baklava is. Maybe even gyros or dolmades. But do we know from straight up about Saganaki (a little frying pan)— a lightly fried Kefalograviera cheese that is crunchy and succulent? Have we been introduced to wondrous fennel sausages or meatballs?

We do know shish kebab and you can get them here laced with about any meat you want. Salads, served with Calamata olives and Feta cheese are what we know, but try this Cafe's Village Salad prepared without lettuce (there is no lettuce in authentic Greek salads). The soup, Avgolemon, an authentic egg and lemon soup will be a surprise for the American taste buds, but pleasing on a brisk day. For lunch the Yemista

(stuffed tomato or pepper) is filled with a savory spiced rice with a few veggies and Feta. This is served with the restaurant's own crisp potato chips and a salad. Vegetarians will also enjoy the Briami (baked veggies) layered and finished with Kefalotiri.

The Greeks wisely have their big meal, which abounds with lemony, tart and garlicky flavors, in the middle of the day. They don't follow the meal with those very sweet desserts until late afternoon. But American palates are ready for the homemade baklava or cheesecakes or tiramisu with a cup of authentic Greek coffee. This strong coffee is prepared with sugar and served in a demitasse cup without cream.

There is a full wine and beer list with an excellent variety of Greek and Italian and California wines, many by the glass. The Cafe also has draft Greek beer and other imported and domestic beers. The Cafe is open for lunch Monday through Friday from 11:30 AM to 2 PM and dinner is served from 5:30 PM to 10 PM Monday through Thursday and until 10:30 PM on Friday and Saturday. Be sure and ask about the restaurant's Comedy-Mystery Dinner Theatre held on Saturday evenings.

Italian Cuisine

AMICI RESTAURANT
Shops at Piper Glen
6414 Rea Rd.   541-8505
$$$$

Amici, Italian for friend, is not exactly on the beaten restaurant track, nor does it fit the traditional mode of a red-checkered-tablecloth

Italian restaurant in any way except the food. Don't look for meatballs and spaghetti here, but you will find superbly prepared Italian cuisine (with a continental twist),

Decorated in pink and green, the restaurant looks more like a sleek country club lounge than an Italian eatery. This means that you'll be comfortable enough, just don't amble in wearing your gym shorts. It serves a great Amaretto Sour, and it offers a broad selection of Italian and domestic wines. If in season, try the soft shell crab appetizer on angel hair pasta. If crab is not in season, check out the French sauteed mozzarella served with anchovy butter or shrimp baked in puff pastry with mushroom, tomatoes and cheese sauce.

Entrees span the continental gamut, featuring rack of lamb, milk-fed veal, chicken, steaks, seafood and pasta. Pasta's are important here. And you have a terrific selection: Tortellini alla Panna, Chicken and Veal filled Tortellini, Tortellini filled with prosciuto and Peas with alfredo cream sauce. Scallops, rack of lamb and chicken Rapieni (stuffed with homemade Italian sausage) are true standouts.

Desserts are equally enticing and diverse. The tiramisu and custard-like rum raisin bread pudding served over raspberries are good selections. But if you want a different type of dessert treat, then order the Coffee Amici. It's blended with Frangelico, Amaretto and whipped cream. The staff will even do a decaf for you. The restaurant is open from 5 PM to 10 PM, Monday through Saturday.

BRAVO!

Adam's Mark Hotel
300 S. McDowell St.   372-4100
$$$

Authentic regional Italian dining is offered in the area's largest hotel. As advertised, every meal makes an entrance with the restaurant's singing waiters. This is the perfect spot to entertain business clients or out-of-town guests. Dinner is served from 6 PM until 10 PM Sunday through Thursday and from 6 PM until 11 PM on Friday and Saturday.

CAFE 521

521 N. College St.   377-9100
$ - $$

Even though located in the Italian section, this new Uptown restaurant straddles the line between Spain and Italy. The restaurant, with its own parking lot, is a kind of minor miracle of its own. That, and the good news that you can have a hot meal until 1 in the morning. From its rose/brown cinder block walls to its tiled floor and ladder back chairs, 521 doesn't try to be a jazzy restaurant. It's the different tasting Italian and Spanish offerings that draw people, particularly after an Uptown performance when folks may not have had time or appetite to eat before.

You can order seafood, veal, Pizza made with sun-dried tomatoes, a host of cheeses, and pasta with sweet tomatoey sauces (Alla Puttanesca) or crisp, biting ones. Garlic chicken or shrimp is a winner especially with a good imported wine or European beer. The restaurant gives special attention to vegetarian dishes. Flan desserts are available. Meals are served daily Tuesday through Friday from 11:30 AM until 2 AM; Saturday, Sunday and Monday the restaurant is open from 5 PM until 2 AM.

CARLO'S OF SOUTH BOULEVARD
6625 South Blvd.   554-0994
$$

Great Italian food is served throughout the day and into the evening. Check out the early-bird special for dinner from 4 PM until 7 PM—only $6.95! Carlo's is open from 11:30 AM until 10 PM Monday through Thursday, 11:30 AM until 10:30 PM Friday, 4 PM until 10:30 PM Saturday and from 4 PM until 10 PM Sunday.

GIORGIO'S NORTHERN ITALIAN RISTORANTE & PIANO BAR
5301 E. Independence Blvd.   535-7525
$$ - $$$

Some of the best Northern Italian cuisine in the city is served here. Specialties include veal, seafood and pasta dishes—the marinara sauce is superb! There's music in the piano bar Monday through Saturday from 7 PM until 1 AM. Lunch is served from 11:30 AM until 2:30 PM Monday through Thursday and dinner from 5:30 PM until midnight Monday through Thursday. Dinner is served from 5:30 PM until 2 AM Friday and Saturday.

ITALIAN ISLES RESTAURANT
5542 N. Tryon St.   596-4681
$$

Wonderful Italian and Greek dishes are featured on the menu. This restaurant is open from 11 AM until midnight, every day, but it oc-casionally closes during the week around 10:30 PM.

LITTLE ITALY RESTAURANT
2221 Central Ave.   375-1625
$

Serving all of your favorite Italian dishes since 1959, this restaurant also offers daily specials available from the incredibly low price of $3.25 to $4.95—and these special prices are good through dinner! Take out is also available. It's open from 11 AM until 11 PM, Monday through Friday and 3 PM until 11 PM on Saturday.

LUISA'S BRICK OVEN PIZZERIA
1730 Abbey Pl.   522-8782
$-$$

Determined to capture the distinctive taste of real Italian pizza that she remembered from her childhood, Luisa imported a wood burning oven from Italy. Now that's determination! She combines the freshest vegetables, the finest meats, unique herbs and the best of cheeses to create this special dining experience, and the same attention to detail goes into the preparation of other menu items. Buon appetito! Luisa's is open for lunch from 11:30 AM to 2 PM Monday through Friday; for dinner from 5 PM until 9:30 PM Sunday through Thursday and from 5 PM until 10 PM Friday and Saturday. You may telephone ahead for take out.

MANGIONE'S RISTORANTE
1524 East Blvd.   334-4417
$$

This wonderful restaurant has become a tradition in the Charlotte area. Enjoy all of your favorite Italian dishes in a warm, friendly atmosphere. Mangione's is open from 5:30 PM until 10:30 PM Monday through Thursday and from 5:30 PM until 11:30 PM Friday and Saturday.

THE OLD SPAGHETTI FACTORY
911 East Morehead St.   375-0083
$ - $$

If you crave spaghetti, this is the place to go—there are eight varieties. The old Cavalaris skating rink has been renovated into this elegant and antique-filled restaurant. Lunch is served from 11:30 AM until 2 PM Monday through Friday and dinner from 5 PM until 9:30 PM Monday through Thursday, 5 PM until 10:30 PM Friday and Saturday and from noon until 9 PM on Sunday.

THE OPEN KITCHEN
1318 W. Morehead St.   375-7449
$$

In business since 1952, this is the kind of place to bring the kids and let them feast on spaghetti while Mom and Dad savor the finer subtleties of Italian cooking. All the dishes have a distinctive flavor so you won't confuse them with anything you've eaten elsewhere. Even if you don't like Italian food, you'll find something to please your appetite—where else but in the South would an Italian restaurant also offer a daily luncheon special with meat, two vegetables and bread? It's open from 11 AM until 10 PM Monday through Thursday and from 11 AM to 11 PM on Friday and from 4 to 11 PM on Saturday. Sunday hours are from 4 to 10 PM.

PIZZARRELLI'S
9101 Pineville-Matthews Rd.   543-0647
$$

This restaurant serves pizza, lasagna, spaghetti, salads, and sandwiches in a casual, comfortable style. There's no scheduled entertainment, but you never know when owner Neil Zarrelli may decide to burst into song. Lunch is served from 11:30 AM until 3 PM Monday through Saturday and dinner from 5 PM until 10 PM Sunday through Thursday and from 5 PM until 11 PM on Friday and Saturday.

SCALINI
Hyatt Charlotte
5501 Carnegie Blvd.   554-1234
$$$$

Scalini, a 3 1/2 star restaurant, serves Northern Italian cuisine in the evening and oversized salads and sandwiches for lunch. Try the weekend country breakfasts for great food at a great price. Breakfast is served from 6 AM until 11 AM Monday through Friday and from 7 AM until 2 PM on Saturday and Sunday. Daily lunch hours are from 11 AM until 2:30 PM and dinner is served from 5 PM until 10:30 PM daily.

...SI!
Quail Corners Shopping Ctr.
8418 Park Rd.   556-0914
$$$

This is a great place for Italian cuisine in the Southeast Charlotte area. Dinner begins with fresh baked Italian bread served with olive oil for dipping and the pasta dishes are all delicious. Lunch is available from 11:30 AM until 2:30 PM Monday through Friday, dinner from 6 PM until 11 PM Monday through Saturday.

THE SPAGHETTI WAREHOUSE

101 W. Worthington Ave.   *376-8686*
$ - $$

This is a large but very reasonably priced and efficient restaurant. Great spaghetti dishes with combinations are available and the excellent Minestrone and Italian Wedding soups are a real treat. The restaurant is open for lunch from 11 AM until 3 PM Monday through Friday and for dinner from 3 PM until 10 PM Monday through Thursday, 3 PM until 11 PM on Friday, noon until 11 PM on Saturday and noon until 10 PM Sunday.

VILLA ANTONIO ITALIAN RESTAURANT

4707 South Blvd.   *523-1594*
$$ - $$$

The restaurant's authentically prepared Italian cuisine is simply delicious and the quiet, romantic atmosphere here helps to make a very special evening. Lunch is served from 11:30 AM until 3 PM Monday through Friday and dinner from 5 PM until 11 PM. Dinner is served from 5 PM until midnight on Saturday. Brunch hours on Sunday are from 11 AM until 3 PM.

Mexican/Spanish

EL CANCUN MEXICAN RESTAURANT

5234 South Blvd.	*525-5075*
3001 E. Independence Blvd.	*376-9424*
5661 Farm Pond La.	*536-7757*
8706 Pineville-Matthews Rd.	
Pineville	*542-6087*
1401 E. Morehead St.	*347-2626*
197 Carowinds Blvd.	
Fort Mill, SC	*(803) 548-6222*
1244 Cherry Rd.	
Rock Hill, SC	*(803) 366-6996*
853 Garison Blvd.	
Gastonia	*843-2855*

$ - $$

The closest thing to authentic Mexican food in the city is served here, as is good Tex-Mex. The restaurant is not fancy and the ambience varies with charm falling rather low on the scale. Nevertheless, what it does right is food. That's why you can now eat at eight different locations. Outdoor dining is available at the Farm Pond Lane location. Take out is also available. Lunch is served from 11 AM until 2:30 PM, Monday through Friday. Dinner is available from 5 PM until 11 PM Monday through Friday, noon until 11 PM Saturday and noon until 10:30 PM Sunday.

LA PAZ

523 Fenton Pl.   *372-4168 or 372-4169*
$$

Located just off Providence Rd., this is probably Charlotte's most popular Mexican restaurant. The food is excellent and there is a great upstairs bar that also serves dinner. It serves a dynamite Margarita and you can order nachos from the bar to satisfy the munchies. If you're dining with the family, there is a full children's menu. Take-out is available and the restaurant will take reservations for parties of eight or more. La Paz is open for dinner from 5 PM until 10 PM Sunday through Thursday and from 5 PM until 11 PM Friday through Saturday.

MONTERREY RESTAURANTE
MEXICANO

Park 51 Shopping Ctr.
10707 Park Rd. at N.C. 51
Pineville   541-6664
Windsor Square Shopping Ctr. 841-8068
Royal Plaza Shopping Ctr.
Harris and Albemarle rds.   535-5497
$$

This is a casual, fun restaurant featuring fantastic Mexican cuisine. If you like large margaritas, this is the place to go because it has an extra-large one, five times the normal size. Lunch is served from 11 AM until 2:30 PM and dinner from 5 until 10:30 PM Monday through Thursday. On Friday, it is open from 5 Pm until 11 PM and from noon to 11 PM on Saturday and from noon to 10 PM on Sunday.

OCHO CAFE

Specialty Shops on the Park
Morrison Blvd.   364-5734
$$ - $$$

A great newcomer in a transformed setting is this authentic looking Mexican-style cantina. Cement floors complete with stacks of drink bottles and chicken coop wire round out the decor. An authentic bar looks very south of the border. Lunch is served from 11:30 AM until 2:15 PM Monday through Saturday; dinner from 5 PM until 10 PM Sunday through Thursday and from 5 PM until 10:30 PM Friday and Saturday. Sunday brunch is served from 10:30 AM until 2:30 PM.

A great newcomer in a transformed setting is this authentic looking Mexican-style cantina, Ocho Cafe.

La Place to be.

"Unarguably the best Mexican Restaurant in Charlotte..."
—Dannye Romine, Food Critic

La paz
Restaurante Mexicano

372-4168
523 Fenton Place

*Off the 700 Block of
Providence Road*

Catering Available

MC • AMEX • VISA • Diner's Club • Discover

Sun - Thurs 5-10 pm • Fri & Sat 5-11 pm

PANCHO & LEFTY'S TEX-MEX CANTINA
Kings Point Shopping Ctr.
601 S. Kings Dr.   375-2334
$$

Nachos, quesadillas, fajitas, mesquite grilled burgers, Tex-Mex chili and much more are featured on the appetizer menu. For dessert, how about a frozen marqarita pie? This exceptional restaurant's chicken fajitas won in the **Best of Charlotte** selection. Or, try out the restaurant's shrimp fajitas for something different and delicious. It's open from 11:30 AM until 10 PM Monday through Thursday, 11:30 AM until 11 PM Friday and Saturday and 4 PM until 10 PM Sunday.

TIO MONTERO
207 Johnston Dr.
Pineville   889-2258
$$-$$$

The original Tio's restaurant on Scott Avenue, the Spanish restaurant that took Charlotte by storm,

earned four stars, and it branched out to Pineville. Unfortunately, the Scott Avenue restaurant has closed, but the remaining location still serves authentic Spanish dishes that most Charlotteans aren't accustomed to tasting such as: Figlo—Eggplant smothered in Spanish cheese, Zarzuela—seafood in tomato sauce, Pescado ala Sal—red snapper baked in salt, served tableside and a great paella. Tex-Mex dishes are also on the menu. Lunch is served from 11 AM until 2 PM Monday through Friday and dinner from 5 PM until 10 PM Sunday through Thursday. The restaurant is open until 11 PM on Friday and Saturday.

Oriental Cuisine

BAODING
Sharon Corners Shopping Ctr.
4722 Sharon Rd.   552-8899
$$$

The restaurant's design looks more like an upscale New York eatery than the typical oriental restaurant. Perhaps that owes to the fact that this isn't "typical." The North Chinese food is chic and matches the decor. You'll know it's oriental, but modern techniques make dining here exceptional. This is without doubt one of the best oriental restaurants in Charlotte. Lunch is served from 11:30 AM to 2:30 PM Monday through Friday and from noon until 3 PM on Saturday and Sunday. Dinner is served from 5 PM to 10 PM Sunday through Thursday and from 5 PM to 11 PM Friday and Saturday. Take out is available.

GINGER ROOT
201 E. 5th St.   377-9429
$$

Oriental restaurants are often swathed in, or at the very least, accented with red and black; the Ginger Root isn't. A design of art

nouveau, decorated with pastels and significant oriental pieces gives this Uptown restaurant a very sophisticated introduction. The food is just as unique and outstanding. Guests begin with a complimentary bowl of Won Ton Soup. All the old favorites will be on the menu, along with a selection of Szechuan, Cantonese and a Mandarin dish from time to time. Lunch is served from 11:30 AM until 2:30 PM Monday through Sunday. Dinner begins at 5 PM and is served until 9:30 PM Monday through Thursday and until 10:30 PM on Friday and Saturday.

CHEF CHEN
The Arboretum
8200 Providence Rd.   541-1678
$$

Formerly the Jade Garden Restaurant, new ownership brings an entirely new style of cooking. The

Half the fun of eating in a Japanese restaurant is watching the show put on by the chefs as they prepare your meal.

wonderfully spicy Sezchuan cuisine is a real pleaser. Try the restaurant's fried dumplings. Chef Chen is open from 11:30 AM until 10 PM Monday through Thursday and from 11 AM to 11 PM on Friday and Saturday. Sunday hours are from noon until 10 PM.

KABUTO JAPANESE STEAK HOUSE
446 Tyvola Rd.   529-0659
1001 E. W.T. Harris Blvd.   548-1219
$$

Watching the chefs is half the fun of eating here. They slice, dice and prepare your meal, with great drama, right before your eyes. Lunch is served from 11:30 AM until 2 PM Monday through Friday and the dinner hours are 5:30 PM until 10 PM. Monday through Thursday, 5:30 PM until 10:30 PM Friday and Saturday and 5 PM until 9:30 PM Sunday.

NAKATO JAPANESE RESTAURANT
8500 Pineville-Matthews Hwy.   543-8899
$$$

Steak, chicken and seafood are cooked right before your eyes by skillful chefs. For a special treat, try the floating sushi bar or the tatami room. Reservations are suggested. Nakato is open from 5 PM until 10 PM Monday through Sunday and open until 11 PM on Saturday.

RESTAURANT TOKYO
4603 South Blvd.   527-8787
$$$

Savor Japanese food at its finest at this wonderful restaurant. Sushi is served a la carte at your table or from the sushi bar. You can't go wrong with the sukiyaki or the outstanding Tokyo Tempura. Open for lunch from 11:30 AM until 2 PM Monday through Friday, for dinner from 5:30 PM until 10 PM Monday through Thursday and from 5:30 PM until 10:30 PM Friday and Saturday. Sunday hours are from 5 until 9 PM.

SHUN LEE PALACE
4340 Colwick Rd.   366-2025
$ - $$

This is a favorite Chinese restaurant for many Charlotteans, with a wide variety of specials to choose from. Shun Lee Palace is open from 11:30 AM until 10 PM Monday through Thursday, 11:30 AM until 11 PM on Friday. Saturday hours are from 5 PM until 10 PM and from noon to 10 PM on Sunday.

THAI TASTE
324 East Blvd.   332-0001
8652 Pineville-Matthews Hwy. 542-6300
$$

We've been complaining for years that Charlotte had no Thai restaurant and now we have several—testimony to the popularity of this tasty food. The curry dishes at Thai Taste are excellent, just let the waitperson know how "hot and spicy" you'd like it to be. Lunch is available from 11:30 AM until 3 PM Tuesday through Sunday and dinner from 5 PM until 11 PM Friday and Saturday.

WAN FU
10719 Kettering Dr.   541-1688
$$ - $$$

Some of the finest Chinese food in the city, everything on the menu is presented beautifully and expertly prepared. This is a terrific bargain for lunch or Sunday brunch.

Lunch hours are from 11:30 PM until 2:30 PM. Monday through Friday and from 11:30 AM until 3 PM on Saturday and Sunday. Dinner is served from 5 PM until 10 PM Sunday through Thursday and 5 PM until 11 PM Friday and Saturday.

Sports Bars

ALL AMERICAN SPORTS BAR
2204 Park Rd.   358-1600
$

Salads, spuds (four varieties) and sandwiches are the main fare here, along with wings, nachos and burgers. Lunch is served from 11:30 AM on Saturday only. The bar is open from 3 PM to midnight Monday through Saturday.

THE PRESS BOX
1627 Montford Dr.   523-4981
$$

One of the first sports bars in the city, it has wide-screen TVs and terrific food. Favorites include the Matheny Burger, the Pita Kabob and the Honey Delight, all served with those famous cottage fries. Don't miss the Hot Fudge Cake for desert! Open every day from 11 AM until 11 PM.

SANDWICH CONSTRUCTION CO.
7801 University City Blvd.   597-0008
$$

Soups, sandwiches, burgers, salads and a variety of daily specials are served alongside NASCAR memorabilia. This casual dining spot is located near UNCC and is open 7 days a week from 11 AM until 11 PM. The bar remains open until 1 AM.

ALL SPORTS CAFE
South Executive Park
6010 Fairview Rd.   366-3663
$ - $$$

This sports oriented cafe is open for lunch and dinner from 11 AM until around 1 AM seven days a week. (It's closed on Sundays during summer months.) All Sports is located near SouthPark Mall and at any given time, you might see a Charlotte Hornet or owner George Shinn getting a bite of seafood.

SEAFOOD

THE HIDE-A-WAY INN
8517 Monroe Rd.   537-4418
$$

This is an old-fashioned family-style fish camp the whole family will enjoy. All entrees are available broiled or fried. Children 5 and under eat for free. The restaurant is open from 5 PM until 9:30 PM Monday through Thursday and from 4:30 PM until 10 PM Friday and Saturday. Dinner is served from 4 PM until 9:30 PM on Sunday.

KEY WEST BAR & GRILL
4544 South Blvd. at Sterling Dr.   522-6100
$$ - $$$

With homage to Hemingway—Ernest, of course—this popular regulars-type hangout restaurant offers great seafood served in casual, fun surroundings. Its soups are dynamite and the chef does special things with seafood that nobody else in town has imitated so far. The outdoor patio and the fresh seafood market make this place a real find. Key West Bar & Grill is open from 11 AM until 11 PM Sunday through Wednesday and from 11:30 AM until 1:30 AM Wednesday through Saturday. The bar stays open until 2 AM daily.

SEAFOOD FACTORY

2920 Central Ave.   *535-3663*
$-$$

Formerly Calabash Cove, this restaurant now offers a new personality. Its patriotic menu explains: "Factories are what made America strong by buying in large lots, using the assembly line...to produce products at low prices." Only food products, beer and wine from America are served. Your best bets here are the steamed shrimp and oysters, fresh from Florida waters, but you can get anything fried or boiled, too. Adventurers should try the 'gator appetizer. Sauteed shellfish, grilled chicken and pastas are also available, but save room for the house-made desserts that feature Key lime pie, peanut butter pie and cheesecake. The restaurant is open from 5 PM until 9 PM Sunday and Monday, and from 5 PM until 10 PM the rest of the week.

SHARK FINNS

6051 Old Pineville Rd.   *525-3738*
$$

This old train station in Pineville gives a new definition to "laid-back." Like, you're not sure if you really want to go in until you do. But you have an idea what you're in for when you see the sign that offers: "Eat, Drink, Be Fat and Drunk."

This is not exactly a low-cal, health conscience place, though its grilled grouper would please any cardiac doctor. Insiders like the combo plate called "Feeding Frenzy." You'll get plenty of snow crab, shrimp, oysters, and crawfish in that. It also offers sandwiches and salads and spicy Jambalaya and gumbo, and of course—shark bites.

We like restaurants where customers get to play games and sing their tin ears off. You can get into it on Crab Race Nights (currently, Thursdays, but check first) when your racing hermit crab crosses the finish line, winning you something cool from the bar or maybe an appetizer.

Formally known as AW Shucks, the specialties, blackened redfish, gumbo and frog legs, are still popular. The live music on Thursday, Friday and Saturday nights is a real "happening." Shark Finns is open from 11:30 AM until midnight Monday through Friday, and 5 PM until midnight on Saturday.

Steak Houses

Charlotte has three traditional steak houses with great food and lots of history. All have been around for years and have a loyal following of Insiders who pass along enthusiastic recommendations to anyone who asks.

HEREFORD BARN STEAK HOUSE
4320 N. I-85 at Graham St.　　596-0854

MEADOWVIEW STEAK HOUSE
9727 E. Independence Blvd.
Matthews　　847-3238

RANCH HOUSE
5614 Wilkinson Blvd.　　399-5411

Other local favorites include:

BEEF 'N BOTTLE
4538 South Blvd.　　523-9977
$$-$$$

If you're looking for an old-time Charlotte steak house with a romantic touch, try this one. Famous for its superb steaks, it also offers excellent seafood dishes and has an extensive wine list. The restaurant is open for dinner from 5:30 PM until 10:30 PM Monday through Saturday.

DUNDEE'S STEAK HOUSE
The Arboretum
8128 Providence Rd.　　543-6299
$$

Served in a casual, Australian decor, the prime rib comes in three sizes and the homemade desserts are a real delight. Dundee's is open from 5 PM until 10 PM Monday through Thursday, from 5 PM until 11 PM on Friday and Saturday and from 5 PM to 9 PM on Sunday. The bar stays open one hour later.

LONE STAR
STEAK HOUSE & SALOON
3101 N. Sharon Amity Rd.　　568-2388
5033 South Blvd.　　523-2388
10610-A Centrum Pkwy.
(across from Carolina Place Mall)
Pineville　　543-1922
$ - $$$

You may have known the Sharon Amity location as Chisholm's or the South Boulevard location as Cripple Creek Steak House & Saloon, but whatever the name, the restaurant features great grilled steaks, seafood, ribs and burgers served in casual surroundings.Each location has different hours, so you may want to call first.

LONGHORN STEAKS
RESTAURANT & SALOON
700 E. Morehead St.　　332-2300
McMullen Creek Market Place　　541-5100
Crown Point Shopping Ctr.
Independence Blvd.　　847-1212
$-$$$

Jeans, steaks and beers are the order of the day here. A free-play jukebox and a lively crowd make for great fun—and perfectly prepared steaks make for great eats. The restaurant is open from 11 AM until 10:30 PM Monday through Thursday, 11 AM until 11 PM Friday, 4 PM until 11 PM Saturday and from 5 PM until 10 PM Sunday.

NICKYO'S RODEO
RESTAURANT & SALOON
731 Providence Rd.　　331-9150
$$

Great times, great fajitas and great steaks are trademarks at Nickyo's. Bessie's filet is always a favorite for dinner. Nickyo's is open from 5 PM until 11 PM Sunday through Thursday and from 5 PM until 1 AM Friday and Saturday.

OUTBACK STEAKHOUSE

1412-A East Blvd.   333-0505
Windsor Square
Matthews   845-2222
$$

A taste of Australia comes to Charlotte and offers more than steaks. The chicken, ribs and fish are also excellent. Try the "Bloomin Onion" appetizer. Dinner is served from 4:30 PM until 10:30 PM Monday through Thursday, 4:30 PM until 11:30 PM Friday, 4 PM until 11:30 PM Saturday and from 4:30 PM until 10 PM on Sunday.

Catering

Just pick up the telephone book and you will find dozens of Charlotte chefs, from A to Z, who will cater to your every wish. But the secret is to find one that can fit the needs of your special event, whether it is a barbecue for 3,000 or an intimate dinner party for your closest friends. Hotels and restaurants are the most likely caters, but you will usually receive a more personalized approach with a business that only does catering. Some include setup and cleanup and everything in between, or you may just want someone to prepare the food and take all the credit yourself. Below is a sampling of a few of Charlotte's established caterers.

CHARLOTTE CATERING & BAKERY

377-8700

Besides the usual weddings, parties and receptions, the owner Libby Glenn will also create a memorable cake for your special occasion.

ELI'S CATERING

529-1400

A well earned reputation has made Eli's one of the city's more prominent caterers. The presentation is as delightful as the food is delicious.

ELLEN DAVIS CATERING

376-9641

For business or pleasure, Ellen Davis will cater to your every delicious whim.

FDY BANQUETS & CATERING

522-8477

This local catering house specializes in parties, weddings and sit-down dinners.

GLORIOUS CUISINE CATERING

847-8331

The husband and wife team of Joseph Falceto and Holly Postle present perfect catering with a European flair. They are particularly well-known for their baked goods.

SERIOUS FUN EVENTS

597-8563

Special event service and production are the specialty of this company. The owners and their staff take their fun very seriously!

SIDE PORCH CATERING

(803) 285-6660

Insiders have trusted Jackie Mackey's originality and flair for deliciously catered food for years. You'll see her team at weddings and major Charlotte events.

Photo by Candee Potter, CPCC © 1992.

*A wide variety of services and activities are available
for Charlotte's growing population of retired citizens.*

Inside
Retirement

*L*ike the rest of the United States, the older population is growing here in Charlotte. The 1990 Census shows that there were 66,617 people over the age of 60 in Mecklenburg County. The Census projected that by the year 2000, there would be 79,653 people over 60. The fastest-growing population segment is for persons 85 and older. Many services are offered in the Charlotte area for this rapidly growing age group.

Both organizations and living communities cater to the active retiree. There are many private, public and church activities to keep senior citizens involved in the community, and organizations that need volunteers always welcome senior citizens to come and share their talents and experiences. For volunteer opportunities call the Volunteer Center at 372-7170.

A resource guide covering almost every aspect of retired life, including adult day care, housing, home health care, employment, nutrition, counseling, clubs and volunteer opportunities is available for $2.00 by calling 347-0400. Here is a sample of some of the programs offered for seniors in the area.

CHARLOTTE-MECKLENBURG SENIOR SERVICES, INC.
1201 Dilworth Rd.   334-4053

The Charlotte-Mecklenburg Senior Services, Inc., provides a broad spectrum of services and programs for all adults age 55 and older. In 1990-91, it supported over 26,000 seniors throughout Mecklenburg County with 64,000 units of service (a unit of service is defined as one service such as health screening, job placement or counseling service). The Centers offer many valuable services such as health screenings, education, employment, Say Y.E.S. (an intergenerational program to link youth and older adults using schools), and the Senior Aides Project which teaches seniors new skills through internships. If you are interested in any of these projects, call the Charlotte-Mecklenburg Senior Services at 334-4053.

COUNCIL ON AGING
1515 Mockingbird Ln.
Ste. 414   527-8807

Funded by the county and the United Way, the Council acts as a resource center, clearinghouse and advocacy group for the elderly. The Council offers workshops, conferences and educational programs for and about seniors and also funds **Ageline** (347-0400), an information and referral hotline for Charlotte-Mecklenburg seniors. If you don't know who to call or where to go, this is a good starting point.

LONG-TERM OMBUDSMAN PROGRAM
1300 Baxter St.   372-2416

The program is made up of regional ombudsmen and volunteer citizen advocates who work to protect the rights of those living in nursing homes, rest homes and family-care homes. They are also available to answer any questions about long-term care and provide information on the options available.

MECKLENBURG COUNTY SENIOR CITIZEN NUTRITION PROGRAM
301 Billingsly Rd.   336-4813

This program offers on-site meals as well as social interaction and activities in 17 different locations. It also provides home-delivered meals and transportation services.

RETIRED SENIOR VOLUNTEER PROGRAM (RSVP)
1201 Dilworth Rd.   334-3053

This is a special program geared for placing volunteers, aged 60 and over, in meaningful positions in nonprofit and public organizations. Volunteer positions are available all over the county, such as Discovery Place, local hospitals, the American Red Cross and libraries. RSVP is unique in that it reimburses its volunteers for mileage and meals and offers liability and accident insurance.

SHEPHERDS CENTER OF CHARLOTTE, INC.
P.O. Box 6052
Charlotte, NC 28207   334-4637

With offices at Myers Park Baptist Church, the Shepherds Center is an interfaith organization sponsored by churches and synagogues and serves older persons with or without religious affiliation. It is a concept, not a place: the concept of able people of retirement age learning and enjoying life and assisting their peers who need help to stay in their own homes. The program has two divisions: education and home service. Call the Shepherds Center to find out more specific information on the variety of programs they offer.

Here is a list of helpful phone numbers:

Ageline (Information and referral 24-hour hotline)	347-0400
AARP	376-2298
Adult Care and Share Center	334-8344
Centralina Area Agency on Aging	372-2416
Charlotte-Meck. Senior Ctrs.	334-3053
CHISS (Community Housing Information Service for Seniors)	347-4637
CPCC Older Adult Program	342-6464
Council on Aging	527-8807
Davidson Senior Services	892-5111
Family Outreach Adult Day Care	332-7037
Friendship Trays	333-9229
Health Department	336-4650
Housing Authority	336-5183
Legal Services For The Elderly	334-0400

Mecklenburg Co. Tax Administrator
(Property tax exemption for elderly)336-2813
Mecklenburg Co. Social Services
(Older and Disabled Adult Services)
Medicare:
Hotline	(800) 672-3071
Information and Applications	336-4812
Mecklenburg Respite Services	393-5914
Mental Health Services	375-3575
Programs for Accessible Living	375-3977
Red Cross (Transportation for Medical Appointments)	376-1661
Retired Senior Volunteer Program	334-3053
Selwyn Life Center	379-5005
Shepherds Center	334-4637
SeniorCare Network at Presbyterian	384-7460
SHIIP (Senior Health Insurance Information Program)	347-4637
Social Security Adm.	(800) 234-5772
Special Transportation Services (Handicapped)	336-3637
Transportation Assistance	336-4547
Travelers Aid	334-7288

Retirement & Life Communities & Homes

Charlotte, like the rest of the state, is coming into its own as a retirement center. North Carolina's population has grown during the past two decades because of its Sunbelt climate and growing job market. Many of these people, who now like calling North Carolina home, have come here to retire. Still retirement living has not yet become a growth industry like it has in Florida, Arizona and southern California.

Some retirees are moving here to be closer to their children, and others have started second careers once they've settled in. When people talk about retirement areas in North Carolina, they usually start with

Pinehurst and Southern Pines, east of Charlotte in the Sandhills where golf courses are considered a local crop. The coast is another popular place to take life easy.

Recent years, however, have seen a substantial increase in retirement areas in Charlotte and Mecklenburg County. These are not nursing homes but rather retirement communities that take the hassles out of everyday life. They offer residents independent living as well as varying degrees of health-care services if the needs arise. Retirement communities offer meals, housekeeping and transportation services as well as many other amenities.

Here is a sampling of a few of Charlotte's retirement communities:

BROOKWOOD
Huntersville   875-7540

This assisted-living facility is associated with the Charlotte-Mecklenburg Hospital Authority and offers cottage living in a country setting.

CARMEL PLACE
5512 Carmel Rd.   541-8012

A rental retirement community, Carmel Place offers a nice South Charlotte location with a terrific amenities package including housekeeping services, a barber and beauty salon, 24-hour security and transportation.

CARRIAGE CLUB
5700 Old Providence Rd.   366-4960

This club-style retirement center has apartments and villas and offers all the amenities in a prestigious South Charlotte location. This center offers a pool, Jacuzzi and an exercise room in addition to all the amenities: kitchens equipped with quality electric appliances, washer/dryer units in all apartments, housekeeping and meals. The Coach House at the Carriage Club offers personalized assisted-living care.

MERRYWOOD

3600 Park Rd.   *523-4949*

This beautiful, wooded site blends well with the history and southern charm of the Park Road and Dilworth neighborhoods that surround it. Close to shopping, next-door to the YWCA and just minutes away from Uptown and hospitals, if you are looking for a convenient location, look here. Merrywood is a 174-unit rental apartment commu-

nity offering active, independent living for senior adults.

THE METHODIST HOME

3420 Shamrock Dr.   *532-3000*

The Methodist Home, which opened in 1948, is located on a 225-acre campus in Northeastern Charlotte. There are three facilities on the campus that provide quality retirement living and top-rated health care. Epworth Place is the Retirement Community, and it offers apartments and cottages with an assisted-living service available for support. Asbury Care Center and Wesley Nursing Center are the nursing care facilities, and residents of Epworth Place are given priority on space in these two centers when needed. All necessities of daily living are available here, as well as many amenities and planned activities.

Photo by John Cress

*Retirement centers like South Charlotte's Carriage Club
take the hassles out of everyday living.*

PINES AT DAVIDSON
400 Avinger Ln.
Davidson   896-1100

This nonprofit retirement community for independent living offers apartments and cottages. Amenities include meals, housekeeping, transportation and three levels of continuing care. Residents also have access to Davidson College, allowing them to audit classes and attend a multitude of cultural events. Residents also receive membership to nearby River Run Country Club.

PLANTATION ESTATES
733 Plantation Estates
Matthews   847-4800

If you enjoy fine dining and super recreational facilities, check out the spacious, Colonial Williamsburg-style apartment homes here. Plantation Estates offers its residents all levels of care from independent living to nursing care for no additional cost.

SHARON TOWERS
THE PRESBYTERIAN HOME AT CHARLOTTE, INC.
5100 Sharon Rd.   553-1670

A retirement community of incomparable style and convenience, Sharon Towers puts its residents at the very heart of Charlotte. Located in the popular SouthPark neighborhood, it is the oldest and most established retirement community in the area, offering independent and long-term care facilities. Sharon Towers is an active community with recreational facilities on-site, a library and a NationsBank branch bank. Sharon Towers offers apartment as well as cottage living, and houses a long-term infirmary for residents who need additional care.

SOUTHMINSTER INC.
8919 Park Rd.   551-6800

In 1983, a distinguished group of sponsors from two of Charlotte's most prominent churches, motivated by the need to find a retirement home for their loved ones, decided to build Southminster. Located on Park Road in South Charlotte, the facility, which opened in June 1987, offers a full range of amenities in a warm, friendly atmosphere. The independent living area contains apartments and cottages equipped with emergency call systems and such options as housekeeping, maintenance, a full-service dining room and scheduled activities and transportation. The Health Center offers three levels of care-assisted living, intermediate nursing care and skilled nursing care.

There is quick response to the emergency call system in each apartment. Two full-time recreation directors plan exciting and varied social activities, classes and sight-seeing trips. Free chauffeured transportation service is offered for regular shopping trips, medical appointments and cultural events. In addition, regular housekeeping service, a barber and beauty salon, general store, First Union National Bank branch and a Presbyterian Hospital wellness clinic are all available.

Charlotte Country Day Concentrates On Scholarly Pursuits

And The Pursuits Of Scholars

CHARLOTTE COUNTRY DAY SCHOOL

For further information contact the Admissions Office at 704-366-1241
or 1440 Carmel Road, Charlotte, NC 28226.

Inside
Schools and Child Care

*T*he Charlotte-Mecklenburg School System is the largest system in the Carolinas and the 27th largest in the nation, serving more than 82,000 students. With 9200 employees, the school system is undergoing some much needed major changes brought about by Superintendent John Murphy. Dr. Murphy began his position as superintendent in July of 1991 and began integrating a new philosophy toward teaching children.

Dr. Murphy has given individual schools more control, and he has adopted a merit bonus pay plan for teachers, based on increased performance from their students. He has also changed CMS policy on firing teachers. Now, if cuts need to be made to reduce the size of the teacher base, they can be made based on performance rather than on seniority, as before. Although many people may have been skeptical of the changes brought on by Dr. Murphy, they now see how the school system has benefited from the changes. Dr. Murphy has proven to be exactly what the Charlotte-

Mecklenburg School System needed—a fresh, new outlook on education.

The vision of the Charlotte-Mecklenburg School System is "to ensure that the Charlotte-Mecklenburg School System becomes the premier urban, integrated system in the nation in which all students acquire the knowledge, skills and values necessary to live rich and full lives as productive and enlightened members of society."

In recent years, CMS has been honored in the Outstanding School Recognition Program sponsored by the U.S. Department of Education with Myers Park High, Carmel Junior High, First Ward Elementary, and Piedmont Open Middle School receiving awards. CMS has also had 12 award-winning programs in the nine-year history of the Governors Program of Excellence.

Students in the Charlotte-Mecklenburg Schools still undergo mandatory bussing to racially desegregate the schools, but one aspect of Dr. Murphy's plan includes integrating the school system in a more equitable, more acceptable way in order to focus on the quality of education, not transportation. Means to accomplish this are stand-alone schools in naturally racially balanced neighborhoods, midpoint schools between predominantly black and white neighborhoods that result in shorter bus rides and magnet schools.

For the last seven years, enrollment in the Charlotte-Mecklenburg Schools has been increasing, and projections show that growth will continue throughout the remainder of the '90s. At current growth rates, the number of students will increase by more than 36,000 by the year 2000.

Mecklenburg County voters have a proud tradition of supporting school construction bonds, most recently in 1985, 1987 and 1989. The 1989 bonds already are funding the construction of 100 new classrooms at existing schools throughout the county, as well as office, cafeteria and library expansions.

Currently, the school system is launching the second phase of classroom construction financed by the 1989 bonds. During this phase, a total of 79 classrooms will be added to 13 schools. School office, cafeteria and library expansions and new cooling systems are a part of the second phase.

To better utilize the taxpayer's money, CMS used modified plans from recently completed elementary schools for two of the new elementary schools. West Charlotte High School's aquatic center is a revised version of the one at Providence High.

Magnet Schools

Beginning in the 1992-93 school year, Charlotte-Mecklenburg Schools added magnet schools to its program. A magnet school features a special program designed to attract students who have interests or talents in a particular area. Magnet schools feature the required curriculum of the Charlotte-Mecklenburg Schools but also provide a range of special subjects, activities and learning opportunities.

Magnet schools are a part of the Charlotte-Mecklenburg Schools Student Assignment Plan, and it is believed that because of shifting populations and the aging of neighborhoods, the magnet concept will better utilize the physical facilities now available. Magnet schools have also been created to improve racial balance and emphasize particular subject matter or particular instructional philosophies.

Students are admitted to the magnet schools through a lottery

Insiders' Tip

Charlotte's magnet schools feature special programs designed to attract students who have interests or talents in a particular area.

Photo by John Cress.

The new South Charlotte Middle School
is part of the classroom construction financed by the 1989 bonds.

program. If one child in a family is admitted, the others are admitted automatically if they are listed on the original application. Once a child is admitted to a magnet school, he or she will continue there through the terminal grade at that school.

You must live in Mecklenburg County to apply to the magnet program, and transportation is provided by the school system. All students, regardless of whether they have attended public or private schools, have equal access to apply to the magnet schools.

For more information about the magnet school program, call 379-7360. The following is a list of magnet schools for the 1994-95 school year:

ACADEMICALLY GIFTED (3-5)
(STUDENTS MUST MEET SPECIAL REQUIREMENTS)
Villa Heights Elementary
Barringer Elementary
Lincoln Heights Elementary

LEARNING IMMERSION (K-2)
Villa Heights Elementary
Barringer Elementary
Lincoln Heights Elementary

YEAR-ROUND WITH EXTENDED DAY
Bruns Avenue Elementary (K-5)
Northwest Middle (6-8)

GERMAN IMMERSION
Bruns Avenue Elementary (K-3)

COMMUNICATIONS AND ACADEMIC STUDIES
Old Providence Elementary (K-5)
David Cox Elementary (K-5)
Marie G. Davis Middle (6-8)

MATH, SCIENCE & TECHNOLOGY
Ashley Park Elementary (K-5)
Oaklawn Elementary (K-5)
Spaugh Middle (6-8)
Harding University High (9-12)

MONTESSORI
Amay James Elementary (Pre K-2)

TRADITIONAL CLASSICAL
Elizabeth Elementary (K-6)
Myers Park Elementary (K-6)
Druid Hills Elementary (K-6)
Hawthorne Middle (7-9)
J.T. Williams Middle (7-9)

OPEN
Irwin Avenue Elementary (K-5)
Piedmont Open Middle (6-9)
Northwest Open Middle (6-9)
West Charlotte High (10-12)

VISUAL AND PERFORMING ARTS
Chantilly Elementary (K-5)
Northwest Middle (6-9)

INTERNATIONAL/GLOBAL STUDIES
Lincoln Heights Elementary (K-6)

INTERNATIONAL BACCALAUREATE, PRE-IB AND MIDDLE YEARS IB
Reid Park Elementary (K-5)
Druid Hills Elementary (K-6)
Marie G. Davis Middle (6-8)
Sedgefield Middle (6-8)
J.T. Williams Middle (6-8)
Alexander/Davidson Middle (7-9)
Harding University High (9-12)
Independence High (9-12)
Myers Park High (9-12)

ACADEMY OF FINANCE
(CONCENTRATED STUDY IN FINANCIAL SERVICES INDUSTRY)
Garringer High School (9-12)

Charlotte/Mecklenburg School Facts

Total number of schools	121
Special programs	9
Elementary schools	78
Middle schools	23
High schools	11
Total number of students enrolled	82,252
Grades K-3	27,909
Grades 4-6	19,278
Grades 7-9	18,706
Grades 10-12	14,952
Evening School	201
Metro School	173
Special Education (Self Contained)	1, 214
Dolly Tate Teen-Age Parent Services	145
Native American	0 .5%
Asian	3.5%
Black	40.5%
Hispanic	1.5%
White	54.5%
Grades K-9 class size Student Average	26
Grades 10-12 class size Student Average	30
Average daily attendance	93%
Graduates continuing their education	83.2%

Garringer High School (9-10)

Board Of Education

The Charlotte/Mecklenburg School System is governed by a nine-member Board of Education, whose members are elected on a nonpartisan basis from the county as a whole to serve rotating four-year terms. One of their duties is to appoint the superintendent.

The Board of Education holds its regular meetings on the second and fourth Tuesdays of each month in the board room on the fourth floor of the Education Center. These meetings are open to the public and follow an agenda available in the board room prior to the meeting. One of the two monthly meetings, normally the one on the second Tuesday, is televised live on WTVI, Channel 42.

BOARD OF EDUCATION MEMBERS

Chairperson: George Battle, Jr.

Vice Chairperson: Jane McIntyre

Susan Burgess
Sharon Bynum
Arthur Griffin, Jr.
John Lassiter
Jan Richards
William Rikard
John A. Tate, III

ADMINISTRATIVE STAFF

Superintendent:
John Murphy

Chief Administrative Officer:
Norman Walsh

Chief Operations and Finance Officer:
Hilton L'Orange

Acting Asst. Superintendent for Human Resources Supporting Services:
Gwendolyn Bradford

Chief Information Officer:
Tom Morris

Asst. Superintendent for Instructional Services:
Daniel Saltrick

Director of Public Information:
David Hains

Asst. Superintendent for Research, Assessment and Planning Services:
Jeffry Schiller

Asst. Superintendent for Student Services:
Calvin Wallace

Registering Your Child

You should contact the Pupil Assignment Office at the Education Center (379-7044) to find out which school your child will attend and then visit the school to register your child. School offices remain open throughout the summer.

Children entering kindergarten must be five years old on or before October 16 of the year in which the child is presented for enrollment. Children entering first grade must be six years old on or before October 16 of the year in which the child is presented for enrollment. However, the law permits enrollment of a child who does not meet these requirements if the child has already been attending school in another state in accordance with the laws or regulations of the school authorities of that state before becoming a resident of North Carolina.

To register, a new student must bring a birth certificate or other acceptable proof of age and an immunization record signed by a physician. This immunization record must include five DTP, four Oral Polio Vaccines, one Rubeola, one Rubella and one Mumps Vaccine. Health assessments are required for all new kindergarten students and include a medical history and physical examination with screening for vision and hearing.

North Carolina law requires all children from ages seven to 16 to attend school. State law requires a minimum of 180 school days per year for grades K-12. Each high school offers assistance to students who are preparing for the Scholastic Aptitude Test. In addition, 10th graders take the Preliminary Scholastic Aptitude Test at no charge.

Transportation

The school system provides buses for students who live at least 1.5 miles from school or who must walk through identified hazard areas. Approximately 54,000 students ride buses every day; 9,000 of them are bused to help maintain racial balance.

For more information about the Charlotte-Mecklenburg Schools, call 379-7010, the School Information Line of the Public Information Office. The Information Center is located at 701 East Second Street near the central business district.

Special Programs

CMS offers a variety of special programs for students. For complete listings and more detailed information, contact the CMS Information Center. Below is a brief description of some of the options available for special needs.

CMS INFORMATION CENTER
701 E. 2nd St.   *379-7010*

Information about schools, including policies, programs and services, is available to parents, students, employees, local citizens, newcomers, agencies, other school systems and communities. The center provides speakers for various programs, displays at special events and tours of the Education Center, schools and other facilities.

The Information Center also serves as a rumor-control center, maintains a file of tutors names, receives calls about concerns/complaints and provides guidance in resolving problems through direct

To register a new student in the Charlotte/Mecklenburg School System, bring a birth certificate or other acceptable proof of age and an immunization record signed by a physician.

Insiders' Tip

assistance or referrals to school system departments or other agencies.

The Center is open from 8 AM to 5 PM. Monday through Friday and maintains a 24-hour service through the use of a recording device after 5 PM. Calls are returned the next working day. Visitors are welcome and encouraged to use the services provided by the Center.

DIAL-A-TEACHER

701 E. 2nd St. 375-6000

Available Monday through Thursday 5 PM to 8 PM, Charlotte-Mecklenburg students can Dial-A-Teacher for homework assistance in mathematics, science, social studies and English/language arts. Staffed by four certified teachers, the program is designed to help students find their own solutions to homework problems. It is not designed to give answers. Dial-A-Teacher is sponsored by the Charlotte-Mecklenburg School System and is open while school is in session.

NORTH CAROLINA ACADEMIC SCHOLARS PROGRAM

(Contact the principal or guidance counselor at your local school.)

The State Board of Education approved the North Carolina Scholars Program starting in 1983. Students who complete the requirements for an academically challenging high school program will receive special recognition.

CMS SCHOLARS PROGRAM

The CMS Scholars Program uses the North Carolina Scholars Plan with a few changes. The student must have a GPA of 4.0 at the end of the first semester of the senior year, with an option of a free elective in lieu of the Vocational Education requirement and four units of science, counting ninth grade science.

THE ACADEMICALLY GIFTED PROGRAM

This state-mandated program is designed for those students who need academic challenge beyond that regularly found in the advanced classes. Emphasis is placed on advanced content, higher-level thinking skills and the development of the individual's critical and creative thinking ability. The Academically Gifted courses are available to those students who meet CMS program eligibility requirements.

MINORITY ACHIEVEMENT PROGRAM

The Minority Achievement Program was started in 1983 in response to the needs of minority students for additional academic support. Aimed at high-achieving minorities, the program seeks to increase the participation of these students in programs for the academically gifted.

ADVANCED PLACEMENT COURSES

More than 400 students are enrolled in Advanced Placement courses. Tested each spring, they may be eligible to move into higher level courses when they enter college. Courses are offered in English language and literature, calculus, biology, chemistry, physics, U.S. history, European history, French language and literature, Spanish language and literature, German, government and politics, music theory and art.

ATHLETICS

Athletics play an important part in the extracurricular life of students. Senior high sports teams participate in the Southwestern 4A Conference/Tri County 4A Conference. Schools offer a wide variety of athletic teams and activities.

FLUORIDE MOUTHRINSE PROGRAM

Charlotte-Mecklenburg Schools, the Mecklenburg County Health Department and the North Carolina Department of Environment, Health and Natural Resources offer a fluoride mouthrinse program to students at school once a week.

DOLLY TATE TEEN-AGE PARENTS SERVICES

1817 Central Ave.   *343-5460*

Teenage Parents Services is a cooperative effort of the Mecklenburg County Department of Social Services, Carolinas Medical Center, Mecklenburg County Health Department and Charlotte-Mecklenburg Board of Education. The organization provides education and comprehensive health services to pregnant junior and senior high girls. Child care services are provided to students to enable them to complete the academic year in which their child is born.

PROGRAM FOR EXCLUDED STUDENTS

Management School-East (6-8)
Management School-West (6-8)
Learning Academy (9-12)

Students who are excluded from senior and junior high and middle school programs may apply for a special program at University Park Center. This program is a basic maintenance one in English, math, science and social studies designed to place students in a corrective environment which allows for learning opportunities.

POSITIVE OPTIONS PROGRAM

Staff Development Center   *343-5400*

Charlotte-Mecklenburg Schools recognize that student substance abuse is a deterrent to effective education and a healthy lifestyle. The Positive Options Program is designed to assess student substance use through an awareness, counseling and intervention process. It provides assistance to parents and students who need further referral services to maintain educational success.

EVENING SCHOOL

Midwood High School

This comprehensive secondary evening program operates from 2:55 until 8:40 PM Monday through Thursday and 2:55 until 6:40 PM Friday. Students in grades 9-12 may attend. The purpose of this alternative program is to ensure that all youth in Mecklenburg County have an opportunity to earn a high school diploma.

PURSUING EXCELLENCE ACHIEVEMENT KNOWLEDGE IN SUMMER (PEAKS)

PEAKS is a summer program for interested and self-motivated students in art, debate, writing, math, SAT preparation, science, French and Spanish.

SUMMER PROGRAM

Summer programs are offered for six weeks at several CMS high schools during June and July. Classes are scheduled five hours a day, and students earn one-half unit of credit during each three-week session.

ACADEMIC INTERNSHIP PROGRAM

This Internship Program offered in all senior high schools gives students an opportunity to explore areas of academic or career interests as they work in the community with government and civic agencies, businesses, industries or individuals. 10th (second semester), 11th and 12th grade students are eligible to participate in the program.

A CHILD'S PLACE

University Park
2400 Hildebrand St.

This is a transitional classroom for homeless children located in First Presbyterian Church in the Uptown area of Charlotte.

CPCC ARTICULATION PROGRAM

A cooperative program with Central Piedmont Community College, this program allows students to sign up for college-level courses.

DROPOUT PREVENTION PROGRAM

This is a system-wide program designed to retain students through graduation and to provide services to alleviate conditions that cause students to drop out of school.

METRO SCHOOL

700 E. 2nd St.   343-5450

A self-contained school for mentally and physically handicapped students, Metro School has a community-based training program that places students in more than 20 businesses and service agencies for on-the-job training.

ENGLISH AS A SECOND LANGUAGE

This is a program designed to provide intensive instruction in English as a Second Language to students whose native tongues are other than English.

INTERNATIONAL STUDIES

The International Studies Program at Independence High School is an interdisciplinary program that provides a foundation of knowledge as well as opportunities for creative thinking and problem solving. Students take International Studies, English, History, Science and a second language course. Students may choose either Chinese, French, German or Spanish. Students take their other courses in the regular program at Independence.

AFTER SCHOOL ENRICHMENT PROGRAM
343-5567

The After School Enrichment Program is an after-school child care program for K-6 children who need supervision beyond the regular school day because their parents work. The after-school program is offered at many sites; a limited number of before-school sites are also available. The program acts as a transition time between the regular school day and home. It offers a safe, nurturing and enriching environment. The atmosphere is relaxed, and choices of activities are available. There is time for talking with friends, playing board games, physical and recreational opportunities or storytime. Homework sessions are supervised, and a snack is pro-vided. Registration fees and weekly fees are involved. Please call the program office for details and site locations.

JUNIOR ACHIEVEMENT OF CHARLOTTE
4632 Holbrook Dr.   *536-9668*

Junior Achievement of Charlotte is an organization devoted to teaching children how America works, its economic system and its private enterprise sector. Experience-based in its programming, Junior Achievement of Charlotte is the 12th largest J.A. operation in the nation. It involves more than 15,200 students and 670 volunteers from the business community and currently provides both private and public schools with programs that range from K-12.

Photo by John Cress.

Myers Park High School is an International Baccalaureate magnet school

Special Schools and Services

Sometimes a child has a particular problem that can't be addressed in a regular public or private school. Fortunately, Charlotte has a number of special schools and services that fulfill these needs. Here's a summary:

ALEXANDER CHILDREN'S CENTER
6220 Thermal Rd. 366-8712

This center's Treatment Program is an intensive 24-hour-a-day therapeutic environment for approximately 24 emotionally disturbed children. Alexander Children's Center is a nonprofit agency. Treatment includes parallel counseling for families or other guardians. Its Child Development Center is an AA-licensed program offering quality child development for children ages 3 months through kindergarten. The Center provides a low staff/child ratio and an expanded curriculum.

CATHOLIC SOCIAL SERVICES
116 E. 1st St. 333-9954

This organization offers many services, including individual, family, adoption, marital and substance abuse counseling and pregnancy support. Fees are based on a sliding scale.

PRESCHOOL EXCEPTIONAL CHILDREN'S PROGRAM
Graham Center
1400 N. Graham St. 343-3655

This program serves three and four-year-olds with identified special needs. It operates by contract-ing with several community service providers who can address a variety of needs for preschoolers with special needs. The program's mission is to promote community efforts to insure all children enter school ready to learn. The program offers free screenings and evaluations.

CHARLOTTE SPEECH AND HEARING CENTER
300 S. Caldwell St. 376-1342

Screening, evaluations, consultation, education and therapy are all a part of the total service available to the community at this nonprofit center. Funded, in part, by United Way, the center is accredited by the Professional Services Board of the American Speech-Language-Hearing Association, and clinical staff are licensed by the state. Help is offered to anyone who has or may have a speech/language or hearing problem. Some services are free; others are on a sliding-fee scale. The center also offers counseling to people in the workplace who have diction problems, a racial, ethnic, or social dialect, or wish to become more verbally assertive. The Center operates a satellite service in Union County.

CHILD AND FAMILY DEVELOPMENT
1316 E. Morehead St. 332-4834
10801 Johnston Rd.
Pineville 542-0317

A private for-profit practice, Child & Family Development offers a number of assessment services for children and their families such as monitoring of high-risk infants and preschoolers, developmental screenings, school readiness assessment, diagnostic evaluations and treatment services, plus special classes that assist children in their development.

THE FLETCHER SCHOOL
1001 Queens Rd.   *376-2032*

The purpose of this special school for learning-disabled children in grades 1-9 is to provide a structured, individualized academic program that will prepare them to return to the regular classroom environment whenever possible. The school has been approved by the N.C. Department of Public Instruction and the Governors Office of Nonpublic Instruction.

MECKLENBURG COUNTY CENTER FOR HUMAN DEVELOPMENT
3500 Ellington St.   *336-7100*

This county agency offers a number of services, including a developmental day preschool for mildly and moderately mentally retarded children, a parent-infant training program, and a developmental evaluation program to determine if an individual of any age has a disability or delayed development. Fees are based on the client's ability to pay.

NEVINS CENTER, INC.
3523 Nevins Rd.   *596-1372*
3127 Kalynne St.   *393-5910*

This Adult Developmental Activity Program provides vocational training, academic training, supported employment and a sheltered workshop for mentally retarded and physically handicapped adults.

OPEN HOUSE COUNSELING SERVICES, INC.
145 Remount Rd.   *332-9001*

This community agency provides counseling and support groups for chemically dependent young people and adults and their families. Services are rendered through the Johnnie H. McLeod Treatment Center, Methadone Medical Services, Outpatient Clinic, Adolescent Outpatient Services and Treatment Alternative to Street Crime.

PERCEPTUAL MOTOR STUDIES
University of North Carolina at Charlotte   *547-4695*

Dr. John Healey, a member of the UNCC faculty, coordinates this unique program for children up to the age of 18 who are experiencing difficulty in their perceptual motor development. Each child undergoes screening before acceptance into the program and is paired with two college students who, under the direction of the coordinator, assist him/her in various activities. The fee for the program is $200 per semester and there is normally a long waiting list.

PRESCHOOL PROGRAM FOR THE HEARING IMPAIRED
North Carolina School for the Deaf
1000 E. Morehead St.   *332-1881*

This total child development program provides comprehensive speech and language development for hearing-impaired preschoolers, newborns to five-year-olds, in Mecklenburg and surrounding counties. Instruction is given on-site and in the home.

ST. MARK'S CENTER
1200 E. Morehead St.
Ste. 200   *333-7107*

This center, established in 1973, offers programs and services to approximately 230 Mecklenburg County residents who have severe or profound mental retardation or are at high risk for a severe disability. Preschool, special education and summer school programs for children and sheltered workshops, developmental activities programs and supported employment programs for adults are offered.

THE RELATIVES
1100 East Blvd.   *377-0602*

This family-oriented crisis counseling center provides emergency shelter (1-14 days) with round-the-clock admittance for young people, ages 7-17, in crisis. Free and confidential services include individual/family counseling, community referral, follow-up and 24-hour assistance by hotline or walk-in visit. Services are available to both parents and children.

UNITED CEREBRAL PALSY DEVELOPMENTAL CENTER
1900 Queens Rd.   *377-6016*

A branch of United Cerebral Palsy of North Carolina, this center, housed in Myers Park Baptist Church, provides education and therapy for children ages 2-5 with cerebral palsy or a similar neurologically based disorder, as well as training for parents in Mecklenburg and surrounding counties. Tuition is based on a sliding-fee scale.

UNITED FAMILY SERVICES
301 S. Brevard St.   *332-9034*

Counseling is offered in marital relationships, personal adjustment, parent/child relationships and family therapy. Fees are based on a sliding scale.

Area Private Schools

There are 35 independent and four special schools within Mecklenburg County. Approximately 10,327 students are enrolled

in these schools in pre-kindergarten through twelfth grade. Some of these private schools are independent in affiliation while others are church-related.

ANAMI MONTESSORI SCHOOL
2901 Archdale Dr.   556-0042

The Anami Montessori School was founded in 1986 as a fully accredited AMI (Association Montessori Internationale) institution. Programs are offered to meet the needs of children ages 2 1/2 to 12 years.

To achieve its goal of providing a quality educational program to aid the natural development of the child's physical, emotional, intellectual and social personality, the school places emphasis on encouragement, respect for the individual, individual choice and personal responsibility. Anami Montessori has small classes and dedicated, caring teachers. An international environment that is warm and loving provides a relaxed, family atmosphere where children often work to the sounds of classical music.

The new, spacious facilities on Archdale Drive back up to the 120-acre Park Road Park. Before- and After-School Day Care programs are offered and the school is certified by the State of North Carolina.

ASCENSION LUTHERAN SCHOOL
1225 E. Morehead St.   372-7738

Founded in 1942, Ascension Lutheran is one of the older private schools in Charlotte and is certified by the state. It is located near the Uptown area. The school provides preschool and extended day care programs, preschool to sixth grade.

BIBLE BAPTIST CHRISTIAN SCHOOL
2724 Margaret Wallace Rd.   535-1694

This school offers K-12 with extended care as well. Offering a traditional curriculum, the school is college-preparatory in mission.

You'll Want To Be A Part of Our Family.

Charlotte Latin School emphasizes the development of the *whole* child, from academics, to athletics, to the arts. We focus on integrity, honor, and citizenship, and believe that family participation is a crucial part of the process. So come get to know us — we'd love for you to be a part of our family!

Charlotte Latin School

9502 Providence Road, Charlotte, NC 28277
Admissions, 704/846-1100 *Grades Pre-K – 12*

CHARLOTTE CATHOLIC HIGH SCHOOL

3100 Park Rd.   *523-5671*

Coeducational, Charlotte Catholic began as part of St. Mary's Seminary in 1877, moving to its present location in 1954. Charlotte's elementary parochial schools feed into Charlotte Catholic, which serves grades 9-12. Non-Catholics may attend. The school is a member of the N.C. Athletic Association and accredited by the Southern Association of Colleges and Schools, the N.C. State Department of Public Instruction and the Diocese of Charlotte.

CHARLOTTE CHRISTIAN SCHOOL

7301 Sardis Rd.   *366-5657*

Charlotte Christian is a non-denominational, independent day school. Founded in 1950, it provides college-preparatory education for more than 700 students K-12. Academic excellence is what Charlotte Christian is best known for. In addition to its full academic program, athletic teams compete within the N.C. Independent Schools Conference. Charlotte Christian is a member of the Association of Christian Schools International, the North Carolina Association of Independent Schools and the Southern Association of Colleges and Schools.

THE CHARLOTTE COUNTRY DAY SCHOOL

1440 Carmel Rd.   *366-1241*

Charlotte Country Day is the oldest independent school in the area and the largest. Celebrating its 50th birthday in 1992, Country Day is known for small classes, dedicated

teachers and a warm and caring environment. The result, along with rigorous athletics, is a well-rounded and academically stimulating program. Country Day is also influenced by its international students whose presence provides an enriching cultural diversity. The school launched a major capital campaign in 1990 to raise funds for expanded athletic facilities and a new stadium. In addition, the monies will be used for renovations, new construction and a faculty salary endowment.

CHARLOTTE LATIN SCHOOL

9502 Providence Rd.   *846-1100*

Charlotte Latin School is a coeducational day school with 1,085 students in grades pre-kindergarten through twelve. Located on 92 wooded acres, Charlotte Latin is one of Charlotte's finest in terms of academic quality and diversity. The curriculum is college-preparatory, and 100 percent college placement is the norm.

Charlotte Latin was founded in 1970, has been named an Exemplary School by the United States Department of Education and is the youngest school ever chartered by the Cum Laude Society. It endeavors to present its students with the challenges and opportunities necessary for the development of leadership qualities and academic excellence. In addition to its well-rounded academic program, 45 Charlotte Latin School teams annually compete in 22 different sports. The school has won 63 state championship titles in various sports in its 22-year history.

THE CHARLOTTE MONTESSORI SCHOOL

2830 Dorchester Pl.	523-6165
212 Boyce Rd.	366-5994

Charlotte's oldest Montessori School was chartered in 1971. The school is affiliated with The American Montessori Society and is approved by the N.C. State Department of Public Instruction. The school offers the child a unique environment that develops self-discipline, independence and an enthusiasm for learning. The school offers programs for Toddlers (ages 15-36 months), primary and kindergarten through grade 5.

COUNTRYSIDE MONTESSORI SCHOOL

9100 Olmstead Pl.	547-1091
9026 Mallard Creek Rd.	549-4253

Chartered in 1975 and affiliated with American Montessori Society, Countryside offers preschool for children ages 2-5 years at the Olmstead location and elementary programs for first through sixth graders at the Mallard Creek site. Day care is available at both locations.

COVENANT DAY SCHOOL

800 Fullwood Ln.	
Matthews	847-2385

Covenant Day School, a ministry of Christ Covenant Church, is a coeducational Christian day school with 450 students enrolled in grades kindergarten through nine. Believing that education feeds the soul as well as the mind, the school offers academic excellence in a nurturing Christian environment.

Beginning with kindergarten, a superior reading program is based on strong phonics instruction and

supplemented with the *IBM Writing To Read* program and classical children's literature. Instruction in French and Latin is combined with modern computer technology to provide a comprehensive academic program.

Extracurricular programs include art, music, journalism, yearbook and band. A varied sports program offers basketball, volleyball, baseball, volleyball, baseball, track and field, soccer, cheerleading and tennis.

DORE ACADEMY
1727 Providence Rd.   365-5490

Dore Academy offers instruction from grades 1 through 12. The school is open to bright students with learning disabilities, offering them a safe, nurturing environment in which to grow and learn.

MECKLENBURG AREA CATHOLIC SCHOOLS
1524 E. Morehead St.   331-1711

Mecklenburg Area Catholic Schools (MACS) is a system of six schools serving 3,000 students in grades pre-kindergarten through 12. The schools' excellent academic programs are the framework of a system in which student test scores consistently rank higher than local and national averages. College placement is the norm for all graduates of Charlotte Catholic High School. MACS is accredited by the N.C. Department of Public Instruction and Charlotte Catholic is fully accredited by the Southern Association of Colleges and Schools as well as the N.C. Association of Independent Schools.

In the tradition of Catholic schools, particular emphasis is placed on the development of spiritual and moral values. Students of all faiths are welcomed.

MONTESSORI OMNI CENTER AMI
9536 Blakeney-Heath Rd.   541-1326

An AMI-affiliated Montessori school, the center opened in 1985 and can serve up to 85 students.

NORTHSIDE CHRISTIAN ACADEMY
333 Jeremiah Blvd.   596-4074

The school serves 800 students, K4-12, and is one of the many ministries of Northside Baptist Church. It shares facilities with the church. Founded in 1962, strict dress codes and behavior guidelines are maintained. College-preparatory

TODAY, A GROUP OF OUR STUDENTS

SENT AN AID PACKAGE TO SOMALIA,

DISCUSSED CREATIVE WAYS TO SAVE THE

RAIN FORESTS, AND EXPLORED THE

REFLECTIVE PATHS OF LIGHT USING

A HELIUM NEON LASER.

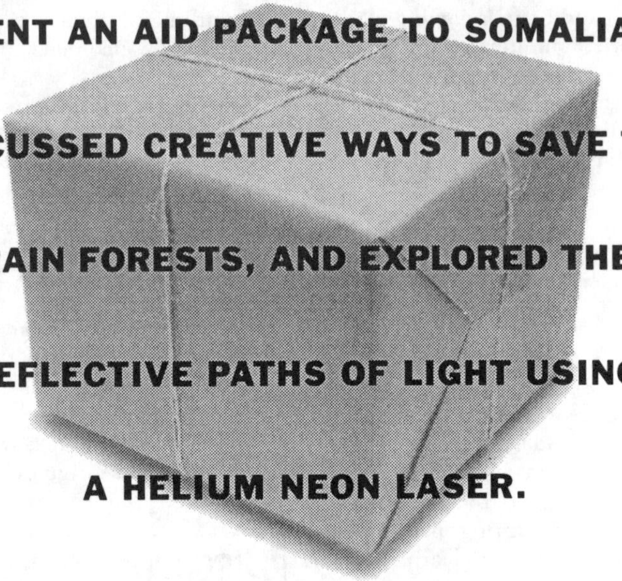

(JUST WAIT TILL THEY ENTER THIRD GRADE.)

PROVIDENCE DAY SCHOOL
5800 Sardis Road
Charlotte, NC 28270
704-362-6080

Contact Susan A. Beattie, Ph.D.

students must complete 24 units and special help is available for slow learners. Families with more than one child in the school receive a discount, as do church members.

PROVIDENCE DAY SCHOOL
5800 Sardis Rd.   *362-6000*

Providence Day School is the only school to be cited for excellence by both the U.S. Department of Education and the National Council of Teachers of English. The school was founded in 1970 and is located on a 35-acre campus in Southeast Charlotte. It serves 1,050 students in grades K-12 and offers a traditional college-preparatory education in a safe, caring environment.

College credit is granted to 70 percent of the school's students who take Advanced Placement tests. Many students receive academic, athletic and special achievement scholarships, and the school is awarded more honors each year than any other school in the regional and state Science Fairs. One hundred percent of the school's graduates attend college.

Tutoring Services

If your child needs special help with homework, a tutor can help. The Charlotte/Mecklenburg School System offers free tutoring via telephone Monday through Thursday 5 PM to 8 PM. Call 375-6000. The best way to find a private tutor is to ask your child's teacher to recommend one. A complete listing of tutoring services is available in the Yellow Pages of the Charlotte telephone directory.

Child Care

There are literally hundreds of child care programs, including child care centers, family child care homes, part-day nursery programs and summer camps. Many churches also offer facilities and programs. Of course, once again, the best source of information for something as important as the welfare of your child, is a trusted friend or neighbor who can give personal testimony as to the competence and reliability of a specific care provider. The following are also good sources for dependable information.

CHILD CARE RESOURCES
700 Kenilworth Ave.   *376-6697*

Child Care Resources Inc. is a private, nonprofit organization. It is a marvelous resource and a great starting point for any parent looking for child care options. Funded by the United Way, it's tied in to all opportunities in and around the community.

CHILDRENFIRST LEARNING CENTERS
2915 Coltsgate Rd.   *365-5863*
6416 W. Sugar Creek Rd.   *598-5858*
Main Office   *365-4550*

ChildrenFirst Learning Centers is a locally owned, private company that offers quality child care services to parents. It serves children ages six to five years and is AA licensed. A unique family services program allows parents to spend quality time with their children.

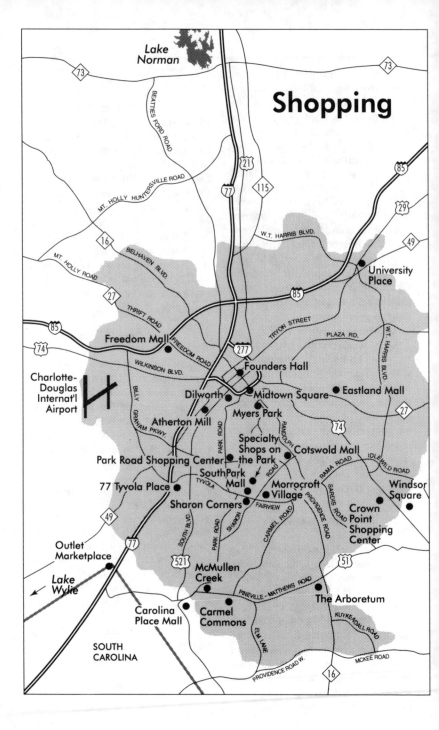

Shopping

Lake Norman

Charlotte-Douglas Internat'l Airport

Freedom Mall

Founders Hall

Dilworth

Midtown Square

Eastland Mall

Atherton Mill

Myers Park

Specialty Shops on the Park

Cotswold Mall

Park Road Shopping Center

SouthPark Mall

77 Tyvola Place

Morrocroft Village

Sharon Corners

Windsor Square

Crown Point Shopping Center

Outlet Marketplace

Lake Wylie

McMullen Creek

The Arboretum

Carolina Place Mall

Carmel Commons

University Place

SOUTH CAROLINA

Inside
Shopping

*A*s you collect your change and head for the door, don't be surprised if you hear, "You have a good one, okay?" At smaller stores this is the colloquial version of the shop worn, "Have a nice day." It's replaced, "Y'all come back, hear?" which was not nearly as grating on the nerves because it implies the owner wants your trade.

The term "trade," not shopping, is how folks once conducted their business, harking back to our bartering days. But no matter what you call shopping or where you do it around town, you'll find that polite attitudes usually prevail. In Charlotte, salespeople won't ignore you, yell or sneer at you. They may hold their sides laughing after you've left, but courtesy and service are still a Southern staple. Visitors are often surprised that good manners remain strong in a city with retail sales of $8.9 billion.

You'll find a good selection of what you need in our 62,000 plus retail stores. Probably most of your dollars will be spent in these shopping forums (mega and mini), buy-ing everything from antiques to animal fabrics; but Charlotte's textile heritage as a mill town gives shoppers a unique advantage not found in states without mills. Nearby textile mills provide two benefits: direct (mill outlets), and indirect (salesman's clothing samples), both discretionary dollar stretchers.

Shopping falls into distinct categories, ask any diehard shopper. First, there's bargain shopping (shopping where you can get the best for the least, no matter how ratty the store, or how far away). Second, there is convenience shopping (usually brought about by necessities of time or transportation). Third and finally, is luxury shopping (the ultimate experience of buying, no matter how much the price tag). Take your pick; all three are available in the Queen City and its satellites.

Uptown

More blossoming has occurred in Uptown's six-story, glass-enclosed **Founders Hall**, located inside NationsBank Corporate Center. You can do your banking in the NationsBank branch. Then, in addition to shopping, you can have an inexpensive deli-cafeteria lunch at **Spratt's Kitchen & Market** or downstairs have the option of lunch, dinner or drinks after work at **Bistro 100**. You can do a little grocery shopping at Spratt's, have your hair done at **Kosta's International Hair**, take your dry cleaning to **Sunrise Dry Cleaning**, have your car cared for at **First Impressions Auto Care**, get some printing done at **Sir Speedy** or mail a package at **Packages Plus II**. Buy a book, a calendar or, for the business traveler, books on tape at the **Bookmark**, choose a pocket, hunting or collectible knife at **Accent on Knives**, have your snapshots developed at **Simpson Photo** or find an original sculpture, painting or that special piece of jewelry that has your name on it at **Pope's Gallery**. The **Performing Arts Center Box Office** is convenient for making reservations or picking up event tickets, or you can work off the stress of the day on state-of-the-art equipment at the Hall's private health club. You don't even have to worry about bringing workout clothes, they are supplied at the **Crown Athletic Club**.

Working women need go no further than the **Express International** for sharp, popular priced suits, dresses and accessories. **Julie Two** also offers great buys for business as well as casual ensembles. Men will appreciate **Jack Wood Ltd.** for their fashionable selection of men's clothing. **David Bernard's** will be on your list for its large variety of men's bet-

ter shoes, and you can stop right next door at **Eastern Lobby Stores** for some of the nation's top newspapers and magazines.

Upstairs, **Grodzicki and Co.** is the store that lets your imagination soar with decorative household accessories and "found nowhere else" fun things. **The Blossom Shop** provides exotic posies flown in from around the world, plus lovely plants and gifts.

But the part of this plan that strikes a warm chord with Insiders is the homage paid to Charlotte's past and future pioneers in artist Ben Long's frescoes. They are beautifully portrayed in Long's triptych fresco decorating the walls inside NationsBank's lobby. And on the first floor in Founders Hall, the hall so named for those brave settlers who laid Charlotte's foundation, stands the touch-video **Museum of the New South**. You can activate the tall, black kiosk by pressing the screen. A selection appears chronicling Charlotte's history, but exactly what you see and learn is up to you. You can take time out from your shopping for a couple of minutes or for an hour, because each segment is presented in short capsules.

Outlet Shopping

Technically, outlets sprang into existence through mistakes made in textile mills. These mistakes, known as seconds and thirds, were sold for a pittance in the mill's storeroom. A few storerooms still exist and these are the best bargains. Stores that have jumped on the out-

Photo by John Cress.

Uptown's six-story, glass enclosed Founders Hall,
located in the NationsBank Corporate Center, offers everything
from a gourmet food market to an upscale health club.

425

let sign bandwagon with cheap, out of date junk won't be mentioned.

There are tucked-away mercantile pockets folks would never know about if not told. A little known one, even among Insiders, is **Woonsocket Spinning Factory Outlet** located at 4701 Monroe Road (no sign on building). Periodically, terrific buys on cashmere coats and jackets can be found here as well as camel hair and cashmere cloth.

Several Insiders' recommendations are about an hour from Charlotte in South Carolina. Remember, Charlotte is only ten miles from the South Carolina border. A good source of information about South Carolina outlets is the South Carolina Welcome Center off I-77. Stop by here for a complete list.

Take N.C. 49 south, crossing Buster Boyd Bridge, into Clover, South Carolina. Turn left on Main Street for 1/4 mile to **Klear Knit** (803-222-3272). The turnoff is well-marked, just follow the signs to the factory store that has great top-name sportswear for men. In Clover, at 123 N. Main Street, **G M Manufacturing Outlet** (803-222-2486) carries knits for women. To find men's dress and knit shirts, try the **Chesterfield Outlet** in Chesterfield, South Carolina. Take U.S. 74 East to Monroe to U.S. 601 south to Pageland, then take S.C. 9E to intersection of Business 9 and Bypass 9. The outlet is open from 9:30 AM to 5:30 PM Monday through Friday and until 4:00 PM on Saturday.

South Carolina has a number of terrific fabric factory outlets. **Interior Alternatives** is the F.S. Schumacher and Waverly outlet in Richburg. Take I-77 south to exit 65, turn right off the ramp onto S.C. 9 and proceed about a half mile to the manufacturer (on the right). To get to Cone Mills' **Printing & Finishing Cloth Store** (803-427-6221) that offers different materials, continue on S.C. 9 into Chester, turn at first stop light, then left onto S.C. 72W and follow signs to the Carlyle plant (about 10 miles). The store is open from 8:00 AM to 4:00 PM Monday through Friday, and the first Saturday of the month from 8:00 AM until 2:00 PM.

For hammocks, embroidery, tassels, etc., scoot out to **Conso** in Union, South Carolina. Take N.C. 49 south to Union and S.C. 215 west on the Duncan Bypass to the Industrial Park. Conso is open from 9:00 AM to 4:45 PM Monday through Friday.

For comforters, curtains, towels, sheets and mini blinds try the Springs Mills **Wamsutta Outlet** in Lancaster, South Carolina (803-286-2491). It's open from 9:00 AM to 6:00 PM Monday through Saturday and 1 to 6 PM on Sunday. Take I-77 and exit at 65 and turn left onto S.C. 9. The store is on the left.

You probably don't think "food" when you're thinking outlet shopping, but quite a few Charlotteans do. **Stouffer's Thrift Store** (803-487-4053) is a little farther down the road, but definitely worth the drive. It carries frozen dishes, including Lean Cuisine. The store is open from 9 AM until 5:30 PM Monday through Friday. Head south on I-85 and take exit 90. The store is located on Hyatt Street in Gaffney.

Also located off exit 90 is **Hamrick's of Gaffney**. This store carries some good buys on a sports brand we're not allowed to mention, but it has a duck in it. They also have seconds on Levi's, Hanes, etc. In the same area (exit 86 off I-85), you'll find **World of Clothing** (803-347-0344). It's a humongous store that is a little overwhelming, but nicely organized. You'll find discounted prices on Levi's, Jordache, Haggar, Botany 500 and Oriental rugs. It's open from 9 AM to 9 PM Monday through Saturday and Sundays from 1 until 7 PM.

For Adidas footwear and apparel, continue south down I-85 to the Spartanburg area (about 1 and 1/2 hours from Charlotte). At exit 69, take I-26 north for short distance to New Cut Road and turn left; continue for about 2 miles to **Adidas American Factory Outlet** (803-587-0700) on your right. Back on I-85 South for approximately 20 minutes to exit 48B in the Greenville area, you'll find **West Point Pepperell** offering an extensive collection of bed and bath merchandise as well as clothing. It's open from 9 AM to 6 PM Monday through Saturday, and from 1:30 until 6 PM on Sunday.

On the living room chairs of a bed and breakfast inn in Pennsylvania, a Charlottean discovered the same unusual fabric she had used to slipcover her own chairs. Knowing her guest was from Charlotte, the grinning owner told her (what any Insider could have told her), the fabric came from **Luxury Fabrics**, just outside of Gastonia. **Luxury** and **Mary Jo's** (primarily a cloth store), both located at the Cox Road exit

off I-85 South, have the best fabric selections and bargains in the area.

Consignment Shopping

Either due to our still sluggish economy, or our more frugal shoppers, more than 80 consignment shops dot the current Charlotte and Matthews scene. Merchandising techniques have changed—the rummage look is "out." "In" is the trendy boutique look that has taken over many of the shops along Dilworth's East Boulevard and East 7th Street. It may take frequent trips, but fashionable styles for women, children and men can be found throughout the city and Matthews.

From the storefront, you would think **Finders' Keepers** at 196 North Trade Street in Matthews (847-1672) to be an expensive retail boutique; however, after checking the merchandise, you will find top quality, designer labels in fine consignment for ladies. Patty Arim has succeeded in maintaining high-quality merchandise, including jeans, sportswear, career dresses and suits as well as manufacturer's samples and below-wholesale jewelry. You can also find a good selection of cocktail/evening wear and maternity clothes.

A particular favorite, now going into its 41st year, is **The Resale Shop** at 1920 E. 7th, Street (376-1312). Susan Fenton not only carries clothing, but also lots of accessories as well as household items. Clothing is attractively arranged by color at **Very Terry Contemporary Consignments** at 310 East Boulevard

(375-0655). At **A Consigning Affair**, 1531-H East Boulevard (358-8919), the owner specializes in bridal, formal and "after 5" wear. Just below, at 1531-D, East Boulevard, is Kay Bartholomew's **The Classy Closet**. **Dilworth Consignment Shop**, 310 East Boulevard #1 and #2 (332-0668), has carefully selected clothing and great vintage jewelry. **Consignment World** has a great selection of women's clothing (children's and men's, too) along with just about anything else you might be looking for. It has two locations, 1821 Norland Road (536-4770), and 10916 E. Independence Boulevard in Matthews (847-2620). **Crickettes Maternity & Children's Consignment** has moved to 4380 Colwick Road (366-0170).

Shopping Malls

Something new is happening in Charlotte shopping malls. For years shopping malls have displayed children's art works and crafts to bring out the crowds. This may not have totally disappeared, but innovative marketing ideas are making their mark. Last summer for example, SouthPark Mall brought in museum-quality sculpture to decorate its corridors during a month-long event entitled "Hot Art - Cool Jazz." This entertaining event provided a dandy way to spend a warm Saturday afternoon. Such well known artists as the delightful Daryle Ryce, Charlotte's own Loonis McGlohon and other jazz notables provided "music to shop by."

EASTLAND MALL

Located at the corner of Central Avenue and Sharon Amity, about 15 minutes from Uptown, Eastland mall serves the retail needs of East Charlotte. Opened in 1975 and renovated in 1990, the mall is anchored by **Belk**, **Dillard's**, **Sears** and **J.C. Penney**. Eastland offers a wide variety of merchandise and pricing with its 125 stores along with a few interesting and locally owned variations on the standard theme. But by far the most remarkable feature of this mall is the **ice-skating rink**, which rests gracefully in the very lower level. When the weather is volcanic outside, it's legal to hop in the car, go to Eastland and cool down with a few laps around the rink. The rink also adds a special touch to shopping during the holidays.

MIDTOWN SQUARE

Midtown was Charlotte's first mall and originally was called Charlottetown Mall. It's had its ups and downs through the years, with competitive SouthPark and Eastland in the forefront. A few years back, the mall revamped, changing its image to Outlet Square. Though the concept of discount shopping still prevails, the mall has changed its name to Midtown Square. There are a variety of clothing stores for all ages, and a convenient food court for shoppers.

SOUTHPARK MALL

SouthPark is located at the corner of Sharon and Fairview Roads, and is probably the best known and most frequented mall in the area, although Carolina Place

SouthPark is located at the corner of Sharon and Fairview Roads, and is probably the best known and most frequented mall in the area

Photo by Thien Nguyen, CPCC © 1994.

Carolina Place Mall opened with much fanfare in July of 1991.

may soon overtake it. As its name implies, this mall is in the epicenter of Charlotte's most affluent neighborhoods. For all that, SouthPark is a remarkably friendly mall, and the stores cater to a variety of wallets and pocketbooks.

Anchors at SouthPark are **Belk, Dillard's, Hecht's** and **Sears**. The mall is single-story, with 115 stores and it is the only place in the 13-county metropolitan area where you can find such upscale retail leaders as **Ann Taylor, Benetton, The Nature Company, The Disney Store, Carroll Reed, Eddie Bauer, Caswell Massey, Lillie Rubin, Cache Laura Ashley** and **Laura Ashley Mother and Child**. The food court offers fast food at its best (or worst), and remains a busy gathering spot. If you prefer heartier fare, try **Charlie's** or **Morrison's Cafeteria**.

The mall management and the owners of the various stores are constantly working to improve the appearance and quality of merchan-

dising. This means that although SouthPark is approaching middle-age by mall standards—it was built in 1969 and renovated in 1987—it's always contemporary in appearance and stock.

And as malls go, SouthPark is a great place for the sport of people watching, except at Christmas when the best advice is to go early, or stay at home. Few people see SouthPark Mall as just a shopping center. There are cinemas and a supermarket. Across Morrison Boulevard, **Specialty Shops on the Park** has a number of fine specialty stores catering to those who demand some of the finer luxuries in life. For a feast to the eyes, try **Treasures Unlimited, The Carriage** and lunch or dinner at the new Mexican Restaurant, **Ocho**.

CAROLINA PLACE MALL
Carolina Place Mall opened with much fanfare in July of 1991. Located in Pineville, it originally was out in the boondocks. No more.

Surrounding the mall on all sides, are stores and restaurants of every description. Predictions that Carolina Place will be the epicenter of more urban sprawl in the already burgeoning Pineville/N.C. 51 area have already become a reality within three short years.

The developers, from Atlanta, managed to attract some big names—**Belk**, **Dillard's**, **Sears** and **J.C. Penny** are anchors. And if the same stores aren't necessarily duplicated, then the same mix is here as you will find at other area malls. Carolina Place must be praised for its architecture. The entrances have a roundish, inviting look and the mall itself curves. Abundant natural light floods the common areas. Parking is plentiful and it is located adjacent to the proposed beltline route which will make it easily accessible once that project has been completed.

Shopping Centers

SHARON CORNERS

Opposite SouthPark Mall, this old strip shopping center has been redesigned into a two-story architectural blend of Georgian and Colonial Williamsburg with open walkways, plantation moldings and cupolas. At the new Sharon Corners, you have a selection of five eateries from a pancake house to a coffee house. The **Original Pancake House** for starters, followed by the always good but hard to get into **Harper's Restaurant**. The high-tech-designed new oriental restaurant, **Baoding**, serves high-tech-designed oriental dishes to match.

This writer's personal favorite (and daily downfall), **White Mountain Creamery** sells the very best fat free/sugar free yogurt. It also serves delicious, fully leaded ice creams and health-conscious muffins, plus a few designer coffees. Of course, many more of the designer, desert-type coffees are available at **Peabody's** located next door to the upscale, **Our Place** boutique for women that has some of the best-looking women's clothes in town. **Men's Wearhouse** for—guess who—and **Chocolate Soup** for children with some original designs. For those who love the out-of-doors, you'll find a great selection at **Jessie Brown's Outdoors**. For people who hate to wrap packages, there's the **P.K.G's Store** and right next door is **Kinko's** for both your black and white and color copying needs. A large **Barnes and Nobles** book store that also has a coffee bar and offers a small luncheon selection has already achieved popularity. **Eckerd Drugs** is one of the few older places that survived the renewal. You will also find a jewelry store, **Lions Ltd. Fine Jewelry**, a tuxedo shop, **American Tuxedo** and bagels, too, at the **Bagel Builders Cafe**, a party store, **The Paper Company**, a place to buy telephones at **Bell Atlantic Mobile**. Those into computers (and who isn't these days) will love **Software, Inc.**, and if you are looking for one of those decorative flags that you see flying from folks' homes, **Banner Ideas** is the place to shop. For hair supplies, check out **Chaz** and to get your pictures and awards framed in a hurry, stop by **FastFrame**. You'll also find a shoe repair and a dry cleaners, but you won't find a grocery store. **Harris Teeter** moved over to the Morrison and Sharon complex in Morrocroft Village off Colony Road.

MORROCROFT VILLAGE

Morrocroft Village wins hands-down as the fanciest, style-setting shopping area in Charlotte. It defies good sense to think of a grocery store as glamorous, but the new **Harris Teeter**, the shopping center's drawing card, certainly has a style worth noting. From basic chicken to a meat counter that often offers rattlesnake meat, this gourmet grocery has it all, including a florist and a self-serve luncheon restaurant. And if folks aren't into self-serve, they can go directly across the parking lot to **L & N's Seafood.** The village is chocked full of fancy to clever boutiques and specialty stores such as **Papitre**, that has stationery, gifts, etc., and old standby's such as **Jos. A. Banks Clothiers** and **Gutmann's.** While selecting china, silver or a baby gift at Gutmann's, you are served coffee, Russian tea or a soft drink. For casual but distinctive women's clothing, stop by **Lynda Reid.** And to make any outfit a little more fun, check out the unusual and classy costume jewelry at **Paula Gold.** For fine jewelry purchases, you'll appreciate **John Rist.** The village also has **London Britches**, a children's shop right next door to **Dan Howard Maternity.** One of Charlotte's better art galleries, **Jerald Melberg Gallery**, has recently taken up residence, and if you need something both traditional and unique for your home, then swing by **De La Maison.** It is true that Harris Teeter

Morrocroft Village wins hands-down as Charlotte's fanciest shopping area.

was the original centerpiece, but **Borders Books and Music** is also commanding equal attention in the village. New shops are moving in all the time, so don't be surprised to find more than have been mentioned.

ATHERTON MILL

Most of us don't realize that in order to go shopping at the turn of the century, Charlotteans had to hop on the trolley to get Uptown. The trolley ended at Tremont and South boulevards in Dilworth, across the street from the 1893 Atherton Mill. Why mention this? Well, the old Atherton Mill has been reclaimed for an entirely new concept in shopping. While the major emphasis is on shopping, a carbarn houses two vintage streetcars and there is an audiovisual center chronicling our transportation history.

Interiors Marketplace at Dilworth is the new decorating splash on the shopping scene. You'll see 83 vignettes (three-walled rooms) subleased to interior designers, antique or architectural dealers decorated with imports from around the world. These rooms that are free for looker/shoppers, are a little akin to the decorated rooms at the Southern Spring Show at the Merchandise Mart. Several new shops that have come into the complex this past year are: **Kitchen Symphony, Busbin Lamps**, a second location for **Redd Sled** and the garden nursery, **Campbell's Nursery**. The upscale restaurant **Palatable Pleasures** (the former gourmet takeout place at Shops on the Park) perfectly complements this unique complex.

Insiders applaud this impressive precedent in preservation. It not only saves two pictures of our past, the mill and the trolley, but it promises a $50 million shot in the arm toward rehabilitating the South Boulevard corridor.

PARK ROAD SHOPPING CENTER

Charlotte's oldest shopping center has remained on top by adding trendy new shops, while its older shops have changed marketing techniques offering new and fashionable interests. Still, shoppers will find a good variety that will fit their pocketbooks. The post office probably does the most business of all, but the grocery stores on either end run a close second. You'll find a well stocked drug store (**Eckerd's**), a pet shop, ice cream and yogurt shop and some old faithfuls such as: **Federal Bake Shop**, with its new emphasis on French, Spanish and European pastries, **L & S Children's** and **L & S Prep Shops**, plus **Julie's** and **Elfrieda's Flowers**. **Little Professor Book Store** continues to serve customers in a number of innovative ways and is an excellent source for books on a variety of subjects. You can even get an extra set of keys made at a little shop in the center of the parking area.

Unfortunately, J.C. Penny has moved to Carolina Place Mall, but **Black Hawk Hardware** has expanded by moving into its spot. It is also home to **Park Terrace Theaters** and the **Charlotte Cafe** that serves breakfast, lunch and dinner. And behind the shopping center is the wonderful Greek restaurant—**Grapevine**

Photo by John Cress.

The 1893 Atherton Milll has been reclaimed for an entirely new concept in shopping.

Cafe. Thrifty shoppers also appreciate the **Junior League's Consignment Store** that is also tucked into this back area behind the laundromat.

FREEDOM MALL
Another well-established shopping center, Freedom Mall at 3205 Freedom Drive houses such stores as **Target**, and **Peeble's**.

77 TYVOLA PLACE
Also home to a **Target** variety store, 77 Tyvola Place has **Kuppenheimer** and the **Dress Barn** as well.

COTSWOLD MALL
Cotswold Mall, 160 S. Sharon Amity Road, houses among others, **Marshalls**, **Stein Mart**, **Blockbuster Video** and **Coplon's**.

MIDTOWN SQUARE
This center is best known for its outlet-type stores such as **Burlington Coat Factory**, **Linens 'N Things**, **Dress Barn** and **Famous Footwear**.

THE ARBORETUM
The newest of the community shopping centers is The Arboretum at the corner of Providence Road and N.C. 51. Power house stores like **Wal-Mart**, **Blockbuster Video**, **Michael's Crafts** and **Kuppenheimer** uniquely blend with some very special boutiques and restaurants like **Sidestreet** or **The Rainbow Cafe**. **Carmen! Carmen!**, a great hair styling salon with locations at Cotswold and at the Arboretum, claims to have the best trained stylists in Charlotte– and they work hard to live up to that

claim. Not only can you have your hair styled, the shop also has skin care products and offers acrylic nails and manicures.

CROWNPOINT SHOPPING CENTER
CrownPoint at the corner of Independence Boulevard and Sardis Road North offers such superstores as **Lowes**, **Office America** and **Baby Superstore**.

WINDSOR SQUARE
Down Independence Boulevard a bit, you will find Windsor Square, which houses the rest of the big boys. **Waccamaw Pottery**, **Sam's Wholesale Club**, **Burlington Coat Factory** and **Home Quarters** are the largest in this power center.

Photo by John Cress.

The newest of the community shopping centers is The Arboretum at the corner of Providence Road and N.C. 51.

Neighborhood Retail Centers

Because Charlotte is so geographically spread out, many people do most of their shopping close to home or work. With new small and medium-sized shopping centers springing up all over the place, this is easy to do—and still find variety and good prices. Smaller than Shopping Centers, Neighborhood Retail Centers are primarily an attraction due to their supermarkets, drug stores, dry cleaners, etc., but are often home to some fascinating retail options. Here are a few of the special ones.

SPECIALTY SHOPS ON THE PARK

Located on Morrison Boulevard across from SouthPark Mall, this center is a unique collection of boutiques in an outdoor, European setting. You'll love such stores as **Talbots, Talbots Kids, The Carriage, Taylor Richards & Conger** and **Williams Sonoma** to name a few.

DILWORTH

From the intersection of South Boulevard to Queens Road, a drive down East Boulevard in the Dilworth neighborhood offers a varied shopping experience. Browse through one-of-a-kind shops, some free standing or clustered together in centers.

Start with the **Dilworth Court** on the corner of East Boulevard and South Boulevard, which has **Rackes, Very Terry's, Berrybrook Farms** and the **Tudor House Gallery**.

At **Kenilworth Commons**, you can take a break at **Dilworth Coffee House**, visit **Honeychile** and browse through **Book Ends**.

The **Shops at Twin Oaks** offers a great variety of shops including, among others, **The Stork's Nest** maternity and children's boutique, **I.C. London** for lingerie, **LTA Travel Services, Cotswold Photographers**, the **Sewing Bird, Belle's** and **Dikadee's Deli**.

Have lunch at **Cafe Verde** in **Talley's Green Grocery** or at the **Outback Steakhouse** before you visit **Danco** at **Dilworth Gardens**.

MYERS PARK

Myers Park offers a veritable mecca of specialty shopping. Along Selwyn Avenue, you'll find the **Fresh Market** and **Cafe Society** in **Selwyn Corners**. Dotted along the street are specialty shops like **The Bride Room, Futons Unfolding, Bicycle Sport, Perris Boutique, Coffee & Tea Emporium, Selwyn Natural Foods**.

Also in the heart of Myers Park along Providence Road are such delights as **The Colony, John Tibbs, Villa Square, Reed's, Grodzicki & Co., Queen Charlotte's Antiques Ltd., Monta's, Mecklenburg Design Center, The Pleating Place** and the **Golden Goose**.

Retail Corridors

Central Avenue, Wilkinson Boulevard, South Boulevard and Independence Boulevard, are the main retail "streets" in Charlotte. Busy, crowded, devoid of trees, and almost unbearably hot in the summer, this is where you'll find stores such as **Wal-Mart, Kmart, Toys R Us, T.J. Maxx** and others of that ilk. But in the shade of these retail behemoths lie some of Charlotte's best specialty stores, attracting customers from many miles around.

Most Charlotte car dealerships make their homes on South and Independence boulevards. There are plenty to choose from, and usually at least two dealers for every marque. If you are shopping for a shiny new ride, remember the car dealer's motto is "We're Dealin'" – and a lot of dealin' takes place on these two streets.

Groceries & Every Day Necessities

Mainstay grocery stores like **Harris Teeter, Winn-Dixie, Giant Genie, Bi-Lo, Food Lion** and **A&P** are just about everywhere in Charlotte. Specialty food stores like the **Fresh Market** and **Talley's Green Grocery** are gaining in popularity as health conscious people look for more specialty foods to grace their tables. You'll appreciate **Selwyn Natural Foods, Berrybrook Farms, Central Sun** and others. Charlotte is well-served with stores catering to basic needs like pharmaceuticals, dry-cleaning, newspapers, etc.

Specialty Stores

The nationwide rise in the popularity and profitability of specialty retail has been spectacular. Twenty years ago, most people shopped at a department store for their every need. Now, specialty stores of all sizes cater to those who want a better selection than is available in the department stores. Charlotte's zoning deities have made a conscious effort to concentrate retail in malls and shopping centers. However, a few stores have been successful by offering really specialized products and services while housing themselves far from the madding retail crowd. These stores are hidden away, so they take some scouting out. There are just too many great stores to do justice to everyone, so the best course of action is to pick a theme, look through the yellow pages and take off for a solid browsing session—you won't be disappointed.

Specialty stores advertise frequently in all the various Charlotte publications. Or better still, ask Charlotte residents about some of their favorite stores: the city is still small enough that people can direct you to wherever you and your wallet feel most comfortable. Here are a few of our favorites.

ANTIQUES
(See Antiques and Home Furnishings in our Homes Section.)

BOOK STORES
Charlotte is full of cozy, little intimate bookstores where the owners and customers know each other like they know their favorite books. They'll order books for you or let you know which new titles will titillate your eccentric reading tastes.

Among these treasures are **Horizon Books** (542-7307), which offers a terrific section of children's books at its store in the Arboretum shopping center at the corner of Providence Road and the

Matthews-Pineville Road, or **Little Professor Book Center** (525-9239) in the Park Road Shopping Center. Little Professor's owner John Barringer and his shop have been a favorite of local bookworms for more than a decade.

The **Intimate Bookshop**, with locations in Eastland (568-3600), SouthPark (366-6400) and University Place (547-7400), offers a great selection of books as well as a comfortable, friendly place to browse to your heart's content.

The national chain, **Waldenbooks**, has added a new store at Carolina Place Mall (544-2810) to existing locations at Eastland Mall (568-5782) and Uptown at 101 N. Tryon Street (376-1574). There is also a **Waldenbooks and More** at 5416 South Boulevard (521-9730). You'll find **Barnes and Noble** at Sharon Corners (554-7906) and at 5837 Independence Boulevard (535-9810), and off Morrison Boulevard is the newly opened **Borders Books & Music** (365-6261). **MediaPlay** has opened three new mega-size bookstores at 4716 South Boulevard in the Woodlawn Market Plaza (525-2416), at Town Center Place 8600 University City Boulevard (595-9956) and at 10011 Independence Boulevard in Windsor Square (847-4103). **Black Forest Books & Toys** at 115 Cherokee Road (332-4838), has a wide selection of children's books as well as many unusual toys.

Newsstand International at Providence Square Shopping Center (365-0910) is the place to go if you're homesick for news from back "home." It carries nearly 40 different Sunday newspapers from around the world and with nearly 5,000 publications (including ones from other countries) in stock, it has the largest magazine selection in the Carolinas. If that doesn't satisfy your reading habit, it also carries hard cover and paperback books.

Another great spot to find newspapers, magazines and paperback books is the **Times Newsstand** in SouthPark Mall (366-2005) It carries over 500 magazine titles and a wide selection of paperbacks. The selection of newspapers includes the *New York Times, Investor's Business Daily, The Wall Street Journal, The Business Journal, National Business Employment Weekly, Barron's* and others. Not your typical newsstand, Times is located inside SouthPark Mall, near the fountain. It is open from 9 AM until 9:30 PM Monday through Saturday and from noon until 5:30 on Sunday.

Poplar Street Books, 226 W. 10th Street (372-9146), is a haven for lovers of used books, sheet music, antique prints and maps. With books and assorted paraphernalia piled up all over the place, it looks like something out of a Dickens novel, but with the aura of old Charlotte instead of Victorian England. Local *literati* and writers' groups hang out here, and poetry readings are often held on Sunday afternoons. **Dilworth Books**, 2238 Park Road (372-8154), is another good source for used and antique books.

If personalized service appeals to you, visit **Bookends** in Kenilworth Commons, 1235-F East Boulevard (332-5137). Owners, Anne Tonissen and Mary McElveen aim to please the browser as well as the serious

Books, Books, Books and More Books!

Enjoy a pleasurable browse at any of The Intimate Bookshops in Charlotte. Books on nearly every topic under the Carolina Blue Sky! Books for every member of the family - for pleasure reading, for reference and for study! PARTNERS save 10% every day on everything and RENT-A-BOOK members read bestsellers at a 70-80% discount! Come browsing!

SOUTHPARK
Sharon & Fairview Rds.
366-6400

EASTLAND
Central Ave. &
Sharon Amity
568-3600

UNIVERSITY PLACE
Harris Boulevard &
U.S. 29 North
547-7400

The Intimate Bookshop

connoisseur and their love of books shows in their friendly, helpful service.

There are a number of specialized book stores in Charlotte such as **Audio Library** at 4736-A Sharon Road (552-TAPE) and 320 S. Tryon Street (333-7600) who rent and sell—you guessed it–books on tape. The **Baptist Book Store**, 5412 South Boulevard (523-5980) and **Byrum's Christian Book Shop** at 2329 The Plaza (331-9717) offer a wide assortment of Christian books and music. For those with a metaphysical turn of mind, **Central Sun Storehouse**, 1825 E. 7th Street (333-9200) or **Unity Bookstore** at 3500 Sharon View Road (553-0756) are the places to check.

All in all, if you enjoy reading, Charlotte has you covered!

CLOTHING

Speaking of being covered... obviously, we can hardly scratch the surface of great specialty shops and boutiques around town, so we will have to settle for mentioning those that are either institutions in Charlotte or special places we are admittedly subjective about.

Two new stores opened last year guaranteed to be on Imelda Marcos's fantasy list; **Designer Shoe Warehouse**, 3531 Tryclan Drive off Clanton Road from South Boulevard and **Off Broadway Shoe Warehouse**. Both are open from Thursday through Sunday and have thousands of shoes. Aisles and aisles of shoes, with few places to sit and try them on, have not deterred customers from flocking to these warehouses by the carload. If you're spending a couple of hundred dollars on a pair of shoes already, you may luck out on some bargains here, but popular priced, reliable label brands are in shorter supply as are some sizes. Still, the variety is dizzying.

And then, there's **Thompson's Bootery & Bloomery**, located at 1024 Pecan Avenue (332-5414). No one in Charlotte will admit to buying seductive lingerie here, but it's not mail order and it's been around for ages, so somebody must be crossing its threshold. Rumor has it that at one time the scantily-clad models in the display window were live, but were replaced by mannequins due to the increased number of car accidents occurring at the intersection.

For classic Charlottean high fashion, you can't go wrong at **The Carriage**, 6401 Morrison Boulevard. The shop offers anything the well-dressed woman about town needs. For classic women's clothing and fabulous accessories, try **Gallant's**, 1033 Providence Road (333-6139). From casual day wear to professional, this shop has it all...and in lots of sizes. **Our Place**, relocated in Sharon Corners, invites you to have a cup of coffee, glass of wine and nibbles while the salespeople put a stunning outfit, including accessories and jewelry, together that will make a clothing statement tailored just for you. You'll feel pampered and have fun with the experience.

If your personal style is more toward trend setting than trend following, let the great folks at **Perris Boutique**, 2907 Selwyn Avenue (338-9011) help you express yourself. With exclusive, one-of-a-kind fashions and accessories, this great little boutique offers a high fashion alternative to the classical look. And if a Hermes scarf is what you're looking for, look no further than **Carl Walker**, which has relocated to 715 Providence Road (334-1003). Carl and his staff cater to women of discriminating taste and carry designer fashions for women of all ages.

Petite Panache at 1041 Providence Road (334-5833) caters to women 5'4" or under who are looking for better-priced clothes. This shop also carries terrific accessories and offers wardrobe planning. Located exclusively at SouthPark Mall, **Benetton** (364-1660) interprets the hottest fashion trends in a combination of colors, style and fabrics. You may think of Benetton as catering to a young clientele, but its mix and match concept offers the flexibility of coordinating classic separates into an exciting new look or blending them into your existing wardrobe. A new Benetton sweater is a sure bet to lift the spirits!

Fairclough & Co. Inc., 102 Middleton Drive (331-0001), is arguably the finest men's clothing store in the city. It offers tailored classics and exquisite styles and fabrics, from formal to casual. But, service is its special strength. From helpful advice to coordinating an entire wardrobe, count on Fairclough for the best of the best. **Jack Wood Ltd.**, relocated in Uptown Founders Hall (332-6566), is known throughout the region for both quality and service that goes beyond the call of duty. Located at Specialty Shops on the Park, **Taylor Richards & Conger** (366-9092) offers elegant lines and classic European cuts. From jackets and fun wear to heavenly ties, formal wear and suits, this store is a treat.

Paul Simon Co. with two locations at 1027 Providence Road (372-6842) and SouthPark Mall (366-4523) offers a wonderful selection of men's clothing in a quiet and comfortable setting. Paul and his staff are always there to offer advice and assistance on everything from ties to shirts, suits to sports coats.

For a fresh splash of unique clothes and furnishings for the itsy bitsy to toddler-four crowd, stop by **Bellini** in the Kings Court Shopping Center at 901 S. Kings Drive (377-6888). New moms and dads can solve their nursery decorating needs here by choosing fabric, etc., that will be made and installed for blessed events. Bellini manufacturers its own whimsically styled furniture, offering handpainted tables, chairs and toy chests. From its beautiful Posies christening gowns to its Trucfuchi, Sweet Potato and Itsy Bitsy fun fashions, junior can sport the haute couture look.

For years, **L&S Children's Fashions**, Park Road Shopping Center (527-5282) and Loehmann's Plaza (567-2006), has carried the widest selection of kid's clothes in

Charlotte—no matter what unusual size your kids may be—at very affordable prices. Competition is fierce however, and there are a number of good children's shops in town now. **Charlotte's Kids Place** at the Arboretum (544-2311) and Providence Square Shopping Center (364-8025) have great selections. And there is a good selection of children's clothes at both locations of **Consignment World**, 1821 Norland Road (536-4770) and 10916 E. Independence Boulevard (847-2620)

The **Stork's Nest** in the Twin Oaks Shopping Center at 1419 East Boulevard (333-BABY) will have what you need whether you are the expectant mother or just looking for that special baby gift. Here you'll find the largest selections of maternity clothes in the area—casual or professional—and you can special-order your nursery bedding and accessories. You will find everything the nursing mother needs as well as christening gowns, books, toys, etc. If you are shopping for a gift, be sure to check out the Baby Register. It's a great way to take the guessing out of the gift giving.

Great Pretender is the perfect name for this unique jewelry store newly relocated to 1419 East Boulevard. Its man-made gem stone copies are so good that you'll squint a lot to try and find the difference between its stones and actual emeralds, diamonds, etc.

FOOD

Coming on strong is a growing international flavor in specialty food stores. Oriental, Mexican,

Greek, Thai, African, Caribbean and others are represented. The greatest concentration of shops is found along Central Avenue. This spreads across Charlotte's Mideastern community, but stores can also be found along South Boulevard, near Uptown and in Matthews. The shops offer too many unusual foods and items to mention, but we'll give you an idea of their offerings. You'll find big vats of Lebanese and Greek Kalamata olives, two roasts of Arabic coffee, tropical fruits, Caribbean spices and sauces, international cheeses, canned goods, frozen foods, flours—even Mideastern video tapes, Spanish language newspapers and magazines. Some even stock party goods and festival garlands. You'll also find clothing such as kimonos and quilted jackets and bolts of cloth to make ceremonial clothes.

Check out: **Viet-My** at 3100 Central Avenue (536-3296); **Kim Long Oriental Grocery and Gifts** at 4421 Central Avenue (532-7509); **Parthenon Gift and Gourmet Shop** at 4328 Central Avenue (568-5262); **Oriental Foods** at 4816-B Central Avenue (537-4281); **Caribbean Foods** at 1403 Eastway Drive (563-5208); **Jasrone Tropicana Mart** at 2315 Central Avenue (342-2098); and **Mid-Eastern Mart** which has moved to 4508 E. Independence Boulevard (536-9847).

Along South Boulevard, look for: **Las Dos Rosas Mexican Food Market** at 7015 (554-9902) or **Park 'n Shop** at 4750 (521-8255). Other stores with an international flavor include **Oriental Dong-Huong-Viet-Nam** at 1407 Eastway Drive (568-8709), **Vietnam Oriental & Seafood Market** at 2417 N. Tryon Street (347-1747), **Far East Oriental Grocery** at 7651 Pineville-Matthews Road (542-1188) and **Payal Indian Groceries & Spices** at 6400 Pineville Road (521-9680).

Other types of specialty shops worth your time include **Arthur's** at SouthPark Mall (366-8610). It is an award winning wine shop, a great restaurant, bakery, gourmet food, gift, coffee, tea, basket, chocolate and candy shop. It's a great place to find that perfect corporate or personal gift. The shop is neatly tucked away on the first level of Belk at SouthPark and features a complete selection of California and imported wines, along with Charlotte's largest wine bar. Arthur's also has shops at Belk Eastland and Carolina Place Mall.

Morehead Seafood at 919 S. McDowell Street, (375-4408), is the best place to buy fresh fish. If you buy snapper here, it was probably still swimming in the Atlantic that morning.

Charlotte Regional Farmers' Market, 1715 Yorkmont Road (357-1269), is the largest in the county and is run by the N.C. Department of Agriculture. Most Saturdays it takes on the atmosphere of a friendly country fair. Originally, farmers brought their crops of vegetables, flowers and crafts, but in the past few years, some savvy farmers have branched out to include many items you'd find in the grocery store such as bananas and pineapples. And the bouquets of farm grown flowers have almost been nosed out by local area nurseries that bring truck loads of plants and shrubs.

On the whole, shopping at farmers' markets is a bit less expensive and a lot more fun. You'll get to know regular crafts people, plus find a revolving number of new ones each time you visit. This market is open during the blooming season from Tuesday through Saturday. There are also several privately owned markets, including **Simpson's Market** at the corner of Kings Drive and E. Morehead Street, which is open Tuesdays and Fridays during the summer.

A few blocks away at 1515 Harding, you'll find one of the oldest farmers' markets in Charlotte— **Mecklenburg County Market**. Open from 7:00 AM to 12:00 PM, Saturday and Wednesday, but the pickin's are freshest and best at 7:00 AM on Saturdays but Insiders have been known to stroll in as late as 11:30 AM and still be able to fill their baskets with home baked goods, fresh vegetables and canned jams and jellies. The brick building is small, but you'd be surprised at the diversity. Bonsai trees, homemade crafts and flowers round out the offerings and you can nip in and out in a few minutes.

Shopping at the **Fresh Market**, 2823 Selwyn Avenue, (332-7753), is a true sensual experience, filled with the sights and aromas of fresh vegetables, freshly ground coffee, cheeses, an old-fashioned butcher's shop, fresh seafood, a bakery that should be declared too good to be legal, wine and all sorts of unusual items for the brave and gourmet.

The **Home Economist**, next to Blockbuster Video at the corner of Independence Boulevard and Idlewild Road, calls itself "a one of a kind food affair" and means it. There really is nothing else like it in Charlotte. This store has literally hundreds of foods that you can buy by the ounce or by the pound and the "bulk buying" concept can save you money by eliminating waste when you really only need an ounce, or assuring a better unit price when you need a ton of something. It also sells natural foods, natural personal care products, vitamins, wines, herb teas, gourmet coffees, baking supplies and more. The new store offers a full-service deli featuring homemade soups, sandwiches and salads.

Talley's Green Grocery is located in the heart of the Historic Dilworth neighborhood at 1408 East Boulevard (334-9200). Charlotte's first whole foods supermarket, Talley's features locally and organically grown produce, antibiotic and hormone-free meats, free range poultry, milk in glass bottles with the cream on top, the freshest seafood— cleaned and cut into fillets in the store, wines, beers, coffees and cheeses from around the world. It has a tremendous selection of bulk items including grains, seeds, nuts, beans, cereal, fancy dried fruits, and gourmet and natural packaged items. Nonfood items include a complete line of nutritional supplements, cruelty-free body care products and environmentally-safe household products. All this, plus the in-house **Cafe Verde**, which features fresh and wholesome meals (see Restaurant section) makes Talley's a popular stop for today's health-conscious shoppers.

If you are into health food, you should also try **People's Natural Food Market** at 617 S. Sharon Amity Road (364-3891). It carries a full line of natural foods, supplements and fitness products. The Eatery serves up a full menu of natural foods and vegetarian dishes, but the sandwiches are great favorites with the restaurant's large and loyal clientele .

HOME FURNISHINGS
(See Antiques and Home Furnishings in our Homes Section)

JEWELRY
Donald Haack Diamonds has two locations—Uptown in the Two First Union Center (372-7720) and at 4611 Sharon Road (365-4400).

The company maintains one of the largest diamond inventories in the Southeast, so when you're looking for that perfect stone this is the place to go. The company has an international reputation for dealing in quality gems.

Perry's At SouthPark, near the Sears entrance to the Mall (364-1391), is one of Charlotte's finest and most unique jewelry stores. As you walk in, you'll be greeted by the exceptionally friendly and professional jewelry experts who can guide you through the beautiful selection of Fine, Antique and Estate Jewelry. The finest quality diamonds and gems are always available, and Perry's can buy, sell on consignment, trade or repair your family treasures.

ETC.

Butterfields, etc. at SouthPark Mall (365-0887) is a gadget lovers dream. You could get lost in time browsing through the great selection of cookware, ceramics, pottery, linens and specialty gourmet items. If you need anything for your kitchen, you're sure to find it here. Gift baskets and special orders are also available.

The **Celtic Trader** at 2400 Park Road (332-2358) is far more than a specialty music store. It's the only store in Charlotte that holds weekly jam sessions. Owner, Rege Malady happens to be a big folk music enthusiast and can help you find about anything you're looking for in folk music. You'll find musical instruments hanging from the walls and ceiling, sheet music, tapes, CD's and even jewelry from the British Isles. Each Thursday around 8:00 PM you'll hear musicians, some from as far away as West Virginia, sit in with the regulars for the weekly session. If you haven't been to this free event, by all means—treat yourself.

There is nothing else in Charlotte like **Central Sun Storehouse**, 1825 E. 7th St. (333-9200). It offers a variety of products and services for the mind, body and spirit, including health foods, herbs, an extensive book department with an emphasis on spiritual self-development and metaphysical topics, tapes to meditate or relax by, New Age music, natural cosmetics and crystals, precious and semiprecious stones. It also has a spiritual astrologer and massage therapist on staff, plus it offers classes on such topics as meditation and astrology.

If you get a headache or stomachache in the middle of the night and have no medicine in the house, or if you suddenly need your prescription filled, **Eckerd Drugs** in the Park Road Shopping Center (523-3031), and **Eckerd Drugs** at 3740 E. Independence Boulevard (536-1010), are open 24 hours. Both stores also carry all sorts of other stuff, such as diapers, greeting cards, some food and beverages, household items and paperback books.

Greenway Gardens, established in 1951 by W. J. Redd, is one of Charlotte's oldest horticultural nurseries. The Garden Shop at 1829 Cleveland Avenue in Historic Dilworth (333-4372), is stocked with quality domestic and imported plants, shrubs, horticultural books, garden tools and accessories, furniture and more. The award winning **Redd Sled Christmas Shop**, open from mid-October until early January, is a fantasy of holiday decorating and gift items. A new location is opening at Atherton Mill on South Boulevard.

M. Grodzicki & Co., 611 Providence Road (334-73000), is delightfully schizophrenic. The front of the shop features sophisticated china, silver and home accessories. The back features unsophisticated, neat and crazy items for parties, as well as cards, stationery, balloons and baskets, plus its own spicy peanuts and Belgian chocolates. This special mix of sophistication and zaniness is now also available at its new store Uptown in Founders Hall.

Metrolina Expo, the flea market at the Metrolina Fairgrounds, U.S. 21 North (596-4643), is a grand way to spend a Saturday or Sunday. Open the first and third weekends of the month, the flea market is the place to go for deals on antiques, jewelry, clothing, furniture, and whatever the vendors come to sell. Be prepared to bargain. If you're new to flea markets, first go to the one held the third weekend to prepare yourself for the madness that occurs on the first weekend!

A Charlotte institution, **Myers Park Dry Cleaners**, 1039 Providence Road (334-0157), is located in the heart of the Myers Park neighborhood. The salespeople make it a point to know their customers and offer that individual service you may have known in your small hometown. It's tough to find a good place to have silk cleaned, but Myers Park is one of the best in town.

It's worth a special trip to Matthews to visit **Renfrow's General Store**, 188 N. Trade Street (847-4088), which provides a step back in time to what a dry goods store was like at the turn of the century. Where else could you find such items as bib overalls and animal feed, as well as garden supplies, kitchen products, hardware and housewares?

Not in any way a traditional hobby shop, **Science Hobbies**, 2615 Central Avenue (375-7684), first opened its doors 30 years ago. It began with rocks, minerals, a few books, some microscopes and telescopes. It has evolved with each new inquiry, about even the most obscure of hobbies, into an eclectic shop where you can find just about anything from lab wares to wooden ship models to beads. The shop specializes in material for science projects and the staff has even been known to share an idea or two with those of us whose imagination doesn't extend beyond growing bread mold! If you want it, you'll find it at Science Hobbies. And if you don't, the sales staff will go that extra mile to find it for you.

While you're in Matthews, drop by **Southern Manner** at 106 N. Trade Street (847-3698). Owned and operated by Matthews native Wayne Haigler, this antique and gift shop opened in 1982 and features such items as Tom Clark Gnomes, baskets and dried flowers, candles, thrown pottery, and antique iron works, pewter and graff.

Soft Spokin' (love the name) **Cycle Shop** between Matthews and Monroe is well worth the trip out to 5803 E. Independence Boulevard (821-8484). The shop offers mountain bikes, Terry women's bikes, tandems and loads of accessories. It also sponsors weekly rides every Sunday and everyone is welcome to join in the fun. Call for information.

Just look for the home with all the kids, and chances are you will find playsets designed and built by Swings-N-Things, Inc. These folks have been manufacturing quality commercial and residential playground equipment since 1986 and you will find it in almost any neighborhood in Charlotte. In addition to its custom designs, Swing-N-Things represents of 40 different vendors, so the possibilities are endless. Swings-N-Things is located in Matthews, across from the Family Dollar Warehouse and its open from 9 AM to 5 PM every day except Sunday.

University Place offers shopping variety for the booming north Charlotte area.

UPTOWN'S PREMIER SHOPPING and DINING LOCATION!

Shopping & dining at Founders Hall is the height of excitement! Visit Uptown's premier shopping & dining location and discover what the excitement's all about!

Founders Hall
NationsBank Corporate Center,
100 North Tryon Street.

The SHOPS At FOUNDERS H·A·L·L

Complimentary Parking (2 hrs.) in NationsBank Corporate Center garage for Founders Hall patrons.

Bistro 100
Unique restaurant with woodburning stoves

Blossom Shop
Fresh cut flowers and plants

The Bookmark
Everything for the book lover

Crown Athletic Club
Elegant membership fitness club

Accent On Knives
All types of knives & cutlery

David-Bernards
Fine men's footwear

Eastern Lobby Shops
International newsstand

The Express
Women's sportswear & accessories

First Impression Auto Care
Auto maintenance, washing & detailing

Grodzicki & Co.
Distinctive & unusual gifts

Jack Wood Ltd.
Fine men's clothing

Julie's Too
Clothing for the career woman

Kostas International Hair Salon
European style hair salon

Package Plus
Package mailing services

North Carolina Blumenthal Performing Arts Center Box Office

Pope's Gallery
Artwork and framing

Simpson Photo Service
Photo equipment, film, photo finishing, etc.

Sir Speedy Printing Center
Full-service printing & copying

Spratt's Kitchen & Market
Delicious, fresh food…fast!

Sunrise Cleaners
Dry cleaning and laundering

Inside
Sports

"I've been covering sports in Charlotte for over 20 years. Needless to say these are exciting times! Growing up around Philadelphia, I was familiar with the excitement pro sports bring to a city. I knew when the NBA came to Charlotte things would never be the same for area sports fans. Suddenly everybody's a coach. I cant wait to see the NFL in the Carolinas. For you sports fans in the Carolinas these are truly the best of times."

-Harold Johnson

(Harold Johnson is a popular local sportscaster for WSOC-TV and has worked in the Charlotte market for over 20 years.)

Nothing else has better reflected Charlotte's pride over recent years than its enthusiasm for sports. The city has attracted all types of sports teams and events, always with lots of support from Charlotteans. Charlotte was awarded its first major league franchise in 1987 with the introduction of the NBA's Charlotte Hornets. The community has since rallied behind efforts to bring the NFL, AAA baseball and professional hockey to the area. The Charlotte Motor Speedway is considered the mecca of motorsports and hosts three of the NASCAR series most popular races. The city lies in the heart of the ACC (Atlantic Coast Conference) and for the past several years, played host to the conference's yearly basketball tournament.

The addition of the new Charlotte Coliseum, with a seating capacity of 24,000, has given Charlotte the needed leverage to secure events of national prominence and attention. In 1991, Charlotte hosted the NBA All-Star game. The event assembled professional basketball's top players, including native North Carolinians Michael Jordan, James Worthy, Brad Daugherty and Dominique Wilkins. The events of All-Star Weekend attracted fans and media attention from across the nation and around the world. The league praised Charlotte's efforts and has expressed interest in staging the event in Charlotte again in the future.

The Coliseum was also the site of the 1994 NCAA Final Four, perhaps the most significant event to be awarded to Charlotte to date. The city pulled out all the stops to entertain the estimated crowd of over 50,000 fans. South Tryon was transformed into the "Street of Champions," a three-block entertainment zone. For four days, five themed restaurants and many street vendors drew crowds of visiting fans and locals to the biggest street party in Charlotte's history. The event was deemed a huge success and created a resurgence of interest in an Uptown entertainment district.

Of course, the biggest news in town is the winning of the NFL franchise. When the National Football League owners unanimously voted in October of 1993 to make the Carolina Panthers the league's 29th franchise, fans throughout the Carolinas celebrated. Within hours, sports paraphernalia with the distinctive panther logo appeared on the streets as if by magic. Long a hotbed of football enthusiasm, the Carolinas impatiently await the first game, an exhibition game against their expansion counterpart, the Jacksonville Jaguars, in the Hall of Fame game in Canton, Ohio on July 29, 1995.

Charlotte's sports scene has changed in recent years, but one thing that hasn't changed is the area's loyalty to the ACC. None of the conference schools are located in Charlotte, but with five member institutions (North Carolina, N.C. State, Wake Forest, Duke and Clemson) no more than a three-hour drive away, it's easy to see why fan enthusiasm stays at a fevered pitch. I-85 stays busy on fall Saturdays as alumni and fans head for the land of tailgate parties and fraternity brunches. The rivalries are strong, but not much is decided on Saturday afternoon. The real rivalries take place on Monday morning at the work place when the hazing of the weekend loser begins.

The ACC's national prominence in football has grown in recent years with the conference naming three national champions in the past 12 years (Clemson in 1982, Georgia Tech in 1991 and Florida State in 1994). With the inclusion of the conference in a national bowl alliance, it appears certain that the ACC will continue to offer the area great football rivalries for years to come.

As collegiate football grows steadily in the area, it is unlikely that it will surpass the region's steadfast attachment to ACC basketball. The conference has been regarded for years as one of the premier basketball conferences in the nation. It has turned out several national champions, most recently Duke in 1991 and 1992 and the University of North Carolina at Chapel Hill in 1993. The Atlantic Coast Conference season culminates each March with the ACC Tournament to decide the conference champion. Although Charlotte has been the site of the tournament for the past several years, it moves to Greensboro in 1995. The Charlotte Coliseum also plays host to NCAA regional and sectional matchups.

Although not members of the ACC, UNC Charlotte, Davidson, Johnson C. Smith and other area schools produce basketball that takes a back seat to no one. UNC Charlotte, which plays in the Metro Conference, fields a basketball team that has established itself on a national level in recent years. Highly acclaimed coach Jeff Mullins is steering the 49ers back to the prominence that led the team to the Final Four in the late 1970s.

One of the hottest sports ticket in town remains the Charlotte Hornets. Season tickets are sold out for the foreseeable future, with a waiting list in place. The city has embraced the NBA team, and fans are eager as the organization augments itself to the competitive life of the NBA. 1991 was a pivotal year for the Hornets as they introduced Larry Johnson, NBA Rookie of the Year, to the Queen City. 1992 was just as exciting with the addition of first-round draft pick Alonzo Mourning. In 1993 the Hornets made their playoff debut. Charlotte was wild during the playoffs as everyone cheered the team on. No one could have ever imagined the Hornets success would have grown to a earn them a place in the playoffs in just five seasons. Injuries slowed the team's progress in the 1993-94 season, but did not dampen the spirits or enthusiasm of the fans.

Another favorite on the Charlotte sports scene is The Charlotte Knights. The AAA team affiliated with the Cleveland Indians, plays just south of Charlotte in the beautiful Knights Castle.

In the following chapter you will find information for the spectator—from professional and collegiate sports teams to the most popular sporting events in the area. For recreational activities and participant sports, see the chapter on **Parks and Recreation**.

Baseball

THE CHARLOTTE KNIGHTS
2280 Deerfield Dr.
Fort Mill, SC
Charlotte Telephone: 332-3746

The Charlotte Knights are the AAA affiliate of the Cleveland Indians and play their games in beautiful Knights Stadium. Knights Stadium is a $15-million facility that was opened for the 1990 season. It seats 10,000 and is located on I-77 South and Gold Hill Road at exit 88, just one mile past Carowinds Boulevard. Yearly attendance exceeds 430,000.

Charlotte successfully lobbied for the AAA team to come to the Carolinas after spending several years as the AA affiliate of the Chicago Cubs. The Cleveland organization is making a major effort to revitalize its farm system. You can see Indians 1991 Second Round draft pick, first baseman Herbert Perry and 1992 Number One Pick, pitcher Paul Shuey who joined the Knights during the '94 season.

Knights ticket prices are $4.50 general admission, $5.50 reserved and $6.50 field and club level. Children up to 12, senior citizens and military personnel with I.D. pay $3.00 for general admission. The stadium has full concession facilities with a wide variety of food. Special group rates as well as skyboxes and tent parties are also available. The season runs from early April until September with the Knights at home for

Photo courtesy of the Charlotte Knights.

The Charlotte Knights are the AAA affiliate of the Cleveland Indians.

72 games. Call the Knights office for schedule and ticket information.

Basketball

THE CHARLOTTE HORNETS
Hive Drive
Charlotte, NC 28217   *357-0252*
Tickets: *357-0489*

"The market is too small," "Fans will never forsake their beloved ACC basketball to support the pros," "If they do get a team, fans will only come out to cheer for their old college heroes," "They could never sell out the new Charlotte Coliseum."

These are just a few of the not-so-flattering accolades that were bounced around by the national sports community when it was announced that Charlotte was pursuing an NBA franchise. These are also just a few of the doubts that were decisively laid to rest when the Charlotte Hornets took to the court for their inaugural season in 1988.

Looking squarely into the face of doubt and skepticism, George Shinn began his quest to bring the sport he loved to Charlotte. With an excellent marketing plan, solid financial backing and the support of a community eager to prove itself, the NBA rewarded Shinn and the city for their efforts on April 22, 1987. The team took to the court for its first game November 4, 1988, amid hoopla and sold-out excitement that turned the game into an event. The event turned into a season of events that captivated a city and led to an NBA first season attendance record. With each successive season Charlotteans embrace the Hornets as everyone plays armchair coach, general manager and owner.

In their first season, 1988-89, the Hornets formed the nucleus of their otherwise young team with veterans Robert Reid, Kelly Tripucka and Kurt Rambis. Along with first-round draft choice Rex Chapman and local favorite Tyrone "Muggsy" Bogues, the Hornets finished their inaugural season with a respectable 20-62 record. Highlights of the season under coach Dick Harter were impressive wins over the Philadelphia 76ers, Utah Jazz and Michael Jordan's Chicago Bulls.

The sophomore jinx may have caught the Hornets in their second season. Enthusiasm for the team remained a picture of consistency as the team itself faced several major changes among key personnel. Veterans Robert Reid and Kurt Rambis were traded away as the team opted for the youth movement. New faces Armon Gilliam and Dick Anderson joined rookie J. R. Reid for the campaign that ended with a 19-63 mark. Dick Harter was replaced by coach Gene Little's, and general manager Carl Sheer was replaced by Allan Bristow. In the 1990-91 season, the Hornets added veteran Mike Gminski and a hot-shot rookie named Kendall Gill en route to the teams then-best season at 26-56. The team set the league attendance record for the second time and pulled off victories against the Boston Celtics, San Antonio Spurs and the defending World Champion Detroit Pistons.

Excitement over the 1991-92 season was at a fever pitch as the team took to the court with the league's Number-One draft choice, Larry Johnson. Johnson, an All-America from UNLV, was college basketball player of the year and continued his outstanding performance as a Hornets player. Johnson made quite an impact with many groups in Charlotte. Not only did he

affect the Charlotte community by leading the Hornets and being named as NBA Rookie of the Year, but also through his generous donation to the United Way, allowing the organization to reach its annual goal.

The Hornets were led by new head coach, former general manager Allan Bristow. Bristow's inaugural season as head coach resulted in a best-ever 31-51 record. Once again the Hornets proved their popularity in Charlotte by selling out every game and leading the league in attendance for the third season.

The 1992-93 season was another attendance breaker. The Hornets made their playoff debut and had a winning season. Allan Bristow signed a five-year contract as head coach of the Hornets and for the third season in a row, Charlotte has done well in the lottery. Charlotte, with the number-two draft pick in 1992, chose 6'10" shot-blocker from Georgetown, Alonzo Mourning. Mourning is the third of Coach Allan Bristow's Big Three. He joined forward Larry Johnson and shooting guard Kendall Gill in forming a powerful force on the court.

Hopes were high for the 1993-94 season. With the outstanding talent on the team, the Hornets were expected to make the 1994 NBA playoffs. Unfortunately, injuries sidelined both Larry Johnson and Alonzo Mourning for much of the season and the team did not perform up to expectations. With a little luck and a lot of talent, the 1994-95 season will meet or surpass the hopes of the Hornet's faithful fans.

The Hornets impact on the area will remain significant for years to come. It has opened the door for other forms of professional sports with an Arena Football League team, a AAA baseball team joining Charlotte in 1992-93 and NFL games just over the horizon. The Hornets are a great attraction and loads of fun.

THE CHARLOTTE THREE ON THREE

This annual tournament allows the basketball junkie to test his or her skills against area players of similar ability. Proceeds go to Habitat For Humanity. The tournament is held in the Uptown streets of Charlotte every August and is open to all ages and skill levels. Each team, made up of four players (only three of whom play at a time) is categorized by height, age, basketball experience and how often the members play. They are then placed together with similar teams in one of several divisions. The two-day, double-elimination tournament has grown to well over 500 teams in recent years and features a slam-dunk contest and a three-point shootout. For more information call the Central YMCA at 333-7771.

Football

THE CAROLINA PANTHERS
Ste. 1600
227 W. Trade St.   *358-7000*
On October 26, 1993, the National Football League owners unanimously voted to make the Carolina Panthers the league's 29th franchise. The award provided the Carolinas, long a hotbed of football enthusiasm, professional sports' crown jewel: an NFL team.

Owner Jerry Richardson's dream of a football team for the Carolinas grew from his own experience in the NFL. A small college football All-America at Spartanburg, South Carolina's, Wofford College (site of the Panthers training camp), Richardson went on to play professionally as a receiver for the former Baltimore colts. With the Colts (now in Indianapolis) he was the 1959 Rookie of the Year, and caught a touchdown pass from Johnny Unitas in the team's 31-16 victory over the New York Giants in the 1959 World Championship game. After playing again in 1960, Richardson took his $4,694 championship bonus and started a single Hardee's restaurant in Spartanburg.

Richardson's fast food business, born of professional football bonus money, now ranks as one of the nation's largest food service operations with more than 120,000 employees and $3.7 billion in annual revenues. Flagstar, Inc. now owns and operates over 500 Hardee's, 200 Quincy's Family Steakhouse restaurants, 1,000 Denny's company restaurants, 375 Denny's franchise outlets and 200 El Pollo Loco restaurants.

"We are looking forward to the challenge of putting a team on the field that the whole region can be proud of," Richardson said. "We feel we have the management team in place to do that."

At the head of that team is team president Mike McCormack. A Hall of Fame offensive lineman with the Cleveland Browns, the legendary Paul Brown called McCormack,

"The greatest offensive lineman I ever coached." His on-field prowess was converted to the sidelines when McCormack climbed the coaching ladder rising from a position as assistant coach to a head coaching job before becoming general manager and finally president of the Seattle Seahawks in 1983.

McCormack joined the Panthers as an executive consultant in April of 1989 before being elevated to president early in 1994. The man who is credited with making the Seahawks a success sees greater opportunities for expansion teams this time around.

"The new Collective Bargaining Agreement says that expansion teams may be entitled to two choices per round in all seven draft rounds for the first three years. If we get that, in addition to opportunities which free agency now may well provide, with very careful planning the Carolina Panthers can do things that would have been impossible in terms of team building under previous expansion rules."

After putting together a Buffalo Bills team that went to four straight Super Bowls, Panthers General Manager Bill Polian is well aware of the challenges involved in building a winner. Says Bills Head Coach Marv Levy, "The Panthers have absolutely hired the best general manager available. They have taken the right step to come into the NFL today."

Polian joined the Bills in 1984 as pro personnel director and was promoted to general manager in 1986. Over the span of his six years as general manager, Buffalo appeared in three Super Bowls, adding another appearance after his 1992 departure. Polian is credited with bringing in 45 of the 47 players who took the Bills to their first Super Bowl.

In 1989 and 1992 Polian was named *The Sporting News* NFL Executive of the Year in voting by his peers. He joins Bobby Beathard and George Young as the only two-time winners of the prestigious award.

Says Richardson of McCormack and Polian: "A strong front office operation gives you the base to build a winning team and we're committed to winning. I think with Mike as president and Bill as general manager, we've taken the key step to building the strongest front office in the NFL."

The Panthers first game is scheduled as an exhibition against their expansion counterpart, the Jacksonville Jaguars, in the Hall of Fame game in Canton, Ohio, on July 29, 1995.

Awaiting completion of a new 72,300 seat stadium, the Panthers will play their inaugural season at Clemson University's Memorial Stadium, home to the Clemson Tigers. With a capacity of over 80,000, a full house each week would enable the Panthers to set an NFL single season attendance record.

The Panthers future home will be Carolinas Stadium on a 33 acre site in uptown Charlotte. The $16 million open-air, natural grass facility was financed through a public-private venture including the sale of Permanent Seat Licenses (PSLs) which give buyers the ability to permanently control and purchase season tickets for all Panthers home games. Over 50,000 PSLs ranging from $600 to $6,300 have been purchased by Panthers fans and all of the money raised will go to build Carolinas Stadium. The total number of PSLs has been regulated to ensure the availability of approximately 8,000 tickets per game for walk-up sales.

In designing and building the 72,300-seat stadium there has been but one goal: to construct the finest stadium in the National Football League.

Fans at the new stadium will benefit from a variety of features designed to make Carolinas Stadium the standard for comfort and enjoyment in the NFL. The stadium itself is designed to offer excellent sight lines from any seat. Fans will have up to twice as many concession stands as normal from which to purchase food and beverages, ensuring quick and efficient service with little waiting. Carolinas Stadium will provide access to 20% more restrooms than a typical stadium. Each end zone will have a major scoreboard display including a large 24' x 32' television-quality color replay video board. Like the Panthers, Carolinas Stadium is a reflection the positive attitude permeating the Carolinas.

While the Panthers are still a year away from playing, the club has already been active in the Carolinas community. Director of Community Affairs Donnie Shell was one of the first staff members hired by the organization. Shell and Director of

Family Programs. B.J. Waymer, conducted the team's first annual Youth Clinic in July and are planning a full range of community programs.

And with the Panthers first game coming up soon, football fans in the Carolinas can look forward to a day right around the corner when NFL football will be a fixture of Carolina Sundays.

CHARLOTTE RAGE
5601-77 Center Dr., Ste. 250
Tickets: (704) 527-RAGE

Beginning in 1992, Charlotte became home to one of the 12 arena football teams, Charlotte Rage. With the Arena Football League's (AFL) preview year in 1987, arena football is still a new concept to many, but is quickly gaining a following. Because the action is so close to the fans, many refer to arena football as "in your face football." Unlike typical NFL football games in which showmanship by the players is discouraged, arena football is a show as well as a sporting event. Rage football is referred to by promoters as Rock 'N Roll Football. Rock music blasts the coliseum adding to the excitement of the fast-paced physical sport.

While many of the rules are the same as NFL football, there are some significant differences. Arena football is played indoors on an astroturf field half the size of an outdoor football field. The goal posts are 9 wide with a crossbar height of 15 (NFL goal posts are 18 1/2 wide with the crossbar at 10). There are also nets which stretch from either side of the goal post to the sideline and allow players to continue play

Only eight players per team are allowed on the field and, with the exception of the quarterback, center and kicker, they play both offense and defense. There is no punting in arena football, but both drop kicks and placement kicks are allowed for field goals and extra points with the difference being that drop kicks give two points for conversions after touchdowns and four points for field goals.

Charlotte Rage features a lot of local talent—11 of the 20 players on the team are from the North and South Carolina area. The team's owner Allan Schwalb is a major motion picture financier from Florida.

The Rage had a great second season doubling their wins and making the playoffs. The Charlotte Rage's 12-game season runs from mid-May through August and offers Charlotteans an exciting, air-conditioned summertime pastime. Games are played on Friday or Saturday nights with ticket prices ranging from $6.00 to $40.00. Rage home arena, the Charlotte Coliseum, seats 21,847. Make sure to grab some friends and head on out to see the Rage battle it out! Season tickets are available.

events of the Tour, The Paine Webber Invitational. Arnold Palmer, who won one of the PGA Tour's first senior championships in 1980, is host of the Paine Webber Invitational and the architect of **The Tournament Players Club at Piper Glen**, the site of the Invitational.

The Paine Webber Invitational attracts a roster of all-time golf greats such as Miller Barber, Bob Charles, Bruce Crampton, Gene Littler, Chi Chi Rodriguez, Orville Moody and the 1994 defending champion Lee Trevino. These and many others vie for a share of the $750,000 purse.

Piper Glen, the 6,774-yard, par 72 championship course designed by Palmer, has long been a symbol of the tradition surrounding The Paine Webber Invitational. Spectacular mounds and amphitheaters provide unrestricted views of tournament action on the tees, fairways and greens, all of which have a reputation for pleasing the thousands of spectators who attend the tournament each year. For those turning 50, the Senior PGA Tour provides a history of exciting tournaments with unmatched competition.

Golf

THE PAINE WEBBER INVITATIONAL
P.O. Box 471693
Charlotte, NC 28247   846-4699

It was in the late '70s that the PGA of America, along with the USGA, decided to establish a Senior Open—that is, a golf championship for 50-and-older senior golfers. Today, there is the Senior PGA Tour, and one of golf's most prestigious

Hockey

THE CHARLOTTE CHECKERS
Tickets: 342-4423

Beginning in October 1994, Charlotteans will have yet another sporting event to attend—hockey. The Charlotte Checkers will be playing their season in the Independence Arena. The team is one of 19 teams in the East Coast Hockey League. The hockey team is sure to be another one of Charlotte's successes!

Racing

CHARLOTTE MOTOR SPEEDWAY
Harrisburg, NC   *455-3200*

Its nearly impossible to mention NASCAR racing and not think of Charlotte. Charlotte and stock car racing go hand in hand. Charlotte is home to tens of thousands of NASCAR enthusiasts and thousands and thousands more when the big races come to town. Even if you have never enjoyed stock car racing before, its hard to resist the excitement that fills Charlotte when the Coca-Cola 600 and Race Week come to the Speedway.

If you have never seen stock cars race before, you owe it to yourself to take a trip to qualifying night the next time the Winston Cup cars come to town. Go to turn number one and stand next to the chicken-wire fence that separates the 3,200-pound machines from the massive grandstands that regularly seat thousands of frenzied fans. Pick the spot where the cars appear destined to join the retaining wall, a spot where the cars become tangent to the spectators before they decelerate from the 170-mph plus speeds to negotiate the ensuing bank turn. It's at that spot where you realize the incredible pace at which these guided missiles are really traveling. Although TV coverage of racing has never been better, it fails to capture the true essence of Winston Cup racing. At that spot you run the risk of being hooked on the sport for years to come.

Twelve miles northeast of Charlotte, in Concord, NC lies the 2,010 acres of Charlotte Motor Speedway. The 1.5-mile oval is home to some of the nation's hottest racing. CMS hosts several different types of racing and auto shows over the course of a year, but the main drawing cards are its three NASCAR Winston Cup events; **The Winston Select, Coca-Cola 600** and the **Mello-Yello 500**. The speedway is Charlotte's largest sports-related economic contributor and was responsible for pumping over $200 million into the economy in 1993. In addition to the tourism-related expenditures, the speedway's leadership position in racing has fostered the development of an affiliated industry. Over 75 percent of stock car racing equipment is manufactured and sold in the Charlotte area, contributing to the region's economy. The speedway is also active in many Charlotte charities for children.

The **NASCAR Winston Cup series** is the world leader in motor sports total attendance, attracting over 4.1 million fans to events in 1993. The tracks operate at well over a 90 percent capacity rate and have justified the sports large amount of corporate involvement. The sport is growing at record pace, and there is no better place to get a taste of it than at the Charlotte Motor Speedway.

The first of Charlotte's major race weekends is centered around **The Winston Select**. Not a part of the regular Winston Cup Series points race, The Winston Select

The Charlotte Checkers play in the East Coast Hockey League.

brings together the past year's winners for a sprint-formatted race of champions. The race has proven to be action-packed and controversial over the years and may better suit the novice race fan that doesn't have the patience to sit through one of the longer, sometimes drawn-out events. In May, 1992 The Winston Select was presented for the first time ever "under the lights" when the Charlotte Motor Speedway added an elaborate lighting system.

May's feature race, the **Coca-Cola 600**, is the highlight of two weeks of racing festivities that begin with The Winston Select. The "Ten Days In May" are culminated with the 600, one of the four Winston Cup "Major's." The Coca-Cola 600 yearly boasts the second-largest single-day paid spectator event in the United States by attracting over 170,000 fans. The race is the NASCAR season's longest of the year (it begins at 5:00 PM and ends around 9:00 PM) and proves to be a grueling endurance test for the teams left to battle on the 400th lap. The race has crowned such notable champions as Richard Petty, Dale Earnhardt and Rusty Wallace and always proves to be a pivotal event in the series' points battle. In October, the Winston Cup cars roar back into Charlotte for one of the year's final competitions. Like the Coca-Cola 600, the **Mello-Yello 500** is often a key in determining the series champion as the teams head for Atlanta and the season finale.

All three races are rich in tradition and provide fender-to-fender racing between heated rivals. The NASCAR series offers a form of racing that is often unequaled in excitement. It is one of few racing series where the aerodynamics of the cars allow the drivers to race within inches of each other. You may even see some friendly contact as the action heats up. Attending a Winston Cup race is a little different from other sports, so if you've never been to a race at CMS there are several things to keep in mind when planing your trip.

• Plan your trip early. Events at the speedway are often sold out in advance.

• The best seats are higher up in the stands on the front-stretch.

• Pack a cooler of your favorite food and beverage. Plenty of concession areas are available at the track, but racing is one of few spectator sports that allows you to provide for yourself.

• Bring a seat cushion. Many of the grandstand seats are made of concrete and get harder as the day grows longer.

• Leave for the track early, real early! The track facilities are second to none, but the traffic can leave something to be desired. If you arrive early, you will also get a chance to see some of the pre-race entertainment that track president Humpy Wheeler has become famous for providing.

• Pledge allegiance to your favorite driver and prepare to cheer until your voice is gone. You're in for a day of excitement that is hard to match.

Have you ever dreamed of being a race car driver? Now you can. A couple of years ago Humpy Wheeler and Eliot Forbes-Robinson, a road racing veteran, made racing affordable again with Legends Car Racing. This new concept in racing has already developed a loyal following and is spreading through the country.

Allison Brothers Racing in Salisbury, North Carolina, builds the cars used in this sport. To date, over 800 5/8 scale models of classic 1937 and 1940 Chevrolet and Ford coupes and sedans which are powered by a 1200CC Yamaha motorcycle engine have been built. No modification is allowed on the engines. Believe it or not, these cars sell for under $12,000.

The Legends Cars race throughout the year at the Charlotte Motor Speedway. The "Summer Shootout Series" is designed for families and runs every Tuesday night June through August from 5 PM until 10 PM. Entertainment is provided by the Speedway's popular new mascot "Lugnut." Admission is $5.00 for adults, $1.00 for children six through 12 years of age and children younger than six are admitted free.

Tours of the Charlotte Motor Speedway are also available Monday through Saturday 9:00 AM until 4:00 PM, and Sunday from 1:00 PM until 4:00 PM. For more information on the Charlotte Motor Speedway, call the track office.

Running

CHARLOTTE OBSERVER MARATHON

The Charlotte Observer Marathon is the largest and most popular of the numerous races held in Charlotte each year. It features the marathon, three 10-K races, a one-mile fun run and a family 5-K leisure walk to accommodate runners of all levels. The event attracts thousands of runners for the events staged during the first half of January each year. Many streets in the area are blocked off to accommodate the participants as they make their way through the different neighborhoods of Charlotte. For more information call *The Charlotte Observer*, 358-5425. For information on other 10-K races and triathlons held throughout the Mecklenburg County area call Larry Frederick of the **Charlotte Track Club** at 358-0713 or your local YMCA.

SOUTHPARK TURKEY TROT
Hyatt Charlotte   *554-1234*

Another annual event is the SouthPark Turkey Trot, an 8-K road race on Thanksgiving Day in the SouthPark area of the city. The race begins at 9 AM at The Hyatt Charlotte at SouthPark and is sponsored by the hotel, SouthPark Mall and others. Proceeds from the race are donated to Special Olympics and Unicef. For more information, call The Hyatt Charlotte at SouthPark at 554-1234.

DILWORTH JUBILEE
Latta Park

Charlotte's oldest road race occurs in August of each year. The 8-K Dilworth Jubilee begins at 8 AM and is run through the beautiful and historic Dilworth area. Since August is typically hot and humid in Charlotte, make sure to dress appropriately. Even if you don't run in the race, volunteers and supporters are always welcomed at this Charlotte race tradition.

Soccer

CAROLINA VIPERS
2700 Independence Blvd.   *349-CISL*

Professional indoor soccer has arrived in Charlotte. As one of the charter members of the Continental Indoor Soccer League (CISL), the Charlotte Vipers began play in June 1994.

Indoor soccer has been referred to as "human pinball" and provides fast-paced action that all sports fans will enjoy. Even the Vipers' ownership group includes action-oriented personalities such as NASCAR drivers Richard Petty and his son Kyle. Majority owner Felix

Photo courtesy of Carolina Vipers.

The Carolina Vipers play action-packed indoor soccer.

Sabates owns two NASCAR teams and was one of the original owners of the NBA Hornets.

If you like excitement, you'll love this sport.

CHARLOTTE EAGLES
2101 Sardis Rd. N., Suite 201   841-8644

The Charlotte Eagles Soccer Club plays in the 72-team, coast-to-coast, United States Interregional Soccer League. This professional development league has the express goal of giving American soccer players an opportunity to play in a high calibre league once their college careers are over. Games are played at Charlotte Latin School and admission is $6.00 for adults, $5.00 for youth 16 and younger and kids under 6 are admitted free.

Swimming

CHARLOTTE ULTRASWIM
Mecklenburg Aquatic Club
9850 Providence Road   846-5335

Every June the Mecklenburg Aquatic Club (MAC) hosts the Ultraswim competition at the Mecklenburg Aquatic Center. Some of the world's best swimmers converge on Charlotte for this nationally recognized competition. Past and future Olympians can be seen competing at this event.

Tennis

THE CHARLOTTE EXPRESS
525-5678

World TeamTennis has returned to Charlotte and has found a new home at Olde Providence

Racquet Club. Jimmy Connors, Martina Navratilova and Bjorn Borg, three of the sport's all-time greats, played in Charlotte in the 1994 season.

For those who haven't had the fortune to see World TeamTennis, the unique format keeps each match fun, exciting and action-packed. Each team is made up to two women and two men. A match consists of one set of women's and men's singles, women's and men's doubles, and mixed doubles. A match is won by the team which has won the most games at the end of the five sets. Prize money is awarded based strictly on performance, both individually and as a team.

The four-week season is played between Wimbledon and the U.S. Open when tennis excitement is at its peak. Seven home and seven away matches are played during the regular season with a playoff and championship match for the top teams at season's end. Nationwide, 12 teams competed for the World TeamTennis Championship in 1994, for a total of $720,000 in prize money.

Collegiate Sports

DAVIDSON COLLEGE
Davidson, NC   *892-2374*
Davidson athletics provide the opportunity for participation at various levels of interest and proficiency. Varsity sports provide outstanding athletes with an opportunity to reach their athletic potential in fiercely competitive arenas. Club sports provide intercollegiate competition at a less intense level, and more than 80

percent of students play on intramural teams.

National recognition was brought to the college in 1992 when the Men's Soccer NCAA Division I National Championship was hosted by Davidson. The tournament was sold out for the first time in history and Davidson was chosen to host the tournament again in 1993 and 1994. Davidson's well known Men's Soccer team were semifinalist in the National Championships in 1992.

Davidson is also known for its nationally competitive men's basketball team and men's and women's tennis teams. Other varsity sports for men include football, baseball, indoor/outdoor track, cross-country, wrestling, soccer, golf, swimming and diving.

Women have varsity teams in field hockey, tennis, volleyball, indoor/outdoor track, cross-country, soccer, lacrosse, basketball, swimming and diving.

The Davidson football team is an Independent Division I-AA (Cost containment) team. All other varsity teams are NCAA Division I and compete in the Southern Conference.

For ticket information call the Davidson College Athletic Ticket Office Monday through Friday, 8:30 AM until 5:00 PM at (704) 892-2375.

JOHNSON C. SMITH UNIVERSITY
100 Beatties Ford Rd.   *378-1297*
The enthusiasm at Johnson C. Smith University has spread from its academic corridors onto the playing courts and fields. The atmosphere is alive with excitement and anticipation. Crowds regularly fill

Jack Brayboy Gymnasium to the rafters during home basketball games. During the 1991-92 season, the Golden Bulls ranked in the final Division II Top 20 after finishing second in its conference, the Central Intercollegiate Athletic Association (CIAA), during the regular season. After reaching the NCAA's Sweet Sixteen in 1992, Coach Steve Joyner's Golden Bulls had a disappointing season in 1993-94. With four returning starters, hopes are high for the 1994-95 season.

In football, Coach Ray Lee brings in an exciting brand of action. JCSU is home to Charlotte's only collegiate football team. Home games are played on campus in the Bullpit stadium, while September's Queen City Classic and October's Homecoming game are played in Memorial Stadium.

JCSU participates in the NCAA's Division II in football, cross-country, volleyball, men's and women's basketball, track, softball, tennis and golf. For ticket information call 378-1297.

QUEENS COLLEGE
1900 Selwyn Ave. 332-7121

Queens College's commitment to athletics is evident in the nine sports now offered for student athletes: men's and women's basketball, men's golf, men's and women's soccer, men's and women's tennis, women's volleyball and women's softball. Queens competes as an independent in the NCAA Division II. In addition, the school's Ovens Athletic Center has proven to be a popular Charlotte sports arena. It serves as the NBA Charlotte Hornets alternate practice site and is home to the Charlotte Pro-Am summer basketball league. Ovens Athletic Center offers a swimming pool and six tennis courts.

UNC CHARLOTTE
Hwy. 49 547-4937

The University of North Carolina at Charlotte offers the city a wide variety of interests with its NCAA Division I, 14-varsity-sport intercollegiate program. The most visible program is men's basketball which plays its home schedule at the Independence Arena. The women's basketball program, that has won over 100 games over the last five seasons, plays on campus in the Belk Gymnasium, a 2,500-seat facility.

The fall sports schedule offers men's and women's soccer, men's and women's cross-country and women's volleyball. One of the top programs in the South, the men's soccer team played in the 1991 and 1992 NCAA tournaments. All fall programs are held on campus.

In November, basketball season heats up. One of the more exciting nights of the season is the party atmosphere offered October 14th at 11:30 PM when the athletic department kicks off the season with Midnight Madness, held in the Belk Gymnasium. The team's first official practice serves as a pep rally for fans as the action continues into the wee hours of the morning. The basketball team has played in four post season tournaments in the past seven years. High-profile coach Jeff Mullins directs the 49ers efforts.

During the spring, UNC Charlotte offers full athletic programs in baseball, softball, tennis, track and golf. All compete on campus (with the exception of golf). The baseball team made its first NCAA appearance in 1993 after winning the Metro Conference Championship, and followed with its first Metro Conference regular season Championship in 1994. All sports compete in the Metro Conference. For any additional information on the schools teams, facilities or schedules call 547-49er. For tickets to athletic events call 547-4949.

Off The Beaten Path

CRICKET

The Charlotte Cricket Club
10820 Independence Pointe Pkwy.
Matthews, NC   *841-2581*

The Charlotte Cricket Club was founded in 1989 by a number of new arrivals to the Charlotte area who missed playing their favorite sport so much that they formed a team. In the five years since the inception of the club, the CCC has made significant progress and has brought the game to the attention of thousands of locals.

Although the game resembles baseball in some respects, those who see it for the first time will find it difficult to understand. But have no fear- the intricacies, grace, aggression and athleticism of the sport will become readily apparent. Each year, the club organizes a game between a team from NationsBank and a team from First Union, both comprised of Americans who have never seen the game before.

The club plays an active spring and fall season at Olde Providence Racquet club. In the spring, the club plays local and regional teams. The club also travels to Philadelphia for a tour. In the fall, the club hosts regional teams, and the season culminates in a three day tournament featuring the Gentleman of Philadelphia, The Mad Dogs from New York, and the Bank of Bermuda.

The Charlotte Cricket Club, which has benefited greatly from the involvement of the local business community, is looking for sponsors and players. No experience is necessary for either. Those who would like to participate in what is the most graceful and civilized of all fair weather sports should call 841-2581 or 362-3857.

POLO

The Charlotte Polo Club
11331 Tom Short Rd.
Charlotte, NC 28277   *846-1010*

Located off Tom Short Road, Southeast of Charlotte, polo is a unique opportunity for a day of family-oriented fun and festivities. The Charlotte Polo Club takes to the field against teams throughout the Carolinas for some divot-stomping excitement. The 9-week Spring season runs from May through June, with the 10-week Fall season running from September through November. The match is played each Sunday with the gates to Cato Farms opening at 1 PM, allowing fans to picnic and tailgate before the 3 PM main event. The Polo matches have proven to be a favored pastime for Charlotteans in the Spring and Fall, with each match attracting several thousand fans.

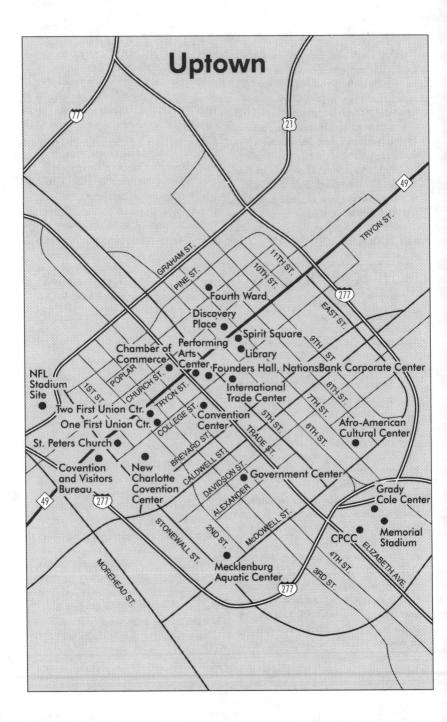

Inside
Uptown

A quick stroll on the streets of Uptown Charlotte will enable you to see and feel the city's spirit. Every aspect of Uptown is a reflection of what the city has come from and where it is going. Uptown is the heart and soul of Charlotte. Recently, one visitor from Washington, D.C., could not stop talking about how clean the city is. "There's no trash around. Everything is so new—but there are still trees too!" Uptown Charlotte is a beautiful area, merging steel, concrete, trees and people in a vibrant environment.

You can find everything in Uptown Charlotte, from the central business district to the government hub to residential neighborhoods. Uptown will also soon house the new Convention Center and an NFL stadium. If you want to know Charlotte's ambitions, you must know Uptown.

The center of Uptown is at the intersection of Trade and Tryon Streets, commonly referred to as Independence Square. It is at this intersection where two Indian trading paths met and the area's first settlers centered their activities. The Square was also the home of Tom Polk's log cabin which was called the courthouse in a successful move designed to convince the colonial legislature to make Charlotte the county seat.

If you are new to this city one of your first questions is probably "why is it called 'Uptown' instead of downtown?" The answer is that the "Uptown" name is a simple marketing ploy. One of the city's strategic marketing moves was to call its downtown jurisdiction Uptown in the belief that its a more distinctive description. Geographically, no matter where you are in the city you must travel uphill to get to Uptown, which is what local folks called the area until after World War II. With the influx of residents from the northern states in the 1950s, however, Downtown became the word of choice. And like most American downtowns, it declined with the postwar boom era and the coming of suburbia. But in the middle 1970s, community and business leaders, along with interested citizens, de-

Photo by John Cress.

The center of Uptown is at the intersection of Trade and Tryon Streets, commonly referred to as The Square.

cided they didn't want the city's nucleus to die. One way to help the area's image was to once again call it Uptown. Then Mayor John Belk officially designated the business district Uptown in 1974 with the backing of the Charlotte Chamber of Commerce.

More than 45,000 people work in Uptown. The city wants that number to increase to 67,000 by the year 2005 and has put an Urban Design Plan into action to market the Uptown area. The goals of marketing Uptown include increasing business by retaining existing businesses and attracting new ones, strengthening Uptown as a cultural center and increasing its residential base. The implementation of this plan is a project of the Central Charlotte Division of the Charlotte Chamber of Commerce.

In the last few years, Charlotte has seen many new additions to its skyline while suffering several failed attempts to secure Uptown as a retail marketplace. During the late 1980s, Charlotte benefited from the new 42-story **First Union Center** with one million square feet, the 12-story **Charlotte-Mecklenburg Government Center**, the **Gateway Center** on Trade Street, College Streets $32-million **Charlotte Apparel Center**, the $10-million expansion and renovation of the **Charlotte-Mecklenburg Public Library**, **Spirit Square**'s renovation, the opening of the 31-story **Interstate Tower** on West Trade Street and the addition of the **Holiday Inn** and **Omni** hotels.

CityFair, the innovative center city mall that closed temporarily in September of 1991 is reopening with a bang. CityFair offers a fun atmosphere with a three-story atrium including a food court, casual dining, retail shops and an Uptown learning center for The University of North Carolina at Charlotte. Great entertainment can be found on weekends during **World Mardi Gras**.

Many Uptown leaders have envisioned the creation of an entertainment zone in Uptown. ARK Management, Inc., which operated the successful Fat Tuesday on the Street of Champions, has developed a new and innovative concept that will help realize this vision. **World Mardi Gras** will be a multifaceted entertainment zone encompassing the first and second floors of the CityFair atrium as well as the arcade hallway extending to and including **Fat Tuesday**. Each weekend and on selected holidays, the atrium will be transformed from a simple food court to an entertainment facility centering around a Mardi Gras theme, complete with full-scale props, costumed employees, live music, theatrical lighting, and a large selection of food and beverages.

The decade of the '90s will see even more commercial growth in the Uptown area that will place Charlotte in the world-class city league. In June 1991 the renovation at the Plaza Park was completed and the stunning new **Carillon** office tower, owned by Hesta Properties, added its jewel to the crown in September of 1991. In October of 1991 Charlotte became one of a few American cities privileged enough to house an **Omnimax Theater** that is now part of the Discovery Place Science Museum (see **Attractions**).

*More than 45,000 people work in Uptown
and enjoy the many inviting outdoor areas to lunch or relax with friends.*

The long-awaited completion of **NationsBank Corporate Center**, **Founders Hall** (see **Shopping**) and the **North Carolina Blumenthal Performing Arts Center** (see **Arts**), transforming a city block, is breathing new life into the retail and entertainment establishments. NationsBank Corporate Center opened in May of 1992 and has dramatically altered Charlotte's skyline. With 60 stories and 1,203,177 square feet, it is the largest office building in the Southeast.

Adjoining the NationsBank Corporate Center is Founders Hall, a grand, six-story glass wintergarden that blends retail stores, fine and casual dining, a first-class health club and a constant array of exciting events and entertainment. Founders Hall features 75,000 square feet of retail space, restaurants and a performance area.

Also adjacent to NationsBank Corporate Center is the Blumenthal Performing Arts Center. This $55-million center features a 2,100-seat performance hall, a 450-seat theater and numerous rehearsal halls. It will provide permanent facilities for the Charlotte Symphony, Charlotte Repertory Theatre, Opera Carolina and many other art groups.

Another great improvement to Charlotte's Uptown will be the new **Convention Center**, which is due to open sometime in January 1995. It should nearly double the present convention business. The new Convention Center will be three times the size of the current center, covering 850,000 square feet—about the size of 430 average homes. The new Convention Center will cater to a national market, spreading its base from the region and raising Charlotte's visibility on the national

Founders Hall and the North Carolina Blumenthal Performing Arts Center, along with NationsBank Corporate Center have breathed new life into Uptown.

The new 850,000 square foot Convention Center is due to open in January 1995 and is expected to double the present convention business.

scene. The Convention Center is expected to generate $275 million annually into the Charlotte/Mecklenburg economy through its activities.

The Uptown addition generating the most excitement presently is the privately funded **NFL Stadium**, which has an Uptown site. Businessman Jerry Richardson succeeded in his bid for an NFL franchise that is expected to bring millions of dollars to the heart of the city (see **Sports**).

Uptown is far more than business and big buildings. Uptown is also a cultural and educational area, hosting the main branch of the public library and Discovery Place, the hands-on children's museum. It is also home to a rich and varied group of cultural organizations.

The **Afro-American Cultural Center** is an art gallery, theater and educational resource for Charlotte's black heritage. **Spirit Square** offers classes, workshops, visual arts, exhi-

The new, privately funded NFL stadium will seat 72,300 football fans.

Charlotte is one of a few American cities privileged to house an Omnimax Theater that is part of the Discovery Place Science Museum.

The conversion of the 70-year-old Ivey's department store
into luxury condominiums will create the only private residences in the heart
of Charlotte's central business district.

Photo courtesy of Ivey's Townhomes.

bitions and performances in its theaters. The new **North Carolina Blumenthal Performing Arts Center** will add even more life to Charlotte's cultural Uptown scene by hosting the symphony, opera and many touring plays and musicals. Uptown is also home to many art galleries and invites the public to experience them through monthly gallery crawls.

In addition, by planning special events, the city works hard to make Uptown available to all who live in Charlotte, not just those who work Uptown during the week. Events ranging from concerts and exhibits to festivals and parades, are held year-round for folks of all ages. Just some of the fun things that happen in Uptown on an annual basis are **First Night Charlotte** (New Year's Eve), **St. Patrick's Day Parade**, **Summer Stage** concerts, **Alive-After-Five** concert series, **SpringFest**, **Jazz Charlotte**, **Kids Day**, **noontime concerts**, **farmers' markets** and **restaurant crawls**. There are more than 150 retail/service businesses Uptown as well as over 45 restaurants.

Not only is Uptown the home to many businesses, it is the home of about 5,700 people. If current trends continue, this total should reach about 7,200 by the year 2005. Several surveys of Uptown workers and of the general population indicate that there is substantial interest in living in the area. A major stimulus for Uptown housing is the planned conversion of the 70-year-old Ivey's department store building into luxury condos. The project, which will create the only private residences in the heart of the central business district,

will also include office space and restaurants. As of April 1994, 35 of the 68 condos had been sold and over half of the commercial space leased. The first commercial tenants are expected to occupy space in **Ivey's Townhomes** project in January 1995, and residential tenants in February.

Some beautiful buildings have been preserved and successfully restored for reuse. The **Afro-American Cultural Center**, 401 North Myers Street, is the former home of Little Rock A.M.E. Zion Church (built in 1911). **Spirit Square**, the regional center for the arts, located in the heart of Uptown at 318 North Tryon, is the former First Baptist Church sanctuary (1909). Other Uptown landmarks that have been restored include the **Dunhill Hotel**, the **Cadillac Building**, **Latta Arcade**, the **Peace Building**, the **United Carolina Bank Building** and the **First Southeastern Center**. If you are interested in learning more about historic Uptown, you can pick up a free guide entitled *Historic Guide to Uptown Charlotte, N.C.* from the Convention and Visitors Bureau.

Even if you don't work Uptown, it is worth frequent visits just to get a glimpse of the changing skyline and Charlotte's future. Pick up a brochure on a self-guided tour of Uptown from the Charlotte Convention and Visitors Bureau at its new location, 122 E. Stonewall Street (371-8700). For a calender of monthly events Uptown or an Uptown guide, contact the Central Charlotte Division of the Chamber of Commerce at 378-1335.

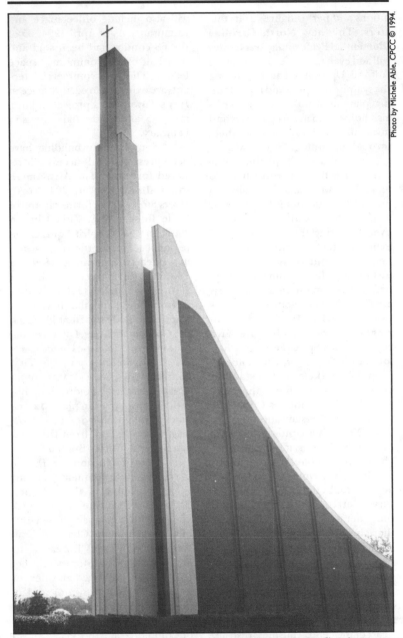

Photo by Michele Able, CPCC © 1994.

With its unique ski-slope roofline, Sharon United Methodist Church
has long been a distinctive landmark in Southeast Charlotte.

Inside
Worship

Don't get in a snit if you're asked: "Where do you go to church? Temple? Worship services?" The inquirer is merely trying to be friendly, not nosy. And if you reply that you don't have a place, don't be surprised if you're invited to attend the inquirer's place of worship. Again, this shows Southern hospitality and good upbringing. Southerners want nothing more than to get you off on—or back onto—the right track. It's easier to understand this attitude if you know that, since the 1740s, the boundaries of Mecklenburg have been defined by eight Presbyterian churches, located near rivers for the agricultural needs of the Scotch-Irish who carved Charlotte out of the wilderness. With livelihood and worship as the cornerstones of the community's value structure, it should come as no surprise that Charlotte's over 600 churches have seated the city at the "buckle" in the Bible belt.

But where you go depends on what you want from your faith. This is the question one of Charlotte's mainstream ministers posed to his congregation a few years back. He wanted to know why poor people sent their social security checks to Jim Bakker's PTL ministry; why many upper-income, well-educated people left the religion they were brought up in to follow the Baghwan. What hunger were those religions satisfying that the mainstream religions were not? He found that the followers of those nontraditional religions, as well as a growing number of people who want to reconnect with God, could care less about where they have to go to do it. Denomination wasn't the deciding factor, no matter how they'd been raised.

Today, many people are looking for a certain atmosphere, an energy and excitement in religion that is powerful enough to make them put the funny papers aside on Sunday morning. They aren't interested in going to church just to be "seen" by their boss or garden club president. They want to go to a place that has meaning for them. A place that is there for them when times are rough—a minister or rabbi who can explain theology (Bible, Koran, etc.)

by relating it to the problems we face with our families and in our jobs today. A place that gives us something that is larger than ourselves.

Armed with this new understanding, many of Charlotte's religious leaders have gone to great lengths to meet the needs of those who are searching and rekindle or ignite that spark of faith missing from their lives. The mission is no longer singly directed with saving souls; it is, for many religious leaders, keeping that soul involved. This is why when Charlotteans are asked why they attend their chosen place of worship, they'll say it is for fellowship and spiritual nourishment. But scratch a little deeper as to why they've chosen this particular church or temple over another, and they'll launch into all the programs going on that make their church special; hence, these are not only spiritual gathering places, they also function as educational centers for self-realization. Mecklenburg Community Church incorporates that attitude in its contemporary approach.

Years ago in the South, Protestants had separate church programs and schools, as did Catholics and Jews, and you better believe—the twain never met. No more. In Charlotte the spirit of ecumenicism among different religions has been dipped in faith and taken root. You'll frequently hear members of different faiths discuss taking a class, or being in a support group, or working out in the gym of a church or temple that is not of their spiritual belief. Insiders know that the **Jewish Community Center's Health Club** is the best bargain in town. The JCC,

in addition to its preschool program, also provides instruction for handicapped children, including summer camp, plus a host of educational and cultural enticements. St., Marks Lutheran and St. Patrick's Catholic Church have joined forces to organize a **"Lunch Pals"** program at Eastover Elementary School. Once a week volunteers have lunch with a child who needs extra tutoring or just a little TLC.

From a purely academic standpoint, religious leaders have discovered that many people are interested in learning what impact the Dead Sea Scrolls have had on the understanding of Christianity, Judaism and the Bible. Parishioners aren't apt to take the time to enroll at UNCC or Winthrop University to find out. To remedy the situation and offer an enticing program to their parishioners and other interested people, St. John's Episcopal, Covenant Presbyterian and other local churches brought three nationally recognized scholars to discuss these questions in four- and seven-week seminars. The free sessions were open to the public and widely attended.

Many churches are reaching inward to provide programs that help people—not just their members. A brand new monthly program called **Parents' Night Out** is sponsored by Midwood Baptist Church for its members and the Midwood neighborhood. This gives young couples a free evening out knowing that their children are cared for in a safe and loving environment. Another bonus feature for young mothers new to Charlotte are varied churches'

"**Mothers Morning Out**" program. Mornings are often difficult times to find baby-sitters and this program provides a place to care for your child for a few hours once a week. Churches throughout the city provide this program on different week days. Almost all of Charlotte's larger churches and synagogues offer day care and programs for children, youth and young adults, but Selwyn Presbyterian provides an innovative program of day care for the elderly.

Outreach programs are the result of Charlotte churchgoers addressing some '90's problems with '90's answers. Since violence has become epidemic in the United States, Charlotte churches have begun to look at its root cause in such programs as "**The Violence in Interpersonal Relationships**." No one would claim that the problems of drugs, homeless, or the environment have been licked, but inroads have been made. A case in point is Myers Park Baptist Church's **North Carolina Harvest Program**. Seventy-five volunteers pick up perishable food from restaurants and caterers and deliver it to such recipient agencies as: Rebound (Christian rehab center), Transition House (for runaways), The Relatives (for troubled teens), George Shinn Homeless Shelter, Salvation Army, Plaza (emergency housing), Crittenton's Tate McCartin (drug rehab for pregnant women), United Family Services (for battered women), MMAE'S (housing for family of hospital patients).

The **Job Hunter's Support Group**, sponsored by St. John's Episcopal Church, teaches thousands of unemployed people how to find work through help with resumes, networking, and the support of each other.

The '92 riots in Los Angeles and elsewhere have shown us that we live in a time that is less than noble. The integrated congregation at Seigle Avenue Presbyterian Church proves that harmony need not be impossible to achieve. These parishioners break stereotypical rules by accepting people for what they are, an attitude that they take with them into the business week. Another example of integrating folks from dramatically different cultures takes place at Spencer Memorial United Methodist Church on East 36th. Street. Since its 1800's founding, this Methodist church has ministered to the working-class in North Charlotte. But in the last few years that ministry has changed to include Cambodians and members of Hmong tribe of Laos who came to America—like many other pioneer Americans—to find religious freedom and live in peace. The church has become a kind of melting pot of people who want to practice their religion while maintaining their native identity.

A couple of years back marked the first time that some members of the Charlotte Area Clergy Association met to explore ways to include the homosexual population in their ministry. There is much work to be done in this area, but the clergy has responded by listening to the struggles of those who have been rejected from other congregations.

Charlotte's concern with substance abuse has seen local churches banding together to stage anti-drug marches, walk for the hungry (Crop Walk), and deal with the growing needs of the poor. A current focus is an overall concern with environmental problems that impact everyone.

For many years the Catholic Church has sponsored a center called **Holy Angels**, a home for seriously deformed infants. And, last year St. Ann's Catholic and St. Peters Catholic Churches, along with Park Road Baptist, began making plans for a preschool for children infected with the AIDS virus. Although the program is designed for HIV-positive toddlers who have not shown symptoms of the disease, church leaders say that children already suffering from the disease will not be turned away. The school is among the first of its kind in the country. Their hope is to enlist other churches to participate in this effort.

Bethlehem Center, a community center, provides child care, educational training, enrichment programs, youth employment training, an alcohol prevention program and many other services. It is sponsored by the United Methodist Home, Wesley Nursing Center, Asbury Care Center and the Methodist Counseling Center. The Presbyterian Church USA supports the **Seigle Avenue Presbyterian Community Ministry**, **South Tryon Day Care Center** and the **Double Oaks Nursery**. A number of other community-wide services are **Goodwill Industries, Shepherd Center, Kinder-Mourn, Alexander Children's Center** for emotionally disturbed children, **Friendship Trays** and the **International House**.

The largest denomination in Charlotte is Southern Baptist, making up over 15 percent of those who attend church. Following Southern Baptist is the AME Zion Church, United Methodist and the Presbyterian Church, each represent over 9 percent of active churchgoers. The Roman Catholic church is the fastest growing church in Charlotte. Charlotte is well represented by Episcopal, Evangelical, Lutheran, Jehovah's Witness, Full Gospel and Church of God houses of worship, and 21 nondenominational groups. Unitarians, Friends, True Lights, Greek Orthodox, Jews and Moslems are all represented with churches or synagogues.

Today, a few individuals are moving outside of mainstream religion, seeking spiritual awakening through Baha'i, Zen, Suffism and AA's twelve-step programs. Often, the movements act to reconnect the person with his/her former religion.

As you may have discerned, religion is important to most Charlotteans, so much so that when they are transferred out of Charlotte, you are apt to hear them moan, "I'll miss my good friends; I'll miss the trees, but most of all, I'll miss my church."

In this edition of *The Insiders' Guide To Charlotte*, we have highlighted a few of Charlotte's churches. We have also listed the denominational headquarters and representative religious groups—resources that may be helpful in locating a church home in Charlotte. The **Charlotte Area Clergy Association**, 2831 N. Sharon Amity Road (537-2663), can also provide assistance. If you are one of the 30,000 internationals that live in Charlotte, a good resource to assist you in finding people of your own faith is the **International House**, 322 Hawthorne Lane (333-8099).

Many area churches hold two worship services on Sunday, plus Wednesday night prayer meetings, Bible studies and a host of other activities throughout the week. For more specific information about a given church, call the church office.

Baha'i

BAHA'I FAITH CHURCH
552-1212 or 537-0164

An informal introduction to Baha'i, begun in 1844 in Persia (Iran), is given each Monday noon at Renaissance Place Restaurant, 631 N. Tryon Street. Each lecture/discussion is based on the teachings of Baha'u'llah (the Glory of God), co-founder of the Baha'i faith. The 100 active member congregation does not have a permanent center for its 19 yearly worship services, which are open only to members. In addition to monthly worship services, the members hold "Firesides" that are informal, intimate meetings held in members' homes to discuss the faith in a personal, nonthreatening way. Sunday schools are also available for children and adults and open to anyone interested in learning about the faith.

The structure of the religion is clergy-less, utilizing the premise that every believer has the obligation to teach. The church's central objective is to spread its "teaching," which is not that easy since members

are forbidden to proselytize aggressively. Prospective members must seek them out.

According to doctrine, members believe in: the oneness of God; the oneness of mankind; individual, independent investigation of truth; the common foundation of all religions is one; the essential harmony of science and harmony of religion; total equality of men and women; elimination of prejudice of all kinds; universal education and job training; universal auxiliary language; a spiritual solution to economic problems; and universal peace upheld by a world government.

Baptist

FIRST BAPTIST CHURCH
301 S. Davidson St.   *375-1446*

On the anniversary of its 156th year in 1988, First Baptist Church moved into a new sanctuary—a 1,600-seat multtiered contemporary structure dominated by beautiful stained glass windows. In 1989, a Casavant Pipe Organ was installed. Sixteen years earlier, the congregation had vacated its space on North Tryon Street (now Spirit Square) and moved to the present location across from the Charlotte/ Mecklenburg Education Center. Since the move, the 2,700-member church has also built a family life center—a facility that is used for recreation programs, physical fitness classes, and other fellowship activities.

First Baptist is known for its outreach programs to the community, including a television ministry, educational and musical programs, and its pastoral care. The church is led by new head minister Dr. Charles D. Page, who was called to the church in 1991. In addition to Dr. Charles, the church has seven other ministers and a full support staff.

Sunday School is at 9:15 AM; worship services at 10:30 AM and 6:00 PM on Sunday; 6:15 PM on Wednesday.

HICKORY GROVE BAPTIST CHURCH
East Harris Blvd. &
Newell Hickory Rd.   *531-4000*

Hickory Grove Baptist Church is the largest church in North Carolina. In 1955 the church began in a barn with about 25 people. Today, its beautiful building, housing 7300 parishioners, sits on 50 acres across the street from its early beginnings.

Senior pastor, Dr. Joe Brown, has a staff of 12 that ministers to the community in many outreach programs. The church has a separate Family Life Center with an indoor track, game room, weight training and fitness area for classes in karate and aerobics. In addition, it has a 20-acre field where 14 different softball teams play. Its strong athletic program offers basketball from ages four to adult, both men's and women's softball and volleyball. It offers a summer sports camp as well as regular camping for boys and girls.

Hickory Grove is proud of its in-depth counseling program that ministers to the problems of single, married and single again. The extensive music department is renowned for both its annual **Passion Play** and **Living Christmas Tree**. Over 16,000 watched 200 participants perform through orchestra, drama and singing for eight free performances.

You can watch this dynamic ministry's *Challenge for Living* on WCNC (36) Sunday at 11 AM or on WCCB (18) at 9:30 AM. Hickory Grove has a strong Bible study and discipleship program. Sunday school hours are: 7:59, 9:15 and 10:45 AM; church services are: 9:15, 10:45 AM and 6:30 PM on Sunday and 6:45 PM on Wednesday.

MYERS PARK BAPTIST CHURCH
1900 Queens Rd.   *334-7323*

The 1,900 parishioners of Myers Park Baptist are among the most committed in their outreach programs of any church in Charlotte. The church's wide range of programs are overwhelming, but a couple of the most outstanding are the **North Carolina Harvest**, a group that recycles food from restaurants and caterers to needy organizations, and the **Shepherd's Center**, an education and help ministry to the elderly (also cofounded and aided by other local churches). The church is also a member of **Bridges for Peace**, an international group whose members visit with peoples in foreign lands, fostering reciprocal invitations.

In conjunction with other local churches, Myers Park Baptist sponsors **Crossroads** seminars that bring in national speakers and are open to the community. Another important outreach program is **Partnership in Tutoring** at the Tuckaseegee Elementary School. The church was one of the founders of **Habitat for Humanity**.

Myers Park Baptist Church has a wide range of outreach programs.

Myers Park Baptist is considered the most progressive Baptist church in Charlotte, often taking difficult stands in its efforts to promote Christianity. The church's beloved minister, Gene Owens, retired last year after 23 years of leadership and the Search committee has not, at this writing, found a new minister.

During the winter, Sunday School is held at 9:45 AM, Sunday worship service is at 11 AM, and there is a family night dinner on Wednesday. During the summer, Sunday worship service is at 9:45 AM and Talk Back or Sunday School is at 10:45 AM.

NORTHSIDE BAPTIST CHURCH
333 Jeremiah Blvd.   *596-4856*

Northside Baptist, led since 1990 by Dr. Bradley Price, is one of Charlotte's largest churches with over 6,000 members. Northside serves the community through its child care center, a Christian academy for K-12 students, a religious bookstore, mission projects and other worthwhile endeavors. The Rev. Jack Hudson led the church for 36 years until his retirement several years ago. Sunday School is at 9:45 AM and Sunday worship service is at 11 AM.

Catholic

ST. PETERS CATHOLIC CHURCH
507 South Tryon St.   *332-2901*

The cornerstone for St. Peter's Catholic Church was laid March 17, 1851, by the Reverend Jeremiah J. O'Connell. Charlotte had just over 1,000 citizens at that time, so the dedication of a new church was a big event, attended by people of many different faiths. The church, including land, cost $1,000—much of it donated by non-Catholics who liked Father Jeremiah when he preached at the Episcopalian Church. For a time, from 1888 until 1892, St. Mary's Seminary, a day and boarding school was held on St. Peter's property until Sacred Heart Academy in Belmont was built.

It was not until after 1892 that Rev. Francis Meyer arrived and the present church was built. Subsequent Catholic churches were built in Charlotte, but St. Peter's is still considered the "Mother" church. St. Peter's was revived in 1986 when the Bishop invited the Jesuit Community to staff the parish. Rev. John C. Houghey S.J., with the aid of Rev. Eugene V. McCreesh S.J., increased the membership from 110 to the current 524 families. The Rev. James Devereux took over the pastorate two years ago.

Since this parish's rebirth, it has made a strong commitment to the poor and was instrumental in establishing, along with other churches, the **Shelter of Homeless Men**. Some of the church's many outreach programs include **St. Peter's Homes,** which is a joint effort with St. Peter's Episcopal Church to help provide housing for the poor, **Prison Literacy**, and mission work in El Salvador, India and Burma.

Within the church there are adult religious education programs and youth religious education programs as well as a Youth Group dedicated to service projects and appropriate fun-type activities. One of St.

Peter's most exciting and enduring undertakings was the **Ben Long Frescoes**. The family of St. Peter's, spearheaded by Rev. Haughey, joined with the entire Catholic community in cooperation with corporate and arts funding to make the commissioning of such an ambitious project possible. The frescoes are a triptych. The left side is The Agony in the Garden, the center is The Resurrection of Jesus, and the right side is The Descent of the Spirit. The frescoes were begun in 1988, completed in 1989, and expected to last for 1,000 years. The inspirational frescoes are open for public viewing from 10 AM until 4 PM Monday through Saturday and from 1 PM until 4 PM Sunday.

Sunday Mass is held at St. Peters at 9 AM, 11 AM and 5 PM. Daily Mass is held Monday through Saturday at 12:10 PM.

Episcopal

ST. JOHN'S EPISCOPAL CHURCH
1623 Carmel Rd.   *366-3034*
St. John's Episcopal Church was built in 1959 and underwent a major reconstruction in 1986. This 1600-member church, with its beautiful contemporary stained-glassed windows, is one of Charlotte's more progressive churches. Former rector Reverend Robert Haden initiated many outstanding programs that have drawn people from throughout the community. Reverend Charles Riddle is the church's interim rector.

Perhaps St. John's is best known for its productive **Job Hunters Support Group** that instructs, networks and supports the unemployed. In the forefront of the environmental problem, St. John's has conducted seminars with varied environmentally oriented speakers, and adopted energy saving programs within the church and among its members. The church has a strong Boy Scout program. St. John's supports the **Bethlehem Center** and works with the Double Oaks Community in many problem areas.

St. John's Arts Ministry encourages expression of the gospel through such art forms as painting, drama, mime, music and liturgical dance. The church has sponsored a commission on AIDS, and St. John's youth group cooks meals monthly for the homeless shelter. The youth group is also very active in **Habitat for Humanity** (as are the adults), and in other service groups. St. John's plays an important part in the **Stephens Ministry**, which is a one-on-one pastoral ministry serving the community.

Sunday worship services are at 8 AM and 10 AM and Sunday School is at 11:15 AM. A prayer-healing and communion service is held on Tuesday at noon.

Greek

HOLY TRINITY GREEK ORTHODOX CATHEDRAL
600 East Blvd.   *334-4771*
The first Greek Orthodox Church was established in Charlotte in 1929 on South Boulevard with only 23 members. The depression years were difficult for the church, but the arrival of Rev. Chrys Papalambrou in 1939 began a resur-

gence that brought in 85 new members. Rev. Papalambrou remained with the church, instigating the building of the Byzantine-style cathedral in 1953-54 to accommodate the growing congregation. The Rev. Papalambrou left Charlotte in 1960 when he was made Bishop. In 1967 a new Hellenic Center was built next to the church that houses the Sunday School which, with its weekly attendance of over 600 children, is one of the largest Sunday Schools in the country. The Hellenic Center also houses a Fellowship Hall and Greek Cultural Center.

Each year the church sponsors a mandatory service project to the community that is undertaken by each adult and young adult Sunday School class. The **Philoptochos Society** (women's group—meaning beloved) conducts its own outreach programs. The **GOYA** (Greek Orthodox Youth of America) organizations also participate in local service projects and there is a separate **Cathedral Foundation** that supports community outreach projects. The church has participated in the **Russian Relief Program**.

Each September, the week after Labor Day, Charlotteans look forward to the **Yiasou Greek Festival** held at Holy Trinity's Hellenic Center. There is much merrymaking, good Greek food specialties, entertainment with Greek dances, crafts displays, a 5 K race and Fun Run to round out the festive doings. Inside the Hellenic Center, you can see a film on the Greek Isles, learn about the Greek religion and the Greek culture. A portion of the proceeds are given to charity.

The Rev. Phaethon Constantinides, affectionately knows as Father C., serves the church with an assistant priest and youth minister. Divine Liturgy is held in English at 9 AM and in Greek at 10 AM.

Interdenominational

CALVARY CHURCH

5801 Pineville-Matthews Rd.   543-1200

Calvary Church, one of Charlotte's larger churches, serves 3,500 members and 1,500 nonmember regular attendees with a ministerial staff of 12. Dr. Ross Rhoads, the Senior Pastor, is very active in the religious life of the community and has written several inspirational books. A multitude of his sermons are available on tape, and he presents a brief daily devotional on WHVN radio.

People come to Calvary from all denominational backgrounds and participate in the diverse educational and social opportunities that are available within the spiritual family of the church. From single's classes to senior adults, from music and drama to international missions, Calvary offers everyone the opportunity to use his or her talents in Christian service. The church also has a Weekday Preschool, Daycare and a Mother's Morning Out program.

The facility, located on 100 acres in south Charlotte, includes a sanctuary with a seating capacity of 6,000 and features the thirteenth largest pipe organ in the world...about the same size as the

Photo by Tina Vito, CPCC © 1994.

The sanctuary of Calvary Church features the 13th largest pipe organ in the world.

Mormon Tabernacle's organ in Salt Lake City. The organ has 11,499 pipes ranging in size from hundreds of tiny pipes smaller than soda straws to pipes over 40 feet tall. It is internationally renowned as one of the great organs built in this century, and visitors from all over the world come weekly to Calvary Church to view and hear this grand instrument. Calvary provides a dozen concerts each year and the Charlotte Oratorio and Symphony use the sanctuary each year for Handel's *Messiah.* Calvary performs a full-scale production of the passion and glory of Easter in its *It Is Finished* spectacular that draws thousands each year to experience a unique interpretation of this biblical play, possibly one of the few Passion plays in the country that gives such dramatic emphasis to Satan.

Sunday School is at 9:15 AM; Worship services at 10:30 AM and 6:00 PM on Sunday; 7:00 PM on Wednesday.

MECKLENBURG COMMUNITY CHURCH
David Cox Road Elementary School Auditorium
4215 David Cox Rd.   *548-9404*

This new interdenominational church, affiliated with the Southern Baptist Convention, is neither typical nor Baptist. Its message is conservative, holding firm to the eternal truth of Christianity, but contemporary in style and method. Basically, the church, similar to Willow Creek outside of Chicago, exists for the unchurched. (Those who generally sit home on Sunday morning reading the funnies or flipping channels.) It also speaks to those who've given up on church. Most churches target what they call the "already convinced." This church ministers to people with questions running the spectrum from religion to life's daily problems.

The unconventional approach for the Sunday morning church service falls into three categories: Music, Drama and Multimedia Event. A full, live band provides contemporary music; "slice of life" dramas provoke question and answer sessions; media events can utilize multi-projectors with dissolves to videos. All three applications are volunteer-led.

Simultaneously, **Sonshine City**, an active, contemporary approach to Sunday School for children from nursery to fifth grade runs during the Sunday morning service. Again, the method in teaching bible study and relationship building focuses on '90's music, interests and happenings. Last year, the church sponsored a **Parenting Seminar** with famed psychologist Dr. John Rosemond. This rapidly growing church, led by Dr. James (Jim) White is embarking on a full menu of social services, including building a Habitat house each year.

Services are at 9 AM and 10:15 AM on Sunday morning. Dress code is casual and relaxed (Bermudas and sneakers).

Jewish

TEMPLE BETH EL
5101 Providence Rd.   *366-1948*

"Temple Beth El offers a special environment, a common ground, where people from varied streams of Judaism can share, ex-

The magnificent new Temple Beth El has been completed at Shalom Park.

change views in an open and honest way and participate in authentic, yet modern, observances of Jewish life cycles and tradition, keeping pace with today's way of life," according to a spokesperson for the membership committee.

The Reformed congregation, made up of approximately 550 members, is affiliated with the Union of American Hebrew Congregations and has been serving the Charlotte community since 1948. The temple offers regular worship services, a religious school, Bar and Bat Mitzvah training, plus organizations for various age groups. Members enjoy an annual retreat each Labor Day at Wildacres in Western North Carolina.

The spiritual leader of the congregation is Rabbi James Bennett. A magnificent new temple has been completed at Shalom Park. Worship service is held on Friday night at 8 PM.

TEMPLE ISRAEL

4901 Providence Rd. 362-2796

Temple Israel has a youth program for grades four through 12 and also conducts an after-school Hebrew School on Tuesdays, Thursdays and Saturdays. The leader of the congregation is Rabbi Murray Ezring. Worship services are at 8 PM on Friday night and 9 AM on Saturday.

Lutheran

ST. MARKS LUTHERAN CHURCH

101 Queens Rd. 375-9185

St. Marks is the oldest Lutheran church in Charlotte. Be-

gun in 1870, it was originally located downtown at 416 North Tryon Street. In the late '50s the congregation decided to move from town to the suburbs. Today, the town has spread and moved out to the church's 1960 address on Queens Road.

St. Marks is not a church that you would pass by without noticing. The massive Christus Victor symbol has been handsomely sculpted into the church's architectural face. The symbol displays a victorious crowned Christ with arms outstretched in benediction as if embracing the world through resurrection.

This liturgical church celebrates the different seasons of the church year as each season depicts a different event in either the life of Christ or the church. The church hosts the **North Carolina Evangelism Conference** every two years. There are three children's choirs and an adult choir, and the church offers a wide Sunday School program with children, young adult and adult classes. The Youth Ministry offers special awareness programs, which have included AIDS, sexuality and environmental concerns. Young people also work in a number of service projects throughout the city and enjoy getaway retreats. Youth groups as well as adults join in the monthly activities that involve softball, basketball and volleyball teams. The church also offers both adult and children's vacation bible schools in the summer.

The church's social ministry supports over 30 different programs. It raised money and built a Habitat house on 16th and Seigle Avenue. In addition it offers the **Hopespring** program with agency offices housed at the church. This program takes up where federal and state governments bow out to help young adults from 18 to 22 years old who have been in foster care homes to find jobs, education and housing. Within the church is a strong **Shepards** group. Core leaders pair church members to pray for and support each other. The Shepherds also minister to the ill or those in crisis. Outreach programs cover local and international concerns. The church is currently developing and supporting a new mission in southwest Charlotte.

St. Marks' senior pastor is Rev. C. Peter Setzer, and assistant ministers are Reverend Paul Cobb, Dr. Robert W. Stackel and Rev. Joseph G. Kovitch. Worship services are at 8:30 AM and 11 AM on Sunday, and at 12:15 PM on Wednesday.

Methodist

LITTLE ROCK AME ZION CHURCH
401 N. McDowell St.   334-3782

Affiliated with the African Methodist Episcopal Zion denomination, this 1500-member black church hosted the denomination's 43rd quadrennial General Conference in 1988, which was attended by the Rev. Jesse Jackson. The present $1.8 million contemporary structure replaced the original church, now the Afro-American Cultural Center, in 1981.

The church's outreach program is primarily concentrated on the Earle Village section. A tutorial program is offered to Earle Village

students during the school year and church volunteers participate in rehabilitating and cleaning the area. Thanksgiving food baskets are also provided for the area's needy families.

The church's current pastor, Dr. James Samuel, was called to the church in 1989. Sunday school is at 9:30 AM and Sunday worship services are at 8 AM and 10 AM.

MYERS PARK UNITED METHODIST CHURCH
1020 Providence Rd.   376-8584

Myers Park Methodist Church is the church with beautiful stained-glass windows that brings cheer to passersby on Providence Road. The church was completed on October 25, 1925, and has 3,650 members. The senior pastor is Lawrence McCleskey, and the associate minister is Melvin McIntosh.

The church has extensive outreach programs, but is probably best recognized for its strong Sunday school program. Even nonmembers attend over 20 different adult and children's classes. Primarily divided along age lines, the classes delve into a variety of biblical as well as relationship and contemporary issues. The church offers an open forum structure for both adult couples and singles classes.

One of the church's local outreach programs is **STEP** (an anagram meaning: Strategy To Elevate People). STEP works in the Wilmore neighborhood and has been instrumental in the **Wilmore Green** project that aids residents in gardening and is active in renovation projects to benefit the community. The church

Photo by Kendra Grubb, CPCC © 1994.

First United Methodist Church at 501 N. Tryon Street
is a beautiful Uptown landmark.

sponsors an awards dinner for resident winners. Last year the church built a Habitat home in Belmont and has raised funds to build another home this year.

The Sunday prior to Thanksgiving, the United Methodist Women sponsor **Harvest of Blessing**, which is a fund raising project that annually raises over $2,000 for the Bethlehem Center. The church sends a number of members on mission-building teams to the Caribbean and Africa, and it supports missionary work throughout the world.

Within the church there is an active music program that works with young adults to produce yearly musical dinner theater performances with the proceeds designated for outreach programs. Last year the youth group went to Jamaica to help paint and rehabilitate a school, and plans are in progress for another venture. The Adults Plus and Best Years senior groups take frequent educational and entertainment trips to varied destinations, including New York City.

Sunday worship services are held at 8:45 AM and 11 AM, and Sunday School is at 9:45 AM.

SHARON UNITED METHODIST CHURCH

4411 Sharon Rd.   *366-9166*

With its unique ski-slope roofline, Sharon United Methodist Church has long been a distinctive landmark in Southeast Charlotte. Beyond the sweeping exterior, however, lies a very down-to-earth multigenerational congregation of 1,500.

First organized in the late '60s on what was then the outskirts of Charlotte, Sharon Methodist has retained the best of its pioneering spirit and draws a regional constituency from southern Mecklenburg County. An energetic staff sets the tone with a full compliment of children's, youth, adult and music ministries. Rev. Jack Yarbrough serves as Senior Pastor and is supported by Associated Minister, Dr. Robert H. Sturge.

Sunday morning worship includes an early service at 8:30 AM, and informal contemporary-style worship at 9:40 (back to back with the Sunday School hour) and a "big music" worship service with a choir of over 60 members at 11 AM. One of the newest outreach program of the church is the Wednesday evening School of Discipleship with its low-cost 6 PM fellowship dinner and courses for all ages.

The church has remained committed to providing a variety of ministries and outreach programs and is involved in many local and international mission projects, including an after school tutorial program, Habitat for Humanity, and an extensive schedule of work mission trips. The most unique of these programs is the Lay Exchange Ministry with Medhodist churches in Great Britain.

The church offers a variety of recorded messages at its 24-hour Communication Center at 551-6799. A free informational cassette tape is available upon request.

Moravian

LITTLE CHURCH ON THE LANE
528 Moravian La.   *334-1381*

Over 2,000 people attend the **Moravian Love Feast** at Little Church on the Lane every Christmas Eve. In the candlelight of the traditional Moravian service, worshipers share in singing carols, reading Scripture and meditation as well as breaking bread and having coffee. The service, held in the warmth and intimacy of the quaint sanctuary, is open to the public.

The church dates back to 1922 when the W. T. Wolford family, who occupied what is now the Harry and Bryant Funeral Home, persuaded the bishop at Old Salem to establish a church in Charlotte. The Rev. Herbert Spaugh served as minister of the congregation until his retirement in 1966 and was responsible for establishing many current Moravian traditions in Charlotte, including an annual Easter sunrise service. Older members of the picturesque church speak proudly as they tell the story of Rev. Spaugh who, in an effort to drum up publicity and interest for what was a new denomination to Charlotte, started a Boy Scout band.

Today the church has about 475 members and is led by the Rev. Robert Peterson at Wolford Chapel, the church's original sanctuary. The church is open to the public every day from dawn until dusk. The quaint chapel is used regularly by anyone who desires to spend some quiet time in personal prayer or meditation. Sunday school is at 9:45 AM and worship service is a 11 AM.

Presbyterian

COVENANT PRESBYTERIAN CHURCH
1000 East Morehead St.   *333-9071*

The large imposing stone structure on East Morehead houses the combination of two Presbyterian churches—Westminster Presbyterian, which first occupied the location, and Second Presbyterian, formerly located Uptown. Since its inception, and due to Covenant's first minister, Dr. Warner Hall, worship and music have been the foundation of the church. The succeeding minister, Dr. Doug Oldenburg, and the current interim minister, Tony Tucker, have also understood how worship is enhanced with music. The same Ministers of Music, Richard and Betty Peek, have been at Covenant from the beginning—now over 40 years. The church's philosophy is like that of Martin Luther, who said that "music takes people one step beyond the spoken word." All children of the church are strongly encouraged to join the choir, and when they become teenagers, they can participate in the choir's **SMART** trip program. The anagram stands for sports, music, art, religion and travel, which are the key components of a 14-day trip to various states. At designated stops, the students play sports, visit museums, see plays and perform at Presbyterian churches throughout this educational journey taken on the church bus.

Covenant realizes that the end result of worship puts us back in the workaday world with all of its attendant problems. Therefore, the emphasis on mission has blazed many trails in Charlotte for the less fortunate. The **Crisis Assistance Ministry** began in the basement of Covenant and continues to be supported. Covenant's holistic five-year commitment to the Seversville neighborhood, in conjunction with four other local churches, is bringing positive results in the community. The church raised $250,000 for this project. Covenant is also the largest donor in the country to the yearly **Crop Walk**, and members also participate in the **Two Cents a Meal** program. A plastic piggy bank-type container is given to each family to deposit two cents per family member, per meal, to remind members that not everyone eats as well as they do. The money is brought to the church monthly and sent to the food bank. Over $1,000,000 has been given in the past eight years. The church also participates in and supports: **Project Uplift, Taps, Relatives, Shepherd's Center, Cities and Schools** and has built two **Habitat for Humanity** houses.

Currently a new recreation center has been built for athletic pursuits and Seniors recreation. Call for worship hours.

FIRST PRESBYTERIAN CHURCH
200 W. Trade St.   *332-5123*

This local church was organized in 1818 and dedicated in 1823. First Presbyterian was originally a community church where all denominations met to worship. Later, as the community grew, different faiths formed their own churches, and the original church became the property of the Presbyterians. The present Gothic Revival style was built in 1857 for $1300. Prominent early settlers include Mrs. Mary Anna Morrison Jackson, wife of General "Stonewall" Jackson and their daughter, Mrs. Julia Jackson Christian. The church's Settlers Cemetery has remained a community graveyard where Tom Polk rests, along with other noteworthy early settlers.

Through the years, First Presbyterian has enjoyed a close association with Queens College, Davidson College, Presbyterian Hospital, and several other Charlotte institutions and has also hosted the denomination's general assembly on four occasions. The church, which has over 1,350 members, has a Sunday 11 AM television ministry on WSOC (9). First Presbyterian continues to serve the Uptown community through current-day ministries such as the **Child Development Center, Community School of the Arts, Loaves and Fishes** and the **Walk-In Ministry**.

Dr. William P. Wood, senior minister, leads the congregation. Sunday School is at 9:45 AM and Sunday worship service is at 11 AM.

MYERS PARK PRESBYTERIAN CHURCH
2501 Oxford Pl.   *376-3695*

Myers Park Presbyterian's Senior Minister, Tim Croft, believes that helping the poor is the call that his church tries to serve, not only in dollars, but in volunteer hours. The 3,200-member church raised $3.5 million dollars last year and pledged 125,000 volunteer hours for this purpose. Worship is this active church's core strength, manifested in caring for each other and others less fortunate.

The primary outreach focuses on helping children through a variety of **mentoring programs**. In a one-on-one relationship, a troubled or problem child assigned to a volunteer adult can count on a relationship filled with tutoring, attending an athletic or entertainment event and problem solving assistance. The church's new gymnasium, with a full time director, provides a bevy of recreational opportunities for parishioners and other groups in the community. The church is also building a residence at **Alexander Children's Center**.

The church also has an **HIV AIDS care team**, which provides help to AID's clients. The church's many programs, including concerts and workshops, are open to the public. Associate ministers are Tyler Downing, Jane Summey and Ray Scott. Sunday school is at 9:45 AM and Sunday worship services are at 8:45 AM and 11 AM.

Unitarian

UNITARIAN CHURCH OF CHARLOTTE
234 N. Sharon Amity Rd.   366-8623

The Unitarian Church of Charlotte is part of the Unitarian Universalist denomination, which emphasizes individual freedom of belief. The 550-member church offers a nationally developed, very inclusive Sunday school for children and youth, a Sunday service, classes and lectures, study and service groups and covered dish dinners.

"An effort is made to be open to Religious truths no matter what tradition they might come from—Judaism, Christianity, Islam, Buddhism and other faiths," states Jim Gronquist, church spokesperson. "Most Unitarian Universalists believe in the oneness of all humanity, the need to protect our fragile environment, and the principle that all people are potentially worthy of dignity and respect, regardless of race, religion, nationality or affectional orientation."

Dr. Doug Reisner ministers to this congregation. Both Sunday School and Sunday worship service are at 10:30 AM.

Denominational Headquarters

ADVENT CHRISTIAN
Contact: Hal Vanhoy, Regional Superintendent
14601 Albemarle Rd.   545-6161

AME ZION
National Headquarters
Contact: The Rev. W. Robert Johnson, III, General Secretary
401 E. Second St.   332-3851

BAPITST
Mecklenburg Baptist Association
Southern Convention
328 W. Carson Blvd.   375-1197

CATHOLIC
Catholic Diocese of Charlotte
Contact: Monsignor John McSweeney
1524 E. Morehead St.   377-6871

CHRISTIAN AND MISSIONARY ALLIANCE
District Office
Contact: The Rev. Gordon Copeland, District Superintendent
10801 Johnston Rd.   543-0470

CHURCH OF GOD

Contact: The Rev. Robert Daugherty
6900 Wilkinson Blvd. 394-6333

EPISCOPAL

Christ Church
1412 Providence Rd. 333-0378
Holy Comforter Episcopal Church
2701 Park Rd. 332-4171
St. John's Episcopal Church
1623 Carmel Rd. 366-3034

LEIGHTON FORD MINISTRIES

6230 Fairview Rd., Suite 300 366-8020

FRIENDS

Charlotte Friends Meeting
2327 Remount Rd. 399-8465

JAARS
(JUNGLE AVIATION AND RADIO MINISTRY)

Service arm of Wycliffe Bible Translators
P.O. Box 248, Davis Road
Waxhaw, NC 843-6000

JEWISH

Temple Beth El
5077 Shalom Park 366-1948

UNITED METHODIST CHURCH

Charlotte District
4108 Park Rd., Suite 101 525-3395
Contact: Bishop L. Bevel Jones
3400 Shamrock Dr. 535-2260

MORAVIAN

Little Church on the Lane
522 Moravian La. 334-1381

N.C. DISTRICT CHURCH OF THE NAZARENE

Contact: Dr. Eugene Simpson
7609 Linda Lake Dr. 537-4017

PRESBYTERIAN CHURCH IN AMERICA

Central Carolina Presbytery
811 Central Ave. 331-9354

PRESBYTERIAN CHURCH U.S.A.

Presbytery of Charlotte
Contact: Dr. H. Alan Elmore
5700 Executive Ctr. Dr. 535-9999

SALVATION ARMY CITY COMMAND

Contact: Lt. Col. David Mikles
534 Spratt St. 334-4731

SEVENTH DAY ADVENTIST

Carolina Conference of Seventh Day Adventist
Contact: Elder Kenneth Coonley
6000 Conference Dr. 535-6720

UNITARIAN

TJ District-UUA
234 N. Sharon Amity Rd. 366-8623

Index Of Advertisers

Index

Symbols

A

C

D

H

M

O

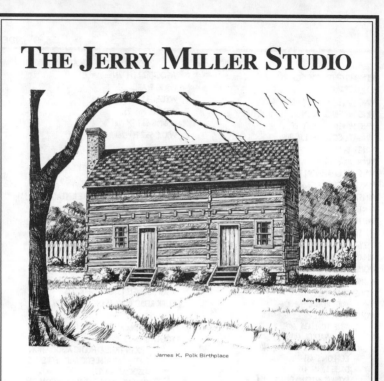

The following coupons
are our gift to you
to help you enjoy Charlotte
and places like the zoo.

— The Publisher

Index of Coupons

Index of Coupons

USING THE COUPONS IN THIS BOOK

• Unless otherwise specified, all coupons are valid through December 31, 1995.

• After reading the coupon carefully, detach and present it. Discounts apply only to the items and according to the terms specified in the offer.

• Coupons may not be used with other promotional discount offers such as: discount-priced daily specials, special discount senior citizens rates, early bird specials, etc. If in doubt, please check with the establishment.

• Neither the Insiders' Guide nor Becklyn Publishing Group, Inc. are responsible if any establishment breaches its contract or refuses to accept coupons.

SPECIAL TIPS
FOR USING RESTAURANT COUPONS

• Select the restaurant you wish to visit, note the value of the offer, the valid days and hours, and any conditions of use (keeping in mind that holidays are often excluded).

• Buy one dinner, entree or menu item and get the second free. The least expensive dinner or entree ordered is complimentary up to the maximum value printed on the coupon.

• The maximum value does not limit your selection, it only limits the amount of discount allowed.

Tips for satisfactory service should equal 15%-20% of the total check before the discount. Please remember the restaurant personnel depend on tips for much of their income.

• If you have questions about the value or terms, check with the establishment before you attempt to use the coupon.

Thank you for your purchase of *The Insiders' Guide to Charlotte.*

6

Mint Museum *of* Art

2730 Randolph Road, 704/337-2000

One free admission with a paid admission

RECEIVE ONE FREE ADMISSION WHEN A SECOND ADMISSION OF EQUAL VALUE IS PURCHASED

Regular Admission (Friday & Saturday) $15.00
Regular Admission (Thursday & Sunday) $10.00

For further information please call:
Box Office: 334-9128 • Business Office: 376-3777

Offer not valid in combination with other discounts and is good thru June, 1995

CHARLOTTE REPERTORY THEATRE

Valid for one complimentary RESERVED SEAT
when a second RESERVED SEAT of equal of
greater value is purchased.

valid wed., thurs. & matinee performances
(subject to availability & not valid with any other discount)

7

Mint Museum *of* Art

Hours: Tuesday 10 am-10 pm; Wednesday through Saturday
10 am-5 pm; and Sunday 12 pm-5 pm

Admission: $4 adults, $3 seniors, $2 students,
children 12 years and under and members are free.

For information on current exhibitions and programs,
call the museum's taped highlights telephone line
at 704/333-6468.

1994-1995 Season Line-up

ASSASSINS...Sept. 8-10, 15-17, 22-25, 1994

THE COMEDY OF ERRORS.......................Nov. 3-5, 10-12, 17-20, 1994

THE CEMETERY CLUB..................................Feb. 2-4, 9-11, 16-19, 1995

A RAISIN IN THE SUN.................March 23-25, 30-31, April 1, 6-9, 1995

A FUNNY THING HAPPENED
ON THE WAY TO THE FORUM.................June 1-3, 8-10, 15-18, 1995

2040 CHARLOTTE PLAZA, CHARLOTTE, NC 28244
(704) 333-8587

Lost in Yonkers	September 7-18, 1994
Someone Who'll Watch Over Me	October 5-16, 1994
The Sisters Rosensweig	November 9-20, 1994
Oleanna	Nov. 30 - Dec. 11, 1994
The 9th Annual Charlotte Festival	Jan. 31 - Feb. 5, 1995
Inherit The Wind	March 1-12, 1995
Signature	March 29-April 9, 1995
Three Hotels	May 10-21, 1995
Five Guys Named Moe	June 7-18, 1995

All performances at Booth Playhouse of
The North Carolina Blumenthal Performing Arts Center

CHARLOTTE SYMPHONY

Peter McCoppin, Music Director

NORTH CAROLINA BLUMENTHAL PERFORMING ARTS CENTER

CALL 704.372.1000

BUY ONE TICKET, GET ONE FREE
TO ANY FRIDAY NIGHT PERFORMANCE

1 FREE TICKET!

CHARLOTTE SYMPHONY

Peter McCoppin, Music Director

NORTH CAROLINA BLUMENTHAL PERFORMING ARTS CENTER

CALL 704.372.1000

BUY ONE TICKET, GET ONE FREE
TO ANY SUNDAY AFTERNOON PERFORMANCE

1 FREE TICKET!

CHARLOTTE SYMPHONY

Peter McCoppin, Music Director

NORTH CAROLINA BLUMENTHAL PERFORMING ARTS CENTER

CALL 704.372.1000

BUY ONE TICKET, GET ONE FREE
TO ANY YOUNG PEOPLE'S CONCERT

1 FREE TICKET!

CHARLOTTE
SYMPHONY

Peter McCoppin, Music Director

704.372.1000

Please call for concert details and to order your tickets.
Present coupon at PAC Box Office.
Orders subject to availability.

CHARLOTTE
SYMPHONY

Peter McCoppin, Music Director

704.372.1000

Please call for concert details and to order your tickets.
Present coupon at PAC Box Office.
Orders subject to availability.

CHARLOTTE
SYMPHONY

Peter McCoppin, Music Director

704.372.1000

Please call for concert details and to order your tickets.
Present coupon at PAC Box Office.
Orders subject to availability.

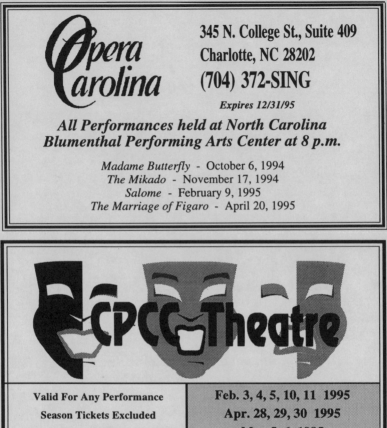

13

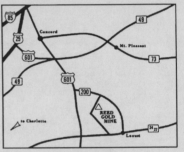
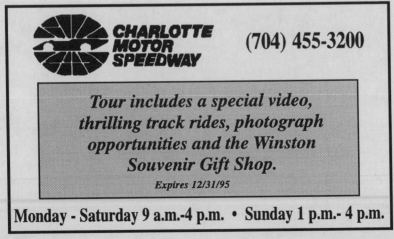

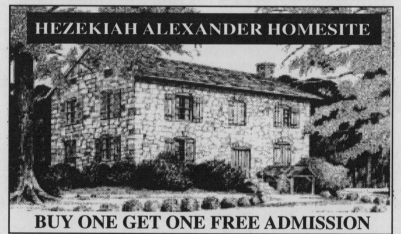

Latta Place, Inc.

Located in Latta Plantation Park, this backcountry plantation home is listed on the National Register of Historic Places.

Guided Tours:
Tues.-Fri 1:30 p.m. & 3:30 p.m.
Sat.-Sun. 1:30 p.m., 2:30 p.m., 3:30 p.m.
Weekend tours only in February

Closed Mondays.
Closed month of January and most major holidays.

Call for special events schedule. • (704) 875-231 • Expires 12/31/95

HEZEKIAH ALEXANDER HOMESITE

3500 Shamrock Dr. • Charlotte, NC

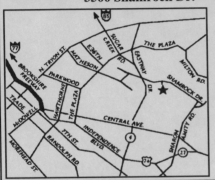

- #1 Historic site in Mecklenburg County
- Oldest existing structure
- Tours highlight daily life of the colonial & early American era
- Special programs & events throughout the year
- Call for hours & tour times

(704) 568-1774

Expires 12/31/95

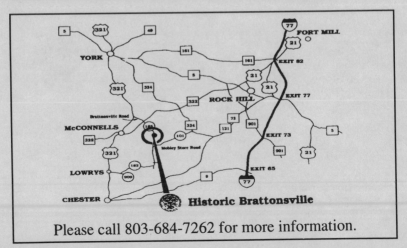

Please call 803-684-7262 for more information.

The Only Place Thrills Are Paramount!™

Paramount's

CAROWINDS ®

**This coupon is worth $5.00
off any general admission ticket.**

170

Located 10 miles south of Charlotte off of I-77 (exit 90)

Take Your Family On A Safari...
At The Museum Of York County!

MUSEUM OF YORK COUNTY

**Valid for one
complimentary
admission when a
second admission of
equal or greater
value is purchased.**

4621 Mt. Gallant Rd. • Rock Hill, SC • (800) 968-2726

SCHIELE MUSEUM
OF NATURAL HISTORY
AND PLANETARIUM, INC.

Buy One Get One FREE!

Buy One Admission And Get One
Admission For Planetarium Cinema
360 Or Any Regularly Scheduled
Program FREE.

Hours: Tues. -Fri., 9 am-5pm • Sat. & Sun, 1 pm-5 pm

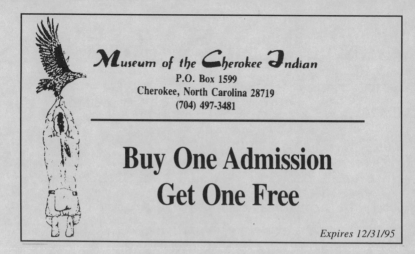

Museum of the Cherokee Indian
P.O. Box 1599
Cherokee, North Carolina 28719
(704) 497-3481

Buy One Admission
Get One Free

Expires 12/31/95

PACK PLACE

Offer expires
12/31/95

Education, Arts & Science Center

A major new attraction located on historic Pack Square in downtown Asheville, North Carolina. The Center is easily accessible. From Interstate 240 take Exit 5A/Merrimon Avenue and follow the signs for Highway 25 South for three blocks to Pack Square. From Interstate 40 take Exit 50 (Highway 25/So. Asheville) and continue on Highway 25 North through Biltmore Village for three miles.

Seasonal Schedule April - December. Call for reservations:
1-800-872-4681 ext. 25 or 1-704-586-8811
Based on availability. Not valid with other promotions.
Not valid on Saturday or Month of October.

21

Appalachian Ski Mountain

P.O. Box 106
Blowing Rock, NC 28605

Snow Reports
704-295-7828

Reservations and Group Information
800-322-2373

Appalachian's season runs from Thanksgiving through mid-March

Lower Early and Late Season Ski Ticket Rates

New Double Chairlift * Nursery (Ages 1-4) * Senior Rates

Super Ticket (Good Day and Night) * Ski School Lesson Guarantee

---

GRANDFATHER MOUNTAIN

Expires 12/31/95

An exciting trip across the Mile-High Swinging Bridge and inspirational views from the highest peak in the Blue Ridge combine to give you an unforgettable vacation experience! Visit Grandfather Mountain and also see majestic native wildlife in six natural habitats. An excellent new Nature Museum, picnic areas, and alpine hiking trails add to your enjoyment.

U.S. 221, 2 miles north of Linville, NC, and 1 mile south of Blue Ridge Parkway

Exit Parkway at Milepost 306 (Linville Exit)
14 miles south of Boone/Blowing Rock, NC

TWEETSIE RAILROAD

Take a step back in time when you step aboard Tweetsie Railroad. After a scenic three-mile ride, you'll stop in an authentic turn-of-the-century railroad town. Here you'll catch a glimpse of life in another era. And don't miss any of the rest of the fun, live musical shows, rides, petting zoo, crafts, and our famous Tweetsie fudge. The fun never stops at Tweetsie—until you do.

Expires 12/31/95

U.S. 321, between Boone and Blowing Rock, NC

Blue Ridge Parkway Milepost 291, Boone Exit

23

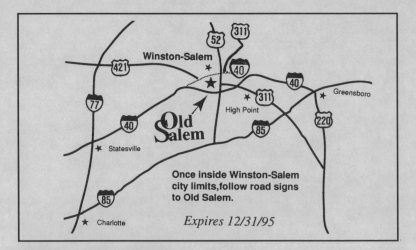

Winston-Salem

Once inside Winston-Salem city limits, follow road signs to Old Salem.

Expires 12/31/95

- **Environmental Park**
- **Hands-on science exhibits**
- **State-of-the-art 120 seat Planetarium**

Exhibit Hours:
Monday-Saturday 10 am - 5 pm
Sunday 1pm - 5 pm
———
Park Hours:
Saturday 11 am - 4 pm
Sunday 1 pm - 4 pm
Wednesday-Friday 11 am - 2 pm

DIRECTIONS

Tryon Palace Historic Sites and Gardens is located in New Bern, North Carolina, at the intersection of US 17 (north-south) and US 70 (east-west). New Bern is approximately 1 1/2 hours driving time east of Interstate 95 via US 70 and is approximately 45 minutes from coastal beaches via US 70.

Expires 12/31/95

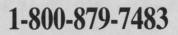
25

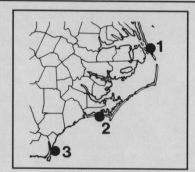

Listen and Remember

Historical Outdoor Drama

Presented by the Waxhaw Historical Festival & Drama Association, this outdoor drama brings to the stage the life and times of Andrew Jackson.

Performances each Friday and Saturday evening in June.

Tickets available at the gate beginning at 7 p.m.

Curtain time: 8:30 p.m.

Waxhaw Amphitheater

Highway 75 E. • Waxhaw, N.C. • (704) 843-2300

Horn in the West

- A musical drama portraying the struggle of Daniel Boone & his men
- Performances held in the outdoor amphitheater located 1/2 mile S. of US 421 near the center of town on Horn of the West Dr.
- Performances start at 8:30 & last 2 hours
- Tues.-Sun. late June to mid-August
- Box office redemption 9 a.m. to 9 p.m. daily except Monday.

Offer expires 12/31/95

FLAT ROCK PLAYHOUSE

THE STATE THEATRE OF NORTH CAROLINA

P.O. Box 310
Flat Rock, NC 28731
704-693-0731

Supported by a
Theatre Section grant
from the
North Carolina Arts Council
a state agency.

The State Theatre of North Carolina, Flat Rock Playhouse is a professional summer theatre that produces 8 shows during 15 weeks. Nationally recognized talent can be seen in the latest Broadway and London hits as well as hot new works.

Sun Mat 2:15pm/ Sun Eve 8:15pm. Offer expires September 4, 1995. Based on availability. Cannot be combined with other discounts.

Directions: Take I–26 to Upward Road. Follow Upward to Hwy 25, take a left, the Playhouse will be on your right 3/4 mile down the road.

29

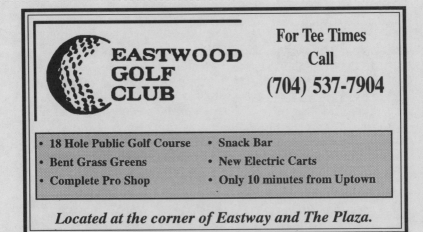
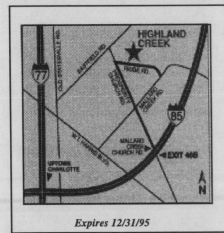

31

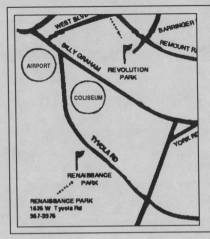

Featuring:

- *18 holes of professional golf*
- *well-manicured greens*
- *well-stocked pro shop*
- *snack bar*

Managed by American Golf Corp.
Owned by Mecklenburg County.

Offer expires 12/31/95

DESCRIPTION

Championship 18-hole golf course with Bent grass greens and Bermuda fairways. The course is nestled around picturesque Lake Wylie. 38,000 sq. ft. clubhouse offers a great atmosphere for any wedding or corporate outing or just a drink after a round of golf.

DIRECTIONS

From Charlotte, take I-77 South to Exit 88 (Tega Cay and Goldhill Road). Take a right at top of ramp and go 7 miles. Clubhouse will be on your left. From Pineville, take HWY 51. Turn left on HWY 21. Go 1.5 miles and make a right onto Goldhill Road. Follow for 12 miles. Clubhouse will be on left.

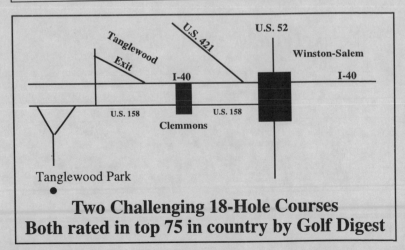

Two Challenging 18-Hole Courses
Both rated in top 75 in country by Golf Digest

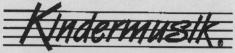

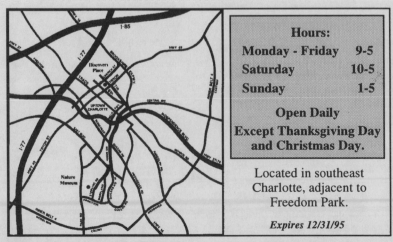

Children's Theatre

**Tickets may be purchased by calling the Box
Office at 333-8983 weekdays from 10am - 5pm.**
Advance reservations must be made 24 hrs. ahead.

Subject to availability.
1017 East Morehead Street

Introduce your child to the joy and enchantment of the world of music!

- *Kindermusik Beginnings*
  *For parents and their children,
  18 months thru age 3*
- *Growing with Kindermusik*
  For children, 3 1/2 to 5 years old
- *Kindermusik for the Young Child*
  For children, 4 to 7 years old
- *Orff Ensemble/Recorder*
  For children, 6 to 8 years old

Kindermusik: The Premier Music Program For Young Children.

Hours:

Monday - Friday	**9-5**
Saturday	**10-5**
Sunday	**1-5**

**Open Daily
Except Thanksgiving Day
and Christmas Day.**

Located in southeast
Charlotte, adjacent to
Freedom Park.

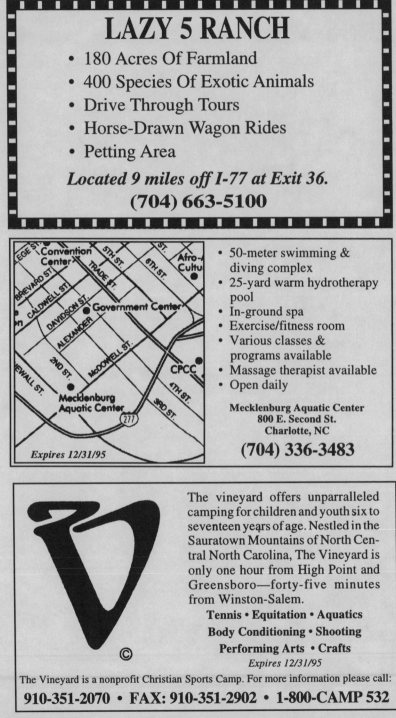

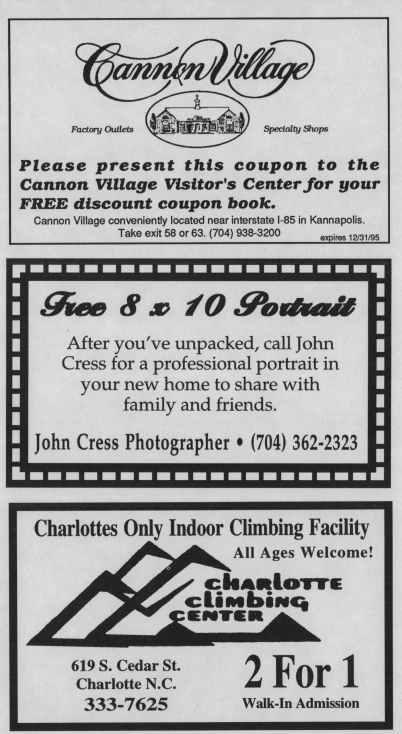

39

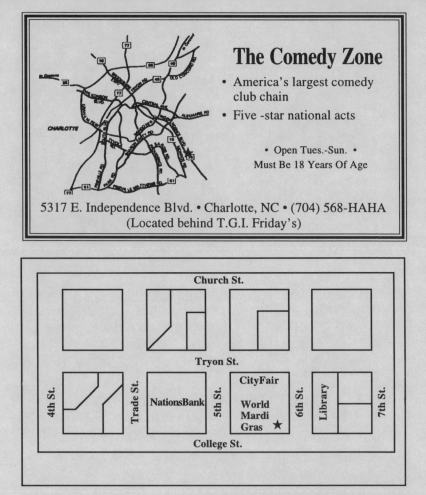
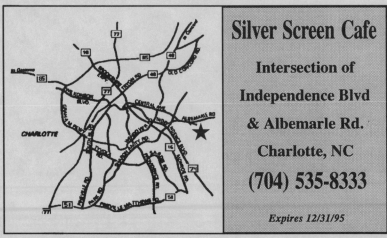
40

41

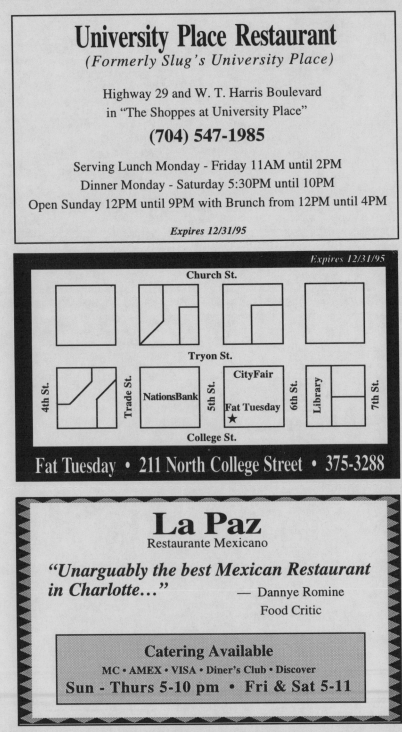

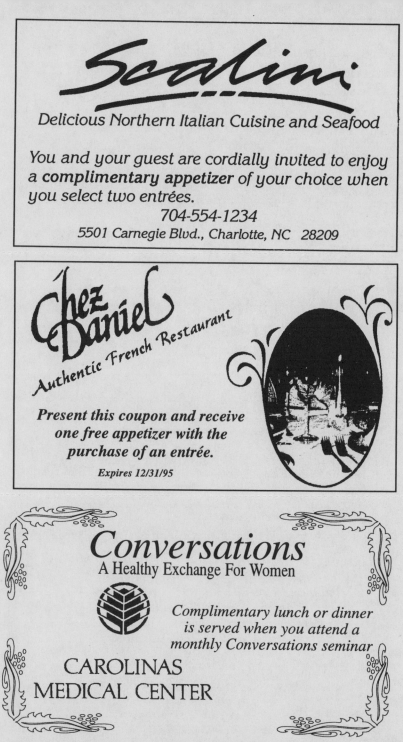

Located in the Hyatt Charlotte hotel in the heart of SouthPark, across Barclay Downs Road from SouthPark Mall.

Enjoy your meal in our 4-story Atrium.

Serving:
Breakfast and lunch from 6:00 a.m. to 2:00 p.m.
Dinner is served from 5:00 p.m. until 10:30 p.m.

Chez Daniel

Authentic French Restaurant

LUNCH: 11:30 am - 2:00 pm
DINNER: 6:00 pm - 10:00 pm

• *Reservations Suggested* •

332-3224

1742 Lombardy Circle • Dilworth Cooperative • off East Blvd.

At "Conversations," local and national experts share useful, timely information that helps you take charge of your health— and make your life longer, happier, and a little easier. Carolinas Medical Center understands that the more you know, the better you feel.

For more information, or to make a reservation for you and a friend, call 355-2229. Seating is limited.

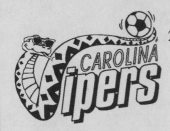

47

MAIL YOUR ORDER TO:
BECKLYN PUBLISHING GROUP, INC.
P.O. Box 14154 • RTP, NC 27709

Please add $3.00 for shipping and handling to the $9.95 special purchase price.
North Carolina residents add 6% sales tax. • One coupon per book.

Name _____

Street _____

City _____ State _____ Zip _____

Phone _____

Enclosed is a check in the amount of $ _____

MasterCard or Visa Account # _____ Exp. _____